WITHDRAWN
UTSA LIBRARIES

The Embedded Firm

The globalization of capital markets since the 1980s has been accompanied by a vigorous debate over the convergence of corporate governance standards around the world towards the shareholder model. But even before the financial and economic crisis of 2008/2009, the dominance of the shareholder model was challenged with regard to persisting divergences and national differences in corporate law, labor law and industrial relations. The present collection explores this debate at an important crossroads, echoing Karl Polanyi's famous observation in 1944 of the disembeddedness of the market from society. Drawing on pertinent insights from scholars, practitioners and regulators in corporate and labor law, securities regulation as well as economic sociology and management theory, the contributions shed important light on the empirical effects on the economy of the shift to shareholder primacy, in light of a comprehensive reconsideration of the global context, policy goals and regulatory forms which characterize market governance today.

CYNTHIA A. WILLIAMS is Professor of Law at the University of Illinois College of Law. From 2007–2009, she held the inaugural Osler Chair in Business Law at Osgoode Hall Law School, York University, Toronto. Professor Williams is a founder and director of the Network for Sustainable Financial Markets, a global collaboration between academics and market participants.

PEER ZUMBANSEN holds the Canada Research Chair in Transnational Economic Governance and Legal Theory at Osgoode Hall Law School, York University, Toronto. Professor Zumbansen is the founder and Director of the Critical Research Laboratory in Law & Society and co-founder and Co-editor-in-chief of the CLPE Research Paper Series (with John Cioffi).

The Embedded Firm

Corporate Governance, Labor, and Finance Capitalism

Edited by

Cynthia A. Williams

and

Peer Zumbansen

CAMBRIDGE UNIVERSITY PRESS
Cambridge, New York, Melbourne, Madrid, Cape Town,
Singapore, São Paulo, Delhi, Tokyo, Mexico City

Cambridge University Press
The Edinburgh Building, Cambridge CB2 8RU, UK

Published in the United States of America by Cambridge University Press,
New York

www.cambridge.org
Information on this title: www.cambridge.org/9781107006010

© Cambridge University Press 2011

This publication is in copyright. Subject to statutory exception
and to the provisions of relevant collective licensing agreements,
no reproduction of any part may take place without the written
permission of Cambridge University Press.

First published 2011

Printed in the United Kingdom at the University Press, Cambridge

A catalogue record for this publication is available from the British Library

Library of Congress Cataloguing in Publication data
  The embedded firm : corporate governance, labor, and finance capitalism /
  [edited by] Cynthia Williams, Peer Zumbansen.
    p. cm.
  Includes bibliographical references and index.
  ISBN 978-1-107-00601-0 (hardback)
  1. Stockholders. 2. Corporations–Investor relations. 3. Capitalism.
  4. Corporate governance. I. Williams, Cynthia A., 1955–
  II. Zumbansen, Peer, 1966– III. Title
  HD2785.E493 2011
  338.6–dc22
                              2011013713

ISBN 978-1-107-00601-0 Hardback

Cambridge University Press has no responsibility for the persistence or
accuracy of URLs for external or third-party Internet websites referred to in
this publication, and does not guarantee that any content on such websites is,
or will remain, accurate or appropriate.

Contents

List of figures	*page* viii
List of tables	ix
Notes on contributors	x

1 Introduction: corporate governance after the 'end of history': investigating the new 'great transformation' 1
CYNTHIA A. WILLIAMS AND PEER ZUMBANSEN

Part I Historical trajectories of business and regulation

2 Corporate governance and financial crisis in the long run 15
SIMON DEAKIN

3 Financialism: a (very) brief history 42
LAWRENCE E. MITCHELL

4 Legitimating power: the changing status of the board of directors 60
DALIA TSUK MITCHELL

5 Engaging corporate boards: the limits of liability rules in modern corporate governance 82
WILLIAM T. ALLEN

6 The primacy of Delaware and the embeddedness of the firm 104
FENNER STEWART, JR.

7 The new embeddedness of the corporation: corporate social responsibility in the knowledge society 119
PEER ZUMBANSEN

Contents

Part II   New interests, new shareholder constellations, new landscapes

8   Beyond the Berle and Means paradigm: private equity and the new capitalist order   151
STEPHEN F. DIAMOND

9   Pension funds as owners and as financial intermediaries: a review of recent Canadian experience   177
SIMON ARCHER

10   Credit derivatives market design: creating fairness and sustainability   205
JANIS SARRA

11   The EU Takeovers Directive: a shareholder or stakeholder model?   233
BLANAID CLARKE

12   "Law and finance": inaccurate, incomplete, and important   256
RUTH V. AGUILERA AND CYNTHIA A. WILLIAMS

Part III   Labor's evolution in the new economy

13   Labor and finance in the United States   277
SANFORD M. JACOBY

14   The conflicting logic of markets and the management of production   318
SUZANNE KONZELMANN AND FRANK WILKINSON

15   Organizing workers globally: the need for public policy to regulate investment   333
JOHN EVANS

16   From governance to political economy: insights from a study of relations between corporations and workers   350
HARRY W. ARTHURS AND CLAIRE MUMMÉ

Part IV   The transnational embedded firm and the financial crisis

17   The intellectual foundations of the global financial crisis: analysis and proposals for reform   383
FRANK JAN DE GRAAF AND CYNTHIA A. WILLIAMS

18	Why executive pay matters to innovation and inequality WILLIAM LAZONICK	413
19	Products, perimeters and politics: systemic risk and securities regulation MARY CONDON	440
20	Modernizing pension fund legal standards for the twenty-first century KEITH L. JOHNSON AND FRANK JAN DE GRAAF	459

Part V Conclusion

21	Conclusion: evaluation, policy proposals and research agenda CYNTHIA A. WILLIAMS AND PEER ZUMBANSEN	477
	Index	483

Figures

15.1	Wage share of national income EU-15, Japan and the United States, 1970–2005	page 336
18.1	Shares of top income recipients in the United States, 1913–2007	414
18.2	S&P 500 and NASDAQ Composite Indices, September 1982–April 2010	429
18.3	Ratios of cash dividends and stock repurchases to net income	431
18.4	Stock repurchases by the S&P 500 (437 companies)	432

Tables

13.1	Financial development and inequality, 1913–1999	page 282
13.2	Distribution of net value added in large European corporations, 1991–1994	295
17.1	The characteristics of governance systems	398
18.1	Total compensation of top executives of US-based corporations, average for 100, 500, 1,500 and 3,000 highest-paid executives, and the proportion of total compensation derived from gains from exercising stocks options	425
18.2	Average annual US corporate stock and bond yields (%), 1960–2009	427
20.1	Main stakeholders in the pension fund service provider supply chain	469

Contributors

RUTH V. AGUILERA, Associate Professor, Department of Business Administration, University of Illinois College of Business and Fellow at the Center for Professional Responsibility, University of Illinois at Urbana-Champaign.

WILLIAM T. ALLEN, Clinical Jack H. Nusbaum Professor of Law and Business, New York University, School of Law.

SIMON ARCHER, Senior Research Associate, Comparative Research in Law and Political Economy Network, Osgoode Hall Law School and Associate, Koskie Minsky LLP, Toronto.

HARRY W. ARTHURS, Professor Emeritus, Osgoode Hall Law School, York University, Toronto and former President, York University, Toronto.

BLANAID CLARKE, Professor of Law, University College Dublin, School of Law.

MARY CONDON, Professor of Law, Osgoode Hall Law School, York University, Toronto.

SIMON DEAKIN, Professor of Law, University of Cambridge; Programme Director in the Cambridge Centre for Business Research; and associate faculty member of the Judge Business School, University of Cambridge.

FRANK JAN DE GRAAF, Professor of International Business, Hanze University of Applied Sciences, the Netherlands and former Advisor for Responsible Investment at PGGM Investments in the Netherlands.

STEPHEN F. DIAMOND, Associate Professor of Law, Santa Clara University, School of Law.

JOHN EVANS, General Secretary for the Trade Union Advisory Council to the Organization of Economic Cooperation and Development (OECD).

SANFORD M. JACOBY, Howard Noble Distinguished Professor, Anderson School of Management, University of California at Los Angeles (UCLA).

KEITH JOHNSON, Program Director for the International Corporate Governance Initiative at the University of Wisconsin Law School and former Chief Legal Officer at the State of Wisconsin Investment Board.

SUZANNE KONZELMANN, Reader in Management, Birkbeck, School of Management and Organizational Psychology, University of London.

WILLIAM LAZONICK, Professor and Director, Center for Industrial Competitiveness, University of Massachusetts.

DALIA TSUK MITCHELL, Professor of Law and Legal History, Faculty of Law, George Washington University.

LAWRENCE E. MITCHELL, Theodore Rhinehart Professor of Business Law, Faculty of Law, George Washington University.

CLAIRE MUMMÉ, Ph.D. Candidate, Osgoode Hall Law School, York University, Toronto.

JANIS SARRA, Professor of Law, Faculty of Law, University of British Columbia.

FENNER STEWART, JR., Ph.D. Candidate and Senior Research Associate, Comparative Research in Law and Political Economy Network, Osgoode Hall Law School, York University, Toronto.

FRANK WILKINSON, Professor of Economics Emeritus, University of Cambridge.

CYNTHIA A. WILLIAMS, Professor of Law, University of Illinois College of Law.

PEER ZUMBANSEN, Professor of Law, Canada Research Chair, Osgoode Hall Law School, York University, Toronto.

1 Introduction: corporate governance after the 'end of history': investigating the new 'great transformation'

Cynthia A. Williams and Peer Zumbansen

Over the last two decades, debates over the convergence or persistence of corporate governance systems have deeply engaged the energies of academics, regulators and investors. These debates have encompassed both the structural mechanisms of corporate decision-making, examining where decision-making authority should lie within the company and which groups should have power, as well as the more politically contested issue of whose interests should matter when corporate decisions are being made. How companies are organized, and what powers their constituents have to influence the corporate enterprise – the core questions of corporate governance – in turn influence capital markets and the investment decisions of managers of huge pools of capital. 'Does the country have an equity culture' is often the question asked by investors and asset managers before massive amounts of money are shifted into, or out of, a country at the click of a 'mouse'.

Debates over the convergence or persistence of corporate governance systems take place in the shadow of at least four significant trends affecting operating companies.

First, there is increased global product market competition caused by improvements in information technology, transportation, standardization and supply chain management. These pressures have forced companies in every economy to cut costs, innovate, adopt new business strategies and develop new alliances. The intellectual habits of product and process innovation have also fuelled financial innovation towards similar goals: a search for yield and thus advantage.

Second, we see the transformation of the world's largest corporations from primarily locally- or domestically-situated enterprises into global networks of supply chains and corporate parent/subsidiary relationships. Such enterprises, held together by webs of contracts, law and the interstitial glue of company history and norms, are subject to competing demands from far-flung regulators, consumers, investors, non-governmental organizations and professionals such as lawyers, investment bankers and accountants.

Third, undergirding these developments are dramatically increased global capital market pressures throughout the developed and developing world. Newly-engaged market participants; new institutional investors and large pools of investible capital; increasing numbers of shareholders with activist agendas; and new types of financial innovation and complex financial engineering have accelerated the transition from industrial to finance capitalism in developed economies. Finance has come to be the dominant contributor to the economic output of such advanced democracies as the United States and Britain, and is of significant importance to the productive capacities of countries throughout the world.

Fourth, these trends are situated in a broader context, which is the emergence of the knowledge society, prompting a reconceptualization of public and private forms of governance. Both political and 'private' actors such as non-governmental organizations, corporations, collectives and individuals operate under conditions of extreme uncertainty, both in terms of procedural and institutional design as well as normative horizon. On the one hand, governments and governmental actors have become increasingly dependent on fragmented, societal knowledge, which leads to an important reconfiguration of the relations between political and civil society actors. The state, in its dependence on constantly updated information, is at the same time implicated in the production of that very information by creating rules and facilitating institutional growth for knowledge production and dissemination. On the other, corporations and other societal actors face pressing governance challenges that in many ways mirror those of contemporary political governing bodies. The dependence of management on expert knowledge, which is generated and communicated both in and outside of the firm, has grown in correlation with the expanding reach of business activities and their impact. With governments and corporations as knowledge actors, producers and consumers, the pressure on law to facilitate and to enable these processes has grown exponentially. No longer clearly situated in an exclusively public or private sphere, 'political', 'private', corporate actors are both authors and receivers of the rules that govern their behaviour.

Given these rapid changes in global operating conditions, it is understandable that there would be pressures on companies to adopt new governance mechanisms in response. Lengthening supply chains, emerging markets such as those in Eastern Europe, Latin America and China becoming part of global production, and increased competition all require different managerial arrangements within the firm, at the least. And yet, we argue, the specific pressures to adopt corporate governance systems that prioritize shareholders' interests – pressures particularly salient in Europe – were as much a product of political ideology as changing economic requirements. In the enclosed chapters we examine those pressures and their effects, both within firms and within societies, evaluating the results of shareholder primacy in light of increasing financialization not only as a matter of theory, but also as a matter of fact.

Thematic overview

The following collection addresses, from a historical and comparative perspective, the changing regulatory landscape for business corporations and financial institutions which has evolved in light of the increasing globalization of the markets and 'financialization' of economies. Taking their cue from political economy studies of national varieties of market regulation, going back to Karl Polanyi and Andrew Shonfield, the contributing authors explore the effect of integrating markets and converging policy strategies on corporate governance, finance and labour market regulation. The collection brings together authors from law, economics, sociology and political science from both North America and Europe to study the evolution of corporate, financial and labour regulation against the background of the continuing global economic – and regulatory – crisis.

Inspired by Sanford Jacoby's book *The Embedded Corporation*,[1] and by institutional and political economy accounts of corporate governance complementarities, the collected chapters bring a number of disciplinary perspectives to bear on the study of the regulatory evolution and relationship between firms, finance and labour in the transformation from industrial to finance capitalism. Part I of the book traces and evaluates this transformation, connecting it to the financial crisis that erupted in 2007. Contributions from Simon Deakin and Larry Mitchell provide a theoretical and historical framework for the book as a whole, discussing, respectively, the shift to shareholder primacy and the transformation to finance capitalism in the United States and United Kingdom. Contributions from William Allen, former Chancellor of the Chancery Court in Delaware, and historian Dalia Tsuk Mitchell analyse some of the implications of this transformation

---

[1] Sanford Jacoby, *The Embedded Corporation* (Princeton: Princeton University Press, 2005).

to finance capitalism on operating companies and their boards of directors, showing the political, historical and sociological forces as work. Fenner Stewart locates these developments within the theoretical debates of leading corporate law scholars today, while Peer Zumbansen provides a broader framework to evaluate the challenges facing both companies and governments within the global knowledge society. Zumbansen's chapter places Polanyi's work on embedded capitalism in the current context of both an intensified process of Europeanization and a global search for regulatory remedies against the dramatic market failures since 2007.

Part II looks more specifically at particular amalgamations of financial power that have formed as the transformation to finance capitalism gathered momentum; particular (and particularly destabilizing) financial instruments; and important regulatory and policy developments in Europe and within international financial institutions such as the World Bank as pressures mounted to adopt more shareholder friendly corporate governance systems. Stephen Diamond, a contrarian on the financialization theme, nonetheless evaluates and highlights the growing influence of private equity investors and hedge funds in the US market. Simon Archer traces changes in the composition, sources of funding and actions within the capital markets of the largest public pension funds in Canada, using that case study as a lens through which to scruitinize the economic role of public pension funds more generally. Janis Sarra discusses credit default swaps and analyses their destabilizing influence on both financial markets and bankruptcy proceedings, providing specific policy advice for regulators to use to address the problems these instruments have caused. Blainaid Clarke's contribution discusses the highly-contested European Takeover Directive, in which the European stakeholder vision of the corporation was supplanted by shareholder-centric rights and pride of place. Her chapter also shows how the political compromises in the Takeover Directive actually operate simultaneously to resist that shareholder perspective. Ruth Aguilera and Cynthia Williams critically evaluate the shareholder bias of noted finance theorists, Rafael La Porta, Florencio Lopez-de-Silanes, Andrei Shleifer and Robert Vishny [commonly referred to as 'LLSV'] from the perspective of economic sociology, while recognizing the important influence on policy LLSV's theories have had at the World Bank. Collectively these authors bring a legal and political economy perspective to bear to carve out the implications of each of these developments for the balance of power within the firm and for the distributions of wealth and risk within developed economies.

There are a number of themes that emerge as we look at the transformation to finance capitalism in Parts I and II. One, which is not unexpected, is that within their different corporate governance structures, labour interests in Europe, the United Kingdom, the United States and Canada have responded to the shift towards finance capitalism in ways characteristic of their home countries' underlying political theories, alliances and power relationships. Thus, labour unions in the United States and Canada have used their pension capital as shareholder activists to advance the interests of their members by using their shareholder voting power, seeking transparency of voting records by their asset managers; board accountability through changes in voting rules; and involvement in limiting executive compensation through the use of shareholder proxy proposals. In these activist uses of pension fund voting power, the expressed corporate governance agenda of labour shareholders has little differed from the corporate governance agenda of shareholder activists generally, including promoting changes in companies' organizing documents that allow the market for corporate control to flourish. Indeed, in an irony little noted in the academic literature (but discussed by Jacoby in this collection), in the United States labour corporate governance activists have been shareholders' most consistent advocate. In Europe, labour has used their more integrated political position as recognized social partners to resist efforts to dismantle works councils and co-determination, but have also responded pragmatically in some cases, such as in Germany, as the economic bargains of the post-war era came under increasing pressure from the demands of finance capitalism. In Part III the contribution from Harry Arthurs and Claire Mummé discusses these differing uses of labour's shareholding power in North America and Europe, using a political economy analysis, while economist John Evans evaluates labour's voice in international public policy by examining the Trade Union's Advisory Council's position within the OECD.

One of the clearest implications of the shift to finance capitalism has been a corollary insistence that the interests of shareholders should predominate in both corporate governance theory and capital market regulation. A second theme of the book is that the underlying premise asserted in favour of the shareholder model of corporate governance, whereby such a shift would enhance social welfare, has not been proven. American legal academics Henry Hansmann of Yale University and Reinier Kraakman of Harvard University have been among the most succinct advocates for the view that there will be (and should be) convergence on the shareholder model of corporate governance, as argued in their iconic article from 2001, 'The End of

History for Corporate Law'.[2] In that article they posited that shareholder wealth maximizing views of the corporate governance relationship would ultimately predominate throughout the world, by virtue of 'the force of logic, the force of example, and the force of competition'.[3] As they put the argument in its strongest form, '[t]he point is simply that now, as a consequence of both logic and experience, there is convergence on a consensus that the best means to this end – the pursuit of aggregate social welfare – is to make corporate managers strongly accountable to shareholder interests and (at least in direct terms) only to those interests'.[4] Yet, the premise that shareholder capitalism enhances social welfare has not been seriously examined as an empirical matter by leading corporate law scholars in the United States. Rather, it has been accepted as an article of faith or has been demonstrated by virtue of high share prices.

In Parts III and IV the premise that shareholder capitalism enhances social welfare is, thus, examined empirically, and is found to be unsupported by the evidence. Contributions by leading labour scholars Sanford Jacoby and Harry Arthurs; by industrial relations economists Suzanne Konzelmann and Frank Wilkinson; and by labour economists William Lazonick and John Evans collectively show that pride of place to finance is correlated with increased economic insecurity and inequality; that shareholder capitalism is inconsistent with highly-productive industrial relations; and that investors' short-term demands, filtered through the stock market or through concentrated pools of investment capital, have often undermined companies' long-term planning and investments in research and development to meet future strategic and social challenges. While the Anglo-American venture capital markets permit rapid innovation, the pressures of finance, within shareholder wealth maximizing corporate governance norms, do not produce

---

[2] Henry Hansmann and Reinier Kraakman, 'The End of History for Corporate Law' (2001) 89 *Georgetown Law Journal* 439 ('End of History I'). Hansmann and Kraakman further elaborate in a related article, also entitled 'The End of History for Corporate Law', in Jeffrey Gordon and Mark Roe (eds.), *Convergence and Persistence in Corporate Governance* (Cambridge: Cambridge University Press, 2004) ('End of History II'). It is significant that Hansmann and Kraakman reiterated their views of the superiority of American-style shareholder-oriented corporate governance in that collection in 2004, notwithstanding the stock market bubble having burst in the United States, which occurred in 2001–2002, and notwithstanding the serious weaknesses of Enron, WorldCom and many other noted failures of corporate governance in the United Sates during 2001–2002.
[3] Hansmann and Kraakman, 'End of History I', p. 441.
[4] Hansmann and Kraakman, 'End of History II', pp. 42–43.

companies that show the same capacity for incremental innovation and learning as do European structures.[5]

The third theme of this book, then, engages with the debates over corporate governance systems. The explicit brief of many of these debates has been to determine whether companies are more efficient and countries more economically successful by prioritizing the interests of shareholders within *liberal* market economies, rather than balancing the claims of a broader range of stakeholders within *coordinated* market economies, using the categories introduced by Varieties of Capitalism scholars.[6] The implicit brief of these debates has challenged European countries and firms, where successful market economies are well-established, to adopt Anglo-American shareholder capitalism, even as advocates did their best to export American-style capitalism throughout the developing world. The contribution by Frank Jan De Graaf and Cynthia Williams in Part IV examines the underlying ideological commitments of liberal market corporate governance theory, and challenges Anglo-American theorists to think more carefully about the benefits of European systems, both for corporate governance arrangements and for capital market regulation. Mary Condon's contribution provides a political economy explanation for international securities regulators' attempts to have greater influence in transnational regulatory efforts after the global financial crisis by strategically deploying the concept of 'systemic risk', but also points out regulatory and definitional problems this concept creates. She also develops the point that securities regulators may need to revisit long-held understandings of the purpose and orientation of disclosure as the preferred regulatory strategy. Part IV concludes with Keith Johnson and Frank Jan De Graaf's recommendations for how understanding of pension funds' fiduciary duties must evolve to take account of the systemic influence these important market actors now have.

Theoretical perspectives

As a general matter, the contributors to this book suggest that what could seem to be politically neutral or merely technical debates about the best systems of corporate governance as a means to the end of creating efficient, well-run companies and economically successful

---

[5] Jacoby, *Embedded Corporation*, p. 19.
[6] Peter Hall and David Soskice (eds.), *Varieties of Capitalism: The Institutional Foundations of Comparative Advantage* (Oxford: Oxford University Press, 2001).

countries are masking, in fact, serious ideological disagreements. This observation should hardly be surprising, and indeed has been the basis for a respected analysis for why European countries have so far failed to create deep, liquid capital markets.[7] Nor should the resistance of countries encompassing stakeholder governance systems towards Anglo-American shareholder governance systems be surprising. Inspired by Karl Polanyi and Mark Granovetter as well as by the more recent revival of economic sociology, spearheaded by scholars such as Richard Swedberg and Jens Beckert, we find that two fundamental dynamics might well explain the persistence of corporate governance systems: the *embedded* nature of companies, corporate governance systems, and markets, as theorized by Granovetter; and the 'double movement' of market liberalization and resistance, as theorized by Polanyi, who himself is regularly associated with designing a theory of embedded capitalism.

In his article 'Economic Action and Social Structure: The Problem of Embeddedness',[8] Mark Granovetter brought a sociological and institutional perspective to bear on a fundamental observation: that markets are embedded within the social and political systems in which they arise. Thus, markets cannot be considered free-standing institutions outside of a society, as the 'free market' often had been, and still is in some contexts. Rather 'the market' must be understood as an embedded institution that manifests the social and political values of the society in which it is embedded, including the professional and transnational networks that affect the market, even as it develops its own logic and values. One implication of this view is that corporate governance reforms cannot be considered in isolation from a thorough understanding of the social and cultural context in which companies arise, and in conjunction with a thorough understanding of the complementarities between companies, corporate governance systems, and the political and institutional frameworks in which companies operate. Since stakeholder corporate governance systems are consistent with the social democratic traditions in the countries in which they've arisen – primarily in Northern and Central Europe, but also to some extent in Japan – it would be naïve to expect they would converge to Anglo-American shareholder capitalism smoothly. Even in the face of global product market competition and institutional investor pressure that will in theory privilege the most

---

[7] Mark Roe, 'Modern Politics and Ownership Separation', in Gordon and Roe, *Convergence and Persistence*, pp. 252–290.
[8] Mark Granovetter, 'Economic Action and Social Structure: The Problem of Embeddedness' (1985) 91 *American Journal of Sociology* 481–510.

efficient system of corporate organization⁹ – believed by many American law professors to be theirs¹⁰ – one would expect exactly the persistence of stakeholder systems that is observed, albeit under pressure.

Indeed, Karl Polanyi's work from 1944 on the double movement of market liberalization and resistance predicts this persistence. In *The Great Transformation* Polanyi argued that as markets expand, so do their undesirable side-effects: instability, monopoly and negative externalities, for instance, and that these side-effects cannot be solved by the market itself. Rather, market expansions are followed by social resistance to 'the pernicious effects of a market-controlled economy'. Polanyi called this the double movement: '[T]he action of two organizing principles in society ... economic liberalism, aiming at the establishment of a self-regulating market ... [and] the other was the principle of social protection aiming at the conservation of man and nature as well as productive organization.'¹¹

The theme of the 'embedded firm' that lies at the core of this volume thus reaches back to a significant return of economic sociology since the 1980s, notably inspired by Granovetter's seminal article.¹² The significance of this reorientation in research lies in its distinct interdisciplinarity. In contrast to the rise in importance of economics in various fields in law, particularly tort, contract, property and corporate law,¹³ the emerging field of economic sociology brings together administrative and regulatory studies in the tradition of Max Weber with scholarship in institutional and new institutional economics, such as that by Ronald Coase, Douglass North and Oliver Williamson.¹⁴ Furthering and

---

⁹ A number of academics have recognized that there can be different ways to organize efficient corporate organizations, and that there can be comparative economic advantage to different corporate governance systems. Jacoby, *Embedded Corporation*, pp. 170–171: 'The Japanese corporate system – governance, strategy, HR, and much besides – facilitates organizational learning and allows companies to specialize in products and processes that are difficult for other companies to imitate. By contrast, the U.S. emphases on flexibility and mobility require general, not firm-specific, skills to facilitate rapid allocation of resources to emergent industries.' Jeffrey Gordon and Mark Roe, 'Introduction', in Gordon and Roe, *Convergence and Persistence*, p. 5 (recognizing the possibility of various paths to efficient corporate organizations).

¹⁰ Hansmann and Kraakman, 'End of History I', p. 441; Hansmann and Kraakman, 'End of History II', pp. 46–48.

¹¹ Karl Polanyi, *The Great Transformation: The Political and Economic Origins of Our Time* (New York: Farrar & Rinehart, 1944), p. 132.

¹² Granovetter, 'Economic Action and Social Structure'.

¹³ See generally Richard Posner, *Economic Analysis of Law* (Boston: Little Brown, 1973), and subsequent editions; Robert Cooter and Thomas Ulen, *Law & Economics*, 4th edn (Boston: Pearson, 2004).

¹⁴ Richard Swedberg, 'The Economic Sociology of Capitalism: An Introduction and Agenda', in Victor Nee and Richard Swedberg (eds.), *The Economic Sociology of Capitalism* (Princeton: Princeton University Press, 2005).

expanding the investigative scope of the law and economics agenda, economic sociology has contributed to an increasingly ambitious intellectual discourse about how to organize, govern and regulate corporations across societies.[15] We recognize this to be another illustration of an encompassing trend towards 'governance studies', which often have their starting point within the framework of a particular discipline but which unfold in an inherently border-crossing manner, drawing on a wealth of different disciplinary perspectives, theoretical foundations and empirical data.[16]

Reflecting on this context, much of the scholarship on comparative corporate governance has been dominated by a law and economics perspective.[17] Two volumes, one edited by John Armour and Joseph McCahery,[18] and the other edited by Jeffrey Gordon and Mark Roe,[19] have attracted considerable attention in enlarging the perspectives on the vivid debate over 'convergence' or 'divergence' in corporate governance principles. Central to all of these volumes, however, is a significantly biased perspective from which the policy and regulatory changes within differently observed countries are studied primarily with view to a very small set of established principles of economically theorized, allegedly technical or, 'good' corporate governance, including enhanced investor protection, capital markets disclosure as a primary regulatory mechanism, an absence of employee co-determination and a reduced interventionist role of the state. This credo is significantly captured in two landmark monographs, one by Mark Roe from 2003, and one from Kraakman et al. in 2004, that each received both explicit praise and criticism.[20]

---

[15] Ruth V. Aguilera and Gregory Jackson, 'International and Comparative Corporate Governance' (2010) 4 *Academy of Management Annals* 485–556.

[16] Peer Zumbansen, 'The Conundrum of Order. The Concept of *Governance* from an Interdisciplinary Perspective', in David Levi-Faur (ed.), *The Oxford Handbook of Governance* (Oxford: Oxford University Press, 2011 forthcoming).

[17] See here, above all the following volumes: Klaus J. Hopt, Hideki Kanda, Mark Roe, Eddy Wymeersch and Stefan Prigge (eds.), *Comparative Corporate Governance. The State of the Art and Emerging Research* (Oxford and New York: Oxford University Press, 1998); Klaus Gugler (ed.), *Corporate Governance and Economic Performance* (Oxford and New York: Oxford University Press, 2001); Joseph A. McCahery, Piet Moerland, Theo Raaijmakers and Luc Renneboog (eds.), *Corporate Governance Regimes. Convergence and Diversity* (Oxford and New York: Oxford University Press, 2002); Klaus J. Hopt and Eddy Wymeersch (eds.), *Capital Markets and Company Law* (Oxford and New York: Oxford University Press, 2003); Klaus J. Hopt et al. (eds.), *Corporate Governance in Context. Corporations, States and Markets in Europe, Japan and the US* (Oxford and New York: Oxford University Press, 2005).

[18] John Armour and Joseph McCahery (eds.), *After Enron. Improving Corporate Law and Modernising Securities Regulation in Europe and the US* (Oxford and Portland: Hart Publishing, 2006).

[19] Gordon and Roe, *Convergence and Persistence*.

[20] Mark Roe, *Political Determinants of Corporate Governance* (Oxford and New York: Oxford University Press, 2003); evaluated in Peter Gourevitch, 'The Politics

At the same time, the economic sociology camp has been extremely prolific: led by thinkers such as Wolfgang Streeck at the Max Planck Institute for the Study of Societies in Cologne, Germany,[21] and by comparative political economists such as Peter Hall and David Soskice, this field has produced an impressive number of critiques of the 'convergence advocates', convincingly arguing for a more layered perspective on the different dynamics of institutional change with regard to path-dependent, historically evolved corporate governance regimes.[22] This work has been published in the intellectually rich context of a renewed interest in the 'embeddedness of market institutions', as originally spearheaded by Karl Polanyi,[23] revived by Granovetter (1985),[24] before receiving more attention from sociologists and political economists in a volume edited by Rogers Hollingsworth and Robert Boyer[25] as well as by scholars such as Neil Fligstein.[26] Related works in this regard have focused on the case of Europe in particular, providing important comparative insights on the different conditions of institutional change and regulatory responses in countries adapting to globally integrated markets, for goods, services, capital and people.[27]

Our collection brings together a diverse group of contributors to challenge the premises of the law and economics perspective with the insights of labour law scholars, economic sociologists and stakeholder

---

of Corporate Governance Regulation' (2003) 112 *Yale Law Journal* 1829–1880; Reinier Kraakman, Paul Davies, Henry Hansmann, Gerard Hertig, Klaus Hopt, Hideki Kanda and Edward Rock, *The Anatomy of Corporate Law. A Comparative and Functional Approach* (Oxford and New York: Oxford University Press, 2004); discussed in David A. Skeel Jr., 'Corporate Anatomy Lessons' (2004) 113 *Yale Law Journal* 1519–1577.

[21] Wolfgang Streeck, *Reforming Capitalism. Institutional Change in the German Political Economy* (Oxford: Oxford University Press, 2009).

[22] Wolfgang Streeck, 'German Capitalism: Does It Exist? Can It Survive?', in Colin Crouch and Wolfgang Streeck (eds.), *Political Economy of Modern Capitalism* (London: Sage, 1997); Wolfgang Streeck and Kozo Yamamura (eds.), *The Origins of Nonliberal Capitalism in Germany and Japan: Cornell Studies in Political Economy* (Ithaca: Cornell University Press, 2001); Hall and Soskice, *Varieties of Capitalism*.

[23] Polanyi, *The Great Transformation*.

[24] See also Mark Granovetter, 'The Impact of Social Structure on Economic Outcomes' (2005) 19 *Journal of Economic Perspectives* 33–50.

[25] J. Rogers Hollingsworth, 'Continuities and Changes in the Social Systems of Production: The Cases of Japan, Germany, and the United States', in J. Rogers Hollingsworth and Robert Boyer (eds.), *Contemporary Capitalism. The Embeddedness of Institutions* (Cambridge: Cambridge University Press, 1997).

[26] Neil Fligstein, *The Architecture of Markets. An Economic Sociology of Twenty-First Century Capitalist Societies* (Princeton: Princeton University Press, 2001).

[27] Steven Weber (ed.), *Globalization and the European Political Economy* (New York: Columbia University Press, 2001); Jonathan Zeitlin and David Trubek (eds.), *Governing Work and Welfare in a New Economy: European and American Experiments* (Oxford and New York: Oxford University Press, 2003).

governance experts. Building on the past twenty-five years of intensive research in the noted fields, the contributors to this volume integrate work done in comparative law, new institutional economics, comparative political economy, regulatory theory, economic sociology and social norms theory in a serious manner. There is no question for these authors that the regulatory landscape of corporate and financial regulation has changed dramatically in an era of post-welfare state market intervention, marked by indirect regulation, soft law and delegation on the one hand and a dramatically integrated global market on the other. Yet the current challenges of the global financial crisis give pause, and call for a re-examination of the premises upon which capital market deregulation and the shareholder primacy viewpoint were based.

In this volume, the contributing authors engage with the concept of 'embeddedness' in a context, where the mainstream view – until very recently – sternly defended the demise of effective governmental interventions into market relations. At the present time, the renewed interest in political economy, and the varied histories of regulation and the notion of embedded institutions, reflects on a wide-reaching awareness of the importance of reassessing the foundations of institutional change.

Conclusion

Written as the financial and economic crises since 2007 continue to destabilize economies around the world, the social vulnerabilities that have been created by the shift in corporate priorities over the past three decades to short-term shareholders' interests are tragically evident. What is less evident is the way forward, from both a theoretical and policy perspective. Studying the trajectory of the past, in careful detail; developing an analysis of the pressures of finance capitalism and implications of those pressures; and examining views of the firm with a broader perspective on the interests to be considered, while attending to the conditions necessary for institutional learning, is the task we've set for ourselves. We bring together the enclosed chapters to challenge, to inspire discussion, and to suggest ideas for that way forward, a way that we suggest must better accommodate broader societal interests within the financial Prometheus that concentrated capital and financial innovation have unbound.

Part I

Historical trajectories of business and regulation

2 Corporate governance and financial crisis in the long run

Simon Deakin

I Introduction

The corporation is the basic organizational unit, and among the most fundamental legal institutions, of a market economy. It should be capable of contributing both to economic growth and, arguably, to human development in a broader sense. There are, however, influential voices which doubt its capacity to do this. Joel Bakan's description of the corporation as a "pathological institution, a dangerous possessor of the great power it yields over people and societies," might have seemed exaggerated to some. Yet Bakan's point was precisely grounded in what he described as the company's "legally defined mandate ... to pursue, relentlessly and without exception, its own self interest, regardless of the often harmful consequences it might cause to others."[1] Behavioral economics defines a sociopath as one who "treats others instrumentally, caring only about what he derives from the interaction, whatever the cost to the other party."[2] Such behavior, while regarded as universal and in some sense "natural" by the axioms of neoclassical economics, is probably confined to a minority of human beings; around a quarter of participants in ultimatum game experiments display entirely self-regarding behavior in this sense.[3] Somehow, at the beginning of the twenty-first century, the corporation had evolved to the point of being a sociopathic institution, at odds with deep-rooted pro-social tendencies in human psychology and behavior.

This chapter is an updated version of my Tanner Lectures, entitled *Corporate Governance and Human Development*, delivered at the University of Oxford in February 2008. I am grateful to the trustees of the Tanner Foundation for permission to draw on that material here.

[1] J. Bakan, *The Corporation. The Pathological Pursuit of Profit and Power* (London: Constable, 2004), at pp. 1–2.
[2] H. Gintis, *The Bounds of Reason: Game Theory and the Unification of the Behavioral Sciences* (Princeton: Princeton University Press, 2009), p. 49.
[3] G. Bolton and R. Zwick, "Anonymity versus punishment in ultimatum games" (1995) 10 *Games and Economic Behavior* 95.

The point was not lost on certain commentators occupying a pivotal position in the contemporary practice of corporate governance. According to Leo Strine, Vice Chancellor of the Delaware Court of Chancery, the subject-matter of corporate governance – the matters which interest the "haves of the corporate governance world" who include institutional investors, non-executive directors, CEOs and activist shareholders – were not addressing the questions "most relevant to ordinary people." These included: "will the economy continue to produce well-paying, decent jobs in the face of international competition? … Can the [American] nation afford to honor the promises made to retirees as the percentage of the population that is elderly markedly increases? How can citizens of Western nations maintain their current lifestyles while reducing their disproportionate consumption of the Earth's natural resources?"[4] Yet, according to Strine, it was "simply silly to believe that questions like these will be fairly and justly considered in the corporate polity itself, in which the only constituency with a vote is capital and in which the only other constituency with real power are the directors and top managers."[5]

The orthodox position of corporate governance theory is that companies exist to maximize shareholder returns. Strine, as "someone from Delaware steeped in the evolution of corporate behaviour during the last forty years," acknowledged a "sweeping victory" for the claim that the purpose of the company is to "maximise corporate profits for stockholders."[6] During the forty years' ascendancy of shareholder value described by Strine, the human person disappeared from the economic theory of the firm. Economic theory had formerly stressed the distinctiveness of the firm as an organizational entity, emerging out of but also separate from market forms of governance, and had seen the employment relationship as the firm's main defining feature.[7] The argument that the firm was after all just a "nexus of contracts," which began to gain ground in the 1970s, represented a turning point.[8] By the mid-1990s the predominant theory was describing employees, or human assets as they had become known, as strictly "non-essential" to the firm, the essence of which was seen as the control of intellectual and physical property by managers acting as the shareholders' agents.[9]

---

[4] L. Strine, "Human freedom and the two Friedmen: musings on the implications of globalization for the effective regulation of corporate behaviour," Torys Lecture, University of Toronto, September 20, 2007, at pp. 41–42.
[5] *Ibid.* [6] *Ibid.*, at p. 26.
[7] R.H. Coase, "The nature of the firm" (1937) 4 *Economica* (NS) 386.
[8] M. Jensen and W. Meckling, "Theory of the firm: managerial behavior, agency costs and capital structure" (1976) 3 *Journal of Financial Economics* 305.
[9] O. Hart, *Firms, Contracts and Financial Structure* (Oxford: Clarendon Press, 1995).

The financial crisis highlighted the fault lines within corporate governance. The growing influence of the shareholder value norm on corporate practice had exacerbated the asset price bubbles of the 1990s and 2000s[10] and heightened the fragility of financial sector firms.[11] Failing firms had not, on the whole, suffered from inadequate governance as that was defined by the consensus of the time; most of them had independent boards, separate chair and CEO roles, and limited defenses, if any, against hostile takeover.[12] Yet, the immediate response of policymakers was to suggest a strengthening of the shareholder value norm, with a growing role for independent directors and external shareholder monitoring proposed as measures likely to prevent future corporate failures.[13] As the immediate crisis receded in the course of 2009–2010, so did the pressure for reform, which in any case had arguably failed to address principal contribution of governance to the crisis, namely the shareholder value norm itself.

This chapter aims to put recent events in a wider perspective by considering the relationship between corporate governance and financial crisis in the long run. Crises and scandals have shaped much of modern company legislation and, more recently, have shaped corporate governance codes. Over the long run, however, the corporate form has responded, if imperfectly, to the context provided by industrialization and the growth of the market economy, and to the functional needs of business organizations to which these developments gave rise.[14] Modern corporate law is the product of these dual pressures, short-term and long-term, and they will both play a role in shaping corporate governance in the post-crisis period. To develop this theme, Section II provides an overview of the relatively recent development of the shareholder value norm in the last decades of the previous century and the first decade of the present one, and contrasts it with the longer-run co-evolution of company law and the industrial market economy. Section III focuses on the anatomy of corporate failure during the 2000s and the role of governance within it. Section IV considers the evolution of corporate governance in the aftermath of the crisis. Section V concludes.

---

[10] See Chapter 13, this volume.
[11] W. Bratton and M. Wachter, "The case against shareholder empowerment" (2010) 158 *University of Pennsylvania Law Review* 653.
[12] B. Cheffins, "Did corporate governance 'fail' during the 2008–9 stock market meltdown?" ECGI Law Working Paper No. 124/2009.
[13] *Walker Review of Corporate Governance of UK Banking Industry* (London: HM Treasury, 2009), available at: www.hm-treasury.gov.uk/walker_review_information.htm (last accessed February 20, 2011).
[14] M. Aoki, *Corporations in Evolving Diversity: Cognition, Governance and Institutions* (Oxford: Oxford University Press, 2010).

II Shareholder value: an aberration in the evolution of corporate law?

The so-called "shareholder value" norm is not simply or even principally a legal rule or principle. It is above all a practice which shapes managerial behavior in large, listed US and British firms, and increasingly those in other jurisdictions. Institutional investors refer to themselves as corporate "owners."[15] Share options account for an increasing proportion of top executive remuneration.[16] Corporate performance is evaluated using shareholder-value based metrics, which are continuously evolving.[17] Hostile takeover bids and the interventions of activist shareholders are designed to ensure that corporate assets are being efficiently used and, if they are not, that they are then redeployed elsewhere in the economy.[18] Employees are encouraged to hold corporate stock in a variety of forms and to see their pensions as investments dependent on stock market performance.[19]

As recently as the 1960s, the mission statements of large companies and the public declarations of industry bodies such as the Confederation of British Industry ("CBI") in Britain and the US Business Roundtable referred to corporate objectives in entirely different terms.[20] Companies should, it was suggested, be providing secure jobs and good working conditions; they should minimize environmental damage; and they should seek close ties with local communities. They should accept their fiscal obligations in a responsible way, knowing that the maintenance of the public space ultimately depended on the surplus which they generated. These corporate mission statements normally did not mention shareholders at all. This was deliberate. Shareholders were seen not just as passive, but as *irrelevant* to the running of the company.[21] In the middle decades of the twentieth century, company law in the UK and

---

[15] The International Corporate Governance Network, an association predominantly consisting of institutional shareholders, refers to "responsible ownership": ICGN Chair Peter Montagnon, quoted in *FT Fund Management*, August 20, 2007.
[16] L. Bebchuk and J. Fried, *Pay without Performance: The Unfulfilled Promise of Executive Compensation* (Cambridge, MA: Harvard University Press, 2004); see also Chapter 18, this volume.
[17] J. Froud, S. Johal, A. Leaver and K. Williams *Financialisation and Strategy: Narrative and Numbers* (London: Routledge, 2006), ch. 3.
[18] L. Summers, *London Stock Exchange Bicentennial Lecture* (London: London Stock Exchange, 2001).
[19] K. Ambachtsheer and D. Ezra, *Pension Fund Excellence: Creating Value for Stakeholders* (Chichester: Wiley, 1998).
[20] S. Jacoby, *The Embedded Corporation: Corporate Governance and Employment Relations in Japan and the United States* (Princeton: Princeton University Press, 2005).
[21] J. Galbraith, *The New Industrial State* (London: Hamish Hamilton, 1967).

the United States took the clear view that management was the responsibility of the board alone.[22] The practice was for the board to delegate that power to a cadre of professional, salaried employees, few of whom would hold stock in the company. The shareholders not only had no legal right to intervene in management issues; they rarely exercised the few voice rights they had. Annual shareholders' meetings were normally formalities.

Notwithstanding the policy focus in recent years on the strengthening of shareholder rights, company law regimes continue to provide that the directors, and not the shareholders, have the principal responsibility for the management of the company.[23] Thus company law sees the corporation as an exercise in group cooperation based on delegation. Property rights are pooled and held in the form of collective assets which are ring-fenced or "partitioned" for the benefit of the organization.[24] The company exists to take advantage of the mutual specialization of the assets thereby placed at its disposal. Without such specialization, it has no comparative advantage over contractual or "market-based" forms of economic organization. For specialization to create a surplus, there must be a governance structure which recognizes that each of the relevant inputs has value to the firm.[25] The principal objective of this governance structure is to avoid mutual defection by the owners of those inputs. The permanence of the corporation as a legal form, and its separation from each of the groups supplying inputs (including the shareholders), is the

---

[22] See Chapters 4 and 5, this volume.
[23] This is formally stated in Delaware law, for example, and may be inferred from the structure of UK company law and from the model articles of association set out in successive Companies Acts (formerly "Table A").
[24] H. Hansmann and R. Kraakman, "Organisational law as asset partitioning" (2000) 44 *European Economic Review* 807.
[25] See R. Rajan and L. Zingales, "The influence of the financial revolution on the nature of firms" (2001) 91 *American Economic Review* 206, discussing the implications of the emergence of firms within which the core specialized assets are not alienable, since they are bound up with human capabilities (as opposed to the alienable non-human assets at the centre of the property-rights theory of the firm (Hart, *Firms, Contracts and Financial Structure*). Rajan and Zingales stress the sense in which firms in which human capabilities represented all or nearly all of the enterprise's value constituted a new phenomenon in the 1990s and 2000s, but from the point of view of the resource-based theory of the firm (originating with E. Penrose, *The Theory of the Growth of the Firm* (Oxford: Blackwell, 1959)), all firms, to some degree, had core capabilities which included the know-how, expertise and loyalty of employees. For analyses incorporating this point of view into a legal framework, see M. Blair, *Corporate Ownership and Control* (Washington, DC: Brookings Institution, 1995); W. Njoya, 2007, *Property in Work: The Employment Relationship in the Anglo-American Firm* (Aldershot: Ashgate, 2007); on the consequences of the financialization of the firm, see also Chapter 7, this volume.

basis for its continuity. This averts the end-game problem and with it the threat of non-cooperation.[26]

Although this core feature of corporate form is sometimes referred to as "permanence," "indeterminacy" might be a better term. Company law and employment law both recognize the importance of indeterminate commitments. Capital is tied up, not permanently, but for an indeterminate period. The shareholders can neither simply demand it back nor is there a sunset clause.[27] Likewise, the so-called "permanent" or "lifetime job" is better understood as the indeterminate-duration contract of employment, with no clear end point identified. In a market economy, no company, and possibly no other organization, can guarantee permanent employment, because reorganization is an ever-present possibility; but neither can a company guarantee to produce returns for its investors. The company is nevertheless more than the sum total of the contracts entered into on its behalf.

Employees are formally absent from Anglo-American company law, by and large, as are creditors, and it is only the shareholders, as members, who have the right to hold the board to account and to replace it if they are not happy with the direction of the company. To say that the directors, let alone the managers or employees, are thereby constituted as the 'agents' of the shareholders, as contemporary economic theory does, is, however, to glide over a complex bundle of rights, obligations and expectations which make up the "default terms" of the corporate contract. Agency implies delegation and, conversely, accountability, but not necessarily unilateral control. Company law traditionally shielded managers and employees from direct shareholder control, using the concept of separate and permanent corporate personality to this end.[28]

---

[26] The theory of non-cooperative games predicts that in a context where the individual parties have strong incentives to "defect" because, in terms of their individual well-being, they will always be better off doing so, in part because they cannot make perfectly enforceable agreements to share in the rents from cooperation (as in the prisoner's dilemma game), the possibility of repeated trading can alter the incentive structure and provide the basis for a stable equilibrium in which aggregate welfare is maximized. Under such circumstances, the role of legal institutions is not to provide perfect contract enforcement (the law cannot supply this on its own if there are positive monitoring and verification costs, which there will be in most situations of complex contracting), but to create an indefinite or indeterminate time horizon for contracting. This is what many of the legal institutions of the firm, including the corporate form and the employment contract, do. See S. Deakin, "Learning about contacts: trust, cooperation and contract law," in R. Bachmann and A. Zaheer (eds.), *Handbook of Trust Research* (Cheltenham: Edward Elgar, 2008) for discussion of this point from a law and economics perspective.

[27] On shareholder lock-in, see M. Blair, "Locking in capital: what corporate law achieved for business organizers in the nineteenth century" (2003) 51 *UCLA Law Review* 51.

[28] See Strine, "Human freedom."

To argue that directors' fiduciary duties were owed to the company and not to the shareholders, as company law did (and in principle still does, although there are a growing number of situations where shareholders are owed duties directly, as in the case of takeover bids), was more than just a rhetorical device. It preserved the autonomy of management, leaving it free to mediate between the different corporate constituencies, with only the most minimal of judicial or regulatory supervision. As long as the enterprise was a going concern, company law had almost nothing to say about the distributional arrangements made to ensure its continuation; intervention was generally confined to end-game situations, such as insolvencies and takeovers.

The corporation or company can therefore be defined as *a legal mechanism for promoting group cooperation in production*. It is important to note that the legal or juridical concept of the company is narrower here than the economic concept of the firm. Thus there are legal aspects of the "firm" as a productive entity which are not captured by company law, but which are to be found in complementary and related fields such as employment law, insolvency law and tax law. Although employees and creditors do not feature much if at all in core company law, they are inescapably present in the economic or organizational entity the "firm." Employment law, insolvency law and tax law may be defined separately from the field of company law, but they interface with company law at numerous points, and the law of the business enterprise cannot be viewed in the round unless the interactions between these areas of law are taken into account.

The legal idea of the corporation is the result of developments, mostly incremental but occasionally involving radical breaks with previous practice, over many centuries. There is a tendency to see the present-day corporate form as a pinnacle of evolutionary fitness – as the culmination, in other words, of a process of institutional selection, which has made it uniquely well suited to its current tasks. The basic features of the modern corporation – separate personality, centralized management, limited liability, free transfer of shares – have come into being, it is said, to meet the needs of the modern business enterprise, and, as such, will be found whenever and wherever that model exists.[29] A historical perspective tells us, however, that the features of the corporate form did not evolve in this way, and that its current features are not inevitably and universally linked to the currently prevailing form of the business enterprise.

---

[29] R. Kraakman, John Armour, Paul Davies, Luca Enriques, Henry B. Hansmann, Gerard Hertig, Klause Hopt, Hideki Kanda and Edward B. Rock, *The Anatomy of Corporate Law* (Oxford: Oxford University Press, 2004; 2nd edn, 2009).

The individual elements of the modern corporate form existed independently of each other, in different contexts, and at different times.[30] Joint stock, in seventeenth- and eighteenth-century England, did not always entail either limited liability or free transferability. In the British industrial revolution, few manufacturing companies had either limited liability or separate corporate personality. Trading companies and utilities, which did have these features, were set up by Act of Parliament and, as a result, tightly regulated, often by reference to what were understood to be "public interest" criteria. Free incorporation with limited liability, once established (only in stages in the 1840s and 1850s in Britain), was, to start with, largely ignored by industrial firms. Enterprises which incorporated as commercial companies had to define their objectives tightly and, for much of the nineteenth century and early parts of the twentieth century, were tightly regulated by the *ultra vires* doctrine and associated judicial techniques.

Thus the modern business enterprise appeared, in Britain at least, at a time when many of the supposedly essential features of the company law of today had not yet been invented; and the emergent corporate forms of that earlier period were buttressed by mechanisms which have since been discarded. Legal institutions develop over time in an uneven and imperfect way. They are as much the product of lock-in and contingency as they are of competitive, *ex post* selection. An appropriate biological metaphor would see them not as evolutionary peaks but as "frozen accidents,"[31] configurations reflecting the original conditions of their emergence, which have only with great difficulty, and at some cost, been adjusted to later environments.

There are good reasons for thinking that the current legal form of the business enterprise is not optimally suited to its environment. The

---

[30] See R. Harris, *Industrializing English Law: Entrepreneurship and Business Organization 1720–1844* (Cambridge: Cambridge University Press, 2000) and J. Getzler and M. Macnair, "The firm as an entity before the Corporation Acts," in P. Brand, K. Costello and W. Osborough (eds.), *Adventures of the Law: Proceedings of the Sixteenth British Legal History Conference, Dublin 2003* (Dublin: Four Courts Press, 2005) for the evolution up to the eighteenth century. On the legal structure of nineteenth-century firms and the nature of managerial techniques in the industrial revolution, S. Pollard, *The Genesis of Modern Management: A Study of the Industrial Revolution in Great Britain* (Cambridge, MA: Harvard University Press, 1965) remains an important reference point.

[31] On the idea of the "frozen accident" in genetics, see F. Crick, "The origin of the genetic code" (1968) 38 *Journal of Molecular Biology* 367, and on its application to legal evolution, see S. Deakin, "Evolution for our time: a theory of legal memetics" (2003) 55 *Current Legal Problems* 1; B. Ahlering and S. Deakin, "Labour regulation, corporate governance and legal origin: a case of institutional complementarity?" (2007) 41 *Law & Society Review* 865.

legal form of the company assumes a set of external conditions (external, that is, to the law) which no longer hold. The company limited by share capital is a structure which locks the shareholders in, in return for conferring upon them, and them alone, voice and decision-making rights which enable them to hold management to account. In such a structure the shareholders are the residual claimants in the sense that they are exposed to the residual risk of the failure of the corporate venture. They are entitled, conversely, to the residue of the surplus if the company is successful.[32] This symmetry between risk and reward explains much about the traditional legal structure of the enterprise, in particular company law's silence on other corporate constituencies, whose interests are left to be protected by contract and by regulation in complementary areas such as employment law. This model is appropriate where there is shareholder lock-in. Examples include founder-controlled or family-owned firms in which the principal shareholders are also contributing their labor and skills to the firm, and larger, listed companies in which the predominant shareholder or blockholder represents a family interest, another enterprise, or a commercial bank either acting in its own right or on a large body of individual shareholders. In the final decades of the nineteenth century and the early decades of the twentieth, a period, like our own, when financial markets were exerting a growing influence over corporate management, most listed companies in Britain and the United States still had significant family or other controlling interests; this was also the case in Germany and to a lesser degree in France.[33] There were debates in a number of countries around this time concerning the dangers of excessive managerial autonomy at a time of increased ownership diffusion. The US debate, associated with Berle and Means' classic work, although it is today the

---

[32] See E. Fama and M. Jensen, "Separation of ownership and control" (1983) 26 *Journal of Law and Economics* 301.
[33] See generally L. Hannah, "The divorce of ownership from control from 1900 onwards: recalibrating imagined global trends" (2007) 49 *Business History* 404. Hannah argues that the British position was closest to one in which the ownership of large companies was dispersed, followed by the French, at this point. In the United States and Germany, family control remained the norm well into the early decades of the twentieth century in the case of most large industrial and financial corporations. Even in the UK, where dispersion of ownership was encouraged by the "free-float" rule of the London Stock Exchange which required two-thirds of the firm's equity to be made publicly available upon a listing, families and other dominant interests retained effective control of boards and hence of companies. Even in industries with widely dispersed share ownership, such as the railway industry, most small shareholders were rentiers or speculators, and boards were entrenched against external control mechanisms such as takeover bids.

best known, was one of the last to begin.[34] Today, although similar concerns are raised within the framework of the debate over ownership and control, there is a degree of liquidity in capital markets which is historically unprecedented. Particularly in the British and US systems, but to a growing extent in France and Germany too along with other civil law or coordinate regimes, family ownership has declined. It was replaced initially by institutional ownership in the form of widely diversified pension funds and mutual funds. More recently, a growing share of publicly-traded equities has been held on a short-term basis by hedge funds, although in forms far removed from any straightforward notion of ownership: share lending, securitized instruments, and various kinds of options and futures contracts.[35]

The traditional legal model of the company is ill designed for such an environment. This is not because of the so-called agency problem which arises from the separation of ownership from control. It is argued, following Berle and Means, that dispersed owners are not in a position to control over-powerful managers. The true problem, however, lies elsewhere: it is that in capital markets characterized by a high degree of liquidity – and above all in the super-liquid capital markets of today – shareholders are no longer the residual risk bearers which the traditional company law model assumes them to be.

The agency costs of dispersed ownership are generally put forward as the justification for corporate governance reforms affecting listed companies. The response to corporate failures and scandals, which have grown in number and significance since the 1970s and in particular since the early 1990s, has been to confer more oversight powers on shareholders, and to impose tighter accountability and reporting requirements on managers.[36] Shareholders have gained significant new powers and influence. This is highly paradoxical: shareholders have

---

[34] See Hannah, "The divorce of ownership from control." The debate over the separation of ownership and control was not phrased in terms of agency costs as it is today, but in terms of the democratization of ownership, at a point when "plutocratic" interests were seen as retaining control through various means despite the wider dispersion of ownership which had occurred in the early decades of the twentieth century. Analogies between the debates of the 1980s and today, on the one hand, and those of the period 1900–1930 can be misleading, when it is remembered, for example, that in many British listed companies, a rule of one person, one vote (not the modern one share, one vote which is a priority of institutional investor interests) was the norm, in part as a consequence of listing rules designed to enhance public access to securities markets.

[35] See generally F. Partnoy and R. Thomas, "Gap filling, hedge funds, and financial innovation," in Y. Fuchita and R. Litan (eds.), *Brookings-Nomura Papers on Financial Services* (Washington, DC: Brookings Institution, 2007).

[36] On boards, see J. Gordon, "The rise of independent directors in the United States, 1950–2005: of shareholder value and stock market prices" (2007) 59 *Stanford Law*

become more powerful at a time when the contribution of equity capital to the financing of the corporate sector has been in decline; and the decline has been greatest in those countries, Britain and the United States, which have spearheaded the corporate governance revolution.

It is well known from empirical studies, but insufficiently recognized by theory, that large firms in almost all countries rely mostly on retained earnings to finance physical investment projects.[37] External finance plays a relatively minor role and new equity issues are even less significant. It is less well known, but again equally clear empirically, that the net contribution of equity finance to new investment projects in the UK and United States has been negative since around 1980.[38] In the early 2000s the trend intensified. The proportion of net equity issues to gross fixed investment in non-financial companies was positive, although never more than around 10 percent, between 1950 and 1979. It turned negative after 1980 and between 1985 and 1989 net issues were fully 25 percent less than investment; parity was almost achieved in the early 1990s but the relationship became negative again, to the extent of nearly 15 percent between 1995 and 1999 and over 20 percent between 2000 and 2006.[39] This change was brought about by increased dividend payments, and in particular through share buy-backs (in which the company itself purchases some of its issued stock from the present shareholders), from the early 1980s onwards. As capital has been retired through share buy-backs and as a consequence of mergers and takeovers, equity has been replaced by debt. As the indebtedness of firms has increased, so has their financial fragility.

There are two ways of interpreting the phenomenon of increasing shareholder power being coupled with decreasing shareholder contribution to the financing of firms.

One is to see it as the vindication of agency theory and of the corporate governance reforms which began in the 1990s. Shareholders are now in a position to ensure that managers do not divert free cash flow.

Review 1465; on takeovers, see J. Armour and D. Skeel, "Who writes the rules for hostile takeovers, and why? The peculiar divergence of US and UK takeover regulation" (2007) 95 *Georgetown Law Journal* 1727, and Chapter 11, this volume. Corporate governance trends in a wider sample of countries are tracked in M. Siems, "Shareholder protection around the world ('Leximetric II')" (2008) 33 *Delaware Journal of Corporate Law* 111.

[37] R. Rajan and L. Zingales, "What do we know about capital structure? Some evidence from international data" (1995) 50 *Journal of Finance* 1421.

[38] J. Corbett and T. Jenkinson, "How is investment financed? A study of Germany, Japan, the United Kingdom and the United States" (1997) 65 *Manchester School* 69.

[39] T. Van Treck, "A synthetic stock-flow consistent macroeconomic model of financialisation" (2009) 33 *Cambridge Journal of Economics* 467.

Projects which do not earn a rate of return at or above the returns available elsewhere on the market, even if they are profitable in themselves and create stable jobs, can be terminated on the grounds that they "destroy shareholder value." Dividend payments and share buy-backs do not just benefit shareholders; they assist in the recycling of capital to growing areas of the economy most in need of it.[40]

Another way of viewing the process is to see it, more prosaically, as rent-seeking by shareholders, exploiting the liquidity which is at their disposal to extract value from the firm. This need not be, but may well be, done at the expense of the company's longer-term organizational goals, and to the detriment of other constituencies. Survey evidence suggests that managers of listed companies in the United States are becoming more reluctant to engage in long-term projects, citing the need to meet earnings targets on a yearly or even quarterly basis.[41] Short-term performance targets are being met at the expense of long-term value maximization. Since this is not in shareholders' interests, how can it be happening? If the capital market were perfectly efficient, it would not be (by definition), but asymmetric information is one possible explanation for investors' short-term focus; shareholders cannot easily evaluate managers' claims to be investing for the longer-term, and managers may not be able to send credible signals of the value-maximizing potential of projects. Less abstractly, fund managers acting as the agents of shareholders have few incentives to look beyond the point at which they are performance-assessed (often the next quarter) while managers remunerated through share options and bonuses linked to share price movements would simply be behaving rationally if they had regard to the same short-term time horizon, at least in cases where share options have short vesting periods.[42]

---

[40] Summers, *London Stock Exchange Bicentennial Lecture*.
[41] J. Graham, C. Harvey and S. Rajgopal, "The economic implications of corporate financial reporting," NBER Working Paper No. 10050 (2005).
[42] The argument put in the text is not inconsistent with the claim that recent corporate governance reforms have empowered an elite of senior managers who have been provided with new opportunities for personal enrichment (R. Monks, *Corpocracy* (Hoboken: Wiley, 2008), ch. 5), but it is inconsistent with the argument that the solution to this problem is to strengthen shareholder rights still further (L. Bebchuk and J. Fried, *Pay without Performance* (Boston: Harvard University Press, 2004)). The growing influence of shareholders within corporate governance has been achieved not at the expense of senior managers, many of whom have directly benefited from the "alignment" of executive pay with share price increases, but at the expense of other stakeholder groups and of governmental influence over corporate behavior. To "reduce boards' insulation from shareholders" (Bebchuk and Fried, *Pay without Performance*, at p. x) would most likely exacerbate the problem.

The current negative contribution of equity finance to physical investment in the United States and UK is a new phenomenon – between the 1950s and late 1970s the contribution of equity finance to investment was positive[43] – and appears to be specific to the Anglo-American economies: equity finance plays a positive if small role in funding investment in continental European and East Asian systems, and in the developing world it plays a positive and substantial role.[44] In Britain and the United States, new firms, start-ups seeking listings, benefit from direct infusions of capital from the stock market. The complex institutional architecture of venture capital funding, with venture capitalists acting as agents of institutional investors and others to oversee a tournament-style competition between start-ups, could not work without a liquid capital market which enables the venture capitalist to cash out its gains and reward the tournament winners.[45] Yet, what works for start-ups at a pre-market stage does not work once the same firms enter the stock market: many of them insert anti-takeover devices and retain weighted voting rights for insiders in an attempt to deflect short-term shareholder pressures.[46] This trend would be troubling if it were indeed the case that venture capital funding for start-ups required the continuous recycling of "free cash flow" from established companies.

What do the capital markets offer mature firms? Agency theory suggests that they provide mechanisms of discipline and evaluation. Shareholders monitor performance and are in a position to discipline weak management by exiting the company. Share price captures expectations of future managerial performance. Failing firms or those likely to fail will be subject to a takeover bid or, in the absence of a direct third party intervention, a restructuring initiated by the existing management team. Successful firms, or those seen as likely to succeed in future, can deploy the liquidity which a rising share price provides them to fund new acquisitions.

According to this point of view, shareholder value extraction works in the public interest, by inducing superior corporate performance, and recycling capital to more highly valued uses. It is far from clear

---

[43] Corbett and Jenkinson, "How is investment financed?"
[44] Ajit Singh, Alaka Singh and B. Weisse, "Corporate governance, competition, the new international financial architecture, and large corporations in emerging markets," in N. Allington and J. McCombie (eds.), *The Cambridge Handbook of Applied Economics* (Cambridge: Cambridge University Press, 2010)
[45] M. Aoki and G. Jackson, "Understanding an emergent diversity of corporate governance and organizational architecture: an essentiality-based analysis" (2008) 17 *Industrial and Corporate Change* 1.
[46] See Google's SEC filing of 2004:www.sec.gov/Archives/edgar/data/1288776/000119312504073639/ds1.htm.

empirically that this is the case. The balance of evidence suggests that hostile takeovers in Britain and the United States do produce added value – just. Firms subject to hostile takeover outperform the industry average, but only by a small margin, and this is an average effect. The variation in outcomes is extreme, in both directions. Hostile takeovers at least do better than agreed ones, which on average lead to a loss of value. Taking agreed mergers and hostile takeovers together, the returns to shareholders in acquiring firms remain negative in a significant proportion of cases. There is also a highly contingent relationship between financial performance and the introduction of 'good practice' corporate governance changes by firms, such as increasing the number of non-executive directors or separating the chair/CEO roles.[47]

Hostile takeovers and restructurings almost invariably lead to asset disposals and hence to downsizing.[48] Downsizing has been linked to higher dividend payouts.[49] Restructuring can lead to more efficient use of labor in the short run, as empirical studies point to productivity improvements post-takeover.[50] It is more difficult to measure the possible longer-term impact of a "breach of trust" on the part of the firm, in the sense of a reneging on implicit contracts entered into by the previous management. The cost of displacement for workers made redundant also has to be taken into account. There is evidence for the UK and United States that job loss through redundancy entails a drop in earnings lasting several years, suggesting that workers dismissed as a result of restructuring lose part of the value of the firm-specific human capital they had previously accumulated.[51]

---

[47] For a recent overview of the evidence, see A. Cosh, P. Guest and A. Hughes, "UK corporate governance and takeover performance," in K. Gugler and B. Yurtoglu (eds.), *The Economics of Corporate Governance and Mergers* (Cheltenham: Edward Elgar, 2008).

[48] S. Deakin, R. Hobbs, D. Nash and G. Slinger, "Implicit contracts, takeovers and corporate governance: in the shadow of the City Code," in D. Campbell, H. Collins and J. Wightman (eds.), *Implicit Dimensions of Contract* (Oxford: Hart, 2003) review this process in the context of the UK takeover wave of the mid-1990s.

[49] See M. O'Sullivan, *Contests for Corporate Control: Corporate Governance and Economic Performance in the United States and Germany* (Oxford: Oxford University Press, 2000); for a more skeptical view on the links between downsizing and shareholder value, which nevertheless points to increases in dividend payouts in the UK from the 1980s onwards (for the United States, distributions go up in nominal terms but not when measured against cash flow), see Froud *et al.*, *Financialisation and Strategy*, ch. 4. L. Uchitelle, *The Disposable American: Layoffs and their Consequences* (New York: Knopf, 2006), gives an account based on case studies of the corporate strategies which linked downsizing to increased profitability and shareholder returns in the United States from the 1980s onwards, which, he argues, are intensifying.

[50] See M. Conyon, S. Girma, S. Thompson and P. Wright, "The impact of mergers and acquisitions on company employment in the United Kingdom" (2002) 6 *European Economic Review* 31.

[51] The evidence is reviewed by W. Njoya, *Property in Work* (Aldershot: Ashgate, 2007).

Downsizing, in general, has been one of the factors behind growing wage inequality in Britain and the United States, where the gap between white-collar and blue-collar wages has been increasing since the 1970s. The growth of shareholder influence over the firm in Britain and the United States has gone hand-in-hand with a historic reversal of the trend for a growing proportion of national income to be taken by labour; since the early 1980s, the factor share of capital has been going up. Wage levels in the United States have been stagnant in real terms across the board during this period, and the median wage has fallen at the same time as CEO pay has risen rapidly, in large part as a result of the growing use of share options and other equity-based remuneration systems in top executive pay. The top 1 percent of earners in the United States saw their pay rise by 181 percent between 1972 and 2001 while median earnings fell by 0.4 percent.[52] More generally, and notwithstanding the importance of institutional share ownership, shares are disproportionately held by groups higher up the income scale, with the effect being particularly skewed at the top.[53] This is partly why the share of national income taken by the top 1 percent in Britain and the United States, which was 20 percent in 1925 and declined to 7 percent and 10 percent respectively by 1980, has risen to 13 percent and 17 percent respectively by 2004. Top income shares were stable over the same period in continental Europe and Japan.[54]

In principle, share price increases, which are not supported by underlying corporate performance, are "virtual wealth" which cannot be accessed without triggering a stock market fall.[55] However, from the mid-1980s, a high and rising share price began to be a source of value in itself for companies, which they could use to lever access to debt finance. Rises in the nominal value of shares were accompanied by increased flows of debt-based finance and consumer credit, enabling firms and households to realize the virtual gains stemming from equity ownership.[56] Companies used a rising share price as collateral and as a cash equivalent in order to raise financing for takeover bids, while households used rising asset values (in equities initially and, more recently, in property) in the same way to increase their indebtedness. In Britain and the United States levels of household debt had reached

---

[52] See Chapter 13, this volume.
[53] J. Froud, C. Haslam, S. Johal and K. Williams, "Accumulation under conditions of inequality" (2001) 8 *Review of International Political Economy* 66.
[54] Chapter 13, this volume.
[55] A. Bhaduri, K. Laski and M. Riese, "A model of interaction between the virtual and the real economy" (2006) 57 *Metroeconomica* 412.
[56] Van Treck, "Financialisation."

unprecedented levels by the mid-2000s, compensating to some degree for falling or stagnant earnings (in the United States); although, again, the effect of this process on household wealth was uneven, and skewed toward the higher income groups. In the United States the highest 20 percent of households by income, which disproportionately benefited from rising share price values, also accounted for most of the rise in household indebtedness and the corresponding overall fall in the personal savings rate.[57]

In part as a consequence of the changes to corporate governance described above, the British and US economies of the 2000s experienced a process of financially-driven growth similar to that of earlier phases of rapid stock market development, such as in the United States in the 1920s: with growing access to credit, asset values were inflated, firms and households took on additional debt, and growing inequality of earnings and wealth were the result.[58] There was economic growth, but on fragile foundations. These conditions set the scene for the corporate failures of the 2000s.

III   Shareholder value and corporate failure: from Enron to the crisis of 2008–2009

In Enron's case, an inflated share price, the result of the bubble in new economy stocks of the late 1990s, distorted the company's priorities beyond the point where its highly ambitious business plan could be maintained. The company, initially a utility, came to act if it was principally a clearing house for energy futures. Enron was the market intermediary for futures contracts and other risk-allocation devices which it claimed to be able to price uniquely efficiently, thanks to its combination of an underlying utility business with a market trading "overlay." It was undoubtedly innovative, as numerous business school case studies of the time pointed out, although some of its claims to have invented "new markets" and a "new corporate model" should in retrospect have been a warning sign. Enron's business plan failed not because its executives were paying themselves huge sums, nor because its non-executive board members were paid high consulting fees, nor even because universities and hospitals to which board members were connected were given generous donations. It failed because it used its rising share price to finance off-balance sheet transactions, the aim of which, in the company's final stages, was to inflate the share price by exaggerating the company's earnings. The strategy could not survive

[57] *Ibid.*   [58] Chapter 13, this volume.

the general stock market fall which began in early 2000: as Enron was using its own stock to capitalize its SPVs, the fall in the value of its shares, made these SPVs, and ultimately the company's own balance sheet position, unsustainable.[59]

Enron was a company "laser focused on earnings per share" to the degree that, in its final stages, the underlying business ceased to matter except as a means of maintaining the impression of high earnings. But Enron was simply taking to extremes a strategy which many other companies were to follow in the course of the 2000s. The lessons of the Enron case were missed in part because the effects of its failure, while catastrophic, were circumscribed. State pension funds which had over-invested in Enron stock suffered significant losses, but institutional shareholders with diversified holdings had limited exposure to the failure of a single firm. Those bearing the greatest residual risk were Enron employees who lost their jobs and also much of their retirement incomes. Enron's practice of pension fund "self-investment," coupled with a pensions "blackout" in force during the weeks prior to its bankruptcy, left these employees doubly exposed to the consequences of the company's failure.

Enron's fall was interpreted as an isolated case of corporate fraud or, alternatively, as a corporate governance failure which stemmed from conflicts of interest among senior managers and board members. The company's collapse undoubtedly revealed fraud and conflicts of interest which would otherwise have remained undiscovered. However, the more fundamental causes were a combination of the context the company was operating in – the dotcom boom and related share price bubble of the late 1990s – and its strategy of pursuing share price maximization through the aggressive use of self-capitalized SPVs.

The view that Enron was a corporate governance "scandal" found clear expression in the Sarbanes–Oxley Act of 2002. But this legislation made the basic problem – the tendency for share price maximization to displace productive activity as a corporate strategy – worse. Almost every change made by the Sarbanes–Oxley Act, from requiring additional and more frequent reporting to loading new obligations upon corporate governance actors from boards to advisers, strengthened the shareholder value norm. Sarbanes–Oxley, and the associated changes introduced to listing rules, reinforced the idea that the board should consist as far as possible of outside directors with limited contact with

---

[59] On the Enron case, see W. Bratton, "Enron and the dark side of shareholder value" (2002) 76 *Tulane Law Review* 1275; S. Deakin and S. Konzelmann, "Learning from Enron" (2004) 12 *Corporate Governance: an International Review* 134–142.

the company whose job was to monitor the executive team. This was despite the absence of any evidence to link ineffective monitoring to the lack of independence of directors, either at Enron or elsewhere. A *better informed* audit committee, when told by Enron's auditors in the late 1990s that its SPV structures were "at the edge" of acceptable practice, might not have replied that they were, instead, "leading edge."[60]

Sarbanes–Oxley followed a familiar pattern in company law. The history of company legislation in Britain in the twentieth century has very largely been one of successive responses to high-profile corporate failures. British Companies Acts have largely been backward looking, and have rarely been successful in anticipating the form of future failures.[61] Shortly after the passage of one such Act, a commentator complained that "one of the evils of the system of 'boom' finance … is the interlocking of companies whose balance sheets are designed to conceal their mutual relations. Under this system it is possible to buttress up the credit of A company of the group by B company of the group operating in A's shares on the Stock Exchange. Such methods of finance cannot always be detected or eliminated."[62] It was unfortunate then that "the new Companies Act … failed to require a holding company to publish a consolidated balance sheet and income account or an interlocking company to publish details of its holdings. It is, of course, impossible to legislate the unscrupulous promoter out of the City, but his operations would be rendered less easy if an amendment to remedy this defect of the Companies Act were brought on the Statute-book."[63]

This commentator was writing about the events not of 2008 but of 1929. The requirement that companies should produce consolidated balance sheets was one of the reforms put in place in the UK by the 1947 and 1948 Companies Acts and which paved the way for the modernization of company accounts and the post-war rehabilitation of stock markets based on a disclosure regime. The same process was a pivotal part of the New Deal reforms to company and securities law in the United States, following the Great Crash. How then was it possible for companies in the early 2000s to be using special purpose entities and other off-balance sheet vehicles to conceal potential liabilities, as Enron did? Financial regulators had been persuaded to accept the relevant changes to accounting auditing principles in order to facilitate

---

[60] See Deakin and Konzelmann, "Learning from Enron."
[61] This process is comprehensively mapped by A. Lee, "Law, economic theory, and corporate governance: the origins of UK legislation on company directors' conflicts of interests, 1862–1948," PhD Thesis, University of Cambridge.
[62] E. Davenport, "After Hatry" (1930) 107 *Nineteenth Century and After* 353.
[63] *Ibid.*

off-balance sheet modes of financing. The move was triggered by the interdependence between rising stock market values and new forms of financial intermediation.

In the more recent financial crisis, the first significant corporate failure was that of the British bank and former building society, Northern Rock. As in 1929, this had been preceded by the adoption of a (huge) Companies Act which turned out to be mostly irrelevant to the crisis. Yet, a failure such as that of Northern Rock had been predicted. At the point when building societies legislation was liberalized in the late 1980s, it was argued (although to little avail at the time) that inadequate controls were being placed over the process of their conversion into listed companies. From their earliest beginnings in the British industrial revolution, building societies were attractive to savers and borrowers alike precisely because they were not commercial banks, which were prone to taking greater risks with deposits and had a much high failure rate. Building societies had unique corporate arrangements, underpinned by legislation from the Victorian period, which were designed to minimize the risks of such failures. Their legal structure ensured that the surplus generated from their operation was preserved for future generations of house buyers. The current depositor-members of a building society, despite being "shareholders" in a formal sense, had no means of accessing that surplus, until the passage of deregulatory legislation in 1989. This allowed building societies to become listed companies and make an almost immediate cash disbursement to their members. Because it was possible to become a member by paying a small deposit into a savings account, and accessing, on conversion, a sum several times the amount of that deposit, it did not take long for building societies to come under pressure to convert to commercial bank status, and many did. Incentives for managers, whose pay rose considerably upon conversion, also helped drive the process. Mass conversion from mutual to commercial bank status took place in the face of evidence that long-term savers and borrowers preferred mutuals for their long-term orientation and local links. It also gave rise to a rare natural experiment for corporate governance forms. The risk of moral hazard posed by deregulatory legislation was much discussed when the conversions of the 1990s were at their height. The failure of Northern Rock demonstrated that these concerns had been more than merely theoretical.[64]

---

[64] For further detail on the points made in this paragraph, see J. Cook, S. Deakin and A. Hughes, "Mutuality and corporate governance: the evolution of UK building societies following deregulation" (2002) 2 *Journal of Corporate Law Studies* 110.

Northern Rock publicly made strong claims for the effectiveness of its corporate governance arrangement as a listed company. After its failure, it was claimed by senior members of its board that the circumstances of its collapse could not have been foreseen. The bank had insufficient reserves to cope with the freezing up of the inter-bank credit market which began in the summer of 2007. While this can be characterized as an unusual event, the point remains that the "straitjacket" of the traditional building society structure had been there to minimize exposure to precisely such risks. The nature of the rescue of Northern Rock was also significant. During the winter of 2007–2008, UK government intervention safeguarded the bank's depositors. The government also went to extreme lengths to safeguard the interests of its shareholders, even those of the speculative funds which purchased Northern Rock stock in the anticipation of a government-led rescue, only accepting after a considerable interval that de facto nationalization of the bank was unavoidable. As in the case of Enron, the residual risk fell mostly on the employees, who were made redundant, and on the taxpayer.

This pattern of deregulation leading to financial fragility and eventually to corporate failure has been repeated several times as the financial crisis developed. The US investment banks most affected by the crisis of 2008 were among those which had lobbied most strongly for the repeal of the Glass–Steagall Act and for the lifting of minimum deposit requirements a few years before. The British bank HBOS, like Northern Rock, was a creature of building society deregulation. As bankruptcy proceedings for Lehman Brothers continued into 2010, documents revealed a familiar pattern of the use of SPVs to give a false impression of earnings growth in the bank's final months.[65] In many of the failed or near-failed banks, there is evidence that managerial incentives were skewed toward the short-term, and executives came under pressure from boards to maintain share-price growth through aggressive trading strategies, increasing leverage, regular restructurings, and participation in mergers and takeovers.[66]

Although by no means the sole cause of the corporate failures of the late 2000s, shareholder-value oriented corporate governance significantly contributed to them, providing an important part of the external context of financial instability, and exacerbating the misalignment of

---

[65] On the use of "form over substance" transactions by Lehman Bros. in the months prior to its bankruptcy, see the report prepared by the bankruptcy examiner, Anton R. Valukas (available online at: http://lehmanreport.jenner.com/, in particular Vol. 3 (last accessed February 22, 2011)).

[66] See Bratton and Wachter, "The case against shareholder empowerment."

incentives within firms. Yet neither the various government-led rescues, nor the wider regulatory response, have addressed the role played by corporate governance norms and structures in precipitating the crisis. In the UK, the Walker review[67] recommended additional powers for non-executive directors and a strengthening of the role of the board in monitoring executive decision-making as means of averting a future crisis. Stricter rules on director independence in the UK and United States have brought about a situation in which many non-executive directors "lack industry-specific experience or knowledge." Thanks also to these same changes, "corporate directors – in contrast to their predecessors of decades past – now have a clear focus on one constituency, the equity holders, and that is the constituency most interested in aggressive risk taking."[68] Thus as with Sarbanes–Oxley earlier in the decade, Walker's response does not address, and indeed is likely to exacerbate, the underlying problem of excessive focus on shareholder returns.

An alternative solution, the remutualization of parts of the banking sector, has been canvassed in the UK,[69] but has yet to be adopted. The rescue of Northern Rock set a pattern of government subsidy for depositors and shareholders, displacing losses on to employees and taxpayers. Scaled up, this is now being repeated as Western governments respond to the costs of the wider economic rescue package of 2008–2009 by cutting welfare state expenditure. Under these unpromising circumstances, what are the prospects for post-crisis corporate governance?

IV   Corporate governance after the crisis

In the absence of a new regulatory framework, corporate governance practice is likely to respond in the near future to developments within financial markets, which include changes in the composition of share ownership and shifts in investment strategy. A first factor to consider is the increasingly rapid disintegration of the defined benefit pension scheme model. This is both cause and effect of shift to shareholder-value oriented corporate governance.

The defined benefit pension scheme has been the standard form of the private-sector occupational pension fund in Britain for most of

---

[67] *Review of Corporate Governance of UK Banking Industry*, available at: www.frc.org.uk/corporate/walker.cfm (last accessed February 22, 2011).
[68] L. Strine, "The role of Delaware in the American corporate governance system, and some preliminary musings on the meltdown's implications for corporate law," lecture to the conference on *Governance of the Modern Firm 2008*, Molengraaff Institute for Private Law, Utrecht University, December 13, 2008, at p. 26.
[69] 'Government considers remutualising Northern Rock', *Guardian*, October 2009, p. 4.

the twentieth century.[70] As recently as the mid-1990s, there was still near-universal support in official and employer circles for the defined benefit model. Unlike the social insurance schemes of the continent of Europe, which, at that stage, were mostly in deficit and facing considerable future liabilities thanks to demographic factors (the so-called "ageing" of the working population), the UK system was thought to be stable and sustainable. The long-term liabilities of the state scheme had been limited by cuts carried out in the 1980s, and employer-based schemes, being funded through investments as opposed to being paid out of current contributions in contrast to the "pay as you go" schemes of the continent, provided an apparently secure basis for future retirement incomes.

Fifteen years on, the UK route no longer appears such an attractive option. Numbers in defined benefit schemes are now only a third of the level they reached at their height in the 1960s, and are falling quickly. Employers are closing defined benefit schemes to new entrants and offering them less secure defined contribution options instead. In some cases, defined benefit schemes are also being closed to future contributions from current members. In others, employers are ending any involvement in their schemes by selling the assests in funds to insurance companies and to pension buyout firms which have recently emerged to specialize in this type of transaction. Liabilities attaching to the vested rights of pensioners and remaining active members are absorbed by the purchaser, who may continue to keep schemes open to current employees on the same terms as before, but generally will not do so.

In the 1980s and 1990s, employers used pension scheme surpluses to take contribution "holidays." In the 2000s, most schemes have been in deficit. A significant factor here has been a tighter regulatory framework coupled with a new accounting standard. Beginning in the 1990s, regulation imposed new costs on funds, requiring limited indexation of benefits with inflation, and tightening reporting and disclosure standards. Shortfalls in schemes were reclassified as debts owed to the fund by the employer. From 2003, it became possible for trustees, backed up by powers granted to the pension regulator, to claim these amounts as a sum due from the employer immediately, even if the employer was paying out and the fund was solvent. Pension schemes now began to appear

---

[70] The account of pension fund governance in the following paragraphs is based on J. Buchanan and S. Deakin, "Pension fund governance: evolution of the trust model," CBR Working Paper series (forthcoming). See also, for background on pension fund governance in the UK, P. Thornton (ed.), *Good Governance for Pension Schemes* (Cambridge: Cambridge University Press, forthcoming).

as serious long-term drains on the financial position of companies, with the potential to affect their share price and credit ratings.

Under the original trust model, the employer had considerable flexibility.[71] It could set the terms of the scheme and reserve discretionary powers both to itself as settlor and to the trustees, both over the level of contributions and over the content of the basic pensions promise. Employees, their contributions notwithstanding, were in the position of passive beneficiaries. While not volunteers (since they did contribute to schemes), their contractual rights were limited, since employment contracts were drafted in such a way as to reserve powers of amendment to the employer in the same way as trust deeds reserved similar powers to trustees. There was little or no standardization of the terms of trust deeds and limited external regulation of their contents. The trustees were normally senior managers and directors of the sponsor. This apparent conflict of interest was perhaps less of a problem than it seemed: trustees and beneficiaries had a common interest in maintaining the viability of the sponsor-employer and in ensuring that it was in a position to continue supporting the scheme, since it could not be legally compelled to do so. Having overlapping membership of the main company and the board of trustees gave expression to an underlying identity of interest between the sponsor and the fund.

The legal nature of the defined benefit pension fund changed decisively in 2003 when new legislation deemed pension fund shortfalls to be debts immediately owing by employers to schemes, with the regulator given extensive powers to oversee their collection. From the government's perspective, such powers were essential if employers were not to load liabilities on to the pension protection fund which had shortly before been set up to meet the liabilities of insolvent schemes. But the problem was that while employers now faced additional liabilities, they still had the option, inherent in the trust model, to end their commitments with regard to rights yet to vest, and this is what they have been doing in increasing numbers.

The fate of defined benefit pension funds casts into sharp relief the wider transformation of corporate governance which has taken place in the UK. In many respects they mark its *terminus ad quem*. Since the 1960s, institutional investors have been to the fore in pressing for corporate governance standards which they saw as necessary to protect their position as residual risk bearers. To safeguard themselves against what they saw as over-mighty managers, they won greater voice for

---

[71] See generally, L. Hannah, *Inventing Retirement: The Development of Occupational Pensions in Britain* (Cambridge: Cambridge University Press, 1986).

external directors, the separation of chair and CEO roles, and a clearer internal audit function. They ensured that shareholders would decide the outcome of takeover bids on financial grounds alone, with the board playing an informational role. Governance and management were not just to be separated, but placed in a clearly hierarchical relationship, with the latter subject to the former. All this was apparently being done in the name of the ultimate beneficiaries of pension funds and other mechanisms for collective saving and insurance. Employees might be made more insecure by the threat of restructuring and the end of expectations of permanent employment, but they benefited from enhanced returns to the pension funds. Insecurity of employment would be compensated for by greater security of savings and retirement income.

That idea has not survived successive takeover waves and the metamorphosis of the market for corporate control into new forms for extracting value from companies, of which the pensions buyout market is one of the recent manifestations along with private equity and hedge fund activism. Shareholder-value led corporate governance has become one of the main drivers behind the erosion of pension fund security. The new accounting standards for pension funds have crystallized risks which, in the recent past, were managed through a combination of fiscal subsidies and supportive regulation. The closure of defined benefit schemes is now being justified in shareholder-value terms.[72]

The decline of the defined benefit model will most likely see a reduced role for pension funds as capital market actors, and a growing one for private equity and hedge funds. In principle, a defined benefit pension fund should take a long-term view of its investments. In practice, pension fund trustees delegated investment decision to specialist asset managers who were set quarterly performance targets. Churning of shares was common. There nevertheless remained a sense in which a defined pension fund (at least before the recent trend in pension scheme abandonment) had an indefinite investment horizon; it had to take a view of the sustainability of the fund based on the returns it would be making when contributors retired in several decades' time. Private equity investment firms, which take listed companies private and then seek to capitalize returns from restructuring via a trade sale or re-flotation, and activist hedge funds, which take medium-sized stakes in companies with a view to triggering

---

[72] As in the case of the BT Pension Fund, whose fund management operation became the corporate governance fund, Hermes: "BT has come under constant pressure from investors to cut its pension scheme free from the business after campaigns to show it acts a barrier to growth" ("Pensions can wipe out BT profits," *Guardian*, July 2008, p. 7).

Corporate governance and financial crisis 39

dividend increases or share buy-backs, again on the basis of restructuring, generally seek to exit their investee companies within a four- to five-year period at most. Their time horizons are therefore relatively short-term by comparison with that of the defined benefit pension schemes, and are finite.

Private equity investment and hedge fund activism are becoming complementary strategies, both of which depend on an approach to value extraction which is justified in shareholder-value terms, but which also results in the displacement of losses on other corporate constituencies.[73] Private equity-led buyouts almost invariably lead to short-term redundancies and a longer-term loss of job security and undermining of collective employee representation. Interventions by hedge fund activists also tend to trigger job losses as companies downsize as part of a restructuring process or divert capital from reserves to pay for increased dividends and share buy-backs. Hedge fund interventions of this kind are associated with short-run abnormal returns for shareholders,[74] but inferior performance, reflected in reduced returns on assets, by target firms over the medium to long term.[75]

These approaches are increasingly becoming part of the corporate governance mainstream. Private equity investment companies may account for as much as a fifth of private-sector employment in the UK.[76] Almost half of US listed companies have a hedge fund investor with 5 percent or more of the company's stock. Although total hedge fund holdings are a small proportion of the overall market, trades by hedge funds just before the financial crisis accounted for 18–22 percent of turnover on the New York Stock Exchange and 30–35 percent of turnover on the London Stock Exchange. In addition they had 55 percent of all credit derivatives trading.[77]

Under these circumstances, it is difficult to be optimistic about the prospects for an investment strategy which would see shareholders playing a role, either directly through activist interventions or indirectly through the information effect of share prices, in monitoring the

---

[73] J. Froud and K. Williams, "Private equity and the culture of value extraction" (2007) 12 *New Political Economy* 405; P. Thornton, *Inside the Dark Box: Shedding Light on Private Equity* (London: Work Foundation, 2008).
[74] A. Brav, W. Jiang, F. Partnoy and R. Thomas, "Hedge fund activism, corporate governance, and firm performance" (2008) 63 *Journal of Finance* 1729.
[75] A. Klein and E. Zur, "Entrepreneurial shareholder activism: hedge funds and other private investors" (2009) 64 *Journal of Finance* 187.
[76] IE Consulting, *The Economic Impact of Private Equity in the UK* (London: British Venture Capital Association, 2008).
[77] See J. Armour and B. Cheffins, "The rise and fall (?) of shareholder activism by hedge funds," ECGI Law Working Paper No. 136 (2009).

effectiveness of firms' human resource strategies, or their approach to wider issues of social and environmental sustainability, over the long run. It is possible to imagine "a different kind of stock exchange, a social stock exchange ... that shows which companies are especially successful in the social arena."[78] Metrics exist by which companies' social and environmental records are ranked and benchmarked.[79] Stock exchanges have developed indices for ethical stocks. The methods developed, initially by private actors, are gradually being incorporated into accounting standards. There is a degree of fusion between corporate governance norms, which focus on accountability, and SRI (socially responsible investment) norms which focus on the financial and reputational risks to companies of social and environmental harm. But in systems which treat the corporation as the shareholders' private property, the highest-valued companies will continue to be those which are most effective in externalizing the costs of their activities on to others.

V   Conclusion

The company is a complex, multi-functional institution. In the fairly recent past it has provided a basis for technological innovation and the recycling of capital, while also offering meaningful, stable employment and long-term financial security. It seems increasingly unlikely that the corporation of the near future will be able to fulfill all these goals. Contemporary economic theory tells us that the human dimension is inessential to corporations, the core of which is the control exercised by property holders over the non-human assets of the firm; and that enduring organizational identities are irrelevant in what is simply a space for contracting. The reality of the contemporary corporation increasingly mirrors this view. Company law retains a vestigial sense of the corporation as an organizational entity which is greater than its constituent parts, but this idea is under pressure from an alternative conception of the corporate form, which sees it as an object of financial arbitrage. The economic growth which shareholder-value based management helped to stimulate has nevertheless turned out to be fragile, and one of its principal consequences, growing inequality, threatens social cohesion.

---

[78] Muhammad Yunus, founder of the Grameen Bank, interviewed in Bertelsmann Stiftung, *Topics: Encouraging Social Change*, January 2008.
[79] S. Lydenberg, *Corporations and the Public Interest: Guiding the Invisible Hand* (San Francisco: Berrett-Koehler, 2005).

Under these circumstances, some urgent rethinking about the goals and modes of operation of corporate governance is required. For the time being, the logic of shareholder value is still playing itself out. A long-run perspective, however, suggests that financial upheavals trigger fundamental changes of direction in company law and policy, and the crisis of the late 2000s is unlikely to be an exception.

3 Financialism: a (very) brief history

Lawrence E. Mitchell

The United States no longer is a capitalist country. It has created a new economic system that appears to be capitalist but no longer performs the functions of capitalism. Capitalism is a system in which wealth is created and sustained by the production of goods and services determined through market supply and demand. A variety of related structures support capitalism, including the institutions of finance, which provide the funds necessary for the production and trade of goods and services.

While capitalism still characterizes a portion of the US economy, it has become subordinated to a new economic order. This economic system is one in which the financial markets exist primarily to serve themselves. In this system, capital is raised for the purpose of creating, selling and trading securities and derivative securities that do not finance industry but rather trade within markets that exist as an economy unto themselves. At the same time, those markets have profound and adverse effects on the real economy.[1] This new economic system is *Financialism*.

Much has been written and said on the US-initiated global financial crisis that began in 2007 and continues today.[2] Only recently has that

---

An earlier version of this chapter was presented as a lecture at Creighton University Law School and published at (2010) 43 *Creighton Law Review* 323.

[1] Lawrence E. Mitchell, "The Morals of the Marketplace: A Cautionary Essay for Our Time" (2009) 20 *Stanford Law and Policy Review* 171; Michael Lim Mah-Hui, "From Servant to Master: The Financial Sector and the Financial Crisis" (2009) 2 *Journal of Applied Research in Accounting and Finance* 12; Robert B. Reich, *Supercapitalism* (New York: Random House, 2007).

[2] See Michael Lewis, *The Big Short: Inside the Doomsday Machine* (New York: W.W. Norton, 2010); Nouriel Roubini, *Crisis Economics: A Crash Course in the Future of Finance* (New York: Penguin Press, 2010); Andrew Ross Sorkin, *Too Big to Fail: The Inside Story of How Wall Street and Washington Fought to Save the Financial System – and Themselves* (New York: Viking, 2009); Brian R. Cheffins, "Did Corporate Governance 'Fail' During the 2008 Stock Market Meltdown? The Case of the S&P 500" (2009) 65 *Business Law* 1–65; David Schmudde, "Responding to the Subprime Mess: The New Regulatory Landscape" (2009) 14 *Fordham Journal of Corporate & Financial Law*

conversation begun to recognize the fundamental change in the function and groundwork of US capitalism that caused the crisis.[3] None of the Administration's efforts to reform the US economy address this fundamental transformation. The massive legislation that, as of the day of this writing, has passed revision in conference committee,[4] seems largely to seek to reform the regulation of existing markets and financial institutions in a manner that institutionalizes financialism and imposes little if any social or economic responsibility on them.[5] Few question whether financialism is a sound model for the sustainable future of US economic health.[6] Yet financialism threatens to rob the patrimony of future generations for the profit of the present, and damages our national security by forcing us to outsource the production of our most essential goods and services.

709; Brian J.M. Quinn, "The Failure of Private Ordering and the Financial Crisis of 2008" (2009) 5 *New York University Journal of Law & Business* 549; Paul Krugman, "How Did Economists Get It So Wrong?" *New York Times*, September 2, 2009; Justin Lahart, "The Great Recession: A Downturn Sized Up," *Wall St. Journal*, July 28, 2009, p. A12; "Recession-Plagued Nation Demands New Bubble to Invest In," *The Onion*, July 14, 2008.

[3] Greta R. Kippner, "The Financialization of the American Economy" (2005) 3 *Socio-Economic Review* 173; Ozgur Orhangazi, "Financialization and Capital Accumulation in the Nonfinancial Corporate Sector: A Theoretical and Empirical Investigation on the US Economy," Political Economy Research Institute Working Paper Series No. 149 (2007), available at: www.peri.umass.edu/fileadmin/pdf/working...101.../WP149.pdf (last accessed February 22, 2011); Lim Mah-Hui, "From Servant to Master"; Thomas I. Palley, "Financialization: What It Is and Why It Matters," Levy Economic Institute Working Paper No. 525 (2007), available at: www.levy.org/vdoc.aspx?docid=971 (last accessed February 22, 2011); Engelbert Stockhammer, "Financialization and the Slowdown of Accumulation," Vienna University of Economics and Business Working Paper No. 14 (2000), available at: http://epub.wu-wien.ac.at/dyn/virlib/wp/eng/showentry?ID=epub-wu-01_18e (last accessed February 22, 2011). See also Lawrence E. Mitchell, "The Legitimate Rights of Public Shareholders" (2009) 66 *Washington and Lee Law Review* 1635.

[4] Edward Wyatt, "House and Senate in Deal on Financial Overhaul," *New York Times on-line*, June 25, 2010.

[5] Restoring American Financial Stability Act of 2010, H.R. 4173 (as of June 10, 2010). Two of the most significant provisions that at least have the capacity to somewhat contain financialism are the so-called "Volcker rule," requiring federally-insured banks to cease proprietary trading, and the Lincoln Amendment, as modified, requiring that bank holding company derivatives trading be placed in a separately-capitalized subsidiary.

[6] Although scholars and policy-makers have begun to recognize this reality. "First Public Hearing of the Financial Crisis Inquiry Commission," 111th Cong. (January 13, 2010); Simon Johnson, "The Quiet Coup," *The Atlantic Online*, May 2009, available at: www.theatlantic.com/magazine/archive/2009/05/the-quiet-coup/7364 (last accessed February 22, 2011); Staff of Congressional Oversight Panel, 111th Cong., "Special Report on Regulatory Reform" (January 2009), pp. 2–5; Paul Volcker, "The Time We Have Is Growing Short," *The New York Review of Books*, June 24, 2010, available at: www.nybooks.com/articles/archives/2010/jun/24/time-we-have-growing-short

I'd like to explain financialism and how it grew in slightly more detail. I know that by trying to cover so much ground, I will almost certainly wind up overgeneralizing and, undoubtedly, leave more questions than I answer. I will use data where I have it, but apologize that this work is in its relatively early stages and I have much to do.

Financialism is grounded principally in two dangerous ideas, ideas not dangerous in themselves but dangerous in practice. These ideas have helped to provide intellectual support for the shift from capitalism to financialism and lie at financialism's foundation. The first idea grew out of the work of Adam Smith. Smith's theory of the invisible hand was designed to show how economic growth could be better stimulated by free market activity than by the dominant practice of mercantilism, while at the same time pursuing the Enlightenment goal of freeing people from oppressive economic and social policies and providing the opportunity for them to improve their own economic conditions.[7] Smith's theory was as much sociological as political and economic, and was grounded in the behavior of the self-interested, but nonetheless morally sensitive, economic man that he had earlier developed in his *A Theory of Moral Sentiments*.[8] Through the nineteenth century, this central idea was transformed by neo-classical economists into a justification for the individual pursuit of maximum utility, and in the twentieth century into the individual pursuit of maximum wealth, stripped of, and abstracted from, Smith's highly contextualized and social ideas and having all but abandoned Smith's emphasis on real economic growth.[9] The abstraction was complete by the last third of the twentieth century, and free market ideology resulted in the substantial deregulation of the US economy.[10] This cleared the way for the growth of financialism.

(last accessed February 22, 2011). Richard Posner, a long-time proponent of neo-classical deregulatory theory, has done a complete volte-face, at the same time revealing a misunderstanding of capitalism itself. Richard A. Posner, *A Failure of Capitalism* (Cambridge, MA: Harvard University Press, 2009).

[7] Adam Smith, *An Inquiry Into The Nature And Causes Of The Wealth Of Nations* (Indianapolis: Liberty Press, 1981).

[8] Adam Smith, *A Theory of Moral Sentiments*, Part I, Section I, ch. I (Indianapolis: Liberty Press, 1982).

[9] Klaus Hennings and Warren J. Samuels, *Neoclassical Economic Theory, 1870 to 1930* (Boston: Kluwer Academic Publishers, 1990); Donald A. Walker and D.E. Moggridge, *Perspectives on the History of Economic Thought* (Aldershot: Published for the History of Economics Society by Elgar, 1989).

[10] Timothy A. Canova, "Financial Market Failure as a Crisis in the Rule of Law: From Market Fundamentalism to a New Keynesian Regulatory Model" (2009) 3 *Harvard Law & Policy Review* 369; Patricia A. McCoy, Andrey D. Pavlov and Susan M. Wachter, "Systemic Risk Through Securitization: The Result of Deregulation and Regulatory Failure" (2009) 41 *Connecticut Law Review* 1327.

The second idea, which depended on the notion of free markets, was the capital asset pricing model.[11] Developed over the course of a decade by economists principally associated with the University of Chicago and MIT, the capital asset pricing model reduced stock selection to a single number, *beta*, which was derived from a regression analysis of a stock price's historical movement in relationship to the market. While the goal of this model was to permit investors to make rational decisions balancing risk and return, its unintentional consequence was to separate the investment decision from any need to be interested in, or concerned with, the underlying corporation issuing the stock, leading to a separation of stock ownership from the underlying business and laying the groundwork for an irresponsible and detached investor class.[12]

Building upon the capital asset pricing model, option pricing theory developed as a way to bring greater certainty to the derivatives market, the market for trading in instruments that in part track the behavior of stocks and bonds without requiring a trader to own the underlying security – as Paul Krugman describes them, "claims on claims."[13] The result was an explosion in over-the-counter derivatives trading and the creation of a bewildering variety of new securities, all of which were further removed from the real economy than even the deracinated portfolios assembled by investors using *beta*.[14]

The complex economic modeling that produced these theories, combined with new technologies, also led to the possibility and proliferation of computer-based trading and its contemporary realization in high frequency trading,[15] further detaching any human element of concern for the real economy while at the same time profoundly affecting real

---

[11] John Lintner, "Security Prices, Risk, and Maximal Gains from Diversification" (1965) 20 *Journal of Finance* 587; Franco Modigliani and Gerald A. Pogue, "An Introduction to Risk and Return: Concepts and Evidence" (1974) 30 *Financial Analysis* 68; William Sharpe, "Capital Asset Prices: A Theory of Market Equilibrium Under Conditions of Risk" (1964) 19 *Journal of Finance* 425. For a hagiographic history of the development of this theory see Peter L. Bernstein, *Capital Ideas: The Improbable Origins of Modern Wall Street* (New York: Free Press, 1992), esp. chs. 2 and 4.

[12] Mitchell, "Morals of the Marketplace."

[13] Krugman, "How Did Economists Get it So Wrong?"; Fischer Black and Myron Scholes, "The Pricing of Options and Corporate Liabilities" (1973) 81 *Journal of Political Economy* 637.

[14] The explosion in the creation and trading of derivatives is, of course, a far more complicated story. See, for example, Gillian Tett, *Fool's Gold* (New York: Free Press, 2009). My point simply is that modern finance theory provided the intellectual underpinning and the tools to support this development.

[15] "SEC Approves New Stock-by-Stock Circuit Breaker Rules," US Securities and Exchange Commission, June 10, 2010, press release available at: www.sec.gov/news/press/2010/2010-98.htm (last accessed February 22, 2011); Charles Duhigg, "Stock Traders Find Speed Pays, in Milliseconds," *New York Times*, July 23, 2009.

economic behavior by affecting the underlying stock prices that drive managerial incentives.[16] The combination of these practices with free market ideas and policies that equated responsibility with selfishness laid the groundwork for a capitalism centered on a financial industry and capital markets that had largely lost touch with the fundamental purpose of capitalism as a system for the production of goods and services and wealth creation and distribution. It laid the groundwork for financialism.

No single factor can describe the development of a complex economic system, but I'd like to provide a brief historical account of the creation of financialism from the early 1950s to the present in an attempt to tie together a number of different trends. These trends include a sharp growth in the number of individual investors, the eventual dominance of institutional investors and the rise in institutional activism, changes in investment goals from dividends to capital gains, dramatic increases in market volatility, changes in executive compensation, and the deregulation of financial institutions in a manner that stimulated speculation by commercial banks and led to the creation of financial instruments that bore little relationship to the real economy. These trends had combined by the turn of the twentieth century to create financialism. I will discuss the most important elements arising from this history in a little more detail as I go along, focusing more on the early stages of the growth of the stock market because that story is perhaps less well-known than more recent developments.

I begin in 1952. Stockbrokers were languishing in a long, desultory market. Turnover, the rate at which share ownership changed hands, was even lower than it had been during the years of the Great Depression. Turnover averaged almost 32 percent from 1931 to 1939.[17] During the following ten years, it averaged half of that. The Depression decade high was 50 percent in 1933, and ranged beyond that from 44 percent to 21 percent. During the 1940s, the high was 24 percent during the short bull market of 1945–1946, but otherwise ranged between 19 percent and 12 percent.[18]

Turnover is an imperfect proxy for market activity, and daily trading volume did increase in the late 1940s. But stock brokers made their money from commissions on trades. With such desultory trading, the

---

[16] For an extended analysis of the relationship between stock prices and managerial behavior see Lawrence E. Mitchell, *Corporate Irresponsibility: America's Newest Export* (New Haven: Yale University Press, 2001).
[17] I leave aside 1930, in which turnover was 64 percent, as an unusual year due to the fallout from the 1929 Crash.
[18] NYSE Factbook Historical Data, nysedata.com/factbook.

Financialism 47

commissions were increasingly few. In fact one historian describes that era as one in which brokers played baseball on the Exchange floor using rolled-up and crumpled quotation sheets as bats and balls.[19] But that was also the year the New York Stock Exchange (NYSE) commissioned a study by the Brookings Institution to determine the number of Americans who owned stock.[20] The surprising result was 4.2 percent of the population.[21] In response, the Exchange instituted a program, "Own Your Share of American Business," a program of advertising, marketing, public relations and educational outreach, which was designed to bring greater numbers of individual investors into the market.[22] But increasing the number of American stockholders was not the NYSE's only goal. In order for brokers to make money, people not only had to buy stock but to trade it as well. In its 1955 Annual Report, the Exchange complained of low turnover, explaining that this was a consequence of an "investment" market in which investors paid cash for their shares. The Report explicitly discussed the NYSE's continuing efforts to persuade the Federal Reserve to lower margin requirements to stimulate borrowing for investment, making more money available for individual shareholders to invest and with a consequent expected increase in turnover and volatility (and thus commissions), even as its "Own Your Share" campaign for individual investors preached prudence and caution.[23]

While it took several decades for turnover and volatility to explode, the results of the NYSE campaign were almost immediate.[24] By 1956, individual share ownership had grown from the 6.5 million of 1952 to 12.5 million, almost doubling in four years. This number continued to grow dramatically through the 1960s, so that by 1965, 20 million

---

[19] Robert Sobel, *N.Y.S.E.: A History of the New York Stock Exchange, 1935–1975* (New York: Weybright and Tally, 1975) p. 321.
[20] Lewis H. Kimmel, *Share Ownership in the United States* (Washington, DC: Brookings Institution, 1952).
[21] Burton Crane, "Brookings' Census Seen Far-Reaching," *New York Times*, July 31, 1952, p. F1; J.A. Livingston, "Share Owners Total 6,500,000 No Matter How You Count," *The Washington Post*, September 24, 1952, p. 30; "Surprises Found in Share Analysis," *The Washington Post*, July 1, 1952, p. 10.
[22] For a good account of the "Own Your Own Share" campaign, and especially its place in the Cold War efforts to promote US capitalism, see Janice Traflet, *"Own Your Share of American Business:" Public Relations at the NYSE during the Cold War, Business and Economic History On-Line,* www.thebhc.org/publications/BEHonline/2003/Traflet.pdf (last accessed February 22, 2011).
[23] "New York Stock Exchange, Annual Report for 1955" (New York: NYSE, 1955), p. 14.
[24] It would be an overstatement to claim that the NYSE's campaign directly caused the growth in stock ownership, and I don't, but the correlation is undeniable.

people, more than 10 percent of the population, owned stock.[25] The trend continued through the end of the century, as, by 2001, more than half of American families, directly or indirectly, owned corporate stock.[26]

At the same time appeared a new type of investor, who would have a profound impact on US capitalism. These were the institutional investors. From almost a standing start at the beginning of the decade, by 1957 *Business Week* was predicting that institutions would become "the most powerful investment group in the world."[27] Twenty-two states had adopted the "prudent man rule" by 1950, allowing fiduciary institutions like pension funds to invest substantial chunks of their assets in common and preferred stocks.[28] The pension funds grew rapidly, increasing in value from $11 billion to almost $40 billion between 1950 and 1957 alone.[29] The book value of the common stock they owned increased from $812 million in 1951 to $2.9 billion in 1955. And, growing almost as quickly, were the mutual funds, which had almost disappeared after the 1929 Crash and had started to make a very slow comeback in the 1940s. From 1940, when mutual funds barely existed, to 1959, between $7 and $8 billion of new money was invested in mutual funds.[30] By 1959, they were adding $4.5 billion in a single year.[31] By 2000, institutional investors owned 61.4 percent of the equities of the 1,000 largest US corporations, growing to an astonishing 76.4 percent at the end of 2007.[32] And with this growth has come worrying concentrations of institutional capital and the financial muscle that goes with it; seventeen of the largest US corporations had 60 percent or more of their

---

[25] The New York Stock Exchange, "Shareownership USA: 1965 Census of Shareowners" (New York: NYSE, 1965).

[26] Ana M. Aizcorbe, Arthur B. Kennickell and Kevin B. Moore, "Recent Changes in US Family Finances: Evidence from the 1998 and 2001 Survey of Consumer Finances" (2003) 89 *Federal Reserve Bulletin* 1–32.

[27] "The Big Board Looks Ahead to a Bigger, Boomier Decade," *Business Week*, January 26, 1957, p. 107.

[28] George Ericson, "Mutual Funds' Big Role in Investment World," *The Christian Science Monitor*, May 20, 1950.

[29] "Pension Funds' Rise Put at 4 Billion a Year," *Chicago Daily Tribune*, February 11, 1958, p. B7.

[30] Overall fund sales should top $2 billion in 1959. ("The Markets Briefs," *Business Week*, December 12, 1959, p. 123).

[31] Total net assets grew $5b 1958–1959 ("Does Merit or a Hard Sell Win?" *Business Week*, April 4, 1959, p. 109).

[32] Carolyn Kay Brancato and Stephan Rabimov, *The 2008 Institutional Investment Report: Trends in Institutional Investor Assets and Equity Ownership of US Corporations*, The Conference Board, September 2008, Report Number R01433–08-RR.; Barry B. Burr, "Institutional Investors Increase Ownership of US Companies to All-Time High," *Pensions & Investments*, September 5, 2008.

stock owned by institutions in 2007, including six that had at least 70 percent institutional ownership.[33]

The next aspect of financialism I'd like to explain is the historical development of its principal institutions, commercial and investment banks, and particularly the shift in the nature of their core businesses that marks the transition from capitalism to financialism.

This part of the story begins with the growth of the investment banking industry from the middle of the century, as the Exchange permitted member incorporation in 1953, which allowed firms to take advantage of limited liability and therefore engage in higher risk activities.[34] The story goes on to a key moment in the development of the financial industry, the public offering of stock in investment bank Donaldson, Lufkin, Jenrette in 1970, and the tectonic shift in the industry created by the existence of publicly held investment banks, a shift which dramatically expanded both the (realized) possibility of high leverage for the banks and the concomitant explosion in profits and compensation.[35] The greater financial resources that public offerings brought to the investment banks also allowed them to automate, first their back offices and then, far more importantly, their trading desks. Eventually the major human contact that traders had with stock was their design of computer programs to trade it.

By the end of the twentieth century, the industry had undergone a dramatic shift in business focus.[36] Where once investment banks made their money underwriting securities, arranging deals and providing financial advice to clients, they now moved in the direction of proprietary trading, that is, trading for their own profits, and the development of what are generally referred to as "new financial products," mortgage backed securities, collateralized debt obligations, other exotic derivatives, proprietary hedge funds and other financial instruments, some

---

[33] Burr, "Institutional Investors."
[34] Vincent P. Carrosso, *Investment Banking in America* (Cambridge, MA: Harvard University Press, 1970). Again, it is not my claim that the reason that the Exchange permitted member incorporation was to increase risky activity. Indeed Carrosso argues that firms incorporated for "[t]ax benefits for partners, continuity of the firm, and greater opportunity to spread ownership," and further notes that "incorporation was made still more attractive after 1953," when the Exchange permitted member incorporation. This, however, does not appear to be a complete explanation, and certainly not an explanation for the change in Exchange rules. The ability to raise capital which limited liability facilitated seems more plausible. In any event, firms did raise considerably more capital, without the risk of partnership unlimited liability, in the decades following increased incorporation.
[35] John Brooks, *The Go-Go Years* (New York: Weybright and Talley, 1973), p. 316.
[36] Mah-Hui attributes a significant proportion of the rise in what I call financialism to the dramatic increase in US debt between 1960 and 2007. "Financial Sector."

of which are aptly described by Warren Buffett as "financial weapons of mass destruction."[37] The development of computerized trading, and especially the recent development of high frequency trading, increased the separation of finance from the real economy. Computers don't care about the companies they trade in; computers don't care about the real economy.

These changes clearly moved the financial industry away from the traditional function of finance as providing funds for productive industry, at the same time that it increased the risk to the nation's credit supply.[38] The new trading-centered finance employed the beautiful minds of Wall Street to help banks and investment banks sell off risk, while keeping most of the profit. The justification for these practices, echoed by Federal Reserve Board Chairman Ben Bernanke, was that they increased liquidity in the US economy and thus the funds available for financing business. This would have been consistent with capitalism, even if much of the profit of this business shift remained with the banks. But the increased liquidity was more commonly used to continue to finance trading and the sale of new financial products like credit default swaps than for financing real economic production. This behavior is financialism, not capitalism.

Another feature of financialism is the relatively recent acceptance of the existence of financial institutions that are too interconnected to be permitted to fail.[39] While not exclusive to financialism (capitalism has sometimes recognized institutions as too big to fail), financialism embraces the existence of such institutions and at least implicitly pledges the continuing willingness of the US taxpayer to sustain their solvency.

The acceptance of the concept of too big too fail is a consequence of misguided free market ideology. While the term often is acknowledged to have originated in the federal bailout of Continental Illinois Bank and Trust Company in 1984,[40] government bailouts had periodically been a feature of US economic policy, including the Chrysler bailout of

---

[37] Warren E. Buffett, Berkshire Hathaway, *2002 Annual Report* (Berkshire Hathaway Inc., 2003), p. 15.

[38] Mah-Hui, "Financial Sector," p. 17.

[39] The financial reform bill in progress largely enshrines the notion. Restoring American Financial Stability Act of 2010.

[40] Harold A. Black, M. Cary Collins, Breck L. Robinson and Robert L. Schweitzer, "Changes in Market Perception of Riskiness: The Case of Too-Big-to-Fail" (1997) 20:3 *Journal of Financial Research* 389–406; Ron J. Feldman and Arthur J. Rolnick, *Fixing FDICIA: A Plan to Address the Too-Big-to-Fail Problem* (Minneapolis: Federal Reserve Bank of Minneapolis, 1998); Carter Golembe, "Too-Big-to-Fail and All That," in *The Golembe Reports No. 1991-4* (Washington, DC: Golembe Associates, Inc., 1994).

1979 and the rescue of Long Term Capital Management in 1998.[41] But it was not until the substantial deregulation of the financial industry with the passage of the Gramm–Leach–Bliley Act in 1999[42] that financial concentration really exploded, creating the monster banks that characterized the US financial sector at the beginning of the twenty-first century.[43] This transformation, among other things, helped to fuel the rise of trading as a major profit center, not only in the investment banks I've just described, but even in the most traditionally conservative commercial banks.[44] Financial liberation continued with the explicit non-regulation of over-the-counter derivatives by the Commodities Futures Modernization Act of 2000.[45]

US capitalism is not well served by the existence of financial institutions that are too big to fail. A larger amount of somewhat smaller financial institutions that, in a very real economic sense, structurally diversify the risk of economic failure across a broader spectrum of banks and reduce, if not eliminate, the need for continual federal intervention in order to protect the nation's credit supply, is almost certainly better suited both to stimulate production in the real economy and to keep our credit supply safe without unnecessarily chilling appropriate risk-taking.[46]

Financialism has diverted economic resources from capitalist production in the real economy to satisfy the demand of financial claimants, primarily stockholders. Data I've collected over several years show the disappearance of corporate equity capital and its replacement by massive amounts of debt, largely done to satisfy the demands of finance.[47] The argument here is that US public stockholders have withdrawn more equity from corporations than they contributed, leaving debt as the real risk capital of US industry. Yet the legal power to control US corporations

---

[41] Barry Ritholtz and Aaron Task, *Bailout Nation: How Greed and Easy Money Corrupted Wall Street and Shook the World Economy* (Hoboken: John Wiley & Sons, 2009), p. 7–50.
[42] Gramm–Leach–Bliley Act, Pub. L. No. 106–102, 113 Stat. 1338 (1999).
[43] See Gary A. Dymski, *The Bank Merger Wave: The Economic Causes and Social Consequences of Financial Consolidation* (Armonk: M.E. Sharpe, Inc., 1999); Jonathan R. Macey, "The Business of Banking: Before and After Gramm-Leach-Bliley" (2000) 25 *Journal of Corporation Law* 691.
[44] Mah-Hui, "Financial Sector."
[45] Commodities Futures Modernization Act, Pub. L. No. 106–554, 114 Stat. 2763 (2001). Mah-Hui notes the five-fold increased notional amount of derivatives between 2002 and 2007. Mah-Hui, "Financial Sector," p. 18.
[46] James F. Bauerle, "Regional Banking Outlook" (2010) 127 *Banking Law Journal* 463; Ann Graham, "Bringing to Heel the Elephants in the Economy: The Case for Ending 'Too Big to Fail'" (2010) 8 *Pierce Law Review* 117.
[47] Lawrence E. Mitchell, "The Legitimate Rights of Public Shareholders" (2009) 66 *Washington and Lee Law Review* 1635; Lawrence E. Mitchell, "Toward a New Law

rests with the stockholders. The result is a disconnect between responsibility and risk, and has destabilized the capital structures of US industrial corporations while leaving stockholders with the power to pressure managers to gamble with industrial credit and economic well-being. While stockholders do continue to take risks, the logic of the capital asset pricing model tells us that the risks they take are casino risks created by themselves, not real financial risks which have been left to creditors. What is true of stockholders is even more true of derivatives traders and the financial institutions that trade for their own accounts.

Here are some facts: from the turn of the twentieth century until the 1960s, US industrial corporations practiced a policy of retaining substantial portions of their earnings for reinvestment in their businesses while paying a reasonable dividend to shareholders and relying upon trade credit and some long-term debt for the balance of their needs. Retained earnings averaged in the range of 50 percent to 60 percent as recently as the early 1960s. By 2007, that average was down to 11 percent, rising from a low in 2002 of just over 3 percent. Almost all of the rest of the money needed to finance production came from debt, increasingly shoved off-balance sheet to conceal corporations' true reliance on borrowing.[48]

How and why did this happen? As more Americans entered the market, which grew at its fastest pace during the great bull market that lasted from 1952 until 1970, investors' desires shifted from steady dividends to making quick capital gains from trading.[49] Approximately 90 percent of listed corporations were paying dividends, and there was a general belief that dividends were what individual investors sought. There was good reason for this. Although dividend payouts were low compared to the 1920s, in 1952, 52 percent of corporate earnings (a post-war high) were paid out as dividends. But dividends did not appear to be the answer. A two-day study of market transactions by the NYSE in 1952

---

and Economics: The Case of the Stock Market," available at: http://papers.ssrn.com/sol3/papers.cfm?abstract_id=1557730 (last accessed February 22, 2011). Mah-Hui provides data showing the dramatic increases of debt across almost all economic sectors (except, interestingly, government debt), while noting the stability of gross corporate investment. Mah-Hui, "Financial Sector," pp. 14–15. These figures are consistent with my own research.

[48] Mitchell, "Legitimate Rights."
[49] This trend was clear as early as 1954. "It's Gains They're After Now," *Business Week*, August 28, 1954, p. 102; "The Payout Keeps Climbing," *Business Week*, January 3, 1953, p. 92; New York Stock Exchange, Annual Report (New York: NYSE, 1952), p. 7. A repeat of this study in 1955 continued to confirm the "investment character of the market." New York Stock Exchange, Annual Report (New York: NYSE, 1955), p. 14.

revealed that 46 percent of individually-purchased shares were bought for long-term capital gains, followed by 25.5 percent for income, 13 percent for capital gains within thirty to 120 days (which the Exchange classified as long-term, although the federal long-term capital gains tax break occurred only after six months) and 6.5 percent for capital gains in under thirty days. Putting together transactions by members and institutions, the Exchange concluded that 75 percent of all transactions had been for investment purposes rather than speculation. But particularly notable is the fact that the vast majority of individual stock purchases were in pursuit of capital gains rather than income.

Prior to the 1960s, those capital gains largely came from the increase in share value caused in large part by the retaining earnings I just mentioned. The investment technology derived from the capital asset pricing model taught investors to see capital gains as coming from the future anticipated cash flows of the corporation, discounted to present value. Thus, instead of selling their stock for money already earned, investors began to sell their stock for money that was to be earned but which may never be earned, and thus, in a sense, shorted future dividends or, to put it differently, stripped the profits of the future for the benefit of the present.[50] This process was exacerbated by the increasing impatience of investors for capital returns, especially the rapidly growing class of institutional investors whose money managers were compensated based on the amount of assets they had under management, and who were beginning to acquire the ability to put pressure on managers to increase stock prices.[51] Even without this, the increased volatility of trading for capital gains that had started to soar in the 1980s gave managers strong incentives to maintain high stock prices in order to maintain the independence of their companies, and later to increase their own compensation as stock option compensation came to dominate due to tax reform in 1993. The result was to put pressure on mangers to manage for stock price, not for long-term sustainability. Perhaps the most trenchant piece of evidence for this is the fact that in a three-year period ending in 2007, the S&P 500 spent more money on stock buybacks (which increases stock prices) than on investment in capital production.[52]

I have thus far shown the development of financialism and its effects upon corporate finance. But financialism also profoundly affects the way that managers of businesses in the real economy define their business

---

[50] Mitchell, "The Case of the Stock Market."
[51] Mitchell, *Corporate Irresponsibility*, ch. 7.
[52] www2.standardandpoors.com/spf/pdf/index/040708_SP500_BUYBACK_ PR.pdf?vregion=us&vlang=en (last accessed February 22, 2011).

goals. In 2006, over 30 percent of the profits of corporations classified as "industrial" came from financial transactions, not from the production of goods and services, and financial assets constituted almost 48 percent of the total assets of non-farm, non-financial corporations.[53] Only a relatively small portion of this is composed of accounts receivable. By far the largest class is identified as "miscellaneous."[54] Industrial corporations, at least pre-crash, had come to rely upon finance rather than their own core businesses to provide profits. This has obvious adverse potential consequences for the future of the economic self-sufficiency of the United States.

Why has this occurred? There are several reasons. The first is the capitulation of industry to the demands of finance that I described earlier. The second, which goes along with this, is a shift in the prior careers of industrial CEOs, from marketing and engineering earlier in the century to finance, which came to be the most common background of CEOs between 1997 and 2007.[55] The training and interests of these chief executives, and the greater profits to be made from finance, inevitably incline them in that direction, and suit the demands of financialism better than those of capitalism. American Can Company is a perfect example. Incorporated in 1901, that important manufacturing corporation acquired a modest midwest insurance company in 1981 and, along with it, Gerald Tsai, Jr., the famous, fallen whiz-kid of 1960s speculative mutual funds. As vice-chairman and then chairman of American Can, Tsai abandoned manufacturing and transformed the company into financial conglomerate, Primerica.[56] General Electric, one of the mainstays of US industry since the late nineteenth century,

---

[53] US Census Bureau, *Statistical Abstract of the United States: 2009* 128 (Washington, DC: US Government Printing Office, 2008), p. 487 (table 729 (assets)). While many real economy corporations hold large amounts of accounts receivable from sales as assets on their balance sheet, the aggregate proportion of these is only about 18 percent of those assets carried as financial assets.

[54] United States Bureau of Economic Analysis, Department of Commerce, National Income and Product Accounts of the United States, Tables 6.16A to 6.17B, 30, March 2007.

[55] Spencer Stuart, "Leading CEOS: A Statistical Snapshot of S&P 500 Leaders," December 2008, available at: www.spencerstuart.com/research/articles/975 (last accessed February 22, 2011); Spencer Stuart, "2004 CEO Study: A Statistical Snapshot of S&P 500 Leaders," 2005, available at: http://content.spencerstuart.com/sswebsite/pdf/lib/Statistical_Snapshot_of_Leading_CEOs_relB3.pdf (last accessed February 22, 2011).

[56] Lisa Belkin, "How American Can Became Primerica," *New York Times*, March 8, 1987; Brian Steleter, "Gerald Tsai, Innovative Investor Dies at 79," *New York Times*, July 11, 2008; *Primerica Corporation*, www.primerica.com (last accessed February 22, 2011).

presents a different type of example. While it continues its manufacturing operations, it now reaps a substantial proportion of its profits from its financial subsidiaries.[57] It isn't difficult to replicate these stories many times over.

A final reason is changes in executive compensation. Executive compensation became largely stock-based beginning in the early 1990s,[58] thus creating incentives for CEOs to engage in financial manipulation in order to achieve higher stock prices.[59] Even in periods of strong industrial production, the profits of industry often pale in comparison to the profits generated by financial transactions. In order to earn the returns that would justify higher compensation, they turned, as the data above suggests, to finance.

I've described the growth of institutional investors, but now would like to address the incentives and behavior of institutions that have contributed to the rise of financialism. Institutional investors are a particularly important cause of financialism, even as a debate continues over giving greater power over corporate affairs to stockholders which, in practical terms, means institutions.[60] Yet institutional investor activism has been one of the principal causes of destructive short-term management in the real economy.

Institutional activism was hailed in the early 1990s as the solution to the longstanding set of problems known as agency costs caused by the separation in the modern corporation of ownership and control.[61] Agency costs are the losses that result when corporate managers favor their own interests over that of the shareholders together with the expense of preventing this. It was widely thought that institutional investors, through their large blockholdings of stock, could provide the

---

[57] General Electric, *2009 Annual Report* (General Electric, 2010), p. 3.
[58] Lucian Bebchuk and Jesse Fried, *Pay without Performance: The Unfulfilled Promise of Executive Compensation* (Cambridge, MA: Harvard University Press, 2004).
[59] Mitchell, *Corporate Irresponsibility*.
[60] See Florence E. Harmon, Securities and Exchange Commission, "Facilitating Shareholder Director Nominations," June 10, 2009 (proposed rule, available at: www.sec.gov/rules/proposed/2009/33–9046.pdf (last accessed February 22, 2011)); William W. Bratton and Michael L. Wachter, "The Case Against Shareholder Empowerment" (2010) 158 *University of Pennsylvania Law Review* 653; Grant Hayden and Matthew T. Bodie, "Shareholder Democracy and the Curious Turn Toward Board Primacy" (2010) 51 *William & Mary Law Review* 2071; Michael S. Kang, "Voting as Veto" (2010) 108 *Michigan Law Review* 1221; Marshall M. Magaro, "Two Birds, One Stone: Achieving Corporate Social Responsibility Through the Shareholder-Primacy Norm" (2010) 85 *Indiana Law Journal* 1149; Mitchell, "Legitimate Rights"; Jia Lynn Yang, "CEOs from Far and Wide Band Against Financial Bill Provision," *The Washington Post*, May 14, 2010, p. A11.
[61] See Lawrence E. Mitchell, "A Critical Look at Corporate Governance" (1992) 45 *Vanderbilt Law Review* 1263, 1269–1271.

shareholder oversight that disappeared with the creation of the large public corporation at the turn of the twentieth century and had been sought since at least the publication of Adolf A. Berle, Jr. and Gardiner Means' *The Modern Corporation and Private Property* in 1932.

That utopia was not to be realized. Some critics, including me,[62] predicted that the natural incentives of institutional money managers would lead them to use their power to push corporate managers to focus on short-term stock prices rather than long-term corporate health and patient profits from production. That prediction has been amply borne out both by observation and in rigorous empirical studies, and many of those who had celebrated institutional activism have since retreated from those views.[63]

Two other kinds of institutional investor flourished in the years before the 2008 market collapse and are likely to remain active after recovery; private equity funds and activist hedge funds. Although very different in their business models and functions, these investors have also contributed to financialism by exacerbating the short-term climate that led to industrial overleveraging, the disappearance of retained earnings and the practice of subordinating the ends of production for the gains of finance.

Few of the developments I've described could have happened without the triumph of neo-classicism and its effects on US law and public policy from the 1980s through the 2008 collapse.

The legal story begins with a variety of measures designed to deregulate the banking industry, starting with savings and loan institutions in the 1980s and culminating in the virtual liberation of commercial banks from New Deal restrictions with the passage of the Gramm–Leach–Bliley Act in 1999.[64] Banking deregulation began with efforts to permit

---

[62] Mitchell, "Critical Look," and Mitchell, *Corporate Irresponsibility*.
[63] John R. Graham, Campbell R. Harvey and Shivaram Rajgopal, "The Economic Implications of Corporate Financial Reporting" (2005) 40 *Journal of Accounting and Economics* 3; John R. Graham, Campbell R. Harvey and Shiva Rajgopal, "Value Destruction and Financial Reporting Decisions" (2006) 62 *Financial Analysis Journal* 27; Philippe Aghion and Jeremy C. Stein, "Growth vs. Margins: Destabilizing Consequences of Giving the Stock Market What it Wants" (2004) 24–25, http://papers.ssrn.com/sol3/papers.cfm?abstract_id=631184 (last accessed February 22, 2011) (concluding that even in an efficient stock market, managers' desire to satisfy stock market demands can "introduce excess volatility into real variables such as output and sales"); Alfred Rappaport, "The Economics of Short-Term Performance Obsession" (2005) 61 *Financial Analysis Journal* 65.
[64] See Macey, "Gramm-Leach-Bliley"; Patricia A. McCoy, Andrey D. Pavlov and Susan M. Wachter, "Systemic Risk Through Securitization: The Result of Deregulation and Regulatory Failure" (2009) 41 *Connecticut Law Review* 1327; Quinn, "Private Ordering."

institutions which had distinctly local or regional business to grow nationally, and increasingly removed restrictions on the businesses in which the regulated institutions could engage. This, along with attractive inducements from states like North Carolina, paved the way for substantial bank consolidation in the 1990s and early twenty-first century.

Traditional small lending institutions thus became further removed from their clients, and banks sought greater profits in the process of securitization, which brought higher profits than mere lending and allowed banks to evade capital restrictions. Securitization, which of course is represented most publicly by mortgage-backed securities and other forms of consumer-debt backed derivatives, allowed loan officers to pay less attention to the safety of their loans, since they were promptly to be sold off and removed from banks' balance sheets (although not entirely from the risk assumed by the banks).[65] The Commodities Futures Modernization Act of 2000 ensured that these instruments would not be regulated.[66] Despite their profound effect on the real economy, these instruments mushroomed in growth while providing financing not for production but simply for more finance.[67]

This process paralleled what happened in the stock market under the capital asset pricing model and its progeny, largely separating (on paper and in practice) the responsibility for, and consequent monitoring of, risk from the real economy that nonetheless was exposed to that risk. The story of credit derivatives has been told many times, and I only mention it here in order to show how it fits into the rest of the story of financialism, and how the law consciously adopted the ideology of free markets in order to permit financialism to develop.

I would be remiss in ignoring the regulatory failings of the Securities and Exchange Commission (SEC), and especially its fateful decision in 2004 to permit largely unregulated investment banks to dramatically diminish their capital requirements (and its inverse, to increase their leverage),[68] eliminating one of the very few regulatory tools available to the SEC to limit the activities of investment banks.

---

[65] Significant risks often were retained off-balance sheet. Mah-Hui, "Financial Sector," p. 17.
[66] Commodities Futures Modernization Act, Pub. L. No. 106–554, 114 Stat. 2763 (2001).
[67] David Mengle, International Swap & Derivatives Association, Inc., Federal Reserve Bank of Atlanta Financial Markets Conference, "Credit Derivatives: An Overview" 11 (2007), available at: www.frbatlanta.org/filelegacydocs/erq407_mengle.pdf (last accessed February 22, 2011); Karen Weaver, Deutsche Bank, "US Asset-Backed Securities Market Review and Outlook," in *Global Securitisation and Structured Finance 2008* (London: Globe White Page Ltd., 2008), pp. 18–211.
[68] 17 C.F.R. § 200, 240 (2004).

In addition, bank regulators, misplacing their trust in the prudence of bankers, also significantly diminished capital reserve requirements.[69] This allowed banks to borrow and gamble with enormous sums of money while maintaining little available cash to help them through financial distress. As the United States implemented an international agreement to lower banks' capital requirements in 2007, New York Senator Charles Schumer said: "There need not be a conflict between being the safest and the most competitive, and this fine agreement proves it."[70] The echoes of economist Irving Fisher's famous early October 1929 statement: "Stock prices have reached 'what looks like a permanently high plateau,' "[71] are all too resounding.

The highlight of deregulation and, I believe, the most foolish piece of economic legislation ever to be passed by Congress and signed by a president, is the Gramm–Leach–Bliley Act of 1999. Its most important consequence was the merging of commercial banking and investment banking functions to permit the growth of enormous financial institutions whose role in protecting the nation's credit system and money supply was now compromised by the huge profits available from speculation in securities and derivatives. This growth was accompanied by increased incentives of well-compensated bankers to earn fortunes from engaging in the creation of new financial instruments and proprietary trading which, just as in the years preceding the Great Depression, exposed that credit system to the possibility of collapse.

It is unfortunate to note that, despite some recognition of these failings, the course of "reform" points in the direction of continuing to institutionalize financialism, which I believe will eventually succeed in destroying US capitalism. Such reforms will do nothing to shift financialism back to capitalism, but rather maintain financialism on perhaps a slightly safer plane.

Restoring US capitalism in the face of growing financialism is urgent, both as a function of US economic well-being, and as a matter of national security, as financialism pushes the production of essential goods abroad. Faced with this urgency, it is short-sighted and irresponsible for lawmakers, regulators, financial professionals, lawyers, and even the investing public, to fail to understand our shift to financialism and the long-term destruction it promises for the economic well-being of the United States.

---

[69] Joshua N. Feinman, "Reserve Requirements: History, Current Practice, and Potential Reform," *Federal Reserve Bulletin*, June 1993, 569, 580–581.
[70] John Poirier, "US Regulators Agree on Basel II Bank Plan," *Reuters*, July 20, 2007.
[71] "Fisher Sees Stocks Permanently High," *New York Times*, October 16, 1929, p. 8.

How do we fix this? I have some preliminary suggestions, some of which have emerged in the reform debate. It is critical to re-enact laws separating investment banking and commercial banking, pass tax law reform to diminish market volatility, consider financial reform that would require demonstrated economic utility before the offering and sale of new financial instruments, create accounting reform that would require all corporations, including financial institutions, accurately to reflect their debt exposure, ensure full tax parity of capital gains and dividends in order to encourage long-term investment and re-introduce the notion of patient capital into US investment practices, restrict the types of compensation contracts corporations, and especially financial institutions, can award their employees (principally accomplished through tax laws), and create disincentives to proprietary trading and incentives for financial institutions to return to their former financing practices (again, most likely through tax changes). All of these changes could be made without unduly aggressive government restructuring of the basic economy. More aggressive suggestions include the use of antitrust law and perhaps new legislation to encourage the development of smaller and more localized financial institutions that monitor their risk because they remain in relationships with their customers, restrictions on the amount, if any, of a financial institution's assets it can securitize, and law and policy statements that disavow the acceptance of institutions that are too big to fail, including a reconsideration of the role of the Federal Reserve in financial disasters.

The need to end financialism and restore capitalism is underscored by the special moral role a sound economic system plays in our society. Perhaps the most important benefit of capitalism is its ability to stimulate economic growth, the creation and distribution of wealth, and the sustaining of that wealth over time. Whatever benefits financialism may have, it lacks these essential characteristics. Indeed, as I hope I have at least preliminarily shown, financialism is a system in which the present generation robs future generations of their economic patrimony and national security and thus is intrinsically immoral. We owe to our children, and our children's children, the benefits of a system that allowed the United States to become the world's most successful and prosperous democracy from its founding until the present. We must destroy financialism for the sake of capitalism.

4 Legitimating power: the changing status of the board of directors

Dalia Tsuk Mitchell

I Introduction

This chapter examines how in the course of the twentieth century the legal community turned from viewing directors as trustees for the community to seeing directors as agents of the shareholders. I argue that academic and judicial definitions of the appropriate status of directors were influenced by different understandings of the role of corporations in society. The early twentieth-century idea that directors were trustees was influenced by the Progressives' concerns about the concentration of private and public power while the late twentieth-century description of directors as agents was influenced by market ideology. Interestingly, while grounded in entirely different worldviews, each assigned status helped legitimate directors' power and limited, if any, liability. The idea that directors were trustees helped legitimate the powerful public corporation while the vision of directors as agents was used by courts to justify their deference to directors' discretion and helped shield them from liability altogether.

The chapter begins with the rise of the giant public corporation during and after the merger wave of the late 1890s. Discussions of the status of the board at that time were situated in a broader public concern about corporate power and its potential abuse. Scholarly focus centered upon the power that the control group (typically controlling shareholders and investment banks) could exercise to manipulate stock prices and market transactions. Legal scholars, seeking to legitimate the large public corporation and its power while eliminating such abuses by the control group, turned their focus on directors; they wanted to vest directors with public power and public trust.

© 2009 Dalia Tsuk Mitchell, thanks and appreciation go to Cynthia Williams and Peer Zumbansen for organizing this collection and for inviting me to participate and to Lawrence Mitchell for comments on drafts and ongoing discussions about corporate legal history. All errors are mine.

By the early 1930s, the vision of the corporate director as trustee seemed to dominate legal discourse, but the victory was short-lived. After the programs of the New Deal were put in place and the Great Depression wore down, concerns about corporate power dissipated. Discussions about directors' status became intertwined with a vision of corporate democracy that rested on the assumption that individual shareholders had to be protected from the manipulative practices of corporate management. In reform literature beginning in the mid-1930s (and through the 1970s) and in courts, directors were described as the shareholders' guardians against managerial abuses of power. This idea, which was developed in large part by New York courts, helped pave the road for the introduction of agency concepts into corporate law.

Beginning in the 1960s, the focal point for analysis shifted to the market. Mainstream legal scholars and economists came to believe that the market was the most effective institution to constrain corporate activities. In addition to the fears of corporate power, which faded after influencing the debates in the early twentieth century, the concerns about corporate hierarchies that dominated the mid-century discussions disappeared. Just as insider professional management became more powerful and the board of directors became ever less involved in managing the affairs of the corporation, scholars used the rhetoric of the laws of contracts and agency to describe directors as the (private) agents of the shareholders. As to the appropriate functions of directors as agents, the legal and business communities converged on the monitoring model of the board of directors. It rested on the assumption that directors could only monitor the executives, and that independent directors were best suited for this task. With this limited role came very limited liability. First, the Delaware courts declared that if the independent directors approved the board's actions, these actions would be shielded from further judicial examination. In addition, the courts collapsed the duty of care into the business judgment rule and made gross negligence a prerequisite for rebutting the presumption of that rule.

Within a few years, these ideas were strongly cemented into US corporate law. Directors' liability at the turn of the twenty-first century seems to be, if anything, an ideal with no practical effect. As the chapter concludes, with power and no liability, and a fixation on share price appreciation, corporate boards have since helped lead the US economy into financial disaster.

II Trust

The turn of the twentieth century witnessed a dramatic growth in the scale of private business organizations. Increasing consumer demand, rising numbers of skilled and unskilled workers, and an expanding pool of capital made the creation of large enterprises possible, while corporate lawyers created a variety of legal devices to help their clients increase the scope of their operations through "cooperation and combinations." Trusts, holding companies and mergers became common, even if often contested in state courts.[1] The nineteenth-century corporation, which was subject to strict constraints on its powers and limitations on its capital structure, was replaced by larger and larger units. Between 1888 and 1893, New Jersey revised its general incorporation statute to eliminate restrictions on "capitalization and assets, mergers and consolidations, the issuance of voting stock, the purpose(s) of incorporation, and the duration and locale of business."[2] Other states followed suit, enacting more enabling incorporation statutes (including Delaware, which by the second decade of the twentieth century would become the revolution's leader).[3] And corporations were quick to use the power that these enabling statutes granted them.[4]

As corporations grew bigger, entrepreneurs found ways to convince the American public to invest in their enterprises, first in bonds and preferred stock and then, by the second decade of the twentieth century, in common stock. Moreover, they found ways to manipulate stock prices as well as to drain the corporation of assets purportedly intended to guarantee the payment of debt.[5] Gradually, these entrepreneurs also helped sustain the growing separation of ownership (having an interest in an enterprise) from control (having power over the enterprise). In the nineteenth century, those who owned all or a majority of a corporation's stock controlled the corporation. But in the early decades of the twentieth century, control came into the hands of minority owners and financial institutions such as investment banks. (Management control also developed at this time but was less significant.[6])

---

[1] William W. Fisher, III, Morton J. Horwitz and Thomas A. Reed (eds.), *American Legal Realism* (Cary: Oxford University Press/USA, 1993) pp. 130–131.
[2] Scott R. Bowman, *The Modern Corporation and American Political Thought: Law, Power, and Ideology* (University Park: Penn State University Press, 1996), p. 60.
[3] *Ibid.*
[4] Melvin I. Urofsky, "Proposed Federal Incorporation in the Progressive Era" (1982) 26 *American Journal of Legal History* 161.
[5] Lawrence E. Mitchell, *The Speculation Economy: How Finance Triumphed Over Industry* (San Francisco: Berrett-Koehler, 2007).
[6] In the early 1930s, Gardiner Means counted five different forms of control – complete ownership, majority control, minority control, control through a legal device without

Control by a minority of the owners – be it a small controlling block or even management – was alarming mostly because of its potential for abuse and manipulation. "Power without responsibility is, philosophically, a perilous matter," Adolf A. Berle, Jr. wrote in 1925, and "the history of minority-controlled corporations during the last thirty years amply demonstrates that the hazard is not imaginary."[7] But the role played by investment banks raised even deeper concerns. For one thing, Berle explained that because management stock would likely be controlled by the investment banking house that served as a promoter for the corporation, "it [was] possible, if not probable, that there [would] be attractive opportunities for manipulation of securities, for negotiating favorable contracts with allied interests, or even for giving value to stock which represent[ed] no real investment."[8] Given the "web of economic interests" which the investment banking house served and from which it made its profits, it was likely that management stock would be voted for transactions that benefited the investment banking house, or even the controlling groups, but not the controlled corporation.[9] Sharing Berle's views, William O. Douglas labeled the interests of investment banking houses "high finance," charging that they were "interested solely in the immediate profit."[10] According to Douglas, the interests of high finance were different from those of small individual shareholders or even the corporation, but with the power of control, high finance was able to profit by siphoning money from other investors.[11]

Berle and Douglas did not stop at critique. Berle's famous *The Modern Corporation and Private Property* (1932), co-authored with Gardiner C. Means, aimed to prevent potential abuses of corporate power by

---

majority ownership and management control. Gardiner C. Means, "The Separation of Ownership and Control in American Industry" (1931) 46 *Quarterly Journal of Economics* 68, 72. The twentieth century witnessed a shift from complete and majority ownership to minority control (often through legal devices) to management control. But see Walter Werner, "Corporation Law in Search of Its Future" (1981) 81 *Columbia Law Review* 1611, 1629–1644 (arguing that individual shareholders never participated in the management of public corporations).

[7] Adolf A. Berle, Jr., "Non-Voting Stock and Bankers' Control" (1925–1926) 39 *Harvard Law Review* 673, 674.
[8] *Ibid.*, p. 676.   [9] *Ibid.*
[10] William O. Douglas, *The Forces of Disorder*, address delivered at the University of Chicago (October 27, 1936) with additions from talks before the Economic Club of Chicago (February 1, 1938) and before the Bond Club of New York (March 24, 1937), in James Allen (ed.), *Democracy and Finance: The Addresses and Public Statements of William O. Douglas* (New Haven: Yale University Press, 1940), p. 9.
[11] *Ibid.*

proclaiming corporate power to be power in trust for the community.¹² Because they feared potential abuses of corporate power, Berle and Means rejected the idea of freeing corporations to act as if they were mere aggregates of individuals or real entities, distinct from their individual members.¹³ Because they celebrated the contributions of corporate power to the modern industrial society, Berle and Means also feared that an overuse of government regulation could eliminate the potential benefits of corporate power. They rejected both the early twentieth-century idea of self-governing associations and the alternative of allowing the state to regulate all corporate activities and instead wanted to subject large economic organizations to limits associated with checks on government power, specifically the requirement that corporations act to benefit the community.¹⁴

Berle and Means' conception of the corporation informed the early New Deal programs, the main focus of which was bringing relief and recovery through government planning and coordination.¹⁵ As Louis Jaffe put it, the different programs were grounded in the realization that, "the most significant and powerful components of the social structure [were] economic groups, competing and complementary in varying degrees";¹⁶ their thrust, as Means described it, was not to "make the

---

[12] Adolf A. Berle, Jr. and Gardiner C. Means, *The Modern Corporation and Private Property* (New York: Commerce Clearing House, 1932), pp. 354–357. For a detailed explanation of Berle and Means' view, see Dalia Tsuk, "From Pluralism to Individualism: Berle and Means and 20th-Century American Legal Thought" (2005) 30 *Law & Social Inquiry* 179. For a different interpretation of Berle's and his contemporaries' ideas see William W. Bratton and Michael L. Wachter, "Shareholder Primacy's Corporatist Origins: Adolf Berle and the Modern Corporation" (2008) 34 *Journal of Corporate Law* 99.

[13] For most of the nineteenth century, corporations were viewed as artificial entities, created by a charter from the state. By the late nineteenth century the fiction paradigm lost much of its credibility as states encouraged incorporation in their territories by reducing the requirement for a state charter into a mere formality. To accommodate the change, legal thinkers adopted either a contractual vision of the corporation or a natural entity one. The contractual paradigm described corporations as mere associations of individuals, similar to partnerships. In turn, the natural or real entity paradigm portrayed corporations as distinct from their individual members, though like them they had a real existence. Ultimately, the natural/real entity vision won over corporate legal theory.

[14] Tsuk, "From Pluralism to Individualism," pp. 195–196. Jurists also believed that the courts could enforce these trust obligations. But the idea of imposing a unified conception of social trusteeship on directors (and corporations) became less feasible after the US Supreme Court decision in *Erie Railroad Co.* v. *Tompkins* (1938) put an end to the idea of federal common law. *Ibid.*, p. 204.

[15] Joseph L. Weiner, "The New Deal and the Corporation" (1952) 19 *University of Chicago Law Review* 724, 724–725.

[16] Louis L. Jaffe, "Law Making by Private Groups" (1937) 51 *Harvard Law Review* 201.

market effective as a coordinator," which would have required "reversing the trend of a century and breaking the large units into a multitude of smaller enterprises." Rather, the thrust of the early New Deal was to keep the large units and increase "the element of administrative coordination of economic activity rather than its elimination."[17]

Still, as far as corporate law goes, the idea that corporate power was power in trust for the community was insufficient as a regulatory tool, a fact that did not escape its main proponents. Fearing that such an abstraction could even help legitimate abuses of corporate power, Berle tried to make the idea of trusteeship concrete. In "Corporate Powers as Powers in Trust," an article published in 1931, "[d]uring the penultimate stage of *The Modern Corporation*'s creation,"[18] he assigned corporate directors the task of guaranteeing the appropriate exercise of corporate power. Ironically, as I conclude, viewing directors as trustees helped ameliorate concerns about corporate power and thus legitimate it.

Berle's "Corporate Powers as Powers in Trust" was an argument designed to eliminate the potential for managerial abuse of its market powers. Berle wanted to protect those who were not in control of the corporate machinery from fraud and manipulative practices that were extremely harmful toward minority shareholders and that, at the time, plagued the securities markets. To that end, Berle surveyed corporate law doctrine with respect to a variety of managerial powers. He concluded, descriptively and normatively, that new stock issuance was allowed only when "the ratable interest of existing and prospective shareholders" was protected,[19] that dividends distribution had to benefit all shareholders,[20] that acquisition of stock in other corporations could not be used "to forward the enterprises of the managers as individuals or to subserve special interests within or without the corporation,"[21] that charter amendments had to "benefit the corporation as a whole, and ... distribute equitably the benefit or the sacrifice, as the case may be, between all the groups in the corporation as their interest may appear,"[22] and that the interests of all classes of shares had to be "respectively recognized and substantially protected" in merger and acquisition transactions.[23] To achieve these goals Berle wanted to

---

[17] Gardiner C. Means, "The Distribution of Control and Responsibility in a Modern Economy" (1935) 50 *Political Science Quarterly* 59, 63.
[18] Jordan A. Schwarz, *Liberal: Adolf A. Berle and the Vision of an American Era* (New York: Free Press, 1987), p. 64.
[19] A.A. Berle, Jr., "Corporate Powers as Powers in Trust" (1931) 44 *Harvard Law Review* 1050–1060.
[20] *Ibid.*, pp. 1060–1063.   [21] *Ibid.*, pp. 1063–1066.
[22] *Ibid.*, pp. 1066–1069.   [23] *Ibid.*, pp. 1069–1072.

make the powers to issue stock, to declare or withhold dividends, to acquire stock in other corporations, to amend the corporation's charter, and "to transfer the corporate enterprise to another enterprise by merger, exchange of stock, sale of assets or otherwise" – each power previously considered a matter of contract law[24] – a matter of the directors' trusteeship duties.

For contemporary scholars, describing corporate directors as trustees for the shareholders, as Berle did in "Corporate Powers as Powers in Trust," seems to be in direct contradiction to describing them as trustees for the community, as Berle and Means suggested in *The Modern Corporation and Private Property*. But for Berle the two positions were complementary. In a follow-up article, he explained that those in control did not see themselves as fiduciaries.[25] Any weakening of their obligations toward the shareholders would thus make their power absolute. As Berle pointedly, albeit perhaps apologetically, put it, "You cannot abandon the emphasis on 'the view that business corporations exist for the sole purpose of making profits for their stockholders' until such time as you are prepared to offer a clear and reasonably enforceable scheme of responsibilities to someone else."[26]

Berle's "Corporate Powers as Powers in Trust" was one of the first attempts to define a role for the board as distinguished from management. Berle wanted the board to mediate the conflicting interests of those in control of the enterprise and the individual shareholders subject to their powers. A few years later, William Douglas' "Directors Who Do Not Direct" followed suit, offering a more elaborate discussion of the function of the board.[27]

"Directors Who Do Not Direct" was published in 1934, shortly after the enactment of the securities acts, and three years before Douglas was to become Chairman of the Securities and Exchange Commission. It began by reiterating the "many different abuses and malpractices" of the 1920s – "secret loans to officers and directors, undisclosed profit-sharing plans, timely contracts unduly favorable to affiliated interests, dividend policies based on false estimates, manipulations of credit resources and capital structures to the detriment of minority interests,

---

[24] Rudolph E. Uhlman, "The Legal Status of Corporate Directors" (1939) 19 *Boston University Law Review* 12, 18.
[25] Adolf A. Berle, Jr., "For Whom Corporate Managers Are Trustees: A Note" (1932) 45 *Harvard Law Review* 1365, 1367.
[26] *Ibid*.
[27] See similarly Lawrence E. Mitchell, "The Trouble with Boards," in F. Scott Kieff and Troy A. Paredes (eds.), *Perspectives on Corporate Governance* (New York: Cambridge University Press, 2010) p. 17.

poor operations, and trading in securities of the company by virtue of inside information, to mention only a few."[28] As Douglas saw it, all these indicated that businessmen had lost sight of their public role.[29]

Douglas believed that the newly enacted federal securities laws offered some protection to shareholders by requiring accurate disclosure in the proxy solicitation process, but he did not think such disclosure was sufficient.[30] Seeking to encourage "the development of a social mindedness ... among business men and their legal advisers,"[31] Douglas' attention focused on corporate law. He wanted to make the board independent of management. While Berle's analysis focused on corporate power, particularly the power of the control group to manipulate the market, Douglas' main concern was management's control of the board, which, he believed, was at the root of the problems of the 1920s.[32]

According to Douglas, the purpose of the board of directors was to protect shareholders from management. To achieve this goal, directors had to be independent of management – they could not be "called in by the managers," drawn from the managers or be subordinate to the managers in any way. In fact, Douglas believed that the independent directors should be elected from among the shareholders. Furthermore, the independent directors were to have a role distinguished from the executives' role. While the executives were to manage the corporation, the independent board of directors was assigned the task of setting the corporation's policies and agenda and monitoring the executives lest they abuse their managerial power to benefit themselves or the control group. As Douglas put it, independent directors, "the representative of the stockholders, would be there, not for the purpose of managing the enterprise, but with the object of supervising those who do and of formulating the general commercial and financial policies under which the business is to be conducted."[33]

In an address delivered five years after the publication of "Directors Who Do Not Direct," Douglas went even further, suggesting that outside, independent directors should be "paid for their work in proportion to the actual contributions made by them."[34] Pay, he suggested, would go a long way toward the creation of a professional director.[35] It would allow

---

[28] William O. Douglas, "Directors Who Do Not Direct" (1934) 47 *Harvard Law Review* 1305, 1306.
[29] *Ibid.* [30] *Ibid.*, pp. 1323–1325.
[31] *Ibid.*, p. 1307.
[32] Mitchell, "Trouble with Boards," p. 25.
[33] Douglas, "Directors," pp. 1314–1315.
[34] Douglas, *Corporation Directors* in *Democracy and Finance*, p. 47.
[35] *Ibid.*, pp. 52–53.

outside, independent directors to protect the interests of the small stockholder as well as the community. "Since the beginning of corporate history – and particularly since corporations began to turn to the public for their funds," Douglas explained, "it has been recognized that the interests of the shareholders could not be adequately served by management alone ... The check of a board of vigilant, well-informed directors is needed to assure that management is always loyal, honest, and prudent."[36]

Lest he be misunderstood, Douglas emphasized that corporate powers were powers in trust. As he put it, "directors are trustees by virtue of business ethics as well as law, and the powers which they exercise are powers in trust."[37] "The paid director," he similarly pointed out in 1939, "would revive and strengthen the tradition of trusteeship ... In a larger sense, he would not be so much a paid director or a professional director as a *public* director, representing not only the present but the potential stockholder, and representing the general public as well."[38]

In the end, while Douglas' focus was not corporate power but corporate internal hierarchies, he, like Berle, saw no contradiction between the directors' role as trustees for the community and their role as representatives of the shareholders. Douglas' and Berle's writings focused on the need to tame and constrain those in control, whether investment bankers, minority owners or management. Demanding that corporations act as trustees for the community and that directors represent the interests of the shareholders were thus complementary requirements.[39]

Berle's and Douglas' arguments did not stimulate a continuing scholarly debate about the role or legal status of the board of directors. The policies of the New Deal seemed to circumscribe the corporation's powers. The federal securities acts regulated the corporation's dealings with its shareholders as well as its creditors, new federal labor laws regulated the corporation's relations with its employees, and antitrust laws affected the corporation's behavior toward consumers and suppliers.[40]

---

[36] *Ibid.*, p. 50.   [37] Douglas, "Directors," p. 1322.
[38] Douglas, *Corporation Directors* in *Democracy and Finance*, p. 53.
[39] Douglas' "Directors Who Do Not Direct" concluded by stressing the need to develop "adequate administrative controls so that the domain of regulation will be neither wholly in the courts nor largely *ex post facto*." Douglas, "Directors," p. 1328. Douglas wanted to see the development of a professional managerial class, "skilled in the technique of business, the art of law, and the skill of government." *Ibid.* Such a class, he believed, could monitor corporations so as to align the interests of the shareholders with the interests of the public – "so that the profit motive will be articulated with the public good" and the investor assured "more protection against the malpractices of management." *Ibid.*
[40] Herbert Hovenkamp, "The Classical Corporation in American Legal Thought" (1988) 76 *Georgetown Law Journal* 1593, 1688. See also E. Merrick Dodd, "The Modern Corporation, Private Property, and Recent Federal Legislation" (1941) 54

Even as corporations continued to gain tremendous power, concerns about the corporation's external power rapidly dissipated while legal scholarship about corporate internal hierarchies focused on the board's control of the proxy machinery and its duty of loyalty.[41]

At the same time, however, the idea that directors were representatives of the shareholders significantly influenced state corporate law, specifically developments relating to the shareholders' ability to sue directors for breaches of their fiduciary obligations. As the following sections explain, viewing directors as representatives substantiated the courts' growing deference to directors' expertise and discretion. Ironically, just as the notion that directors were representatives of the shareholders was disassociated from the idea that they were trustees for the community, the courts' deferential approach paved the road for the erosion of directors' duties toward their corporations and their shareholders.

III   Representation

The early 1940s witnessed growing fascination with corporate democracy, mirroring perhaps "the emergence of democracy as a basic concept in American constitutional law" at the same time.[42] With totalitarianism in Europe, American social scientists, who in the early decades of the twentieth century focused on challenging absolutist theories in law, politics and morals, were left to wonder why the United States had been spared the ravages of European dictatorship. Political and legal theorists beginning in the late 1930s thus struggled to explain the contrast between democratic and non-democratic societies. As Morton Horwitz notes, "this new obsession with democratic theory was designed to show how America had managed to avoid succumbing to European totalitarianism."[43]

Two versions of corporate democracy vied for scholarly attention: the first one focused on enhancing shareholders' participation rights (leading, among others, to the enactment of the shareholder proposal rule);[44] the second one described corporate democracy as representative democracy. In a corporate law that was dominated by the ideology of

---

Harvard Law Review 917 (discussing the impact of the New Deal legislation on the relationship between management and security holders).

[41] Mitchell, "Trouble with Boards," p. 26.
[42] Morton Horwitz and Orlando do Campo, "When and How the Supreme Court Found Democracy – A Computer Study" (1994) 14 *Quinnipiac Law Review* 1, 28.
[43] *Ibid.*, pp. 28–29.
[44] For a detailed history of the shareholder proposal rule, see Dalia Tsuk Mitchell, "Shareholders as Proxies: The Contours of Shareholder Democracy" (2006) 63 *Washington and Lee Law Review* 1503.

managerialism at least since the 1930s, it is perhaps not surprising that the latter won over.

Take, for example, Robert A. Kessler's provocative 1960 article entitled "The Statutory Requirement of a Board of Directors: A Corporate Anachronism." Having reviewed numerous court decisions, Kessler concluded that in a majority of jurisdictions, the board of directors was regarded as "a kind of a group of Platonic guardians whose right to rule was a legislative mandate."[45] Accordingly, shareholders could not "give orders to the directors, or act for the corporation, unless by unanimous vote or agreement."[46] As Kessler pointedly put it:

> Although the cases do not make it express, they indicate that the status of the board of directors is analogous to that of a legislative body under a "delegative" theory of democratic government. The directors have been held to be the "representatives" of the entire body of shareholders and hence not subject to the dictates of even a majority of their "constituents," the shareholders. Their decisions are required to be made at a board meeting, at which they may not be represented by proxy, although each director individually consents to the proposed action. Such a requirement can be justified only on the ground that the deliberative body of "the elect," analogous to the conception held by the founding fathers for the United States Senate.[47]

The leading jurisdiction was New York where cases in the 1930s typically demonstrated "respect for the board of directors as an inviolable institution" with whose actions the shareholders could not intervene.[48] Take as one example *McQuade* v. *Stoneham*, a case involving an agreement between a majority of the shareholders of the National Exhibition Company to ensure that all three of them continued to serve as directors and officers and to receive a set amount of salary, or dividends, from the corporation. Writing for the majority, Judge Pound of the New York Court of Appeals declared the agreement void. As he explained: "the stockholders may not, by agreement among themselves, control the directors in the exercise of the judgment vested in them by virtue of their office to elect officers and fix salaries ... Directors may not by agreements entered into as stockholders abrogate their independent judgment."[49]

Beyond their refusal to allow shareholders to control the board (even in closely held corporation), courts were also disinclined to evaluate

---

[45] Robert A. Kessler, "The Statutory Requirement of A Board of Directors: A Corporate Anachronism" (1960) 27 *University of Chicago Law Review* 696, 697.
[46] *Ibid.*, p. 700.   [47] *Ibid.*, p. 701.   [48] *Ibid.*, p. 698.
[49] *McQuade* v. *Stoneham*, 189 N.E. 234, 236 (N.Y. 1932). According to Kessler, the only exception to this rule was *Clark* v. *Dodge*, 199 N.E. 641 (N.Y. 1936), which involved a closely held corporation in which the only two shareholders were the officers and directors of the corporation. *Ibid.*, p. 698.

directors' decisions. Since the turn of the twentieth century, New York courts expanded the nineteenth-century rule that exempted directors from liability for honest mistakes, that is, mistakes that even a prudent person might make,[50] to include all matters entrusted to directors' discretion. For example, in 1914, Judge Cardozo wrote that mere disagreement about the expediency of particular transactions was not a reason for "the court ... to revise the judgment of the directors, and substitute its conclusion for theirs."[51] In a similar manner, in 1931, in *City Bank Farmers' Trust Co. v. Hewitt Realty Co.*, a case involving a request to compel directors to declare dividends, the New York Court of Appeals drew a distinction between situations where directors breached their trust, or acted in bad faith, or engaged in fraud, which warranted the court's intervention, and "questions of expediency" which the courts should not evaluate as "such questions are confided by the Legislature in the directors."[52]

It was not long before the courts refrained from evaluating directors' actions in matters entrusted to their discretion even when the directors' errors were gross. Take as one example *Everett v. Phillips*, a suit by a minority shareholder of Empire Power Corporation to compel directors sitting both on its board and on the board of Long Island Lighting Company to demand payment of indebtedness from the lighting company to the power company. In determining that the directors did not violate their trust to the power company or its shareholders, the Court of Appeals of New York noted that not merely innocent mistakes but also gross mistakes were protected from *ex post* intervention by the courts. As Chief Judge Lehman put it, "[H]owever high may be the standard

---

[50] Perhaps the earliest articulation of this exemption was found in *Percy & Al. v. Millaudon & Al.*, 8 MART. (n.s.) 68, 77–78 (La. 1829) ("[T]he adoption of a course from which loss ensues cannot make the [director] responsible, if the error was one into which a prudent man might have fallen ... The test of responsibility therefore, should be, not the certainty of wisdom in others, but the possession of ordinary knowledge and by showing that the error of the [director] is of so gross a kind that a man of common sense, and ordinary attention, would not have fallen into it"). For further discussion see S. Samuel Arsht, "The Business Judgment Rule Revisited" (1980) 8 *Hofstra Law Review* 93, 99–100.

[51] *Holmes v. St. Joseph Lead Co.*, 147 N.Y.S. 104, 107 (Sup. Ct. 1914). For a more elaborate, and often quoted, description of the rule, see *Pollitz v. Wabash R.R. Co.*, 100 N.E. 721, 724 (N.Y. 1912) ("Questions of policy of management, expediency of contracts or action, adequacy of consideration, lawful appropriation of corporate funds to advance corporate interests, are left solely to [the directors'] honest and unselfish decision, for their powers therein are without limitation and free from restraint, and the exercise of them for the common and general interests of the corporation may not be questioned, although the results show that what they did was unwise or inexpedient").

[52] *City Bank Farmers Trust Co. v. Hewitt Realty Co.*, 177 N.E. 309, 311 (N.Y. 1931).

of fidelity to duty which the court may exact, errors of judgment by directors do not alone suffice to demonstrate lack of fidelity. That is true even though the errors may be so gross that they may demonstrate the unfitness of the directors to manage the corporate affairs."[53]

Gradually, exemptions to directors' liability encroached upon the standard of care applicable to their actions. As Justice Bernard Shientag of the New York Supreme Court noted in 1944, "although the concept of 'responsibility' is firmly fixed in the law, it is only in a most unusual and extraordinary case that directors are held liable for negligence in the absence of fraud, or improper motive, or personal interest."[54]

Also gradually, the idea that directors were representatives of the shareholders was replaced by the notion that they were the shareholders' agents, a seemingly minute but in practice rather significant difference. Take *Bayer v. Beran*, a case involving a derivative suit brought by the shareholders of the Celanese Corporation of America against their directors for alleged breaches of their fiduciary duties. These allegations focused on the directors' approval of a radio advertising campaign in which the president's wife, a professional opera singer, was sometimes featured. The shareholders argued, first, that the directors were negligent in approving the campaign and, second, that the campaign was engaged in to further the career of the president's wife.[55]

Addressing the appropriate obligations of directors to the corporation and its shareholders, Shientag proclaimed: "Directors of a business corporation are not trustees and are not held to strict accountability as such." Rather, as he put it, "directors are agents; they are fiduciaries."[56] As such, they had two obligations: "responsibility and loyalty."[57] The level of care and diligence required of directors as agents or fiduciaries was "proportioned to the occasion."[58]

---

[53] *Everett v. Phillips*, 43 N.E.2d 18, 19–20 (N.Y. 1942). While *Everett* involved a duty of loyalty claim, the statement quoted above applied both to duty of loyalty and duty of care situations. See also *Rous v. Carlisle*, 26 N.Y.S.2d 197, 200 (App. Div. 1941) ("If a director exercises his business judgment in good faith on the information before him, he may not be called to account through the judicial process, even though he may have erred in his judgment. It is necessary, therefore, for the stockholder to allege facts showing more than error in business judgment").

[54] *Bayer v. Beran*, 49 N.Y.S.2d 2, 6–7 (Sup. Ct. 1944). It is important to note that *Bayer v. Beran* also helped shift the focus of discussion of breaches of duty of loyalty from trust to fairness, thus helping to bring about the erosion of the directors' and officers' duty of loyalty. For an intriguing discussion of the twentieth-century devolution of the duty of loyalty, see Lawrence E. Mitchell, "Fairness and Trust in Corporate Law" (1993) 43 *Duke Law Journal* 25.

[55] *Bayer*, 49 N.Y.S.2d, at p. 5.   [56] *Ibid.*, at p. 5.

[57] *Ibid.*, at p. 2.   [58] *Ibid.*, at p. 3.

Interestingly, Shientag labeled directors agents even though he viewed their status as analogous to the status of democratically elected representatives. He stressed that the power to manage the corporation was vested in the board and that the judicial role was to discourage shareholders from interfering with the directors' "free and independent judgment."[59] (If directors were agents of the shareholders, the latter, as principals, would determine the scope of their power.)

Beyond labels, Shientag also changed the requirements that the description of directors as representatives of the shareholders implied. With a nod to the general rule that directors as agents of the stockholders (and, more accurately, as their representatives) "are given by law no power to act except as a board,"[60] Shientag was willing to validate corporate decisions that did not follow this requirement. As he put it, "the failure to observe the formal requirements is by no means fatal."[61] In *Bayer*, despite the fact that no formal meeting was held to approve the advertising campaign prior to its introduction, Shientag proclaimed that the directors fulfilled their care and diligence responsibilities.[62]

A decade later, albeit in a different context, the Court of Appeals of New York went even further in eroding the status of directors as representatives. *Auer* v. *Dressel* was an action by stockholders to compel the corporation's president to call a special meeting, among other things, so that the shareholders could vote on a resolution endorsing the conduct of Mr. Auer as president and requesting that he be reinstated. While the selection of officers was within the realm of the directors' discretion, the court held that the shareholders could call a special meeting to express "their approval of Mr. Auer's conduct as president and their demand that he be put back in that office."[63] "It would be preposterous," the court reiterated, "to leave the real owners of the corporate property at the mercy of their agents."[64]

Judge Van Voorhis, in dissent, continued to endorse the notion that the directors' status was analogous to the electorate in democratic governments. As he announced, the statute provides that "the business of a corporation shall be managed by its board of directors."[65] Having been elected by the shareholders "for stated terms which have not expired," the board, not the stockholders, had the power to appoint the officers of the corporation. Accordingly, "for the stockholders to vote on the proposition would be an idle gesture."[66]

---

[59] *Bayer*, 49 N.Y.S.2d at p. 6.
[60] *Ibid.*, at p. 11.   [61] *Ibid.*   [62] *Ibid.*, at p. 10.
[63] *Matter of Auer* v. *Dressel*, 118 N.E.2d 590, 593 (N.Y. 1954).
[64] *Ibid.*, at p. 593 (quoting *Rogers* v. *Hill*, 289 US 582, 589 (1933)).
[65] *Ibid.*, at p. 595 (Van Voorhis J., dissenting).
[66] *Ibid.*, at p. 594.

Despite Van Voorhis' and similar critiques, the tides were rapidly shifting. For purposes of allowing directors to act without interference from the shareholders, the vision of directors as representatives of the shareholders seemed to survive. But it was supplemented by a new set of ideas that helped shield the board from liability almost absolutely. By the 1970s the emergence of a new economic theory of the corporation, which recognized no internal power or hierarchy, gave rise to the idea that directors were not representatives but merely the shareholders' agents whose task was limited to monitoring the executives. Independent directors were seen as best suited for this task. With a limited role came very limited liability. By the mid-1980s, the Delaware courts collapsed the duty of care into the business judgment rule; they declared that the business judgment rule altered the standard of care from negligence to gross negligence and made gross negligence a prerequisite for rebutting the presumption of the business judgment rule. Moreover, the Delaware courts declared that if a majority of the independent, disinterested directors approved the board's actions (including conflict of interest transactions), such actions would be protected from *ex post* judicial examination. For all practical purposes, directors were shielded from liability for their decisions and actions.

IV Legitimacy

Beginning in the late 1930s and continuing until the mid-1970s, Keynesian economics gained wide acceptance among American scholars. Predicated upon the belief that governments should not choose among competing, individual visions of the public good, it helped legitimate a regulatory shift from "planning" to "accepting existing consumer preferences" and "manipulating aggregate demand."[67] Both those who criticized the early New Deal as only increasing the concentration of power in a few hands and those who criticized it as increasing government power found in the new consumer ideology a point of convergence. The former wanted to expand the regulatory functions of the administrative state to protect consumers and promote full production, while the latter wanted the state only to redress "weaknesses and imbalances in the private economy without directly confronting the internal workings of capitalism" – to "manage the economy without managing the institutions of the economy."[68]

---

[67] Alan Brinkley, "The New Deal and the Idea of the State," in Steve Fraser and Gary Gerstle (eds.), *The Rise and Fall of the New Deal Order, 1930–1980* (Princeton: Princeton University Press, 1989), pp. 85, 92, 98.
[68] *Ibid.*, pp. 94, 87–97.

In the 1940s, with totalitarianism in Europe, and scholars' growing concerns about the relationship between statism and tyranny, the compensatory, fiscal vision of the state, which entailed only limited power, became the more appealing one. At the same time, the economic boom produced by the war effort made the need for regulation less urgent. The economy seemed to do well without government interference. A vision of a free market, corrected on rare occasions by the state's fiscal hand, began to dominate economic thought.[69]

The growing academic faith in the power of economic markets to produce and serve the common good opened a door for the introduction of economics into corporate law. Neo-classical economists, who thus far had focused their theorizing efforts on markets, turned to the corporation's internal structure. Their new economic theory of the firm offered a picture of the corporation that fit the market-centered economic policies of the postwar years. Rather than putting management hierarchies or the need to constrain corporate power at the center of the corporate paradigm, the new economic theory of the firm found a way around hierarchical power and its consequent need for regulation. Drawing on microeconomics, it painted a picture of the corporation as a nexus of private, contractual relationships. This cleared the way for presumably egalitarian economic markets to become the relevant focal point.[70] The corporation was a collection of "disaggregated but interrelated transactions" among individuals or the convenient fiction of corporate entity in free and efficient markets.[71]

The new theory of the firm supported a shift of focus in scholarly debates from questions of power, influence, sanctions and legitimacy to issues of cost reduction and profit maximization.[72] Its proponents reframed the problems of corporate power and hierarchies as the problem of the separation of ownership from control (or agency costs) and sought to demonstrate how capital markets could eliminate the concerns about efficiency associated with this separation.[73]

---

[69] On these developments, see *ibid.*, pp. 97–121; Alan Brinkley, *The End of Reform: New Deal Liberalism in Recession and War* (New York: Alfred A. Knopf 1995), pp. 154–165; Michael J. Sandel, *Democracy's Discontent: America in Search of a Public Philosophy* (Boston: Harvard University Press, 1996), pp. 250–273.

[70] William W. Bratton, Jr., "The 'Nexus of Contracts' Corporation: A Critical Appraisal" (1989) 74 *Cornell Law Review* 407, 416–420.

[71] *Ibid.*, p. 420.

[72] William W. Bratton, Jr., "The New Economic Theory of the Firm: Critical Perspectives from History" (1989) 41 *Stanford Law Review* 1471, 1498.

[73] See, for example, Daniel R. Fischel, "The Corporate Governance Movement" (1982) 35 *Vanderbilt Law Review* 1259. See also Tsuk, "Pluralism to Individualism," pp. 212–215 (discussing the new economic theory of the firm).

Interestingly, the Delaware courts, whose claim to fame was their analysis of the hostile takeover cases of the 1980s, refused to legitimate the market, specifically the market for control, as a means of constraining directors and executives. In *Unocal Corp. v. Mesa Petroleum Co.*, the seminal takeover case, the Delaware Supreme Court drew upon the board's "fundamental duty and obligation to protect the corporate enterprise" to create the power of the board to adopt defensive tactics that would thwart hostile takeovers (and the market for control).[74] A decade later, in *Unitrin, Inc. v. American General Corp.*, the Delaware Supreme Court went as far as to empower directors to fight all-cash, all-shares premium tender offers and, for all practical purposes, eliminated the market for control.[75] As the court saw it, as long as a proxy contest was a possibility, even a remote one, the market for control remained viable.[76]

Yet, while the Delaware courts seemed to continue to embrace the 1940s conception of representative democracy, they also strongly endorsed one of the ideas that followed directly from the new economic theory of the firm and that substantially undermined the conception of representative democracy, namely, the idea that directors were agents of their shareholders. Chancellor Allen's decision in *Blasius Industries, Inv. v. Atlas Corp.* illustrates this point. *Blasius* involved a conflict between Atlas's board and Atlas's largest shareholder, Blasius. In an attempt to prevent or at least delay Blasius from placing a majority of new directors on the board, Atlas's board increased its size by two and filled the newly created directorships.[77] Chancellor Allen began by stressing that corporate law "does not create Platonic masters."[78] Rather, the shareholders, as principals, could view issues differently than did the board and "[i]f they do, or did, they are entitled to employ the mechanisms provided by the corporation law and the ... certificate of incorporation" to advance their views.[79] Moreover, the shareholders, in Chancellor Allen's opinion, were entitled "to restrain their agents, the board, from acting for the principal purpose of thwarting that action."[80]

---

[74] *Unocal Corp. v. Mesa Petroleum Co.*, 493 A.2d 946 (Del. 1985). The court enumerated several provisions of the Delaware General Corporations Law as sources for the board's power but none of these provisions was explicitly meant to address takeovers.
[75] *Unitrin, Inc. v. American General Corp.*, 651 A.2d 1361 (Del. 1995).
[76] See *ibid.*, at pp. 1382–1383. For a critique of this approach launched by an ardent advocate of the new theory of the firm (albeit prior to the cases discussed here), see Henry G. Manne, "Cash Tender Offers for Shares – A Reply to Chairman Cohen" (1967) 16 *Duke Law Journal* 231; Henry G. Manne, "In Defense of the Corporate Coup" (1984) 11 *Northern Kentucky Law Review* 513.
[77] *Blasius Industries, Inv. v. Atlas Corp.*, 564 A.2d 651, 652–656 (Del. 1988).
[78] *Ibid.*, at p. 663.   [79] *Ibid.*   [80] *Ibid.*

One would be mistaken, however, to assume that Chancellor Allen (or the Delaware courts) fully embraced the idea that directors were agents of the shareholders. If such were the case, directors would not be able to act without the explicit or, at least, implied consent of their principals. But, while Chancellor Allen would not allow directors to affect the shareholders' ability to elect their agents, he was fully content to permit directors to prevent shareholders from selling their stock to a hostile bidder (a more meaningful action).[81] Indeed, the issue was one of legitimacy. Chancellor Allen used agency theory to legitimate the status of directors as, ironically, Platonic masters. As he put it, the "shareholder franchise" was "the ideological underpinning upon which the legitimacy of directorial power rests."[82] The shareholders' vote, often dismissed "as a vestige or a ritual of little practical importance," was a means of legitimating management's exercise of power. As Allen noted, whether the vote was "seen functionally as an unimportant formalism, or as an important tool of discipline," it "legitimate[d] the exercise of power by some (directors and officers) over vast aggregations of property that they [did] not own."[83]

Directors, in short, were neither trustees nor representatives, but agents of the shareholders. Yet, the obligations derived from their status as agents were limited to allowing shareholders to exercise their voting power, a meaningless ritual at best.

---

[81] See, for example, Chancellor Allen's decision in *Paramount Commc'ns, Inc. v. Time, Inc.*, 1989 Del. Ch. LEXIS 77, at 89–90 (July 14, 1989) ("[T]he financial vitality of the corporation and the value of the company's shares is in the hands of the directors and managers of the firm. The corporation law does not operate on the theory that directors, in exercising their powers to manage the firm, are obligated to follow the wishes of a majority of shares. In fact, directors, not shareholders, are charged with the duty to manage the firm ... That many, presumably most, shareholders would prefer the board to do otherwise than it has done does not, in the circumstances of a challenge to this type of transaction, in my opinion, afford a basis to interfere with the effectuation of the board's business judgment"). See also Robert B. Thompson, "Shareholders as Grown-Ups: Voting, Selling, and Limits on the Board's Power to 'Just Say No'" (1999) 67 *University Cincinnati Law Review* 999, 1011–1014 (noting the apparent inconsistencies between the Delaware courts' disempowerment of shareholders in the hostile takeover cases and their approach in cases such as *Blasius*). Thompson concludes that "Delaware has long preferred a corporate governance system that is very indirect. Directors, elected by the shareholders make almost all corporate decisions, including those relating to takeovers. Shareholders have a limited say by a limited ability to replace the directors. Just as shareholder views about a takeover can be channeled away from a selling decision and into a proxy decision, so can voting decisions be channeled into an annual meeting or perhaps requiring action at two annual meetings before shareholder decision-making can prevail. The growth in the role of institutional investors as shareholders has not been enough to move Delaware from its long-stated preference of indirect democracy." *Ibid.*, at p. 1020.
[82] *Blasius*, 564 A.2d at p. 659.   [83] *Ibid.*

The Delaware courts went further. First, accepting that the role of the board was to monitor the executives (rather than to manage the corporation), the Delaware courts turned their attention to the growing numbers of independent directors serving on boards (independence narrowly defined as lack of control or domination by an individual interested in the transaction).[84] Just as boards began adopting a wide range of anti-takeover tactics, the Delaware courts declared that if a majority of the independent, disinterested directors approved the board's actions (including conflict of interest transactions and defensive tactics), such actions would be shielded from further judicial inquiry.[85] As Lawrence Mitchell writes, the "cleansing effect" or "protective effect" of the independent directors allowed the courts to look not at the substance of the actions but the procedures pursuant to which they had been taken. Good process – decision-making by reasonably informed, rational, independent boards – allowed the courts entirely to bypass the substance of the decision-making.[86]

As to the duty of care, the Delaware Supreme Court collapsed it into the business judgment rule and proclaimed that to invoke the business judgment rule's protection directors had a duty merely to inform themselves, prior to making a business decision, of all material information reasonably available to them.[87] Without precedent to support its holding, the Delaware Supreme Court further announced that "under the business judgment rule director liability is predicated upon concepts of gross negligence."[88] Unless a plaintiff arguing a breach of the duty of care demonstrated that the directors were grossly negligent (that is,

---

[84] *Grobow v. Perot*, 539 A.2d 180, 188–189 (Del. 1988). For an insightful analysis of "independence" under Delaware law, see Usha Rodrigues, "The Fetishization of Independence" (2008) 33 *Journal of Corporation Law* 447.

[85] *Moran v. Household Int'l, Inc.*, 500 A.2d 1346, 1356 (Del. 1985); *Revlon, Inc. v. MacAndrews & Forbes Holding, Inc.*, 506 A.2d 173, 176 n.3 (Del. 1986); *Paramount Commc'ns, Inc. v. Time Inc.*, 571 A.2d 1140, 1154 (Del. 1989).

[86] Mitchell, "Trouble with Boards," p. 55.

[87] See *Aronson v. Lewis*, 473 A.2d 805, 812 (Del. 1984); Dalia Tsuk Mitchell, "Status Bound: The Twentieth-Century Evolution of Directors' Liability," (2009) 5 *New York University Journal of Law & Business* 63. See also Lyman Johnson, "The Modest Business Judgment Rule" (2000) 55 *Business Law* 625, 641–642. According to Johnson, *Aronson* changed the traditional presumption that directors acted "in good faith, in the exercise of their best judgment, for what they believed to be the advantage of the corporation and all its stockholders" into a presumption that "in making a business decision the directors of a corporation acted on an informed basis, in good faith and in the honest belief that the action taken was in the best interests of the company." *Ibid.*, at p. 640. For the traditional formulation of the rule see, for example, *Bodell v. Gen. Gas & Elec. Corp.*, 140 A. 264, 268 (Del. 1927).

[88] *Aronson*, 473 A.2d at p. 812. See also Johnson, "Business Judgment Rule," p. 643 n.81 (noting that this sentence captured "*Aronson*'s functional conflating of the duty of care and the business judgment rule").

grossly negligent with respect to the requirement to be informed), the directors would have the presumption of the business judgment rule and the court would not second-guess their actions.[89] In short, a rule that originated in an understanding of human fallibility, and transformed into a rule of deference to expert opinion, had become, by century's end, a defense precluding judicial inquiry into the directors' challenged actions.[90]

Conceptually, this new vision of the business judgment rule was the logical result of treating directors as agents. While the idea that directors were representatives of the shareholders correlated well with a rule of deference to their expert judgment, the notion that directors were agents undermined such deference. As agents, directors could not be presumed to be experts. They could only be described as performing the tasks assigned to them by their principals, the shareholders. In such a context, the business judgment rule could only be a means of protecting directors from their principals when the latter challenged how the task was performed; it could only be a rule shielding directors from liability.

At any rate, if up to the 1980s directors might have been held liable for violations of their fiduciary obligations (although they seldom were),[91] by the end of the decade such possibility was virtually nonexistent.[92] As long as directors, insiders and outsiders alike, followed the scripts that the Delaware courts had provided them throughout the 1980s, the

---

[89] *Smith v. Van Gorkom*, 488 A.2d 858, 873 (1985).
[90] See Arsht, "Business Judgment Rule Revisited," at p. 100 ("[T]he business judgment rule was not conceived as a defense that, once asserted, precluded judicial inquiry into the procedures and methodologies followed by the directors in making their challenged decision." Rather "the business judgment rule was a starting point for inquiry into the directors' decisionmaking process").
[91] Before the 1980s, only in "a handful of cases outside the context of financial institutions ... directors of business corporations had been found liable for breach of their duty of care." Henry Ridgely Horsey, "The Duty of Care Component of the Delaware Business Judgment Rule" (1994) 19 *Delaware Journal of Corporate Law* 971, 978. For the most part, commentators agree that "the business judgment rule has historically proved to be 'a very potent defense for corporate directors and officers against claims primarily asserted by shareholders for loss resulting from decisions that went awry.'" *Ibid.*, at pp. 978–980.
[92] It is important to note section 102(b)(7) of the Delaware General Corporation Law which was enacted shortly after the Delaware Supreme Court's decision in *Van Gorkom* and which allows corporations to include in their charters provisions that limit, or even eliminate, the personal liability of directors for almost all breaches of the duty of care. (Other jurisdictions followed suit. See Mark A. Sargent and Dennis R. Honabach, *D & O Liability Handbook* (New York: Thompson West ed., 2008).) Ironically, even without section 102(b)(7), the Delaware courts would have been able to shield corporate directors and officers from liability.

Delaware courts would not re-evaluate their decisions. In corporate law at the turn of the twenty-first century, managerial power is absolute power.

V Epilogue

The 1980s increased focus on the independent directors' monitoring role went hand-in-hand with the rise of shareholder-valuism as the norm governing corporate law. With directors having limited time and knowledge, stock price appreciation became the metric for a board's success, and investors – apathetic individuals and institutions alike – demanded it. The Delaware courts' decisions validated such demands by advising directors as the shareholders' agents to maximize shareholder profit so as not to trigger their principals' fury. Accommodating agents as the courts encouraged them to be, corporate boards have since helped lead US industry into a deep recession.[93]

The financial collapse, at the turn of the twenty-first century, of companies as divergent as Enron, WorldCom and, more recently, American International Group and General Motors have brought the board of directors back to the front pages of newspapers around the country while scholars draw upon century-old ideas of agency and representation (or expertise) to suggest ways to reform corporate America.

Some find hope in empowering shareholders, first and foremost by making their vote real. Seemingly accepting the notion that directors are the shareholders' agents, Lucian Bebchuk, one of the leading voices in this campaign, further advocates allowing shareholders "to amend the corporate charter or to change the company's state of incorporation," as well as to play a role in "specific business decisions of substantial importance."[94]

Responding to such calls, in 2007 North Dakota enacted its Publicly Traded Corporations Act, which allows shareholders to propose the adoption, amendment or repeal of a bylaw, as well as gives shareholders access to the ballot to nominate directors and demands that the corporation's proxy materials reflect such nominations.[95] In 2009 the SEC approved a proposal to give shareholders the ability to nominate

---

[93] Lawrence E. Mitchell and Dalia T. Mitchell, "The Financial Detriments of American Corporate Governance: A Brief History," in H. Kent Baker and Ronald Anderson (eds.), *Corporate Governance* (Robert W. Kolb series: 2010) p. 19.
[94] Lucian Arye Bebchuk, "The Case for Increasing Shareholder Power" (2005) 118 *Harvard Law Review* 833, 837.
[95] Publicly Traded Corporations Act, N. Dak 10–35–01 to 10–35–33 (2007).

directors via company proxy materials.[96] Even Delaware has modified its laws to permit corporations to provide greater participation rights to shareholders.[97]

The efforts to increase shareholder power face opposition, however, from scholars who argue that directors, as distinguished from managers, should be empowered to control the affairs of their corporations. In words that resonate with the 1940s model of representative democracy, Stephen Bainbridge, who best elaborated this model of director primacy, writes:

> the board of directors is not a mere agent of the shareholders, but rather is a sort of Platonic guardian serving as the nexus of the various contracts making up the corporation. As a positive theory of corporate governance, the director primacy model strongly emphasizes the role of fiat – i.e., the centralized decisionmaking authority possessed by the board of directors.[98]

Assessing which model – the shareholder-centric model or the director primacy model – is likely to be more effective in preventing financial scandals of recent magnitude is beyond the scope of this chapter. But it is interesting to use these models to illustrate how the developments described in this chapter have helped limit our conception of the directors' role. With shareholder-valuism as the norm governing corporate law, advocates of either the shareholder-centric model or the director primacy model claim to offer the model of corporate governance that holds the greatest promise for enhancing firm – in fact, shareholder – value.

Having legitimated the modern public corporation and its power in the first half of the twentieth century, having shielded directors from liability in the second half of the twentieth century, scholars and jurists at the turn of the twenty-first century have come to accept that corporations and their directors serve a rather limited role. With power, no liability, and an extremely limited definition of their role, one that, incidentally, had nothing to do with business as business, perhaps we should not be surprised when financial crisis strikes.

---

[96] Facilitating Shareholder Director Nominations, Securities Act Release No. 9046, Exchange Act Release No. 60,089, Investment Company Act Release No. 28,765, 74 Fed. Reg. 29024 (proposed June 10, 2009) (to be codified at 17 C.F.R. pts. 200, 232, 240, 249, 274).
[97] 8 Del. Gen. Corp. L. 112, 113 (2009).
[98] Stephen M. Bainbridge, "Director Primacy: The Means and Ends of Corporate Governance" (2003) 97 *Northwestern University Law Review* 547, 605.

5 Engaging corporate boards: the limits of liability rules in modern corporate governance

William T. Allen

I Introduction

The financial crisis that the global economy has endured since 2008 has led to a renewed focus on the corporate governance of banks and related financial institutions.[1] Boards of directors of large financial institutions have been justly criticized in some instances for paying insufficient attention to the operations of their firms, especially to the financial risks that their business models engendered and to the incentive that their compensation practices created. Indeed these criticisms particularly were cited by US Senator Charles Schumer in introducing his Shareholders Bill of Rights Act in May 2009, which would have imposed a host of mandated corporate governance practices or structures on all US public companies.[2] They were emphasized too by the Chair of the Securities and Exchange Commission [SEC], Mary Shapiro, in announcing a revised version of the SEC's proposed rule change that would, under stated circumstances, permit shareholders access to company proxy solicitation statements for purposes of nominating a limited number of company directors.[3] While, given the significant governmental policy failures that stood behind the crisis, one might conclude that such attributions by public officials were merely opportunistic, or meant to deflect public attention, nevertheless they do remind us that control over the internal affairs of large scale business corporations is a matter of substantial public concern.

---

[1] See Peter O. Mülbert, *Corporate Governance of Banks After the Financial Crisis – Theory, CEvidence, Reform*, ECGI Working Paper No. 130/2009 (2010), available at: http://ssrn.com/abstract=1448118 (last accessed February 22, 2011).
[2] See http://schumer.senate.gov/new_website/record.cfm?id=313468 (last accessed February 22, 2011). That bill was superseded by Senator Dodd's bill on financial regulation, which continued some but not all of Schumer's corporate governance mandates.
[3] See www.sec.gov/news/press/2009/2009-116.htm (last accessed February 22, 2011).

Even considered apart from the unique public concerns that surround the operation of the banking and finance industry,[4] the modern business corporation is an institution of immense public significance.[5] The business corporation is the instrumentality within which the greatest part of our economic activity occurs, a major locus of jobs and wealth creation, and through which, to a large extent, our national competitiveness is maintained.[6] It is largely within the corporate form that all of the great scientific discoveries from the time of the second industrial revolution forward have been shaped into useful products or services and brought to markets to improve human lives. The legal rules and practices and the economic techniques we deploy to incentivize and to control the various individuals playing roles within these institutions matters to their efficiency and thus matters to our wealth production. Thus to the extent corporate governance rules and practices affect the productivity of these instrumentalities they deserve our close attention.[7]

---

[4] For a timely comparative study of banking regulation in the United States, the United Kingdom, Germany and Switzerland, see Andreas Busch, *Banking Regulation and Globalization* (Oxford: Oxford University Press, 2009).

[5] Cynthia Williams and Ruth Aguilera, "Corporate Social Responsibility in a Comparative Perspective," in A. Crane, A. McWilliams, D. Matten, J. Moon and D.S. Siegel (eds.), *Oxford Handbook of Corporate Social Responsibility* (Oxford: Oxford University Press, 2008), p. 452; see Edward S. Mason, "Introduction," in Edward Mason (ed.), *The Corporation in Modern Society* (Cambridge, MA: Harvard University Press 1960), p. 1.

[6] US government statistics suggest that from the period following the close of World War II through 2005 the proportion of the nation's GDP that was produced within the corporate form rose from slightly above 50 percent to something above 60 percent. See William Allen, Reinier Kraakman and Guhan Subramanian, *Commentaries & Cases on the Law of Business Organization* (New York: Aspen Press, 2009), p. 81.

[7] In just what way they matter, however, is not simple to establish. In fact, the extent to which particular corporate governance practices or structures do contribute to economic productivity, measured by accounting data or financial market returns, has been a challenging subject for empiricists. Most of the widely accepted "best practices" of modern corporate governance cannot consistently be shown to be associated with improved corporate performance under these measures. See, respecting director independence: Jeffrey E. Gordon, "The Rise of Independent Directors in the United States 1950–2005: Of Shareholder Value and Stock Market Prices" (2007) 50 *Stanford Law Review* 1465; Sanjai Bhagat and Bernard Black, "The Non-Correlation between Board Independence and Long Term Firm Performance" (2001) 27 *Journal of Corporation Law* 231; separating of the positions of chairman and CEO: Maria Carapeto, Meziane Lasfer and Katerina Machera, "Does Duality Destroy Value?" January 2005, available at http;//ssrn.com/abstract=686707 (last accessed February 22, 2011) ("Our results suggest that, contrary to the market's expectations, the split/combination of the roles of the CEO and the COB does not actually mitigate or exacerbate the agency conflicts"); Brian K. Boyd, "CEO Duality and Firm Performance" (1995) 16 *Strategic Management* 301; removing or installing a "poison pill" takeover defense: Lynn A. Stout, "Do Antitakeover Defenses Decrease Shareholder Wealth? The Ex Post/ Ex Ante Valuation Problems" (2002) 55 *Stanford Law Review* 845; John C. Coates, "Empirical Evidence on Structural Defenses: Where Do We Stand?" (2000) 54 *University of Miami Law Review* 783.

In legal theory, these institutions are governed "by or under the direction of"[8] a shareholder-elected board of directors. The legal system has long encouraged these elected directors to be attentive to the business and affairs of the corporation by the imposing upon them a legal duty to exercise the care that a reasonably prudent man would do in circumstances of same or similar character – the so-called "duty of care." As every law student knows, however, any discussion of the duty of care is incomplete unless the judicially created "business judgment rule" is also taken into account. While the duty of care and the business judgment rule together constitute just a detail in the network of rules and practices that confer and constrain power over the internal affairs of business corporations, that detail is significant. This chapter focuses upon the problem that the duty of care and the business judgment rule together treat. That question is: how can we encourage boards to be engaged in the work of monitoring and directing corporate business, without destroying more value than we create? In examining this question, this chapter reviews the role played by corporate boards over time within a framework shaped by the supra-legal social forces that have transformed US corporate governance over the last century. In this context I seek to explain the limited utility of the corporate directors' fiduciary duty of care as a liability rule and to identify the other sources of discipline operating on corporate boards today that continue to justify a robust business judgment rule as sound public policy.

In looking at this aspect of the role of the corporate board, this chapter consists of four substantive sections in addition to the introduction. Section II lays out a skeletal description of the legal regime of US corporate governance in order to make the chapter useful to non-lawyer readers. Section III describes the structure of US corporate governance and role of the corporate board during the period 1920–1980 (the "age of managerialism") and identifies the deep social forces that eroded that model of governance.[9] Section IV turns to corporate law proper and discusses the role of the duty of care and the business judgment rule as well as the limitations that a liability rule for attention will inevitably encounter in a rational capital market-centered system of corporate governance. Section V concludes with a review of the non-liability constraints on corporate boards that make the existence of a powerful

---

[8] The language comes from Section 141 (a) of the General Corporation Law of the State of Delaware, the section of the Delaware Code that confers basic power over the corporation to its board of directors. In the United States, the corporation law of the state of Delaware is chosen by a large majority of new firms as a locus of incorporation at the time of their initial public offering of stock.
[9] See also Chapter 4, this volume.

business judgment rule consistent with effective governance in the US system.

II Foundational corporate governance concepts in the United States

By the term corporate governance I refer to the complex of legal rules and widely-shared social practices that allocate and constrain power over the internal affairs of a business corporation. National systems, even those using similar production technology, differ in these rules and practices. Convergence in corporate governance systems will, for the foreseeable future, always be foreseen but not observed.[10] Focusing in this chapter upon the corporate governance of the United States, I assume that the primary functional purposes of corporate governance practices are two: first, to facilitate the efficient management of firms by professional managers and thus to improve the ability of firms to engage in commercial activity[11] and, second, to provide sufficient protections to those possessing risk capital to induce them to freely commit their savings to the corporate enterprise. The first of these purposes is advanced chiefly through the empowerment of an effective, centralized corporate board that is authorized to direct the operations of the firm. The second is advanced chiefly by providing default legal rules that empower equity investors to designate the members of that board and to remove them from office.[12] It is too often not acknowledged

---

[10] For a review of strikingly different corporate governance practices than those deployed in the United States, see William Allen and Han Shen, "Assessing China's Top Down Securities Markets," in J. Fan and R. Morck (eds.), *Capitalizing China* (Chicago: University of Chicago Press, forthcoming 2011).

[11] This is done principally by locating power over all of the business and affairs of the company in a single body – the elected board of directors. It is the board, inevitably comprised of individuals who dedicate only part of their time to the enterprise, that designates the full-time senior management, who possess or should possess specialized skill in the firm's business.

[12] See Section 141 (k) of Delaware General Corporation Law, Title 8 of the Delaware Code. In referring to the dominant corporation law in the United States I refer to the General Corporation Law of the State of Delaware. Under US law, a business corporation may (indeed must) be incorporated under the company law of one of the fifty states of the federal union. For reasons that have been controversial for decades, the Delaware statute has been and continues to be especially attractive for the organization of publicly financed corporations. This has given rise to the most discussed (often polemically) topic in US corporate law: whether the system of decentralized incorporation has led to a "race to the top" in governance standards or a race to the bottom. The literature is huge, well-known and leads finally to the conclusion that simple generalizations are impossible. Compare, for example, Rob Daines, "Does Delaware Law Improve Firm Value?" (2001) 62 *Journal of Financial Economics* 525 (empirical

that in practice optimizing the joint product of these two foundational functions will not be simple or apparent.[13]

The governance priority accorded to equity investors under traditional US law (so-called shareholder primacy norm) has been justified in the dominant theory by the fact that all other major constituencies of the corporation have available non-governance means to protect their investment in the firm.[14] Thus workers – who generally do not have great capacity to bear financial risk – have a contractual right to their return (wages) and that contract usually calls for periodic (often weekly) payments. Moreover, in the event of failure of the firm, wages that are due almost always receive a statutory priority over claims of other claimants on the firm. Thus the investments of workers in the firm, while not perfectly protected, are extensively protected by law and contract.[15] Likewise, commercial and financial creditors of the firm have contractual claims against the firm, which by their nature are senior to any return that equity investors may receive.

Equity investors receive no statutory or contractual right of return. Instead, they receive five things: first, and most importantly, the right to vote and thus, collectively, the right to designate the board of directors; second, the unconditional right to sell their shares, should they find a willing buyer; third, the right to receive dividends, but only if and as when declared by the board; fourth, the right to sue directors in the name of the corporation should the directors act in violation of their open-ended fiduciary duties of care and loyalty; and finally in the event of the dissolution of the firm, the right to any residual value after all other claimants on the firm have been fully satisfied.

---

study finding statistically significant positive returns to Delaware incorporation) with Guhan Subramanian, "The Disappearing Delaware Effect" (2004) 20 *Journal of Law Economics & Organizations* 32 (unable to find same effect for later period). See Marcel Kahan and E. Kamar, "The Myth of State Competition in Corporate Law" (2002) 55 *Stanford Law Review* 679. For whatever reason, those choosing jurisdictions for incorporation at the IPO stage continue to pick Delaware disproportionately. See Rob Daines, "The Incorporation Choice of IPO Firms" (2002) 77 *New York University Law Review* 1559; M. Boulton, "Venture Capital and the IPO Decisions of Venture Capital Backed IPO Firms", http://ssrn.com/abstract=1147785 (2009).

[13] What this means is simply that the typical conception of the task of corporate governance in modern scholarship – the reduction of agency costs of management – is inadequate. In principle, actions that in fact reduce agency costs may so impair effective management of the enterprise as to reduce corporate wealth creation and shareholder value.

[14] See, for example, Michael C. Jensen, "Value Maximization, Stakeholder Theory, and the Corporate Objective Function" (2001) 7 *European Financial Management* 317; for a critique, see for example Simon Deakin, "The Coming Transformation of Shareholder Value" (2005) 13 *Corporate Governance* 11.

[15] For a discussion, see Chapter 13, this volume.

The fourth of these elements of consideration received by equity investors – the shareholders' right to sue for breach of the corporate directors' fiduciary duties – is somewhat distinctive to the US system.[16] It is not the case that no other system recognizes the possibility of such suits, but rather that no other system in fact observes suits of this character to such an extent. In the United States these suits are relatively frequent and while measuring their *ex post* value to investors is problematic,[17] it is likely that they do have a positive *ex ante* effect on the conduct of corporate boards.

Derivative suits, as such suits are called, may either assert that directors have breached the fiduciary duty of loyalty (usually by engaging in some form of unfair related party transactions[18]) or that they have violated their duty of care; that is, that the board has been insufficiently attentive in its oversight of management and that its inattention has resulted in injury to the firm. But as part of the protection required with regard to the interests of equity investors, the fiduciary duty of care is deceptively simple. In fact, enforcement of the corporate directors' duty of care, in a capital market centered system of corporate governance, can hurt as easily as it helps investors' interests. We will return to this aspect of our corporate governance discussion in Section IV.

Let me turn now from the barest fundamentals of the legal structure of corporate governance system in the United States to the *evolution* of that system in the United States

III A brief sketch of the evolution of US corporate governance

The modern business corporation developed with the technology of the second industrial revolution.[19] That technology, whether in early railroads that made mass markets feasible, or in later steel and industrial machinery manufacture, required both the massing and dedication of

---

[16] Suits by shareholders brought on behalf of and for the benefit of the corporation itself are called derivative suits and have a number of procedural complexities. For a general introduction, see Allen *et al.*, *Commentaries and Cases*, ch. 10.
[17] See R. Romano, "The Shareholder Suit: Litigation Without Foundation?" (1991) 6 *Journal of Law, Economics and Organization* 55.
[18] For a general description see Allen *et al.*, *Commentaries and Cases*, ch. 9.
[19] Oscar Handlin and Mary F. Handlin, "Origins of the American Business Corporation" (1945), 5 *Journal of Economic History* 1; James Willard Hurst, *The Legitimacy of the Business Corporation in the Laws of the United States 1780–1970* (Charlottesville: University of Virginia Press, 1980). Of course, even in the United States, the history of the legal form substantially predates the second industrial revolution, but we here emphasize the modern business corporation as an organizational form, not as a legal entity alone.

great amounts of capital and the deployment of specialized managerial skill to coordinate enterprises of a new scale.[20] For the most part, in the United States corporations satisfied their need for the riskiest tranche of their capital structure by resort to securities markets. The use of this technique to fund the equity portion of modern business corporations had significant, and well understood, corporate governance consequences.[21] The collective action disabilities that diversified stock market investors experienced was not the only factor in creating de facto managerial control of large business enterprises. The specialization of senior managers in the information relevant to effectively managing such enterprises would certainly have empowered such managers even in the presence of a powerful non-operating owner. But the transformation of nineteenth-century "owners" into diversified twentieth-century investors, with quick exit options into a liquid market, was itself perhaps the most powerful factor in creating the governance structure of the paradigm of the mid-twentieth century US business firm.[22] That paradigm, of course, was one in which full-time managers, with specialized knowledge of the firm and its industry and default control over the company's proxy solicitation mechanism, were largely free from supervision of equity investors. The period following the close of World War I and extending well into the 1970s or early 1980s might helpfully be characterized as the *Age of Managerialism* in US business.

A   *Boards of directors in the age of managerialism*

While in legal theory shareholder-elected boards are ultimately responsible for welfare of the corporate enterprise, for much of the last century, for those directors who were not officers of the corporation, the title director was more, but not much more, than an honorific. Typically boards

---

[20] Alfred DuPont Chandler, *The Visible Hand: The Managerial Revolution in American Business* (Cambridge, MA: Harvard University Press, 1977).

[21] It is the financing of the required equity tranche of the capital structure through securities markets, of course, that creates the environment in which the so-called agency problem of management can grow to be a substantial problem for investors. But such funding also provides substantial systemic economic benefits. Namely, it permits cheap diversification of investment risk and thus allows savers rationally to accept greater risk in their investment decisions (and can reduce the costs of capital). Thus despite the attention long drawn to the "agency problem" of management, one continues to observe the formation of business corporations and their funding through initial public offerings of stock as an apparently preferred style of finance. The foundational empirical study of the extent of the shareholder collective action problem is, of course, Adolf A. Berle and Gardiner C. Means, *The Modern Corporation and Private Property* (New York: Commerce Clearing House, 1932).

[22] See Chapter 3, this volume.

of that time were composed of senior managers of the firm and of outsiders related by business to the company – bankers, lawyers or suppliers. Independence, the characteristic that seems to hold the highest value in today's corporate governance[23] discourse, was not very prominent. In this world, corporate directors acted chiefly as advisors to the corporation's chief executive officer. Certainly boards had a formal role in selecting and compensating the CEO, overseeing his succession plans, and reviewing strategic planning, but in the ideology of board service of the time, boards were not deemed primarily responsible even for these things. From the time of the rise of large capital markets and the disappearance of family owners,[24] until forces described below began to stir them after 1985, boards of US public companies have been largely passive entities. Many scholars thought board passivity was inevitable, given the directors' tiny ownership stakes and the part-time involvement with the company.

We might call this model of a limited board the *Advisory Board Model* of the corporate board. From the period when family control of large enterprise was replaced by professional managers who raised equity on public markets until, say, 1985, the Advisory Board conception provided the business model for how legal scholars thought boards did and businessmen thought boards *should* work. Once the Great Depression subsided, this situation was not seen as problematic. The success during this period of the US economy and its corporate actors made questions of corporate governance seem largely irrelevant. This was especially true for the decades following the conclusion of World War II. For the United States the 1950s and 1960s were halcyon days in economic terms at least. That period was marked by high growth rates, moderate unemployment and stable prices. At the center of this economy were the large, powerful and seemingly permanent US business corporations, which dominated global markets.

These large corporations – General Motors, AT&T, US Steel, etc. – seemed such a permanent feature of the social landscape that in 1967 the Canadian-born economist John Kenneth Galbraith, writing in the tradition of Adolf Berle, claimed in a popular book, *The New Industrial State*, that they represented a new and dangerous challenge

---

[23] Gordon, "Independent Directors," p. 1465.
[24] It is an exaggeration of course to refer to the disappearance of family ownership. A significant minority of publicly funded business corporations continue even today to have very sizable and even controlling family ownership. In the US Koch Industries, Inc. and Cargill, Inc. are among the most prominent examples of very large firms in private hands. Family ownership however did disappear as the characteristic form of business control in the United States by the very early part of the twentieth century.

to democratic government.²⁵ He asserted that these business corporations had succeeded in freeing themselves from the constraints of competitive product markets largely through manipulative advertising; that they were in fact free from capital markets constraints, through their internal generation of capital; and, through revolving door employment practices, were largely free of unwanted government interference. At the same time, as was widely agreed, publicly funded corporations were free from effective shareholder monitoring because of the collective action disability that diversified shareholders face. Controlling these powerful institutions Galbraith saw not a system of corporate governance, but only self-perpetuating senior managers who selected and dominated the corporate boards that nominally supervised them. With a mystery writer's flair he dubbed this unanswerable control group the "technostructure."

B   *Social forces that destroyed the manageralist model of corporate governance*

This dark 1967 vision of an emerging corporatist society was plausible to many at the time, but, in fact, events were to prove this vision badly incorrect. For even as *The New Industrial State* was being written, deep social forces were at work that over the next thirty years would transform what Professor Galbraith had seen as an impregnable permanent economic power structure.

The first of these forces was the emergence by the 1970s of powerful global competition in product markets far beyond the controlling power of an entrenched US "technostructure." Two facts drove this heightened product market competition. The first was technological innovation, the primal driver of so much change in our times. As Joseph Schumpeter famously understood, technology has the capacity, while creating great new opportunities, to rapidly, if not instantly, render whole product lines simply irrelevant.²⁶ Silicon chips, the computer, miniaturization, materials science and bio-technology were perhaps the greatest drivers of this more competitive world. The transformations that they occasioned changed existing business structures along with every part of our lives.

The second factor creating more competitive product markets was the emergence onto the international scene *circa* 1975 of powerfully

---

[25] John K. Galbraith, *The New Industrial State* (Boston: Houghton Mifflin, 1967).
[26] Joseph Schumpeter, *Capitalism, Socialism and Democracy* (London: Allen & Unwin, 1943), with a new introduction by Thomas McCraw (2008).

renewed national economies. World War II had resulted in the destruction of the industrial infrastructure of the axis nations and weakened others. North America, by contrast, came out of the war not only intact, but muscular with wartime growth. The United States stood as the only modern fully developed economy of size in the decade following 1945. US firms dominated international markets by default.

By the mid-1970s, however, Japan and Germany had largely rebuilt their industrial capacity with state of the art technology and were seeking global markets. Thus, by the close of the 1970s foreign produced goods were challenging the dominance of US corporations not only in foreign markets, but in a variety of important US product markets – cars and electronics being early and notable examples. The United States ceased to be king of the hill and henceforth would have to fight even for the ground necessary to stand upon.

General Motors was the paradigm. In the 1950s and 1960s GM had been the proud prototype of the power and control that caused Galbraith to sound an alarm. But by the mid-1980s General Motors was becoming the most public of object lessons in the failure to understand and thus to meet product market competition. Entering the 1980s GM controlled more than 50 percent of the US automobile market, but that position eroded more or less steadily to reach approximately 35 percent by 1990.[27] This product market disaster did generate a governance response: in 1991 the GM board of directors did the unimaginable: it fired the CEO. While in the end that early governance response proved ineffective, the firing of the CEO of the paragon company of the United States was deeply shocking. It was a harbinger of fundamental change.

Cars and electronics were of course only the first product markets in which global competition pushed US firms into patterns of change, including ultimately changed relationships between the CEO, the directors and the company's shareholders.

The second foundational change that contributed to the evolution of a new corporate governance model was ideological: the historic shift in the dominant political ideology of business regulation. Students today may not fully appreciate just how regulated large parts of the US economy still were in the 1950s and 1960s. But over a relatively short period from approximately 1970 to 1990 the United States moved from an approach to business and economic regulation marked by heavy emphasis on government administration of price and entry and terms of service for a large part of the economy to a model that placed

---

[27] See, for example, www.ft.com/cms/s/0/655892fa-4c83-11de-a6c5-00144feabdc0.html (last accessed February 22, 2011) (chart of distribution of US auto sales).

principle reliance upon market competition. This evolution too became first noticeable in the 1970s.

Interestingly, criticism of the then-dominant regulatory state was supported early on by a left-of-center critique that claimed that the regulatory apparatus had too often been captured by the regulated industries themselves and was used by them as a technique to dampen price competition. The critics proposed a deregulatory solution as a way to encourage consumer-friendly price competition.[28] The earliest success of these critics was the US Securities Acts Amendments of 1975, which deregulated the fixed brokerage fees that had existed for 183 years on Wall Street. Almost at a stroke the brokerage business was transformed from one of fixed prices in which the most important feature of a broker was his social connection, into a business in which the most important feature of a broker was the speed and price of execution of a trade. Commissions dropped and evidence suggests that prices thereafter on markets were more efficiently set.[29] Thus presumably everyone, except perhaps the affable but dull-witted sons of the well-to-do, thought this was a big improvement. This change was followed by the highly successful US Airline Deregulation Act of 1978, which introduced wide-ranging deregulation of the airline industry. It thus made price competition and thus cheap flights available to the traveling public. Both of these acts were seen as having been notably successful in lowering prices and were thus able to win converts to the deregulatory approach. After the 1980 election of Ronald Reagan to the US Presidency, the political right took up the deregulatory banner with enthusiasm. The Reagan administration led a broad attack on regulation of business that, in the end, transformed the US market economy. Air, truck and rail transportation were deregulated; oil and gas prices, electricity, telecommunications and of course banking and finance. Suddenly – or not so suddenly actually – markets were a whole lot freer and lot more competitive.

The Zeitgeist must have been reading Milton Friedman, not J.K. Galbraith. The attraction of using greater market competition as a technique of organizing economies seemed to be in the air. About the same time that Ronald Reagan led the assault on regulation in the

---

[28] In the US Senate Senator Edward Kennedy was a leading supporter of the 1978 legislature to deregulate air transportation that became the Airline Deregulation Act (PL 95–504). A leading spokesman in this connection was the economist Alfred Kahn who was named Chair of the Civil Aeronautics Board to oversee its dismemberment.

[29] Charles Jones and Paul Sequin, *Transaction Costs and Price Volatility: Evidence From Commission Deregulation*, http://ssrn.com/abstract=6428 (1998) (last accessed February 22, 2011).

United States, Margaret Thatcher began her beneficial privatization of the British economy; and most remarkably, about the same time Deng Xiaoping started leading the People's Republic of China away from Mao Tse Tung's planned and administered economy and toward greater use of market prices in the allocation of capital and products in the operation of the Chinese economy. Later even the European social democratic and socialist parties were reluctantly introducing privatization programs in their domestic economies, albeit with a certain scorn for what then and now they refer to as the Anglo-Saxon model.[30] At any rate, the rise in less regulatory, more "market" centered political ideology in the 1980s, which was an important contributor to the increasingly competitive environment for US businesses both domestically and globally, pressed powerfully on the status quo of management and governance techniques.

The last fundamental force of change acting on corporate governance was the emergence of institutional investors.[31] As the great Chicago economist Frank Knight had noted early in the twentieth century, later documented by Berle and Means, the disaggregation of investors that was a natural consequence of the rise of large public equity markets, had had the effect of freeing managers of the supervising presence of "owners." In the absence of monitoring owners, management became free, to the extent product markets permitted, to be less efficient, particularly to build enterprises that were uneconomically large. But the disaggregation of ownership created by the large securities markets

[30] A substantial part of the polis in Europe resisted what was seen as the harshness of the effects that more competitive markets may impose. One characteristic *cri de coeur* made in 2003 read like this: "There is an important distinction between Rhine capitalism and Anglo-Saxon capitalism. What we are now experiencing is essentially an absolute dominance of this Anglo-Saxon model … If Rhine capitalism that still has at least a social tradition is now steamrolled by Anglo-Saxon capitalism, we must take sides since Rhine capitalism is far better. Bismarck's Rhine capitalism is better than capitalism without a social tradition … What we have here in Europe is worth defending. There are essential differences. One difference is that there are social security nets everywhere in Europe, in all countries of the European Union. These nets do not exist in America. The second difference is that the socially disadvantaged are not stylized as losers in our attitudes but are people who somehow need help. This is anchored in our thinking. The attitude is very different in America where there are simply winners and losers … I have never understood why this Anglo-Saxon model had to be adopted economically. The New Economy in the 1990s should be recalled. The New Economy was a flop, a propaganda success of the Anglo-Saxon model that actually accomplished nothing." Eberhard Richter, "Rhine Capitalism, Anglo-Saxon Capitalism and Redistribution," October 19, 2004, available at www.indymedia.org.uk/en/2004/10/299588.html (last accessed February 22, 2011).
[31] See, for example, J. Coffee, Jr., "Liquidity versus Control: The Institutional Investor as Corporate Monitor," in Klaus J. Hopt and Eddy Wymeersch (eds.), *European Takeovers: Law and Practice* (London: Butterworths, 1992), p. 315.

in the United States began slowly to abate and perhaps reverse in the 1950s, with the development in the United States of large institutional investors, especially pension funds and mutual funds. By the mid-1980s institutional investors owned almost 50 percent of the traded equity in the United States[32] and by the early 1990s agents of institutional voice and coordination for these investors – such as Institutional Shareholder Services[33] – began systematically and effectively to reduce the costs of collective action and to press corporate boards and management for changes in governance that they deemed beneficial to shareholders.

Finally a force that we might not characterize as fundamental in the same way that we have characterized technology, political ideology and the emergence of institutional shareholders, but which we ought to nevertheless consider an important feature of the evolution of corporate governance, was the development of two ideas or theories. The first is the often described (and criticized) *efficient capital market hypothesis*[34] (ECMH) and the related if secondary "agency theory" of modern financial economics.[35] These theories are significant not for their power to describe the social world, but rather for the normative or ideological power they exerted over the large group of scholars that accepted them. That is, each of these now very familiar theories had importantly been deployed to help shape and justify a certain vision of beneficial power in modern corporate governance; in that vision the principal problem that corporate governance must be designed to address is the divergence between the incentives of managers and the financial interests of equity investors. Accordingly a fundamental tenet is the existence of a close,

---

[32] See, for example, The Conference Board Commission on Public Trust and Private Enterprise: Findings and Recommendations 25 (2003) (reporting that institutional investors owned 46.6 percent of the shares of the largest 1,000 US corporations in 1987 and 46.9 percent in 1990).

[33] Later acquired by Risk Metrics Group (www.riskmetrics.com (last accessed February 22, 2011)).

[34] See, for example, Eugene F. Fama, "Efficient Capital Markets: A Review of Theory and Empirical Work" (1970) 25 *Journal of Finance* 383; Eugene F. Fama, "Efficient Markets II" (1991) 25 *Journal of Finance* 1557. In law, see for example Ron Gilson and Reinier Kraakman, "The Mechanisms of Market Efficiency" (1984) 70 *Virginia Law Review* 549; R. Gilson and R. Kraakman, "The Mechanisms of Market Efficiency Twenty Years Later: The Hindsight Bias" (2003) 28 *Journal of Corporation Law* 715; William T. Allen, "Securities Markets as Social Products: The Pretty Efficient Market Hypothesis" (2003) 28 *Journal of Corporation Law* 551.

[35] The literature is vast. The oft-cited foundational article is M. Jensen and W. Meckling, "The Theory of the Firm: Managerial Behavior, Agency Costs and Ownership Structure" (1976) 3 *Journal of Financial Economics* 305. Famously, the agency idea – the divergence in incentives between owners and agents – was first noted in 1776 by Adam Smith, who thought that it would inevitably limit the growth of non-owner managed businesses. Adam Smith, *An Inquiry into the Nature and Causes of the Wealth of Nation* (Oxford: Clarendon Press, 1776), p. 741.

if not perfect correspondence, between current share optimization and achievement of optimal social welfare.[36] The practical impact of these economic theories, other than on the teaching and writing of academic lawyers and financial economists, in corporate governance has been in providing to the voices of institutional shareholders a powerful coherent theory in which shareholder empowerment is linked with the public good.[37]

Thus by the 1970s the environment that provided the culture in which the modern manageralist model of corporate governance had grown to dominance was changing in significant ways. It seems hardly an exaggeration to say that together change in these primal forces – the intensity of global product market competition, the application of scientific and technological discovery to new products and product improvements, the emergence of a market centered political ideology, and the growth and organization of institutional investors – have driven change in corporate governance as in much else in our social life. For corporate governance specifically one of the remarkable effects of this interaction of forces was the considerable growth in importance and scale of capital markets. The computer and all that it made possible, deregulation and innovative in banking and finance, deployment of ideas of financial economics, and growth in the global economy together changed the scope, richness and scale of capital markets and the players in that market became larger and more specialized. These deep sources of change have massively changed corporate governance – largely for the better I think – but notice that I have not yet mentioned law or liability rules in particular in talking about forces that have driven change in corporate governance. I point this out because one of the points I wish to emphasize is the secondary nature of the law of directors' duties and liability

---

[36] The literature is huge but most descriptive is the academic work of Judge Frank Easterbrook and Daniel Fischel. For example, *The Economic Structure of Corporate Law* (Cambridge, MA: Harvard University Press, 1991). Most triumphalist is the 2001 work of Professors Henry Hansmann and Reinier Kraakman, "The End of History in Corporation Law" (2001) 89 *Georgetown Law Journal* 439. See also Henry Hansmann, "How Close is the End of History?" (2006) 31 *Journal of Corporate Law* 745.

[37] An even more significant effect of widespread acceptance of the ability of ECMH to accurately describe the way financial markets work, however, was in its use, together with subsidiary ideas such as the Black–Scholes (or later) option pricing models, to create "designer securities" or derivatives. The purported ability to model financial risk more or less accurately (premised on ECMH) provided the tools that allowed for the creation of a wide array of complex derivative securities that in turn played a critical role in creating the conditions for the recent financial crisis. See, generally, Joseph E. Stiglitz, *Freefall: America, Free Markets, and the Sinking of the World Economy* (New York: W.W. Norton, 2010).

rules – especially in regulating corporate governance. But changes in law did play a part in the evolution of modern corporate governance.

Among the secondary effects of the changes in the product and capital markets was the massive hostile takeovers phenomenon in the United States in the 1980s. These leveraged transactions in turn created massive pressure on corporate law and governance. In 1985 – in the famous *Van Gorkom*,[38] *Revlon*[39] and *Unocal*[40] cases – the Delaware courts in responding to these very significant transactions began a process of modification of their interpretation of corporate directors' fiduciary duties. The focus of these legal changes were two ideas. First, in these cases the Delaware Supreme Court made it very clear that it took very seriously the formal allocation of ultimate corporate power to the board of directors that had been winked at throughout the age of managerialism. It did not adopt the "realistic" view of the academic community at that time, which saw boards as inevitably passive. In these change of corporate control cases, the Delaware Supreme Court demanded to see board engagement, not the CEO domination that Professor Galbraith had noted.

The second thrust of these opinions was the willingness of the Delaware Supreme Court to push the business judgment rule aside in order to more actively review board engagement in these cases. No single event jarred complacent directors into a new mindset more than did the Delaware Supreme Court opinion in the *Van Gorkom* case. It was the first time in memory that non-executive directors, who faced no financial conflict of interest, had been held to be negligent in approving a corporate merger. These judicial expressions of changing expectations of corporate directors were among the earliest changes in contemporary corporate governance standards.

IV Board engagement and the directors' duty to be attentive

Now let me put this large-scale historical framework aside for the moment and focus more specifically on corporate law itself. I wish to focus on the advisory board model of corporate governance that existed at least in the United States until the forces we have just identified began to force change. I especially want to focus on the legal obligation

---

[38] *Smith* v. *Van Gorkom*, 488 A.2d 858 (Del. 1985).
[39] *Revlon* v. *MacAndrews and Forbes Holding Company, Inc.*, 506 A.2d 173 (1986).
[40] *Unocal Corp.* v. *Mesa Petroleum Co.*, 493 A.2d 946 (Del. 1985).

of directors, then and now, to exercise reasonable care and attention and on the business judgment rule.

It seems entirely reasonable to assert that those occupying positions of responsibility on corporate boards exercise a reasonable degree of care and attention in that role.[41] Moreover, enforcement of such a mandate with a potential liability for breach presumably strikes positivistic lawyers as essential for such a mandate to have meaning. But, confoundingly, while threatening directors with potential liability for insufficient attention should make directors more careful, we cannot tell whether it would make them too careful for the shareholders' own good. Recall that with respect to public companies almost inevitably any director will own what will proportionately be a very small part of the company's shares (and thus its net returns). In exercising power, directors will of course also recognize that the judicial system is inescapably imperfect. If there is a loss arising from some decision that they considered carefully, perhaps a court authorized to do so might nevertheless conclude that a careful board might have thought longer or harder. After all judicial systems cannot perfectly discriminate between a sensible decision to accept risk, which turned out to be unlucky in execution, and a decision that was taken imprudently.

Undoubtedly, diversified equity investors would be ill served should directors become less tolerant of rational acceptance of risk by reason of perceived risk with regard to their own possible liability. Diversified shareholders in a stock market-centered system are the corporate constituency that is best situated to bear financial risk.

It would be only a slight exaggeration to say that during the period in which the advisory board conception of governance dominated popular understanding of the nature of the corporate board, that Delaware courts addressed this problem by announcing one rule respecting directors obligations of due care and applied another rule when push came to shove. That is courts announced but did not enforce the duty of care. It was deployed largely as an exhortation – albeit without a liability punch. Except for a few nineteenth-century and Depression era examples of bank directors who failed to detect a fraud that caused bank failure,[42] there were essentially no cases that imposed liability on directors' absent self-dealing or suspected fraud. If directors were charged in a shareholder suit with carelessness that proximately caused

---

[41] See, for example, *The Charitable Company* v. *Sutton*, 2 Ark 400, 406 (Ch. 1742), 26 Eng. Rep. 642 (1742).
[42] For example, *Godbold* v. *Branch Bank*, 11 Ala. 191 (1847); *Hodges* v. *New England Screw Co.*, 1 R.I. 312 (1850); *Bates* v. *Dresser*, 251 US 524 (1920).

a corporate loss, absent a conflicting interest or some unusual circumstance, it would be expected that such suit would be dismissed on motion under the business judgment rule.[43] The business judgment rule is the doctrinal technique used by courts to protect directors from the risks they would face were juries permitted to answer the question: "did this director when he approved this loss-making transaction breach his duty of care" or, more specifically, "did this director act as a reasonable person in the same or similar circumstances would have acted when he approved this loss-making action?"[44]

But a system that effectively denies to investors a right of action for breach of the duty of care does not leave investors unprotected. The effective and low-cost systematic protection against director inattention has little to do with the legal regulation of directors' duties. That protection resides in investors' ability cheaply to diversify their risks of loss in the stock market. That protection extends to risks of bad judgments that arise from all sources – from director decisions that are ill-advised or even negligent to decisions that are prudent but risky and prove to be losers in the end perhaps because of macro-economic factors.

So in offering strong protection against liability for breach of the duty of care, the business judgment rule would appear to be beneficial to investors. But undeniably this strong protection appears to have its dark side. It is that public company directors, having neither substantial investment risk nor liability risk, might well tend to become passive. In theory of course the board stands in for the disaggregated investors as directors are asked to pay the attention that owners might do. The goal is for corporate directors to be engaged, attentive monitors of management performance.

Indeed it is in trying to assure these things that the law imposes a fiduciary duty of care in the first place. The business judgment rule thus deals with one of the core problems of corporate governance: how can the law offer to directors reasonable protection from liability for claims of insufficient attention (and thus encourage them to authorize risky transaction), while still offering sufficient incentives to assure

---

[43] As a judge I elaborated on the important shareholder protective role of the business judgment rule in the case of *Gagliardi* v. *Trifoods, Inc*, 683 A.2d 1049 (Del. Ch. 1996). The history of the rule is discussed in S. Samuel Arsht, "The Business Judgment Rule Revisited" (1979) 8 *Hofstra Law Review* 93, 130–133.

[44] William T. Allen, "The Corporate Directors' Duty of Care and the Business Judgment Rule in U.S. Corporate Law," in K. Hopt, M. Roe, E. Wymeersch, H. Kanda and G. Prigge (eds.), *Comparative Corporate Governance: The State of the Art* (Oxford: Oxford University Press, 1998), p. 307.

investors that directors act in an engaged, monitoring role. That balance is an art not a science.[45]

Over the last twenty years we can observe in Delaware corporation law a tendency in some settings to review the reasonableness of director decisions. This first occurred in Van Gorkom, mentioned above, which involved a change in corporate control transaction; later a willingness to closely review the reasonableness of board processes and decisions was seen in the famous Disney case in which high executive compensation was challenged.[46] This tendency for courts to be willing to second-guess board decisions or processes when there is no financial conflicting interest is, I think, worrying and likely in the end not to be beneficial to investor interests. Importantly, I think, once we take account of the deep changes in the environment of corporate governance that have evolved over the last thirty years, I would urge that we can see that investor interests have much more effective and less risky techniques available to assure reasonable director attentiveness than the imposition of *ex post* liability for breach of a duty of care.

When we lawyers think of controlling behavior we tend to think in terms of liability rules. To a man with only a hammer, too much is said to seem like a nail. But there is much more than liability rules at work in the world. I mention three non-legal factors that shape director conduct: the first is the set of moral beliefs shared by members of the groups from which directors are drawn and the desire of normal persons to secure a good reputation among such people in terms of these beliefs. Second is the set of economic incentives that directors face and the third change is in the institutional setting of the exercise of shareholder voice.

The most general of these supra-legal forces is group-based norms of appropriate behavior. Whether one is a corporate director, a member of a sports team or a school child at recess, well socialized persons hold developed ideas of right conduct that at least absent financial self-interest tend more or less powerfully to induce conduct consistent with those ideals. In restraining ourselves we may be motivated in part to avoid the shame of discovery of transgressing behavior, or we may be

---

[45] For reasons of limited space I will skip over the doctrinal developments of this law in the context of corporate takeover cases. In that area Delaware courts have shown a slightly greater willingness to sanction directors deemed insufficiently active and engaged or to issue preliminary injunctions holding up transactions that courts determine preliminarily appear to have resulted from a want of due care. See *Omnicare, Inc. v. NCS Healthcare Inc.*, 818 A.2d 914 (Del 2003).
[46] *In Re The Walt Disney Company Derivative Litigation*, 2005 WL 2056651 (Del. Ch. 2005).

motivated by a genuine commitment to behave in accordance with our developed and usually shared view of right behavior.

Social control that operates through a commitment to a shared belief system and its informal enforcement, is a very powerful if highly imperfect form of social control. Given the unspecified nature of the core fiduciary duty of loyalty, one of the important roles of the Delaware Court of Chancery has been, through the use of its rhetoric, to try to teach corporate directors what constitutes conduct consistent with duty in that office. In doing so it exploits for a good purpose some directors' natural tendency to prefer to do the right thing. Expert practitioners and scholars have long noted the generalized preaching that occurs in some of these judicial opinions.

Group moral codes are "enforced" through a variety of social techniques, but perhaps most salient for corporate directors is reputation. Certainly the willingness of the business press to publicize directors who appear to have badly minimized their board engagement has had an effect on director attitudes. No one successful enough to be invited onto a public company board wants his or her photograph in *Business Week* or the *Financial Times* as the stooge that slept through board service while the enterprise was destroyed. Admittedly this form of discipline is sometimes unfair. Nevertheless it can be and indeed has been a powerful force for positive change in governance.

In my experience, there has been over the last twenty years a marked change in the dominant board ideology among the sorts of people who are invited onto boards. Board ideology has morphed over the years to emphasize cooperation, as traditionally, but also to emphasize independence and to stress monitoring of corporate performance. In part this may be a response to greater emphasis on the board's independence, especially on the nomination or governance committee, mandated by the 2002 amendment of the NYSE listing standards. But more deeply it reflects the combined effect of business journalism, active shareholder lobbying and judicial exhortation.

A second non-liability force for shaping director conduct is the deployment of economic incentives established through property right designation, or by contract. Incentives are not usually intended to inhibit conduct, as a liability rule does, but to elicit it. Incentives arrangements, such as director share ownership or stock based compensation, when well designed, have the advantage of being prospective in operation and capable of detailed customization. Thus, for example, at Berkshire Hathaway, Warren Buffett only nominates for the board individuals with very substantial stock investments in the company. These investments are thought by him to offer greater assurance of appropriate attentiveness than any liability rule is apt to provide. Moreover these incentives have the powerful advantage of being self-enforcing. Thus the costs of such a scheme of social control should be relatively low, at least if the contract is well designed.

A third range of non-liability techniques for inducing heightened director attentiveness has come from efforts to make shareholder voting more effective. These efforts include organizational or coordination efforts by shareholder advocates and legal change. Several legal system changes, having nothing to do with liability rules, have had the effect of inducing greater director attentiveness. I will mention four. The first was the US SEC's important 1992 amendment of its rules enabling institutional investors to communicate with each other respecting forthcoming corporate votes, without costly SEC filings. The second rule change involved the 2002 change in NYSE listing standards that mandated that board nominations be in the hands of a wholly independent board committee. A third significant change is the current effort in the United States to enhance shareholder voting power by changing the director election standard from plurality of those voting to a majority of those voting and to eliminate staggered boards.[47] Both of these changes which have come about not by legal rule changes but by shareholder pressure on boards, have been adopted by a majority of public companies. Finally, it is expected that the SEC will shortly announce a new rule giving qualifying shareholders access to the company's proxy statement.

While this access right will be highly conditional, it must be noted that control over the Company's proxy statement has been a foundational power upon which managerialist control was erected. Thus the power of active shareholders to influence board decisions wholly apart from liability rules has dramatically increased.

These efforts to enhance shareholder voice have had a notable effect. No longer does one find CEOs of especially prominent firms defending the view – as they often felt inclined to do in public speeches during the managerialist age – that shareholders are just one of several corporate constituencies – all of which are to be treated fairly by senior management. Now directors, and senior officers as well, appear to believe that shareholder welfare is the metric of success, even if the board has discretion about how and over what period to do that. For most people

---

[47] See, for example, Lucian Bebchuk, "The Case for Increasing Shareholder Power" (2005), 118 *Harvard Law Review* 833, and Leo Strine, Jr., "Toward a True Corporate Republic: A Traditionalist Response to Bebchuk's Solution for Improving Corporate America" (2006), 119 *Harvard Law Review* 1759.

whether this constitutes progress or not, probably turns on their view of rough accuracy of the ECMH or on the size of their investment portfolio.

V   Conclusions

Once we raise our gaze from the lawyer's tool box of positive and negative incentives that can be judicially enforced, we will see a social environment that can assist us – and has been used by the Delaware courts – to help to move corporate boards to a more active engagement, but which can do so without creating the tension that the liability/business judgment rule tension creates.

Power over the great institutions of our productive economy is in fact being reallocated today. Not only have product markets become more competitive, but within firms CEOs are losing power to boards, while – even more strikingly – corporate management and boards are losing power to shareholder representatives. Legal changes such as the movement to change shareholder access to the proxy and the successful effort to change the voting standard for corporate elections are part of this. Equally significant are political efforts by institutional agents of ultimate owners of stock. These representatives of investors are forcing the gradual reduction in staggered boards for example and the rescission of poison pill rights plans. Perhaps even more importantly event-driven investors are growing in size and importance. The line between hedge funds who invest in financial instruments and seek short-term returns, and private equity funds who seek to invest in control positions and seek longer horizon gains, is growing obscure. The growth in market discipline that started with airline deregulation in 1978 and Mrs. Thatcher, continues to grow.

But we academics, who in thinking about corporate governance focus exclusively on the agency problem of centralized management and ways to reduce it, must recall that the heroes of our account (the residual risk bearers) are imperfectly represented by those who present themselves as the voice of shareholders. The human actors who pull the strings of the institutional investors and the governance entrepreneurs are agents, too. We have not thought enough about how the actual incentives of the human actors who act for these institutions may differ from the social interest in long-term wealth creation. We all know that Risk Metrics is a for-profit business with its own conflicts. We understand that hedge funds, who claim to be owners, may sometimes have hedged away the true economic risk of their position. We know that the average mutual fund has an annual turnover rate in its portfolio of more than

100 percent – which seems consistent with excessive trading driven by an internal agency problem. But what do we corporate law academics make of these facts? They do not fit well into the theory that structures the conventional academic view.

One way to look at the current corporate governance scene is to reflect on a contest for the trust of the men and women of the country who have accumulated savings, often to fund their retirements. On the one hand there are agents of the real economy – decentralized senior management teams and boards in control of the institutions of the real private economy. On the other hand are certain agents of the financial economy – particularly hedge fund entrepreneurs, portfolio managers, investment banks and governance entrepreneurs. So the question is "who do you trust?" Who is more aligned with your long-term interests?

Sensible corporate governance public policy no doubt lies in some balance of power between the agents of the real economy and agents of the financial economy. But there is no science to discover or to deduce that balance point. When matters of great importance to the welfare of the people are concerned and uncertainty is present, modesty and caution in making changes to facilitate one group or the other is usually prudent. At the very least I suggest that the agents of shareholders who have gathered a great deal of influence and power into their hands do not appear to require a liability lever against corporate boards, when those boards act without a conflicting interest. Thus at the very least I commend to courts and commentators a continuation of a strong business judgment rule.

6 The primacy of Delaware and the embeddedness of the firm

Fenner Stewart, Jr.

I Introduction

The concept of *embeddedness* can be traced to Karl Polanyi's *The Great Transformation*.[1] The book is a history of the commoditization of English society from the eighteenth century forward, recounting how markets became unstitched from the fabric of society. As markets became more distinct from everyday life, society began to change in order to meet the needs of markets. One example of this transformation was the enclosure of English farmlands and the end of the ancient system of farming on land that was considered free for the use of all. This created a radical disruption in social function. Without farmland, thousands were forced to move to sites of industrial production, generating a radical shift in society from traditional agrarian life to one that was dominated by factory work. In other words, the book explains how markets became dis-embedded from society and then how these dis-embedded markets altered social activities as they became embedded into market function.[2]

Polanyi never believed that society could become completely embedded within the market function, concluding that society's members would never tolerate a market function which completely overwhelmed their other social needs. This resistance to market pressures is what Polanyi called the "double movement." Simon Deakin has elaborated on Polanyi's idea of the double movement, explaining how it also operates in reverse.[3] In other words, market actors will resist projects for

---

I am grateful to Peer Zumbansen and Cynthia Williams for comments on this chapter, and also to Stephen Bainbridge and Mark Roe for their comments on an earlier version.

[1] Karl Polanyi, *The Great Transformation: The Political and Economic Origins of Our Time* (New York: Farrar & Rinehard, 1944).
[2] Mark Granovetter, "Economic Action and Social Structure: The Problem of Embeddedness" (1985) 91 *American Journal of Sociology* 481, 482.
[3] Simon Deakin, "The Rise of Finance: What Is It, What Is Driving It, What Might Stop It? A Comment on 'Finance and Labor: Perspectives on Risk, Inequality and Democracy' by Sanford Jacoby" (2008) 30 *Labor Law & Policy* 67.

greater equality, when these social demands compromise market function. The balance between favoring the needs of markets or the needs of society has fluctuated throughout the twentieth century.[4] According to Deakin, the pendulum is swinging toward the needs of markets today, as societal governance is evermore closely tied to the expectations of investors.[5] Today, certainly, the pendulum appears to swing in a different, yet still unknown, direction.[6]

In his seminal article of 1985, Mark Granovetter elaborated upon Polanyi's dis-embedded market theory and expanded it into a more complete sociological theory of how embedded social behavior affects economic institutions.[7] He argued that to adequately study economic institutions, like corporations, one must take into consideration how the behavior of such institutions is "constrained by ongoing social relations."[8] In other words, one must take into consideration the social embeddedness of such institutions. Granovetter's central contention was that when economic reasoning ignores an institution's social embeddedness, such reasoning is blind to the actual social relationships within the institutions and will be unable to understand how a particular institution functions or fails to function.[9]

Granovetter's recognition that social relationships affect an organization's function has been seen as a call for a sociology explaining *why* institutions behave as they do. He criticized the assumptions of New Institutional Economics by highlighting how actual social networks inside and outside of the corporation operate in ways that such economic thinking cannot explain. Specifically he took issue with Oliver Williamson's theory of transaction costs, arguing that while there was a certain analytical value to Williamson's – eventually highly influential – market/hierarchy model of the corporation,[10] it remained blind to the *social reality* of corporate function.[11]

Up until now, Granovetter has served as something of a connector between Polanyi's work and current, ongoing investigations into the concept of embeddedness.[12] Certainly, the new interest in economic

---

[4] Fred Block, "Introduction," in Polanyi, *Great Transformation*, pp. xxvii–xxvix.
[5] For instance, Deakin, "Rise of Finance," pp. 67–68.
[6] See the observations by Lawrence Mitchell in Chapter 3, this volume.
[7] Granovetter, "Embeddedness."
[8] *Ibid.*, p. 482.   [9] *Ibid.*, pp. 481–482.
[10] See Oliver E. Williamson, "The Modern Corporation: Origins, Evolution, Attributes" (1981) 19 *Journal of Economic Literature* 1537; Oliver E. Williamson, "The New Institutional Economics: Taking Stock, Looking Ahead" (2000) 38 *Journal of Economic Literature* 595.
[11] Granovetter, "Embeddedness," pp. 493–504.
[12] Jens Beckert, "The Great Transformation of Embeddedness. Karl Polanyi and the New Economic Sociology" (2007) Max-Planck-Institut für Gesellschaftsforschung/Max-Planck-Institute for the Study of Societies, MPIfG Discussion Paper 07/1.

sociology and its relevance in bridging discourses in sociology, legal theory and political economy[13] contributes to a better understanding of the merits and boundaries of "economic governance," something of particular importance at a time of fundamental challenges to the financial credo of the last two decades.

Legal theory, itself, records early beginnings of such critical engagement with an exclusively economistic bias. John Dewey, in a famous inquiry into the law's constitution of the corporation,[14] identified the law as a powerful tool with the ability to take an abstract idea (such as the suggestion that the corporation was a "person") and to transform it into something more concrete and real (by, for example, granting a corporation the right to contract or equipping it with constitutional protections). Such legal reification, according to Dewey, shapes not only how people think about a corporation, but also shapes people's behavior within, and in relation to, corporations.

Sociologists have long focused on sites where law is produced as sites of contestation between influential groups, attempting to maintain or change the embedded patterns of social relationships. In "Competition as a Cultural Phenomenon," Karl Mannheim detailed how preferences become entrenched (embedded) within society through social processes (like law-making), and in particular through the competition between influential social groups within these social processes.[15] From this perspective, Mannheim can be seen as providing a promising approach for connecting Polanyi's and Granovetter's ideas of embeddedness with Dewey's understanding of the legal reification of business ideas. Building upon this connection of ideas,[16] this chapter explores one of the most important sites of contestation between influential business groups, namely the place that over time has triumphed in attracting the highest number of Fortune 500 business incorporation in the United States: Delaware – the regulatory laboratory of the United States for de facto "national" corporate law.

---

[13] Jens Beckert and Wolfgang Streeck, "Economic Sociology and Political Economy. A Programmatic Perspective" (2008) MPIfG Working Paper 08/4 www.mpifg.de/pu/workpap/wp08 (last accessed February 22, 2011).

[14] John Dewey, "The Historical Background of Corporate Legal Personality" (1926) 35 *Yale Law Journal* 655.

[15] Karl Mannheim, "Competition as a Cultural Phenomenon (1929)," in Paul Kecskemeti (ed.), *Karl Mannheim, Essays on the Sociology of Knowledge* (London: Routledge and Kegan Paul, 1952), pp. 197–198.

[16] For more on the interconnections between the thought of Polanyi, Granovetter, Dewey and Mannheim in relation to the study of the corporation and the law, see Fenner Stewart, Jr., "Socio-Legal Constructivism, the Embeddedness of the Firm, and the Embedding Process," CLPE Working Paper (forthcoming 2010–2011).

The primacy of Delaware 107

The social process of how preferences become entrenched/embedded within US corporate charters is of particular importance to understanding embedded behavior within the US corporation. If Dewey was correct and the law shapes the behavior of actors within the business world, then the corporate charter is a central tool in this process. The corporate charter is the foundational contract of the corporation, establishing the distribution of wealth and power between its members and between these members and others outside of the corporate organization. In other words, it is a form of contract which formalizes social relations between the constituents of a corporation. Although the charter does not dictate all social relations within the corporation, it does set a standard for expectations for social relations and is highly influential in the embedding process.

This chapter provides a history of the legal debates over the corporate charters in the US context, starting with a famous dispute, originating in a series of contesting law review articles in the 1970s. A brief literature review will recount the academic arguments that have provided the intellectual support for sustaining Delaware's primacy over corporate law-making in the face of constant attack. By understanding the debates that have sustained Delaware's ability to lead the US competition for incorporation, this chapter provides insight into what is regarded as the most important legal instrument for maintaining the status quo for actual social relationships within the US corporation: the "market for incorporation."

However, the chapter will also draw attention to the growing skepticism over Delaware's ability to generate optimal corporate law. This skepticism is most clearly evident in the federal government's growing willingness to design and to pursue corporate law policies in the face of corporate governance scandal, notwithstanding the fact that corporate law in the United States is "state law." The consequences of these developments are at present subject to scrutiny and discussion. In sum, this chapter provides an example of how shifts in law-making networks outside of the firm hold the potential to shift the embeddedness of behavior of social relationships inside the firm.

II   The first wave: drawing the distinction

As is well known, in one of the most influential articles ever published by the *Yale Law Journal*,[17] William Cary reconsidered the trends in

---

[17] It was called the most influential piece ever published by the *Yale Law Journal*, see Fred R. Shapiro, "The Most-Cited Articles from the Yale Law Journal" (1991) 100 *Yale Law Journal* 1449.

federalism and corporate law from the nineteenth century forward and declared that modern state corporate law was a product of state competition. Most importantly, this competition was attempting to attract incorporation to increase state revenues, creating a "race-to-the-bottom" for corporate governance standards.[18] His focus was on the by-then leader of the pack in this race, Delaware. Cary opined that Delaware's motivation for keeping ahead in this never-ending race was that a considerable portion of the small state's budget depended upon revenues from incorporations, making the state beholden to corporate managers selecting to incorporate in Delaware. This compelled the state to offer corporate legal arrangements that would advantage these managers by allowing them a broad and unchecked authority, often making it easy for them to engage in behavior that resulted in less than optimal corporate performance.[19] Cary argued that it was time for the federal government and the judiciary to "import lifting standards" that would set a level beyond which corporate standards would not be allowed to "deteriorate."[20]

Three years later, in 1977, Ralph K. Winter published a reply to Cary's position, which by this time had almost universally become endorsed as a matter of fact. In the face of this general consensus, Winter boldly rejected Cary's position, arguing that state competition should "tend toward optimality so far as the shareholders' relationship to the corporation is concerned" and thus state corporation codes, like those of Delaware, "are optimal legal arrangements."[21] Put differently, what Cary regarded as a "race-to-the-bottom," Winter regarded as a "race-to-the-top."

Borrowing from the ideas of Henry Manne,[22] Oliver Williamson[23] and Armen A. Alchian,[24] Winter constructed an argument suggesting that

---

[18] William L. Cary, "Federalism and Corporate Law: Reflections Upon Delaware" (1974) 83 *Yale Law Journal* 663, 666.
[19] *Ibid.*, pp. 668–669.   [20] *Ibid.*, p. 705.
[21] Ralph K. Winter, "State Law, Shareholder Protection, and the Theory of the Corporation" (1977) 6 *Journal of Legal Studies* 251, 254.
[22] See Henry Manne, "Mergers and the Market for Corporate Control" (1965) 73 *Journal of Political Economy* 110; see also Henry Manne, "Our Two Corporation Systems: Law and Economics" (1967) 53 *Virginia Law Review* 259.
[23] Oliver Williamson, "Corporate Control and the Theory of the Firm," in Henry Manne (ed.), *Economic Policy and the Regulation of Corporate Securities* (Washington, DC: Enteprise Institute, 1969), p. 281.
[24] Armen A. Alchian and Reuben Al. Kessel, "Competition, Monopoly, and the Pursuit of Pecuniary Gain," in National Bureau of Commercial Economic Research, *Aspects of Labor Economics* (Princeton: Princeton University Press, 1962), p. 156; Armen A. Alchian, "Corporate Management and Property Rights," in Manne, *Economic Policy and the Regulation of Corporate Securities*; and Armen A. Alchian and Harold Demsetz, "Production, Information Cost and Economic Organization" (1972) 62 *American Economic Review* 777.

since corporations need to attract capital by selling bonds and equity capital, this placed management in a position where they needed to take the interests of such financial actors into consideration. Winter wrote, "the state which 'rigs' its code to benefit management will drive debt and equity capital away,"[25] although Cary was correct in assessing that managers ultimately had the power to decide in which jurisdiction to incorporate, managers would not select a jurisdiction that would cause their business to: (1) earn lower-than-normal returns, and/or (2) have a higher cost of capital. On the contrary, managers would select jurisdictions that did the opposite, for the sake of self-preservation. Thus, state competition (also called the charter market) produced an optimal corporate law regime, which accurately reflected the demands that corporate constituents had for corporate governance.[26]

The rationale for the charter market that causes the race-to-the-top can be restated as follows. If the corporate legal regime is structured so that management cannot maximize the corporate output (profits), debt holders may make it more expensive to: (1) hold debt and (2) raise new debt. Such a corporate legal regime will also depress stock price potential, making it more expensive to raise new capital as well as maintain optimal relations with shareholders and creditors. Such underperforming firms will become targets for takeover. The threat of takeover will create a market for managerial control. Thus, managers will have ample incentive to demand an off-the-rack default statutory model of corporate governance that encourages the shareholder maximization norm. Since such a default model can be assumed to be what managers are shopping for when they select a jurisdiction to incorporate, this is what state competition provides. Thus, the charter market creates a race-to-the-top. And not only a race-to-the-top, but a system of legal innovation that is not compromised by political interference, which would ultimately be the result of Cary's recommendation for federal government intervention.

In conclusion, with the two sides of the Cary/Winter debate delineated, the stage seemed set for the next three decades with the advocates of Cary's position representing: (1) anti-managerialism, (2) federal intervention in state competition and (3) more centralized planning; and with the advocates of Winter's position representing: (1) managerialism, (2) unfettered state competition and (3) more decentralized market rationality.[27] Underpinning both positions was an understanding

---

[25] Winter, "State Law," p. 289.   [26] *Ibid.*, p. 290.
[27] For representatives from the Winter camp, see Roberta Romano, "Law as a Product: Some Pieces of the Incorporation Puzzle" (1985) 1 *Journal of Law, Economics,*

that the firm is a distinct market actor, which focused squarely upon finding an optimal solution to the shareholder-management problem.

III   The second wave: event studies and the attempts to settle the Cary–Winter debate

Winter's economic analysis of charter markets forced those from the Cary camp to adjust their arguments, by taking a more economically sophisticated position in order to counter Winter's arguments. Following Winter's lead, they employed more economically savvy arguments to suggest that shareholders (and creditors) had much less control over managers' incorporation preferences in practice than Winter's charter market theory suggested, and thus the race-to-the-top argument was flawed.[28] In response, others became inspired to settle this theoretical tit-for-tat once and for all by engaging in empirical research in the form of "event studies," which they hoped would settle the debate. Event studies were empirical tests, which gauged market responses to corporate law amendments.[29] These studies established that many stocks affected by the amendments rose in value when the markets learned of the amendments, bolstering Winter's position that state competition was good for shareholders.

Those defending Cary's position fired back. Melvin Eisenberg rejected these event studies, arguing that they had "only limited usefulness" in the context of the Cary–Winter debate.[30] He contended that if a uniformly low-grade corporate law regime existed, as Cary suggested, then

---

and *Organization* 225; Roberta Romano, *The Genius of American Corporate Law* (Washington, DC: American Enterprise Institute, 1993); Stephen M. Bainbridge, *The Creeping Federalization of Corporate Law*, Regulation 26 (Washington, DC: The Cato Institute, 2003); Leo E. Strine, Jr., "Toward a True Corporate Republic: A Traditionalist Response to Bebchuk's Solution for Improving Corporate America" (2006) 119 *Harvard Law Review* 1759, 1775; and Stephen M. Bainbridge, *The New Corporate Governance in Theory and Practice* (New York: Oxford University Press, 2008). For representatives from the Cary camp, see Melvin A. Eisenberg, "The Structure of Corporation Law" (1989) 89 *Columbia Law Review* 1461, 1508; Lucian Arye Bebchuk and Allen Ferrell, "Federalism and Corporate Law: The Race to Protect Managers from Takeovers" (1999) 99 *Columbia Law Review* 1168, 1170; Lucian Arye Bebchuk and Assaf Hamdani, "Vigorous Race or Leisurely Walk: Reconsidering the Competition over Corporate Charters" (2002) 112 *Yale Law Journal* 553; and Lucian Arye Bebchuk, "The Case for Increasing Shareholder Power" (2005) 118 *Harvard Law Review* 833.

[28] For instance see Eisenberg, "The Structure of Corporation Law."
[29] Peter Dodd and Richard Leftwich, "The Market for Corporate Charters: 'Unhealthy Competition' vs. Federal Regulation" (1980) 53 *Journal of Business*; Romano, "Law as a Product"; and Jeffry Netter and Annette Poulsen, "State Corporation Laws and Shareholders: The Recent Experience" (1989) 18 *Financial Management* 29.
[30] Eisenberg, "The Structure of Corporation Law," p. 1508.

the notice of an amendment from "one low-grade regime to another would not be a significant event."[31] He also suggested that Delaware's mature case law increased predictability, helping to countervail potentially suboptimal rules and amendments to rules. More importantly, Eisenberg emphasized that other contributory factors may have skewed the results of the event studies, which were not taken into consideration. Examples of such factors included packaging negative amendments to existing law with positive ones. Eisenberg suggested that such event studies were limited because the economic analysis was so superficial that it could not adequately appreciate the complexity of the US "charter market";[32] Lucian Bebchuk made similar arguments, arguing how negative information can be packaged with positive information in order to maintain or improve stock value,[33] and re-emphasizing the arguments, which suggested that Cary's position was still correct.

Within four years of Eisenberg's reply, Romano published what would become the landmark statement from the Winter camp.[34] Aiming at responding to Eisenberg's demand for "deeper economic analysis,"[35] Romano employed the lenses of: (1) financial risk management within equity markets, (2) agency cost theory and (3) the relational understanding between socio-legal norms and market forces, which – taken together – helped to better understand the mechanics of the charter market. In the end, this deeper economic analysis led both Eisenberg and Romano closer to a centrist position, with Eisenberg leaning toward Cary's position[36] and Romano toward Winter's.[37]

IV The third wave: post-Enron

The debate was not dead, however. Bebchuk took Cary's side and warned that state competition encouraged a race-to-the-bottom, given the state's obvious inclination to make rules attractive to managers and controllers.[38] In 1999, Bebchuk and Allen Ferrell illustrated how anti-takeover statutes were inefficient and reduced shareholder wealth,[39] providing one clear example of how states provided default rules that

---

[31] *Ibid.*, p. 1508.   [32] *Ibid.*, p. 1509.
[33] Lucian Bebchuk, "Federalism and The Corporation: The Desirable Limits on State Competition in Corporate Law" (1992) 105 *Harvard Law Review* 1437.
[34] Romano, *The Genius of American Corporate Law*.
[35] Eisenberg uses this language to level his criticism of the superficial nature of the event studies, see Eisenberg, "The Structure of Corporation Law," p. 1509.
[36] *Ibid.*, p. 1509.
[37] Romano, *The Genius of American Corporate Law*, p. 148.
[38] Bebchuk and Ferrell, "Federalism and Corporate Law."
[39] *Ibid.*

benefited only managers to the detriment of all other constituents, and "should lead the many who offer unqualified support of state competition to reassess their position."[40] But in 1999, the US economy was hot, the inflation-adjusted aggregate output was up, real gross domestic product was up, corporate profits were up, employment was up, and everyone was making money. Bebchuk's concerns were inaudible over the sound of investors' portfolios filling with money. The corporate United States seemed to be anything but broken.

All that changed in 2001, when the Enron scandal outraged Americans and pulled corporate governance under the microscope.[41] In step with this change in climate, Bebchuk reiterated his position that the empirical evidence supported the view that state competition offered harmful incentives, which privileged managers to the detriment of all other corporate constituents.[42] Building on this critique, Bebchuk went on to argue that Delaware's position in the charter market was so strong that assumptions about the operation of state competition were false. In order words, Delaware was more sheltered from the influence of other state's actions than was assumed in the literature, producing suboptimal corporate rules and justifying federal intervention.[43]

In the summer of 2002, the federal government induced aggressive measures to appease populist reactions to the Enron scandal. Suddenly, there was a rash move toward Cary's federal intervention that may have been procedurally pleasing to some corporate governance observers, but was ultimately substantively disappointing to most. With this came renewed interest in the Cary–Winter debate.

In this vein, Mark Roe set out to offer some fresh insight,[44] building on Bebchuk's suggestion that Delaware was in fact insulated from state competition, not its driver. Roe concluded that the nature of corporate regulatory competition had been "misconceived – and badly so," arguing that Delaware's chief competition was never other states, but the federal government.[45] Other states did not have the constitutional authority to trump Delaware's default rules for corporate governance, but the federal government did. In other words, Delaware's incorporation regime existed because the federal government tolerated it. So, the results of corporate

---

[40] *Ibid.*, p. 1199.
[41] See only William W. Bratton, "Enron and the Dark Side of Shareholder Value" (2002) 76 *Tulane Law Review* 1275.
[42] Lucian Bebchuk, Alma Cohen and Allen Ferrell, "Does the Evidence Favor State Competition in Corporate Law?" (2002) 90 *California Law Review* 1775.
[43] Bebchuk and Hamdani, "Vigorous Race."
[44] Mark J. Roe, "Delaware's Competition" (2003) 117 *Harvard Law Review* 588.
[45] *Ibid.*, p. 591.

The primacy of Delaware 113

law evolution may have been due in part to state competition, but the ever-looming threat of federal intervention was also a major factor. Which of these two factors affected the evolution of corporate law was difficult to determine because the world of Delaware policy-making was opaque.

Roe further suggested that if federal–Delaware competition was taken into consideration when attempting to understand the traditionally conceived mechanism of state competition, the state race debate did not play out the way charter market analysis had been assuming all along.[46] He suggested that a new theory was necessary to explain how policy networks forged US corporate law, arguing that top-down "centralized strategic" planning had as much responsibility for corporate law outcomes as did lateral state competition.[47] This would give support to the idea that the federal political dimension compromises the narrow quest for solely understanding state competition through the assumed model of charter markets as constructed during the second wave of the debate.

A year into Sarbanes–Oxley, in 2003, Stephen Bainbridge took a position as far to the Winter end of the continuum as Bebchuk had taken to the Cary end of it.[48] Bainbridge blasted the federalization of corporate law, calling the actions of Congress and other regulators "deeply flawed."[49] He argued that since the Enron scandal, the actions of the federal government represented "the most dramatic expansion of federal regulatory power over corporate governance since the New Deal."[50] Rejecting the federal reforms as an unnecessary encroachment on state jurisdiction he pointed to Romano's event study in support of his claim that state competition and Delaware's default rules favored shareholders by maximizing shareholder wealth.[51] When addressing Bebchuk's 1999 argument about the negative effects of state competition upon shareholder wealth by legislating anti-takeover statutes, his response was "so what … nobody claims that state competition is perfect."[52] He also proclaimed that "even if Bebchuk could prove that state competition is a race-to-the-bottom, basic principles of federalism would still counsel against federal preemption of corporate law," because the potential for regulatory innovation would be seriously compromised.[53]

In 2005, Roe re-emphasized that American scholars ought to recognize that the presumptions on state competition were skewing their perception, arguing that instead of looking at the results of horizontal state competition, observers needed to understand when the federal

---

[46] Ibid., p. 646.   [47] Ibid., p. 646.
[48] Bainbridge, *The Creeping Federalization*.
[49] Ibid., p. 26.   [50] Ibid., p. 26.
[51] Ibid., p. 30.   [52] Ibid., p. 30.   [53] Ibid., pp. 30–31.

government decided to leave such authority in the hands of the states and when it decided to claw back such authority for itself.[54] Instead of Delaware being the product of market pressures, Roe viewed Delaware as a political group with a narrowly defined range of concerns within the larger policy network of corporate law development.[55] In this light, Delaware's policy-making network was like a caucus of managers and investors. Within this caucus, Roe deemed that managers clearly had the "upper hand" in guiding policy development, but they also appeared to exercise self-constraint, because they understood "the game could move to Washington" if the scales were pushed too far toward managerialism.[56]

Also in 2005, Leo E. Strine, Jr., Vice Chancellor of Delaware's Court of Chancery, set out to "take some of the mystery out of Delaware's role in the governance of American public corporations."[57] When discussing the politics of state competition, he was reserved. He alluded to the fact that Delaware was and will be in the lead for some time to come in the state race for corporate law.[58] In defining the boundaries of state competition, he stated that the issues of competition, labor, trade and disclosures to public investors were generally regulated federally, while Delaware governed the "internal affairs of the corporation."[59] He never more than tacitly acknowledged that the federal government had full authority to regulate in this area as well, if it so chose.[60] In other words, he failed to directly acknowledge that Delaware's power was a privilege granted to the state by the federal government and not a constitutional right. Accordingly, Strine does not elaborate on this federal power other than to say that present interventions like the Sarbanes–Oxley Act and the amendments to listing requirements were suboptimal reforms.

In an exchange in the *Harvard Law Review*, the issue of federal intervention in the Delaware caucus was raised again. Bebchuk argued that managers were too powerful and were in fact blocking shareholders from maximizing shareholder value.[61] Accordingly, he asserted that since managers dominated state law, the federal government had to intervene.[62] In response, Strine entertained Bebchuk's proposal,[63] but emphasized that

---

[54] Mark J. Roe, "Delaware's Politics" (2005) 118 *Harvard Law Review* 2491, 2494.
[55] Ibid., p. 2494. [56] Ibid., p. 2542.
[57] Leo E. Strine, Jr., "The Delaware Way: How We Do Corporate Law and Some of the New Challenges We (and Europe) Face" (2005) 30 *Delaware Journal of Corporate Law* 673, 673.
[58] Ibid., pp. 673–674. [59] Ibid., p. 674. [60] Ibid., p. 686.
[61] Bebchuk, "The Case for Increasing Shareholder Power."
[62] Ibid., p. 874.
[63] Strine, "Toward a True Corporate Republic," p. 1775.

such reform "must emanate from state policymakers";[64] Delaware (and not the federal government) ought to be "the primary source of substantive corporate law" reform.[65] Bainbridge, in his response to Bebchuk, did not exhibit any of the potential flexibility that Strine did. He flatly rejected Bebchuk's call for greater shareholder empowerment by arguing that if Bebchuk's proposal could really enhance the value of the firm, why did it not already exist? In challenging Bebchuk in this manner, Bainbridge employed a classic Winteresque race-to-the-top argument.[66] Bainbridge rejected any changes to Delaware's law and law-making capacity.

In reply, Bebchuk was somewhat encouraged by Strine's opinions (although he believed they did not go far enough).[67] Bebchuk attacked Bainbridge's race-to-the-top argument by referencing a Winteresque argument from 1983, which was opposed to federal intervention to better regulate insider trading. The 1983 article argued there was nothing wrong with the existing standards, since charter competition would have corrected them if they were suboptimal. This example illustrated the error of assuming that state competition already provided optimal corporate governance arrangements like Bainbridge was suggesting.[68] In an interesting twist, Bebchuk pointed out that the innovative nature of state competition implied state law was subject to improvement in an evolving context.[69] Thus, even if one assumed Delaware produced optimal corporate law, it did not mean his proposition ought to be rejected outright. But after his brief flirtation with state competition, Bebchuk laid out a number of arguments in support of federal intervention.

The recent Bebchuk/Strine/Bainbridge debate helps to confirm Roew's observation that the true motivator for corporate governance innovation is the threat of federal intervention. Bebchuk's call for such intervention caused a defense of Delaware from both Strine and Bainbridge, and also a willingness on Strine's part to seriously entertain various shareholder empowerment initiatives. This reflects what is at stake in these debates over Delaware: the spectrum of embedded relationships between public and private power in US society.

V   Lessons from the Delaware debate

The power to influence the development of the corporate charter within the Delaware caucus is the power to potentially influence Granovetter's

---

[64] *Ibid.*, p. 1777.   [65] *Ibid.*, p. 1780.
[66] Stephen M. Bainbridge, "Director Primacy and Shareholder Disempowerment" (2006) 119 *Harvard Law Review* 1735, 1737–1742.
[67] Lucian Arye Bebchuk, "Reply: Letting Shareholders Set the Rules" (2006) 119 *Harvard Law Review* 1784, 1796.
[68] *Ibid.*, p. 1805.   [69] *Ibid.*, p. 1808.

actual and ongoing social networks inside and outside of the corporation and hence underscores its embeddedness. The above narrative highlights the levels of contestation between managers and shareholders for control over future reforms. To date, managers have dominated the caucus, marginalizing efforts by the advocates of shareholders, who want shareholders to have greater direct participation within US corporate governance structures. Historically, the Delaware caucus has weathered tremendous economic transformations, remaining relatively unchanged, when compared to the reforms taken, say, by Britain and Australia over the last twenty-five years.[70] Delaware has been less prone to amendment, partly because its corporate law regime is regarded to be the result of an innovative and inspirational regulatory lab which harnesses the power of state competition.[71]

With view to the still open questions regarding state competition, Bebchuk petitions for more federal intervention challenging whether the market for charters inspires the optimal law-making which is claimed to exist. He called for greater power-sharing between the federal and state governments in this process, hoping this will crack open the Delaware caucus and result in more direct shareholder influence over corporate decision-making. In response to Bebchuk, Vice Chancellor Strine argued that greater power-sharing with the federal government would be a mistake because Delaware's regulatory machinery was not influenced by managers to a degree that would prevent greater shareholder participation within corporate governance – if such reforms were what shareholders really wanted and what US corporate governance really needed. Meanwhile, this dialogue between two highly regarded and influential discourse participants – the Vice Chancellor of Delaware's Court of Chancery and the United States' top legal academic advocate of shareholder empowerment – has been unsettling to the avid champions of Delaware's present status quo.

Confidence in Delaware, like that heralded by Professor Bainbridge, has made US corporate observers less likely to look beyond national borders for inspiration in corporate reforms and also less likely to assume that such reforms are necessary.[72] In this way, the charter competition argument has been very successful at maintaining a status quo in which corporate managers (as the end consumers of this charter market competition) have greater control over corporate governance policy

---

[70] For more on this, see Jennifer G. Hill, "Regulatory Show and Tell: Lessons From International Statutory Regimes" (2008) 33 *Delaware Journal of Corporate Law* 819, 823.
[71] *Ibid.*, pp. 821–829.   [72] *Ibid.*, pp. 819–820.

than similar managers have in either Britain or Australia – countries that have both seen an increase the participatory rights of shareholders.[73] However, US corporate governance can be said to be in transition: there has clearly been a shift of power away from the Delaware caucus in response to its "modest and incremental"[74] approach to reform. Starting with the post-scandal regulatory responses (such as the Sarbanes–Oxley Act), the federal government has been more willing to interfere with the presumed preeminence of the charter market.[75] This may prove to be the harbinger of the demise of the monopoly which Delaware has enjoyed for the past century,[76] providing new opportunities to increase the participatory rights of shareholders.

Today, corporate managers are under attack for having failed to provide for adequate monitoring and oversight of their firms' investments before the Credit Crisis. The situation has called into question the balance between managerial authority and managerial accountability. Eyes are on the capacity of state level legal mechanisms (in particular Delaware) to deal with these corporate governance failures.[77] Meanwhile, federal reforms (such as "say on pay" and other shareholder empowerment initiatives) have either been established[78] or are in the works.[79] Such federal interventions demonstrate a continued willingness to intercede in corporate regulatory development at the state level.

It is difficult to foretell the long-term impact of such federal interventions in the area of corporate governance. If the interventionist attitude prevails, the federal government would likely face increased pressures from a number of interest groups – not just shareholder groups – pushing for further corporate governance reform. Is this a Pandora's box in the making? Alternatively, Delaware may want to answer the sort of pressures that prompted the federal government's activity in the first place. It seems that either way more shareholder participation rights in US corporate governance is a likely outcome.

The likelihood of such an outcome brings this argument full circle. As noted in the beginning, the British corporate governance expert Simon Deakin observed how Polanyi's double movement had in recent

---

[73] *Ibid.*, p. 826.   [74] *Ibid.*, p. 823.
[75] *Ibid.*, pp. 824–825.   [76] *Ibid.*, pp. 841–842.
[77] Anne Tucker Nees, "Who's The Boss? Unmasking Oversight Liability Within The Corporate Power Puzzle" (2010) 35 *Delaware Journal of Corporate Law* 199.
[78] "Nay on Pay: America's Shareholders Find a Voice to Condemn Undeserved Compensation," *The Economist*, May 13, 2010.
[79] "The Rewards of Virtue: Does Good Corporate Governance Pay? Studies Give Contradictory Answers," *The Economist*, April 26, 2010.

times been offset to favor market interests to the detriment of society, driven predominantly by the power exercised by investors in this era of financialization. Now, with the regulatory responses against the crisis still forthcoming, one of the questions arising out of the foregoing is whether increases in shareholder participatory rights are likely to further increase the movement toward the financialization of the firm in the US context? While, only a few years ago, we would have found it hard to see how it would not, the current crisis and the emerging regulatory responses[80] might suggest otherwise. This uncertainty hints at what the political stakes are in the Delaware debate.

Of course, the issue is more complex. Greater shareholder participation may not be bad thing. As Adolf A. Berle argued in response to E. Merrick Dodd in the classic US debate over managerialism: although shareholder empowerment may not be an adequate solution to managerial opportunism, enforcement of property rights is the only legal tool available to safeguard against managerialism[81] – but how much has changed almost eighty years later? In 1932, Berle was hopeful that new theories in sociology would soon provide the theoretical support for legal innovations which would better regulate corporate governance.[82] The law is still waiting.

---

[80] Julia Black and Robert Baldwin, "Really Responsive Risk-Based Regulation" (2010) 32 (2) *Law & Policy* 181.
[81] Generally see Adolf A. Berle, Jr., "For Whom Corporate Managers are Trustees: A Note" (1932) 45 *Harvard Law Review* 1365.
[82] Adolf A. Berle, Jr. and Gardiner C. Means, *The Modern Corporation and Private Property*, (New York: Harcourt, Brace and World Inc, 1968, 1st edn, 1932), pp. 219–220.

7 The new embeddedness of the corporation: corporate social responsibility in the knowledge society

Peer Zumbansen

I Introduction

Reflections on corporate social responsibility (CSR) in the midst of a financial crisis are likely to have several starting and turning points. The current instabilities of the financial markets dramatically put into perspective the almost religious wars fought over the last twenty years between shareholder value proponents and stakeholder capitalism defenders, carried out as a dispute over global convergence or divergence of corporate governance standards. The expansion of global corporate finance,[1] particularly since the collapse of communism, dramatically changed our perspective on the business corporation, from industrial, embedded capitalism to financial capitalism. This change in perspective tells a story about the way in which we attribute different categories of responsibilities to the business corporation. While we are seemingly well acquainted with the 'classical' segments of that story,[2] its continuation is anything but clear. The history of corporate social responsibility as an ideal, concept, dream, ideology or illusion is as intertwined in the larger political economy of capitalist development[3]

This chapter forms part of a larger research project on corporate governance in the knowledge society. Financial assistance from the Social Sciences and Humanities Research Council of Canada (Grant # 410–2005–2421) and from the International Bar Association in conjunction with their 2008 Annual Conference in Buenos Aires is gratefully acknowledged.

[1] Chapter 13, this volume; Ronald Dore, 'Financialization of the Global Economy' (2008) 17 *Industrial and Corporate Change* 1097–1112.
[2] See, for example, Lord Wedderburn of Charlton, 'The Legal Development of Corporate Responsiblity: For Whom Will Corporate Managers Be Trustees?', in Klaus J. Hopt and Gunther Teubner (eds.), *Corporate Governance and Directors' Liabilities: Legal, Economic and Sociological Analyses on Corporate Social Responsibility* (Berlin and New York: Walter de Gruyter, 1985), pp. 3–54.
[3] Earl Latham, 'The Body Politic of the Corporation', in Edward S. Mason (ed.), *The Corporation in Modern Society* (Cambridge, MA: Harvard University Press, 1961), pp. 218–236: 'The great corporations are political systems in which their market, social, and political influence go far beyond their functional efficiency in the economy.' *Ibid.*, p. 218.

as it has a particular idiosyncratic history of its own.[4] The following observations aim at illustrating this history with reference to three larger paradigms regarding the theory of the business corporation – and associated theories of corporate (social) responsibilities.

This chapter proposes to reflect on the history and on the prospects of CSR through the study of its evolution by focusing on three paradigms: the *organizational–industrial paradigm* of the corporation, which evolved over the first seventy-five years of the twentieth century, views the corporation as an object for competing concepts of market intervention, for both conflicts over the appropriate role of business enterprises and for the scope of legal regulation of business in the context of Keynesian economics and welfare statism. Within the first paradigm, the relevance of contested 'social responsibilities' of the business corporation can only be understood when seen against the larger background of a radically unfolding market economy,[5] a critique of formal law[6] and a deep-reaching deconstruction of political, legal and economic power.[7] For corporate law, this phase is marked by heated normative debates over the *social* status of business corporations, which centred around ideological disputes over the 'public' or 'private' nature of the corporation.[8]

This period of the 'social' is succeeded, within legal and social theory, by an amalgamation of competing assessments of social structures more generally, a development that unfolds in the 1970s and 1980s and is characterized by a surge in interdisciplinary and comparative research and an overall push for both critical and empirical studies throughout the social sciences.[9] In the comparably confined field of corporate theory, the second, *financial paradigm* of the corporation is fuelled by what can be coined the most successful 'law & society'

---

[4] J. (Hans) van Oosterhout and Pursey P.M.A.R. Heugens, 'Much Ado about Nothing: A Conceptual Critique of Corporate Social Responsibility', in Andrew Crane, Abagail McWilliams, Dirk Matten, Jeremy Moon and Donald S. Siegel (eds.), *Oxford Handbook of Corporate Social Responsibility* (Oxford and New York: Oxford University Press, 2008), pp. 197–223.
[5] K. Polanyi, *The Great Transformation: The Political and Economic Origins of Our Time* (Boston: Beacon Press, 1944).
[6] Oliver Wendell Jr. Holmes, 'The Path of the Law' (1897) 10 *Harvard Law Review* 457.
[7] Robert L. Hale, 'Coercion and Distribution in a Supposedly Non-Coercive State' (1923) 38 *Political Science Quarterly* 470–494; John P. Dawson, 'Economic Duress – An Essay in Perspective' (1947) 45 *Michigan Law Review* 253–290.
[8] Adolf A. Berle, 'Corporate Powers as Powers in Trust' (1931) 44 *Harvard Law Review* 1049–1074; E. Merick Dodd, 'For Whom are Corporate Managers Trustees?' (1931) 45 *Harvard Law Review* 1145–1163.
[9] Duncan Kennedy, 'Two Globalizations of Law and Legal Thought: 1850–1968' (2003) 36 *Suffolk Law Review* 631–679.

movement, namely *law and economics*, which shifts the focus from management's *balancing* of competing *societal interests* towards a fundamental transformation of the corporation into a contractualized investment vehicle whose success is measured almost exclusively with reference to its returns to stockholders. In a context which until recently was marked by the seemingly unlimited availability of funds on a global basis, the firm became a vehicle for strategic investment placements. Spurred by a series of financial innovations in the last three decades, the financialization of the corporation became a central aspect of global markets. As a consequence, every element of a business firm became subjected to varied processes of securitization,[10] involving a fast proliferating landscape of investment actors.[11] Far-reaching deregulation of capital controls during the 1980s facilitated an unprecedented flow of capital across national boundaries, allowing for securitizations, often repeatedly, of a large number of assets, including mortgages, credit card debt, and commercial claims. With companies designing corporate strategies with stock performance firmly in mind, shareholder value became the dominating principle in assessing corporate performance. The international competition over investment and the innovation of ever-new and more flexible financial instruments consolidated this fundamental transformation of corporate governance, frequently referred to as a rise of 'financialism'.[12] It has led to a far-reaching change in the understanding of the business corporation from an organizational entity geared towards economic growth to an investment vehicle with a very particular set of expectations attached to it.[13]

Yet, the pressure brought about by the credit crisis suggests companies are undergoing a transition towards another paradigm. The first two paradigms are telling of particular political economy constellations that provided the context for the distinct relationships political regulators were striking between individual freedom on the one hand and the political-legal promotion of the public good on the other. This

---

[10] Ronald Dore, 'Financialization of the Global Economy' (2008) 17 *Industrial and Corporate Change* 1097–1112, 1099: 'The basic financial innovation on which the pyramid of ever more arcane financial instruments is built is securitization.'
[11] Frank Partnoy and Randall Thomas, 'Gap Filling, Hedge Funds and Financial Innovation', in Yasuyuki Fuchita and Robert E. Litan (eds.), *New Financial Instruments and Institutions: Opportunities and Policy Challenges* (Washington, DC: Brookings, 2007), pp. 101–140.
[12] Lawrence E. Mitchell, 'Financialism – A (Very) Brief History', in Cynthia A. Williams and Peer Zumbansen (eds.), *The Embedded Firm: Corporate Governance, Labor and Financial Capitalism* (Cambridge: Cambridge University Press, 2011); Simon Deakin, 'Corporate Governance and Financial Crisis in the Long Run', in *ibid*.
[13] William Lazonick, *Business Organization and the Myth of the Market Economy* (Cambridge: Cambridge University Press, 1991), ch. 3.

'double-movement', as depicted by Polanyi,[14] came increasingly under strain, with the balance decidedly tipping towards the pursuit of individual freedom. In the centre of the first paradigm stood the manager,[15] whose role was fundamentally reconceived under the second paradigm, which saw him turn into an agent responsive above all to the watchful eyes of a globally active institutional investor class.[16]

While much in the current debate in response to the financial crisis suggests a turn against the undesired consequences of financialism,[17] this chapter argues that we need to see beyond this form of framing a regulatory response. In light of the longstanding assertions of a growing public role of the corporation in the provision of services, infrastructure and, notably, knowledge, the analysis proposed here suggests that the current debate about re-regulation and a new financial regulatory framework is not exhaustive in capturing the evolving nature of the firm.

By revisiting the legal theoretical debates around the contested, 'public' or 'private' nature of the firm before and during the financialist paradigm, the chapter argues for a longer-term perspective on the corporation and its law. The role of corporate management must be reconceptualized from the perspective of the third frame of analysis, an emerging *knowledge paradigm*. The knowledge paradigm suggests that the corporation has evolved into such a complex entity that we must combine an inside with an outside view of the firm to adequately assess its functions, performances and responsibilities.[18] In light of the

---

[14] Polanyi, *The Great Transformation*.
[15] Alfred D. Chandler, Jr., *The Visible Hand: The Managerial Revolution in American Business* (Cambridge and London: Harvard University Press, 1977).
[16] Dore, 'Financialization', p. 1103; see also William Lazonick and Mary O'Sullivan, 'Maximizing Shareholder Value: A New Ideology for Corporate Governance', in William Lazonick and Mary O'Sullivan (eds.), *Corporate Governance and Sustainable Prosperity* (London: Palgrave Macmillan, 2002), pp. 11–36; and Chapter 3, this volume.
[17] For an astute discussion, see Timothy A. Canova, 'Financial Market Failure as a Crisis in the Rule of Law: From Market Fundamentalism to a New Keynesian Regulatory Model' (2009) 3 *Harvard Law & Policy Review* 369–396; see also the analysis by Brian R. Cheffins, 'Did Corporate Governance "Fail" during the 2008 Stock Market Meltdown? The Case of the S&P 500' (2009) 65 *Business Lawyer* 1–62, and by Franklin A. Gevurtz, 'The Role of Corporate Law in Preventing a Financial Crisis: Reflections on In Re Citigroup Inc. Shareholder Derivative Litigation' (2009) 23 *Pacific McGeorge Global Business & Development Law Journal* 113–155, who argues that US state-based corporate governance is still more lenient in regulating managerial risk taking as compared to what currently emerges in banking regulation.
[18] Stan Davis and Jim Botkin, 'The Coming of the Knowledge-Based Business', in Dale Neef (ed.), *The Knowledge Economy* (Woburn, MA: Butterworth, 1998), pp. 157–164, highlighting the technological and behavioural drivers of the shift from data to information to knowledge; Dore, 'Financialization', p. 1102, noting 'a shift in power from

dramatically changed socio-economic functions of the corporation in an era of transnationalization and privatization, any sustainable trajectory for a corporation's (social) responsibilities must build on an adequate assessment of a corporation's environment. The knowledge paradigm points to a fundamental transformation of what corporate management does[19] and how the law sanctifies or sanctions its actions. Our interest in the knowledge paradigm is motivated by the assumption that, under conditions of the continuing radical transformation of the institutional and normative environment of post-Keynesian economics and post-welfare state governance, future attention has to be directed to both corporations and the state as emblematic representations of this changing environment.

II The death of contract and the rise of finance

For almost a century the quest into the nature of the firm had been determined by the negotiation of competing social interests. These were institutionalized along very different patterns in capitalist countries around the world. In both Western Europe and the United States until the 1920s, there was a clearly discernable nexus between industrial expansion and welfare politics, in many cases driven by large corporate actors. 'The question of social responsibility was whether corporations should be treated as public institutions with obligations to mitigate the system's inherent instability, even if these obligations conflicted with maximizing shareholder returns.'[20] Divergence began most obviously with the emergence of the 'Speculation Economy'[21] in the United States in the 1920s, as the role of finance became increasingly important in the organization and regulation of business corporations, leading to Berle and Mean's famous observations about the tension between management and shareholders,[22] a question that remained, however, still couched within a larger debate about the relationship between

---

managers whose expertise lies in their intimate knowledge of the operations of the organization they run, to owners and representatives of owners who closely monitor their activity with an eye to maximizing the returns to capital'.

[19] Peter F. Drucker, 'From Capitalism to Knowledge Society', in Neef, *Knowledge Economy*, pp. 15–34.
[20] William W. Bratton and Michael L. Wachter, 'Shareholder Primacy's Corporatist Origins: Adolf Berle and the Modern Corporation' (2008) 34 *Journal of Corporation Law* 99–152, 102.
[21] Lawrence E. Mitchell, *The Speculation Economy: How Finance Triumphed over Industry* (San Francisco: Berrett-Koehler Publishers, 2007).
[22] Adolf A. Berle, Jr. and Gardiner C. Means, *The Modern Corporation and Private Property* (New York: Harcourt, Brace & World, 1967), pp. 128–140.

business and society. By comparison, in Western Europe, the corporation was still seen as embedded in a tightly regulated system of company, employment and social welfare law, with the business corporation as the anchor point for an ongoing assessment of private power in a fast unfolding market society.[23]

A Corporations and finance

For lawyers, in particular in private law, this situation presented a formidable opportunity to reflect on the nature of legal regulation of the market.[24] The next, obvious step was to understand a critical assessment of the role of law in the context of political market intervention as only one example of a much more fundamental analysis of law as such. Beginning with a critical deconstruction of the legal arguments pertaining to the autonomy of the firm[25] to the continuing dispute over a corporation's ownership and control questions,[26] sociologists of law suggested a radical examination of the relation between law and facts, law and social reality.[27] In this rich context, the business corporation first became the subject of intensive legal analysis and social theory critique.[28]

In light of the fast-evolving and expanding market society at the turn of the twentieth century, the legal imagination of corporate organization was distinctly political. Eventually, though, with the 'prairie fire' of law and economics,[29] spreading in the late 1960s in the United States to revive Ronald Coase's theorem of the firm's economic primacy over market contracting,[30] the business corporation can be seen to have receded into an amorphous, purportedly apolitical realm of

---

[23] Franz Böhm, 'Das Problem der privaten Macht', in Franz Böhm (ed.), *Reden und Schriften* (Karlsruhe: C.F. Müller, 1960), pp. 25–45.

[24] Rudolf Wiethölter, 'Artikel Bürgerliches Recht', in Axel Görlitz (ed.), *Handlexikon zur Rechtswissenschaft* (Darmstadt: Wissenschaftliche Buchgesellschaft, 1972), pp. 47–55; Peter Behrens, *Die ökonomischen Grundlagen des Rechts* (Tübingen: Mohr Siebeck, 1986).

[25] John Dewey, 'The Historic Background of Corporate Legal Personality' (1926) 35 *Yale Law Journal* 655–673.

[26] John Parkinson, Gavin Kelly and Andrew Gamble (eds.), *The Political Economy of the Company* (Oxford and Portland: Hart Publishing, 2000).

[27] Eugen Ehrlich, *Fundamental Principles of the Sociology of Law* (orig. published in German as *Grundlegung der Soziologie des Rechts*, 1913) (New York: Russell & Russell, 1962), p. 495; Georges Gurvitch, *Sociology of Law* (orig. published in French as *Problèmes de la Sociologie du Droit*) (London: Routledge and Kegan Paul, 1947).

[28] Dewey, 'Corporate Legal Personality'; David Sciulli, *Corporations vs. the Court: Private Power, Public Interests* (Boulder: Lynne Rienner Publishers, 1999).

[29] Brian R. Cheffins, 'The Trajectory of (Corporate) Law Scholarship' (2004) 63 *Cambridge Law Journal* 456–506.

[30] Ronald Coase, 'The Nature of the Firm' (1937) 4 *Economica* 386–405.

the market, itself conceived as a sphere of private agreement, rational profit seeking and economic efficiency. In historiographical perspective, the life of the corporation as a public, political actor,[31] was of short duration.

Of equally confined nature was the time-horizon against which the success of a firm came to be measured: with stock performance as the sole determinant of a company's value, it became increasingly difficult to represent other aspects of a corporation. The focus on short-time volatility of corporate shares to evaluate a company's merits and prospects would quickly become the only perspective from which we would try to understand a firm.[32] But this narrowing of gaze came at the price of blocking the view on how the firm's environment had dramatically been transformed over the course of a few decades. To the degree that the advancement of communication and information technology revolutionized corporate organization and finance across vast strategic spaces, the attention given to stock performance eventually removed the firm from its geographical environment by elevating it into a purely ethereal realm. What architects of synthetic credit instruments call the reference asset, which can be the original subject of a loan or security, became radically virtualized in relation to the business corporation. The corporation, in turn, was reduced to an anchoring point for continuously refined financial programmes. It was as if the corporation was increasingly removed from the real economy only to be repositioned in an artificial space of financial engineering.

In the end, the firm as we have come to understand it over the past twenty years, has outgrown even the ideal model of a nexus of contracts.[33] In order to remain operational, the model had to be adapted to the processes of financial engineering, which – at least partially – moved the corporation out of the centre of the labyrinth of contracts in which it, or its securities, are entangled. The financialization of the corporation entailed a radical separation of the corporation itself from the instruments that represent claims in, of or against the corporation. The corporation had become a nodal point for an ephemeral crossing,

---

[31] See only Edward S. Mason, 'Introduction', in Edward S. Mason (ed.), *The Corporation in Modern Society* (Cambridge, MA: Harvard University Press, 1961), pp. 1–24; Adolf A. Berle, *The 20th Century Capitalist Revolution* (New York: Harcourt, Brace & World, 1954); Sciulli, *Corporations vs. the Court*.

[32] Lazonick and O'Sullivan, *Corporate Governance*, pp. 11–36.

[33] Arman A. Alchian and Harold Demsetz, 'Production, Information Costs, and Economic Organization' (1972) 62 *American Economic Review* 777–795; Michael C. Jensen, *A Theory of the Firm: Governance, Residual Claims, and Organizational Forms* (Cambridge, MA and London: Harvard University Press, 2000).

interlinking and overlapping of financial vectors, with almost no relation to the original 'business' of the corporation: the corporation had become a virtual realm for investment.

The financialization of corporate governance is powerfully reflected in the fast rise in importance of financial experts in the board of directors, the importance of financial expertise in the making of business decisions and, finally, in the transformation of the educational environment for the supporting professions – including lawyers, consultancies and accountants. The flip-side of this is the dramatic erosion of labour interests' representation in the contemporary business corporation. Where corporate activity had for a long time been marked by a lively public political discussion of different constituencies' interests in the firm, its financial and physical virtualization[34] increasingly erased the reference points for a general assessment of what corporations were doing.

B   Transformations of capitalism and the law

This context, albeit only sketched out here, is of crucial importance for any inquiry into the prospects of corporate social responsibility (CSR). One of the reasons for the dismal history of CSR has been the disjuncture between the by-then-attained complexity of corporate activity on the one hand and the comparably crude regulatory attempts with regard to the corporation and its financialization, on the other,[35] which characterized the larger part of the twentieth century. As the contestation of the firm and the inquiry into its duties and obligations continued, decade after decade, along over-simplified and yet politically and normatively highly charged dividing lines,[36] there were but few attempts at stepping back from the lines of attack to take a fresh perspective on what a business corporation is all about.[37] All observers of the firm were too immersed in the evolving environment of industrial capitalism to

---

[34] See, for example, William H. Davidow and Michael S. Malone, *The Virtual Corporation: Structuring and Revitalizing the Corporation for the 21st Century* (New York: HarperCollins, 1992); for the foundations, see Manuel Castells, *The Rise of the Network Society, The Information Age: Economy, Society and Culture*, Vol. I. (2nd edn, 2000) (Cambridge, MA and Oxford: Blackwell, 1996).

[35] Henry Mintzberg, 'The Case for Corporate Social Responsibility' (1983) 4 *Journal of Business Strategy* 3–15, 14.

[36] Archie B. Carroll, 'A History of Corporate Social Responsibility: Concepts and Practices', in Andrew Crane, Abagail McWilliams, Dirk Matten, Jeremy Moon and Donald S. Siegel (eds.), *Oxford Handbook of Corporate Social Responsibility* (Oxford and New York: Oxford University Press, 2008), pp. 19–46.

[37] But, see Christopher D. Stone, *Where the Law Ends: The Social Control of Corporate Behavior* (New York: Harper & Row, 1975), and the contributions to Gunther Teubner,

recognize it as anything other than a vehicle of wealth-enhancing, general social progress. In the heated dispute between 'shareholder value' and 'stakeholder capitalism', in particular in light of the self-proclaimed triumph of the former as representing the 'end of history in corporate law',[38] those who wanted to hold on to a system of an embedded system of corporate governance[39] thus long remained on the losing side of the argument. In this context, most of the arguments pointing to the *political* nature of the firm as a public or quasi-public actor were never seen to carry much weight.[40] With the state, seen domestically, in a strange to-and-fro between retreat and re-regulation and, perceived globally, as desperately trying to maintain its regulatory reach towards actors and processes which had long been powerfully unfolding in the transnational space,[41] the long-recognized anchor-point for a political theory of the firm seemed lost – and with it the place of corporate governance within a larger project of critical regulatory inquiry.[42]

C   *Crisis – what crisis?*

Since 2008, much of this debate appears in a different light, with exorbitant values being 'wiped out' at breathtaking speed.[43] Starting at the

---

Lindsay Farmer and Declan Murphy (eds.), *Environmental Law and Ecological Responsibility: The Concept and Practice of Ecological Self-Organization* (London: Wiley, 1994).

[38] Henry Hansmann and Reinier Kraakman, 'The End of History for Corporate Law' (2001) 89 *Georgetown Law Journal* 439–468; see the more recent reassertion: Henry Hansmann, 'How Close is the End of History?' (2006) 31 *Journal of Corporate Law* 745–750; for a critique see Antoine Rebérioux, 'The End of History in Corporate Governance? A Critical Appraisal' (2004) *Amsterdam Research Centre for Corporate Governance Regulation, Inaugural Workshop 17–18 December 2004* www.arccgor.nl/uploads/File/Reberioux%20Amsterdam%202.pdf; Simon Deakin, 'Squaring the Circle? Shareholder Value and Corporate Social Responsibility in the U.K.' (2002) 70 *George Washington Law Review* 976–987.

[39] See, for example, Ronald Dore, William Lazonick and Mary O'Sullivan, 'Varieties of Capitalism in the Twentieth Century' (1999) 15 *Oxford Review of Economic Policy* 102–117.

[40] For a sobering account, see Harry W. Arthurs, 'The Administrative State Goes to Market (and Cries "Wee, Wee, Wee" All the Way Home)' (2005) 55 *University of Toronto Law Journal* 797–831.

[41] Charlotte Villiers, 'Corporate Law, Corporate Power and Corporate Social Responsibility', in Nina Boeger, Rachel Murray and Charlotte Villiers (eds.), *Perspectives on Corporate Social Responsibility* (Cheltenham: Edward Elgar, 2008), pp. 85–112; and Dennis Patterson and Ari Afilalo, *The New Global Trading Order: The Evolving State and the Future of Trade* (Cambridge: Cambridge University Press, 2008), chs. 2 and 3.

[42] Peer Zumbansen, 'The Parallel Worlds of Corporate Governance and Labor Law' (2006) 13 *Indiana Journal of Global Studies* 261–312.

[43] See Nouriel Roubini and Stephen Mihm, *Crisis Economics* (New York: Penguin, 2010), pp. 110–114. See also Carmen M. Reinhart and Kenneth S. Rogoff, *This Time*

end of September 2008 the drama of a federal bailout programme in the United States began to embark on a breath-taking course, and its long-term effects, after two years now, is anything but certain.[44]

Yet, what does seem certain is that this extreme value destruction speaks to the similarly overwhelming, 'irrationally exuberant'[45] creation of value that marked the last two decades.[46] In light of the *securitization mania*,[47] the long emerging impression that we were witnessing an irrevocable, fundamental shift from industrial to financial capitalism appears questionable now. A host of rescue teams is waiting on the sideline, but where are these suggestions directing us? Polanyi's return?[48] What would have appeared, just a few years ago, at best as an inopportune attempt at applying a purportedly outdated political economy approach to a host of economic processes that seemed to defy political regulation in the name of a boastingly triumphant market fundamentalism, might today be able to critically inform a disparaged discourse over the future of financial market regulation. It is against this background that today's search into the soul of the market and the company is unfolding.

D   Re-embedding capitalism?

Hence, the suggestion to take three points of departure for a new look at the idea and concept of corporate social responsibility. By looking at the corporation through the lens of the three paradigms – organization, finance and knowledge – it might be possible to contextualize the place of CSR against the background of finance, corporate governance and labour regulation.

---

is Different: Eight Centuries of Financial Folly (Princeton: Princeton University Press, 2009), pp. 223–239.

[44] M. Landler and E.L. Andrews, 'For Treasury Dept., Now Comes Hard Part of Bailout', *New York Times*, 3 October 2008, available at:www.nytimes.com/2008/10/04/business/economy/04plan.html (last accessed 22 February 2011); see also Canova, 'Financial Market Failure'.

[45] Robert J. Shiller, *Irrational Exuberance*, 2nd edn (New York: Currency Doubleday, 2005).

[46] See only Joseph Stiglitz, *The Roaring Nineties: A New History of the World's Most Prosperous Decade* (New York: W.W. Norton, 2003).

[47] George Soros, *The New Financial Paradigm: The Credit Crisis of 2008 and What It Means* (New York: Public Affairs, 2008), xvii.

[48] See, for example, Michael J. Piore, 'Second Thoughts: On Economics, Sociology, Neoliberalism, Polanyi's Double Movement and Intellectual Vacuums' (2008) *Society for the Advancement of Socio-Economics, Presidential Address* 22 July for an intriguing inquiry into the possibility of framing regulatory challenges today through the lens of Polanyi's 'double movement'.

III Industrial organization and corporate governance (paradigm 1)

The study of the first paradigm is fairly straightforward. It includes a revisiting of the well-known dialectics between mainstream corporate governance and CSR promoters. Let us call this paradigm the 'Organizational-Industrial or, the *Economic* Paradigm'. From this conceptual viewpoint, the dispute is one about conflicting ordering values for political economy models. It is here, where a comparative perspective is of crucial importance[49] in light of the fact that CSR discourses form part of highly path-dependent, historically evolving and socio-culturally defined negotiations over the role of business in society.[50] Like a red thread running through the twentieth-century's history of CSR we see the eternal negotiation and renegotiation of the rights and duties that structure the relation between a company and its employees.[51] This history reaches back, in fact, deep into the nineteenth century: already in the 1800s the negotiation of workers' rights suggested the conceptualization of holistic concepts of workers' workplace and employment relations, expanding from the contract of employment to the establishment of supporting institutions,[52] albeit with considerable variations.[53]

A *The corporation and its stakeholders*

These fragments can be seen as early representations of later institutionalized prominent elements of the employee–company relation, for

---

[49] Cynthia Williams and Ruth Aguilera, 'Corporate Social Responsibility in a Comparative Perspective', in Crane *et al.*, *Corporate Social Responsibility*, pp. 452–472.
[50] Very instructive in this regard: David R. Levy and Rami Kaplan, 'Corporate Social Responsibility and Theories of Global Governance: Strategic Contestation in Global Issue Arenas', in *ibid.*, pp. 442–445.
[51] See, for example, Richard F. Bensel, *The Political Economy of American Industrialization, 1877–1900* (Cambridge: Cambridge University Press, 2000); Sanford M. Jacoby, *The Embedded Corporation: Corporate Governance and Employment Relations in Japan and the United States* (Princeton and Oxford: Princeton University Press, 2004).
[52] Carroll, 'A History of Corporate Social Responsibility', p. 21, mentioning hospital clinics, bath houses and lunch rooms, among others.
[53] Lawrence E. Mitchell, *The Speculation Economy: How Finance Triumphed over Industry* (San Francisco: Berrett-Koehler Publishers, 2007); Daniel T. Rodgers, *Atlantic Crossings: Social Politics in a Progressive Age* (Cambridge, MA: Belknap Harvard, 1998).

example in Germany,[54] but also in France[55] and Japan.[56] With significant differences between various national economies, the institutionalization of workers' rights took distinct forms, allowing economists and social scientists to study these differences through the lens of 'varieties of capitalism'.[57] The comparative historical narrative of these varieties became, over the course of the twentieth century, a crucial element in an increasingly global discourse over the competitive features of national economies on a global scale. As markets continued to follow the course of disembeddedness,[58] the regulation of business enterprises fast became a strategic token in the global race for resources. With corporations being increasingly able to take their domestic regulators hostage by threatening to take their business elsewhere in search of a more supporting regulatory environment, governments soon had to recognize that their approach to corporate governance regulation was inseparable from its policies in the areas of taxation, employment law, social insurance law, industrial relations and, eventually, environmental law. From this perspective, company law came to be recognized as an integral part of a government's politics of market regulation. But, to the degree to which this realization rendered regulators more sensitive – and humble – with regard to the fragile constitution of a complex regulatory field, governments also became painfully aware of the limits of their interventions.

In this context, CSR was deeply entangled in the right–left negotiations of which direction political regulation of this comprehensive field of corporate governance was to take.[59] At the core of this negotiation

---

[54] Gregory Jackson, 'The Origins of Nonliberal Corporate Governance in Germany and Japan', in Wolfgang Streeck and Kozo Yamamura (eds.), *The Origins of Nonliberal Capitalism* (Ithaca: Cornell University Press, 2001), pp. 121–170; Kathleen Thelen, 'Varieties of Labor Politics in the Developed Democracies', in P. Hall and D. Soskice, *'Varieties of Capitalism'* (New York: Oxford University Press, 2001), pp. 71–103.

[55] Mark J. Roe, *Political Determinants of Corporate Governance* (Oxford and New York: Oxford University Press, 2003); Jean-Philippe Robé, *'L'entreprise oubliée par le droit'* (2001) 32 *Journal de l'École de Paris du management* 29–37, available at: http://www.ecole.org (last accessed 22 February 2011); James Fanto, 'The Role of Corporate Law in French Corporate Governance' (1998) 31 *Cornell International Law Journal* 31–91.

[56] Ruth Aguilera and Gregory Jackson, 'The Cross-National Diversity of Corporate Governance: Dimensions and Determinants' (2003) 28 *Academy of Management Review* 447–465; Luke Nottage, 'Japanese Corporate Governance at a Crossroads: Variation in "Varieties of Capitalism"' (2001) 27 *North Carolina Journal of International Law and Commercial Regulation [NCJILCR]* 255–299.

[57] See Hall and Soskice, *Varieties of Capitalism*.

[58] Polanyi, *The Great Transformation*.

[59] Gregory Jackson, 'Comparative Corporate Governance: Sociological Perspectives', in John Parkinson, Gavin Kelly and Andrew Gamble (eds.), *The Political Economy of the Company* (Oxford and Portland: Hart Publishing, 2000), pp. 265–287.

was the tension between the firm as a real, economic, social entity on the one hand and a legal person on the other. Reaching back deep into the social philosophies of the nineteenth century, the negotiation of the nature of the corporation presented an opportunity to revisit and contest the evolving nature of a country's political economy.[60] The high point of this inspection was the early twentieth-century dispute over the duties of management. At the centre of the dispute was nothing less than a political theory of the business corporation. Yet, with the dramatic expansion of the market and the crucial role of the firm within it, the political nature of the business corporation became re-channelled into an assessment over how much else the corporation should be doing with regard to protecting a wider range of interests: as a result, a new dispute opened up that would, as we know, shift the focus away from the firm as such towards a firm with considerable philanthropic duties. Early litigation tells a fascinating story of these changing shifts in perspective.[61]

B   *The corporation in a welfarist 'mixed economy'*

Against the background of the expanding regulatory and welfare state in the West, CSR experienced an important revitalization and further consolidation in the second half of the twentieth century. As the state continued to reach deeper and deeper into every corner of society, corporations consolidated their role as vitally important actors in the fast-progressing 'mixed economy' that had already taken its beginnings in the mid-nineteenth century[62] and that would become characteristic

---

[60] Franz Klein, *Die neueren Entwicklungen in Verfassung und Recht der Aktiengesellschaft* (Wien: Manzsche k.u.k. Hof-Verlags- und Universitäts-Buchhandlung, 1904); Walther Rathenau, *Vom Aktienwesen* (Berlin: S. Fischer, 1918).
[61] See *Lochner v. New York*, 195 US 45 (1905); *Dodge v. Ford Motor Co*, 204 Mich. 459, 170 N.W. 668 (1919); but see Lynn Stout, 'Why We Should Stop Teaching Dodge v. Ford' (2008), 3 *Virginia Law and Business Review* 163, for the argument that US corporate law does not in fact mandate a management's legal duty to maximize shareholder value despite dicta to the contrary in *Dodge v. Ford*.
[62] With regard to France, see Prosper Weil, *Le Droit Administratif (9ême éd. 1980)* (Paris: Presses Universitaires de France, 1964), ch. II. (reflecting on the way that the mixed economy affected the choice of regulatory instruments of administrative agents); see also Francois Ewald, *L'Etat Providence* (Paris: 1986), p. 111: 'Le rêve d'une société où chacun ne dépendrait plus que de lui-même, de sa volonté et de sa liberté, l'utopie d'une société de prévoyance avaient vécu. Le patron devait maintenant, dans la conduite de ses affaires, viser l' "amelioration morale et matérielle" de ses ouvriers.' With a view to the concurring, staged triumph of laissez-faire in Britain and the United States, see R.H. Tawney, *The Acquisitive Society* (New York: Harcourt, Brace & World, 1920); Polayni, *Great Transformation*, pp. 135, 139 (concerning Britain).

of political economy,⁶³ where corporations played a pivotal part in the state's pursuit of full employment, universal education and health care.

At the same time, the concept of a mixed economy remained anything but uncontested.⁶⁴ It was clear that its mobilization constituted an invitation, if not a provocation, to either critically assess the relation between state and market or to deconstruct the allegedly neutral role of the state and the 'private' nature of the market. One illustration of this unresolved, dormant dispute was the lingering doctrinal and conceptual ambiguity, which surrounded legal regulatory fields such as 'economic' or 'social' law.⁶⁵ The contested categorization of different fields to belong to either 'private' or 'public' law could either be seen as a significant (or, bizarre) manifestation of civil law private lawyers' obsession with formal-doctrinal distinctions, or as a far-reaching critique of the unquestioned political normative foundations of legal regulation.⁶⁶

---

[63] Heinz-Dieter Assmann, *Wirtschaftsrecht in der Mixed Economy* (Königstein: Athenäum, 1980); Günter Frankenberg, 'Shifting Boundaries: The Private, the Public, and the Welfare State', in Michael B. Katz and Christoph Sachße (eds.), *The Mixed Economy of Social Welfare* (Baden-Baden: Nomos, 1996), pp. 72–94.

[64] See Andrew Shonfield, *Modern Capitalism: The Changing Balance of Public and Private Power* (London, New York and Toronto: Oxford University Press, 1965), pp. 82–84 (regarding France); Ha-Joon Chang, 'Kicking Away the Ladder: An Unofficial History of Capitalism, Especially in Britain and the United States' (2002) 45 *Challenge* 63–97, 77 (Britain); see also Niklas Luhmann, 'Capitalisme et Utopie' (1997) 41 *Archives de Philosophie du Droit* 483–492, at 488: 'L'utopie qui permet une coexistence du système politique et du système économique, sous reserve de la différenciation fonctionelle, porte le nom d' "économie sociale de marché" Du point de vue politique cette formule indique que l'on veut et que l'on peut réaliser en un seul système les objectifs du système capitaliste et du système socialiste.' See the acid refutation by Friedrich A. Hayek, *The Mirage of Social Justice [Law, Legislation and Liberty. A New Statement of the Liberal Principles of Justice and Political Economy, vol. 2]* (Chicago: University of Chicago Press, 1976), pp. 62–106 ('Social' or Distributive Justice), p. 101: 'It seems that among the younger generation the welfare institutions into which they have been born have engendered a feeling that they have a claim in justice on "society" for the provision of particular things which it is the duty of that society to provide. However strong this feeling may be, its existence does not prove that the claim has anything to do with justice, or that such claims can be satisfied in a free society.'

[65] Rudolf Wiethölter, 'Die Position des Wirtschaftsrechts im sozialen Rechtsstaat', in Helmut Coing, Heinrich Kronstein and Ernst-Joachim Mestmäcker (eds.), *Wirtschaftsordnung und Rechtsordnung, Festschrift für Franz Böhm zum 70. Geburtstag* (Tübingen: Siebeck Mohr, 1965), pp. 41–62; Ernst-Joachim Mestmäcker, 'Das Verhältnis der Wirtschaftswissenschaft zur Rechtswissenschaft im Aktienrecht', in Ludwig Raiser, Heinz Sauermann and Erich Schneider (eds.), *Das Verhältnis der Wirtschaftswissenschaft zur Rechtswissenschaft: Soziologie und Statistik* (Berlin: Duncker & Humblot, 1964), pp. 103–119.

[66] Rudolf Wiethölter, 'Artikel Wirtschaftsrecht', in Axel Görlitz (ed.), *Handlexikon zur Rechtswissenschaft* (Darmstadt: Wissenschaftliche Buchgesellschaft, 1972), pp. 531–539.

Despite this, the next period was marked by a number of noteworthy contributions to the polemical debate over the scope of a company's obligations and duties 'to society'.[67] Let us briefly turn our attention to the famous, infamous statement by Milton Friedman, which since then has haunted CSR proponents: in response to the question, 'What does it mean to say that the corporate executive has a "social responsibility" in his capacity as businessman?', Friedman posited that wherever management attempted to orient corporate output around a public interest, for example, by making 'expenditures on reducing pollution' or by 'hiring "hardcore" unemployed instead of better-qualified available workmen to contribute to the social objective of reducing poverty', it would inevitably lead to the spending of 'someone else's money'.[68] Friedman concluded that: 'The difficulty of exercising "social responsibility" illustrates, of course, the great virtue of private competitive enterprise – it forces people to be responsible for their own actions and makes it difficult for them to "exploit" other people for either selfish or unselfish purposes. They can do good – but only at their own expense.' The central point for our purposes is Friedman's rejection of the corporation – as an artificial entity – having the competence to act responsibly.[69]

CSR proponents have often proven unable to effectively counter this argument. And yet, against the background of the late nineteenth-, early twentieth-century political economy with the creation of the corporation in law as legal person, a defence against Friedman's attack should have have been relatively simple: Friedman's refutation of any attempt to attribute general social obligations to the business firm is grounded in the idea that a corporation is a physical entity, created and structured through a series of private agreements among individual business people. Attributing a general social responsibility to a corporate manager

[67] See only Milton Friedman, 'The Social Responsibility of a Corporation is to Increase its Profits', *New York Times Magazine*, 13 September 1970, available at: www.colorado.edu/studentgroups/libertarians/issues/friedman-soc-resp-business.html (last accessed 22 February 2011).
[68] The quotes in this paragraph are excerpted from Joel Makover, 'Milton Friedman and the Social Responsibility of Business', *World Changing.com*, 19 November 2006, available at: www.worldchanging.com/archives/005373.html (last accessed 22 February 2011).
[69] This is dramatically echoed in the decision by the US Court of Appeals for the Second Circuit of 17 September 2010 in *Kiobel* v. *Royal-Dutch-Petroleum*, 06–4800-cv, 06–4876-cv, holding that the Alien Tort Claims Act does *not* apply to corporations, as 'legal persons', but only applies to the individuals acting within the corporation. See Andrea Bottorff, 'Federal Appeals Court Upholds Verdict for Shell in Nigeria Protest Deaths', available at: http://jurist.org/paperchase/2010/09/federal-appeals-court-upholds-verdict-for-shell-in-nigeria-protest-deaths.php (last accessed 22 February 2011).

would, in Friedman's view, constitute both an unwarranted expansion of his duties and a non-permissable violation of management's duties to its employers – that is the firm's shareholders. Friedman comes dangerously close to recognizing the firm's legally constructed artificial reality when comparing a manager to a civil servant. Friedman here suggests that were a manager to be likened to a civil servant, which would inevitably include an assignment of additional and different duties, then there ought to be, for starters, a different appointment or election process. It is here where Friedman not only recognizes the concept of the legal person, but is effectively exploiting it, implying that it is in the prerogative of the legislator to change these ground rules. But, as long as they remain in place, it is not in the purview of judges (or scholars) to arbitrarily expand the existing range of obligations.

That this argument is tautological is fairly obvious. At the heart of the argument is the view that management's duty exhausted itself in meeting shareholders' demands since that is what the law requires.[70] The first paradigm for CSR, which embeds its concept and idea in a larger political economy has, in the end, to run dry, because it cannot effectively penetrate the black box of corporate law regulation, which remains sealed with a thick layer of inconclusive statements over duties and obligations. The crux of the problem is the following: on the one hand, the corporation is perceived as simply a contractual arrangement through which it channels its own and so-called 'residual' interests.[71] On the other hand, the corporation is constituted as a juridical person, that is, the corporation is the result of an artificial construction, which shields the owners from the corporation's creditors.[72] As such, however, it is the subject of legal construction, regulation and interpretation. Put bluntly, the corporation as a legal framework exists *only through authority of the law*, and it is through law that the conflict between distance and care, between public intervention and private autonomy, is constantly being renegotiated. The firm becomes the laboratory, in which

---

[70] This assumes that shareholder interests are uniform, notwithstanding type of owner, structure of ownership, risk preferences or time-frame for investment. An assessment of shareholder interests simply cannot be made in the abstract, however. This is an important lesson to be learned from taking a closer look at Berle and Means' 1932 book *The Modern Corporation and Private Property*. See William W. Bratton and Michael L. Wachter, 'Shareholder Primacy's Corporatist Origins: Adolf Berle and the Modern Corporation' (2008) 34 *Journal of Corporation Law* 99–152.
[71] Eugene Fama and Michael C. Jensen, 'Agency Problems and Residual Claims' (1983) 26 *Journal of Law and Economics* 327–349.
[72] Reinier Kraakman, Paul L. Davies, Henry Hansmann, Gérard Hertig, Klaus J. Hopt, Hideki Kanda and Edward B. Rock, *The Anatomy of Corporate Law: A Comparative and Functional Approach* (2nd edn 2009) (Oxford and New York: Oxford University Press, 2004).

Polanyi's double movement of market liberalization and market control is seemingly inescabably intertwined. Certainly, this does not in any way solve the problem of how to negotiate the principle of private autonomy and legal construction within the company, unless one chooses to collapse the distinction between the allegedly private sphere of contractual arrangements here and the public sphere of political intervention there. This move is well known and has been made again and again throughout the twentieth century.[73] But, because it re-engages the concept of the corporation in a debate, which is at once legal, political and moral, this debate is necessarily open-ended. It would already be an advance to view CSR as reflective of this open-ended dispute, not as its solution.

C   Beyond right and left?

As we will see in the following section, the political economy paradigm, as discussed up until now, has been seriously undermined and relativized by the increasing disempowerment of certain parties' interests in the corporation. The degree to which the received nexus-of-contracts model fails to explain the financial flows, subdivisions and re-shaping of business corporations today reflects on the differentiation of the corporate form. As the modern business corporation became, on the one hand, the intersection for investments, and, on the other, a dramatically decentralized, 'networked' firm,[74] its traditional organizational structure began to dissolve. We are only beginning to understand the consequences this has for our analytical apparatus. As regards the former, the dramatic rise of financial instruments, special investment vehicles and funds suggests a far-reaching erosion of the traditional, publicly held stock corporation as regards the interest pluralism concept of the corporation. The emerging networked firm poses formidable challenges

---

[73] Duncan Kennedy, 'Legal Formality' (1973) 2 *Journal of Legal Studies* 351–398; Duncan Kennedy, 'Form and Substance in Private Law Adjudication' (1976) 89 *Harvard Law Review* 1685–1778; William W. Bratton, 'The "Nexus of Contracts" Corporation: A Critical Appraisal' (1989) 74 *Cornell Law Review* 407–465; William W. Bratton, 'Welfare, Dialectic, and Mediation in Corporate Law' (2005) 2 *Berkeley Business Law Journal* 59–76.

[74] Walter W. Powell, 'Neither Market nor Hierarchy: Network Forms of Organization' (1990) 12 *Research in Organizational Behavior* 295–336; Laurel Smith-Doerr and Walter W. Powell, 'Networks and Economic Life', in Neil J. Smelser and Richard Swedberg (eds.), *Handbook of Economic Sociology*, 2nd edn (Princeton, Oxford and New York: Princeton University Press and Russell Sage, 2005), pp. 379–402; C.K. Prahalad and M.S. Krishnan, *The New Age of Innovation: Driving Co-Created Value Through Global Networks* (New York: McGraw-Hill, 2008).

for traditional political economy concepts of the corporation and its stakeholders.[75]

We are increasingly facing the dilemma of having to describe a fast-evolving, complex structure without the appropriate vocabulary. From the political economy perspective described above, the combination of a sophisticated, critical legal perspective and a yearning sociological description seems to be all we have at our disposition. The promise of trying to rescue the political economy perspective into the next evolutionary stage, a more radically *financial* phase of corporate organization, is that we might be able to translate our inquiry over the meaning of public and private in corporate law into an adequately critically agenda for the corporation in an era of financial capitalism. The danger of studying the corporation through the lens of political economy is that we are likely to apply the same distinctions as we used to, without, however, being able to develop them against the former political, regulatory and socio-economic framework. While early critics of legal formality with regard to the corporation believed in the validity of re-politicization,[76] this is anything but certain today. For one, the institutional framework of political market regulation has been undergoing dramatic changes, effectively eroding the demarcation lines between the market and the state.[77] While

---

[75] See, for example, Luc Boltanski and Ève Chiapello, *Le nouvel esprit du capitalisme* (Paris: Gallimard, 1999), p. 291 [English edition 2002, p. 217], Katherine V.W. Stone, 'The New Psychological Contract: Implications of the Changing Workplace for Labor and Employment Law' (2001) 48 *UCLA Law Review* 519–659; Harry W. Arthurs and Claire Mummé, 'From Governance To Political Economy: Workers As Citizens, Stakeholders and Productive Social Actors' (2007) 45 *Osgoode Hall Law Journal* 439–470 (and reprinted in this volume as Chapter 16), and Richard Sennett, *The Culture of the New Capitalism* (New Haven: Yale University Press, 2006) with regard to the challenges for labour and employment rights; but see Colin Scott, 'Reflexive Governance, Meta-Regulation and Corporate Social Responsibility: The "Heineken Effect"', in Nina Boeger, Rachel Murray and Charlotte Villiers (eds.), *Perspectives on Corporate Social Responsibility* (Cheltenham: Edward Elgar, 2008), pp. 170–185, whose concept of reflexive governance requires us to treat the network as a 'learning' entity for which 'law' can only be seen as one part of an evolving normative framework that is created by different state and non-state actors and out of which the identification of CSR obligations takes place; compare with a varieties-of-capitalism approach to a hybrid governance model of the innovative and the learning firm: William Lazonick, 'Varieties of Capitalism and Innovative Enterprise' (2007) 24 *Comparative Social Research* 21–69 and Peer Zumbansen, 'Varieties of Capitalism and the Learning Firm: Corporate Governance and Labour in the Context of Contemporary Developments in European and German Company Law', in Boeger et al., *Corporate Social Responsibility*, pp. 113–143.

[76] Robert L. Hale, 'Coercion and Distribution in a Supposedly Non-Coercive State' (1923) 38 *Political Science Quarterly* 470–494; Adolf A. Berle, *The 20th Century Capitalist Revolution* (New York: Harcourt, Brace & World, 1954).

[77] Alfred C. Aman, Jr., 'Administrative Law for a New Century', in Michael Taggart (ed.), *The Province of Administrative Law* (Oxford and Portland: Hart Publishing,

one, in critical tradition, might want to continue to discredit the validity of these boundaries in the first place, there is, however, another element which seriously challenges the critical project: the transnationalization of legal regulation leads to a complex co-existence of legal and non-legal forms of governance and self-regulation, which political science, law and sociology have been trying for some time already to fully grasp. With the de-territorialization of societal activities on the one hand and the proliferation of norm-entrepreneurs designing norms and regulatory regimes for these cross-jurisdictional spaces of societal activity on the other, the space of political action is being redefined.[78] With law having become unearthed, the chances for survival of a nation-based concept of legal regulation have to be reassessed and newly mapped within a changed regulatory landscape.[79]

IV What makes and what comes after financial capitalism? (paradigm 2)

Let us briefly turn to the second, financial paradigm. Given the emphasis on the financial strategies that business corporations have been pursuing on global markets, the 'financial paradigm' offers important insights into the way in which the corporation has been transformed from a fairly straightforward investment, production and dissemination organization into a complex amalgamation of financial strategies. One element of this transformation is that financial decisions in the recent past have been driven by an increasingly short-term orientation in mind, as regards the maximization of shareholder value in response to highly volatile investor constituencies who, at any time, could 'take their money elsewhere'.

The consequences for corporate law and policy of this shareholder orientation have been occupying scholars and practitioners in a truly global debate over corporate governance.[80] Emerging from this

---

1997), pp. 90–107; Orly Lobel, 'The Renew Deal: The Fall of Regulation and the Rise of Governance in Contemporary Legal Thought' (2004) 89 *Minnesota Law Review* 342–469; Richard B. Stewart, 'Regulation, Innovation, and Administrative Law: A Conceptual Framework' (1981) 69 *California Law Review* 1256–1377.

[78] Gralf-Peter Calliess and Peer Zumbansen, *Rough Consensus and Running Code: A Theory of Transnational Private Law* (Oxford: Hart Publishing, 2010).

[79] Niklas Luhmann, *Law as a Social System* (trans. K. Ziegert, ed. F. Kastner, D. Schiff, R. Nobles and R. Ziegert) (Oxford and New York: Oxford University Press, 2004), p. 497.

[80] See, for example, John W. Cioffi, 'State of the Art: A Review Essay on Comparative Corporate Governance: The State of the Art and Emerging Research' (2000) 48 *American Journal of Comparative Law* 501, and Jan von Hein, *Die Rezeption US-amerikanischen Gesellschaftsrechts in Deutschland* (Tübingen: Mohr Siebeck, 2008).

development was the insight (and challenge) about how models and strategies of corporate governance and corporate finance became intricately interlinked and intertwined. And because of this intertwining of different approaches to defining the 'core business' of the corporation,[81] financialism offers a tremendous opportunity to investigate the context and environment of corporate organization today. Financialism, as we will see, did not foreclose the possibility of the reconceiving of the 'embedded firm'. It can instead be seen as already being able to grasp the demands of a highly diversified knowledge economy, which bears substantial potential to better synergize governance and finance strategies in a sustainable way.

V   What managers do depends on what they know (paradigm 3)

A   The place of knowledge in management

What then might be the 'lessons' of the current crisis of financialism? Is there more at stake today than a 'return of the state', a call for 'more', 'tighter', 'more effective' regulation? Much suggests that these proposals are very narrowly construed and inapt to capture the complexities of corporate organization and regulation today. While the reform of financial market regulation heads today's regulatory to-do list, the unanswered questions about the role of corporate governance in the financial crisis still linger painfully.[82] It is here where we can see the emergence of a new paradigm, putting into sharp relief the complex entanglement of the corporation in a radically transformed regulatory, organizational, but also epistemological environment. The challenges of the corporation today are no longer constituted by what it can do, but what it *knows*. The knowledge paradigm aims to capture the particular challenges that management faces when confronted with decision-making challenges in a global market, which is characterized by a great degree of uncertainty and risk. This paradigm opens up a new perspective on the way that management engages on a day-to-day basis in the negotiation of short-term and long-term perspectives in a context that is both highly artificially constructed with view to the financial instruments, which management operates with, but

---

[81] C.K. (Coimbatore Krishnarao) Prahalad and Gary Hamel, 'The Core Competence of the Corporation' (1990) 68 *Harvard Business Review* 79–91.
[82] Brian R. Cheffins, 'Did Corporate Governance "Fail" during the 2008 Stock Market Meltdown? The Case of the S& P 500' (2009) 65 *Business Lawyer* 1–62; Gevurtz, 'Reflections on Citigroup', pp. 113–155.

is also deeply embedded in an evolving transnational political economy. This context is, on the one hand, marked by a radical decline in publicly available funding for central infrastructure needs. On the other hand, this context is undergoing dramatic transformations with regard to its longstanding forms of political–legal regulation and market governance. As domestic welfare states are continuing to struggle with the aftermath and development prospects of privatization and deregulation politics since the late 1970s, Western nations have meanwhile been active in shaping the emerging economies in the East and the South, as illustrated, inter alia, by the World Bank's Development Agenda.[83]

B   *From individuals to organizations to networks? From industrial captains to managerial revolutionaries to the 'end' or 'future' of management?*

While many might agree, in theory and practice, that the successful operation of business of such highly volatile and risky transnational markets continues to depend crucially on the persons behind the wheel, the modes of management are a matter of deep concern.[84] At the same time, organizational sociologists and management theorists are pointing to the amorphous status of *knowledge* as a subject of scientific assessment and strategic exploitation: as knowledge begins to both transform and constantly re-shape the global economy, the need arises for a sophisticated conceptual apparatus to assess this development. Needed are economics of knowledge[85] as well as a theory of knowledge management that does not isolate business knowledge from questions of governance under conditions of uncertainty.[86]

As global companies struggle to maintain their position in the market, the need to transnationalize management becomes crucially felt. With the biggest US multinationals either still being 95 per cent run

---

[83] See, for example, the World Bank Report: 'Building Knowledge Economies' (2007), available at: http://go.worldbank.org/851HK6EUHO (last accessed 22 February 2011).
[84] Gary Hamel, *The Future of Management (with Bill Breen)* (Cambridge, MA: Harvard Business School Press, 2008), ch. I.
[85] See Dominique Foray, *The Economics of Knowledge [Paris: L'économie de la connaissance, 2000]* (Cambridge, MA and London: MIT Press, 2004).
[86] Helmut Willke, *Systemisches Wissensmanagement*, 2nd edn (Stuttgart: Lucius & Lucius, 2001), pp. 65–66; Helmut Willke, *Smart Governance: Governing the Global Knowledge Society* (Frankfurt and New York: Campus, 2007), ch. 3; regarding the distinction between risk and uncertainty, see already Frank H. Knight, *Risk, Uncertainty and Profit* [unabridged republication of the 1957 edn of the orig. 1921 edn] (Mineola: Dover Publications, Inc., 1921), p. 197.

by Americans and/or losing their trained and groomed foreigners to aggressively poaching 'emerging markets' firms, the issues surrounding a volatile 'market for management' tend to eclipse the important questions regarding the transformation of management today. What does management need to know? How is that information generated, processed and utilized? How is that information turned into quality knowledge that informs corporate management today? How have the issues arising from a transformation of global markets identified above – first, the arrival of the emerging economies' actors on the scene and, second, the erosion of financial markets and the need to revisit the foundations of the much-hailed financialization of corporate governance – begun to inform the scope of management responsibility?

Against this background, we must assess the emerging challenges to our traditional concepts of a company's responsibilities from a different angle. CSR is today on the agenda of business leaders, policy-makers and activists because it relates to questions of regulating corporate behaviour in a time where it has become a formidable challenge to identify what it is that a company does – admittedly a necessary prerequisite for any proposal of how companies should be regulated, to whom they owe which kind of responsibilities. Where companies are invested in domestic and transnational infrastructure provision projects pertaining to telecommunications, road construction, health care and old age care provision, energy services and urban development, among others, their identification as 'private' actors seems increasingly inadequate. Of course, such a distinction can only hold where we fail to recognize that allegedly private agreements are embedded in a legally constructed system of rights allocation.[87] The same holds true for our assessment of the corporation: if we look beyond the business corporation as an economic actor, we recognize that it is at home in two worlds: besides its emergence as an economic entity, its other nature is legal.[88] Here, we see that a company exists by grace of the law that called it into being. This observation is an important starting point for any assessment of a company's

---

[87] Morris R. Cohen, 'The Basis of Contract' (1932) 46 *Harvard Law Review* 553–592. And yet, the identification of a contract as a 'private arrangement' continues to illustrate the liberal core of Western legal order, which recognizes the individual's freedom of engaging in her private affairs, where and as long as this exercise of freedom does not infringe the rights of other members of society. The price to pay for such a theory of contract is of course the denial of any valid foundation to the distinction between public and private in the first place. The Realist critique, then, only points out what has forever been the basic architecture of the Western positivist legal order.

[88] Dewey, 'Corporate Legal Personality'; Charles Perrow, *Organizing America: Wealth, Power, and the Origins of Corporate Capitalism* (Princeton and Oxford: Princeton University Press, 2002), pp. 22–47.

responsibilities. Recognizing that a company is a legal construct, it becomes possible to ask and to answer questions regarding its nature, goals, and eventual limitations with respect to its double nature.

But, it can be said that the continuing contestation of the business corporation's *responsibilities* stems from the insight that the recognition of the legal nature of the firm does not resolve the normative questions arising out of the *reality* of the firm. The challenge facing all attempts at designing a comprehensive and effective CSR strategy today results from the fact that neither of these reconstructions offers much of a guidance here: the myriad contexts and markets in which companies operate today, the host of different societal functions, domestically and transnationally, which are driven deeply by the powerful transformations of today's Western societies, constitute a dramatically changed environment for business corporations. In the second half of the twentieth century, we had only slowly begun to conceptualize the changing governance forms for corporate entities as companies began to assume an ever-growing amount of formerly public functions. For a long time, the experiences of corporate governance reform were still very much embedded in a domestic, nation-state framework of market regulation. Even with a dramatic rise of privatization of virtually all sectors of public function, corporate regulation was still conceived of as occurring within a constellation made up of company, taxation and securities regulation on the one hand, and social welfare and labour/employment regulation on the other. With the winds of globalization blowing hard and cold over the last few decades, the nation-state has increasingly lost its singular role as market regulator. As firms began spanning their activities across the globe, the state has been at odds in effectively governing this development.[89] On the other side, from the perspective of many emerging market governments, it is their insatiable infrastructure needs that companies are lining up to satisfy. Companies such as Cisco and GM are offering governments a comprehensive infrastructure development programme, along with the promise of themselves building some or even all of it.[90] Moving jobs and capacities, human and financial, around the globe, according to identified needs and promises

---

[89] See Dennis Patterson and Ari Afilalo, *The New Global Trading Order: The Evolving State and the Future of Trade* (Cambridge: Cambridge University Press, 2008), chs. 1 and 2.

[90] 'A Survey of Globalisation – The Empire Strikes Back: Why Rich-World Multinationals Think they can Stay ahead of Newcomers', *The Economist*, 18 September 2008. For example, GE in 2006 signed an memorandum of understanding with China's National Development and Reform Commission geared towards collaborating on meeting some 200 second tier Chinese cities' need of electric and physical infrastructure – cities with a minimum population of 1 million each. In the context of the

of growth, so-called globally integrated enterprises today assume myriad organizational forms, that fundamentally challenge traditional concepts of legal regulation.

The role of law in this transnational regulatory environment has become ambiguous, as it is no longer clear whether the self-governing normative regimes that structure global corporate activity are attached to a particular state. It is against this background that we have to reconsider a conceptual approach that associates legal and political regulation with the state, while continuing to position the corporation in an ambiguously private sphere of self-regulation.

C *The corporation as state: corporate social responsibility in the knowledge society*

In the knowledge society, the main protagonists are the post-modern state and the business corporation. Both actors occupy a central and yet highly ambivalent place within an increasingly complex, transnational regulatory space. The parallel observations on the state and the corporation are inspiring a historical–theoretical inquiry into the trajectories that sociologists have been tracing from the late eighteenth century into the present with regard to the notions, concepts and understandings of 'society'. The idea of society here functions as a backdrop for a host of contentions as to the nature and goals of political, legal, state (societal) order. Emerging with the nineteenth century, such ordering paradigms provided for an increasingly eminent role of the 'state' within the architectural imagination. Today, in light of the state's changing role in the growingly interconnected, transnational regulatory landscape, the very idea of 'society' begins to forcefully contest a number of the state's formerly held institutional and normative claims.

With a dramatic reconfiguration of public and private governance modes at the end of the twentieth-century Western welfare state, there arises an urgent need to reassess the foundations on which our concepts of legal governance have come to rest.[91] The case of the business corporation, studied through the paradigm of the transnational knowledge society, promises to offer rich insights into the foundations

---

company's engagement in Vietnam, with 'huge problems facing the country in water, oil, energy, aviation, rail and finance', the GE president met with three Vietnamese leaders who had participated in GE's leadership programme in the United States, a coincidence the company described as a 'transfer a lot of learnings between us and we end up friends for life'.

[91] Peer Zumbansen, 'The Conundrum of Order: Governance from an Interdisciplinary Perspective', in David Levi-Faur (ed.), *Oxford Handbook on Governance* (Oxford: Oxford University Press, 2011).

and directions of these ongoing changes precisely because the traditionally privately conceived firm has been assuming such a central place in the transformation of society from public to private ordering. Whereas public governance at the outset of the twenty-first century is being described today by formulas ranging from the 'enabling' or 'moderating state' to the 'risk' or 'knowledge society', modern corporate governance in many ways resembles this fundamental concern with the transformation of regulation. The defining mark of contemporary governance is its radical dependency on dispersed, fragmented societal knowledge. As political scientists, sociologists and legal scholars alike are engaging in a theoretical–historical assessment of the regulatory prospects after the decline of the Western welfare state, the question of what might succeed the state as a central reference point within a decentralized knowledge society becomes central.

A parallel challenge can be discerned with regard to the large business corporation, which has in many ways been assuming formerly public functions. No wonder, then, that the debate among corporate lawyers, activists, philosophers and social scientists over CSR continues with no end in sight.[92] Seen through the sociological lens of the knowledge society, CSR functions as a powerful magnifying glass through which we gain a clearer view not only on the wide-ranging concerns over management power in today's large corporations, but also on the parallels between the information and knowledge generation and administration challenges in both firms and contemporary governments. Succeeding an early twentieth-century pluralist formulation of corporate conflicts that focused on the opposed interests of owners, employees and creditors within and around the business corporation, an adequate conceptualization of CSR must begin to incorporate and internalize a radically more complex perspective on corporate governance. A more promising concept of CSR would thus suggest focusing on the different fields in which the company exerts itself. Such 'fields' may be identified through a regulatory lens[93] or by identifying the 'things companies do' and

---

[92] A powerful assessment of the corporation's assumption of the governance of citizenship is now offered by Andrew Crane, Dirk Matten and Jeremy Moon, *Corporations and Citizenship* (Cambridge: Cambridge University Press, 2008), pp. 50–87.
[93] Cynthia A. Williams, 'The Securities and Exchange Commission and Corporate Social Transparency' (1999) 112 *Harvard Law Review* 1197–1311; Cynthia Williams and John Conley, 'Is there an Emerging Fiduciary Duty to Consider Human Rights?' (2005) 74 *University of Cincinnati Law Review* 75–104; Aaron Dhir, 'Realigning the Corporate Building Blocks: Shareholder Proposals as a Vehicle for Achieving Corporate Social and Human Rights Accountability' (2006) 43 *American Business Law Journal* 365.

'why'.[94] Using an approach that seeks to integrate a sociological theory of society into the identification of the content and scope of the corporation's various responsibilities one might gain a better understanding of the nature of the corporation *in* that society.

Where traditional CSR concepts are often conceptualized in opposition against something that had been taken as the dominant and exclusive definition of the corporation (as profit maximizer),[95] the here-proposed CSR approach is likely to provide an analysis of the way in which the corporation's economic performance, embedded in a more comprehensive assessment of the different functions the corporation assumes in society, forms part of the corporation's role in different social systems. As the corporation passes through the three paradigms, CSR in turn can no longer be understood as the counter programme or add-on to corporate governance,[96] but must be seen as a lens through which to study the reconceptualization of corporate governance. From this perspective, the parallels between the early twenty-first century state and the contemporary business corporation can help us understand the challenges that face both concepts in light of a complex, transnational knowledge society. The state in a functionally differentiated society has been described as the evolving institutionalization of the political system, which itself is merely one of several communications taking place in society.[97] In turn, the corporation can be seen as being determined by the processes of functional differentiation of the economic system. This observation has been used in fact to sketch a radically expanded, more complex concept of the corporation than would have been possible under either the industrial-organizational or the financial paradigm.[98] As the contours of the knowledge society and

---

[94] Ruth Aguilera, Deborah Rupp, Cynthia A. Williams and Jyoti Ganapathi, 'Putting the S Back in Corporate Social Responsibility: A Multi-Level Theory of Social Change in Organizations' (2004) 32 *Academy of Management Review* 836–863.

[95] Harry J. Glasbeek, 'The Corporate Social Responsibility Movement – The Latest in Maginot Lines to Save Capitalism' (1988) 11 *Dalhousie Law Journal* 363–402.

[96] See the critique by Robert B. Reich, 'The Case Against Corporate Social Responsibility' (2008) UC Berkeley Goldman School of Public Policy Working Paper 08–003, http://ssrn.com/abstract=1213129 (last accessed 22 February 2011).

[97] Niklas Luhmann, 'Metamorphosen des Staates', in *Gesellschaftsstruktur und Semantik. Studien zur Wissenssoziologie der modernen Gesellschaft* (Frankfurt: Suhrkamp, 1995), pp. 101–137.

[98] Gunther Teubner, 'Enterprise Corporatism: New Industrial Policy and the "Essence" of the Legal Person' (1988) 36 *American Journal of Comparative Law* 130–155; Gunther Teubner, 'The Invisible Cupola: From Causal to Collective Attribution in Ecological Liability', in Gunther Teubner, Lindsay Farmer and Declan Murphy (eds.), *Environmental Law and Ecological Responsibility: The Concept and Practice of Ecological Self-Organization* (London: Wiley, 1994), pp. 17–47.

the actors, actants[99] and networks associated with it become increasingly clear, the concept of the corporation evolves at breathtaking speed and with daunting complexity. Mirroring the blurring and erosion of its physical and legal boundaries, the corporation's nature is once again seemingly beyond grasp. The persistently growing sophistication of organizational and management theory allows us at least to better appreciate the task. Building on theories of the innovative firm[100] in the context of an expanding understanding of the knowledge society is likely to provide us with a more adequate concept of the corporation today.

D   *What is the knowledge society?*

Its defining marks can be seen in the overriding, crucial role played by the generation, dissemination and application of knowledge – as opposed to mere information. Following a distinction introduced by Joel Mokyr, the difference between propositional knowledge (describing existing constellations) and prescriptive knowledge (applied with the goal of shaping outcomes)[101] matters because while the basis of the former grows, the latter is part of a much more complex institutional framework. Knowledge gathered, developed and assessed for future-oriented development becomes embedded in a dramatically *transformed* environment, governed – above all – by conditions of complexity and uncertainty.[102] To the degree that it has become increasingly difficult to clearly associate a particular legislative, regulatory initiative with one or the other political partisan camp, former invocations or contestations of redistribution in the name of 'social justice' or 'freedom' ring strangely faint today. In a fast-evolving context of a globally merging market and knowledge society a reconceptualization of public and private forms of governance becomes necessary, but the orientation points are hard to

---

[99] Bruno Latour, *Reassembling the Social: An Introduction to Actor-Network Theory* (Oxford and New York: Oxford University Press, 2005).
[100] William Lazonick, 'The Innovative Firm', in Jan Fagerberg (ed.), *Oxford Handbook of Innovation* (Oxford and New York: Oxford University Press, 2005), pp. 27–55; William Lazonick, 'Varieties of Capitalism and Innovative Enterprise' (2007) 24 *Comparative Social Research* 21–69.
[101] Joel Mokyr, 'The Knowledge Society: Theoretical and Historical Underpinnings' (2005), available at: faculty.wcas.northwestern.edu/~jmokyr/Unitednations.PDF, 2.
[102] Ulrich Beck, 'From Industrial Society to Risk Society: Questions of Survival, Social Structure and Ecological Enlightenment' (1992) 9 *Theory, Culture & Society* 97–123; Michael Power, 'From Risk Society to Audit Society' (1997) 3 *Soziale Systeme* 3–21, available at: www.soziale-systeme.ch/leseproben/power.htm (last accessed 22 February 2011).

identify. In contrast to the depictions rendered by Weber or Polanyi, we are urged to understand the boundaries between politics and society as having been artificially drawn with reference to historically evolved patterns of institutional development and depicted as political institutions on the one hand, market institutions on the other: patterns that have meanwhile come to seem extremely blurry, as both political and 'private' actors such as non-governmental organizations, corporations, collectives and individuals operate under conditions of extreme and uncertainty and can hardly be depicted through references to either 'public' or 'private', 'political' or 'market'.[103]

Governments and corporations alike are dependent on increasingly fragmented, societal knowledge, which leads to an important reconfiguration of the relations between the different actors within and outside of their organizational boundaries.[104] As sociologists describe the state as the emblem of the political system in a functionally differentiated society without centre or pinnacle (Luhmann), we see this society emerging as a society that is complex and marked by 'a multiplicity of independent and parallel regulations'.[105] The state, in its dependence on constantly updated information, is at the same time implicated in the production of that very information by creating rules and facilitating institutional growth for knowledge production and dissemination,[106] which raises again far-reaching legitimacy problems, that democratic and legal theory only insufficiently have been trying to address through enhanced 'participation' models.[107]

---

[103] See most recently Willke, 'Smart Governance'.
[104] Dominique Pestre, 'Science, Society and Politics: Knowledge Societies from Historical Perspective' (2007) *Report to the Science, Economy and Society Directorate at the European Commission*, http://ec.europa.eu/research/science-society/document_library/pdf_06/historical-perspectives_en.pdf, 911 (last accessed 22 February 2011); regarding the consequences for urban governance and the reconfiguration of institutional settings, see the intriguing report by Stefan Bergheim on the Deutsche Bank Research Project of 2 October 2008 on the 'broad basis of societal progress', available at: www.dbresearch.com/PROD/DBR_INTERNET_EN-PROD/PROD0000000000232129.pdf (last accessed 22 February 2011).
[105] *Ibid.*, p. 9.
[106] Karl-Heinz Ladeur, *Der Staat gegen die Gesellschaft* (Tübingen: Mohr Siebeck, 2006)
[107] Pestre, 'Science, Society and Politics', expressing deep scepticism about the viability of such approaches in light of the high-level scientific knowledge that is today used to support political decision-making; with regard to an emphasis on 'participation' as a cure for the legitimacy problem of contemporary domestic and transnational decision-making bodies, see critically Nico Krisch, Benedict Kingsbury and Richard B. Stewart, 'The Emergence of Global Administrative Law' (2005) 68 *Law and Contemporary Problems* 15, and Carol Harlow, 'Global Administrative Law: The

Meanwhile, corporations, like other societal actors involved in market identification, creation and consolidation, in investment and redistribution activities as well as in R&D and 'knowledge management',[108] face pressing governance challenges that in many ways mirror those of contemporary political governing bodies.[109] The dependence of management on expert knowledge, which is generated and communicated both in and outside of the firm, has grown in correlation with the expanding reach of business activities and their impact. With governments and corporations as knowledge actors, producers and consumers, the pressure on law to facilitate and to enable these processes has grown exponentially. Not adequately captured as being situated in an either exclusively public or private sphere, 'political', 'private' corporate actors are both authors and receivers of the rules that govern their behaviour. While this new view on the embeddedness of societal activity in a decentralized, de-territorialized and de-hierarchized knowledge society suggests a paradigmatic move beyond distinctions based on institutional manifestation ('state'/'market') or political, normative demarcation ('public'/'private'),[110] the place to ask the original CSR questions becomes increasingly elusive.[111] These questions

Quest for Principles and Values' (2006) 17 *European Journal of International Law* 187–214.
[108] Olivier Bouba-Olga, *L'économie de l'entreprise* (Paris: Éditions du Seuil, 2003), pp. 170–173; Foray, *Economics of Knowledge*, p. 217; Dirk Baecker, *Studien zur nächsten Gesellschaft* (Frankfurt: Suhrkamp, 2008), p. 22: 'The innovative corporations of the coming society will have bid the nervous self-confidence farewell, in accordance with which they understood their fate to be exclusively determined by the economy, meaning that it would be sealed on markets, where corporations compete with each other for the demands of affluent consumers. The corporation's fate does, indeed, decide itself here, but, at the same time, it decides itself in the laboratories of science, in the praying halls of churches, in court rooms, in the backrooms of politics and in the editing offices of newspapers, television broadcasters and internet hosts' [translated by Zumbansen].
[109] Peer Zumbansen, 'The Conundrum of Corporate Social Responsibility: Remarks on the Changing Nature of Firms and States', in Rebecca Bratspies and Russell Miller (eds.), *Transboundary Harm: Lessons from the Trail Smelter Arbitration* (Cambridge: Cambridge University Press, 2006), pp. 274–289.
[110] See the contributions to Helmut Kitschelt, Peter Lange, Gary Marks and John D. Stephens (eds.), *Continuity and Change in Contemporary Capitalism* (Cambridge: Cambridge University Press, 1999); J. Rogers Hollingsworth and Robert Boyer (eds.), *Contemporary Capitalism: The Embeddedness of Institutions* (Cambridge: Cambridge University Press, 1997).
[111] Mokyr, 'Knowledge Society'; Willke, *Smart Governance*, p. 35, describing the need to translate institutions governing 'normative decision-making', involving assertions that decisions about the future are based on norms and normative considerations, into institutions facilitating 'cognitive' decision-making based on knowledge.

must turn to 'culture'[112] and to the corporation's place and nature in the 'coming society'[113] just as the inquiry into the nature of the state must reach beyond the narrow choice between the state's waning or 'returning'.[114] This is the challenge of corporate governance in the knowledge society.

[112] John M. Conley and Cynthia A. Williams, 'The Corporate Social Responsibility Movement as an Ethnographic Problem' (2008) Working Paper http://papers.ssrn.com/sol3/papers.cfm?abstract_id=1285631 (last accessed 22 February 2011); see also Aaron Dhir's Research Project at Osgoode Hall Law School's CLPE Comparative Research in Law & Political Economy Network on 'Canadian Corporate Governance, Law and Racial Diversity', available at: http://papers.ssrn.com/sol3/papers.cfm?abstract_id=1340726 (last accessed 22 February 2011).

[113] Dirk Baecker, *Studien zur nächsten Gesellschaft* (Frankfurt: Suhrkamp, 2008).

[114] Susan Strange, *The Retreat of the State* (Cambridge: Cambridge University Press, 1996); Adam Harmes, *The Return of the State* (Toronto: Douglas & McIntyre, 2004).

Part II

New interests, new shareholder constellations, new landscapes

8 Beyond the Berle and Means paradigm: private equity and the new capitalist order

Stephen F. Diamond

I Introduction

The collapse of the credit markets that began to roil the global financial system in the late summer of 2007 hit more than just the homebuilding and mortgage sectors of the economy. As interest rates increased, private equity, or "PE," an important new form of financial capital, also felt the shockwave. PE funds have grown substantially in size as well as in political and financial significance in the last decade. The Blackstone Group, for example, one of a handful of top tier PE funds, took over the Hilton Hotels Corporation for $26 billion in 2007. Cerberus Capital, another major PE player, surprised many when it announced plans to buy the troubled Chrysler Group from DaimlerChrysler – a pioneering venture into the top ranks of industrial United States.

KKR, one of the oldest PE funds, currently owns such a large number of independent businesses that it is, indirectly, the second largest employer in the United States with 560,000 employees, twice as many as GM, ahead of MacDonald's and just behind Wal-Mart. Today's PE fund managers have been hailed widely in the business press as the new "masters of the universe," pushing aside bond traders and investment bankers, not to mention lowly CEOs. The managers of the largest funds are billionaires. Henry Kravis, the second "K" in KKR, has a wing named after him at New York's Metropolitan Museum of Art.

Since the credit freeze, however, the major banks that had made billions in loans to PE funds to finance their leveraged buyouts ("LBOs") of companies like Chrysler, Clear Channel or the UK's Alliance Boots retail pharmacy giant, have been unable to re-sell those loans into the wider capital markets, thus drying up the liquidity upon which PE funds depend. In turn this caused the critical flow of capital to PE funds to seize up, leading some to predict a quick end to the recent "LBO boom." The *Financial Times* wondered whether PE might turn out to be "a cyclical phenomenon of finite duration and questionable wisdom."[1] Indeed, Bloomberg News concluded: "Private-equity firms have been hunkered down since the onset of the credit crisis about 16 months ago, scarred by broken deals and frustrated by the evaporation of debt financing crucial to buyouts."[2]

These difficulties contributed to another problem for private equity. In order to raise more capital and gain currency to finance expansion, several private buyout funds, ironically, turned to the stock market themselves, "going public" by selling a small percentage of their management firms to outside investors. Most prominently, the Blackstone Group went public in 2007 at a price of $31 a share in order to raise $4 billion for its partners and for expansion. The initial public offering (IPO) placed a value on Blackstone of more than $33 billion. But within a few weeks the fear of a credit crunch and possible tax hikes caused the price of Blackstone shares to drop 22 percent, making it the worst performing IPO of 2007. In addition, investor advocacy groups including the AFL-CIO complained about the opaque governance structure that Blackstone used to shield its business operations from scrutiny by its new shareholders.[3] The structure seemed designed to avoid the oversight provisions of the federal Investment Company Act, put in place in the New Deal era as a firewall to protect investors from speculative activity by investment firms such as buyout funds. In other words, Blackstone was recreating within its own firm the very separation of ownership and control that it attempts to eliminate when it buys out other corporations. Other major PE funds that had planned to follow Blackstone's lead into the public markets began to have second thoughts.

Despite the downturn, however, cash has continued to flow to PE funds. At the end of the summer in 2007, according to the *Wall Street Journal*, Blackstone announced it had raised the largest buyout fund in history "despite the recent red flags in the debt markets," raising a total of $21.7 billion. This included a $1 billion commitment from the California State Teachers' Retirement System "along with a host of other big public pension funds."[4] This was soon followed by an announcement by the Carlyle Group in early September that it had successfully raised 5.3 billion euros for its European based buyout operations. The pace in 2008 indeed slowed, but fundraising secured

---

[1] "The End of LBOs," *Financial Times*, July 27, 2007.
[2] Jason Kelly, "Paulson's Capital May Bring Blackstone, Carlyle Back," Bloomberg, October 17, 2008.
[3] This author advised the AFL-CIO on concerns with regard to the Blackstone IPO.
[4] Laura Kreutzer, "Blackstone Closes Record Buyout Fund," *Wall Street Journal*, August 8, 2007.

slightly more than $100 billion in the first nine months of the year relative to the $118 billion raised in the same period the year before.[5] In 2009, KKR led the IPO of one of its portfolio companies, the semiconductor firm Avago, raising $650 million.[6] KKR increased its overall return by acting as deal manager and underwriter simultaneously. It also completed a second IPO of Dollar General in 2009, a discount retailer that KKR took private in a $7.2 billion LBO in 2007. That deal generated a $239 million dividend for KKR and its partners.[7] By acting as co-lead underwriters with Goldman Sachs and Citigroup, KKR also shared in the $64 million transaction fees generated by the deal.[8] KKR had originally put in some $2.8 billion of its own money to take the company private and that stake was valued in advance of the IPO at about $4.75 billion, "indicating a windfall for KKR," according to the *Wall Street Journal*.[9] Meanwhile, Blackstone founder Stephen Schwarzman told an investors' conference in October 2008 that "the best returns in private equity have come in a period like the one that we're just entering. This is an absolutely wonderful time."[10] By mid-2010, "private equity firms ... sit atop an estimated $500 billion" in cash that has been raised from pension funds, endowments and foreign governments.[11]

This chapter will assume that, in fact, private equity as an institutional form is here to stay. More significantly, I will argue that private equity attempts to solve one of the perennial problems long associated with the Anglo-American form of capitalism, the separation of ownership and control. The resolution of this issue now takes on even greater importance with the collapse, at least for the time being, of the investment banking model that has long been at the heart of modern financial capitalism. As I argued recently in a paper with economist Jennifer

---

[5] "PE Fund-Raising Still Going Strong. Buyout Shops, Not So Much," *Wall Street Journal*, October 7, 2008. Although fund-raising and deal flow were down significantly in late 2008, nonetheless PE funds had some $2.5 trillion under management at the end of 2008. Marko Maslakovic, *Private Equity 2009*, IFSL Research, London, August 2009.
[6] Peter Lattman, "KKR Affiliate Sees Value Increase, Strong Performance Comes as Buyout Firm Prepares for Its Own Listing," *Wall Street Journal*, August 19, 2009, p. C3.
[7] C. Thomas Keegel, International Sec'y-Treas., Int'l. Bro. Teamsters, Letter to Duncan Niederaurer and Richard Ketchum, June 16, 2010.
[8] *Ibid.*
[9] Peter Lattman, "KKR To Stage IPO of Dollar General," *Wall Street Journal*, August 21, 2009, p. B4.
[10] Kelly, "Paulson's Capital."
[11] Julie Creswell, "On Wall Street, So Much Cash, So Little Time," *The New York Times*, June 24, 2010, p. 5

Kuan,[12] the hidden infrastructure established by investment banks on the regulated stock exchanges was a critical backstop to policing the problems caused by the separation of ownership and control. With that infrastructure now seriously damaged, the future health of capitalism will depend on the emergence of new forms of oversight and management of the issues that inherently plague financial capital.

A cautionary note is in order: I come forward neither to praise Caesar nor to bury him. This chapter is an attempt to assess this critical institutional player so that the current playing field of global capitalism can be better understood. As a critical supporter of corporate social responsibility efforts such as those proposed by the international labor movement[13] and European social democratic parties, it is important to have a clear understanding of the nature of the institutions that dominate our economy and that I believe will be, in some form, a key part of the response to the current crisis.

The chapter will proceed in five parts. First, I will attempt to describe the world as managers of private equity funds as well as some of their critics see it. Second, I will summarize the structure and mechanics of PE funds, including the importance of leverage to their success. Third, I will discuss what I have referred to here as the separation of ownership and control problem, including its modern formulation as an "agency" problem, first clearly formulated by Berle and Means. Fourth, I will critically assess the "counter-attack" on PE funds from labor and the left, which I believe is wrongly rooted in the concept of "financialization." I will conclude with an attempt to summarize what I consider to be the "real" nature of private equity.

II PE's worldview

PE fund managers argue that they offer a potential solution to what many have long argued is the core problem of the modern corporation: the ability of insiders of public companies to take advantage of outside shareholders. This tension between corporate managers and public investors has become a key factor in post-Enron debates about

---

[12] Stephen Diamond and Jennifer Kuan, "Ringing the Bell on the NYSE: Might a Nonprofit Stock Exchange Have Been Efficient?" (2007) 9 *Duquesne Business Law Journal* 1.

[13] The leading advocate for reform of the private equity sector in the international labor movement has been the International Union of Foodworkers, a global labor umbrella group based in Geneva. See www.iuf.org/buyoutwatch (last accessed February 22, 2011). The substance of my critique of the limitations of the labor attack on PE will become clear in the chapter.

corporate governance and finance on Wall Street and in Washington, DC. The labor movement is playing a crucial role in these debates through traditional lobbying but also through its newly established shareholder activism programs at the AFL-CIO and the breakaway group "Change to Win" and at several major union affiliates such as AFSCME, the Teamsters and SEIU. These and other critics of corporate behavior argue that the *"financialization"* of the modern economy lies behind the distorted behavior of corporations. But this is a misguided view of modern capitalism and largely irrelevant to an assessment of PE funds. For the new corporate responsibility movement to reach its full potential, a new approach is required.

Typically, PE funds take companies private by buying up the publicly traded stock of a target firm and, arguably, because of their complete control of the company, they can then more effectively deploy firm assets to productive and profitable uses.[14] After an LBO, the senior inside managers have one boss – the PE fund – to whom they must respond rather than thousands of dispersed public shareholders. This appears to allow firms to act more decisively. For example, Robert Nardelli, the controversial new CEO of the auto giant Chrysler, which was taken over by Cerberus Capital, told the *New York Times* that the company has "become more nimble" and that a new slogan at the company is being used to describe decision-making: "Either a yes or a no but not a slow maybe." Thus, a recent decision on cutting production was made in "several minutes," he said, while it would have taken months at a publicly traded firm.[15]

Once a firm's managers have generated the benefits from this new decisiveness and flexibility, the PE fund will eventually re-sell the target firm to another private owner or back to the public in an initial public offering (or "IPO") of their common stock. These re-sales can generate huge profits for the PE funds' professional staff, outside investors and the managerial teams put in place at the target firm. Jay Ritter calculates that over a twenty-year period some 666 companies with annual revenues at or above $50 million generated three-year buy and hold returns of more than 45 percent for buyout fund backed IPOs.[16]

---

[14] The large buyout funds such as Blackstone and KKR are now diversified alternative asset managers engaged in a range of businesses in addition to the traditional corporate buyout market. A discussion of this diversification is outside the scope of this chapter.
[15] Associated Press, "Chrysler CEO Pleased With Labor Contract," in *The New York Times*, October 30, 2007. Of course, the Chrysler buyout hit huge headwinds with the recession that followed the credit collapse.
[16] Jay Ritter, "Some Factoids About the 2007 IPO Market – Long-run Returns," available at: http://bear.cba.ufl.edu/ritter (last accessed February 22, 2011). Market adjusted and style adjusted returns are lower.

PE funds also find ways to generate returns when the IPO window is closed. In a recent, albeit extreme, example, the $4.3 billion buyout of British company Travelport, owner of the online travel website Orbitz, returned 100 percent of the $1 billion in equity invested in the company by its new PE owners, Blackstone and Technology Crossover Ventures, in less than a year. The firm used a new technique called a "dividend recapitalization" – it borrowed more money once taken over and issued that borrowed money as a dividend to the PE funds. Of course, that rewards the PE fund and its limited partners by increasing the debt burden weighing on the target company.

At the large UK clothing retailer Debenhams, some £2 billion (1.4 billion in debt and 600 million in equity) was used by a consortium of private equity firms including CVC, TPG and Merrill Lynch Private Equity to take over the company. A dividend recapitalization yielded £1.2 billion to the three firms, a 200 percent return on their original equity, and that was followed by a profitable IPO. According to the *Financial Times*: "Merrill – along with the other buy-out firms – has made a handsome return on the investment regardless of the share price performance following the float. The three private equity firms made more than three times their collective initial £600m equity investment in less than three years."[17] In a discussion over whether the Debenhams deal was a "flip" or "flop" the *Financial Times* explained their profit calculations:

> While the exact profits from the deal have never been disclosed, the FT has calculated that TPG invested about £250m and made an estimated return of £675m, excluding the 14 per cent stake it kept after the flotation. CVC put in about £215m and made close to £580m with a 9.7 per cent stake, while Merrill Lynch Private Equity invested £135m to earn about £365m and an 8.5 per cent stake. Staff are thought to have made close to £50m from their 4 per cent stake. John Lovering, Rob Templeman and Chris Woodhouse, Debenhams' top executive team, made estimated profits of £21m, £41m and £41m respectively and retained combined stakes worth about £60m at the time of the float.[18]

Whether the restructuring put in place at such companies is rational or destructive is a hotly debated issue. Travelport laid off hundreds of workers in its first year under new private ownership but contends it has both hired hundreds of new workers (no doubt at much lower wages), and invested heavily in new technology. Although cash flow improved, cost-cutting and real estate sell-offs were blamed, in part,

---

[17] "Debenham's Shares Tumble over Merrill's Departure from Buy-out?" *Financial Times*, March 27, 2008.
[18] "Debenham's – Flip or Flop?" *Financial Times Alphaville Blog*, August 6, 2007, on file with the author.

for the poor performance of Debenhams after its re-listing. At Chrysler PE decisiveness was used to pressure the United Auto Workers union into unprecedented concessions that led to a dramatic downsizing of the workforce as well as huge wage cuts. The ratification vote of a new collective bargaining agreement by union members was very close, with opposition led by one of the UAW's own lead negotiators, Bill Parker, head of a large Chrysler union local.[19] CEO Nardelli, however, called the agreement "revolutionary" claiming it is "a major step forward" to restoring the company's competitiveness.[20]

What is not at issue, however, is that PE funds mark a potentially dramatic change in the ownership structure of US businesses with important implications for labor and society as a whole. Yet the reaction to this development varies widely across the left and the trade union movement. Some view the emergence of PE funds as a source of new profitability for labor managed pension funds, while others argue that the funds represent another step in the emerging dominance of "financial" capital that undermines job security and union power.

The arrival of a potentially new stage in the history of capitalism is, without doubt, an unusual and perhaps perplexing event. The last such moment was marked seventy-five years ago by the publication of *The Modern Corporation and Private Property* in 1932 by legal scholar Adolf Berle and economist Gardiner Means.[21] Their book is now recognized as a critical, if flawed,[22] study of the publicly traded corporation, which was then still a relatively new and little understood institution. Their analysis of the potential tension between inside managers and outside investors remains relevant to the dysfunction that, to this day, often can plague the public corporation. Berle and Means argued that when corporations sell shares to the wider public it enables the firm's inside managers to control the day-to-day operations of the business, often taking advantage of that privileged position to enrich themselves at the expense of outside investors. Now, seventy-five years later, it appears that PE funds offer a different approach to managing businesses, definitely still capitalist but distinct from the Berle–Means paradigm firm with its separation between ownership and control. Because PE funds close the gap between ownership and control they presumably

---

[19] Tiffany Ten Eyck and Chris Kutalik, "Opposition Swells Against Concessionary Auto Contracts," *Labor Notes*, December 14, 2007.
[20] Associated Press, "Chrysler CEO Pleased."
[21] Adolph A. Berle and Gardiner C. Means, *The Modern Corporation and Private Property* (New York: Commerce Clearing House, 1932; 1991).
[22] Clifford Holderness, "The Myth of Diffuse Ownership in the United States" (2009) 22 *Review of Financial Studies* 1377.

eliminate the damage that gap can generate. Thus, PE funds mobilize hundreds of billions of dollars in the capital markets with the purpose, it is argued, of resolving the failings of public corporations that Berle and Means first identified

III How do private equity funds work?

By what alchemy of financial engineering or corporate restructuring do PE funds carry out their magic? Private equity is a subset of a larger division within the financial world called "alternative assets." Alternative assets typically are defined to include private equity funds, hedge funds and real estate funds. Over the last twenty years large institutional investors such as pension funds, insurance companies, foundations and university endowments have turned to this asset class as a means to diversify away from the lower average returns found in traditional stocks and bonds. Until the late 1970s the fiduciary standards applied to pension funds and other large institutional pools of capital required them to stick largely to what were then considered secure investments such as bonds. However, financial theorists began to argue that diversification across a wider range of assets could allow investors to secure greater returns without necessarily taking on too much risk. Soon, trustees of pension funds were allowed to move out of bonds, first into the larger equity markets and then into newly emerging "alternative asset" classes like PE funds. In fact, to fail to make such investments was soon viewed as, potentially, a violation of a trustee's fiduciary duty to maximize a fund's returns.

Some large institutions now allocate as much as 20 or 30 percent of their assets to alternative investments. In fact, public sector pension funds, including those jointly managed with union representatives, are among the largest and most important investors in buyout funds. The Oregon Investment Council, which manages that state's public employees pension fund, began investing in KKR as early as 1980. The California Public Employees Retirement System (CalPERS), the nation's largest institutional investor, has approximately $240 billion under management on behalf of 1.5 million current and future retired public employees. Currently, it allocates more than $42 billion of its assets, or about 24 percent, to alternative investment and real estate funds, including buyout funds, venture capital and hedge funds.[23] Together, California, Oregon and Washington public sector pension

---

[23] Asset Allocation, CalPERS at www.calpers.ca.gov/index.jsp?bc=/investments/assets/assetallocation.xml (last accessed February 22, 2011).

plans have invested more than $50 billion in private equity alone in the last decade.[24]

The subset of private equity itself consists of several different types of funds including buyout funds (the class that includes KKR, Blackstone, Carlyle and others), venture capital funds, mezzanine funds and distressed securities. Each has a different investment strategy but they share certain basic characteristics. They are all typically structured as "limited partnerships," where a general partner raises money from investors who will be limited partners, or "LPs," of the fund. The general partner, or "GP," then manages the money raised, usually through a separate management company, choosing where to invest and how to best monitor those investments. The LPs have only a "limited" role in the day-to-day life of the fund, waiting, instead, patiently for an eventual return of their investment, hopefully with a significant profit. In return for the sacrifice of active oversight, the LPs gain limited liability protection – liable only for losses up to the value of their investment in the fund. By definition LPs must be large institutional players or wealthy individuals because the GP will raise the money for the fund through a "private" placement where the LP interests being sold will not be accompanied by the disclosure of information that public corporations provide their shareholders. The LPs are thought to be capable, in the words of the US Supreme Court, of "fending for themselves" without the disclosure requirements applied by the Securities and Exchange Commission to public companies.[25]

The magic of leverage

To better understand the potential returns a private equity fund can generate, consider a hypothetical example: Private Equity Fund I, or "PEF I," which proposes to raise a relatively small fund, perhaps $100 million, to engage in "leveraged buyouts." The general partner of PEF I will prepare an offering memorandum providing basic information to potential LPs about the background of the professionals that work for the GP, as well as a description of the fund's proposed investment strategy. Assume that ten LPs will each invest $10 million in the fund. Unlike a mutual fund or a hedge fund, the money that the LPs invest is committed at the time the fund is legally established, called the "close" of the fund, but it will not yet be actually invested. As the GP decides on investment

---

[24] Jason Kelly and Jonathan Keehner, "Pension Plans' Private Equity Cash Depleted as Profits Sink," Bloomberg News, August 20, 2009.
[25] *SEC v. Ralston Purina*, 346 US 119 (1953).

targets it will issue a "capital call" to the LPs who then will turn over the requisite percentage of their prior cash commitment. However, the GP will need operating capital from the start-up of PEF I so it receives, typically, a 2 percent management fee annually from the LPs. Thus, for a relatively small $100 million fund, the GP will receive $2 million per year to pay the salaries of its professional staff.[26] The management fee is paid even if the fund does not actually make any investments, although that is relatively rare. Most funds are set up to last for ten years but most of the $100 million is likely to be "called" and invested within three or four years of the start of the fund.[27] Then, the money is put to work and the LPs wait for an "exit" when the GP decides to liquidate an investment and pay off the LPs.

For a leveraged buyout, or "LBO," fund, the GP typically looks for "undervalued" publicly traded corporations that can be bought with the funds invested by the LPs but with the added leverage of debt borrowed through commercial and investment banks. The meaning of "undervalued" can vary from fund manager to fund manager, but usually it means that the GP's analysis of the available public information about the target company indicates that with certain changes in the way the company is managed its value could be increased significantly. The basis of that conclusion, of course, is proprietary. The managers of PEF I will offer the target's current public shareholders a price that is usually at a significant premium to the current market price but not as high as the GP thinks it is potentially worth. In theory, the current shareholders will accept because they are unable to earn the same return with the existing management.

In fact, this financial strategy is of central importance to those supporters of "agency theory" who carry on the work begun by Berle and Means in the 1930s. This kind of takeover is part of the "market for corporate control" that is thought to force managers of companies either to run them profitably on behalf of shareholders or face a potential takeover by buyout funds like PEF I. To carry out an acquisition on the scale of the $26 billion takeover of Hilton Hotels by Blackstone, however, requires far greater resources than even the largest funds, which

---

[26] PE league tables indicate that the top fifty funds raised $810 billion between 2003 and 2008, with the lowest amount $5.9 billion and the highest, $32 billion. Private Equity International, *PEI 50* (2008).

[27] The call represents, in theory, a monitoring device for the protection of the LPs. If an investor is not happy about the fund's performance or management there is an opportunity for exit. However, tightly negotiated investment agreements as well as the potential reputation effect limit severely the opportunity for early LP exit. Thus, ironically, there remains a potential agency problem inside the fund itself even as it tries to address that problem in its target firms.

now can run to more than ten billion dollars, can raise directly from LPs. Hence the concept of leverage: once it has its initial $100 million committed by the ten LPs, our PEF I will identify buyout targets and then turn to commercial and investment banks to raise additional funds to follow through on its acquisition strategy. These funds are usually raised initially as bridge loans from banks which are in turn sold off to investors in the wider capital markets. These loans look very much like the bonds offered by large public companies – they are so-called "fixed income" instruments with an interest payment due every six months. Because there is somewhat greater risk associated with many of these transactions than in the bonds issued by, for example, traditional investment grade companies like GE, that interest rate can be relatively high. Many of these bonds are so-called "junk" bonds, the very same type of instrument made famous by Michael Milken in the 1980s, although they are now called, euphemistically, "high yield debt."

Assuming the availability of $500 billion committed to buyout funds in the United States currently and a potential 4:1 leverage ratio, the sector can wield $2.5 trillion to search for corporate targets. This capital base competes for investment opportunities with several other major players, including the $2 trillion sitting in hedge funds,[28] the approximate $4 trillion in sovereign wealth funds of major governments[29] and a relatively small $250 billion in venture capital.[30] One way to consider the potential socio-economic impact of buyout funds is to compare the $2.5 trillion figure with the value of the sector's potential targets. The market capitalization – the total value of outstanding shares at the current price – of US publicly traded companies on the New York Stock Exchange and NASDAQ is approximately $15 trillion.[31] Thus, in theory, at current levels the buyout sector could take over more than 13 percent of all publicly traded companies. In fact, to make good on the promises to its LP investors, PE funds *must* engage in something close to that volume of takeovers or else it must release its LPs from their capital commitments – something that LPs are not likely to be pleased about. While that percentage may seem low, the existence of LBO funds of this magnitude affects many more companies than those that become actual targets. In theory, every public company is a potential target and thus must take measures to improve share prices to avoid a takeover.

[28] Bei Hu, "Hedge Fund Assets to Hit $2 Trillion by Year-End, Survey Says," *Bloomberg/Business Week*, April 6, 2010.
[29] IFSL Research, Sovereign Wealth Funds 2010, March 2010.
[30] National Venture Capital Association at www.nvca.org (last visited June 30, 2010).
[31] World Federation of Exchanges, 2009 Market Highlights at www.world-exchanges.org/statistics (last accessed February 22, 2011).

Thus, all public companies are under pressure to engage in the kinds of aggressive restructurings that an LBO fund would carry out.

Leverage, of course, also helps magnify the returns to the fund because the interest on the debt raised through the banks is fixed. Therefore, as long as the rate of return on the capital used to buy out target companies is higher than that interest rate the fund is earning free cash flow. If our hypothetical PEF I can leverage itself 4:1 and raise another $400 million through its banks, then it will be in a position to command $500 million. Then the GP can begin its search for appropriate targets, buying them up usually through "friendly" deals negotiated with the current management team, although so-called "hostile" tender offers made directly to the shareholders of targets are possible as well.[32] After restructuring the company in a manner that the GP believes will increase its profitability, the GP will look for an "exit" opportunity. This usually means returning to the public capital markets and selling shares in the company back to the public, at a price far higher than was paid to take the company private. Alternatively, and today often a more common tactic, is a so-called "trade" sale where the company is sold to another corporation for either cash or shares in the new company.

For a buyout fund the 2 percent annual management fee is attractive and can be quite important in lean times but it is not "real money." The real money for the GP is in the "carried interest," or "carry." Buyout funds typically receive 20 percent of the returns to the fund above the initial investment by the LPs. So, let's say PEF I uses its $500 million war chest to buy a small auto parts company in Ohio. If the market had valued the company at $400 million, then PEF I will have bought out the existing shareholders at a 25 percent premium. Now the GP of PEF I must find a way to increase the value of the company. They might do it by "slashing and burning" – laying off workers, moving plants to Mexico or China; or they might do it by renegotiating labor contracts with the company's unions that in turn allows

---

[32] Many deals in the first wave of LBOs in the late 1980s were done as "hostiles." A "hostile" refers to a takeover where the acquiror meets resistance from the target company management and thus makes a tender offer directly to shareholders to buy their shares, typically at a premium to the then current market price. A "friendly" takeover occurs when the proposed acquisition is met with favor by existing management who often intend to stay with the company after the transaction is completed, often in return for a significant equity stake in the business. Lobbying by labor and incumbent managers helped usher in the end of the "hostile" era with the passage of state level anti-takeover legislation in the late 1980s and 1990s. Takeovers continued nonetheless as buyers simply allocated larger percentages of the takeover consideration to target management to motivate them to back the offers as "friendly." The current wave of PE buyouts can be seen as an evolutionary response to the resistance to hostile transactions.

management to deploy new labor-saving technologies to lower costs; or, more likely, a combination of both. As a result of these changes, if all goes as planned, perhaps four years later the company might be valued at $750 million. PEF I's GP may then decide to return to the stock market for an IPO. Ignoring for simplicity fees and interest payments, PEF I will have made a profit of $250 million after paying off the $400 million in debt it incurred as well as the original $100 million investment by the ten LPs.

This will make the GPs very happy: the "carry" is commonly 20 percent of the return to the fund so the GPs will walk away with $50 million on top of their $4 million in management fees collected during the two-year period. Buyout funds run lean organizations so this $54 million payday will be distributed among a handful of professionals. KKR, for example, has only 139 investment professionals who manage the investment of more than $50 billion in assets. The remaining 80 percent of the return from the sale, or $200 million, is returned to the ten LPs who are presumably happy, too, assuming they don't look too closely at the social cost of the layoffs or plant closures imposed on that small town in southern Ohio in order to "turn the company around." The pension funds have earned a 50 percent annual return on their original investment, far above the expectations for their mainstream investments in, for example, the stock of Microsoft or GE. Of course, that is a relatively high return exaggerated to illustrate the operations of buyout funds. But such returns are not unheard of or impossible for a single investment. Funds formed by GPs like KKR and Blackstone have regularly returned 20–30 percent per annum or more to their LPs while typical returns in the stock market are in the single digits.[33]

While PE funds may respond to a genuine and deep problem inherent in the nature of the public corporation, they bring with them, however, their own peculiar set of problems, some of which may be more destabilizing and socially destructive than any wrought by Enron and its progeny. And while many on the left and in the labor movement may appear to comprehend the nature of these new funds, their perspective is limited by the intellectual impact today of the framework put in place by Berle and Means in the 1930s. Does the story that PE funds tell about insider mismanagement make sense? Should we welcome the PE buyout strategy as a necessary pill to swallow? An effective response to the new capitalism requires a reconsideration of the dominant Berle–Means paradigm.

[33] Ritter, "Factoids."

IV The problem with the public corporation

It is not well known today, although more recently a handful of legal scholars have begun to remind us,[34] that Berle and Means had two aims with their 1932 study: to explore what they felt was the central governance problem of the public corporation as described here but also to situate a solution to that problem within their social democratic vision of governance. The former has lived on, even in the mainstream law and economics scholarship that dominates much of the academic and policy debate about corporate behavior. But the latter has gone down the memory hole.

Berle and Means argued that while the public corporation solved one problem for capitalism it created yet another for society at large. The demands of the rapid industrial growth of the late nineteenth and early twentieth centuries required massive amounts of capital that individual businessmen, even if they were as wealthy as J.P. Morgan or Andrew Carnegie, could not provide. Sometimes this was a "push" process: family controlled firms began to sell off ever-larger portions of their firms to outside investors. Sometimes it was a "pull" process: Wall Street firms engineered the roll up of small family owned entities into larger, more efficient and, thus, profitable entities, earning sizeable fees in the process. The food retail giant known today as Safeway began its life this way when Charles Merrill (the founder of banking giant Merrill Lynch) engineered the merger of thousands of smaller local stores into a new entity that he then "took public" in 1928 through the issuance of shares that were soon listed on the New York Stock Exchange. For the first time in US history, the business of the United States was genuinely a public endeavor. While 4.4 million Americans owned shares in 1900 by 1928 the number had risen to 18 million.[35]

The growing weight of publicly traded companies raised an alarm for Berle and Means. They argued that the modern corporation "has brought a concentration of economic power which can compete on equal terms with the modern state."[36] The potential social damage that could be done by the new institution was sharply highlighted by the collapse

---

[34] See William W. Bratton, "Berle and Means Reconsidered at the Century's Turn" (2001) 26 *Journal of Corporation Law* 737; William Bratton and Michael Wachter, "Shareholder Primacy's Corporatist Origins: Adolf Berle and *The Modern Corporation*" (2008) 34 *Journal Corporation Law* 99; Dalia Tsuk, "From Pluralism to Individualism: Berle and Means and 20th-Century American Legal Thought" (2005) 30 *Law and Social Inquiry* 179; Cynthia Williams, "The Securities and Exchange Commission and Corporate Social Transparency" (1999) 112 *Harvard Law Review* 1197.
[35] Berle and Means, *Corporation and Private Property*, p. 56.
[36] *Ibid.*, p. 313.

of the capital markets in 1929. For these New Deal intellectuals this triggered the need for a "constitutional" approach to the governance of the corporation that would re-generate legitimacy to the decision-making processes of what was to them as much a socio-political institution as an economic one.

Driving this political approach was their insight into the inherent problem of the corporation: that it was plagued, as suggested here, by a fundamental separation of ownership and control. Smith and Marx, among others, had mentioned this issue in passing but in eras when the "joint stock" company, as it was largely known in the nineteenth century, had nowhere near the importance it took on by the early twentieth. Since Berle and Means viewed that separation as a permanent and serious disability, it required a new doctrinal approach to corporate law. In fact, their argument presented a deep challenge to then-dominant free market liberalism: if the corporate form contained within it *two* competing interest groups, managers and investors, then this tore asunder the notion of a civil society of competing individual businesspersons with clear and unambiguous property rights to their business assets generating efficient, and socio-politically legitimate, outcomes through arm's-length trading in the marketplace. The emergence of the modern publicly traded corporation, then, arguably triggered a larger crisis in political theory.

As they wrote in 1932:

The separation of ownership from control produces a condition where the interests of owner and of ultimate manager may, and often do, diverge and where many of the checks which formerly operated to limit the use of power disappear ... New responsibilities towards the owners, the workers, the consumers and the State thus rest upon the shoulders of those in control. In creating these new relationships, the quasi-public corporation may fairly be said to work a revolution. It has destroyed the unity that we commonly call property – has divided ownership into nominal ownership and the power formerly joined to it. Thereby the corporation has changed the nature of profit-seeking enterprise.[37]

To help solve this problem – and to do so within the boundaries of some form of "capitalism" – the authors looked to the already established law of trusts to argue that corporate managers, those who "controlled" the corporation, had to behave with as much rectitude on behalf of outside shareholders, the "owners" of the corporation, as the trustees of a trust fund did for the beneficiaries of the trust. As then Judge, and later Justice, Benjamin Cardozo wrote in a widely cited 1928 opinion issued just as Berle and Means were conducting their initial

[37] *Ibid.*, p. 7.

research: "A trustee is held to something stricter than the morals of the marketplace. Not honesty alone, but the punctilio of an honor the most sensitive is the standard of behavior."[38] This approach proved too much for most New Deal era politicians who backed away from the most radical proposals coming out of FDR's brain trust, but the federal securities laws put in place then, including the Investment Company Act, which regulates private equity funds, did create new forms of oversight of corporations and financial institutions that remain in place today, if in muted form.

Today's agency school

While Berle and Means' more radical vision of the corporation as a social entity did not survive, their image of the conflict between inside managers and outside investors is imprinted in the psyche of every business and law school graduate in the United States. It is widely believed that most of our corporate law and financial structures are aimed at solving the problems that result from this conflict. Today, they are known as "agency problems" – with inside managers of the public corporation cast as "agents" of the outside shareholders, or "principals." There are costs associated with this principal–agency relationship known as "agency costs."[39]

These agency costs include the time and money that principals must spend to negotiate contractual protections with agents and to monitor the agents during the life of the contract. If the contractual terms are violated or the contract proves, as is often the case, incomplete, further costs will be incurred by the need to engage in *ex post* gap-filling through dispute resolution or judicial or legislative intervention. Some theorists of the agency school go so far as to suggest that the corporation itself is merely a "nexus of contracts" between all of the suppliers and purchasers of corporate inputs and outputs, right up to the CEO's office where a "labor market" sets the price and terms under which senior corporate personnel will work. The advantage of this view is that it appears to solve the legitimacy problem that the Berle and Means argument highlighted because it finds a way to insert the market mechanism back into the corporate structure.[40]

---

[38] *Meinhard v. Salmon*, 164 N.E. 545 (N.Y. 1928) (Cardozo, Ch. J.).
[39] On agency costs, see the classic statement by Michael Jensen and William Meckling, "Theory of the Firm: Managerial Behavior, Agency Costs and Ownership Structure" (1976) 3 *Journal of Financial Economics* 305–360.
[40] A good summary can be found in Richard Posner, *Economic Analysis of the Law* (New York: Aspen, 1977).

Together, these agency costs add to the cost of capital and thus to the cost of "doing business." But, agency theorists argue, if laws and contracts are efficiently designed, these costs can be minimized, and, in fact, the resulting predictability can make investing in such an environment more attractive. Thus, in today's debate about competition between national financial markets such as London and New York, some argue that the higher cost of regulation in the US markets is, ultimately, worth paying; while others argue that the mix of legal intervention and private ordering through contractual arrangements has gone awry with post-Enron reforms such as the Sarbanes–Oxley Act raising the costs of managing a public corporation in the United States to an intolerable level.

But what if you could design a corporate or financial structure that would eliminate so-called "agency costs"? The result would be truly revolutionary: potentially, at least, it could mean the elimination, or at least dramatic minimization, of costly contractual negotiations over the complex relationships that exist today among senior corporate management, boards of directors, Wall Street financial analysts, individual and institutional investors and government regulators. Enron, WorldCom, Tyco – all are considered examples of the problems that arise when agency problems are not adequately resolved.

This is, in part, the justification used to form private equity funds – they hold out the promise of eliminating the modern corporation's agency problems by concentrating ownership and control in a single institution. Voila! A problem that has plagued Anglo-American capitalism for more than a century might just disappear. Interestingly, continental European and Asian capital has largely avoided this issue by continuing to rely on state, family or closely networked ownership forms. However, they have also, it can be argued, lost the opportunity to take the kinds of risks that the use of "other people's money" allows one to take with the public corporate form. Nonetheless, private equity is aggressively entering those markets as well with an agenda that is similar to that found in the United States and the United Kingdom.

V   The labor–left counter-attack

Trade unions have an ambivalent attitude toward the rise of private equity. On the one hand, many US labor unions have representatives on the boards of the same pension funds that are largely responsible for the steady flow of capital into PE funds and, of course, that means some union members have benefited handsomely from the funds' above average returns.⁴¹ On the other hand, over the last decade organized labor has developed a relatively sophisticated program of investor activism through the Office of Investment at the AFL-CIO, the Capital Strategies Group of Change to Win and similar groups at key union affiliates. This effort relies on labor's pension fund investments in public companies to raise concerns about corporate social responsibility, excessive CEO pay, workers' rights and internal corporate governance.

But labor does not seem to have made up its mind whether or not PE funds raise or lower corporate standards of behavior. When it was clear in spring of 2007 that German auto giant Daimler was looking to sell off its troubled Chrysler division, United Auto Workers union president Ron Gettelfinger said he would oppose a PE bid for the company because such an investor would "strip and flip" the company.⁴² A few weeks later, after a meeting with Cerberus Capital, which had by then announced a deal with Daimler, Gettelfinger sang a completely new tune. Without any internal discussion, debate or vote by the UAW membership at Chrysler, he announced that the takeover bid by Cerberus Capital for the car company "was in the best interest of our membership, the Chrysler Group and Daimler."⁴³ Reacting to Gettelfinger's endorsement of the deal, Canadian Auto Workers union leader Buzz Hargrove initially told the *New York Times* "the history of private equity has been to buy, then slash and burn a lot of jobs, and then get out with a lot money for a handful of people."⁴⁴ But in very short order, after a meeting with Cerberus Capital's CEO, Hargrove too reversed course, telling reporters, according to *Edwards Auto Observer*, "he was convinced Cerberus was 'not about slice and dice ... they're in it for the long term.'"⁴⁵ The *New York Times* reported that Chrysler rank and file workers expressed surprise and confusion at the change in tune from union leaders.⁴⁶ Some Canadian labor groups have gone even further than verbal endorsements of PE deals. The Ontario Teachers Pension

---

⁴¹ Michael J. de la Merced and Peter Edmonston, "Cerberus Goes Where No Firm Has Gone Before," *The New York Times*, May 15, 2007 ("Big pension funds of public employees like Calpers are among the biggest institutional investors in private equity firms, and public pension money accounted for about a quarter of all new money raised by private equity last year").
⁴² Kevin Krolicki and Poornima Gupta, "UAW Presses Daimler to Call Off Chrysler Sale," *Reuters*, April 18, 2007.
⁴³ Michelle Krebs, "Cerberus Charms Chrysler's Unions," *Edmunds Auto Observer.com*, May 16, 2007.
⁴⁴ Nick Bunkley, "Chrysler Workers Surprised After Union Backs Sale," *The New York Times*, May 15, 2007.
⁴⁵ Krebs, "Cerebus Charms."
⁴⁶ Bunkley, "Chrysler Workers Surprised."

Fund has its own PE arm and engineered a bid to buy out Bell Canada in 2007, only to find the deal first delayed and then fall apart altogether in the face of the credit crisis.

The leadership of Unite Here!, an amalgam of unions representing hotel, restaurant and clothing industry workers, was effusive in its praise for the multi-billion dollar bid by Blackstone for Hilton Hotels, stating in a press release issued as soon as the deal was announced that it "welcomed" the transaction contending "Blackstone has demonstrated its commitment to fair treatment for thousands of hotel workers."[47] But when Blackstone announced its intention to sell shares to public investors in an IPO, the AFL-CIO and SEIU, though not working together, each criticized the transaction. The AFL-CIO wrote to the SEC in a call for the enforcement of the governance requirements of the Investment Company Act against Blackstone. Both labor groups began campaigning to raise tax rates on PE partners' income from the carried interest in their funds.[48]

Unlike North American unions, European labor has been largely united in a campaign against private equity. In a 2007 report entitled "Private Equity's Broken Promises," the Central Executive Committee of the UK's GMB, the century old general workers union with more than 600,000 members, blasted PE funds.[49] The report lists dozens of examples of British companies taken over by PE funds using debt to replace equity followed by layoffs and then exit transactions that led to huge paydays for the partners and investors in the funds. In 2004 the "AA," the British automobile insurance and roadside protection association, was bought from its corporate parent by buyout funds CVC Capital and Permira. The GMB had voted AA Employer of the Year in 2003, but under PE ownership one-third of its workforce was laid off with disabled workers apparently a particular target, wages were cut, the workday at call centers was increased from 8 to 11.75 hours, and the GMB was forced out and replaced by a company union. Meanwhile, the company took on close to 2 billion dollars of new debt and paid Permira and CVC a special dividend of nearly a billion dollars.

A second report issued by the Geneva based IUF, the international trade union body that represents 12 million workers in 336 unions in the

---

[47] "Hotel Workers Union Applauds Blackstone-Hilton Combination," Unite Here! Press Release, PR News, July 3, 2007.
[48] AFL-CIO, Statement for the Record, United States Senate Committee on Finance, Hearing on Carried Interest Part III: Pension Issues, September 6, 2007 ("the AFL-CIO sees no valid justification for the individuals who manage private equity, real estate, and hedge funds to receive tax subsidies that leave the burden of paying ordinary tax rates to working people").
[49] GMB, "Private Equity's Broken Pension Promises" (2007).

food, farm and hotel sectors around the world, highlighted the impact of debt financing by PE groups.[50] The report noted that while public companies may have a debt to equity ratio of 1:10, once bought out by a PE fund that ratio is often reversed. Frequently, PE funds then cause the companies they take over to take on additional debt in order to pay out a dividend to their investors because an exit opportunity seems too far away. In a presentation to British Labour Party MPs the IUF's Director of Communications, Peter Rossman, noted that KKR and Carlyle shared in a $250 million dividend only a month after closing on the $4 billion debt financed buyout of satellite operator PanAmSat.[51] The Trade Union Advisory Committee (TUAC) to the OECD joined in the European campaign, noting in a report last spring that "the high rates of return required to finance private equity debt-driven buy-outs can jeopardize target companies' long-term interests and provision of decent employment conditions and security for employees." The TUAC called for regulatory reform of tax rates, corporate governance, transparency, risk management and workers' rights.[52]

"Financialization" or pluralism redux?

The focus by unions on the role of debt in PE-led deals is critical but the impact of debt on the governance of a firm is not well understood. For several years, labor and left-wing critics of globalization have promoted the concept of "financialization" as a leading symptom of the post-Cold War capitalist economy. The late Marxist economist Paul Sweezy argued in *Monthly Review* that by the end of the 1980s the world economy "had given way to a new structure in which a greatly expanded financial sector had achieved a high degree of independence and sat on *top of the underlying production system.*"[53] Robin Blackburn, a socialist, took a similar approach recently in the *New Left Review* where he wrote: "It is not household names like Nike or Coca-Cola that are the capstones of contemporary capitalism, but finance houses, hedge

---

[50] International Union of Food, Agricultural, Hotel, Restaurant, Catering, Tobacco and Allied Workers' Associations (IUF), *A Workers' Guide to Private Equity Buyouts* (2007).
[51] Peter Rossman, Presentation to Trade Union Sponsored Labour MPs on Private Equity and Leveraged Buyouts, February 27, 2007.
[52] Trade Union Advisory Committee to the Organization for Economic Cooperation and Development, "Growth With Equity," Trade Union Statement to the OECD Ministerial Council Meeting, May 15–16, 2007, at p. 9.
[53] Paul M. Sweezy, "Economic Reminiscences" (May 1995) 47:1 *Monthly Review* 8–9, cited in John Bellamy Foster, "The Financialization of Capitalism" (April 2007) 58:11 *Monthly Review* (emphasis added).

funds and private equity concerns, many of which are unknown to the general public. In the end even the largest and most famous of corporations have only a precarious and provisional autonomy within the new world of business – ultimately they are *playthings of the capital markets*."[54] The IUF's Rossman calls "financialized capital" "extremely impatient," "volatile, highly mobile, and linked to a variety of new financial instruments based on debt." In an article for the ILO's journal *Labour Education* Rossman and his IUF colleague Gerard Greenfield defined "financialization" as "both the enhanced importance of *financial versus real capital* in determining the rhythm and returns expected from investments, and the increased subordination of that investment to the demands of global financial markets."[55]

As should be clear, each of these analysts, although they come from different political traditions, defines the current capitalist period as one in which finance dominates the so-called "real economy." This would appear to be a relatively simple reprise of the longstanding populist view that what all too often plagues what would be an otherwise healthy capitalism is a tension between, on the one hand, the interests of "real," "productive" capitalists who roll up their sleeves and build companies and, on the other, those who merely "speculate" using financial assets like so many chips in a casino. As such, this view is, in fact, a restatement of the original Berle–Means paradigm of the separation of ownership and control, only in reverse.

Berle and Means were working in a period when it was widely believed that corporate managers had triumphed over the financial markets. Keynes famously spoke favorably in his *General Theory* published in 1936 of the potential for the "euthanasia of the *rentier*, of the functionless investor."[56] In Stalin's Russia, that policy was in fact carried out with unparalleled brutality. Berle and Means' book was followed in 1941 by James Burnham's hugely popular *The Managerial Revolution* that caught the mood of the day when it argued that the United States, Germany and Russia were all suffering from the imminent global triumph of a new bureaucratic post-capitalist class.[57] In this intellectual and political milieu it was not a surprise that Berle and Means compared the new

---

[54] Robin Blackburn, "Finance and the Fourth Dimension" (May–June 2006) 39 *New Left Review* 42 (emphasis added).
[55] Peter Rossman and Gerard Greenfield, "Financialization: New Routes to Profit, New Challenges for Trade Unions" (January 2006) 142 *Labour Education* 55.
[56] John Maynard Keynes, *The General Theory of Employment, Interest and Money* (New York: Harcourt Brace, 1936).
[57] James Burnham, *The Managerial Revolution* (orig. 1941) (Westport: Greenwood Press, 1972).

boards of directors of public corporations to "a communist committee of commissars" and cast the corporate director as someone who "more nearly resembles the communist in mode of thought than he does the protagonist of private property."[58] Nor was it shocking for Gardiner Means to write of a new "collective" capitalism emerging in the United States.[59] Berle and Means' work was critical because it described a method by which these managers appeared to have triumphed from within capitalism itself aided by a newly expanded Wall Street apparatus of lawyers, bankers and brokers, leaving the corporate entity in the hands of technocrats.

As it turned out, of course, Berle and Means were wrong, as were Burnham and Keynes. Capitalism was not morphing somehow into a Stalinist post-capitalist nightmare. It was true that the capital markets took many years to recover from the trauma of 1929 and to learn how to function within the new regulatory framework that New Deal legislation imposed on the economy. But the capital markets never disappeared and neither did competition within the modern capitalist economy. As recent research by Barry Holderness concludes, Berle and Means, in fact, radically overstated the number of companies with powerless dispersed shareholders.[60] Many publicly held US businesses retain sizeable shareholders with "control blocks" that enable them to influence managerial decision-making.[61] Thus, most takeovers of public companies are friendly transactions, with existing management induced in various ways to agree to the acquisition. Indeed, today's PE funds often are able to engage in soft landing takeovers with handsome premiums paid to shareholders as well, who are then free to redeploy their capital in other parts of the economy.

In other words, it may have looked as if outside investors had no weight inside the corporate boardroom, but to have written off that possibility altogether would have meant to argue that competition itself was no longer operating inside the US economy. No matter how much influence government regulation or spending may have had at the height of the Cold War, US corporations continued to compete with each other, often bitterly, in capital, labor and product markets. New companies

---

[58] Berle and Means, *Corporation and Private Property*, p. 245.
[59] Gardiner Means, *The Corporate Revolution in America: Economic Reality vs Economic Theory* (New York: Crowell-Collier Press, 1962).
[60] Holderness, "Myth of Diffuse Ownership," p. 1377 ("Although Berle and Means offer considerable empirical evidence, upon close examination their evidence is not as supportive of diffuse ownership as is often believed"). I am grateful to Henry Manne for bringing the work of Holderness to my attention.
[61] *Ibid.* ("The ownership of U.S. firms is similar to and by some measures more concentrated than the ownership of firms in other countries.")

were formed, financed by Wall Street and prospered; other older companies faltered, lost support in the financial markets and went out of business. Workers fought for and organized unions, engaged in collective actions and pushed for higher wages, sometimes successfully, in other cases unsuccessfully.

But if in their assessment of reality Berle and Means had failed, on the ideological front they succeeded in helping to redraw the framework within which US capitalism was understood. An emerging real world battleground in the 1930s where, on the one hand, managerial *and* financial capitalists together were pitted against, on the other hand, a militant new labor movement with ideas about radical reorganization of economic activity, was recast as a need to (socially) democratize the principles that governed the behavior of the new managerial class. This technocratic analysis became the basis of the dominant postwar ideology of industrial pluralism, with interest groups competing in the "space" left open between giant business and labor organizations.[62] It is a similar Cold War pluralist ideology that is used by some in US labor and business groups today to promote "constructive engagement" with an authoritarian regime like that of China, arguing that a new "space" is being opened up by the regime's market reforms. In fact, there is even less space there for a genuine labor movement than there was, or is, in a United States dominated by the ever-evolving alliance of managerial and financial capitalists.

Thus, the left – from socialist to social democratic – was completely unprepared intellectually for the restructuring of US capitalism underway over the last twenty years. Its thinkers remained, and largely remain, compelled by the apparent progressive promise of the liberal pluralist ideology that took hold as earlier labor militancy was beaten back by war, repression and new legal structures such as the Taft–Hartley Act of 1947. The recent capitalist restructuring has included downsizing, outsourcing and dramatic technological change alongside growth in the financial markets. The attempt to cast these recent developments as just the "financialization" of capitalism is a non sequitur. This view ignores what capitalists actually do. Instead, whether or not consciously, it gives credence to a populist argument that focuses on apparent power shifts within the economy – and, of course, a focus on "power" is part

---

[62] Among those legal scholars with a revived interest in Berle and Means, Tsuk focuses most closely on the pluralist dimension of their work but without discussing the wider context of class conflict and only a limited concern with the influence of Stalinist and fascist elements in the New Deal itself. Normatively, Tsuk laments the defeat of the "lasting meaning" of Berle and Means' concern with corporate power by the law and economics school, which may explain her focus. See Tsuk, "Pluralism."

174   S.F. Diamond

and parcel of a pluralist worldview. We are not in a corporatist world of interest groups competing for power, but in a world where owners of capital employ highly specialized managers, who also have an opportunity to become owners of capital, to generate and appropriate value in production.[63] Where workers organize, economically and politically, they must do so in opposition to the organizational intent of both those managers and financiers, who share a mutual interest in the continuing dynamic of restructuring.[64] This is the very heart of the capitalist process – in China as well as in the United States, as true in 2010 as in 1932.

VI   Conclusion: the real nature of private equity

It is particularly inapt to cast private equity funds as a form of "financialization" of capitalism. Private equity actually concentrates in a new institutional form the resources and abilities of investors together *with* the on-the-ground knowledge of managers. While it is true that PE funds rely heavily on debt and other financial instruments to engage in ever larger deals and magnify their returns, their success in this effort depends on very careful attention to the details of how to operate the targeted businesses so that the financial instruments used to take over control are appropriate to the task.

Thus, some may properly criticize the new CEO of Chrysler, Robert Nardelli, for his outsized pay packages while overseeing a decline in profitability at his previous company, Home Depot. But to ignore his deep understanding of the production process would be foolish – prior to joining Home Depot, where, of course, he picked up a first class education in the consumer goods segment of the economy, he ran the highly respected locomotive production operations of GE. And the debt instruments used in PE-led deals actually embody in a detailed set of heavily negotiated contracts the terms of a complex new social relationship between investors, PE fund managers, investment bankers and managers of the target companies.

Thus, the PE fund must have within it a concentration of very specialized talent to coordinate the takeover process and access to and

---

[63] See Dan Krier, *Speculative Management: Stock Market Power and Corporate Change* (Albany: State University of New York, 2005).
[64] The ever-present problem at the heart of capitalism is the tension between increases in productivity on a social scale and the heteronomic ownership structure of individual business units. Thus, managers (financial and production based) must constantly face the readjustment of their cost and profit estimates as new technology undermines yesterday's assumptions.

relationships with senior managerial talent in a range of industries. The partners of PE funds also tend to have backgrounds in the financial markets and are very sensitive to the concerns of the professionals who invest on behalf of large institutions such as pension funds. In turn – and this is crucial – today's buyouts, as I suggested, are largely *friendly* transactions where the buyout fund plans to work closely with existing management because the PE fund partners know these executives have crucial inside knowledge about the target firm. A clear example of this is the Cerberus buyout of Chrysler: the new owners announced their intention to keep Thomas LaSorda on board as president because he was thought to have a good relationship with the leadership of the UAW.[65] Because significant concessions from the UAW were and will continue to be a major goal of the buyout that relationship would be highly valued both by Cerberus and by the investors in the billions in debt needed to carry out the transaction. In addition, the buyouts are friendly with respect to the major shareholders who dominate US corporations. Rather than riding to the rescue of helpless dispersed shareholders, then, PE funds must engage skillfully the complex alliance between managerial and operational employees, on the one hand, and the large institutional investors like pension funds and hedge funds that together own today's public corporations.

We are not witnessing in the early twenty-first century some kind of *coup d'etat* by "finance" against the "real" economy, any more than the agency problems of the publicly traded corporation meant that a new class of managers took power in the mid-twentieth century. The rise of some widely traded public corporations in the era of Berle and Means should, instead, have been seen as a successful effort to marry financial resources with managerial talent in a new capitalist form. But even then many large companies retained concentrated ownership among a few large shareholders. Today, we might be witnessing what Harvard Business School's Michael Jensen predicted in 1989 would be the "eclipse of the public corporation."[66] But perhaps that should read the "eclipse of those still remaining widely traded public corporations."

Private equity led buyouts represent an evolution in the effort by a significant fraction of sophisticated players in the economy to forge new methods of managing and controlling the process of creating and

---

[65] Micheline Maynard, "Latest Chrysler Twist Adds Mystery to LaSorda's Fate," *New York Times*, September 6, 2007 ("Mr. LaSorda is overseeing Chrysler's negotiations with the United Automobile Workers union, familiar territory for him, since his father and grandfather were officials of the Canadian Auto Workers").
[66] Michael C. Jensen, "The Eclipse of the Public Corporation" (September–October 1989) 67 *Harvard Business Review* (revised 1997).

appropriating value from the labor force on behalf of investors. By concentrating expertise in finance with operational know-how, it is possible that the ability of capital to engineer greater returns will be enhanced. To recognize the magnitude of the accomplishment of PE funds is not to support, normatively, the result. Instead it helps to highlight the challenge for labor and the left. Private equity funds are doing what capital has always done and will continue to do unless an alternative form of organizing economic activity is established. A misguided populist fear of "financialization" does not bring us any closer to beginning the exploration of that alternative.

9 Pension funds as owners and as financial intermediaries: a review of recent Canadian experience

Simon Archer

I Acting like owners?

In the spring of 2007, a venerable Canadian corporation, Bell Canada Enterprises (BCE), became an acquisition target, and an acquisition agreement was subsequently signed. Until the deal was unwound on a technical valuation clause, it was the biggest proposed leveraged buyout in Canadian history: it was big news. Some of the features of this transaction were the size and nature of the target (formerly a regulated monopoly) and the identity of the primary purchaser, Ontario Teachers' Pension Plan (OTPP, an occupational pension plan for elementary and secondary school teachers). It might not have attracted much more attention – pension funds had been purchasing and controlling companies in Canada for a decade or more – but then in August 2007, about two months after the deal was made, the Canadian and then global credit markets seized up, and the General Financial Crisis (GFC), as it has come to be known, ensued. About a year later, the deal was unwound, but only after the bondholders of BCE visited the Supreme Court of Canada complaining of their treatment through the whole process.[1]

Forgotten now are some of the more curious local aspects of this deal: OTPP (or any other pension fund) was prohibited from owning BCE – at least on paper – by Ontario pension legislation. The CEO of OTPP, a public sector union pension plan, publicly mused that it may restructure BCE, which implied tackling the unionized BCE employees. Indeed, it was said anecdotally that OTPP had a policy of not investing in businesses that sponsored defined benefit pension schemes – of which OTPP was one of the biggest in Canada. Contrary to past practice, in this deal, a major Canadian pension fund sought to own a local

---

[1] *BCE Inc.* v. *1976 Debentureholders* [2008] 3 SCR 560. The bondholders lost and so the transaction could have gone forward but the deal collapsed when a valuation term could not be met in the midst of the GFC.

business, instead of purchasing, say, privatized UK utilities, far from the concerns of local pensioners.

None of these features was new, but together and in the largest transaction of the decade, they suggested that these pension funds had reached a pivotal size and stage in their development.

When examined as financial intermediaries, the questions asked of pension funds are predominantly about their function in relation to their ultimate – if estranged – beneficiaries. These questions are of performance as investment vehicles,[2] relative efficacy of administrative arrangements and, more broadly, the possibility for "democratization" of these institutions.[3]

A second, more recent, group of questions revolves around the role of these funds in capital markets as financial intermediaries. For example, their influence on depth and liquidity of markets in certain securities,[4]

---

[2] For example, see the debate about the persistence of above-benchmark returns (or the lack thereof) in G.L. Beebower and G.L. Bergstrom, "A performance analysis of pension and profit-sharing portfolios: 1966–1975" (1977) 33 *Financial Analysts Journal* 31–42 and J.A. Christopherson, W.E. Ferson and D.A. Glassman, "Conditioning manager alphas on economic information: another look at the persistence of performance" (1998) 11 *Review of Financial Studies* 111 and J. Busse, A. Goyal and S. Wahal, "Performance persistence in institutional investment management" (2010) 65 *The Journal of Finance* 765–790. Finding no such effect, see J. Lakonishok, A. Schleifer and R.W. Vishny, "The structure and performance of the money management industry" (1992) *Brookings Papers on Economic Activity: Macroeconomics* 339; W. Ferson and K. Khang, "Conditional performance measurement using portfolio weights: evidence for pension funds" (2002) 65 *Journal of Financial Economics* 249; R. Wermers, "Mutual fund performance: an empirical decomposition into stock-picking talent, style, transactions costs, and expenses" (2000) 55 *The Journal of Finance* 1655. To the author's knowledge, there are no comprehensive studies of Canadian defined benefit pension funds.

[3] See traditional treatments by A. Berle, *Power Without Property: A New Development in American Political Economy* (New York: Harcourt Brace & Co., 1959), P. Druker, *The Unseen Revolution: How Pension Fund Socialism Came to America* (New York: Harper & Row, 1976) and more recently by K. Ambachtsheer, *Pension Revolution: A Solution to the Pension Crisis* (Toronto: John Wiley & Sons, 2007). For variations see R. Davis, *Democratizing Pension Funds: Corporate Governance and Accountability* (Vancouver: UBC Press, 2006), G. Clark, "Pension fund governance: expertise and organizational form" (2004) 3:2 *Journal of Pension Economics and Finance* 233; J. Zanglbein, "Public pension funds: the need for federal regulation of trustee investment decisions" (1985) 4 *Yale Law & Policy Review* 188; S. Fogdall, "Exclusive union control of pension funds: Taft-Hartley's ill-considered prohibition" (2001) 4:1 *University of Pennsylvania Journal of Labor and Employment Law* 215; R. Nobles, "Conflicts of interest in trustees' management of pension funds – an analysis of the legal framework" (1985) 14 *The Industrial Law Journal* 1.

[4] See, for example, E.P. Davis, *Pension Funds, Retirement Income Security and Capital Markets: An International Perspective* (Oxford: Oxford University Press, 1995). Davis and Yuwei Hu have explored the questions set out in this book in subsequent work, including the efficiency of prudential regulation versus "bright-line" or quantitative limit regulation.

their influence on "innovation" in the financial service sector,[5] their influence on the balance sheets of their sponsors (especially those who are also issuers of securities), and of course, their role as "active owners," seeking to influence management in their investments, and occasionally, enforcing their rights as shareholders through litigation have all attracted attention. In contrast to their traditional (though still pervasive) characterization as passive investors, there has been some discussion of their influence as corporate monitors[6] and litigators.

These questions are often concomitant with policy questions about the appropriate regulation of pension funds themselves: should, and when should, they be required to meet diversification and passive investment norms enforced by quantitative rules? When do public policy concerns, such as equitable treatment of cohorts of members, justify intervention? What is the appropriate set of governance norms for pension funds, given inherent agency conflicts in their decision-making?[7]

The basic observation of this chapter is that pension funds' sources of revenue have changed over the past twenty years, and this has led to a predictably greater activity in – indeed, "embededness" in – capital markets, to such an extent that we can reasonably ask whether these institutions have fundamentally changed in purpose and function.

The reasons for the change in revenues are twofold, one of demographics and one of design. As pension schemes become more mature

---

[5] Z. Bodie, "Pension funds and financial innovation" (NBER) Working Paper No. W3101 (1989).
[6] See, for example, B. Richardson, "Do the fiduciary duties of pension funds hinder socially responsible investment?" (2007) 22:2 *Banking & Finance Law Review* 145; J. Hendry, P. Sanderson, R. Barker and J. Roberts, "Responsible ownership, shareholder value and the new shareholder activism" (2007) 11:3 *Competition and Change* 223; J. Coffee, "Reforming the securities class action: an essay on deterrence and its implementation" (2006) 106 *Columbia Law Review* 1572; J. Cox and R. Thomas, "Does the plaintiff matter? An empirical analysis of lead plaintiffs in securities class actions" (2006) 106 *Columbia Law Review* 1587; G. Yaron, "Acting like owners: proxy voting, corporate engagement and the fiduciary responsibilities of pension trustees" (June 28, 2005), available at SSRN: http://ssrn.com/abstract=772184 (last accessed February 22, 2011); D. Smith, "Ethical investing by union pension funds" (2006) 44:1 *Canadian Business Law Journal* 158–172; J. Zanglein, "High performance investing: harnessing the power of pension funds to promote economic growth and workplace integrity" (1995) 11 *The Labor Lawyer* 59.
[7] Perhaps the biggest policy question of all – should tax-favored private savings be provided through occupational pension plans at all, or provided through a state-sponsored arrangement – is once again being raised in Canada with some vigor. This chapter does not address the other major social dimension of the "maturing" of pension plans and funds. That is, a declining percentage of the paid labor force in Canada participates in private occupational pension plans each year. This is the "coverage question," the causes and effects of which is addressed in other work.

they rely more on income from investments than from new contributing members. For some mature plans, their assets will be greater in value than the value of the entity sponsoring them. When such a large asset is present on a balance sheet, it draws attention in many dimensions: from accountants, regulators, shareholders, unions and, not least, the direct beneficiaries. Such assets need stewardship, and the ways in which these funds have been designed and administered has led to an increased reliance on exposure to capital markets, and results, it seems, in deals like the attempted BCE leveraged buyout.

Some tentative conclusions can flow from these simple observations. Size matters: large pension plans have become very different institutions than they were ten years ago. Smaller and mid-sized plans are disappearing, or more likely, will be absorbed into large plans where permitted. The "market" in pension funds is shrinking, and has a tendency toward concentration in a few very large players. This reflects in part the decline in defined benefit pension provision in the common law world, but also a dynamic within sectors that have seen relatively little decline (e.g. public sector plan provision).[8]

Sponsors face increased scrutiny, which in part explains the decline in the prevalence of occupational plans, particularly in the private sector. The risks inherent in the equity-driven investment strategies of these funds (or funds' sponsors) in the past, strategies that seek to lower costs of benefits, were being priced into the sponsor's share prices and credit ratings. This led to the "funding question": are these plans affordable anymore, at least as part of employment-centric benefits? The answer has by and large been "no," which has led to the primary policy question, should employers be in the "pension business" at all?

The largest pension funds – which are clustered in the public sector (sector matters too) take on more bank-like or insurance-company-like features. They are the largest institutional investors in many markets. They have dozens to hundreds of staff, mandated to seek risk-adjusted returns within the confines of prudential regulation and tests for solvency. These objectives require specialized financial service skills difficult to distinguish from investment banks or hedge funds.

There are follow-along effects to the consolidation of funds and the specialization in staff: their primary service providers have also undergone similar consolidation and specialization processes.

---

[8] Defined benefit funds and plans are increasingly a public sector phenomenon. This raises the question of whether defined benefit pensions are "private" and "market based" in any sense at all.

II Background to Canadian pension funds

Occupational pension plans grew out of an industrial relations policy dilemma. In the early 1960s in Canada the decision was made to provide a significant portion of retirement income through employer-centric plans. In this respect pension plans are the product of social policy forming one of three "pillars" of the retirement income system in Canada.[9]

There are a relatively stable number – 3,800 – of "trusteed pension funds" in Canada.[10] They range in size (as measured by assets under management) from a few million to over $100 billion in size. However, the industry is characterized by a smaller number of very large funds. The 140 largest funds (3.8 percent of total number of funds) account for over $720 billion (80 percent of total assets under management).[11] Within this 140, there are a smaller number of "super-large" funds – those with over, say, $10 billion in assets under management. These

---

[9] The retirement income system is often divided into three main pillars following the World Bank's nomenclature and conceptual divisions: mandatory minimum public income support programs, mandatory public wage-based occupational pension plans and voluntary wage-based group or individual retirement savings programs. In Canada, public programs are usually thought to include Old Age Security (OAS) and Guaranteed Income Supplements (GIS), the Canada/Quebec Pension Plans (C/QPP) is the mandatory public wage-based plan, occupational pension plans include employer and jointly employer-and-employee sponsored pension plans, and individual retirement savings includes a variety of investments and "registered retirement savings plans." The conceptual division into three pillars is for convenience: C/QPP is an employment-based defined benefit plan associated with a large, independently-run pension fund; Group Registered Retirement Savings Plans (RRSPs) sponsored by employers are closely akin to occupational pension plans, and not individual retirement savings. Pension plans are the most important source of retirement income for middle-income earners in Canada, they are the second largest asset for households lucky enough to have them, they are focal point of conflict and cooperation in employer–employee relations, and lately in retiree–employer relations, they are a significant aspect of social policy (the second-largest tax expenditure in Canada), and as will be demonstrated below, they are significant capital market actors.

[10] In the pre-funded pension plan context, pension funds are the pools of assets that fund pension plans. Statistics Canada tracks pension funds through its survey of Trusteed Pension Funds in Canada. All figures and tables referred to in this chapter are on file with author and easily reproduced through public data sources. Statistics Canada produces two main surveys of pension funds, a biennial survey of all funds registered with the Canada Revenue Agency, most recently available in 2004, and a quarterly review of a smaller sample of that population, for which data is available to the end of 2007. Trusteed pension plans does not necessarily refer to a board of trustees, but to the statutory requirement that pension fund assets be segregated from the sponsoring entity's assets, typically but not necessarily in a trust instrument. There are many more pension plans than pension funds, as usually more than one plan will be associated with a pension fund

[11] These figures drawn from the Pension Investment Association of Canada, available at: www.piacweb.org (last accessed February 22, 2011).

very large funds are all associated with public sector or para-public sector defined benefit plans, and these funds are the core group exhibiting the change in characteristics that will be discussed in more detail below.

In aggregate, Canadian pension funds had about $900 billion in assets under management in 2007. We can compare the size of these assets under management to other closely-regulated financial institutions. As financial institutions, pension funds are second only in size to the chartered Canadian banks (about $1.7 trillion in assets). They are larger than other financial institutions with similar functions: mutual funds as a sector have just under $600 billion under management, and life insurance about $200 billion under management. Other major regulated financial institutions are all significantly smaller in size.[12]

By Statistics Canada measures, Canadian pension funds held $370–400 billion in equities in 2007, or about 20 percent of the Toronto Stock Exchange (TSX) market capitalization – although there is reason to be cautious with these estimates.[13] Other estimates of the size of pension funds to market capitalization show a much higher ratio, some as high as 50 percent of total market capitalization.[14]

Compared to gross domestic product, Canadian funds appear even more significant: in Canada, a ratio of nearly 50 percent of total pension fund investments to GDP, versus an OECD average of about 5 percent, but again, these comparisons do not account for differences in retirement savings systems.[15] For example, in countries with a comparable public/private retirement income system to Canada, the ratio of total pension fund investment to GDP is higher: in the United States, over 50 percent, and in the UK, perhaps 70 percent.[16] Other reviews of pension fund importance have found similar results for some time. Pension fund

---

[12] These include property and casualty insurance, mortgage, loan and trust businesses, credit unions, *caisses populaires*, investment dealers and other consumer loan and finance businesses.

[13] Statistics Canada asset allocation data do not always clearly break out fund holdings, by, for example, equities held through pooled funds. Comparison of Statistics Canada sources to that collected privately by Benefits Canada and the Pension Investment Association of Canada suggest a slightly higher weighting to equities.

[14] See the Organization for Economic Cooperation and Development's Global Pension Statistics Project, a description of which is available at: www.oecd.org/dataoecd/28/31/33865642.pdf (last accessed February 22, 2011).

[15] These and other figures quoted in this chapter compiled by the author using Statistics Canada surveys.

[16] Note that these comparisons are assets under management at market values: two qualifiers are necessary. Asset values fluctuate relatively quickly and across a small period of time, and these comparisons of size should not be confused with estimates of, say, a "net worth" value of pension plans, which takes into account the liabilities these assets are intended to meet.

Pension funds 183

investment grew from one-sixth of gross national product (GNP) in the 1960s to about one-third in 1977.[17] In 1984, the Economic Council of Canada predicted that pension funds would grow to four-fifths of gross national product by 2030.[18] It was estimates such as these that motivated labels like "creeping socialism" and "power without property."

A   Sources of revenues of pension funds

Originally the largest sources of pension fund revenues were contributions from sponsors and members of the pension plans associated with the funds. Weitz traces the early size and trajectory of these revenues, showing that even early on, there was extraordinary growth in revenues in the early years.[19]

From about 1993 to present emerged a more significant source of revenue: profits from the sale of securities. This source of revenues fluctuates: it was 10 percent of total revenues in 1980, 22 percent in 1988, 50 percent or more of total pension fund revenues in 1995 and in the years 1999–2000. Over that period the net income of pension funds was strongly linked to the net loss or profits on sales of securities: pension funds' expansion through the 1990s was financed through capital gains.[20] The comparison to individual retail investors in the same period is tempting, such as a possible "wealth effect" that is considered a contributing factor to the now-overextended appetite for debt among Canadian and US households and, latterly, governments.

These overview statistics of pension fund revenues suggest observations about the funds. First, they are significant pools of capital in relation to other capital market institutions and in relation to the markets they invest in. This is not a new observation (Berle made it in 1959, Drucker again later), but it still pertains. Any change in these funds is likely to have an impact upon broader capital markets (in addition to their immediate stakeholders). Some of these impacts are discussed in the next section.

---

[17] As quoted in H. Weitz, *The Pension Promise, The Past and Future of Canada's Private Pension System* (Scarborough, Ontario: Carswell, 1992), p. 230.
[18] Economic Council of Canada, *One in Three: Pensions for Canadians to 2030* (Ottawa: ECC, 1984).
[19] Weitz, *Pension Promise*, pp. 267–268. It should also be noted that while experience varies, public sector plans are typically "contributory," that is, requiring some employee contributions, but not private sector plans.
[20] It is relevant to note that since the first capital market correction in 2001–2003 and again in the GFC, contributions to pension funds were increased significantly, although they still represent a fraction of the total revenues.

The internal tensions in these funds have also changed. The two factors that characterize the late 1970s and 1980s – investment income meeting costs of the plans and resulting asset accumulation – meant that in the late 1980s, a generation of high-nominal-return investments created significant surpluses in many pension funds.[21] Although surpluses are cyclical as much as engineered, income tax regulation requires that they be used in some way, or, over certain limits, contributions lose their tax deductible status. These surpluses formed the basis – and when they recur, still form the basis – for some significant conflicts between stakeholders in pension funds: employees, retirees and sponsor businesses. In Canada litigation over surpluses began in earnest in 1986, and dominated the 1990s, leading to an awkward exploration of the application of nineteenth-century trust law principles to pension plans and funds, which has attracted much comment in industry literature and some academic literature.[22]

The profit from trade in securities fluctuates and appears to be strongly cyclical – at least on the basis of the past fifteen years' evidence.[23] Pension funds appeared to become very active in short- and medium-term trading of securities. Such activity is inconsistent with the standard view of passive long-term investment, and is one indication of the shift in pension funds from passive vehicles focused on capital preservation to more active traders focused on short-term capital gains.

In fact, capital gain appears to have been the motive for shifting from "matched" assets – that is, assets with payment streams roughly equivalent to the obligations of the pension plan – into equity markets. In this sense, risk was added to balance sheets of sponsors while freeing up cash flow, usually without the complete understanding (let alone consent) of other stakeholders including beneficiaries. The evidence suggests that the equity premium "paid off" in the late 1990s and again in the period 2004–2007, but the risks associated with assuming an equity portfolio "landed" from about mid-2001 to 2004, and from 2007 to

---

[21] These surpluses arise in part because indexation for inflation, which drove high nominal returns, is not usually built into the liability structure of private sector pension plans, or if it is, on an ad hoc basis. As a result, high nominal returns are matched against inflation-eroded real benefits, generating surplus funds to requirements.

[22] See, for example, E. Gillese, "Pension plans and the law of trusts" (1996) *Canadian Bar Review* 75.

[23] This period is a difficult period to generalize about: it was perhaps the most unusual period in US and Canadian capital markets since the 1920s. Equity prices were far higher than valuations warranted (price to earnings ratios were three and four times higher than the historical average of fifteen) and interest rates traveled from historical highs to thirty-year lows during that period.

mid-2009. The earlier period saw markedly reduced revenues from the sale of securities. Data from the latter period are not available.[24]

There are some clear conflicts in these positions that engage directly the decision-making of the plan sponsor–employer over its available cash flow. Investment in equities reduced the costs of employers' current contributions and so diverted internal resources to other uses, although the additional risk taken on may have been "priced in" to sponsor securities when they are listed companies, and there is some evidence of this effect.[25] This use of equities also meant that the "animal spirits" of capital markets (primarily in the form of equity prices and interest rates) directly enhance or diminish different stakeholder fortunes, volatility to which those stakeholders were less exposed in prior decades.[26]

In summary, the evolution in the sources of revenue of these funds has shown pension funds increasing their participation in equity markets, and as a result, produced some tensions in the way the costs of participation in equity markets are distributed across stakeholders, and even suggests periodic but ever diminishing importance of those stakeholders as funds mature. This evolution is also evidence that capital markets – particularly equity markets – have become more important to pension funds as they grow larger and more mature. As noted above, this has led to a group of questions about pension funds' interventions as "owners," seeking to promote better behavior in their investments, however that behavior may be defined.

B   *Investment patterns of pension funds*

Bonds and equities are the largest proportion of pension funds' asset allocations. The traditional view is that there has been decreasing allocations in bonds over time, shifting investments into equities, and that there has been a slight increase in real estate holdings and a significant

---

[24] It is also a question for financial economists, who question whether equities really do outperform bonds in the long run (it appears to vary significantly with the period examined) and therefore whether there is an "equity premium" justifying some level of risk-taking in investments, and whether there should be that level of risk-taking given the nature of the liabilities the assets of a pension plan are intended to meet. See L. Bader and J. Gold, "Perspectives: the case against stock in public pension funds" (2007) 63:1 *Financial Analysts Journal* 55.

[25] For example, J. Rubin, "Impact of pension freezes on firm value," Pension Research Council Working Paper (2007) and E.P. Davis, S. Grob and L. de Haan, "Pension fund finance and sponsoring companies: empirical evidence on theoretical hypotheses" (DNB) Working Paper No. 158 (2007).

[26] In this context, stakeholders are not only beneficiaries, but plan sponsors, their shareholders (if applicable) and governments, each of whom have something to gain or lose from the configuration of the plan and fund.

increase in "other" assets such as hedge funds and private equity, more about which below.

It is difficult to come to clear conclusions about any detail of the composition of pension fund portfolios based on the available Statistics Canada. According to standard sources, the largest Canadian pension funds allocate something over 50 percent of their portfolios to equities; bonds and mortgages are about 30 percent; real estate about 7 percent; venture capital, private equity, infrastructure and "other" assets about 10 percent. Given the concentration in a small number of funds, these averages are quite misleading, however. Very large public sector funds (whose asset allocations are available through annual disclosure) includes some with alternative asset allocation of up to 30 percent of the totals assets – that is, infrastructure and private equity allocations over several billion each. These funds or the subsidiaries managing these allocations can be quite significant market "players" in their own right. On the other end of the scale, smaller pension funds tend to allocate more traditionally and through fund portfolios maintained by asset managers which mirror more closely retail portfolio products.

More detailed portfolio tracking by Statistics Canada would be a valuable research tool, and to this effect some provincial regulators have begin tracking more detailed composition and changes in pension fund portfolios.[27]

III Factors driving change

A *Size and concentration*

The most notable theme through this quick review of pension funds is that both size and concentration are important. It has long been observed that in the provision of pensions, and associated pension activities, economies of scale accrue significantly to larger players. In just one often-quoted statistic, large defined benefit plans and funds such as the OTPP have expense ratios of perhaps fifty basis points, compared to expense ratios in retail mutual funds of 250 basis points, or higher. This is one way in which size matters and it is uncontroversial.

Another way that size and scale matter is as one answer to declining incidence of occupational pension plans. It has been observed in Canada, the United States and UK that occupational pension *plan*

---

[27] See, for example, Ontario's requirement of registered pension plans to submit an annual filing (the "Annual Investment Summary") with details of the fund's portfolio and market values.

coverage is declining as a percentage of the labor force. Absent a reversal of industrial relations of the past twenty years, or some massive regulatory intervention, there does not seem to be a prospect of organic growth in the sector. At the same time, this decline in incidence (or pressure to exit the provision of a defined benefit plan) has led to proposals to create larger plans, such as sectoral or industry-specific plans, that permit the provision of benefits to groups of employers (also known as multi-employer pension plans and funds). Similarly, public sector plans have mooted providing third party capital investment services to smaller plans, a form of collectivizing the investment function. Other OECD countries have adopted similar "industry-wide" models.

The third way in which size matters is in relation to external economies: the size of funds relative to their domestic and increasingly global capital markets. Here, pension funds appear to be in a similar position to other Canadian financial institutions: increasingly exposed or intertwined with global capital markets. In the domestic market, pension funds exerted comparatively more leverage than in foreign markets, and investing in foreign markets, though much easier than twenty years ago, is easier to justify by larger funds. The interaction of domestic financial service regulation and global markets is a key tension: the former is seen, by actors, as restricting their ability to merge and compete for investments in other capital markets.

B   *Public and private sector plans*

In the 1960s and 1970s, governments issued special non-fungible bonds to pension funds. By 1990s these funds were becoming increasingly independent of government and at times jointly-sponsored or trusteed by members and government employers. Their assets were transferred out and invested in capital markets. In 1998, the Canada Pension Plan Investment Board (CPP-IB) was established which assists in funding the Canada Pension Plan (CPP), the mandatory public pension plan.[28] These funds are not only the largest in Canada, they are the funds engaging in the most sophisticated investment and capital market behaviors. The major phase in "pension fund activism" (in a very broad sense) is co-terminal with the entry of more and larger public sector pension funds into the capital markets.

---

[28] Note that the CPP-IB is the fund of an occupational pension plan, CPP, but sometimes classified as a public plan along with Old Age Security/Guaranteed Income Supplement benefits, because it is compulsory. CPP is approximately 20 percent pre-funded through CPP-IB.

As sponsors, public and para-public employers have very different risk profiles and pressures than their private sector equivalents. They are not at risk of insolvency or fundamental transformations of their businesses; they have taxpayers, not shareholders, as stakeholders. This may be a factor in their ability to engage in a wider array of investment behaviors and maintain some level of stability in the rate of new participants. It has also been accompanied by a focus on the equality of treatment as between groups of participants (inter-generational in/equity) and less on outside stakeholders (that is, a focus on contributions of cohorts moving through to retirement who benefited from the "equity premium" not available to newer members). In recent years, public sector plans have also been the focus of criticism for the relatively high level of benefits they provide compared to private sector employer funds, which are slowly disappearing. This is from time to time expressed as private sector tax rage, which again may be an indirect political influence on the management of the public funds' assets.

Private pension funds are in comparison smaller in size (in Canada, typically less than $1 billion under management), and these plans are administered or managed by Chief Financial Officers. These plans are clustered in particular in the mature manufacturing sector. The cost and balance sheet pressures on these plans are leading, to some extent, to conversion to defined contribution (DC) plans or closing them altogether. (In other jurisdictions such as the UK, there is a developing industry in the purchase of liabilities from closed private sector plans and running them at a profit, but that industry has not yet developed in Canada.)[29] In short, private pension funds appear to be a declining part and therefore influence on the sector as a whole. This "pension gap" is primarily a coverage issue, but leads to periodic widespread criticism of the public sector plans and funds as a whole.

C Demographics

A third and much-observed factor driving change is the demographics of plan populations. The effect of these demographic changes is the subject of significant commentary already, and often used to justify policy changes or law reform. Briefly, plan populations have, typically, an

---

[29] This business is feasible, apparently, because mortality assumptions required by regulation are often too conservative given the nature of the actual plan population (recall, they tend to be clustered in mature manufacturing industries). The model assumes that payouts will be lower than projections and a profit can be generated in the difference, which forms the basis for the insurer to acquire capital to fund the business, which capital, ironically, would likely involve investments from pension funds.

Pension funds 189

increased average age, reflecting two trends: longer life expectancies on one hand and an increasing ratio of retiree to active members of pension plans. Longer life expectancies increase liabilities owed by a plan to someone who is no longer contributing to the plan (to the extent these liabilities are not immunized). Fewer active participants in relation to retirees means that there is a lower proportion of contributions relative to other sources of income (from investments). This has put pressure on investments to produce the revenues required to meet these increasing liabilities. These demographic changes put two contradictory pressures on revenues and investment behavior: they increase the annual payout costs of plans and lower the revenues available from current members. This results in contradictory investment impulses: on the one hand, to seek to immunize the liabilities associated with a larger pool of retirees, and on the other, the impulse to seek higher returns to meet cash flow needs through, for example, greater exposure to risk in private equity investments. The data reviewed for this chapter do not help flesh out the details of the effect of these changes, except to support the contention that plans are seeking equity premia (they have not reduced equity exposures significantly) but also seeking investments with profiles closer to liabilities (e.g. alternative assets) in greater proportion. The ability to seek the latter is contingent, it seems, on size, and so this presents a significant barrier to small- and medium-sized funds.

D   *Changing legal and regulatory environment*

A fourth factor facilitating change is the changing regulatory environment in Canada. In 1993 the current investment rules, which involved quantitative restrictions forcing diversification and passive behavior, were introduced in the federal jurisdiction, and adopted by reference in most provinces across Canada.[30] While these quantitative restrictions allow significant ownership positions – up to 30 percent of the voting

---

[30] Schedule III of the Pension Benefits Standards Act, R.S.C. 1985, c. 32 (2nd Supp.). These rules are prohibitions on: investing more than 10 percent of the book value of the plans' assets in any one "person" or group of affiliates (with some limited exceptions) (the "10 percent rule"); owning more than 30 percent of the voting securities of an issuer, except certain resource, real estate and investment corporation issuers (the "30 percent rule"); owning 5 percent of the book value of a real estate or resource property, and; investing more than an aggregate 15 percent of the book value of the pension fund in resource properties, and 25 percent of the book value of the fund in resource and real estate investments combined. Aside from quantitative restrictions, the investment rules also prohibit other forms of transaction by the pension fund: self-dealing and related party transactions (with some exceptions). Investments must be registered to clearly show they are held in trust for a pension fund, and rules about record-keeping.

stock except in resource, real estate and investment company issuers, which are somewhat more restrictive – some of the very large Canadian pension funds would like fewer quantitative restrictions.

There is debate over the cause-and-effect relationships between investment regulation and investment patterns, and the way these relationships have changed over time. Weitz cites several studies from the 1970s (e.g. Conway's) that argue that the prudence standard in combination with self-regulation is the most important influence on investment patterns;[31] research on more recent periods suggest that quantitative and regulatory restrictions are too costly and are a driver of investment inappropriate (or suboptimal) behaviors. The regulatory issues in the OTPP deal for BCE are a case in point.

Large funds have in some sense "outgrown" the existing regulatory framework and have challenged it.[32] Large pension funds have lobbied the federal regulator to provide them with exemptions from these rules, but have not met with success, perhaps because the federal regulator (the Office of the Superintendent of Financial Institutions) maintains that these regulations are appropriate to pension funds as special financial institutions with assets backing guarantees (not speculative investment), akin to insurance companies or banks.

OTPP's attempted purchase of BCE is an example: although prohibited by regulation from owning more than 30 percent of the voting shares of a single issuer, OTPP structured the deal such that it would have owned 51.6 percent of the non-voting shares of BCE (Class B and C), and no more than 30 percent of the Class A voting shares. The title to the balance of the Class A voting shares would have been owned by Morgan McCague, a former OTPP executive, who had agreed to vote the shares according to OTPP instructions and agreed that he wouldn't nominate directors. This structure is common to these types of deals, effectively circumventing the quantitative restrictions in the pensions statute.[33]

The deal was subject to a review by the Canadian Radio and Telecommunications Commission (CRTC) in order to establish that it met certain public interest minimum standards, including Canadian ownership and control (the merits of the CRTC mandate can be debated). In order to meet CRTC standards, the deal would effectively

---

[31] Weitz, *Pension Promise*.
[32] The argument is usually presented that these rules are appropriate and efficient in young capital markets and developing capital markets (e.g. "emerging markets") but less so in mature and sophisticated capital markets.
[33] Also note that in 2005, the limit on holding foreign property by pension funds was repealed, and since that time, foreign property holdings have steadily increased.

have to contravene limitations to ownership in the quantitative rules. The pension regulator's opinion was obtained, which, in a very formal analysis, did not find contravention of the quantitative rules. The CRTC Commissioner publicly expressed his skepticism about this opinion and found that BCE was in effect owned and controlled by the OTPP, which permitted him to approve the deal for CRTC purposes.

If the question is whether or not investment rules and the broader regulatory environment influence the investment behaviors of pension funds, the answer must be yes, but not in the way intended, as discussed in the next section.

E   Economic theory

The quantitative rules mentioned above are an expression of an underlying logic of investment: modern portfolio theory. Since about 1990 developments in the field of "financial economics" have challenged portfolio theory (which had become orthodox theory by which to ground investment policy and practice). Briefly, portfolio theory suggests the risk–return profile of a portfolio will be optimized if it is appropriately diversified. Prior to this logic, pension funds had been confined to a "legal list" (literally, a list) of high-quality investments in government debt and "blue chip" issuers. Diversification became the norm through the amendment of the "legal list" to permit prudent investment in a diversified portfolio. Today, mid-sized pension funds have perhaps between thirty and seventy-five individual holdings in their equity portfolios. One result of this approach was the increased attention to – and hope for – the "equity premium" over riskless assets discussed above.

Beginning in the 1990s, driven by work from financial economists like Zvi Bodie the theory and practice of pension plans seeking equity premiums in diversified portfolios was challenged on several bases, including the argument that pension funds ought to be "de-risking" through investment in bond-only portfolios, and that in the long-term, there were reasons to believe that equities did not in fact outperform bonds, and therefore the additional risk of equities was unrewarded.[34]

As a result, financial economic theory *may* be informing the asset allocation of pension funds, and thereby, who they do business with and when. There are some anecdotal examples in the UK and British Columbia of such strategies (shifting from stocks to bonds) being adopted by pension funds, but the statistical review above suggests

[34] On other pension investment issues, see Bodie, "Innovation."

that "de-risking" pursuant to this new economic logic is not yet being robustly adopted by pension funds.

It is interesting to note that in the 1980s and early 1990s, outside academic circles there was very little discussion or critique of the propositions of financial economics, notably that (1) equities outperform bonds or (2) where things like retirement income are at stake, investment profiles ought to closely match liability profiles. After two strong market corrections, such propositions now seem self-evident. The sad irony of the belated application of this "corrected" economic logic is that the new cohorts will be required to pay more into a pension fund and receive less for it, forming a real disincentive to participate in the scheme.[35]

IV Implications for pension funds as owners and financial intermediaries

The immediate concerns of this chapter are pension funds as intermediaries and as institutions in capital markets. Three relevant aspects of these roles will be considered: monitoring and control of investments; liquidity, volatility and stability in capital markets; and pension funds' impacts on real and financial sectors.

A Monitoring and control

The increase in equity holdings completes a trend identified in prior eras (1960s, 1970s and 1980s) and appears to have reached a steady state in terms of proportion of assets allocated in the 1990s. The main motive and implication of holding these equities has already been mentioned above: trading in equities as a source of revenue. This type of trading betrays a "short-termism" not typical of passive investors. Pension funds take advantage of broader market trends when able.

The second major implication of the increased holding in equities is that, where they are held for some length of time, pension funds may become more interested in monitoring and influencing their investments. This was a much-hoped-for stabilizing influence of pension funds after the leveraged buyout era of the 1980s, and also in the movement to "democratize" capital through greater control over both

---

[35] The argument that there should be inter-generational equity asserts that cost and benefits of cohorts should roughly equal. This argument is situated within a larger question of appropriate social discounts given policy objectives and expectations about future performance.

investment decisions and use of security-holder's rights to influence investments. The possibility and measurement of these potential influences has been the focus of research.

There are probably four main channels for effecting influence over investments: shareholder proposals, shareholder or securities litigation, industry coalitions promoting certain policies and informal moral suasion. Each of these channels has been much better developed in the United States than in Canada, which may reflect different temporal stages in development, or an altogether different path or variety.

Pension funds became significant institutional investors in Canadian corporations over the past twenty years. Their influence was initially channeled through informal suasion, which later developed into the promotion of "good governance" and even, but rarely, litigation.

Currently, the most robust form of "active ownership" is the promotion of certain characteristics in investments, including the elimination of multi-voting shares and abusive use of dual-class shares, monitoring of executive compensation, and rejecting poison pill defenses, among others.[36] There is a Canadian coalition of institutional investors led by major pension funds, and there is evidence of coordinated action of pension funds using shareholder proposals. (It should be noted that contrary to the recent trend in the United States, the main institutional investor coalition in Canada, the Canadian Coalition for Good Governance, has decided not to promote "say on pay" proposals through Canadian pension funds holdings, despite the coalition's consistent observation that executive compensation is an issue for institutional investors to monitor to promote good governance. This position itself may be an effect of concentration in the financial service industry.) There has even been some limited securities litigation by pension funds in Canada, although it is significantly less developed than in the United States.[37]

It seems that the promise of robust institutional investor activism, in the sense of democratized capital and even corporate monitoring, has not yet been fulfilled, however. It has certainly not had the same growth or development that has characterized the US experience despite increasingly integrated financial sectors and real economies.[38] The

---

[36] As this chapter is sent to the publisher, two major public pension funds have actively opposed a significant and "abusive" payout to the founder of a major Canadian auto parts manufacturer as part of a transaction eliminating a dual class share structure.

[37] At the date of writing, there have been perhaps fifteen cases brought pursuant to relatively new secondary market disclosure legislation. Most Canadian pension funds participate in US proceedings against issuers where appropriate, but there is no clearly developing pattern of litigation by Canadian funds against Canadian issuers.

[38] See, for example, M. Faccio and M. Lasfer, "Do occupational pension funds monitor companies in which they hold large stakes?" (2000) 6:1 *Journal of Corporate Finance* 71.

reasons for this lack of growth and divergence from the US experience are of significant interest for further study. One common suggestion is that moral suasion is the primary and most effective method of intervention in the Canadian context, characterized by block holders and a small, oligopolistic financial sector. This type of influence is inherently difficult to measure, and so it may be passed over by many types of empirical study. Litigation has not been a method funds have used in Canada: "loser pays" cost-recovery rules discourage litigation, and only very recently has a statutory cause of action been introduced in Ontario that facilitates claims based on secondary market disclosure. Whatever the reason, there does not appear to be a widespread or large-scale influence on asset allocation by pension funds, and on the subsequent management or monitoring of those investments.

The second major development in equity holdings was the increasing use of pooled funds. The growth in the use of pooled funds reinforces the "passive investor" model. It is difficult to decompose the use of pooled funds on the data available: they may be used by smaller funds, not the larger funds that are the leaders in new developments. They may also be a preferred way to enter foreign and lesser-known markets, to reduce risks through pooling. The use of pooled funds is not inconsistent with the churning noted above, but it does – to use a Berlian term – further separate ownership from ownership through the introduction of yet another level of management of assets.

Finally, the examination of pension funds' performance as monitors invites, if only for symmetry, the consideration of pension funds' own governance. Where funds are arm's length and managed by professionals, managers and their governing boards are effectively independent stakeholders in the funds, with interests and conflicts that have been the subject of a large corporate governance literature. It is also generating an equivalent pension governance literature.[39] This literature criticizes the deviations from the "trust paradigm" and examines methods to separate sponsorship of a fund from management of a fund, and provides metrics to measure performance.[40] Several aspects of governance are being studied,[41] including effective member representation on

---

[39] See, for example, research program at the International Centre for Pension Management, University of Toronto.

[40] See, for example, K. Ambachtsheer, K.R. Capelle and H. Lum, "The state of global pension fund governance today: board competency still a problem" (Toronto: ICPM Working Paper, June, 2007) and G. Clarke, "Best practice pension fund governance" (2008) 9 *Journal of Asset Management* 2.

[41] The Harvard Worklife Program has generated about five years' research presented at annual conferences into a series of related issues in capital stewardship,

boards, the impact of corporate governance norms on pension fund governance and the relationship between labor and management in governance.

B   *Depth, liquidity, price and volatility*

The literature on pension funds and capital markets examines stability in other ways: the impact on overall savings, creating liquidity and volatility, and enhancing efficient use of market information.

The net increase in securities held by pension funds, particularly equities, combined with their size relative to domestic capital markets, suggests that pension funds are significant providers of demand for securities in Canada. It is said anecdotally that the high yield bond market in Canada died when institutional investors decided not to participate.

The churning through the sale of securities seen in the 1990s and in the most recent three years also suggests that they are significant sellers as well, providing liquidity to capital markets. This impressionistic review is confirmed by other studies and by anecdotal evidence.

The demand side of this liquidity and depth is that pension funds appear to stimulate innovation in capital markets – a word that has both positive and negative connotations. Other literature suggests that due to pension funds' specific demands (glossed above in discussing asset-liability matching), they stimulate the development of financial products, especially bond-like products which have characteristics of low risk or steady returns. These include such products as zero coupon bonds, indexed linked mortgages and other guaranteed income products. Bodie, Partnoy and Bookstaber have all noted in different contexts that pension and insurance funds have stimulated demand and innovation in collateralized mortgage obligations (among other structured products).[42] These became a topic of some interest in the summer of 2008 when credit markets froze, and have led to a widespread reconsideration of their development, regulation and, not least, pricing.

The allocation data presented above also suggest the increased use of derivative products, and more complicated portfolio insurance strategies, such as "portable alpha" and most recently "130/30" long–short

---

labor-management participation in pension funds and capital markets and changing investment practices.
[42] Bodie, "Innovation"; F. Partnoy and R. Bookstaber both provide popular accounts in, respectively, *Infectious Greed: How Deceit and Risk Corrupted the Financial Markets* (New York: Times Books, 2003) and *A Demon of Our Own Design: Markets, Hedge Funds and the Perils of Financial Innovation* (New Jersey: John Wiley & Sons, 2007).

strategies. The merits of these innovations may be denied, but not the fact of them. Although it appears to have driven capital gains for funds in the 1990s (and for a brief period in 2003–2007), one of the criticisms of this investment strategy is the (unnecessary) fees generated by churning. Profitless churning has been the subject of criticism in the United States and Canada and in other markets as well, including retail mutual funds. The data reviewed for this study are not sensitive enough to explore these propositions, but anecdotal or indirect evidence suggests a number of areas for future consideration.[43]

The first is that pension funds are such significant purchasers and sellers that they can move market prices by the nature of their transactions, and not on the basis of some new information about that security. In this way, when pension funds buy or sell securities for internal reasons (e.g. to meet liabilities or as a result of their internal allocation management), they can, temporarily at least, move prices. In this situation, price movements are not reflecting more or better information, but instead idiosyncratic changes in a large buyer. This may not be an entirely harmful outcome of necessary decision-making; it may even provide nimble market actors with a price arbitrage opportunity, but it is not increasing the distribution of information efficiently, but the opposite.

This situation can become more problematic, however, when coupled with thinly-traded securities or complex and inflexible investments, creating what has been termed "tight coupling" between events that are otherwise not usually correlated or that would otherwise not result in poor outcomes. This is now better understood as one of the causes of single-day price movements during the 2008–2009 GFC, and from time to time since then. The phenomenon is not new, however, having been first observed in the implementation of "portfolio insurance" in the late 1980s, which was really a more complex program of dynamic hedging that required automatic portfolio adjustments given changes in market prices. When unusual circumstances arise (e.g. the crash in equities in the late 1980s) these strategies can exacerbate price movements. The uncertainty about the extent of losses related to sub-prime investments (or in Canada, asset-backed commercial paper) was partly as a result of these features. Indeed, it is anecdotally reported that one single public sector pension plan was the sole purchaser of non-bank asset-backed commercial paper in the months leading up to the freeze in that market in August 2007, and held over 30 percent of that entire

---

[43] See, for example, Davis, *Pension Funds*, p. 166.

market at that time. When it decided to slow purchasing, the market for short-term paper collapsed.

More generally, commentators have noted the effects of both immunization strategies and "herding" in causing market volatility, such as closely matching portfolios so as to meet a prudence standard, and that these features tend to become more exaggerated in mature funds in which investment income and capital gains are more significant than other sources of revenues.[44] Pension funds have also lowered unit costs of investment for the contributors to pension funds, especially as compared to their near-substitutes in retail mutual funds.[45]

Finally, most broadly and fundamentally, pension funds aggregate savings. As pools of capital, they make savings available for investment. Whether they increase savings or merely displace it is a key question, and this continues to be disputed.[46] There is evidence that the correlation of the size of pension funds to national savings rates is low, and where those pension funds are major holdings of equities, it is even lower. However, where pension plans are mandatory (in Canada, plans are voluntary to provide, but where provided, they typically require employee participation) these plans appear to increase savings.

C   *Alternative assets and the real and paper economies*

Pension funds' increase in the use of alternative assets has several implications, some of which are particularly worth examining. The impact of these allocations is on both the financial service sector and, potentially, on the integration of the broader economy.

These investments are difficult to discuss generically. They include stakes in infrastructure projects like roads, hospitals, water treatment plants, railways and airports. There is a small but growing sector in "urban regeneration," largely spurred by experience in Europe and somewhat in the United States. They are sometimes structured as public–private investments, the "P3s," and may be privatized or formerly public businesses or assets. Some themes that emerge from a summary review of them suggest that they involve a much more active role for the pension fund than would a traditional purchase of securities.

---

[44] *Ibid.*
[45] Ambachstsheer has described these differences in detail: Ambachtsheer, *Pension Revolution*. One annual study consistently finds Canadian mutual fund fees (MERs) to be the highest in the world; causes are not certain.
[46] See, for example, J. MacIntosh and D. Cumming, "Crowding out private equity: Canadian evidence" (2006) 21 *Journal of Business Venturing* 569.

First, in these deals, pension funds are making direct investments in businesses with a (potentially) long-term perspective. Pension funds are not merely making investments in an issuer through a private placement, for instance, but are leading or actively collaborating in the structuring of these deals, sometimes as investments in a new business, and sometimes as takeovers. Because these deals are non-standard, they require greater expertise and resources to develop and to perform due diligence and monitoring. As such, they require a more intense use of either internal but more likely external service providers, again, driving innovation and financial sector producers, which appears to be shifting activity, if not decisions, outside Canada.

This kind of deal-making is outside the classic "passive" paradigm and much closer to the practices and behavior of the typical co-investors in these deals: hedge funds and private equity houses. This comparison should give pause: hedge funds and private equity investors grew out of the LBO era in the 1980s, and out of the massive expansion in financial sector instruments and methods in the 1990s; they have sometimes been on the sell-side when pension funds were on the buy-side, and, like pension funds, they have as classes both been implicated in speculation, short-termism, moving markets and financial crises.

Third, these types of deals can come with very significant stakeholder conflicts, notably among the P3s which have involved a privatization of a public service or asset. Here, investee funds are conflicted where the investment prospectus and business plan can or will involve savings or efficiencies at the cost of organized labor, social services or "public" values. These politics may actually explain pension funds' relatively low levels of, but nonetheless contested, infrastructure investments in Canada, but their routine purchase of infrastructure assets in other jurisdictions, where political conflict can be muted.

The political economy of the P3 deals is indicative of a broader set of conflicts that will arise if these types of allocations continue. If pension funds become in effect controlling owners of these businesses, they will face ongoing potential for conflicts of interest. This argument is, in a sense, an extension of the conflict over the legal principle in the old *Cowan* v. *Scargill* case.[47] When a pension fund owns and controls a business, would an undivided loyalty to the beneficiaries' financial interests operate to require layoffs, off-shoring or other practices that

---

[47] *Cowan* v. *Scargill* [1985] Ch. 270. This is considered the leading case on the paramountcy of a pension trustees' duty to consider the "financial best interests" of a beneficiary to the exclusion of other possible interests. The influence of this case has been significant – probably more than is warranted given later developments in US and Canadian law. See, for example, Yaron, "Acting like owners."

could result, in effect, in there being fewer members of the pension plans themselves? This shift in position and decision-making, brought about by direct ownership, may be an extension of degree or a qualitatively different type of conflict than that in *Cowan*; the implication is the same. It places a new set of decisions in the hands of the controlling owner, the pension fund, that had to date been avoided through passive investment stances or mediated through the channel of moral suasion.

Finally, these new types of deals are a change in pension funds' involvement in the "paper economy" (short-term trading in securities) versus the productive "real economy" (real economy investment). As the size of the financial sector grew, especially in the 1990s in Canada and the United States, some economists began to observe and argue that there was a disjunction or uncoupling of the financial markets and real productive economy.[48] This argument took several forms, and rested in part on the modest levels of reinvestment of corporate savings in research, development, plant improvements and training. It was argued that these savings were being used instead to obtain returns in non-core investments, finance expensive mergers and acquisitions, buy-back shares or take corporations private, move companies offshore, and other such "non-productive" uses. In some respects, the churning of pension funds' investments in equities is an example of this "paper economy" that saw income generated through methods other than through investment and growth in a productive economy.

These new direct investments by pension funds appear to have the opposite effect: they can be direct investments in production, and potentially new production. There is some early research into these types of deals, typically by studying the short- or medium-term influence of one type of investors, for example hedge fund investments. At least one line suggests that these investments appear to be long-term and have positive corporate outcomes.[49] However, whether the long-termism (it is not possible to test some of these predictions for at least

---

[48] For a popular account, see J. Stanford, *Paper Boom: Why Real Prosperity Requires a New Approach to Canada's Economy* (Toronto: J. Lorimer & Co., 1999). For alternative approaches to finance's role in the "real economy" from a similar analytical perspective: see, for example, M. Konings and E. Engelen, "Financial capitalism resurgent: comparative institutionalism and the challenges of financialization," in G. Morgan, Colin Crouch, Ove Kai Pedersen and Richard Whitley (eds.), *The Oxford Handbook of Comparative Institutional Analysis* (Oxford: Oxford University Press, 2010).

[49] W. Bratton, "Hedge funds and governance targets" (2007) 95 *Georgetown Law Journal* 1375; F. Partnoy, A. Brav, W. Jiang and R. Thomas, "Hedge fund activism, corporate governance, and firm performance" (2008) 63 *Journal of Finance* 1729.

one business cycle) translates into higher real or productive corporate investment is not clear.

Viewing pension funds in this way – as conduits for saving to investment – brings up a fundamental comparison in corporate theory. Corporations were and still are characterized as having the same basic purpose: to aggregate otherwise disparate savings into productive and risk-taking investment. Although much corporate theory has gone on to qualify or deny this proposition, it remains one of the fundamental rationales for corporations and the public policy that creates and supports them.[50] Do pension funds meet this purpose?

One of the statistics cited above is suggestive of an answer. Pension funds in Canada might aggregate $20 billion a year on a cash flow basis.[51] They must invest this money, and do so. Although that is a significant amount of total savings, corporate savings were $118 billion during the same year, nearly six times the size.

Corporations' internal resources, even by this crude measure, appear much more significant than other capital market sources including pension funds – and internal savings are often the best form of capital for corporations because they come with the fewest new obligations and in theory at the lowest cost. This observation has been made in other places over time,[52] and it presents a fundamental challenge to the proposition that corporations use shareholders (their "owners") as a primary source of financing, or, put another way, aggregation of disparate shareholder savings to common productive risk capital.

Pension funds are, though, aggregators of individual savings for the purpose of investment. Whether it is because of their inherent

---

[50] See, for example, a standard Canadian corporate law text by A. Van Duzer, *The Law of Partnerships and Corporations*, 2nd edn (Toronto: Irwin, 2003).

[51] We might also note they provide about $8 billion in cash payments to individuals per year, an amount which, as it is being paid to retirees, ought to be mostly or totally spent in the period, and as such, have a "multiplier" effect in the broader economy.

[52] For a modeling of this observation, see S. Myers and N. Majluf "Corporate financing and investment decisions when firms have information that investors do not have," (NBER) Working Paper Series, Vol. 1396 (July, 1984); T. Jenkinson and J. Corbett, "The financing of industry, 1970–89: an international comparison," CEPR Discussion Papers 948 (1994) and "How is investment financed? A study of Germany, Japan, UK and US," (CEPR) Working Papers 16, American Institute for Contemporary German Studies (1997); M. O'Sullivan, "The expansion of the U.S. stock market, 1885–1930: historical facts and theoretical fashions" (2007) 8:3 *Enterprise and Society* 489. Henwood has noted that in the United States, the model of dispersed share markets, corporations have been retiring more shares than they have been issuing for the past twenty years – in effect, shedding shareholders. (Note though the opposite is true of Canada, which saw net retirement of shares for the first time in twenty years in 2006). Berle also measured the source of capital for corporations for the period 1919–1956, finding 80 percent of it to be from internal resources, somewhat higher than prior estimates (70 percent).

efficiencies (pooled assets improve leverage, diversification and otherwise spread risks across a greater number), or because of their coercive nature (pension plans are typically mandatory, where they are provided), or their incentive effects (tax policy defers tax paid on pension fund income), they have formed large pools of individuals' savings. The immediate question for corporate theory is, where do these funds fit in the savings-to-investment cycle?

It is difficult to form a single response to this question. Pension funds are mandated not to take extraordinary risks with investments, and have been, in large part, passive investors in only the safest equities and fixed income instruments. This is certainly how Berle described them in 1959, and that description has been borne out by the allocation patterns of pension funds between the 1960s and 1990s. Even in this characterization, however, Berle viewed pension funds as the "fission" of property from its owners – completing the work of corporate structures that he (and Gardiner Means) first observed in 1932.

Pension funds effectively speculated in capital gains starting during the 1980s and in earnest in the 1990s – the prudence of these investments does not matter, only the destination of the capital – and this may have fueled some actual direct investment in young and new corporate activity. The largest pension funds did compete in the venture capital and start-up financing, and there was some study of the crowding-out effects of this behavior when it extended into larger private equity plays. However on the whole pension funds "rode the market" in a long bull phase.

Finally, the direct investments in alternative assets sketched out above are much more like productive risk-taking capital, and not paper trading. The increasing allocations to alternative assets could be a significant opportunity to re-couple a fundamental purpose of capital markets in funding corporations. The data available for this study do not assist greatly in understanding the details of this coupling, but suggest it is a useful area for study.[53] Given the nature of the relationship to be studied – the flow of capital from pension fund through to alternative asset class and particular issuers, and the allocated use of that capital – it may require more in-depth and descriptive case studies in addition to empirical evidence. Some of this work has been done, although it does not typically extend into a broader "political economic" analysis.[54] This

---

[53] It would be useful, for example, to know how long pension funds hold assets in different classes, and a range of outcomes derived from the financing provided by the fund.
[54] See, for example, D. Cumming, "Private equity, leverage buyouts and governance" (2007) 13:4 *Journal of Corporate Finance* 439.

type of study would not only help describe the economics of the relationship between pension funds as aggregators of savings and issuers as recipients, but help to build an analysis of the political economy of the decision-making and relationship between pension funds and corporate investment. Corporations and pension funds appear in this view as a combination of command structures and networked relationships, nodes and relations. The merits of this descriptive lens are debatable, but the relationship to productive economic relations is perhaps the key element to understand for the purpose of corporate theory, and perhaps capital market theory.

V   Conclusions

Pension funds have become more active investors, but this has not translated into what is sometimes termed the "democratization of capital": there is not yet evidence that Canadian pension funds' investment behaviors are fundamentally altered by adopting corporate social responsibility or responsible investment screens, there is little evidence that pension funds are better or more active monitors than other investors, and in Canada at least, little evidence of pension funds making shareholder proposals or engaging in securities litigation. It has sparked a debate between those who would seek to close the perceived gap between ownership and control – in other words, those who seek to have beneficial owners exercise more control over the decision-making of intermediaries – on one hand, and those who view that very gap as essential to good corporate governance and proper decision-making by professional management.[55]

Traditionally, pension funds are thought to contribute to the stability of financial markets. They can provide "depth" and "liquidity" by being significant purchasers and sometimes sellers of securities. The aggregate statistical evidence suggests that pension funds still provide depth and liquidity to capital markets by virtue of their size and demand relative to other institutional investors and particularly relative to Canadian capital markets. During periods of crisis, like the recent one, pension funds also provide stability in their role as large securityholders. The intervention of a large provincial pension fund led to the restructuring of the asset-backed commercial paper market in Canada, for instance.

---

[55] L. Strine, Jr., "Toward common sense and common ground? Reflections on the shared interests of managers and labor in a more rational system of corporate governance" (2007) *Journal of Corporation Law*.

The difference in the role of pension funds between normal and unusual market conditions also suggests that the analysis of each set of conditions will differ: by definition in anomalous conditions it is much more difficult to study generalized behavior of markets and actors within them. Responses to crises, especially by state policy and regulators, tend to be ad hoc. In order to understand the role of pension funds (or any actor) under unusual conditions, it is necessary to engage in closer analysis by case-study or, where a set of power and decision-making relationships can be established, a political economy analysis. It is the characterization of unusual market events that draws attention to the need for research and policy analysis and frames or conditions the normative (regulatory and self-regulatory) responses to both normal and unusual market conditions.

However, there may be ways to resolve this paradox. There is some evidence that the (increasingly) sophisticated investment choices of pension funds, combined with their large positions and comparatively slow board-level decision-making, may be an important structural feature and catalyst of these financial crises. Pension funds' demand for more and sophisticated synthetic financial products, designed under normal conditions to mimic riskless, bond-like investments or investment strategies, may actually exacerbate some aspects of financial crises. More fundamentally, pension funds' size relative to domestic capital markets, and especially, the size of their positions relative to some securities, can itself move prices in the market for certain securities. In this respect, the liquidity pension funds provide to markets may not reflect new information and may distort price signals, at least in the short term.

Pension funds' changing source of revenues reveal two contrary observations about the connection between real and financial sectors. On one hand, pension funds in Canada became much more active traders of equities during the 1990s, and expanded their use of pooled funds. This trend shows greater participation in the "paper economy" of trading existing securities over the short-term, and suggests that pension funds are not acting as "patient capital" or long-term monitors, and do not provide significant direct investment to the real economy. On the other hand, it appears that where size and prudence permit, allocations to alternative asset classes are increasing. These investments provide a much closer connection to real economy investment and reinvestment, and as a result, bring up a series of "active management" and even political questions, particularly in infrastructure investment, but also in private equity placements and real estate.

The size and concentration of pension funds is perhaps the most easily observed factor driving their evolution. The declining prevalence of defined benefit pensions economy-wide and the economics of scale both indicate pressures to consolidate the provision of pensions and the administration of their assets. This creates a small group of very large capital market institutions that have evolved from passive investors to very active ones, and no longer merely investors – they are now also sellers of financial services. This consolidation (termination of small plans and merger of others) leads in all likelihood to a rationalization or consolidation of service providers to pension funds. This includes a consolidation in legal but particularly in actuarial services, such as the recent merger of Towers Perrin and Watson Wyatt in Canada. It also leads to new business lines for large pension funds in providing institutional and perhaps even eventually retail investment management services and benefit provision.

Each of these features of pension funds brings up a fundamental purpose and function of both corporate theory and capital markets: what are the implications for the funding of corporations? Back in 1959 Adolph Berle argued that pension funds completed the "fission" of shareholders from their "property," and, in that context, noted that capital markets provide perhaps less than 25 percent of the capital used by corporations. The experience of Canadian pension funds in the 1990s is consistent with this observation, the implication being that corporations (and capital markets) do perform valuation functions such as sending price signals and providing a mechanism to change patterns of ownership and control, but on the whole they did not aggregate disparate investors' capital toward productive real economy investment. However, as pension funds increase allocations to alternative assets, this characterization erodes.

10 Credit derivatives market design: creating fairness and sustainability

Janis Sarra

I Introduction

Now that the first wave of the financial crisis has been resolved through the coordinated efforts of regulators and banks, it is important to address some of the systematic weaknesses of the current financial system. One such weakness is the inappropriate incentive effects of the market for credit derivatives, and in particular, for credit default swaps. As a risk management tool, credit derivatives were originally an effective means of diversifying lending risk. Credit derivatives have worked to cover exposures where there have been credit events of the underlying reference entities.

However, as products proliferated in number and complexity, they have caused some negative consequences, increasing risk of losses for less sophisticated investors, creating excessive exposures for banks and other entities, and creating negative incentives in respect of financially distressed companies. In part, the risks arose because of the expansion to markets involving asset-backed commercial paper, residential mortgages and other products where some of the underlying assets had been inappropriately valued or rated and thus risk mispriced. In part, these risks arose when derivatives became part of the "originate and distribute" model of lending; and in part, they arose from the speculative market for these products, which has shifted derivatives to some extent from their original risk diversification purposes.

To date, the global market for derivatives has operated largely without regulatory oversight; yet it is increasingly evident that deficiencies in the market contributed, at least in part, to the liquidity crisis in the financial sector, resulting in massive injections of public funds in numerous jurisdictions. As structural adjustments are being made to

My sincere thank you to George Triantis, Edward Waitzer, Michael Mainelli, Ronald B. Davis, Eric Talley, Sam Robbins and Cynthia Williams for their thoughtful comments on the draft. Originally written for distribution by the Network for Sustainable Financial Markets, Consultation Paper No. 2, 2009.

ensure long-term financial stability, the credit derivative market needs timely, targeted and effective adjustment, with a measure of regulatory oversight.

Credit default swaps (CDS), by far the most common form of credit derivative, are illustrative. There are two critical points at which intervention is required. The first is at the purchase and sale stage, where there is a serious lack of transparency regarding both material adverse risks associated with the reference entity and material risk in respect of the protection seller's ability to settle the CDS if a credit event occurs. There is also a lack of due diligence and disclosure by those who are recommending CDS products to less sophisticated purchasers. Second, at the point of settlement and restructuring proceedings, there is a threat to current public policy goals of rehabilitating financially distressed businesses where they are viable, given structural and incentive effects for derivatives that are both physically and cash settled. The disconnection between economic interest and legal interest runs contrary to fundamental insolvency law principles adopted by numerous jurisdictions. In this respect, there needs to be a balancing of public law principles, those advancing the goals of insolvency law and those advancing the effective operation of capital markets. At times they align, at others, they are in sharp discord.

This brief chapter addresses these two issues, offering ten recommendations for immediate action. More fundamentally, there needs to be public debate regarding the "casino" aspect of the current market for credit derivatives.

II   Credit derivatives, distinguishing risk management tool from speculative market

Credit derivatives are financial instruments that allow parties to manage credit exposure. There are numerous kinds of credit derivatives, such as credit default swaps, collateralized debt obligations (CDO), full and index trades, and credit-linked notes. Credit derivatives are classified as either single or multi-name (basket) products. Single-name credit derivatives are targeted on the creditworthiness of a single reference entity. Multi-name products hedge the risk of clustered defaults in a portfolio.[1] A credit derivative can be a privately negotiated agreement that explicitly shifts credit risk from one party to the other; or it can be

---

[1] Elizabeth Murphy, Janis Sarra and Michael Creber, "Credit Derivatives in Canadian Insolvency Proceedings, the Devil will be in the Details" (2006) *Annual Review of Insolvency Law* 187–234.

collateralized and housed within a special purpose vehicle that resells debt contracts in various tranches at differing prices, quality and risk. CDO can be cash flow based, whereby the vehicle issues its own financial instruments to finance purchase of debts of different corporate entities, ensuring a fixed flow of loan repayments that are used to pay investors in the various tranches; or CDO can be synthetic, whereby the entity does not directly purchase debts but, rather, enters into credit default swaps with a third party, creating synthetic exposure to the debt of a number of corporate entities.[2]

The most common credit derivative, a credit default swap (CDS), is a credit derivative contract in which one party, the "protection buyer," pays a sum of money periodically to the "protection seller," usually referable to the amount of protection provided by the contract. The protection seller's obligation to pay arises on the occurrence of a credit event, most frequently, the reference entity's failure to pay, bankruptcy or restructuring. The reference entity is not a party to the credit default swap. The protection buyer that is a creditor of the reference entity hedges the risk of default by that entity, and takes on the risk of default by the protection seller. The protection seller acquires the default risk of the reference entity. Unlike insurance, the amount of compensation that can be claimed under a credit derivative is not related to the actual losses suffered by the protection buyer.[3] Credit derivatives do not require either the protection seller or protection buyer to actually hold an interest in the referenced asset; therefore the protection purchased by the protection buyer can be more than, less than, or completely unconnected to its underlying exposure to the reference entity.

Credit derivatives emerged in the early 1990s as a tool for banks to manage their credit risk in respect of entities that they had directly invested in through their lending activities, diversifying their risk on loan default. In this respect, credit derivatives were initially effective in cushioning the commercial banks' losses in notable cases such as Enron and Parmalat. The market grew in less than two decades to an estimated USD 62 trillion in CDS alone at the end of 2007. During this period, three significant changes occurred in the market.

First, the original objective of banks managing risk of direct investment under lending portfolios was overtaken by a speculative market for buying and selling derivatives in multiples of the value of the

---

[2] International Swaps and Derivatives Association (ISDA), 2006, www.isdadocs.org/index.html (last accessed February 22, 2011).
[3] The protection buyer need not suffer an actual loss to be eligible for compensation if a credit event occurs.

underlying reference assets or entities, resulting in a significant trading market involving a greater number of market participants.

Second, global credit derivatives exposures by ratings shifted downward. In 2002, 36 percent of all credit derivatives globally were rated at AA or AAA, whereas only 8 percent were rated as below investment grade. Just four years later, in 2006, only 17 percent of credit derivatives globally were rated at AA or AAA, whereas 31 percent were now rated as below investment grade.[4] Counterparty risk was heavily concentrated among the top twenty global banks and broker dealers, including Bear Sterns, Lehman Brothers, AIG, Merrill Lynch and Royal Bank of Scotland.[5]

Third, the banks' market share declined as hedge funds increasingly took a greater share of both the buy side and sell side of the market. In 2000, banks accounted for 81 percent of the buy side and 63 percent of the sell side of market share, that number dropping to 59 percent and 44 percent respectively by 2006. Hedge funds went from 3 percent of the market on the buy side in 2000 to 28 percent market share in 2006. As a seller, their market share grew from 5 to 32 percent market share in the same period.[6] Those derivatives were then hedged in further credit derivatives in multiples of the value of the originating reference entities. The hedge funds were a major driver of change in the market. The reasons for the move down the credit curve included tight spreads; as margins squeezed at the upper end of credit curve, to maintain returns, investors shifted to more speculative investment grades and unrated exposures.

Together, these changes altered the credit derivatives market significantly, without any jurisdiction seriously assessing the public policy implications. The risks associated with these products were highly opaque, given the complexity and constantly changing nature of the products. Market participants have had varying reasons for involvement in the credit derivatives market, often on both the buy and sell side. Protection buyers may use credit derivatives to manage portfolio uncertainties, including to hedge over concentrations in loan portfolios, free up economic or regulatory capital, and avoid sales of bond holdings. Protection sellers may be in the market to increase exposure to sectors, diversify investment portfolios, enhance relative value of trades, exploit yield alternatives, and provide capital arbitrage.[7] As a

---

[4] Fitch Ratings, discussed in Murphy *et al.*, "Credit Derivatives."
[5] *Ibid.*
[6] British Bankers Association, *Credit Derivatives Report*, 2006.
[7] As this chapter is being finalized, the United States is in the process of enacting the Restoring American Financial Stability Act of 2010, under which Title VII, the Wall Street Transparency and Accountability Act of 2010, accords regulatory oversight of over-the-counter swaps markets and a number of other structured financial products to the Commodities and Futures Exchange Commission (CFTC) and the SEC.

risk management tool, CDS could continue to be effective, with some adjustment to the market. As a speculative market product, there needs to be a more fundamental regulatory shift, given the social and economic harm they can cause.

While the appeal of CDS is ostensibly that they can be tailored to the individual contract, the reality is that most are now off-the-shelf standardized products with industry wide standard terms developed by the International Swaps and Derivatives Association (ISDA), with tuning primarily in respect of the reference entity and only a few business terms. Most credit derivative transactions, including most CDS, are not funded, but may be subject to margin and collateral arrangements depending on the counterparty. The ISDA standard form CDS is silent on obligations of the protection buyer regarding its knowledge of material adverse information in regard to the reference entity.

Although there is some jurisdictional lack of clarity, derivatives have been found to be covered by financial services or securities legislation where they trade in public markets in some jurisdictions, but had been often viewed by regulators as part of the exempt market, assuming sophistication of parties. Other jurisdictions, such as the United States and its Securities and Exchange Commission(SEC), did not have any regulatory control over CDS or other swaps.[8] In the absence of regulatory oversight, courts have generally looked to the wording of the derivative contract or industry standards, creating considerable incentives for parties to dispute the meaning of contract terms when a credit event occurs.[9]

Hedge funds and other derivatives traders have engaged in market trading that speculated heavily on the reference entity's risk. The reselling of that risk, in tranches that moved progressively down the rating scale, to purchasers with little or no information of the underlying risk of the derivative, created a serious disconnect between the value of the reference entity and its assets and the derivatives written on them. There is asymmetry of information between the knowledge of risk of the originating lender and the credit risk transferred to subsequent investors because there is no obligation to disclose material adverse risk on either the buy or sell side of protection.

Many outstanding derivative contracts can aggregate five to ten times the amount of creditor claims.[10] For example, the insolvency of Delphi

---

[8] Except under anti-fraud powers where they are considered securities. SEC Chair Christopher Cox, presentation to the US Senate Banking Committee, September 23, 2008; Securities Exchange Act 1934, 15 USC 78.
[9] For a discussion, see Murphy *et al.*, "Credit Derivatives."
[10] *Ibid.*

in the United States revealed that there was USD 25 billion in outstanding credit derivatives on USD 2 billion of Delphi bonds. While the liquidity of the products assisted in hedging risk in a number of instances, the CDS evolved from being a risk management tool to a primarily credit trading tool and the volume of CDS trades began to outpace the outstanding bond issuance of that credit. Hence CDS outstanding were greater by multiples than the volume of bonds. Where there was a requirement for physical settlement on occurrence of a credit event, protection buyers would have to go to the open market to source bonds.[11] Professor Mainelli has also observed that "slicing and dicing tranches" led to abnormal bucket distributions and greater sensitivity to rating changes.[12] When the financial markets began to seriously deteriorate, the CDS exposures of counterparties became evident, creating a major crisis in the ability of protection sellers to ensure coverage. One immediate cause of the AIG Insurance liquidity crisis, for example, was a requirement that its financial products subsidiary post additional cash collateral on its outstanding CDS obligations due to its over-exposure.[13] At the point of the US government bailout, AIG had outstanding more than USD 446 billion of CDS liabilities.

Equally significant, protection buyers are relying on the financial viability of the protection seller so that their claims can be met at the point of a credit event in respect of the reference entity, yet there is no disclosure required by the protection seller of its capacity to settle the derivatives if the specified credit event occurs. In this respect, credit derivatives differ from other bilateral contracts where the creditworthiness of a counterparty is typically dealt with through negotiated credit controls, including collateral requirements, covenants, representations and warranties, and the oversight of a credit officer. In order to facilitate their liquidity, many such terms are not negotiated in CDS and there is a lack of oversight. The ISDA has observed that swaps and related over the counter (OTC) derivatives combine characteristics of loans with those of traded capital market instruments; the swap transaction creates a credit relationship between the counterparties, the terms of which are documented just as the terms of a traditional loan, but unlike a loan, swaps are traded in the market and renegotiation of credit terms for each transaction would be costly in a system of repeated interaction between counterparties, creating a drag on trading

---

[11] ISDA, "2006 report."
[12] Michael Mainelli, email correspondence to the author, October 10, 2008.
[13] AIG Insurance was required to begin to book billions of dollars of losses as the risk exposure on CDS sold by it rose in price with the deteriorating credit position of the reference entities.

activity.¹⁴ Consequently, the ISDA Master Agreement contains the "non-economic" terms such as representations and warranties, events of default and termination events, leaving counterparties to negotiate only the "economic" terms such as rate or price, notional amount and collateral.¹⁵

While standardization of terms in derivatives can reduce transaction costs and create a more liquid market for derivatives, the standardized terms have been developed by industry participants, arguably with their own interests in mind. Proprietary and confidentiality agreements mean that there is little public exposure to, or debate regarding, the risks and benefits associated with the terms. Standards developed solely though the participation of a small number of industry participants can lead to further information asymmetries, collective action problems for end-purchasers of derivatives, and arguably, risk of self-dealing conduct by those setting the standards. To date, the judiciary in Canada and elsewhere have simply deferred unquestioningly to industry set standards because of the lack of counterparties with the information, skill or resources to argue that the standards may not always be the appropriate measure of parties' agreed upon risk.

Credit derivatives also pose challenges for regulatory oversight in some jurisdictions such as the European Union (EU), where insider trading prohibitions are considerably robust.¹⁶ The EU Joint Market Practices Forum has published recommendations for the handling of material non-public information by credit market participants, including recommending that prohibitions on insider dealing should apply to dealings in any security-related credit derivative, specifically, a financial instrument "whose value depends on a publicly-traded security."¹⁷ The working group sought to maintain compliance with the principles of the EU's Market Abuse Directive; suggesting that lenders that hedge credit risk by purchasing CDS referencing their borrowers may possess material non-public information and may be found subject to a duty of trust and confidence owed to their borrower.¹⁸ As with other

---

[14] ISDA, "2006 Report."
[15] The ISDA Master Agreement includes provisions that facilitate payment netting and close-out netting.
[16] Joint Market Practices Forum, *Statement of Principles and Recommendations regarding the Handling of Material Non-Public Information by Credit Market Participants*, European Supplement, 2005. Henry Hu and Bernard Black, "Debt, Equity and Hybrid Decoupling; Governance and Systemic Risk Implications" (2008) 17 *European Financial Management* 1 briefly discuss insider trading and cross-market manipulations.
[17] Joint Market Practices Forum, *Statement of Principles*.
[18] *Ibid.*

financial services markets, failure to disclose material adverse risk can affect the credibility of the derivatives market, and arguably, the creation of standards to require such disclosure in the credit derivative market would assist in preventing some aspects of the current financial instability.

Arguably, there are two significant aspects of the credit derivatives market that require immediate attention. The first is how to address the principal-agency problems generated by the disconnection between legal interest and economic interest. The second is how to address the recent shift in externalities associated with credit derivatives.

III   Principal-agency issue

There are significant agency issues that have arisen with respect to credit derivatives. First, there are inappropriate incentives created by the use of CDS in multiple values of the original debt. Traditionally, a creditor's interest in a debtor company was to receive return of its capital plus interest and fees, often premised on encouraging an ongoing credit relationship with the business enterprise. The introduction of CDS in some instances has created a misalignment between the creditor's and debtor's interests. A creditor can lend an amount to a debtor company and then purchase CDS many times the value of the underlying reference asset or entity. Thus the creditor has an incentive to have the debtor company fail, triggering a credit event in which the value to the creditor from settlement of the CDS is greater than repayment of the loan. If the creditor is a senior lender, it may be able to precipitate the credit event. Some of the previous willingness by lenders to not enforce covenants for a limited period in order to allow a debtor time to devise a business plan may be less likely now that the lender is not only fully hedged, but over hedged.[19]

Second, there are agency issues between tranches of creditors under originate and distribute lending. Securitization of debt through CDOs and other derivatives creates incentives for the originating lender not to be duly diligent in its lending decisions, as it can offload the risk to the purchasers of various tranches of the debt.[20] Under this model, there are few incentives for the originating lender to exact protective

---

[19] Hu and Black, "Hybrid Decoupling." They call this over-hedging of debt "negative economic ownership." They observe that there can also be "hybrid" decoupling, whereby investors short their shares, buying protection with credit default swaps or use a long equity position to hedge a short debt position, *ibid.*, at pp. 2, 19.

[20] The sub-prime mortgage lending in the United States and consequent crisis is an example of this agency problem.

covenants or undertake monitoring on an ongoing basis, given that risk of default is borne by other parties. Over multiple similar transactions, these disincentives can cause a market crisis. Yet for derivatives markets to function, the incentives of originators should be better aligned with those of end purchasers. A third agency issue is with respect to incentives in insolvency restructuring proceedings, discussed below.

These incentives shift credit decisions away from the merits of a company's business plan and create risks for less senior creditors. One option to address the issue would be to require that a proportion of the exposure be left on the originating lender's balance sheet or that a seasoning period be required before the debt can be sold. Such requirements could address some of the immediate agency issues associated with the speculative market.

There is another agency aspect of the credit derivatives market; the problems associated with credit ratings, particularly in respect of synthetic derivatives. In brief, there are at least two potential explanations. The first is that credit rating agencies developed inadequate valuation methods to assess these products, valuing the debt in various tranches higher than the cost of the underlying asset, making them attractive to sellers, but creating new counterparty risks, or that the agencies accepted the methodology developed by investment banks structuring CDOs without separate assessment. The other explanation is the "regulatory license" explanation offered by Professor Partnoy, specifically, that credit rating agencies served as gate-openers rather than gatekeepers by actively promoting synthetic derivatives in a conflict of interest situation as their fees come from those that they are rating, and those entities have no real choice of rating agency, given the closed market created by regulators.[21] There were few incentives to properly value the products. The sales-driven nature of the financial services sector exacerbated these conflicts of interest, including commission driven remuneration and entrenched concentration on short-term returns. Mainelli would resolve the problem by requiring indemnification by parties promoting products, using liability risk as the motivating factor in enhancing market transparency.[22] Since credit rating agencies are paid by the banks or other entities issuing derivatives, either they

---

[21] Frank Partnoy, "How and Why Credit Rating Agencies are Not Like Other Gatekeepers," May 2006, http://ssrn.com/abstract=900257 (last accessed February 22, 2011). See also M. Zelmer, "Reforming the Credit-Rating Process," *Financial System Review* 51 (Ottawa: Bank of Canada, December 2007).

[22] Michael Mainelli, "Standards Markets? The Free Market Response to Regulation," October 16, 2006, www.gresham.ac.uk/event.asp?EventId=513&PageId=108 (last accessed February 22, 2011).

should be required to disclose the fees they are receiving for the ratings, including any additional consulting fees from the same entity, or there should be a prohibition on payment for ratings.[23] On a more fundamental basis, there is a public policy question as to whether credit ratings are the appropriate vehicle to control risk. Credit rating agency incentives must be aligned more closely with those of derivatives purchasers as investors.[24] New legislation creating oversight regimes is being adopted in the EU, Japan and elsewhere.[25] In the United States, the SEC is proposing creation of a more robust regulatory framework for credit rating agencies, designed to improve the quality of ratings by requiring greater disclosure, addressing conflicts of interest, shedding light on rating shopping and promoting accountability.[26]

IV   Shifting externalities

Historically, there were positive externalities associated with commercial bank lending.[27] Banks assisted in correcting governance problems of firms, such as managerial slack, through their monitoring activities, given their superior access to information under loan covenants, and through direct intervention with corporate officers or exiting the relationship, signaling to other creditors that there were problems with the debtor company.[28] Stakeholders benefited from the bank's governance role in this respect. A fundamental assumption underlying this theory of interactive corporate governance, developed by Professors Triantis and Daniels, was that all stakeholders shared the goal of firm-value maximization.[29] The positive externality for corporate stakeholders was that they could be confident that the bank was engaged in a measure of monitoring and oversight of the firm's solvency, an important benefit for trade suppliers, employees and others that did not have the

---

[23] Michael Mainelli, "Assessing Credit Rating Agencies: Quis Aestimat Ipsos Aestimatores?," "Balance Sheet," *The Michael Mainelli Column*, Volume 11, Number 3, pp. 55–58, MCB University Press (August 2003); www.zyen.com/Knowledge/Articles/Balance%20Sheet%200803.pdf (last accessed February 22, 2011).
[24] Mainelli, "Standards Markets?" would encourage markets that would use innovative regulation to achieve multiple societal goals and enhanced quality through reputational risk and competition.
[25] Financial Stability Forum, *Improving Financial Regulation*, September 25, 2009, www.financialstabilityboard.org/publications/r_090925b.pdf.
[26] Mary Shapiro, Chair, SEC, February 5, 2010.
[27] Externalities occur when an economic activity causes an external benefit or cost to third party stakeholders that were not directly involved in the transaction.
[28] George C. Triantis and Ronald Daniels, "The Role of Debt in Interactive Corporate Governance" (1995) *University of California Law Review* 83, 1073–1113.
[29] *Ibid.*, p. 1081.

bargaining power to extract disclosure and default control rights. To the extent that the bank's monitoring deterred debtor misconduct or shirking, it reduced the risk on all the firm's debt. For companies that relied increasingly on the public debt markets, while the indenture trustee often had limited responsibility to monitor compliance, issuers frequently were required to back their commercial paper with lines of credit from banks, with the banks serving a similar governance role.[30]

Hence, the screening and monitoring activities of a lender produced externalities that benefited numerous stakeholders with an interest in the corporation, through the bank's decision to lend, which signaled to potential and existing stakeholders the quality of the borrower; through the imposition of fixed obligations under the loan agreement that prevented managerial slack; through security rights that constrained the ability of managers to liquidate non-cash assets or unilaterally sell more debt; and through loan covenants and monitoring of specified prohibited types of behavior.[31] Triantis and Daniels called this feature "interdependent screening" to describe externalities that flow not only among creditors, but also from lenders to shareholders, employees and other stakeholders.[32]

The exponential growth in use of credit derivatives has shifted the externalities in a way that may contribute to market destabilization. First, the disconnection between economic interest and residual control rights can create new incentives, in that originating lenders may be less willing to expend the time and resources to undertake due diligence in undertaking credit arrangements, as risk is laid off through derivatives under the originate and distribute model. Hence the signaling to the market that occurred with the decision to lend is no longer reliable as a measure of the firm's value. Second, in the purchase and sale of credit derivatives, parties have frequently given up the negotiation of terms and conditions, including monitoring, restrictive covenants and default control rights, because they know that they will offset their own risk through other structured financial products. Hence that prior positive externality may be lost as senior creditors no longer undertake

---

[30] *Ibid.*, pp. 1084, 1088–1089.
[31] *Ibid.*, p. 1079.
[32] Triantis and Daniels observe that a "bank's choice between exit and voice is based on a self-interested evaluation of the relative net benefits from each option. A bank that exits enjoys the benefit of a more certain recovery of its investment. However, it bears transaction and regulatory costs of exit, incurs search and transaction costs in entering into new lending arrangements, and may forgo the opportunity to finance a revitalized borrower in the future. In addition, bank management may be reluctant to abandon a sunk investment, even if a prospective cost-benefit calculation favors exit." *Ibid.*, p. 1084.

monitoring and strategic intervention. When the firm begins to slide into financial distress, corporate stakeholders no longer share a common goal of maximizing firm value and constraining managerial slack because the originating lender has hedged its risk through its derivatives, and multiple subsequent counterparties have done the same. Stakeholders that could previously rely on the governance role of banks can no longer do so; yet given the diverse nature of their interests, information asymmetries and collective action problems, they are unlikely to be able to fill this governance gap.

This shift in how parties purchase and sell debt may not be significant for a single swap transaction, but multiplied many times through complex derivative transactions and multiple swaps, previous positive externalities are lost and new negative externalities are created, creating more systemic risks across the market. The move to standardize derivatives contracts, while arguably efficient in terms of controlling transaction costs, may exacerbate this risk through the reduction or elimination of debt governance covenants. Moreover, the signaling that occurred through exit or other creditor reactions to the debtor's decisions is diminished because banks and other significant lenders may be fully hedged. Yet that fact is not transparent to other stakeholders, who may still look for such signaling. Given the global nature of credit derivatives, the externalities may create systemic problems that require more broad-based intervention than merely improving disclosure.

There may be additional externalities. Hu and Black have observed that when credit derivatives impede the normal negotiations between creditors and debtors in that borrowers can less easily renegotiate terms and conditions with lenders, there is heavier reliance on liquidity and the ability to refinance.[33] Spread across the economy, the freezing of such relationships may increase systemic financial risk as it increases the economy's exposure to liquidity shocks.[34]

What targeted intervention in the credit derivatives market might look like is difficult to discern. Imposition of some sort of fiduciary obligation on either one or both counterparties presents formidable challenges in determining what the scope of such an obligation would entail and how it would be enforced, particularly when end purchasers are widely dispersed and face serious collective action problems. If one restricts the supply of derivatives products, the products will simply relocate to other jurisdictions, given their high degree of mobility. Increased transparency is one necessary measure; however, enhancing

---

[33] *Ibid.*
[34] Hu and Black, "Hybrid Decoupling."

disclosure alone does not ensure that purchasers can properly interpret the information, nor does it assist in offering remedies for misconduct.

One possible way to compensate for potential negative externalities is to set a price for participation in the market. For example, one could tax credit derivatives on a per transaction basis. A small amount on each transaction could be placed in a central trust fund in the domestic jurisdiction in which the credit derivative is being purchased. That fund would be available to counterparties that had been unfairly harmed by failure to disclose or other misconduct by market participants, or could be restricted to payments during financial crises. Not unlike deposit insurance funds or pension guarantee funds, the fund would be available, to some specified cap, to cushion such losses. The fund could possibly be empowered to then impose risk-based levies on the counterparties causing the losses, in an attempt to partially recover where the counterparty was solvent. On insolvency, such a claim by the fund would be eligible for debt to equity conversion along with other creditors' claims. Such a strategy would spread the cost of misconduct across parties most actively buying and selling CDS and other derivatives, would allow cost recovery against specific counterparties in some cases, and would diminish the risk of unfair losses to end purchasers.

V   Central counterparty clearing facilities

The recent introduction of the first central counterparty clearing platform (CCP) is aimed at increasing transparency for derivatives market participants and offer a means of imposing risk controls such as robust margin requirements to hinder the accumulation of large and uncollateralized CDS positions.[35] The existence of a sufficiently capitalized CCP means that counterparties do not have to rely on the capacity of the counterparty to settle the swap when a credit event occurs. The "risk" is shifted to the CCP, but it has controlled this risk through capital adequacy and other requirements for parties to be eligible to clear on the CCP. The UK financial authorities have observed that "a CCP can impose consistent and robust risk management practices as well as act as a circuit breaker to the default of a member. In addition, greater use of CCP clearing can aid market liquidity and efficiency, be a motivating force behind contract standardisation, and reduce systemic

---

[35] Press Release, US Dept. of the Treasury, Regulatory Reform Over-The-Counter (OTC) Derivatives (May 13, 2009), www.ustreas.gov/press/releases/tg129.htm (last accessed February 22, 2011).

risk."[36] CCPs are now available to financial institutions to allow for purchase and sale of derivatives and fluidity of settlements. They do not, however, address any of the incentives that were driving the market at the time of the failure, and arguably, they continue to support the speculative aspects of the market by facilitating the transactions. While CCPs do address some important aspects of systemic risk, their entry into the market may have short circuited a broader normative public policy discussion about the need for a speculative market on top of the risk management benefits of the market, as well as the discussion about the ability of financial products markets to seriously undermine real economic activity.

The introduction of CCPs will reduce settlement risk for financial institutions. The premise is that there are adequate capital adequacy requirements in place to hedge against counterparty failure and that access to the CCP is based on a measure of experience and sophistication. CCPs do not yet address non-financial derivatives participants, nor are they aimed at any normative determination of the risks associated with particular products or the downstream harms that may occur from particular products being in the marketplace.[37] Moreover, to date there is little regulatory oversight, approvals largely taking the form of exemptions from particular market requirements as opposed to active oversight to reduce systemic risk. There continues to be a serious lack of transparency in respect of the products in the market, their settlement and any specific or systemic risks posed. To date, regulators have only limited access and limited authority to information from CCPs, arguably posing new kinds of systemic risks. Globally, regulators are working to try to agree on data reporting from CCPs, but to date there are few requirements and no harmonization.

There are three further public policy issues that need to be considered, but which are beyond the scope of this discussion. The first is how mark-to-market accounting has influenced and been influenced by the credit derivatives market and whether or not it should be adjusted to

---

[36] Financial Services Authority & HM Treasury, *Reforming OTC Derivative Markets, A UK Perspective*, December 2009, p. 11.
[37] The UK Treasury and the FSA have proposed measures to address systemic shortcomings in OTC derivative markets, including greater standardization of OTC derivatives contracts to enhance the efficiency of operational processes; facilitating the increased use of CCP clearing and trading on organized trading platforms; and supporting greater comparability of trade information. IOSCO and the Basel committees are discussing revision of existing standards and the European Commission (EC) is considering a Clearing Directive as a tool to mitigating any risk. Financial Services Authority & HM Treasury, *Reforming OTC Derivative Markets*.

account for current financial uncertainty.[38] Mark-to-market accounting requires that asset price shocks be reflected on balance sheets, creating their own shocks and raising the question of whether market prices appropriately reflect economic value or whether this approach fosters greater uncertainty for investors.[39] Second, there should be public policy discussion as to whether any regulatory intervention should distinguish between sophisticated and less sophisticated derivatives market participants. Arguably, more sophisticated purchasers can price risk in future derivatives agreements or bargain particular governance and monitoring controls. If so, perhaps regulation needs to focus on ensuring that risk moves to those parties that have the capacity for such risk bearing, protecting the more vulnerable market participants. Third, given the clear connection between financial services market design and operation and its impact on real economic activity and social security, there should be new strategies developed that promote long-term wealth generation, including consideration of incorporating environmental, social and governance issues in financial product design.[40]

Some ideas for addressing problems in the credit derivatives market are innovative and far reaching, requiring broad-based public discussion that allows for measured and effective change to be developed, which can be broadly endorsed by multiple jurisdictions. In the interim, some initial steps could be taken to enhance the fairness of

---

[38] Under current mark-to-market, some long-term investors face pressure to sell their CDS because of short-term funding requirements. The opacity of structured financial products has made them harder to value, thus negatively affecting secondary market liquidity. For a discussion, see J. Sarra, "Restructuring of the Asset-Backed Commercial Paper Market in Canada" (2008) *Annual Review of Insolvency Law*. Essentially, by reflecting market moves, fair value accounting increases the volatility of reported earnings. Arguably, officers' incentives to realize mark-to-market losses are also influenced by the extent to which their investors will reward or penalize them for how they value downside risk.

[39] The Financial Stability Forum has made recommendations regarding accounting and valuation procedures for financial derivative instruments that are difficult to price in times of market stress. Current accounting rules do not allow valuation to be expressed as a range of potential outcomes, yet allowing such disclosure could offer greater information to market participants; www.fsforum.org (last accessed February 22, 2011). The Forum suggests that banks' disclosures of their on- and off-balance sheet risk exposures have been materially improved in the past year. New disclosure standards for banks have been issued covering valuation and liquidity risk, securitization and off-balance sheet activities; *Improving Financial Regulation*, September 25, 2009, www.financialstabilityboard.org/publications/r_090925b.pdf (last accessed February 22, 2011).

[40] See, for example, FSA *Retail Distribution Review Consultation Paper*, December 2009; Australia *Parliamentary Inquiry into Financial Products and Services* (Ripoll Inquiry), www.aph.gov.au/Senate/committee/corporations_ctte/fps/media_releases/feb09.pdf (last accessed February 22, 2011).

the credit derivatives market, in turn increasing the sustainability of financial markets, while dampening the negative speculative aspects of the market. While these steps alone would not have prevented the market meltdown, they could have mitigated the degree of harm to end purchasers. Aspects of the derivatives market resemble a securities market more than a traditional loan relationship, and disclosure reduces information asymmetries and risks associated with the inability to negotiate covenants and other protections. A few initial changes could facilitate the appropriate analysis and pricing of risk. As a general principle, regulation should be principles-based and outcomes focused, intervening where the market itself has failed to adequately produce standards of fairness, transparency or sustainability. There needs to be space to develop alternate standards or approaches where there is a problem identified in the market, and the current structure does not allow for full consideration of the public policy implications of changes made by the industry.

VI Recommendations for point of purchase and sale

1. Information asymmetries in the OTC market must be reduced through disclosure requirements that are targeted, and measured against potential outcomes. The underlying principle is that there must be sufficient disclosure of material information to allow market participants to make informed choices about credit derivative investment.
    i. Protection buyers should be required to disclose, at the time of purchase, any material adverse risk in the reference entity that they are aware of or ought reasonably to be aware of, in order that protection sellers can appropriately price the contract. Materiality in this respect could be based on a standard of whether the facts in respect of the adverse risk reasonably would be expected to have a significant effect on the protection seller's valuation or pricing of the derivative.
    ii. Protection sellers should be required to disclose any material adverse risk to their financial health at the time of the sale and/or renewal of a derivative contract, and could have an ongoing disclosure requirement regarding material adverse change to their ability to settle the derivative at the point of a credit event occurring.
    iii. Publicly traded companies should be required to disclose the effect of credit derivatives on their risk exposure, including how their credit risk has affected valuation of derivative liabilities and

any resulting gain or loss included in earnings statements, and any known information on how counterparty credit risk may have affected their valuation of, or ability to collect on, derivative assets. While some jurisdictions may now require such disclosure as part of their financial services requirements, it should be more broadly and consistently available.

The outcome sought by this recommendation is to reduce the potential for unnecessary and unfair financial loss for market participants through greater transparency regarding material risk. It would require plain and timely disclosure of such information to retail and other purchasers as an investor protection measure. In essence, it is a principle or standard, with the mechanics of how that disclosure is to occur left to market participants to develop.

2. Financial institutions and other parties that create new tranches of derivatives must disclose underlying material risks to the derivatives to counterparties. Counterparties and retail investors purchasing derivatives should have enforceable remedies for the failure of these entities and individuals to disclose material adverse risks at the point of sale of the derivatives. Materiality could be based on a standard of whether the facts in respect of the adverse risk reasonably would be expected to have a significant effect on the potential counterparty or retail investor's valuation or pricing of the derivative.
   i. Improve the usefulness and accessibility of disclosure, offering purchasers alternatives, industry benchmarks, comparative information on price and risk, and a more comprehensive understanding of the range of risk associated with different products.

The outcome sought is to ensure that a standard of greater transparency is applicable to new products as they develop, allowing for market innovation while trying both to ensure that there is sufficient information in the market to assess and price risk, and ensure that those making the products available are providing a type of indemnification in respect of the product in terms of assurances that the material adverse risks are known by the counterparties at the time of sale. However, transparency is only one measure, and in itself will not eliminate conflicts of interest, particularly in jurisdictions that impose minimal rules based compliance rather than a culture of responsible activity and compliance.

3. Financial services advisors, credit rating and other entities that recommend investment in derivatives should meet a due diligence standard in examining and disclosing material adverse risk in the derivative products being sold in the public market, including having

research standards and processes that generate appropriate rating of products.
   i. There should be a fiduciary obligation imposed on financial advisors, particularly in respect of advice to non-sophisticated market participants.
   ii. Credit rating agencies should be required to disclose all fees associated with a rating, as well as consulting and other fees received from the bank or other entity selling the derivatives, disclosure that enable purchasers to understand conflicts of interest and other factors that influence the robustness of the advice given, and transparency in respect of the range of fee structures that are available for advice.
   iii. There should be effective remedies for purchasers and other market participants from failure of those individuals and entities recommending or rating derivatives to meet due diligence and disclosure obligations.
   iv. The level of professionalism and competency needs to be augmented to ensure that financial advisor delivers appropriate advice on derivatives.
4. There should be strategies that promote long-term wealth generation, including consideration of incorporating environmental, social and governance issues in financial product design.
   i. Design of such strategies must involve a public policy debate that encompasses a broad number of participants, not solely financial products market players.
5. Any central exchange and clearing facility that is being created needs to be subject to regulatory oversight, and work toward standardized transparent trading procedures, consistent standards of conduct and disclosure, and transparency in the valuing and settlement of derivatives. The purpose of an exchange would be to manage systemic risks to the derivatives market.[41]
   i. Credit derivatives documentation should be made public, either through a common database of trading information, a central registry or public disclosure vehicle similar to SEDAR in Canada or exchange disclosure requirements in UK and elsewhere.
   ii. There should be public reporting of credit default swaps, including trading and position reporting by OTC dealers and credit default swap clearing data.

---

[41] Not unlike futures exchanges, standard portfolios could be defined through pools of various types of assets and derivatives contracts could then be defined relative to such portfolios and traded on the exchange, creating one measure of investor protection.

Credit derivatives market design 223

iii. There should be a requirement that a portion of exposure be left on the originating lender's balance sheet or that the debt require seasoning for a period of time before it can be repackaged and resold.
iv. Best practices standards must be developed for OTC derivatives through collaboration between regulators and market participants, including in respect of counterparty credit risk management, oversight, liquidity management and netting.
v. One option is to require registration of all derivative trades in a trade repository, allowing regulators access to the information to be able to meet their regulatory responsibilities, including assessment of aggregated risks for asset classes and market instability, addressing any potential issues of costs and data fragmentation.[42]
vi. There is a need for transparency of information across jurisdictions to ensure that manipulation of information does not create unfairness or harm in the market.[43] The move toward CCP requires a rethinking of how trading and settlement can become more transparent to parties, so that they can properly assess and price derivatives products. Access to meaningful information can allow parties to appropriately price risk and allow regulators to monitor market participants and intervene where conduct violates standards.
vii. Where CCP clearing is not available, counterparties to derivatives need to manage their counterparty risk, including netting agreements. There should be regular valuation and margin call processes; strong legal and operational frameworks; and appropriate capital requirements. Capital requirements should be proportionate to the risk they assume and bilateral arrangements, due to their higher risk, should be subject to higher capital requirements.[44]
viii. Increased standardization of products would help ensure that parties understand the derivatives products they are purchasing

---

[42] Financial Services Authority & HM Treasury, *Reforming OTC Derivative Markets*, p. 22. Some regulators have suggested that mandating the creation of data repositories for smaller market segments could be disproportionately costly; and that there could be data fragmentation if there is more than one trade repository for any asset class, *ibid.*, p. 23.
[43] The FSA reports evidence to suggest that derivative contracts can be used to manipulate the price or exploit inside information of the underlying securities that are within scope of its market abuse regime, *ibid.*, p. 25.
[44] Financial Services Authority & HM Treasury, *Reforming OTC Derivative Markets*, p. 17.

and would assist in development of clearing and auction activities, in turn likely reducing operational risk.[45] Standardization should extend to derivatives products that are bought and sold at significant volumes, whether or not they can be cleared through a CCP. Standardization, however, requires global consensus on terms of contracts, so that regulators can appropriately monitor and enforce, and so that parties have certainty in their remedies wherever the derivative settles.[46]

ix. In recognizing central clearing facilities for multiple credit derivatives, there must be regulatory oversight and transparency. All OTC derivative trades, whether or not centrally cleared, should be subject to robust arrangements to mitigate counterparty risk, including bilateral collateralization arrangements and appropriate risk capital requirements.[47]

---

[45] The ISDA has recently published "Big Bang" and "Small Bang" protocols that adopt the cash settlement auction mechanism globally to settle most CDS contracts following a credit event. The protocols incorporate auction settlement terms into standard CDS documentation, referred to as "hardwiring," which will require auction settlement of contracts after a default or other credit event on a company referenced in credit default swap transactions. It includes provision for the ISDA Determinations Committee to now make binding determinations for issues such as whether a credit event has occurred; whether an auction will be held; and whether a particular obligation is deliverable. The auction settlement will eliminate the need for credit event protocols to cash settle CDS transactions. ISDA, 2009 ISDA Credit Derivatives Determinations Committees and Auction Settlement CDS Protocol ("Big Bang" Protocol). ISDA Release, April 8, 2009, "ISDA Announces Successful Implementation of 'Big Bang' CDS Protocol"; "Determinations Committees and Auction Settlement Changes Take Effect", www.isda.org/press/press040809.html (last accessed February 22, 2011). The ISDA has published a further Supplement (the "Restructuring Supplement") to the 2003 ISDA Credit Derivatives Definitions to extend the auction hardwiring provisions to restructuring credit events.

[46] Private dispute resolution processes have often proved effective and efficient in timely resolution of commercial disputes. However, the ISDA determinations mechanism will also be used for more complex determinations that may impact systemic risk or implicate public interest issues. There must be a mechanism to ensure that parties still have recourse to impartial non-industry adjudicators where the issue implicates a public policy concern. To date, there is little regulatory or legislative provision to ensure such access. The UK financial authorities have also pointed out the differences between standardized contracts and "clearing eligible," suggesting that the latter should be determined having regard for availability of price information, sufficient depth of liquidity and whether the product contains inherent risk attributes that can be mitigated by the CCP, while the former should be a goal of most derivatives even where not eligible for CCP. UK financial authorities are attempting to find the linkage between risk reduction and the use of CCP, suggesting that standardization alone is not sufficient reason to require CCP clearing; rather, the CCP's ability to manage the risks associated with the product is a more important consideration.

[47] The UK regulatory authorities advocate risk-proportionate capital charges being applied to bilateral counterparty exposures in order to motivate firms to adopt the identified best practices associated with bilateral collateralisation arrangements, *Reforming OTC Derivatives Markets*.

Credit derivatives market design 225

The development of standards should be a combination of state and market driven initiatives. The market is able to more quickly adapt standards and measurement of risk to new product developments, but solely industry-dominated standard setting failed recently to adequately assess risk, and in the future may create somewhat self-serving standards given the closed nature of the industry. Given the global nature of the market, a move to create shared definitions of derivatives terms and shared standards and overarching principles is desirable. Current initiatives by industry participants could be enhanced by participation of regulatory authorities and investor protection or other NGOs, in order to ensure public interest concerns are included in the development of standards.

6. Regulators should consider requiring public disclosure of "no economic interest at risk" derivatives and prohibiting actions by these derivatives holders that lead to default events, in order to address the moral hazard issues of financial products imperiling the real economy.

Many insurance statutes require the insured have at least a factual expectation of loss if the object of the insurance suffers pecuniary damage, loss or destruction; and the factual expectation requires a lawful or substantial economic interest in the preservation of the insured property. The same approach should be considered for credit derivatives in terms of requiring that a creditor that has hedged its claims through a derivative discloses the real quantum and nature of its remaining economic interest, if any, before it has decision or control rights in proceedings involving the reference entity.

VII   Financial distress of the reference entity and implications for restructuring

Globally, in the past decade, jurisdictions have been moving their insolvency law systems toward rehabilitation of financially distressed companies, adopting restructuring regimes that allow for the development of viable business plans that maximize enterprise value, preserve economic activity and save jobs. The premise is that there is frequently value lost when businesses are liquidated prematurely. All insolvency systems are premised on the notion that creditors with claims should be the ultimate decision-makers as to whether a financially troubled company restructures, as they are the parties with the real economic interest in the entity. Hence most restructuring law facilitates negotiations between debtor companies and their creditors with a view to maximizing firm value. A number of jurisdictions also place considerable value on the public interest associated with restructuring debtor companies, with the concomitant benefits to suppliers, employees and other stakeholders and to economic activity more generally. However, the existence of credit derivatives may perversely affect the motivation and behavior of stakeholders of a financially distressed entity, and may cause greater complexity and uncertainty in a restructuring proceeding, as the real economic interests of claimants are not transparent.

Commercial banks as operating lenders traditionally had a strong role in monitoring the financial status of debtor companies, particularly in the period leading up to insolvency. However, their hedging of risk through derivatives has reduced the incentive to engage in oversight and monitoring, notwithstanding that they are best placed through loan covenants, access to information and in-house resources to engage in that monitoring. While arguably that hedging of risk freed up capital for other market participants seeking to borrow, the previous reliance that creditors and other market participants often had on banks to engage in such monitoring and the resultant signaling of a firm's financial health, have diminished considerably. Given the weaker covenants under which some debtor companies have financed their operations in recent years, creditors may be unable to assert control over a debtor until there has been a significant deterioration in its financial position, leading to deferred liquidation or restructuring and consequent lower recovery to creditors. It may no longer be feasible for the bank or other traditional operating lender to take a lead in restructuring negotiations, given that they have little or no remaining economic interest due to their credit default swaps.

On insolvency, one moral hazard is that a creditor that has material holdings of credit derivatives may have economic interests that encourage it to cause a default to occur so that there is a credit event. There are many factors that can affect the motivation and behavior of stakeholders in an insolvency restructuring, given their economic interests; yet the creditor that has hedged its risk through a credit derivative is arguably in a different position in the restructuring proceeding, as there is a lack of transparency in respect of whether in fact there are economic interests at risk. This observation is not to suggest that credit derivatives drive behavior in all cases; rather, it is a growing phenomenon with the move to cash settlements and growth of the market.

Under physical settlement of a CDS, the single institution from which a debtor company borrowed and believed it had a relationship results now in multiplicity of intermediaries and counterparties as CDS settle. The insolvent company may not even appreciate before commencing a restructuring proceeding that it is a reference entity. Cascading swaps means multiple rapid changes to who holds the claim, making it difficult for a debtor company to establish who has a claim. It can suddenly be dealing with literally hundreds of new claimants. Given settlement time lags where the protection seller with each physical settlement becomes the party at the restructuring bargaining table, the company's ability to devise a viable business plan can be hindered, particularly problematic if there is urgency in devising a plan because of a liquidity crisis or the need to maintain customer goodwill. Physical settlement of multiple CDS has the potential to cause a revolving door effect, making it hard for the company to build consensus and garner requisite support of creditors for a going forward viable business restructuring plan.

A number of jurisdictions have granted exemptions for derivatives from stays under insolvency laws because of the important public policy goal of global financial stability. However, the continued trading of derivatives can cause further financial instability of the market in the name of preserving liquidity and makes restructuring increasingly difficult for particular debtors. In this respect, there is a tension between two broader public policy goals. On the one hand, Basel II capital rules require the ability to terminate, net and realize on collateral in order to allow institutions to take offsetting transactions into account for capital purposes.[48] If parties cannot close out, they face exposure on their offsetting trades, which can cause greater financial problems in the market. On the other hand, the move toward rehabilitation in insolvency laws globally is driven by the recognition that liquidation can often leave value on the table that would have meant greater realizations for subordinated secured creditors, unsecured creditors and employees, as well as positive ripple effects in the local economy that can be realized by preservation of economic activity in the community. Both are important public policy goals and both require consideration in devising a going forward structure of the market.

Many restructurings are substantially negotiated before any formal proceedings are taken, the UK being one such jurisdiction where this practice occurs. Yet creditors who may be obliged to assign their claims to protection sellers may not be able to bind their claims to an agreed restructuring plan, removing a valuable public policy tool to preserve economic activity.

---

[48] Basel Committee on Banking Supervision, *International Convergence of Capital Measurement and Capital Standards: A Revised Framework*, June 2004, www.bis.org/publ/bcbs107.htm (last accessed February 22, 2011) (Basel II).

Cash settlement of CDS poses different kinds of challenges for restructuring. Unlike insurance, no title to the claim passes and there is no right of subrogation. With cash settlement, the protection buyer that is a creditor of the insolvent company continues to be the party with the legal claim, although at a reduced or eliminated financial exposure.[49] The debtor and other creditors have no notice or knowledge of the reduced exposure. If the creditor is fully hedged, there will be little incentive to engage in constructive negotiations for a restructuring plan. This level of disengagement may be problematic for the restructuring. While in some cases, there can be an active market for derivatives during a restructuring where credit derivatives holders are also direct creditors and take an active and constructive role in workout negotiations, the converse can also occur. The financial institution with which the debtor company has had an operating lending relationship may be less interested in advancing further credit in form of post commencement or exit financing if it has no ongoing financial interest in the debtor. The creditor may actually have over-coverage and thus a negative economic interest, materially benefiting if the restructuring fails. Yet parties to the restructuring currently have no information on the economic interest held by those parties hedged through a credit derivative.

Accordingly, a debtor company may find the creditor that is hedged under a CDS adamant in its refusal to agree to amendments to its credit documentation such as a payment change or deferral and changes to covenants that would otherwise trigger a default or obligation acceleration. In addition, protection buying creditors will be unlikely to consent to the extension of the maturity date beyond the protection period unless a credit event has already occurred or the extension itself qualifies as a credit event. These motivations may complicate the efforts of distressed companies to negotiate arrangements with their creditors at the early stages of distress in an attempt to restructure outside of formal insolvency proceedings. Moreover, a claims trader creditor may be seen as having a new, speculative and short-term interest in the debtor. Having acquired its position when the debtor company is already in financial difficulty, it is often hedging against the speculative outcome

---

[49] Where there are cash settled credit default swaps, on occurrence of a credit event, the CDS may be settled by determining the value of the underlying debt instrument through an ISDA-run or similar auction, whereby the protection seller pays the protection buyer for its estimated loss based on the value established in the auction or where a value can be determined based on post credit event bids for the debt product.

of the restructuring process. Such a creditor, perhaps holding a deciding vote, has little interest in the long-term viability of the company.

Moreover, the normative justification for carving out derivatives from stays under restructuring proceedings is unclear, given the shift from their risk management function to speculative product. It creates a statutory preference for particular creditors, over the claims of traditional secured creditors, employees, trade suppliers and tort claimants. Considering the general insolvency law goals of transparency, timeliness and certainty, such exclusion must be revisited. As the bailouts of 2008–2009 illustrated, there is a broader public interest in how the global derivative market is to operate effectively, and adjustments to the system must be made after public policy discussion among stakeholders broader than industry participants. Interests affected are beyond capital markets participants, and regulation is needed to ensure that there is transparency in the nature of economic exposure and underlying risk. There should be a public policy debate on whether there is a need to design new principles to account for the separation of economic and legal interest in the context of insolvency proceedings.

These observations are not to suggest that the market has failed to address some of its flaws itself. CDS protocols and index auctions have helpfully assisted in facilitating cash settlements. The purpose of such protocols is to offer market participants an efficient way to settle credit derivative transactions referencing.[50] For example, when Collins & Aikman filed for bankruptcy in 2005, there were concerns that there were not enough deliverable bonds to settle all the existing index-related contracts. To address this issue, the ISDA published the first protocols to amend the existing contracts for index-related trades to cash settlement from physical settlement on a multi-lateral basis, rather than through counterparty to counterparty negotiations, and to participate in an auction to determine the cash-settlement price of the defaulted bonds.[51] With the CDS outstanding greater by multiples than the volume of bonds issued, the bonds would have to be bought and sold numerous times in the market to settle the CDS, which would have created pressure to source bonds, raising the price of the bonds higher than the likely recovery value. Hence, the market developed credit event auctions, first to facilitate cash settlement and, more recently, to allow for physical settlement on net open positions.[52]

---

[50] ISDA, "2006 report."
[51] Nomura, CDS Recovery Basis, ISDA, 2006.
[52] ISDA Auction Process, 2008, www.isda.org (last accessed February 22, 2011).

The protocol mechanism facilitates industry-wide net settlement of CDS referencing an insolvent entity. The Lehman Brothers Holdings' auction illustrated that the market can price the value of CDS and allow cash settlement for counterparties to CDS trades. The auction set a price and resulted in protection sellers paying 91 cents on the dollar to protection buyers.[53] More than 350 organizations adhered to the 2008 Lehman CDS Protocol, which provided a settlement procedure for approximately USD 6 billion of net CDS exposures.[54]

While these innovations are important, they address only one aspect of the settlement process. There continues to be a lack of transparency as to who is bearing the ultimate costs of the deficiencies in value when all the CDS settlements are completed. The dealer firms tend to have less net exposure as they frequently buy protection to offset the risk of the protection they have sold. The same may not be the case for end purchasers. The Financial Services Authority in the UK has reported that "there is a risk that the greater complexity facing creditors could, in the immediate aftermath of a credit event on a heavily traded security or multiple concurrent defaults, lead to disorderly markets for related securities."[55] Any move toward central clearing facilities requires a rethinking of how such trading and settlement becomes more transparent to parties, so that they can properly assess and price their risk. Moreover, protocols also do not resolve the issue of strategic behavior where there is no longer economic interest in a debtor company.

Not all issues canvassed above require regulatory intervention; resolution of some issues could be contractual. Credit derivatives going forward may involve negotiation of new covenants regarding disclosure or insolvency control rights in light of recent market problems. If protection sellers, who bear the risk of default, want a voice in insolvency restructuring proceedings, presumably they can contract for acquisition of such rights on a credit event through agreeing to physical settlement in the CDS. However, such contractual protection may not be possible once the derivative is resold. In those cases, do cash settled protection sellers have any interest in a restructuring proceeding such that they should be recognized in any way by the court? Such recognition, if it could be established, poses another set of challenging issues

---

[53] *Ibid.*
[54] ISDA 2008 Lehman CDS Protocol, www.isda.org (last accessed February 22, 2011).
[55] FSA, *Financial Risk Outlook 2008*, www.fsa.gov.uk/pubs/plan/financial_risk_outlook_2008.pdf, pp. 52–53 (last accessed February 22, 2011).

for timely and fair insolvency restructuring proceedings and requires further public policy debate.[56]

Some jurisdictions have statutorily created unsecured creditors' committees, where representative creditors have a role in the negotiations for an insolvency workout, paid out of the insolvency estate, and such committees often have strong normative sway with the court.[57] In some jurisdictions, courts recognize ad hoc committees of creditors for similar purposes. In thinking about the disconnection between economic interest and legal claim, it may be that the price for participation on such committees should be that such creditors are required to disclose the extent to which their economic risk has been hedged, with the court given authority to refuse to let the creditor participate where there is little or no economic interest.

VIII Recommendations at the point of settlement and insolvency restructuring proceedings

1. There should be mandatory disclosure during a restructuring proceeding of the real economic risks at stake, including disclosure of the amount of debt that has been hedged by creditors that seek to exercise their voting or oversight rights in a restructuring proceeding. Lack of transparency now means that the debtor company and other creditors are not aware of who is bearing the real economic risk of firm failure, inhibiting the potential for a viable business restructuring plan.
    i. The court should be granted authority to determine the scope and timing of disclosure, including making determinations in respect of confidentiality, limiting access only to parties in the proceeding, and determining any exceptions, such as for *de minimus* holdings.
2. The court's consideration of any restructuring plan should take account of economic interests at stake. This weighing of interest could be accomplished in two different ways:
    i. Voting on a restructuring plan could be premised on the real economic interests in the firm's insolvency. Currently, our voting system globally is based on provable claims. However, the growth

---

[56] For example, if it could be established that there was some sort of interest in the proceedings, there would remain collective action problems in many cases, and thus there is a question of whether a representative agent, not unlike an indenture trustee, could represent the collective interests of cash settlement protection sellers.
[57] See for example, Rule 2019, US Bankruptcy Code.

of credit derivatives means that the voting power of financial institutions that have partial or full credit default swap coverage may be disproportionately large compared with the amount of economic risk, skewing voting outcomes and harming the potential for restructuring of an economically viable company. This alternative would require some recognition of the rights of cash settled swap holders, who are now the residual risk holders.

   ii. Alternatively, legal voting rights could be unaffected, but the court could be granted authority to weigh actual economic interests when considering parties' positions and exercise of voting rights. In Canada, this exercise is a balancing of prejudice and equities in the proceedings. In civil law jurisdictions, some codification of both the authority and the criteria would have to be enacted.
3. Amend insolvency restructuring legislation to include credit derivatives within the mandatory stay of proceedings, except with leave of the court on the basis of unfair prejudice, the standard currently used for other creditors to be exempted from the stay. The court could then exercise oversight of the clearing process in a measured way that assists with the risk management aspects of the products and slows the speculative market. Such an approach could ensure that derivatives continue to settle where they are not adversely affecting the workout process, but could be stayed where the court was persuaded that it would prevent inappropriate conduct or would preserve going concern value pending negotiations for a restructuring plan.
4. Create timely claims bar dates, so that for CDS with physical settlement, the debtor need only bargain with parties as of that date, and not face a continually revolving door of CDS settlements that make the negotiating parties a moving target. While some jurisdictions have established such dates in proceedings, there is currently no widespread established practice or rule in this regard.

These recommendations are first steps toward creation of a fair and sustainable credit derivatives market. Their implementation would pave the way for more extensive debate regarding reform of the market, so that it advances the broad public policy goals of many jurisdictions of effective, fair and sustainable capital markets.

11 The EU Takeovers Directive: a shareholder or stakeholder model?

Blanaid Clarke

I Introduction

The year 2009 marked the fifth anniversary of the adoption of the EU Takeovers Directive 2004/25/EC ('the Directive'). This affords us an opportunity to contemplate its contribution to corporate governance generally and stakeholder welfare in particular and also to consider its continuing fitness for purpose. In this chapter, the impact of the Directive on non-shareholder stakeholders will be considered. While the stated purpose of the Directive is to coordinate certain safeguards required by Member States of listed companies 'for the protection of the interests of members and others',[1] the emphasis in the Directive is clearly on shareholders. The main substantive provisions deal with the protection of minority shareholders by means of the mandatory bid (Article 5) and the squeeze out and sell out rights (Articles 15 and 16), restrictions on the target board denying shareholders the opportunity to decide on the merits of a bid (Article 9) and restrictions on the transfer of securities and on voting rights (Article 11). This focus in takeover regulation on shareholders almost exclusively is not restricted to transnational regulation but is also typical of national regulation. For example the City Code on Takeovers and Mergers in the UK similarly acknowledges its primary responsibility to be the protection of shareholders.[2] This concentration on shareholders in the Directive is symptomatic of a wider trend in corporate governance to confer pride of place to shareholders. The Directive also exemplifies the manner in which non-shareholder stakeholders are included in European corporate governance regulations. The only other group of stakeholders

---
[1] Recital 1, Directive 2004/25/EC on Takeover Bids.
[2] The Introduction to the City Code states 'The Code is designed principally to ensure that shareholders are treated fairly and are not denied an opportunity to decide on the merits of a takeover and that shareholders of the same class are afforded equivalent treatment by an offeror' (The City Code on Takeovers and Mergers, Introduction A1).

expressly referred to in the Directive is employees and the only rights conferred on this group are information rights.

Of course the environment in the wake of the global financial crisis is substantially different from that in 2004. Although the crisis was the result of 'a perfect storm of economic conditions'[3] which included the sub-prime mortgage crisis, the property collapse, the liquidity crisis, market volatility and an accommodating accounting and regulatory environment, most commentators agree that corporate governance failings played a contributory role. In particular, the chronic and reckless risk-taking by the management of banks has been criticized.[4] The banks' remuneration policies both created the high risk environment and rewarded managers and directors for their role in it. As a result there have been calls for greater corporate accountability and increased controls over public companies. The crisis has also highlighted the dangers of focusing exclusively on shareholder return as opposed to adopting a wider stakeholder perspective. The chapter thus considers whether it would be appropriate and indeed possible for the Directive to accommodate a more 'enlightened' shareholder approach.

II   Background to the Directive

The corporate governance literature typically divides the corporate world into two models.[5] The Anglo-American model (which is applied also to Ireland) is a shareholder focused model. It features a strong equity market with dispersed ownership and strong investor protection regimes.[6] Labour markets in this model are perceived as flexible and shareholders are viewed as interested in short-term returns. This model

---

[3] M. Lipton, S. Rosenblum and K. Cain, 'Some Thoughts for Boards of Directors in 2009' (2008), p. 1, available at: www.wlrk.com/docs/ThoughtsforDirectors2009.pdf (last accessed 22 February 2011).

[4] See, for example, C. Plath, 'Corporate Governance in the Credit Crisis: Key Considerations for Investors' (20 November 2008), available at: www.ssrn.com/abstract=1309707 (last accessed 22 February 2011); G. Kirkpatrick, 'Financial Market Trends OECD' (OECD, 2009), available at: www.oecd.org/dataoecd/32/1/42229620.pdf (last accessed 22 February 2011) and the *G20 Declaration of the Summit on Financial Markets and the World Economy* (Office of the White House, Press Secretary, 15 November 2008).

[5] It is important to note that the US and UK models differ from each other in important aspects – see S. Toms and M. Wright, 'Divergence and Convergence within Anglo American Corporate Governance Systems: Evidence from the US and UK, 1950–2000' (2005) 47 *Business History* 267–295 or R. Aguilera, C. Williams, J. Conley and D. Rupp, 'Corporate Governance and Social Responsibility: A Comparative Analysis of the UK and US' (2006) 14 *Corporate Governance: An International Review* 147.

[6] J. Franks, C. Mayer and S. Rossi, 'Ownership: Evolution and Regulation' (2009) 22:10 *Review of Financial Studies* 4009–4056.

involves an active market for corporate control and a strong belief in the value of this market in controlling agency costs. The market for corporate control originally advocated by Henry Manne in 1965 suggests that inefficient management leads to share price decreases as shareholders seek to exit these companies. Opportunities thus arise for other persons to acquire the companies cheaply, to install new management and to achieve greater returns for the new shareholders. The theory suggests that not only do takeovers lead to the removal of underperforming directors but also that the threat of such takeovers encourages directors to perform to the best of their abilities in order to avoid losing their jobs following such takeovers. Thus takeovers or the threat of takeovers act as a stimulant to encourage directors to adopt an optimal governance structure.[7] By contrast, the continental European model is traditionally characterized by a stakeholder-oriented approach, a reliance on long-term debt finance, ownership by large blockholders, weak markets for corporate control[8] and rigid labour markets.

One of the challenges in agreeing a common framework for the regulation of takeovers in Europe was in agreeing a directive which would be appropriate for all Member States whichever model of corporate governance applied and yet which would 'prevent patterns of corporate restructuring within the Community from being distorted by arbitrary differences in governance and management cultures'.[9] The rationale for a directive was to coordinate the safeguards which Member States require of listed companies in order to protect 'members and others' with a view to making such safeguards 'equivalent' throughout the EU.[10]

The Directive, which started life as the 13th Company Law Directive, was based on the regulatory system applying to takeovers in the UK. The reason for this was that when a directive was first considered, few European countries had detailed rules regulating takeovers. Levels of takeover activity varied dramatically from one Member State to another

---

[7] H. Manne, 'Mergers and the Market for Corporate Control' (1965) 73 *Journal of Political Economics* 110; M.C. Jensen and W.H. Meckling, 'Theory of the Firm: Managerial Behaviour, Agency Costs and Ownership Structure' (1976) 3 *Journal of Financial Economics* 305; E.F. Fama, 'Agency Problems and the Theory of the Firm' (1980) 88 *Journal of Political Economics* 288.

[8] Despite this, empirical research has indicated that as of the mid-1990s, an unprecedented number of hostile takeovers occurred in continental Europe. This has been attributed to political changes, regulatory reforms and changes in the business environment during this period. See M. Martynova and L. Renneboog, 'Mergers and Acquisitions in Europe: The Fifth Takeover Wave', in L. Renneboog (ed.), *Advances in Corporate Finance and Asset Pricing* (Amsterdam: Elsevier, 2006).

[9] Recital 3, Directive 2004/25/EC on Takeover Bids.

[10] Recital 1, Directive 2004/25/EC on Takeover Bids.

with the United Kingdom experiencing a substantially greater number of takeovers, particularly hostile takeovers, than other Member States.[11] As a result of a recognized need for regulation, the United Kingdom's self-regulatory Code on Takeovers and Mergers ('the Takeover Code') had been introduced in 1968 and the London Panel on Takeovers and Mergers (the London Panel) was established then to implement and enforce it.[12] The Takeover Code was said to represent the collective opinion of those professionally involved in the field of takeovers as to good business standards and how fairness to shareholders could be achieved.[13] It took the form of a series of detailed rules and a number of General Principles. These General Principles were described as 'statements of good standards of commercial behaviour'. The Takeover Code successfully provided an orderly framework within which takeovers could be conducted. As the London Panel had developed a recognized expertise and an international reputation in regulating takeovers, the Takeover Code was the natural model for European regulation. Not unsurprisingly thus, the focus of the early drafts of the Directive was on management control and the primary regulatory focus was on shareholder value. This caused significant tension between Member States and led to numerous iterations of the Directive at drafting stage. It was only thus in 2001, sixteen years after the original White Paper, that the Commission and the Parliament actually reached a common agreed position on a proposal.[14] Cioffi described this proposal as 'the clearest and most far-reaching attempt to introduce Anglo-American concepts of shareholder value, and shareholder capitalism generally, into the European political economy'.[15]

Although in earlier stages of the drafting process, the mandatory bid provision had been the most contested provision in the Directive, by 2001 agreement had been reached as to the necessity to include such a provision in the final Directive. At this stage, the most controversial provision was the proposed board neutrality provision. The 2001 proposal contained a prohibition on frustrating actions by the board of the target company ('the offeree') unless shareholder

---

[11] J. McCahery, L. Renneboog, P. Ritter and S. Haller, 'The Economics of the Proposed European Takeover Directive', in G. Ferrarini, K. Hopt, J. Winter and E. Wymeersch (eds.), *Reforming Company and Takeover Law in Europe* (Oxford: Oxford University Press, 2004).
[12] *Weinberg & Blank on Takeovers and Mergers* (Sweet & Maxwell), Part III B at para. 3.502.
[13] The City Code on Takeovers and Mergers, Introduction A1.
[14] [2001] OJ C23/1.
[15] J. Cioffi, 'Restructuring "Germany Inc": The Politics of Company and Takeover Law Reform in Germany and the European Union' (2002) 24 *Law & Policy* 355, 381.

approval was obtained. In Germany in particular, managers of companies such as Volkswagen, DaimlerChrysler and BASF viewed the proposed directive as a threat to their own positions and that of German corporations generally. Concerns were expressed that shareholder pressure would lead to redundancies and plant closures and that German companies would become more vulnerable to a takeover in the increasingly global environment.[16] In particular, the hostile takeover of Mannesmann by British Vodafone in 1998 weighed heavily on German corporate minds. A further problem was that the German industrial unions opposed what they viewed as 'the importation of Anglo-American forms of law, governance, and economic organization'. The proposed directive was seen as a means of shifting both power and income from employees to shareholders, as had been the case in the United States and United Kingdom since the 1980s. In particular, it was considered to pose a threat to German co-determination, which provided employees with a significant institutionalized voice in corporate governance. The Rapporteur for the proposed directive, Klaus Heiner Lehne, opposed its introduction. He recommended that board neutrality could only be justified if a level playing field existed for European companies facing a takeover bid and that since this was not then the case the agreement should be rejected. He maintained that the proposal failed to achieve a level playing field with the United States. He also argued that the protection for employees of companies involved in the bid was insufficient. A tied vote ensued and the proposed directive was rejected. It took until late 2003 to resolve these differences and to reach agreement on a compromise text which was introduced in 2004. The manner in which this agreement was reached will be discussed now in the context of the Directive's substantive provisions.

III   Board neutrality/level playing field

Following upon the rejection of the proposed directive, the European Commission established a High Level Group of Company Law Experts under the chairmanship of Jap Winter to advise it inter alia on the issue of board neutrality. In January 2002, the Committee published a report ('the Winter Report') which noted that 'in the light of available economic evidence … the availability of a mechanism which facilitates

---

[16] Under pre-existing domestic legislation, Germany already prohibited golden shares and shares with differential voting rights though these were not matters dealt with by the proposed directive.

takeover bids is basically beneficial'.[17] In part, it attributed this benefit to the market for corporate control.[18] It stated categorically that 'such discipline of management and reallocation of resources is in the long term in the best interests of all stakeholders and society at large'.[19] A natural conclusion thus is that the market for corporate control should be protected by prohibiting directors from engaging in actions to pre-empt or frustrate hostile bids. Such protection is necessary because as the Winter Report noted:

> managers are faced with a significant conflict of interests if a takeover bid is made. Often their own performance and plans are brought into question and their own jobs are in jeopardy. Their interest is in saving their jobs and reputation instead of maximising the value of the company for shareholders.[20]

The Winter Report concluded that even if board resistance might in some circumstances be justified, 'any regime which confers discretion on a board to impede or facilitate a bid inevitably involves unacceptable cost and risk'.[21] It thus suggested that a guiding principle of any European company law regulation aimed at creating a level playing field should be the right of shareholders to make the ultimate decision in respect of whether to tender their shares and at what price. This is the view which at first glance appeared to find favour in the Directive when it was finally introduced. Recital 16 states that

> in order to prevent operations which could frustrate a bid, the powers of the board of an offeree company to engage in operations of an exceptional nature should be limited, without unduly hindering the offeree company in carrying on its normal business activities.

This theme is continued in Article 3(1)(c) which includes a General Principle providing inter alia that 'the board of an offeree company ... must not deny the holders of securities the opportunity to decide on the merits of the bid'. Article 9(2) giving effect to this principle requires the specific prior authorization of shareholders for 'any action ... which may result in the frustration of the bid other than seeking alternative bids' and specifically 'before issuing any shares'. Under Article 9(2) approval is required at least from the time the offeree is approached but it may be earlier if Member States so choose.

---

[17] Report of the High Level Group of Company Law Experts on Issues Related to Takeover Bids (2002), p. 19.
[18] The exploitation of synergies and the opportunity to sell at a premium on market price were identified as the two other benefits.
[19] Report of the High Level Group, p. 19.
[20] Report of the High Level Group, p. 21.
[21] Ibid.

Of particular importance to the board neutrality debate is the fact that it does not accommodate any responsibility of directors to non-shareholder stakeholders such as employees. The debate concerning the value of a shareholder versus a non-shareholder stakeholder approach continues to rage. Manne noted that corporate voting 'is premised on the not illogical view that shareholders are interested exclusively in maximizing their return on investment and not in social causes, political movements or the reallocation of wealth'.[22] He noted that 'some shareholders may put these interests above profit maximization – but the laws of corporate governance should not countenance interference by those activists with the contractually established expectations of the vast number of investors'. It is argued by many academics that increasing shareholder power may actually harm non-shareholder stakeholders.[23] Shareholders may further their own special and possibly short-term interests and not act in the interests of the wider group. In the context of a takeover, for example, shareholders may sell to the highest bidder despite the fact that this is not generally in the interests of employees, consumers, etc. Acceptance of this view may suggest that managerial discretion rather than shareholder power is necessary to prevent shareholders from making decisions that would take value away from other stakeholders. As noted above, this argument played an important role in persuading members of the European Parliament to vote against the proposed directive in 2001. Yet the importance of affording employees this protection is disputed. Bebchuk argued that even if one assumes that stakeholders should get some protection beyond that provided by their contracts, it does not follow that boards should be insulated from shareholder intervention.[24] He suggests that the overlap between the interests of management and non-shareholder stakeholders is hardly such that management can be relied upon to use its powers to protect these stakeholders. Indeed he notes that, if anything, management's interests are more likely to be aligned with shareholders' interests than non-shareholder stakeholders' interests. Whereas managers usually hold a significant portion of their wealth in the form of shares and options, they do not usually have much of their wealth tied

---

[22] H. Manne, 'The "Corporate Democracy" Oxymoron', *Wall Street Journal*, 2 January 2007, p. A23, available at: www.law.harvard.edu/programs/olin_center/corporate_governance/MediaMentions/01-02-07_WSJ.pdf (last accessed 22 February 2011).

[23] M. Blair and L. Stout, 'A Team Production Theory of Corporate Law' (1999) 85 *Virginia Law Review* 247, 253; M. Lipton and S. Rosenblum, 'Election Contests in the Company's Proxy: An Idea Whose Time Has Not Come' (2003) 59 *Business Law* 67.

[24] L. Bebchuk, 'The Case for Increasing Shareholder Power' (2005) 118 *Harvard Law Review* 833.

to employee wealth. Thus, he argues, 'if we expect management to be an imperfect agent for shareholders, we can expect management to be an even less reliable agent for stakeholders'. Furthermore, managers for self-serving reasons, may actually avoid decisions that would benefit non-shareholder stakeholders or make decisions that would cause them losses. For example managers might recommend a bidder which would safeguard their positions but would involve substantial job losses. A common argument which is made is that managers will use their powers to frustrate a bid in order to serve their own interests.[25] Where managers do so, it will be difficult to prove that they have acted improperly. Bebchuk concluded that 'limits on shareholder power should be viewed not as supporting the interests of employees and other stakeholders, but rather as enhancing the power of management relative to shareholders'. Consequently, the resulting increase in management slack might well operate to the detriment of both shareholders and stakeholders. Roe too agreed that shareholder wealth maximization may be the best rule of corporate governance because 'a stakeholder measure of managerial accountability could leave managers so much discretion that managers could easily pursue their own agenda, one that might maximize neither shareholder, employee, consumer, nor national wealth, but only their own'.[26]

Although the board neutrality rule deals with a particular type of agency problem – that of managers versus shareholders – a further agency problem which jeopardizes the level playing field objective was dealt with in the Winter Report – that of minority versus majority shareholders. Although this was not a feature of the 2001 proposed directive, the Winter Report addressed it as part of the need to ensure proportionality between risk-bearing and control.[27] Article 11 introduces the breakthrough rule which was designed to increase the number of takeovers in the EU by eliminating these corporate governance arrangements which might otherwise impede takeovers.[28] The Winter Report argued that the presence of differentiated voting rights, voting caps, pyramid structures and other such structures in Member States' company law was generally inconsistent with the principles of shareholder decision-making and proportionality between risk-bearing capital and control. The rule's desired effect thus was to transform a bid

---

[25] R. Walking and M. Long, 'Agency Theory, Managerial Welfare and Takeover Bid Resistance' (1984) 15 *Rand Journal of Economics* 54, 54–55.
[26] M.J. Roe, 'The Shareholder Wealth Maximization Norm and Industrial Organization' (2001) 149 *University of Pennsylvania Law Review* 2063, 2065.
[27] Report of the High Level Group, p. 20.
[28] Report of the High Level Group, p. 29.

on a company where there is one dominant blockholder into a bid for a company with dispersed ownership. It allows the bidder thus to acquire control without necessarily persuading the dominant blockholder to sell. Article 11(2) and (3) dis-apply certain restrictions when a bid has been made public. During the acceptance period, Article 11(2) disapplies vis-à-vis the offeror restrictions on the transfer of securities provided for in the articles of association of the offeree and restrictions on the transfer of securities in contracts between the offeree and its shareholders or between shareholders entered after the adoption of the Directive. Article 11(3) provides that restrictions on voting rights provided for in the articles of association of the offeree and restrictions on voting rights in contracts between the offeree and its shareholders or between shareholders who entered after the adoption of the Directive shall not have effect at the general meeting of shareholders 'deciding on any defensive measures' in accordance with Article 9. In addition, Article 11(3) provides that multiple-vote securities will carry one vote each at the general meeting of shareholders which 'decides on any defensive measures' in accordance with Article 9. Article 11(4) provides that where following a bid, the offeror holds 75 percent or more of the capital carrying voting rights, none of the above restrictions and none of the 'extraordinary rights' of shareholders in the articles of association concerning the appointment/removal of board members shall apply. Furthermore, multiple-vote securities will carry one vote each at the first general meeting of shareholders following closure of the bid, called by the offeror to amend the articles or appoint/remove directors. The offeror is entitled to call such a meeting on short notice once at least two weeks' notice is given. Article 11(6) and (7) provide an exception to the application of Article 11(3) and (4) if the restriction on voting rights is compensated for by 'specific pecuniary advantages' or if the rights are held by Member States. The Winter Report noted that the application of such a rule after a successful bid was designed to strike a balance between, on the one hand, the need, at least for the time being, to allow differences in the capital and control structures of companies in view of the current differences between Member States, and on the other hand, the need to allow and stimulate successful takeover bids to take place in order to create an integrated securities market in Europe.[29]

The concerns of Klaus Heiner Lehne and those who voted against the 2001 proposed directive were not ignored. In order to reach agreement, a compromise was suggested – a compromise which, it is submitted, undermines entirely the spirit of, and indeed the rationale for, the

---

[29] Report of the High Level Group, p. 30.

Directive. Article 12(1) provides that Member States may decide not to require companies registered in their jurisdiction to apply Article 9 and Article 11. The only concession is that if Member States 'make use of this option' they must still grant companies the reversible option of applying the Articles.[30] This decision must be taken by the shareholders in a general meeting in accordance with the rules applicable to the amendment of their articles of association. A further weakening of Articles 9 and 11 is introduced by the reciprocity provision in Article 12(3). This allows Member States 'to exempt companies which apply' the Articles 'if they become the subject of an offer launched by a company which does not apply the same Articles as they do', or a company controlled by such a company. To do so, however, Article 12(5) provides that they need the authorization of their shareholders at a meeting granted no more than eighteen months before the bid. The introduction of these optionality and reciprocity provisions allows Member States to resist the pressure to move towards a shareholder dominated system of corporate governance. Having achieved their first goal in incorporating these provisions, Member States proceeded to make full use of them.

By February 2007, eighteen of the twenty-seven Member States had introduced, or were expected to introduce, Article 9. Of these, only Malta had not previously provided for the board neutrality obligation in domestic legislation.[31] All the other Member States which had no strict board neutrality obligation before the implementation of the Directive, decided not to introduce one. What is more telling however is that in five[32] of the eighteen Member States where the obligation pre-dated the Directive, the reciprocity exception discussed above has also been introduced. Thus, in these five Member States managements' power to take frustrating measures without the approval of shareholders has actually increased as a consequence of the Directive.[33] The Commission noted that this development 'will very likely hold back the emergence of an open takeover market, rather than promote it'.[34] The vast majority of Member

---

[30] Article 12(2), Directive 2004/25/EC on Takeover Bids.
[31] European Union Commission Staff Working Document, *Report on the Implementation of the Directive on Takeover Bids*, SEC (2007) 268, 21/2/07, 6, available at: http://ec.europa.eu/internal_market/company/docs/takeoverbids/2007-02-report_en.pdf (last accessed 22 February 2011).
[32] France, Greece, Hungary, Portugal and Slovenia.
[33] A further two of the Member States which currently have board neutrality in place but had not transposed the Directive by the time of the publication of the report, Cyprus and Spain, informed the Commission about their intention to implement the Directive by introducing reciprocity.
[34] EU Commission Staff Working Document, *Report on the Implementation of the Directive on Takeover Bids*, p. 6.

States have not imposed the breakthrough rule, choosing to make its application merely optional for companies. It is expected to be imposed only by the Baltic States and thus a mere 1 percent of listed companies in the EU will apply this rule on a mandatory basis.[35] However, the majority of Member States have chosen to adopt the reciprocity provision in Article 12(3). The Commission pragmatically concluded thus that, taking into account the modalities of implementing the reciprocity rule, 'the main "benefit" of reciprocity seems to be the fact that it gives management new powers to take frustrating action and makes it easier for companies to disapply the board neutrality or breakthrough rule'.[36] In the UK, the prohibition on frustrating action contained within the Takeover Code was retained. The UK did not utilize the reciprocity provision[37] or introduce a mandatory breakthrough rule. However, it seems clear that the implementation by a large number of other Member States of the Directive in a protectionist manner[38] appears to have impeded the market for corporate control rather than facilitated it.[39] The previous Internal Market Commissioner McCreevy has admitted that the 'protectionist attitude of a few seems to have had a knock-on effect on others' and that if this trend continues increased barriers to takeovers will result.[40] The Commission is required by Article 20 of the Directive to examine the Directive in light of the experience acquired in applying it and, if necessary, propose its revision. In furtherance of this, it has commissioned a study, the results of which are expected to be published in late 2011.[41]

In the run-up to the crisis it is clear that the market for corporate control did not operate to control banks' inefficient management. One of the reasons for this is that the fundamental prerequisites for the operation of this disciplinary force were not in place.[42] The share prices of the banks did not reflect the inefficiencies which subsequently proved so costly to the global market. There were no opportunities to acquire

---

[35] *Ibid.*, p. 7. [36] *Ibid.*, p. 9.
[37] It may be argued, however, that the effect of the implementation of the Directive into national law has weakened the prohibition on frustrating action in the UK and Ireland. See B. Clarke, 'Articles 9 and 11 of the Takeover Directive (2004/25) and the Market for Corporate Control' (2006) *Journal of Business Law* 355–374.
[38] EU Commission Staff Working Document, *Report on the Implementation of the Directive on Takeover Bids*, p. 10.
[39] See B. Clarke, 'Takeover Regulation – through the Regulatory Looking Glass' (2007) 8:4 *German Law Journal*.
[40] Press Release 27 February 2007 (IP/07/251).
[41] European Corporate Governance Forum, Minutes of the meeting of 11 February 2011.
[42] This argument is expanded in B. Clarke, 'Where was the "Market for Corporate Control" when we Needed it?' (17 December 2009), UCD Working Papers in Law, Criminology & Socio-Legal Studies Research Paper No. 23/2009, available at SSRN: http://ssrn.com/abstract=1524785 (last accessed 22 February 2011).

the banks cheaply and even if there had been it is not clear that there would have been support for a change in risk management structures either at board or at investor level. The UK's Turner Review on banking regulation concluded that: 'A strong case can be made that the events of the last five years have illustrated the inadequacy of market discipline: indeed, they suggest that in some ways market prices and market pressures may have played positively harmful roles.'[43] Although it is not suggested that the market for corporate control cannot operate as an effective form of corporate governance in certain cases, clearly it is not a complete solution to this agency problem.

IV Duty to employees

Following the rejection of a first proposal for a directive in 1989 involving detailed and prescriptive rules, it was agreed that a framework directive should be introduced. Thus the second proposal in 1996 set out General Principles but allowed Member States a significant degree of discretion in their implementation.[44] Article 5 listed five General Principles and required Member States to ensure that the rules made pursuant to the directive respected them. Article 5(c) stated purely that:

the board of the offeree company is to act in the interests of the company as a whole.

The obligation was not thus linked either with advice or frustrating action. Furthermore, the notion of identifying specific groups of stakeholders was avoided and instead the phrase well known to common law lawyers, 'the company as a whole', was used. Subsequently, the Economic and Social Committee[45] and the European Parliament gave their opinions on the text. The Legal Affairs Committee advised the European Parliament that the concept of acting in the interests of the company as a whole 'also entailed protecting jobs'.[46] It proposed rewording the General Principle (c) as:

the board of an offeree company is to act in the interests of the company as a whole, including safeguarding jobs.[47]

---

[43] Financial Services Authority, 'The Turner Review, a Regulatory Response to the Global Banking Crisis' (2009), p. 45.
[44] COM/95/0655 FINAL – COD 95/0341 OJ C 162 6/6/1996, p. 5.
[45] Official Journal C 295, 07/10/1996, p. 0001.
[46] COD/1995/0341: 21/05/1997.
[47] Official Journal C 222, 21/07/1997, p. 0020.

This was accepted by the European Parliament.[48] As a consequence, the Commission's proposal was amended in November 1997[49] and Article 5.1(c) provided:

> the board of an offeree company is to act in all the interests of the company, including employment.

The use of the term 'employment' was awkward and it was not clear whether it extended beyond the suggestion of the Legal Affairs Committee and could for example be said to include other employees' interests such as their terms of employment. Furthermore, the inclusion of a duty to act in the interests of an identified group of non-shareholder stakeholders caused consternation in certain Member States, most notably the UK and Ireland. In the UK, the House of Lords Select Committee noted:

> The general principle at Article 5.1(c) has been recast so that the board of the offeree company is to act in all the interests of the company, including employment. The Minister considers that although this is consistent with the general principles of the Takeover Code, it seems likely to provide fertile ground for litigation because it is cast in very general terms.[50]

Similar views were expressed at the Council Working Group meetings. The Council Working Party in September 1998 suggested reverting to 'the company as a whole' and deleting the reference to 'including employment'. This change was explained on the basis that 'the contents of Amendment 11 ("including safeguarding jobs")' had been included in Article 9(1)(b), which requires the board of the offeree company to give its opinion on the possible effects that the takeover bid may have on employment.[51] While this of course assumes a very narrow interpretation of the original duty, the change was accepted by the Presidency and a modified presidency proposal reflecting this wording was issued in December 1998. The new text thus stated:

> the board of an offeree company is to act in the interests of the company as a whole, and must not deny the holders of securities the opportunity to decide on the merits of the bid.

The same text was used in all subsequent proposals including the final text agreed in late 2003. It is also worth noting that this is a mandatory requirement.

---

[48] COD/1995/0341: 26/06/1997C 222 21.07.1997, pp. 0012–0020.
[49] COM/97/0565 final C 378 13.12.1997, p. 0010.
[50] The House of Commons Select Committee on European Legislation, Twelfth Report (18557) par.3.3. (January 1998), available at: www.publications.parliament.uk/pa/cm199798/cmselect/cmeuleg/155xii/el1205.htm (last accessed 22 February 2011).
[51] In the Statement of the Council's reasons for the Common Position adopted by it – 8129/00 ADD 1 22/5/2000.

The first question to be asked is what do the terms 'interests' and 'company as a whole' mean and how are they likely to be interpreted by the supervisory authorities? At first glance, it appears to amount to a restating of the traditional common law fiduciary duty. In the UK, the courts traditionally interpreted the term 'company as a whole' in that context as meaning acting in the interests of shareholders.[52] This is consistent with the development of corporate theory and stakeholder theory in these jurisdictions. Davies has noted however that:

a requirement ... that directors must act *in the interests of* 'the company' comes close to being meaningless. This is because the company is an artificial legal person and it is impossible to assign interests to it unless one goes further and identifies with the company the interests of one or more groups of human persons.[53]

Thus for Member States with different cultural backgrounds that have traditionally possessed strong employee protection values at the core of their corporate governance systems, a different interpretation of this provision may be applied, one that is broader than that in the shareholder-centric model. In addition to interpretation problems, there will be difficulties in monitoring and enforcing the proper application of this duty. Stout and Blair argue that 'the phenomenon of trust behavior suggests that fiduciary relationships are created by the law in situations where it is efficient or otherwise desirable to promote other-regarding, trusting and trustworthy behaviour'. They note that the key to a successful fiduciary relationship lies in 'framing both economic and social conditions so as to encourage the fiduciary to make a psychological commitment to further their beneficiary's welfare rather than their own'.[54] In the context of a takeover, this may be difficult.

The question which has taxed academics since Berle and Means first introduced the concept of a separation of ownership and control, is in whose interest should the company be run? Often, the shareholder versus non-shareholder stakeholder debate concludes with an acknowledgement that the interests of shareholders are served by taking into account the interests of stakeholders. Acting in the interests of employees, for example, may have a direct effect on profitability through enhanced reputation; more effective working practices; greater focus on strategic operations; increased employee loyalty; and more successful recruitment drives. In the UK, the enlightened shareholder value

---

[52] See for example *Greenhalgh* v. *Arderne Cinemas Ltd* [1950] 2 All ER 1120.
[53] P. Davies, *Gower and Davies Principles of Modern Company Law* (London: Sweet & Maxwell, 2008), p. 507.
[54] L. Stout and M. Blair, 'Trust, Trustworthiness, and the Behavioural Foundations of Corporate Law' (2001) 149 *University of Pennsylvania Law Review* 1735–1810.

principle has been enshrined in the Companies Act 2006.[55] This duty, though based on shareholder primacy and requiring directors to act in the collective best interests of shareholders, emphasizes not exclusive concern for short-term gains but rather an approach which values the building of long-term relationships.[56] In the context of a takeover, however, there is often no long-term company interest to be considered. Where a cash offer is made, the decision for the shareholders becomes more straightforward. Should they act in their own economic interest or act in the interests of a third party in a purely altruistic manner? That said, the company is clearly continuing but under completely new ownership. In such circumstances thus the long-term focus will involve the interests of the offeror and the employees. The question arises then as to whether directors are being required to act in the interests of future shareholders (i.e. the offeror) or employees to the detriment of current shareholders.

It seems that in the wake of the financial crisis, there has been a wider appreciation of the impact of corporate decisions on stakeholders. In June 2010, Hector Sants, the Chief Executive of the UK Financial Services Authority and Deputy Governor of the Bank of England, advocated amending the Companies Act 2006 to include 'a stronger and more explicit obligation to wider society'. He suggested that 'there must be clear recognition of the need for institutions to contribute to the common good'.[57] Given that the Directive is a framework directive, it is submitted that if there was a consensus that Sants' approach was correct, there would be nothing to prevent Member States from interpreting the reference to 'the interests of the company as a whole' in General Principle (c) of the Directive in this manner and implementing it accordingly.

To date, in implementing the Directive, the UK has avoided defining the term 'interests of the company' by importing the provision directly

---

[55] S.172(1) of the Companies Act 2006 provides that a director of a company must act in the way he considers, in good faith, would be most likely to promote the success of the company for the benefit of its members as a whole, and in doing so have regard (amongst other matters) to – (a) the likely consequences of any decision in the long term (b) the interests of the company's employees (c) the need to foster the company's business relationships with suppliers, customers and others (d) the impact of the company's operations on the community and the environment (e) the desirability of the company maintaining a reputation for high standards of business conduct, and (f) the need to act fairly as between members of the company.
[56] A. Keay, 'Tackling the Issue of the Corporate Objective: An Analysis of the United Kingdom's "Enlightened Shareholder Value"' (2007) 29 *Sydney Law Review* 577.
[57] Speech by H. Sants to the Chartered Institute of Securities and Investments Conference on 17 June 2010, available at: www.fsa.gov.uk/pages/Library/Communication/Speeches/2010/0617_hs.shtml (last accessed 22 February 2011).

into the implementing legislation. However, the London Panel's Code Committee indicated that the Panel's primary focus in considering breaches of the Code is, and will continue to be, the consequences for shareholders. However, 'on reflection' it noted that breaches of the Code might also have consequences for other people.[58] The failure to provide a clear meaning for this term is likely to cause difficulties for companies seeking to comply with this General Principle and for supervisory authorities seeking to enforce it. In this regard, it is worth noting Hertig's comment that true convergence in corporate governance depends upon the extent to which legal rights and duties are enforced to an equivalent degree across jurisdictions.[59] Finally, it should be noted that the orthodox view has always been that company directors owe fiduciary duties to the company itself rather than the shareholders. The rationale for this is that the breach of such a duty results in a wrong to the company. The Directive is silent on this point. It obliges Member States to ensure that the General Principle is protected but does not expressly bestow any rights on shareholders, employees or other stakeholders in respect of enforcement of this duty. This too may add to the enforcement problems.

V   Information to employees

The only express rights conferred on employees in the Directive are the right to receive information and within limits the right to have their views published. Article 6(2) provides that when the offer document is made public, the boards of the offeree and the offeror must communicate it to the representatives of their respective employees or, where there are no such representatives, to the employees themselves. Article 6(3)(i) provides that the offeror must include in the offer document:

the offeror's intentions with regard to the future business of the offeree company and, in so far as it is affected by the bid, the offeror company and with regard to the safeguarding of the jobs of their employees and management, including any material change in the conditions of employment, and in particular the offeror's strategic plans for the two companies and the likely repercussions on employment and the locations of the companies' place of business.

---

[58] Panel Response Statement, *The Implementation of the Takeovers Directive*, RS2005/5, 21 April 2006, p. 15.
[59] G. Hertig, 'Convergence of Substantive Law and Convergence of Enforcement: A Comparison', in J. Gordon and M. Roe (eds.), *Convergence and Persistence in Corporate Governance* (Cambridge: Cambridge University Press, 2004).

Article 9(5) then requires the board of the offeree to set out its views on:

the effects of the implementation of the bid on all the company's interests and specifically employment, and on the offeror's strategic plans for the offeree and the likely repercussions on employment and the locations of the companies' place of business as set out in the offer document.

At the same time, this opinion must be communicated by the board of the offeree to the representatives of its employees or, where there are no such representatives, to the employees themselves. Where the board of the offeree receives in good time a separate opinion from the representatives of its employees on the effects of the bid on employment, that opinion must also be appended to the document. The Winter Report noted that such provisions were adequate and that any further concerns for the interests of employees should be addressed by specific legislation providing for information and consultation of employees and for their protection in the event of a bid leading to restructuring.[60]

Does this represent a significant improvement on the pre-existing situation for employees?[61] In the UK prior to the implementation of the Directive, the offeror was required to provide information in the offer document of: its intentions regarding the continuation of the business of the offeree and its subsidiaries; its intentions regarding any major changes to be introduced in the business, including any redeployment of the fixed assets of the target and its subsidiaries; the long-term commercial justification of the offer; and its intentions with regard to the continued employment of the employees of the offeree and of its subsidiaries.[62] The offeree board was also required 'insofar as is relevant' to comment upon the statements made in the offer document regarding the offeror's intentions in respect of the offeree and its employees.[63] Although there was no requirement to deliver copies of the offer document or the response document to employees directly, the latter clearly had access to them. Furthermore, the only employees referred to in the Takeover Code were the employees of the offeree or its subsidiaries. The offeror's employees, though likely to be affected by the acquisition, were not mentioned. The inclusion of the offeror's employees in explicit disclosure is a welcome amendment brought about by the Directive.

---

[60] Report of the High Level Group, p. 16.
[61] It should also be noted that industrial relations legislation applied at this time. For example, the regulations implementing Council Directive 2002/14/EC established a general framework for improving information and consultation rights of employees.
[62] The Takeover Code, Rule 24.1.
[63] The Takeover Code, Rule 25.1.

The informational requirements in the pre-existing rules were not quite as far-reaching as those stipulated in the Directive. In most cases, they were met by the inclusion of a formulaic note to the effect that it was the intention of the offeror to safeguard the employees' existing contractual rights. The fact that this will not suffice under the Directive has caused its own problems. Particularly in the case of a hostile bid, the offeror may not have access to sufficient information to allow it to make any meaningful proposals as to its future strategy for the offeree's employees. It may not possess accurate information about staffing numbers and levels. The offeree board thus cannot comment on any substantive plans. There is no requirement in the Directive to provide this information to an offeror. In the Takeover Code such an obligation arises only if the information has been made available to an alternative offeror and specifically requested.[64] In many cases, the offeree will be understandably reluctant to make this information available without being mandated to do so. For example, the offeror may be a competitor and any information given may provide a competitive advantage in the future either in the context of the takeover or otherwise. In practice, thus, the information provided tends to be detailed enough to be useful to employees only in the case of an agreed bid.

Kraft Foods Inc.'s (Kraft) acquisition of Cadbury plc (Cadbury) in the UK in 2010 provides a stark example of the problem. In October 2007, two years before this hostile bid was made, Cadbury had announced its plan to close its Somerdale factory with the loss of 500 jobs. It announced that production at the factory would be transferred to its Bournville plant in Birmingham and, by 2010, to a plant in Poland. When the Kraft offer was announced in September 2009, Kraft's CEO Irene Rosenfeld stated in a letter to Cadbury shareholders that 'We believe we would be in a position to continue to operate the Somerdale facility, which is currently planned to be closed and to invest in Bournville, thereby preserving UK manufacturing jobs'. A similar statement was repeated in its offer document in December and its revised offer document in January 2010. In February 2010, one week after the offer was declared wholly unconditional, Kraft announced that following extensive talks with senior management, it had reluctantly accepted that Cadbury's plans to close the Somerdale plant were too far advanced and that it was unrealistic to reverse them. It explained that the investment required to reverse the closure programme would be so significant as to be unviable. Kraft explained that it had believed the transfer was not scheduled until the latter part of 2010. It had planned to continue existing operations

---

[64] The Takeover Code 20.2.

at the Somerdale plant and to use the Polish plant to meet its need for additional capacity in continental Europe. Kraft also emphasized that the statement was merely one of belief and was expressed as such. It subsequently emerged that the first time representatives from Kraft had even touched upon the Somerdale closure was on the night before the Cadbury board publicly recommended the bid. At that meeting, Cadbury informed Kraft that it considered that it would be difficult to continue to operate the Somerdale plant. Later Kraft discovered that more than £100 million had been invested in the Polish facilities. The hostile nature of the bid deprived Kraft of the information necessary to make a correct assessment of the situation. Let us be clear though, it was not that Cadbury could not disclose this information to Kraft, it was that it chose not to do so. Of course, given the fact that Kraft was one of its major competitors and the bid may not have been successful, there were sound commercial reasons why the board would have been reluctant to hand over sensitive or even useful information of this kind.[65] Although the London Panel subsequently criticized Kraft for its statement on the basis that it did not meet the standard of care and accuracy required by the Takeover Code, no further action was taken. The Kraft case illuminates the weakness of the information provisions in the Directive. However, it must be acknowledged that even if this information had been publicly available, its value would be questionable. It is hard to sustain the argument that it would have mattered to shareholders given that this was a cash bid, and the company itself had decided to let these employees go just two years before. Similarly, while the unions may have used this information in their discussions with Kraft, their negotiating power was limited. As Lord Mandelson, the then UK Secretary of State for Business, Innovation and Skills, complained, 'the fate of a company with a long history and many tens of thousands of employees was decided by people who had not owned the company a few weeks earlier, and probably had no intention of owning it a few weeks later'.[66] This reflects the hard facts of the marketplace.

VI   Payments to employees

Article 3(1)(a) of the Directive sets out as the first General Principle the requirement that 'all holders of the securities of an offeree company

---

[65] Panel Statement, Kraft Foods Inc. Offer for Cadbury Plc 2010/14.
[66] Lord Mandelson, Secretary of State for Business, Innovation and Skills, Speech at the Trade and Industry dinner, Guildhall, the Mansion House, London (1 March 2010), available at:http://webarchive.nationalarchives.gov.uk/+/http://www.bis.gov.uk/news/Speeches/mandelson-mansion-house (last accessed 22 February 2011).

of the same class must be afforded equivalent treatment'. This too was based on an equivalent General Principle in the Takeover Code. Rule 16 of the Takeover Code gives effect to this principle by prohibiting an offeror or concert party from making any arrangement with any shareholder or intending shareholder of the offeree which relates to shares in the offeree if the same arrangement is not being extended to all shareholders. This would thus prohibit the offeror making a payment to employees of the offeree in order to compensate it for any breach of the implicit contracts or for job losses if those employees were also shareholders. Although an exception is made for payments which incentivize employees who are to play a continuing role, this again focuses on financial performance and resultant shareholder value.

Similarly, the prohibition on frustrating action by the offeree board referred to above restricts the ability of the offeree to enter into contracts otherwise than in the normal course of business. Where the payment is of such a level that it may result in the frustration of an offer or possible offer, shareholder consent is required before it may be agreed. This will be discussed further below.

VII   Impact of ESOPs

The special status of shareholder in employee stock ownership plans (ESOPs) merits particular consideration. These plans straddle the two corporate governance options. For shareholder focused economies such plans are popular as a means of aligning the interests of employees and shareholders and providing an economic incentive which will increase employee productivity to the ultimate benefit of the shareholders. Tax advantages flow to companies forming an ESOP and they constitute an efficient means of contributing to the pension plans of their employees. For those keen to promote the interests of non-shareholder stakeholders, ESOPs are viewed as a means of empowering employees. Often the shares are held through an employee share ownership trust (ESOT). This has given rise to a new category of shareholder with interests which may diverge from those of other shareholders. As in the case of the institutional shareholder group, the ESOT possesses unique strengths and powers and operates subject to its own objectives and its own regulations. Empirical research confirms that individual members of the ESOPs benefit from ESOPs. The evidence of benefits to the companies themselves is more mixed, however.[67]

---

[67] J. Blasi, D. Kruse and A. Bernstein, *In the Company of Owners: the Truth about Stock Options* (New York: Basic Books, 2003); S. Freeman, 'Effects of ESOP Adoption

As a shareholder, the ESOT has a typical shareholder's interest in maximizing share value and share premiums. However, the ESOT can transfer its involvement from one company to another less easily than other shareholders or other stakeholders such as consumers. In addition, many ESOT members also possess a strong employment interest in the company which makes them more sensitive to the interests of the employees. The question then arises as to how the ESOT balances these often conflicting interests. The risk that a large shareholder might try to influence corporate decisions in a self-serving way that harms other shareholders is well-recognized in closely held firms. In the context of a takeover where the consideration is cash, the primary concern of the ordinary shareholders is likely to be increased share premium possibly at the expense of long-term job security or social responsibility. A conflict of interest thus arises. A second problem is that a concern exists that ESOPs can be used to frustrate a takeover bid by placing substantial numbers of shares in the hands of employees who are more likely to resist a takeover offer. Polaroid was the first company in the United States to successfully use an ESOP as a frustrating action.[68] While a sale of stock to a newly created ESOP was acknowledged to be a deliberate anti-takeover device, the Court found that the transaction satisfied the standard of proportionality applied in Delaware to takeover defences and thus was not a breach of the board's fiduciary duties. Under the Directive, the squeeze out provision cannot be utilized until 90 percent of the shares are acquired or promised. This gives a reasonable sized ESOT a significant element of control over the success or failure of a bid.

The Directive addresses only the second problem. As noted above, the prohibition on frustrating action expressly applies also to the issuance of shares. Shareholder approval would thus be needed before a contract was entered into to provide these rights to employees. There are two provisions, however, which may lessen the impact of the prohibition. First, the prohibition applies only during the course of a takeover or when a bid is imminent. Such plans could be introduced outside the takeover period and the Directive would not have any effect. In such a case it would fall to the courts to determine whether their introduction

---

and Employee Ownership: Thirty Years of Research and Experience', University of Pennsylvania, Centre for Organizational Dynamics Working Paper 07–01 (2007), available at: www.community-wealth.org/_pdfs/articles-publications/esops/paper-freeman.pdf (last accessed 22 February 2011).

[68] *Shamrock Holdings, Inc* v. *Polaroid Corporation*, 559 A.2d 257 (Del. Ch. 1989). See R. Bruner, 'Leveraged ESOPs, Wealth Transfers and "Shareholder Neutrality"': The Case of Polaroid' (1990) 19 *Financial Management* 59.

was appropriate in terms of the proper exercise by the company board of their corporate powers and their fiduciary duties. This is a particularly difficult task as such plans may be designed to benefit the company or solely to avoid a change of ownership.[69] Second, Article 9(3) appears to exempt from the prohibition 'decisions' to take certain action where (1) the decisions have been 'partly or fully implemented' before the beginning of this period or (2) where the decisions, though not yet partly or fully implemented, are in the normal course of the company's business. A number of unanswered question arise in this context – are decisions to introduce an ESOP or to issue shares under such a plan made 'in the normal course of business'? At what stage are the decisions 'partly implemented'?

VIII Conclusion

Hansmann and Kraakman in the context of takeover regulation suggested that while they could not predict where 'the equilibrium point' would lie, 'it is a reasonable conjecture that the law on both sides of the Atlantic will ultimately converge on a single regime'.[70] While they might have suggested a gradual shift of corporate priority from a stakeholder consensus model to a model based on shareholder values, it is submitted that the Directive met the challenge of responding to the two different corporate governance models by offsetting many of the elements of each. There was less stakeholder empowerment and stakeholder rights than continental Europeans might have originally hoped. There were also less mandatory shareholder primacy provisions than the UK might have expected. The Directive in the end did not rock any political boats. It might thus be said to be less effective in shaping corporate governance than might have been predicted originally.

As this chapter has shown, the position of employees did not change dramatically as a result of the Directive. In the aftermath of the crisis, there have been calls for the priorities of companies to be realigned to a greater extent with values supported by all stakeholders and, in the context of takeovers, for directors to be 'equipped to be stewards rather than

---

[69] See E. Grannis 'A Problem of Mixed Motives: Applying "Unocal" to Defensive ESOPS' (1992) 92 *Columbia Law Review* 851.
[70] H. Hansmann and R. Kraakman, 'The End Of History For Corporate Law', in J. Gordon and M. Roe (eds.), *Convergence and Persistence in Corporate Governance* (Cambridge: Cambridge University Press, 2004), p. 55. See also J. Hill, 'The Persistent Debate about Convergence in Comparative Corporate Governance' (2005) 27 *Sydney Law Review* 743.

just auctioneers'.[71] While this is clearly not mandated by the Directive, a broad interpretation of the Directive's duty to act 'in the interests of the company as a whole' would not prevent such an interpretation at national level. Although regulators and legislators in many individual Member States have advocated such an approach, it is submitted that introducing specific measures to adopt a stakeholder view is some way off. First a political consensus would need to be reached, investors would need to be persuaded that this was in their long-term interests and decisions would need to be made as to the appropriate form of regulation and the manner in which it would interact with existing corporate governance rules. Though not insurmountable, these are significant barriers to change. Thus we can expect the continuing ambiguity and equipoise in Member States between shareholder and stakeholder approaches that the Directive allows.

[71] Lord Mandelson, Mansion House Speech.

12 "Law and finance": inaccurate, incomplete, and important

Ruth V. Aguilera and Cynthia A. Williams

> On the face of it, shareholder value is the dumbest idea in the world. Shareholder value is a result, not a strategy ... Your main constituents are your employees, your customers and your products.[1]
> – Jack Welch, former CEO of General Electric

I Introduction

While virtually all scholars of corporate governance agree that there exist national differences in corporate governance practices and their efficacy, there is an ongoing debate about the relevant dimensions of difference and how they may best be explained. In this chapter, we argue that the strong conceptual and empirical link between law and finance as proposed within the legal origins theory and fully launched in a series of articles by LLSV[2] is inaccurate, incomplete, and yet important. At the least, it is important to get a clearer view of the field such that we may better understand the broader scope of the "law–finance" relationship, particularly as the law and finance theory has had demonstrated effects on international policy developments.

A number of scholars have effectively demonstrated the key shortcomings of this theoretical and empirical unidirectional linkage from law to finance.[3] We do not need to review that literature here, but

---

This chapter originally appeared as an essay in the 2009 *Brigham Young Law Review* Symposium on Law and Finance. We appreciate the permission of the *Review* to reprint the essay.

[1] Francesco Guerrera, "Welch Condemns Share Price Focus," *Financial Times*, March 12, 2009, p. 1.
[2] We use the acronym "LLSV" to refer to the four authors of the first legal origins papers, which include Rafael La Porta, Francisco Lopez-de-Silanes, Andrei Shleifer, and Robert Vishny. See generally Rafael La Porta, Florencio Lopez-de-Silanes, and Robert W. Vishny, "Corporate Ownership Around the World" (1999) 54 *Journal of Finance* 471; Andrei Shleifer and Robert W. Vishny, "A Survey of Corporate Governance" (1997) 52 *Journal of Finance* 737.
[3] See generally Mark J. Roe, "Corporate Law's Limits" (2002) 31 *Journal of Legal Studies* 233; Mathias M. Siems, "Shareholder Protection Around the World ('Leximetric

find it convincing. And, in response to some of their critics, La Porta, Lopez-de-Silanes, and Shleifer have rectified some of their strong and prescriptive former claims.[4] In this chapter, we discuss in Section II what we have learned from this agitated debate with so many policy and real-life ramifications, why it is important to conceptualize a larger and more complex picture of the proposed law–finance causality, what we can learn from existing research on comparative systems in social science, and what we need to study next in the field of research of legal systems and economic sociology. In Section III, we discuss why it is important to get "law and finance" right.

II   The view from economic sociology: law as a partial view

A   Complementarities matter

One could take multiple routes to illustrate the principle that looking simply at the characteristics of the legal system to explain economic outcomes is *incomplete*. One limitation is, perhaps, the methodological tools we use to analyze these questions. For instance, it seems rather narrow to summarize the advanced industrialized countries into two stylized systems: liberal market economies and coordinated market economies, which happen to correspond nicely to the common and civil law dichotomy. Perhaps the explanation for simplicity is the methodological limitations we face in comparative corporate governance research and comparative law – namely, a large number of potential explanatory variables and a small number of cases.

Organizations are widely conceived as complex systems of interdependent factors, but empirical methodology often poorly reflects such interdependence. For example, standard linear models, such as regression analysis, treat variables as competing to explain variation in the outcome rather than focusing on how causes may combine in specific *cases* to create outcomes. Meanwhile, case studies have an important tradition in organizational research, but such studies face the challenge of generalizing across cases or using cases effectively to better "contextualize" the boundary conditions of existing theories. Recently, new innovations in comparative research methods have been developed and

---

II')" (2008) 33 *Delaware Journal of Corporate Law* 111; Mathias M. Siems, Simon Deakin, and Priya Lele, "The Evolution of Labour Law: Calibrating and Comparing Regulatory Regimes" (2007) 146 *International Labor Review* 133.

[4] See generally Rafael La Porta, Florencio Lopez-de-Silanes, and Andrei Shleifer, "The Economic Consequences of Legal Origins" (2008) 46 *Journal of Economics Literature* 285.

applied to the comparative study of corporate governance at the organizational or national level. In particular, a number of newer small-N and set-theoretic methods, such as Qualitative Comparative Analysis (QCA), have been applied to cross-national data (where N is small)[5] or to organizational analysis where causation is complex and there is more than one path to an outcome.[6] Kogut and Ragin put it well when discussing the limited diversity within varieties of capitalism and their empirical rejection of the hypothesis of a direct relationship between rule of law and financial development. They state that "[c]ontrary to silver bullet theories, many studies recognize that economic systems are varied and that there is more than one path to wealth."[7]

Jackson and Aguilera have used this comparative methodology to study why the twenty-two OECD[8] countries show such diverse ownership structures and how these ownership structures have shifted over time – from the 1990s to the 2000s.[9] They were able to systematically explore various existing explanatory factors *in conjunction* (law, financial systems, labor markets, political system, board composition, etc.).[10] They demonstrate, for example, that law is necessary but not sufficient to explain economic organization.[11] More specifically, their analysis rejects the sweeping conclusions drawn from most of LLSV's studies.[12] They show that the quality of law does prove to be necessary for ownership dispersion, at least at a minimum threshold, but that the reverse case (concentrated ownership is a reflection of poor quality of law) is not necessarily true.[13] That is, Jackson and Aguilera uncover that not all cases of concentration are the result of bad law.

---

[5] See generally Bruce Kogut and Charles C. Ragin, "Exploring Complexity When Diversity is Limited: Institutional Complementarity in Theories of Rule of Law and National Systems Revisited" (2006) 3 *European Management Review* 44, 50.

[6] See generally Charles C. Ragin, *Redesigning Social Inquiry: Fuzzy Sets and Beyond* (Chicago: University of Chicago Press, 2008).

[7] Kogut and Ragin, "Exploring Complexity," p. 50.

[8] OECD stands for Organisation for Economic Co-operation and Development. The OECD is an organization of thirty countries committed to democracy and the market economy. See "About OECD," www.oecd.org/pages/0,3417,en_36734052_36734103_1_1_1_1,00.html (last accessed February 22, 2011).

[9] Gregory Jackson and Ruth V. Aguilera, "Some Determinants of Diversity on Cross-National Corporate Ownership: A Fuzzy Sets Approach," Working Paper, Research Institute of Economy, Trade and Industry, Tokyo, 2009.

[10] Jackson and Aguilera, "Some Determinants of Diversity," pp. 4–5.

[11] *Ibid.*, p. 2.   [12] *Ibid.*, p. 20.

[13] *Ibid.* For further discussion of the many variables that interact to shape corporate governance systems, see Ruth V. Aguilera and Gregory Jackson, "Comparative and International Corporate Governance" (2010) 4 *Annals of the Academy of Management* 485–556.

The need to study driving factors in conjunction to obtain a more comprehensive yet systematic understanding of relationships is also true for the political hypothesis based on Gourevitch and Shinn[14] and Roe.[15] The political factors influencing ownership structure, as discussed by Roe and Gourevitch, do appear to be important, but they are missing interesting nuances if not explored in combination with other explanatory factors, such as the structure of labor forces, law, finance, etc. That is to say that strong law and weak majoritarian institutions are sufficient for ownership dispersion but not necessary for dispersion. The main point from this research is *equifinality*, suggesting that there are multiple paths to any given outcome. For instance, if strong law is not present then there might be substitutes (strong labor and left-wing politics) that in complementarity lead to the same outcome that strong law would lead. It also claims that there is not one best Pareto optimal solution in institutional settings or one-model-fits-all best practice of corporate governance.

B   *The difficulty of transplantation and the reality of translation*

It is particularly illuminating to explore nonpure models, such as examining what happens when archetypical "Anglo-Saxon" shareholder value oriented practices are implemented in non-Anglo-Saxon institutional environments. Examining the transplantation of such corporate governance practices allows us to get a deeper understanding of how countries, industries, and firms are selective in their adoption of "pure" corporate governance practices and even more often how some effort is invested into translating those practices so they fit into their environment. A good illustration of the diffusion of practices is the globalization of Anglo-American institutional investors in the mid-1990s, which shocked the recipient host countries' established norms and practices but did not manage to fundamentally transform them. We will draw on two empirical examples to be more specific.

First, Goyer's research comparing foreign investment in France and Germany demonstrates that law and ownership structures cannot account for the disparities in the investment allocation by short-term investors in those two countries.[16] He looks at the different patterns of

---

[14] Peter A. Gourevitch and James Shinn, *Political Power and Corporate Control: The New Global Politics of Corporate Governance* (Princeton: Princeton University Press, 2005).
[15] Roe, "Corporate Law's Limits."
[16] Michel Goyer, "Capital Mobility, Varieties of Institutional Investors, and the Transforming Stability of Corporate Governance in France and Germany," in

investment by short-term institutional investors in France and Germany and finds that for stakes above the 5 percent level, short-term investors are twice as likely to invest in France as compared to Germany.[17] Why? Because Germany's work councils and organized labor make it more difficult to set in motion short-term oriented strategies to extract shareholder value, while labor is less powerful in France.[18]

Second, the translations that occur with transplantation are not only ideological but also structural, as illustrated in the research by Ahmadjian and Robbins.[19] They show that the foreign (mostly US) ownership of Japanese firms grew from 5 percent in 1990 to 20 percent in 2001; these foreign investments led to a clash of capitalism between foreign share-owners and local owners (mostly banks and other local firms).[20] Foreign owners were interested in establishing shareholder-oriented (short-term) practices such as downsizing and asset divestitures.[21] Ahmadjian and Robbins are able to show that the presence of foreign capital determined the levels of downsizing and divestitures in this period in Japan – practices highly inconsistent with Japanese stakeholder capitalism and challenging traditional lifetime employment.[22] When Japanese owners maintained control, however, these shareholder-friendly practices still occurred, but much slower.[23]

C   *The relationship of law and politics*

Roe argues that legal institutions are a direct derivative of politics because countries have different preferences concerning the legitimacy of shareholder value.[24] If shareholder value is considered legitimate, institutions are then built to protect minority shareholders.[25] By contrast, the absence of institutional arrangements that would protect the rights and promote the interests of minority shareholders in some countries reflects the lack of legitimacy about caring only for shareholders. Thus, the question is not about the technical issue of building an

---

Bob Hancké, Martin Rhodes, and Mark Thatcher (eds.), *Beyond Varieties of Capitalism: Conflict, Contradictions, and Complementarities in the European Economy* (Cary: Oxford University Press, 2007), p. 195.

[17] Goyer, "Capital Mobility," p. 205.
[18] *Ibid.*, pp. 206–215.
[19] See generally Christina L. Ahmadjian and Gregory E. Robbins, "A Clash of Capitalisms: Foreign Shareholders and Corporate Restructuring in 1990s Japan" (2005) 70 *American Sociological Review* 451. See also Roe, "Corporate Law's Limits;" Gourevitch and Shinn, *Political Power and Corporate Control.*
[20] Ahmadjian and Robbins, "A Clash of Capitalisms," p. 452.
[21] *Ibid.*   [22] *Ibid.*   [23] *Ibid.*
[24] Roe, "Corporate Law's Limits," p. 267.
[25] *Ibid.*, pp. 262–266.

efficient system of corporate law, but whether or not there is political will to do so.

Roe further argues that it is simplistic to think that legal institutions which were introduced 700 years ago, such as the civil law code-based jurisprudence, are as important in influencing economic life as regulations that were introduced fifty years ago such as the 1933 US Glass–Steagall Act or the 1936 Italian Banking Law introduced in reaction to the 1930s financial crisis and World War II.[26] We find these arguments persuasive.

D Ownership structures – dispersed is not necessarily optimal

The implicit assumption of the legal origins theory is that dispersed ownership within corporations is the ownership structure most likely to produce the best economic outcomes. Yet, most firms in the world are not owned by dispersed shareholders but are firms with controlling shareholders, mainly family-owned firms or firms owned by either large institutional investors or the state.[27] Even in the United States – the archetypical Anglo-Saxon shareholder-oriented country with dispersed ownership – between 1992 and 1999, one-third of the largest firms (the Standard & Poor 500 Industrial) that accounted for 18 percent of the S&P 500 equity stake had family ownership control structures.[28]

Yet, the legal origins research and some finance scholars argue (sometimes quite forcefully) that continued family ownership generally leads to poor performance; hence, they recommend that a more efficient ownership structure aligning management with shareholders' interests is dispersed ownership with strong minority shareholders' protection.[29] The jury is still out within the corporate finance literature on whether family-owned firms perform worse – or better – than firms with

---

[26] Mark J. Roe, "Juries and the Political Economy of Legal Origin" (2007) 35 *Journal of Comparative Economics* 294, 295–308.

[27] Stijn Claessens, Simeon Djankov, and Larry Lang, "Disentangling the Incentive and Entrenchment Effects of Large Shareholdings" (2000) 57 *Journal of Finance* 2741, 2742–2744; Mara Faccio and Larry H.P. Lang, "The Ultimate Ownership of Western Corporations" (2002) 65 *Journal of Financial Economics* 365, 366; Julian Franks and Colin Mayer, "Corporate Ownership and Control in the U.K., Germany, and France" (1997) 9 *Journal of Applied Corporate Finance* 30, 32–37; La Porta *et al.*, "The Economic Consequences of Legal Origins," p. 287; Andrei Shleifer and Robert Vishny, "Large Shareholders and Corporate Control" (1986) 94 *Journal of Political Economy* 461, 462–465.

[28] Ronald C. Anderson and David M. Reeb, "Founding-Family Ownership and Firm Performance: Evidence from the S&P 500" (2003) 58 *Journal of Finance* 1301, 1302.

[29] See generally Randall Morck, *Concentrated Corporate Ownership* (Chicago: University of Chicago Press, 2000).

nonfamily ownership, however. For example, Anderson and Reeb state, "[C]ontrary to the notion that family ownership is detrimental, we find stronger firm performance in family than in nonfamily firms."[30] Amit and Villalonga report similar results.[31] As argued by agency scholars, concentrated ownership can be advantageous to minimize managerial expropriation because it combines ownership and control.[32] Of course, as uncovered by Faccio *et al.*, in the case of East Asian markets or the Adelphia US case, this monitoring will only work when there are transparent financial markets and non-fraudulent accounting, respectively.[33]

Another dimension of corporate ownership to be understood is not so much the type of owner but how much they own (i.e., concentration). We do not equate the owner's identity with the firm's responsibility as one did fifty years ago with the Fords, the DuPonts, and the Rockefellers of Chandler's multidivisional firms, probably because firms have become so large and because there is a mix of ownership (for instance, in the United States). It is also arguable that US corporate governance has shifted from "managerial capitalism" with dispersed retail ownership where managers made the key decisions, to "investor capitalism."[34] As Davis argues in his book, *Managed by Markets: How Finance Reshaped America*, the arrival of post-industrial society, predicted by Daniel Bell, in which the great majority of jobs are in the service sector, accompanied by a weaker relationship between employers and employees and a shift in pension financing from defined benefit company pensions to "defined contribution plans" (401(k)), has triggered the massive growth of the mutual fund industry.[35] Mutual funds and other institutional investors are growing in size and ownership concentration. Davis states that "Nearly three quarters of the average Fortune 1000 corporation's shares were owned by institutional investors in 2005, with mutual funds making up the most concentrated block."[36] Yet, these

---

[30] Anderson and Reeb, "Founding-Family Ownership," p. 1303.
[31] Raphael Amit and Belen Villalonga, "How Do Family Ownership, Control and Management Affect Firm Value?" (2006) 80 *Journal of Financial Economics* 385.
[32] Harold Demsetz and Kenneth Lehn, "The Structure of Corporate Ownership: Causes and Consequences" (1985) 93 *Journal of Political Economics* 1155.
[33] Mara Faccio, Larry H.P. Lang, and Leslie Young, "Dividends and Expropriation" (2001) 91 *American Economics Review* 54, 72.
[34] Michael Useem, *Investor Capitalism: How Money Managers Are Changing the Face of Corporate America* (New York: Basic Books, 1997), pp. 5–8; Gerald F. Davis, "A New Finance Capitalism? Mutual Funds and Ownership Re-Concentration in the United States" (2008) 5 *European Management Review* 11, 13–21.
[35] Gerald F. Davis, *Managed by Markets: How Finance Reshaped America* (Oxford: Oxford University Press, 2009).
[36] Gerald F. Davis, "The Rise and Fall of Finance and the End of the Society of Organizations" (August 2009) 23 *Academy of Management Perspective* 27, 33.

portfolio shareholders show a remarkable lack of engagement ("voice") as shareholders, primarily exercising exit, having high ratios of share turnover in their portfolios, both in the Anglo-Saxon countries as well as in Europe.[37] This is explained in part because it is very expensive to express voice, and second, even very large shareholders such as Hermes in the UK rarely have enough control to discipline managers.[38] As a result, investor capitalism still presents the problem of potential managerial expropriation.

E   *Future research*

The development of capitalism in the twenty-first century, particularly after the US financial collapse and its subsequent recession, is entering a new era where there is a conflict between the increasing globalization of markets, finance, regulation, corporate activity, managers, and knowledge, and the many economic activities that are very much grounded at the state level. The state has played a much more central role in economic life in Europe and Asia until recently, either through regulation or through direct firm ownership and strategic intervention. The state's active role in economic and social life, including welfare state provisions, has been for the most part sustained despite the strong 1990s shareholder-oriented pressures from the US. These pressures resulted in an international hybridization process ranging from full adoption of some practices, such as antitrust regulation, to complete rejection of some practices such as compensation disclosure, as documented in an edited book by Morgan *et al.*,[39] and in a book by Djelic[40] on the "Americanization" of European firms, and in an article on how national culture might buffer organizational level innovation and institutional change,[41] among many others. The pattern emerging now in the US shows a more proactive and monitoring role in the economic, governance, and regulatory relationship between markets and firms.

---

[37] Gregory Jackson, "A New Financial Capitalism? Explaining the Persistence of Exit over Voice in Contemporary Corporate Governance" (2008) 5 *European Management Review* 23, 24–25.
[38] Jackson, "A New Financial Capitalism?," p. 24.
[39] Glenn Morgan, Richard Whitley, and Eli Moen, *Changing Capitalisms: Internationalism, Institutional Change, and Systems of Economic Organizations* (Oxford: Oxford University Press, 2006).
[40] Marie-Laure Djelic, *Exporting the American Model* (Oxford: Oxford University Press, 1998).
[41] Trevor Buck and Azura Shahrim, "The Translation of Corporate Governance Changes Across National Cultures: The Case of Germany" (2005) 36 *Journal of International Business Studies* 42.

This is particularly so after the government interventions in some of the largest US companies that were striving to achieve maximum shareholder value and yet now are partially or majority state-owned, such as AIG and Citigroup.

The institutional legal and economic environment has triggered movement from firms in emerging or developing countries looking to reach higher levels of legitimization in their corporate governance. For example, many firms from middle income, developing, and emerging markets are listed in the New York or London Stock Exchange to prove to their stakeholders that they seek to meet the highest economic and governance standards. The movement in the other direction also occurs, when firms from the industrialized world operate in less developing or emerging markets. These firms make such a move, among other things, to take advantage of institutional arbitrage – such as weak enforcement of global environmental regulations, cheaper labor, or favorable government incentives. Both of these very common internationalization patterns expand beyond the ideas in the legal origins literature in showing that it is almost impossible to attribute economic advantages to merely one single legal or economic system when most firms operate multiple layers of legal systems and their value chain is affected differently. Today, the analogy is that firms are often born simultaneously in multiple countries (e.g., KPMG) or they are born global or born-again global, they grow in multiple countries around the world, yet they must die in one country (e.g., Lehman Brothers, Enron, Arthur Andersen).[42]

A recent trend which challenges even more directly the idea that a certain legal system is best for economic development or that legal systems are ultimately constraining development is the concept of the "New Multinationals" as suggested by Guillén and Garcia-Canal.[43] This concept is probably the strongest robustness test to refute the hypothesis that strong country level institutions, and particularly the legal environment, is a necessary condition to economic development. The new multinational enterprises from emerging, upper-middle income, and rich oil countries have overcome the so-called liability of foreignness in the different markets by entering developed and developing countries simultaneously from the first stages of their international

---

[42] Jim Bell, Rod McNaughton, and Stephen Young, "Born-Again Global Firms: An Extension to the Born-Global Phenomenon" (2001) 7 *Journal of International Management* 173.

[43] Mauro F. Guillén and Esteban Garcia-Canal, "The American Model of the Multinational Firm and the 'New' Multinationals from Emerging Economies" (May 2009) 23 *Academy of Management Perspectives* 23.

expansion.[44] In this context, as suggested by Cuervo-Cazurra and Genc, new multinationals tend to posses critical political capabilities enabling them to succeed in countries with weak institutional environments and compensate for their lack of resource endowment.[45] In sum, this research in the internationalization field shows that MNEs' success, such as that of Inditex of Spain (Zara) or Haier in China, can be achieved almost irrespective of the institutional environment.

To conclude, we think that legal scholarship could benefit a great deal by drawing a bit more on research on national business systems,[46] on the comparative capitalism approach,[47] and more historically oriented institutional analysis.[48] We also need to think more systematically on how employees contribute to the value-added in the firm, from a stakeholder perspective as suggested in the UK–US comparison[49] and from the perspective of the knowledge economy.[50] Other authors have stressed the role of employees in the finance–legal relationship by studying the political power of workers[51] or the economics of human assets.[52] This previous research shows that bringing labor into the equation helps us

---

[44] *Ibid.*, p. 43.
[45] Alvaro Cuervo-Cazurra and Mehmet Genc, "Transforming Disadvantages into Advantages: Developing-Country MNEs in the Least Developed Countries" (2008) 39 *Journal of International Business Studies* 957, 963–966.
[46] Richard Whitley, *Divergent Capitalisms: The Social Structuring and Change of Business Systems* (Cary: Oxford University Press, 1999).
[47] Masahiko Aoki, *Toward a Comparative Institutional Analysis* (Cambridge, MA: MIT Press, 2001); Ronald Dore, *Stock Market Capitalism: Welfare Capitalism: Japan and Germany Versus the Anglo-Saxons* (Cary: Oxford University Press, 2000); Peter A. Hall and David Soskice, *Varieties of Capitalism: The Institutional Foundations of Comparative Advantage* (Cary: Oxford University Press, 2001); Bob Hancké, Martin Rhodes, and Mark Thatcher, *Beyond Varieties of Capitalism: Conflict, Contradictions, and Complementaries in the European Economy* (Cary: Oxford University Press, 2007).
[48] Gourevitch and Shinn, *Political Power and Corporate Control*; Arndt Sorge, *The Global and the Local: Understanding the Dialectics of Business Systems* (Oxford: Oxford University Press, 2005); Kathleen Thelen, "Historical Institutionalism in Comparative Politics" (1999) 2 *Annual Review of Political Sciences* 369–404.
[49] Ruth V. Aguilera, Cynthia Williams, John M. Conley, and Deborah Rupp, "Corporate Governance and Social Responsibility: A Comparative Analysis of the U.K. and the U.S." (2006) 14 *Corporate Governance: An International Review* 147; Howard Gospel and Andrew Pendleton (eds.), *Corporate Governance and Labour Management: An International Comparison* (Oxford: Oxford University Press, 2009).
[50] Chapter 7, this volume.
[51] Marco Pagano and Paolo F. Volpin, "The Political Economy of Corporate Governance" (2005) 95 *American Economic Review* 1005.
[52] Margaret M. Blair, "Firm-Specific Human Capital and Theories of the Firm," in Margaret M. Blair and Mark J. Roe (eds.), *Employees and Corporate Governance* (Brookings, MA: Brookings Institution Press, 1999); Margaret M. Blair and Lynn A. Stout, "A Team Production Theory of Corporate Law" (1999) 85 *Virginia Law Review* 247; Raghuram G. Rajan and Luigi Zingales, "The Governance of the New Enterprise," in Xavier Vives (ed.), *Corporate Governance: Theoretical and Empirical Perspectives* (Cambridge: Cambridge University Press, 2000).

examine what might seem a remote link between employees, company resources, and national and global financing "machines" as Davis has shown with the securitization of mortgages and the takeoff of pension plans with the emergence of weaker and more flexible labor contracts in the post-industrial United States.[53]

Firms and markets co-evolve, institutions change, not only at the regulatory level, but also within technological and knowledge spheres, and these processes are shaping economic life in a reciprocal and evolutionary way. Economic sociology captures and illuminates much of this co-evolution; law and finance does not.

III Why is LLSV nonetheless important?

The above sections referred to or have made the following points: first, careful longitudinal studies and studies using more accurate evaluations of the components of countries' legal systems have failed to support the central claim of LLSV – that a country's legal origin is an important exogenous determinant of its capacity for financial development. That is to say, LLSV is based on an inaccurate view of the law. Second, more nuanced institutional analyses and comparative political economy analyses of corporate governance arrangements than those of LLSV can contribute valuable insights into the central question of the relationships between financial markets and economic development, and therefore provide a more considered view. That is to say, LLSV is based on an incomplete view of what matters for economic outcomes. Why, then, does LLSV still matter?

At least in part, LLSV matter because their original contributions – their data-rich descriptions of ownership patterns around the world – have given rise to provocative research questions and spawned engaging academic debates and comparative analyses.[54] They have established and defined the field of law and finance, and then elaborated upon it with prodigious productivity. Few academics can point to similar accomplishments.

Yet, as a number of contributors to this volume discuss,[55] LLSV matter for at least two additional reasons that go beyond academics: first,

---

[53] Gerald Davis, *Managed by Markets: How Finance Reshaped America* (Cary: Oxford University Press, 2009).
[54] La Porta *et al.*, "Corporate Ownership"; Shleifer and Vishny, "A Survey of Corporate Governance."
[55] John Armour, Simon Deakin, Viviana Mollica, and Mathias Siems, "Law and Financial Development: What We Are Learning from Time-Series Evidence" (2009) 1435 *Brigham Young University Law Review*.

because their ideas have been adopted in international development initiatives by the World Bank as the basis for one set of its policy prescriptions for economic development in emerging markets; and second, because their ideas are indicative of, and have supported, the virtually unrelenting pressure on European countries to adopt more market-dominated systems for organizing their economic life.

While one could think that perhaps LLSV's ideas have simply been misused in these regards, their own ten-year retrospective analysis of the significance of their work, published in 2008, ends with a clear policy preference: "our framework suggests that the common law approach to social control of economic life performs better than the civil law approach. When markets do or can work well, it is better to support than to replace them."[56] (Replacing markets, in LLSV terms, includes civil law countries continuing "to resort to 'policy-implementing' solutions to newly arising problems," such as "using state mandates to solve social problems, such as the thirty-five hour work-week in France," rather than adopting "market-supporting" solutions.)[57] It is because LLSV's preference for market solutions has had such powerful reverberations in global policy developments and European debates that it is important to examine their analysis in more depth.

A LLSV and the World Bank's Doing Business Initiative

LLSV's work is consistent with and has provided intellectual support for a complex of policy prescriptions that are considered important in allowing financial markets to flourish – introducing clear property rights to facilitate exchange; protecting principles of freedom of contract; and perhaps most central in their writing, enhancing the legal protections for outside investors and outside senior creditors. As described by leading law and development scholar David Trubek, reform initiatives implementing these kinds of broad policy goals have been incorporated into the World Bank's rule of law initiatives over the last two decades.[58] These programs derive from the Washington Consensus: the view that promoting economic development through export-led growth, attracting foreign investment, and encouraging capital market development and integration is the most effective way to alleviate poverty.[59] Between

---

[56] La Porta *et al.*, "Economic Consequences of Legal Origins," p. 327.
[57] *Ibid.*
[58] David M. Trubek, "The 'Rule of Law' in Development Assistance: Past, Present, and Future," in David M. Trubek and Alvaro Santos (eds.), *The New Law and Economic Development: A Critical Appraisal* (Cambridge: Cambridge University Press, 2006).
[59] See generally John Williamson, "A Short History of the Washington Consensus" (2009) 15 *Law & Business Review of the Americas* 7.

1990 and 2005, the World Bank has therefore supported 330 "rule of law" initiatives at a cost of $2.9 billion.[60] (As Professor Trubek also discussed, as the consensus over the Washington Consensus has started to dissolve, the World Bank has begun to develop a broader range of policy approaches to poverty alleviation that provides more latitude to attending more directly to social and economic development efforts of a "bottom-up" nature.)[61]

Based in significant part on LLSV's methodology for quantifying law, one strand of rule of law projects that is still emerging is the World Bank's Doing Business Initiative, begun in 2004.[62] That initiative is an ambitious attempt to collect information on the ease of doing business in (now) 183 countries in order to quantify and benchmark "the scope and manner of regulations that enhance business activity and those that constrain it."[63] In 2004, five types of business activities were evaluated in 133 countries: (1) starting a business; (2) hiring and firing workers (the "Employing Workers' Index," which became particularly controversial); (3) enforcing a contract; (4) getting credit; and (5) closing a business.[64] In 2005, two more measures were added for (6) registering property; and (7) protecting investors.[65] In 2007, additional measures evaluating (8) business taxes; (9) trading across borders; and (10) dealing with licenses were added.[66] From these submeasures the World Bank produces an ordinal ranking of countries on the ease of doing business, a ranking that suggests in 2010 the rather counterintuitive view that it is better to do business in Thailand, Georgia, Saudi Arabia, Malaysia, or Estonia than in Germany, the Netherlands, Austria, France, or Spain.[67]

Initial exposition by the World Bank of the premises of the project show the close intellectual affinity to LLSV's work, as the Bank concluded in 2004 that "[h]eavier regulation of business activities generally brings bad outcomes, while clearly defined and well-protected property rights enhance prosperity."[68] Lest one misses the point, the Bank also emphasized that "[c]ommon law countries regulate the least. Countries in the French civil law tradition the most."[69]

---

[60] Trubek, "The 'Rule of Law'," p. 74.
[61] Ibid.
[62] See generally Kevin E. Davis and Michael B. Kruse, "Taking the Measure of Law: The Case of the Doing Business Project" (2007) 32 *Law & Social Inquiry* 1095.
[63] Ibid., p. 1096.   [64] Ibid., p. 1097.
[65] Ibid., p. 1098.   [66] Ibid.
[67] World Bank Report, *Doing Business 2010*, available at: www.doingbusiness.org/economyrankings (last accessed February 22, 2011).
[68] Davis and Kruse, "Taking the Measure of Law," p. 1102.
[69] Ibid.

In a thoughtful evaluation of the Doing Business Initiative, Davis and Kruse praise the project for its attempt to systematically evaluate business environments. However, they also express concerns over the methodology, given that "law is inherently difficult to measure in quantitative terms,"[70] and given the lack of empirical evidence that the parameters they have chosen to evaluate have a clear relationship with important social and economic outcomes in developing economies.[71] Moreover, some of the elements being evaluated are ideologically charged, such as those giving high scores to countries in which it is easy to hire and fire workers and in which business taxes are low.[72] Seeing how the World Bank describes changes in its methodology in 2009 for "scoring" labor gives a good indication of the concern:

> The methodology for one of the Doing Business topics – employing workers – was updated this year ... The scope of the question on night and weekly holiday work has been limited to manufacturing activities in which continuous operation is economically necessary. Legally mandated wage premiums for night and weekly holiday work up to a threshold are no longer considered a restriction. In addition, the calculation of the minimum wage ratio was modified to ensure that an economy would not benefit in the scoring from lowering the minimum wage to below $1.25 a day, adjusted for purchasing power parity. This level is consistent with recent adjustments to the absolute poverty line. Finally, the calculation of the redundancy cost was adjusted so that having severance payments or unemployment protections below a certain threshold does not mean a better score for an economy.[73]

These revisions were inspired, in part, by a report by International Labor Organization researchers showing that, in many instances, countries whose labor laws reflected Internal Labor Conventions scored worse than if their national labor legislation violated those treaties.[74]

Clearly there are political forces at work much beyond LLSV's analysis to make these kinds of assumptions palatable to some people (but by no

---

[70] *Ibid.*, p. 1104.
[71] *Ibid.*, pp. 1109–1112. See also David E. Pozen, "The Regulation of Labor and the Relevance of Legal Origin" (2006) 28 *Comparative Labor Law and Policy Journal* 43, 45–55 for a related methodological critique.
[72] Alvaro Santos, "Labor Flexibility, Legal Reform and Economic Development" (2009) 50 *Virginia Journal of International Law* 43–106, 53–55 provides a comprehensive discussion of this topic, as does Benito Arrunada, "Pitfalls to Avoid When Measuring the Institutions: Is Doing Business Damaging Business?" (2007) 35 *Journal of Comparative Economics* 729, 735–744.
[73] The World Bank Group and International Finance Corporation, *Doing Business 2010: Reforming Through Difficult Times* (New York: Palgrave Macmillan, 2009).
[74] Janine Berg and Sandrine Cazes, Int'l Labour Org., "The Doing Buiness Indicators: Measurement Issues and Political Implications" (2007) *Economic & Labour Market Paper 2007/6*, at p. 3, available at: www.ilo.org/empelm/what/pubs/lang – en/docName – WCMS_113905/index.htm (last accessed February 22, 2011).

means all people) working in an institution like the World Bank, whose primary goal is to eradicate poverty. It is surprising that a development agency's metric would reward pay levels below the absolute poverty line or would reward lowering social protections for workers who are fired or are unemployed. Prior to the changes in methodology in 2009, that was precisely the direction that countries' reform efforts could take in order to increase their score in the Doing Business Initiative, and to increase their likelihood of attracting funding from the World Bank. Further research should evaluate the extent to which other more direct World Bank development initiatives with proven potential to reduce poverty, such as educating girls in rural societies, were sacrificed on behalf of the Doing Business Initiative.

To the extent that LLSV's work informs both the methodology and assumptions of the Doing Business project – and their own retrospective discusses their involvement and the reforms the project has encouraged – then concerns over the reliability of LLSV's methodology and results (as discussed above and by Armour et al.[75]) are heightened. Some of the legal reforms that the Doing Business Initiative promotes presumably do have positive consequences for enhancing social welfare outcomes, such as reforms that shrink the size of the unofficial economy or permit extremely low-income people to advance ownership claims over property. But by failing to untangle those reforms that improve the lives of the poor from those that simply mesh with the political commitments of economists such as LLSV, though, the World Bank risks undermining both its efficacy at achieving its core mission and its reputation.

B   LLSV and the promotion of shareholder-oriented corporate governance

It is beyond the remit of this short chapter to demonstrate the various ways in which European countries and companies have been under virtually unrelenting pressure over the last three decades to adopt so-called Anglo-American concepts of corporate governance and finance; that is, until August 2007 when the global financial fabric began to unravel. When the intellectual history of this era is written, these authors have no doubt that it will show that a "west wind was blowing" as cadres of professors, asset managers, shareholder activists, and institutional investors from the US enjoyed European hospitality on a quite regular basis even as they encouraged European leaders, countries, and companies to adopt US values,

---

[75] Armour et al., "Law and Financial Development."

specifically US "shareholder value," rather than stakeholder value, as the touchstone of proper corporate governance. At a macro level, a deeply held belief in the superiority of market mechanisms relatively unconstrained by government regulation for solving important social coordination problems underlies much of this promotional activity, influenced by three decades of deregulatory political and economic theory.[76]

LLSV's thesis shares this faith in markets, and their work supports legal rules, such as those protecting minority shareholders, to encourage financial markets to flourish. As they summarize:

> In sum, there is by now a great deal of evidence that legal origins influence legal rules and regulations, which in turn have substantial impact on important economic outcomes – from financial development, to unemployment, to investment and entry, to the size of the unofficial economy, to international trade. Much of this evidence suggests that common law is associated with better economic outcomes than French civil law.[77]

Even so, they point out that "it is less clear that legal origins predict aggregate growth."[78] The authors expound:

> [The finding that it is uncertain whether legal origins predict aggregate growth] resonates with the obvious observation made by LLSV (1998) that countries like France and Belgium achieved high living standards despite their legal origin. One possible explanation of the aggregate growth evidence is that civil law countries have found compensating mechanisms to overcome the baggage of their legal tradition in the long run.[79]

Indeed, as the authors stated in a footnote, "[w]e note, however, that the evidence on the relationship between institutions and aggregate growth more generally, which seemed substantial a few years ago, has been crumbling."[80]

This last admission is the point at which one wonders if the asserted superiority of the common law system for "better economic outcomes" is also crumbling. If the financial development that is encouraged by common law legal origins is not leading to higher aggregate economic growth, then on what basis is financial development a useful measure of better economic outcomes? And on what basis is a high level of financial development per se a good thing and demonstrative of institutional superiority if it *does not* lead to higher aggregate growth

---

[76] Frank Jan De Graaf and Cynthia A. Williams, "The Intellectual Foundations of the Global Financial Crisis" (2009) 32 *University of New South Wales Law Journal* 402–405, reprinted in this volume as Chapter 17.
[77] La Porta *et al.*, "Economic Consequences of Legal Origins," p. 302.
[78] Ibid., p. 302.   [79] Ibid.
[80] Ibid., n. 11.

in the real economy? These are questions policy-makers are posing today in light of the global financial crisis. An example is found in the Turner Review for the Financial Services Authority (FSA) in the UK, where Lord Turner observed that in the UK and the US, from the 1980s on, "[t]he evolution of the securitised credit model was accompanied by a remarkable growth in the relative size of wholesale financial services within the overall economy, with activities internal to the banking system growing far more rapidly than end services to the real economy."[81]

It seems likely that the measure of financial development LLSV use as their indicator of better outcomes from common law legal origins, stock market capitalization per GDP,[82] is simply a measure of the degree of financialization of a particular economy. This view is consistent with the data LLSV present in Table 7 of their ten-year retrospective, which shows that most countries experienced an increase in stock market capitalization per GDP between 1990 and 1999,[83] a time when the technology bubble in stock prices was developing in many advanced economies, pushing stock market values higher generally. Table 7 also shows that in a number of countries, the ratio of stock market capitalization to GDP grew dramatically from 1990 to 1999, most notably in the United Kingdom (from 0.81 to 2.25) (English legal origin); the United States (0.54 to 1.52) (English legal origin); the Netherlands (0.50 to 2.03) (French legal origin); Switzerland (1.93 to 3.23) (German legal origin); and Sweden (0.39 to 1.77) (Scandinavian legal origin).[84]

If, as it seems, the legal origins measure of stock market capitalization to GDP does not relate to or predict aggregate growth but perhaps does measure financialization, then this outcome measure may, *in more market economies*, be inversely related to better economic outcomes. While this is frank speculation, it is based on the view that the underlying strengths and stability of European social democracies perhaps ameliorated the worst excesses and instabilities of financialization even where financialization was well advanced (such as in the Netherlands, Switzerland, and Sweden).

If, as we have argued, financialization per se is not a useful measure of "better economic outcomes," and with debate amongst economists concerning the value to countries' economies of foreign direct

---

[81] Financial Services Authority, *The Turner Review: A Regulatory Response to the Global Banking Crisis*, March 2009, available at: www.fsa.gov.uk/pubs/other/turner_review.pdf (last accessed February 22, 2011).
[82] La Porta *et al.*, "Economic Consequences of Legal Origins," pp. 316–318.
[83] *Ibid.*, p. 317.   [84] *Ibid.*

investment in predicting better economic outcomes for developing economies,[85] LLSV need to concentrate on higher unemployment levels and a larger informal economy in civil law countries to make the case that "common law is associated with better economic outcomes."[86] These are undoubtedly important measures of real economic benefits or detriments from systems of laws, regulations, and norms, and so it is here that LLSV's analysis seems persuasive. Yet, LLSV seem to be engaging in academic cherry-picking. A more comprehensive look at other measures of the economic benefits of the European systems of social and economic organization suggests as much.

In his recent book, *Common Wealth: Economics for a Crowded Planet*, economist Jeffrey Sachs compares data on various measures of economic health between the social welfare states of Denmark, Finland, Norway, and Sweden; the mixed economies of Austria, Belgium, France, Germany, Italy, and the Netherlands (the latter has aspects of both social welfare and mixed economy); and the more free market countries of Australia, Canada, Ireland, New Zealand, the United Kingdom, and the United States.[87] Professor Sachs presents data showing lower poverty rates in the social welfare states (5.6 percent) compared to the mixed economies (9 percent), compared to the free market states (12.6 percent), with the United States showing a poverty rate of 17.1 percent.[88] The poverty rate is defined as the percentage of people living at less than half the average national household income.[89] The Gini coefficient, which measures how equally wealth is distributed within countries, where 0 is perfectly equal and 100 is perfectly unequal, was determined by Professor Sachs to be 24.7 for social welfare states; 28 for the mixed economies; and 32 for the free market economies, with the United States at 35.7.[90] Average per capita income is higher in the social welfare states as compared to the free market economies, with the mixed economies placing third.[91] And, contrary to LLSV's conclusions, Professor Sachs presents data showing that "the social-welfare states have an even higher employment rate (number of workers as a

---

[85] See, for example, Joseph E. Stiglitz, "Capital-Market Liberalization, Globalization, and the IMF" (2004) 20 *Oxford Review of Economic Policy* 64–65. LLSV use higher levels of foreign direct investment as a positive measure of a countries' economic health, but as the Stiglitz article shows this view is not universal among economists: foreign direct portfolio investment is associated with higher levels of economic and currency volatility and political instability.

[86] La Porta *et al.*, "The Economic Consequences of Legal Origins," p. 302.

[87] Jeffrey D. Sachs, *Common Wealth: Economics for a Crowded Planet* (New York: Penguin Press, 2008), p. 258.

[88] Sachs, *Common Wealth*, p. 261.

[89] Ibid.   [90] Ibid., p. 261.   [91] Ibid., p. 262.

share of the working-age population) than the free-market countries."[92] He concludes that "the social-welfare states have achieved high levels of incomes, low rates of poverty, and a more equal distribution of incomes than the free-market societies."[93] These conclusions provide a sharp contrast to LLSV's incomplete picture of the economic outcomes asserted to flow from legal origins, and suggest that the debates over the superiority of different capitalist systems of economic organization cannot be considered over.

IV   Conclusion

LLSV's research purporting to demonstrate the importance of the legal origins of a country for its stock market development and ownership dispersion, mediated through the protection of minority shareholders as against directors, has been subjected to enough further, careful analysis that we can see the inaccuracies, but also the importance, of their research.

In this chapter, we have suggested that economic sociology has much to add to the raw facts of ownership patterns within countries. There are provocative hints that companies with controlling shareholders can actually outperform companies without, contingent on the nature of the owners (family, state, bank, parent company, etc.), the type of industrial sector, the stage of the firm's life cycle, and the other institutional arrangements in the country. Putting ownership patterns on the agenda of academic inquiry was clearly an important contribution by LLSV. Understanding what those patterns imply for firm performance, within different institutional arrangements and complementarities, is yet to be fully addressed, either in their work or in comparative corporate governance generally.

We have also suggested that it is important to uncover the contributions, if any, of legal origins to positive *economic* measures of a country's health, fully conceived. Financial measures alone do not suffice to provide that understanding. In light of the collapse of innovative financialization over the past few years, and the resulting global recession, we should re-examine LLSV's fundamental conceptions – and perhaps misconceptions – of the value of stock market capitalization per se as a measure of healthy economies.

[92] *Ibid.*, p. 261.
[93] *Ibid.*, p. 262.

Part III

Labor's evolution in the new economy

13 Labor and finance in the United States

Sanford M. Jacoby

I Introduction

We live in an era of financialization. Since 1980, capital markets have expanded around the world; capital shuttles the global instantaneously. Shareholder concerns drive executive decision-making and compensation, while the fluctuations of stock markets are a source of public anxiety. So are the financial scandals that have regularly occurred in recent years: junk bonds in the 1980s; lax accounting and stock manipulation in the early 2000s; and debt securitization today.

We also live in an era of rising income inequality and employment risk. The gaps between top and bottom incomes and between top and middle incomes have widened since 1980. Greater risk takes various forms, such as wage and employment volatility and the shift from employers to employees of responsibility for pensions and, in the United States, for health insurance.

There is an enormous literature on financial development and another on inequality. But relatively few studies consider the intersection of these phenomena. Standard explanations for rising inequality – skill-biased technological change and trade – account for only 30 percent of the variation in aggregate inequality.[1] What else matters? We argue here that an omitted factor is financial development. This study explores the relationship between financial markets and labor markets along three dimensions: contemporary, historical, and comparative. For the world's industrialized nations, we find that financial development waxes and wanes in line with top income shares. Since 1980, however, there have been national divergences between financial development – defined here as the economic prominence of equity and credit markets – and

---

This chapter is dedicated to Lloyd Ulman: scholar, teacher, mensch. It is a revised version of a previous paper, "Finance and Labor," which first appeared in *Comparative Labor Law & Policy Journal* (2008).

[1] IMF, *World Economic Outlook: Globalization and Inequality* (Washington, DC, 2007), p. 48.

inequality. In the United States and the UK, there remains a strong positive correlation but in other parts of Europe and in Japan the relationship is weaker.

What accounts for swings in financial development and inequality and the relationship between them? Economic growth is one factor. Another is the politics of finance. The model presented here is simple but consistent with the evidence: upswings in financial development are related to political pressure exerted by elite beneficiaries of financial development. Political objectives include policies that favor financial expansion – and finance-derived earnings – and the shunting of investment gains to top-income brackets. Against financial interests is arrayed a shifting coalition that has included middle-class consumers, farmers, small business, and organized labor, upon which we focus here. When successful, these groups cause a contraction in the economic and political significance of finance, which registers in the distribution of income and wealth. In other words, politics drives the swings in financial development and mediates the finance–labor relationship.

Political contests occur not only in the public arena but also within firms. We expand the politics of financial development to include contests over corporate resource allocation through the mechanisms of corporate governance. Corporate governance affects the distribution of a firm's value-added among shareholders, executives, workers, and retained earnings. Here too, organized labor is an important player. In both public and private arenas, labor wields influence via its bargaining and political power and, more recently, via its pension capital.

Our historical framework draws from Karl Polanyi's classic study of markets and politics in the nineteenth and early twentieth centuries. Polanyi challenged economic liberalism by showing that market expansion in the Western countries was not a natural development; it was embedded in politics and society. He also showed that markets are not self-regulating. Undesirable side-effects – instability, monopoly, externalities – cannot be rectified by the market itself. As a result, every market expansion is followed by spontaneous countermovements to "resist the pernicious effects of a market-controlled economy." Polanyi called this the double movement "the action of two organizing principles in society ... economic liberalism, aiming at the establishment of a self-regulating market ... [and] the other was the principle of social protection aiming at the conservation of man and nature as well as productive organization." Writing in the early 1940s, Polanyi could not foresee the relevance of his ideas to our present age. Today, laissez-faire ideas, including those relating to financial markets, again are with us as are countermovements to contain the market's failings.[2]

The focus of this study is on financial markets in the world's richest nations. Much of the material is based on the American experience, although there are comparisons to Europe and Japan. Section II analyzes the mechanisms that link contemporary financial development to rising inequality and risk. Section III considers the political and ideological bases for post-1980 financial development and corporate governance. Section IV is historical, tracing political movements to contain finance and emphasizing the contributions of organized labor. Section V takes us back to the present. It considers the efforts of organized labor to re-regulate finance and reshape corporate governance, in part by using its pension capital.

II Labor and financial development since 1980

Financial development since 1980 is unprecedented. The value of financial assets – bank assets, equities, private and public debt securities – increased from $12 trillion in 1980 to $140 trillion in 2005. Equities alone drove nearly half the rise in global financial assets during those years, with stock market capitalizations reaching or exceeding levels not seen since the 1920s.

Along with this has come abundant capital that lowers debt costs, thereby permitting banks, hedge funds, and private equity funds to leverage small asset bases.[3]

Although financial development is global, the wealthiest regions of the world – the United States, the UK, the Eurozone, and Japan – account for 80 percent of world financial assets. Finance has become a key sector of the American and British economies, representing over 15 percent of their GDPs and over 40 percent of total corporate profits before the financial implosion that started in 2008.[4]

Finance is vital to economic growth. It provides capital to sustain firms and households, and mechanisms to mitigate risk. The relationship

---

[2] Karl Polanyi, *The Great Transformation: The Political and Economic Origins of Our Time* (New York: Farrar & Rinehart, 1944), p. 132.
[3] Bank for International Settlements, *Semiannual Over-The-Counter (OTC) Derivatives Markets Statistics* (Basel, 2008).
[4] Raghuram Rajan and Luigi Zingales, "The Great Reversals: The Politics of Financial Development in the 20th Century" (2003) 69 *Journal of Financial Economics* 13–15; Charles R. Morris, *The Trillion Dollar Meltdown: Easy Money, High Rollers and The Great Credit Crash* (New York: Perseus Book Group, 2008); Diana Farrell, Susan M. Lund, and Alexander N. Maasry, "Mapping the Global Capital Market," McKinsey Global Institute (2007), p. 8.

between financial development and growth is ambiguous, however. The effects vary by a nation's GDP level and the type of financial development – credit markets, equity markets, or financial openness – under consideration.[5] Other aspects of finance are more controversial. Investors are prone to herd behavior and to mercurial speculation about an uncertain future. Because perceptions of the future are constantly changing and because speculation involves leveraging, capital markets are prone to volatility and periodic crises that can damage the real economy, as with the recession that started in 2008.

There is also the problem that financialization raises risk. Optimism – animal spirits – and the opportunities for diversification associated with financial development raise the risk-tolerance levels of investors. Wall Street asserts that derivatives and other instruments have mitigated the problems that this poses. But the events of 2008 suggest the opposite: that hedging amplifies, rather than reduces, risk. Until recently, it was claimed that we were at the end of history – that financial crises, at least in advanced economies, were a thing of the past thanks to savvy central banking and savvier derivatives. Today the assertion appears to be another case of irrational exuberance.[6]

Another problematic aspect of financial development is its relation to inequality.[7]

---

[5] Levine and Zervos find that stock market liquidity is positively associated with growth but that stock market size has no effect. Arestis *et al.* show that the contribution of stock markets to growth is modest and that the effect attenuates in developed countries. An IMF (2006: 16) review of the evidence on financial openness concludes that "it remains difficult to find robust evidence that financial integration systematically increases growth, once other determinants of growth are controlled for," a finding replicated by Rodrik. M. Ayan Khose, Eswar Prasad, Kenneth Rogoff, and Shang-Jin Wei, "Financial Globalization: A Reappraisal," IMF Staff Papers 56, 8–62 (April 2006); Dani Rodrik and Arvind Subramanian, "Why Did Financial Globalization Disappoint?" IMF Working Paper (March 2008). See also Ross Levine and Sara Zervos, "Stock Markets, Banks, and Economic Growth" (1998) 88 *American Economic Review*; Philip Arestis, Panicos O. Demetriades, and Kul B. Luintel, "Financial Development and Economic Growth: The Role of Stock Markets" (2001) 33 *Journal of Money, Credit, and Banking*; Philip Arestis, Georgios E. Chortareas, and Evangelia Desli, "Financial Development and Productive Efficiency in OECD Countries" (2006) 74 *The Manchester School.*

[6] Philip T. Hoffman, Gilles Postal-Vinay, and Jean-Laurent Rosenthal, *Surviving Large Losses: Financial Crises, the Middle Class, and the Development of Capital Markets* (Cambridge, MA: Bellknap Press, 2007); David Skeel, *Icarus in the Boardroom: The Fundamental Flaws In Corporate America And Where They Came From* (New York: Oxford University Press, 2005); Charles Kindleberger and Robert Aliber, *Manias, Panics, and Crashes: A History of Financial Crises* (Hoboken: John Wiley and Sons, 2005).

[7] The literature on finance and inequality largely deals with developing, not developed, countries: Clarke *et al.* and Beck *et al.* find a negative association between financial development and inequality, although they examine credit provision, not equity markets; Baddeley finds a positive association between financial development and inequality;

The finance–inequality link occurs via the concentration of finance-derived incomes in the top brackets. Since 1980, the top 1 percent doubled its income share in the United States, reaching levels not seen since the early twentieth century (see Table 13.1). Atkinson estimates that a rise of 8 percentage points in the top 1 percent share – which occurred in the United States since 1980 – can account for nearly all of the Gini coefficient's increase during this period. Of course, this does not prove that the former caused the latter. But the difficulty of demonstrating causality is endemic to studies of inequality, as with the well-known example of the returns to computer usage.[8]

A   Wealth ownership

After remaining stable during most of the postwar period, top wealth shares recently have trended upward in the United States. The average

---

Das and Mohapatra show that stock market liberalization is followed by rising inequality, especially through the effects on top-income shares; and Goldberg and Pavcnik find that trade openness, which is correlated with financial openness, is positively associated with inequality. Claessens and Perotti find that the relationship between financial openness and consumption smoothing by the poor is mediated by politics: when the rich have political control, the relationship is negative, which is consistent with our argument. Aghion et al. explain how growth is hampered by inequality. George Clarke, Lixin Xu, and Heng-fu Zou, "Finance and Income Inequality: What Do the Data Tell US?" (2006) 72 *Southern Economic Journal*; Thorsten Beck, Asli Demirguc-Kunt, and Ross Levine, "Finance, Inequality, and the Poor," Working Paper (2007); Michelle Baddeley, "Convergence or Divergence? The Impacts of Globalisation on Growth and Inequality in Less Developed Countries" (2006) 20 *International Review of Applied Economics*; Mitali Das and Sanket Mohapatra, "Income Inequality: The Aftermath of Stock Market Liberalization in Emerging Markets" (2003) 10 *Journal of Empirical Finance*; Pinelopi Goldberg and Nina Pavcnik, "Distributional Effects of Globalization in Developing Countries" (2007) 45 *Journal of Economic Literature*; Stijn Claessens and Enrico Perotti, "Finance and Inequality: Channels and Evidence" (2007) 35 *Journal of Comparative Economics* 748–773; Philippe Aghion, Eve Caroli, and Cecilia Garcia-Penalosa, "Inequality and Economic Growth" (1999) 37 *Journal of Economic Literature*. A recent paper, however, focuses on financial development in wealthy countries over the past century and finds a positive association between financial development and top-share incomes, the same relationship considered here. Jesper Roine, Jonas Vlachos, and Daniel Waldenstrom, "What Determines Top Income Shares? Evidence from the Twentieth Century" (2007) Social Science Research Network (SSRN) Working Paper 1018372, Research Institute of Industrial Economics (IFN), forthcoming.

[8] A.B. Atkinson, "Measuring Top Incomes: Methodological Issues," in A.B. Atkinson and T. Piketty (eds.), *Top Incomes over the Twentieth Century: A Contrast between Continental European and English-Speaking Countries* (New York: Oxford University Press, 2007), pp. 18–42; John DiNardo and Jorn-Steffen Pischke, "The Returns to Computer Use Revisited: Have Pencils Changed the Wage Structure Too?" (1997) *The Quarterly Journal of Economics*. In contrast to the Kuznets inverted-U curve charting inequality against industrialization over time, the post-1980 data look like the first part of a subsequent inverted-U.

Table 13.1 *Financial development and inequality, 1913–1999*

	Financial development				Inequality	
	Stock market capitalization as GDP share		Gross fixed capital raised via equity		Top 1% income share	
	US & UK	Eur. & Japan	US & UK	Eur. & Japan	US & UK	Eur. & Japan
1913	0.74 (0.39)	0.55	0.09	0.15	0.19 (0.18)	0.19
1929	1.07 (0.75)	0.65	0.37	0.30	0.19 (0.20)	0.16
1938	0.85 (0.56)	0.64	0.05	0.27	0.16 (0.15)	0.15
1950	0.55 (0.33)	0.14	0.06	0.01	0.11 (0.12)	0.10
1970	1.15 (0.66)	0.22	0.04	0.20	0.08 (0.08)	0.09
1980	0.42 (0.46)	0.16	0.04	0.02	0.08 (0.09)	0.07
1999	1.89 (2.3)	1.32	0.11	0.21 [0.08]	0.16 (0.18)	0.08
1980/1929	0.39 (0.61)	0.27	0.11	0.07	0.39 (0.45)	0.46
1999/1980	4.5 (4.9)	8.3	2.8	10.5 [3.4]	2.1 (2.0)	1.1

Notes: the European nations and Japan include two using the French legal system (France and Netherlands), two using the Germanic system (Germany and Japan), and one following the Scandinavian system (Sweden). Figures in parentheses are for the United States; figures in brackets exclude the Netherlands.

Sources: financial data are from Raghuram Rajan and Luigi Zingales, "Great Reversals: The Politics of Financial Development in the Twentieth Century" (2003) 69 *Journal of Financial Economics* 13–15. Top share sources are as follows.

UK: A.B. Atkinson, "Top Incomes in the U.K. over the 20th Century" (2005) 168 *Journal of the Royal Statistical Society*. US: Emmanuel Saez website, http://elsa.berkeley.edu/~saez/. France: Thomas Piketty, "Income Inequality in France, 1901–1998," CEPR Working Paper 2876 (2001). Germany: Fabien Dell, "Top Incomes in Germany and Switzerland over the 20th Century" (2005) 3 *Journal of the European Economic Association*. Netherlands: A.B. Atkinson and Wiemer Salverda, "Top Incomes in the Netherlands and the U.K. over the 20th Century" (2005) 3 *Journal of the European Economic Association*. Sweden: Jesper Roine and Daniel Waldenstrom, "Top Incomes in Sweden over the 20th Century," Stockholm School of Economics, working paper 602 (2005). Japan: Chiaki Moriguchi and Emmanuel Saez, "The Evolution of Income Concentration in Japan, 1886–2005," Working Paper, Northwestern University (2007). Data do not include capital gains.

net worth (wealth minus debt) of the top 1 percent wealth class grew by 78 percent from 1983 to 2004, while for the middle 20 percent, net worth grew by 27 percent. Financial development is related to wealth accumulation at the top. Non-residential assets are relatively unimportant for the median wealth bracket (24 percent of net worth), but for the top 1 percent they constitute 91 percent of net worth. The top 1 percent owns 42 percent of net financial assets; the bottom 90 percent owns 19 percent. Wealth appreciation and income flows derived from owning financial assets have risen in recent years, much more so than for residential housing, the primary asset held by the less wealthy. Corporate payouts are up, as are opportunities for capital gains. (A dollar invested in an S&P index fund in 1980 would be worth $1,500 today.) In 2004, the top 10 percent accounted for 61 percent of all unrealized capital gains. To the extent that the wealthy get better (including inside) information and realize larger financial returns than the less wealthy, their share of wealth-derived income will be greater than their total share of wealth.[9]

B Financial occupations

Forty-five percent of the income going to the top 1 percent bracket derives from wages and salaries, 25 percent from business income, and 30 percent from wealth (dividends, interest, capital gains, and rents). One might think that the last figure is an upper limit on the contribution of finance to top income shares. But the top 1 percent contains a large number of individuals who earn their salaries or their business incomes in financial occupations. These include but are not limited to investment bankers, commercial and trust bankers, managers of hedge, venture, private equity, and mutual funds, financial advisors and consultants, and attorneys specializing in financial transactions. Consider that the fifty highest-paid hedge fund managers in 2007 earned a total of $29 billion. Then there is the well-known phenomenon of skyrocketing compensation for CEOs and other executives. The lion's share derives from capital gains via stock options. In 1980, less than a third of CEOs were granted stock options; today options are universal for top US executives. Individuals in finance-dependent occupations are estimated to account for as much as 40 percent of those in the top income

---

[9] Lawrence Mishel, Jared Bernstein, and Sylvia Allegretto, *The State of Working America: 2006/2007* (Ithaca: Cornell University Press, 2006); *Financial Times*, February 22, 2007; Harry De Angelo, Linda De Angelo, and Douglas J. Skinner, "Are Dividends Disappearing?" (2003) 72 *Journal of Financial Economics*; Edward N. Wolff, "Recent Trends in Household Wealth in the U.S.," Economics Department, NYU (2007); Wojciech Kopczuk and Emmanuel Saez, "Top Wealth Shares in the United States: 1916–2000: Evidence From Estate Tax Returns," National Bureau of Economic Research (NBER) Working Paper 10399 (2004); "Recent Changes in U.S. Family Finances," *Federal Reserve Bulletin* (2006), pp. A1–A38.

brackets. In fact, the figure likely is higher because the estimate excludes some capital gains and many financial occupations.[10]

C Risk

Investors affect the level of risk in the real economy and its allocation among owners, creditors, suppliers, executives, and employees. A firm's financial structure influences outcomes in this area. Debt, for example, interferes with cyclical risk insurance for employees (e.g. via wage smoothing and job guarantees). Ownership dispersion also matters. Blockholders, more prevalent in continental Europe, are relatively undiversified so their risk preferences will be closer to those of similarly undiversified employees, whose main asset is their illiquid firm-specific human capital. As owners become more diversified, they can tolerate greater risk.

In fact, this is what has happened with the rise of institutional investors, a heterogeneous group including mutual funds, trusts, insurance companies, and pension funds, the largest category. Institutional composition varies across nations, with pension funds more important in the United States and the UK than other countries. US institutional investors in 1960 owned 12 percent of US equities; by1990 they owned 45 percent and the share rose to 61 percent in 2005. Institutions today own 68 percent of the 1,000 largest US public corporations. Although institutional holdings rose over a long period, it was in the 1980s that institutions began to flex their muscles as shareholder activists.[11]

---

[10] Data from Emmanuel Saez, tables A7 and A8 at http://elsa.berkeley.edu/~saez (last accessed February 22, 2011); *New York Times*, June 21, 2007; *Los Angeles Times*, April 25, 2007, April 16, 2008; Lucian Bebchuk and Jesse Fried, *Pay without Performance: The Unfulfilled Promise of Executive Compensation* (Cambridge, MA: Harvard University Press, 2006); Gerald Epstein and Arjun Jayadev, "The Rise of Rentier Incomes in OECD Countries," in Gerald Epstein (ed.), *Financialization and the World Economy* (Cheltenham: Edward Elgar Publishing, 2005); Steven N. Kaplan and Joshua Rauh, "Wall Street and Main Street: What Contributes to the Rise in the Highest Incomes?" NBER Working Paper 13270 (2007). The change in executive pay after 1993 is not explained by changes in firm performance or size. Bebchuk and Fried, *Pay without Performance*. Problems with stock options recently have caused a modest decline in the share of CEO compensation based upon them. *Wall Street Journal*, April 14, 2008.

[11] Margaret Blair, *Ownership and Control: Rethinking Corporate Governance for the 21st Century* (Washington, DC: Brookings Institution Press, 1995), p. 46; Conference Board, "2007 Institutional Investment Report" (2007); IMF, *Global Financial Stability Report* (2005), p. 68. Total US institutional assets of $24 trillion are owned by corporate pension funds (28 percent), public pension funds (11 percent), mutual funds (25 percent), trusts (11 percent), and insurance companies (25 percent).

Institutional investors are highly diversified; they rarely own more than 1 percent of a company. They also supply much of the capital for the M&A market: raiders in the 1980s and private equity today. Hence they can and do cause companies to pursue riskier business strategies such as heavier debt, the regular payment of which can endanger a firm when markets turn down, as is presently the case with many debt-laden companies owned by private equity. Institutions also press firms for a larger share of corporate resources. As a result, institutional activism statistically is associated with asset divestitures and with layoffs. This does not mean that institutions push firms to the edge of bankruptcy but even a bankruptcy now and then would not do serious damage to their portfolios.[12]

Institutional investors have never been the paragons of long-term investing that some claim them to be. In the 1980s, one CFO said that institutional investors "have the short-term, total-return objective as their primary objective" (short-termism). Pension funds have always had myopic tendencies in some degree because of the short tenures of in-house fund managers. Recent changes in portfolio composition have accelerated short-termism. Active trading of equities is increasing; indexed equities are now only 30 percent of all pension fund assets. To raise returns above those provided by equities, institutions are also putting more money into "alpha" (riskier) investments, illiquid and/or leveraged. These include private equity, venture, and hedge funds; real estate and real estate CDOs; commodities; and micro-cap stocks. Some pension funds and private endowments have 50 percent or more of their assets in these alternative investments, a mistake for which they suffered during the financial crisis. Private equity and hedge funds come with much shorter time horizons than for indexed equities. On average, private equity's purchase-to-sale process takes around four years. Hedge funds, which make more than half the trades on the NYSE, have even shorter time horizons, sometimes less than a second.[13]

---

[12] Michael Firth, "The Impact of Institutional Investors and Managerial Interests on the Capital Structure of Firms" (1995) 16 *Managerial and Decision Economics*; Sanford M. Jacoby, "Convergence by Design: The Case of CalPERS in Japan" (2007) 55 *American Journal of Comparative Law* 249.

[13] Quote from Michael Useem, *Investor Capitalism* (New York: Basic Books, 1996), p. 82; Gary Gorton and Matthias Kahl, "Blockholder Identity, Equity Ownership Structures, and Hostile Takeovers," NBER Working Paper W7123 (1999); *Pensions & Investments*, November 15, 2004, April 17, 2006, August 21, 2006; *Business Week*, September 17, 2007; Stephen J. Choi and Jill E. Fisch, "Beyond CalPERS: Survey Evidence on the Developing Role of Public Pension Funds in Corporate Governance," Working Paper, Fordham Law School (2007); World Economic Forum, *Globalization of Alternative Investments* (Geneva, 2008). The institutions that had the greatest

Thus institutional investors and their alpha investments raise a firm's risk levels and shorten its time horizons. For workers this induces wage and employment volatility and the shifting of other risks, such as health insurance and pension costs. What is telling is that volatility is greater in public than private firms; the latter have exhibited a *decline* in employment volatility, suggesting an association with financial markets. Another result is that investment projects with long-duration payoffs, such as employee training, are adversely affected. The decline in employee job duration is attributed by many economists to technology-driven shifts from specific to general technology that permit labor mobility. But it is also likely that changes in investor time horizons have undermined the viability of career-type employment systems. In fact, there is an empirical association between greater shareholder control and a reduction in employee tenure levels.[14]

D Corporate governance

Finance enthusiasts assert that giving shareholders a larger role in corporate governance promotes efficiency. When shareholders lack influence, executives build overstaffed empires, pay themselves too much and, to avoid conflict and enjoy a quiet life, overpay and coddle employees. When shareholders gain power, the effects are attenuated. Measures of shareholder power are statistically associated with downsizing and with lower levels of executive and worker compensation, outcomes that allegedly are efficient.[15]

But owners, too, can exacerbate inefficiency. They may seek excessive payouts and burden firms with ill-conceived practices like stock

---

exposure to alpha suffered sharp declines in portfolio value in 2008, including Ivy League university endowments such as Harvard's and Yale's.

[14] Robert A. Moffitt and Peter Gottschalk, "Trends in the Transitory Variance of Earnings in the U.S." (2002) 112 *Economic Journal*; Clair Brown, John Haltiwanger, and Julia Lane, *Economic Turbulence: Is a Volatile Economy Good for America?* (Chicago: University of Chicago Press, 2006); *The Economist*, July 14, 2007; Boyd Black, Howard Gospel, and Andrew Pendleton, "Finance, Corporate Governance, and the Employment Relationship" (2007) 46 *Industrial Relations*; Steven J. Davis, John Haltiwanger, Ron Jarmin, and Javier Miranda, "Volatility and Dispersion in Business Growth Rates: Publicly Traded vs. Privately Held Firms," NBER Working Paper 12354 (2006).

[15] Marianne Bertrand and Sendhil Mullainathan, "Enjoying the Quiet Life? Corporate Governance and Managerial Preferences" (1999) 111 *Journal of Political Economy*; Henrik Cronqvist and Rudiger Fahlenbrach, "Large Shareholders and Corporate Policies" (2009) 22 *Review of Financial Studies* 3941–3976; Michael C. Jensen, "Agency Costs of Free Cash Flow, Corporate Finance, and Takeovers" (1986) 76 *The American Economic Review*. Note that the "lazy executive" view is an analogue to the view that employees are shirkers. Both assume that the pursuit of

options, which promote instead of inhibit executive malfeasance.[16] The new field of behavioral finance, which applies psychological concepts to executive and investor behavior, calls into question assumptions of investor rationality. It shows that investors are prone to cognitive distortions such as myopia, overconfidence, and biased self-attribution. The findings undermine the claim that share price is a reliable criterion of performance and that shareholders know better than executives and boards how to create value. Behavioral finance provides justification for practices that limit shareholder influence, such as takeover defenses.[17]

Institutional activism generally brings a larger share of value-added to owners but this is not the same as an increase in value-added. In fact, activism can undermine value creation. First, downsizing does not boost productivity, although it raises shareholder returns and reduces labor share of value-added, especially when downsizing is aggressive (i.e. when it occurs during periods of profitability). Second, cutting compensation undermines the efficiency wage effect, which is the rise in productivity induced by above-average wages and that occurs via a decline in employee turnover and a rise in effort. Third, attempts by activist investors to reduce takeover barriers may harm, rather than help, efficiency. The average takeover is not associated with pre-existing performance defects or with subsequent profitability gains, even nine years after the event. Instead, the average takeover is driven by arbitrage of price imperfections and by tax benefits associated with leverage. Hence when

---

self-interest leads individuals to the suboptimal quadrant of the prisoner's dilemma, an idea that originates in classical liberalism. For a different and more empirical view, see Robert M. Axelrod, *The Evolution of Cooperation* (New York: Basic Books, 1984).

[16] Bronwyn Hall, "Corporate Restructuring and Investment Horizons in the U.S., 1976–1987" (1994) 68 *The Business History Review*; Brian J. Bushee, "The Influence of Institutional Investors on Myopic R&D Investment Behavior" (1998) 73 *The Accounting Review*; Julian Franks and Colin Mayer, "Capital Markets and Corporate Control" (1990) 5 *Economic Policy*; Clayton Christensen and Scott Anthony, "Put Investors in Their Place," *Business Week*, May 28, 2007; *The Economist*, April 23, 2005, p. 71. Note that Michael Jensen recently recanted his faith in stock options. See http://papers.ssrn.com/sol3/papers.cfm?abstract_id=480401 (last accessed February 22, 2011).

[17] A sampling of behavioral finance includes: Russell Korobkin and Thomas Ulen, "Law and Behavioral Science: Removing the Rationality Assumption from Law and Economics" (2000) 88 *California Law Review*; Andrei Shleifer, *Inefficient Markets: An Introduction to Behavioral Finance* (New York: Oxford University Press, 2000); Robert J. Shiller, *Irrational Exuberance* (Princeton: Princeton University Press, 2000); Ray Fisman, Rakesh Khurana, and Matthew Rhodes-Kropf, "Governance and CEO Turnover: Do Something or Do the Right Thing?" SSRN Working Paper (2005).

managers oppose takeovers, it is not always to preserve their empires but sometimes because of skepticism that takeovers make economic sense.[18]

Earlier we observed the high proportion of individuals in the top 1 percent who come from finance-dependent occupations. Why have their salaries been rising so quickly? The standard explanation has to do with market forces: returns to skill of corporate and financial elites. Surely there is some truth in that. But finance-related incomes not only reflect value creation; again there is also value extraction in the form of rising payouts to shareholders.[19] Owners, who include top executives, appropriate resources that otherwise would have been reinvested or returned to other factors of production, including employees, whose share of productivity gains has declined in recent years. Resources also come from taxpayers who subsidize the tax benefits associated with debt, capital gains, compensation of private equity and hedge fund managers, and more.[20]

True, a portion of shareholder payouts find their way back to middle-class households via retirement plans. But even including these plans, the flow is a trickle. The wealthiest 10 percent owns about 80 percent of all equities, including pension assets. And when shareowners receive larger payouts, less is left for non-executive employees, which is one reason – albeit

---

[18] Bebchuk and Fried, *Pay without Performance*; William J Baumol, Alan Blinder, and Edward N. Wolff, *Downsizing in America* (New York: Russell Sage Foundation Publications, 2003), p. 261; Gunther Capelle-Blancard and Nicolas Couderc, "How Do Shareholders Respond to Downsizing?" SSRN Working Paper 952768 (2007); David I. Levine, "Can Wage Increases Pay for Themselves? Tests with a Production Function" (2007) 102 *Economic Journal*; Julian Franks and Colin Mayer, "Hostile Takeover and the Correction of Managerial Failure" (1995) 40 *Journal of Financial Economics*; Andrei Shleifer and Lawrence H. Summers, "Breach of Trust in Hostile Takeovers," in Alan J. Auerbach (ed.), *Corporate Takeovers: Causes and Consequences* (Chicago: University of Chicago Press, 1988); Andrei Shleifer and Robert Vishny, "Stock Market Driven Acquisitions" (2003) 70 *Journal of Financial Economics*; William W. Bratton, "Is the Hostile Takeover Irrelevant? A Look at the Evidence," Working Paper, Georgetown Law Center (2007); Lynn Stout, "Do Antitakeover Defenses Decrease Shareholder Wealth?" (2002) 55 *Stanford Law Review*.

[19] See text at note 33.

[20] Regarding the effect of takeovers on labor's share of value-added, see Shleifer and Summers, "Breach of Trust in Hostile Takeovers"; Jagadeesh Gokhale, Erica Groshen, and David Neumark, "Do Hostile Takeovers Reduce Extramarginal Wage Payments" (1995) 77 *The Review of Economics and Statistics*; Martin J. Conyon, Sourafel Girma, Steve Thompson, and Peter W. Wright, "Do Hostile Mergers Destroy Jobs?" (2001) 45 *Journal of Economic Behavior & Organization* 427–440. The claim also is made that high pay for private equity and hedge fund managers is a return to skill and to risk-taking. Bear in mind, however, that hedge and private equity principals – regardless of their skill or lack thereof – are guaranteed 2 percent in management fees. Compensation of fund managers also derives from a guaranteed 20 percent of any earnings ("carried profit"), which is taxed not as income but as capital gains, a favorable provision that also applies to venture capital and real estate partnerships.

only one – that labor's share of GDP has fallen and is smaller now than at any time since the mid-1960s. Within labor's share, there also has been a reallocation to top brackets. From 1972 to 2001, the top 0.01 percent saw their real earnings rise by 181 percent, whereas real earnings for the median worker fell by 0.4 percent. The result is a combination of rising inequality along with stagnant incomes for the less affluent.[21]

III   Origins of modern financial development

It would be naïve to think that financial development was due only to market forces unleashed by globalization. The financial industry is a paradigmatic example of a lobby that secures for itself political benefits whose costs are borne by other, often unsuspecting, parties. The workings of finance are recondite, unlike trade, and for this reason it is difficult to mobilize consumers and workers around financial policy. The result is regulatory capture.

The current era of financial development can be traced back to the mid-1950s, when London bankers sought to expand their business by weakening capital controls associated with Bretton Woods. Initially the effort was rebuffed by British governments committed to Keynesian policies. Wall Street also sought weaker capital controls but it too failed. Eventually the bankers realized that it was easier to do an end run around regulations than to change them and the result was the Euromarket, an offshore and unregulated foreign currency market that emerged in the 1960s and was a challenge to Bretton Woods. President Kennedy allegedly said that it was "absurd" to shrink government spending for the sake of facilitating private capital flows. But elite financiers had access to top monetary officials, who often were former colleagues, and throughout the 1960s they lobbied steadily for financial deregulation. Wall Street's persistent complaints about the SEC led Richard Nixon to criticize the agency for its "heavy-handed bureaucratic schemes." Nixon's choice to head the SEC in 1969 was a diehard libertarian who favored relaxation of Glass-Steagall.[22]

---

[21] Ian Dew-Becker and Robert J. Gordon, "Where did the Productivity Growth Go? Inflation Dynamics and the Distribution of Income" (2005) 2 *Brookings Papers on Economic Activity* 67–127; Richard Freeman, *America Works: Critical Thoughts on the Exceptional US Labor Market* (New York: Russell Sage Foundation Publications, 2007), p. 39; *New York Times*, August 28, 2006; Alan B. Krueger, "Measuring Labor's Share" (1999) 89 *American Economic Review* 45–51.

[22] Eric Helleiner, *States and the Reemergence of Global Finance: From Bretton Woods to the 1990s* (Ithaca: Cornell University Press, 1994), pp. 81–122; James Hawley, "Protecting Capital from Itself" (1984) 38 *International Organization* 131–165; Joel Seligman, *The Transformation of Wall Street* (Boston: Aspen Publishers, 1982), p. 382, p. 441.

Economic stagnation in the 1970s made it easier for banks (and other industries) to press for deregulation. Major financial institutions like First National City Bank and Morgan Trust lobbied for deregulation, including repeal of Glass-Steagall. Their argument was that New Deal regulatory policies were strangling growth, a claim that became conventional wisdom not only for Republicans but also for centrist Democrats like Presidents Carter and Clinton. Carter kicked off a "deregulatory snowball" when he signed a bank deregulation act in 1980. Under Ronald Reagan, financial deregulation intensified. The virtual demise of antitrust enforcement encouraged hostile takeovers and permitted the emergence of financial powerhouses like Citibank. Following their historic 1994 Congressional victory, the Republicans placed on their agenda proposals to scrap restrictions on margin buys by large investors and to limit lawsuits against allegedly fraudulent underwriters, executives, and accountants.[23] Although a Republican Congress repealed Glass-Steagall, it was Clinton's Treasury Secretary, Robert Rubin, who plied the halls of Congress to line up Democratic support. (The 1999 Financial Services Modernization Act that repealed Glass-Steagall came to be known as the Citigroup Authorization Act. Shortly after its passage, Rubin resigned to become chairman of Citigroup.) With Glass-Steagall out of the way, commercial banks like Citigroup were free to move into relatively unregulated domains such as securitization.[24]

Tax policy is crucial to finance and to top incomes, a fact that has never been lost on the financial industry. For example, the industry worked closely with other business organizations to secure passage of the 1981 tax reform act. The main lobbying group was the newly formed Business Roundtable, which included on its board financiers such as David Rockefeller of Chase Manhattan and Walter Wriston of

---

[23] In 1995, Congress passed the Private Securities Litigation Act with near-unanimous support from Republicans and also from some liberal Democrats. Treasury Secretary Rubin favored the bill and, initially, so did Clinton. But Clinton later made a symbolic concession to consumers by vetoing the bill, knowing that Congress had the votes to override him, which it did. *New York Times*, December 20, 1995; David Leinsdorf and Donald Eltra, *Citibank: Ralph Nader's Study Group Report on First National City Bank* (New York: Grossman Publishers, 1973); Ernie Englander and Allen Kaufman, "The End of Managerial Ideology: From Corporate Social Responsibility to Corporate Social Indifference" (2004) 5 *Enterprise & Society* 417; Charles Geisst, *Undue Influence: How the Wall Street Elite Puts the Financial System at Risk* (Hoboken: John Wiley & Sons Inc, 2005); Thomas H. Hammond and Jack H. Knott, "The Deregulatory Snowball: Explaining Deregulation in the Financial Industry" (1988) 50 *The Journal of Politics* 3–30.

[24] Robert Kuttner, *The Squandering of America: How the Failure of Our Politics Undermines our Prosperity* (New York: Knopf, 2007), p. 105; *New York Times*, May 14, 1998; Robin Blackburn, "The Subprime Crisis" (2008) 50 *New Left Review*.

Citibank. Citing supply-side theories, the Roundtable argued that tax cuts rather than government spending would remedy economic stagnation. The act contained a cornucopia of tax goodies, including more favorable treatment of corporate debt. The provision underwrote the decade's leveraged buyouts, which were touted as a tonic for US competitiveness but proved a chimera when the junk bond market collapsed in the late 1980s and again during the financial crisis that occurred twenty years later.

The 1980s also saw a decline in top marginal income-tax rates. Two-thirds of the decline in tax progressivity between 1960 and 2004 occurred during the Reagan presidency. Additionally, there were cuts in personal tax rates related to finance, including a 29 percent reduction in the capital-gains tax. It is Republicans – going back to 1954 – who consistently favor low rates on unearned incomes. In the Anglo-Saxon nations, a 10 percent cut in the top investment rate is associated with a 0.4 percentage point increase in the top 1 percent income share.[25]

Shareholder primacy asserts that maximizing shareholder value is the corporation's sole objective. It is a break from previous legal doctrines that the corporation is an entity distinct from its shareholders. The earlier view held that boards were legally autonomous from shareholders and could exercise independent business judgment on behalf of the enterprise. Promotion of the shareholder-primacy doctrine, starting in the 1970s, came in tandem with a surge in hostile takeovers that circumvented boards and made direct appeals to shareholders to tender their shares. Economic justification for the doctrine was provided by agency theory, an old idea that now received scientific grounding. The theory

---

[25] J. Craig Jenkins and Craig M. Eckert, "The Right Turn in Economic Policy" (2000) 15 *Sociological Forum* 307–338; Thomas Piketty and Emmanuel Saez, "How Progressive is the U.S. Federal Tax System?" (2007) 21 *Journal of Economic Perspectives*; *Business Week*, June 14, 2004; Dennis P. Quinn and Robert Y. Shapiro, "Business Political Power: The Case of Taxation" (1991) 85 *American Political Science Review* 851–874; A.B. Atkinson and A. Leigh, "Understanding the Distribution of Top Incomes in Anglo-Saxon Countries over the 20th Century," Working Paper, Australian National University (2004). In the 1980s, wealthy businessmen endowed tax-related think-tanks such as Grover Norquist's Americans for Tax Reform, launched in 1985, which received support from the Olin and Scaife Foundations. Even the Brookings Foundation swung from liberal to centrist as business donations rose from $95,000 in 1978 to $1.6 million in 1984. Brookings' fund-raiser at the time, a conservative Republican named Roger Semerad, said the gifts demonstrated that Brookings was "no longer tied to decades of ideology." A 1984 Brookings report advocated a cash-flow tax, the first step towards the long-sought conservative goal of substituting consumption taxes for progressive income taxes. The chief economist for the US Chamber of Commerce said that the report "shows that we have won the philosophical revolution." *Boston Globe*, March 31, 2006; Peter Bernstein, "Brookings Tilts Right," 110 *Fortune* July 23, 1984, p. 96.

did not constitute a rebalancing of the relationship between shareholders on the one hand and boards, executives, and other stakeholders on the other; it simply cut off the latter part of the scales. Agency theory offered an economic rationale for hostile bids, stock options, and other governance changes intended to boost shareholder influence. As the Council of Economic Advisers opined in 1985, takeovers "improve efficiency, transfer scarce resources to higher valued uses, and stimulate effective corporate management." The self-regulating market was born again.[26]

Agency theory and deregulatory dogma became increasingly influential in law schools and the courts. They traveled from economics to law over a bridge erected by conservative philanthropists. The annual "Pareto in the Pines" retreats were started in the 1970s to educate legal scholars about the applicability of economic concepts to antitrust law, corporate law, and other topics. The concepts were technocratic, such as cost-benefit analysis, as well as normative, such as agency theory and public choice. Later the students included regulators and jurists. By 1991 the Law and Economics Center at George Mason had given economics training to nearly a thousand state and federal judges. Funding for the seminars and for academic research in law and economics came from wealthy libertarian ideologues like Richard Scaife and John M. Olin. The intent was to offer a platform to academic "norm entrepreneurs" whose ideas would confer legitimacy on shareholder primacy in the private sector and deregulation in the public sector. Institutional investors took these ideas as their own and embedded them in codes of corporate governance that were thrust upon stock exchanges and foreign governments in the 1990s.[27]

---

[26] Morton J. Horwitz, *The Transformation of American Law, 1870–1960: The Crisis of Legal Orthodoxy* (New York: Oxford University Press, 1992); Stephen M. Bainbridge, "Director Primacy and Shareholder Disempowerment" (2006) 119 *Harvard Law Review*; Margaret Blair and Lynn Stout, "Specific Investment and Corporate Law" (2006) 7 *European Business Organization Law Review*; Simon Deakin, "The Coming Transformation of Shareholder Value" (2005) 13 *Corporate Governance*; Connie Bruck, *The Predators' Ball: The Inside Story of Drexel Burnam and the Rise of the Junk Bond Raiders* (New York: Penguin Classics, 1988), p. 261.

[27] Michael C. Jensen and William Meckling, "Theory of the Firm: Managerial Behavior, Agency Costs, and Ownership Structure" (1976) 3 *Journal of Financial Economics*; Cass Sunstein, "Social Norms and Social Roles" (1996) 96 *Columbia Law Review*; Sanford M. Jacoby, "Economic Ideas and the Labor Market: Origins of the Anglo-American Model and Prospects for Global Diffusion" (2003) 25 *Comparative Labor Law & Policy Journal*; J.P. Heinz, A. Southworth, and A. Paik, "Lawyers for Conservative Causes" (2003) 37 *Law & Society Review* 5–50; *USA Today*, May 3, 2006. Many of the governance reforms spawned by agency theory and pressed by shareholder activists turn out to have little or no relationship to performance; some even have negative effects. One explanation is that optimal governance is endogenous

Law and regulation establish boundaries for another type of political contest, this time played at the corporate level. Here the players – workers, executives, and owners – press singly or in coalition for alternative forms of corporate governance with different allocations of value-added. Following Gourevitch and Shinn, one may identify three games, each with a winner and loser: (1) owners + executives vs. workers, (2) executives + workers vs. owners, and (3) owners + workers vs. executives. The first game, which Gourevitch and Shinn label "class conflict," was prevalent in the early decades of the twentieth century, with workers usually the losers. The second game, which I term "producerism," gained currency during the postwar decades when managers and workers, many of them unionized, replaced class conflict with cooperation to raise productivity; owners got the short end of the stick. The third coalition, "institutional capitalism," emerged after 1980 as institutional owners pressed executives to focus on share price, thereby creating a bond between owners and worker-shareholders who own stock directly or through pension plans. But institutional capitalism is not the only game being played today. There is nascent class conflict because the median worker owns but a pittance in equities and many executives, encouraged by stock options, have cast their lot with owners. Another prevalent game today is the "war of all against all": executives exploit owners and workers; owners try to do the same to executives and workers. The vast majority of workers, however, are powerless.[28]

What about the situation outside the Anglo-American world? Northern Europe and Japan since 1980 have experienced rapid financial development, with growth rates exceeding those in the UK and the United States, although Northern Europe and Japan started and remain at lower levels. What is crucial, however, is that despite recent financialization, their top income shares have not increased to the same extent as in the United States and the UK (see Table 13.1). Why?

---

to a firm's idiosyncratic characteristics; the activists' formulaic approach ignores this fact. See Jacoby, "Convergence by Design," pp. 250–254; Sanjai Bhagat, Brian Bolton, and Roberta Romano, "The Promise and Peril of Corporate Governance Indices" (2008) 109 *Columbia Law Review* 1803–1882.

[28] Note that multiple games can be played in the same country at the same time, although one game is likely to be more prevalent than others. This has caused endless debates in the Varieties of Capitalism literature over how to classify a nation's type. Peter Gourevitch and James Shinn, *Political Power and Corporate Control: The New Global Politics of Corporate Governance* (Princeton: Princeton University Press, 2005); Sanford M. Jacoby, *The Embedded Corporation: Corporate Governance and Employment Relations in Japan and the United States* (Princeton: Princeton University Press, 2005).

First, Northern European and Japanese unions have shrunk less in size and influence than their US and, to a lesser extent, British, counterparts. Japanese and Northern Europeans have relatively cooperative relations among workers, executives, and owners. This is relational capitalism, or what David Soskice calls the "coordinated market economy" (CME). It is a fifth type of game, the obverse of the war against all. In CMEs, there remains support for the idea that the corporation is beholden to all of the stakeholders who have invested in it, not only shareholders. Hostile takeovers and private equity are resisted in European CMEs and remain rare in Japan. Foreign norm entrepreneurs, chiefly US investors, have been less successful than at home in molding CME law and regulation to their purposes, although they have found a more receptive audience in the European Commission.[29]

Table 13.2 shows the allocation of value-added at the firm level under different corporate-governance regimes in Europe. Labor's share is relatively low in the United Kingdom and Ireland, where governance coalitions changed after 1980 in the direction of shareholder primacy. Conversely, labor's share is higher under the CME coalitions found in Europe and in Japan. Since the mid-1990s, German companies have shifted shares away from labor, although this tends to be the result of a union-sanctioned reallocation from wages to investment, with relatively less flowing to shareholders than in the United States. The United States has seen a huge jump in payouts to shareholders, from 58 percent of after-tax profits in 1981 to 89 percent in 2000. In Japan, allocations have changed only modestly. Hence politics, broadly defined, drives a wedge between finance and labor in CMEs but tightens the connection in liberal economies.[30]

---

[29] David Soskice, "Reinterpreting Corporatism and Explaining Unemployment: Coordinated and Uncoordinated Economies," in Renatta Brunetta and Carlo Dell'Arringa (eds.), *Labour Relations and Economic Performance* (New York: New York University Press, 1990); Ronald Dore, *Stock Market Capitalism, Welfare Capitalism: Japan and Germany vs. the Anglo-Saxons* (New York: Oxford University Press, 2000); Jonas Pontusson, *Inequality and Prosperity: Social Europe vs. Liberal America* (Ithaca: Cornell University Press, 2005); Gregory Jackson and Hideaki Miyajima, "Varieties of Capitalism, Varieties of Markets: Mergers and Acquisitions in Japan, Germany, France, the UK, and USA," Research Institute of Economy, Trade and Industry Working Paper (June 2007). In 1999, American Federation of Labor and Congress of Industrial Organizations (AFL-CIO) president John Sweeney issued a statement opposing Vodafone's hostile bid for Mannesmann and endorsing the CME approach to governance: "The AFL-CIO," he said, "believes value is created over the long-term by partnerships among all of a corporation's constituents – workers, investors, customers, suppliers, and communities. Mannesman, and the European model of corporate governance under which it is structured, has allowed just those kinds of value creating partnerships to flourish." Statement by AFL-CIO President John Sweeney on Mannesmann Takeover, November 22, 1999.

[30] Henk von Eije and William Megginson, "Dividends and Share Repurchases in the European Union" (2008) 89 *Journal of Financial Economics*; Gregory Jackson,

Table 13.2 *Distribution of net value added in large European corporations, 1991–1994*

	Labor	Capital	Government	Retained Earnings	Dividends
Anglo-Saxon	62.2	23.5	14.3	3.2	15.0
Germanic	86.1	8.8	5.1	5.2	3.0
Latinic	80.3	14.4	5.3	3.0	4.7
Average	79.0	13.7	7.3	3.6	6.1

Note: dividends and retained earnings do not equal the capital share because net interest payments and third-party shares are not included.
Source: Henk Wouter De Jong, "The Governance Structure and Performance of Large European Corporations" (1997) 1 *Journal of Management and Governance.*

IV Financial development in the past

Another way of gauging the relationship between finance and labor is to consider earlier periods of financial development. From the 1870s through to the 1920s the industrialized world experienced an expansion of trade and finance that rivals today's. Before World War I, trade growth averaged 3.8 percent annually. The share of trade in GDP for the Western economies reached a high point in 1913 that was not exceeded until the 1970s (and for some countries not until the 1990s). Trade and finance were positively related but it was finance that was the more dynamic. Between 1870 and 1913 foreign investment flows, including portfolio investments, grew faster than, and exceeded the level of, trade-related flows. After 1918 the financial sector grew larger and more concentrated as banking and the security industries converged. The number of US national banks with securities affiliates increased from ten in 1922 to 114 in 1931.[31]

"Stakeholders Under Pressure: Corporate Governance and Labour Management in Germany and Japan" (2005) 13 *Corporate Governance*; Takeshi Inagami, "Managers and Corporate Governance Reform in Japan: Restoring Self-Confidence or Shareholder Revolution?" in D. Hugh Whittaker and Simon Deakin (eds.), *Corporate Governance and Managerial Reform in Japan* (Oxford University Press, 2009); J. Fred Weston and Juan Siu, "Changing Motives for Share Repurchases," UCLA Anderson Working Paper (December 2002). Data on labor's share and on corporate payouts that are derived for roughly comparable companies are a more reliable indicator of distributional outcomes at the firm level than aggregate measures of labor's share of value-added, which comprise a changing mix of firms and have the added problem of including income from self-employment.

[31] Angus Maddison, *The World Economy, vol. 2 Historical Statistics* (Paris: Organization for Economic Co-operation and Development, 2006), p. 362; Barry Eichengreen,

Financial development was related to industrialization. But the relationship went in both directions: finance serviced industry, and owners poured their wealth into financial assets. Hence income concentration in the late nineteenth century rose in tandem with financial development. Top income shares in Germany increased from 1870 to 1900; British top 5 percent shares declined in nominal value but rose in real value between 1867 and 1911; and top wealth shares in France rose after 1880. As compared to the United States in 1913, Europe and Japan had more developed stock markets and a slightly larger share of income going to the top 1 percent. The United States caught up on both dimensions by 1929 (see Table 13.1). US wealth concentration did not match that of previously feudal countries until the 1980s. Yet it hardly was egalitarian: the top 1 percent in 1912 held about 56 percent of US wealth. The rich invested their assets through financial intermediaries such as trust banks that grew rapidly after the turn of the century. Stock ownership was concentrated; many of the wealthy were company founders and their descendants. After World War I, however, stockholding became more diffuse. The initial reason was progressive income taxation, which induced the rich to shift assets into municipal bonds. Wall Street brokers responded with campaigns to persuade less affluent individuals to buy stock directly or through employer stock purchase plans. The 1920s were an era of exuberance. On the eve of the crash, a series of articles in the *Saturday Evening Post* described the preceding decade as one in which "buying [of stock] ... was not based on reasoning but simply on the fact that prices had risen; a rise led the public to expect more and more returns."[32] The magazine presciently warned that excessively optimistic speculation would lead to depression and unemployment.[33]

Globalizing Capital: A History of the International Monetary System (Princeton: Princeton University Press, 1996); Paul Bairoch and Richard Kozul-Wright, "Globalization Myths," UNCTAD Discussion Paper 113 (1996); Charles Kindleberger, *A Financial History of Western Europe* (New York: Oxford University Press, 1993); Richard F. Bensel, *The Political Economy of American Industrialization, 1877–1900* (New York: Cambridge University Press, 2000), pp. 418–442; Larry Neal, "Trust Companies and Financial Innovation," (1971) 45 *Business History Review*.

[32] *Populists, Plungers, and Progressives: A Social History of Stock and Commodity Speculation 1890-1936*, by Cedric B. Cowing (Princeton University Press, 1965), p. 170.

[33] Emmanuel Saez, "Income and Wealth Concentration in a Historical and International Perspective," in Alan Auerbach, David Card, and John Quigley (eds.), *Public Policy and Income Distribution* (New York: Russell Sage Foundation Publications, 2006); Peter Lindert, "Three Centuries of Inequality in Britain and America" and Christian Morrisson, "Historical Perspectives on Income Distribution: The Case of Europe," in A.B. Atkinson and F. Bourguigon (eds.), *Handbook of Income Distribution* (New York: Elsevier, 2000), 179; Thomas Piketty, Gilles Postel-Vinay, and Jean-Laurent Rosenthal, "Wealth Concentration in a Developing Economy: Paris and France, 1807–1994" (2006) 96 *The*

Despite more dispersed shareholding in the 1920s, ownership remained concentrated. Fifty-five percent of the 200 largest US companies were controlled by their owners in 1929, either through total or majority ownership, or through minority control and various legal devices. The top 1 percent in 1927 had around 60 percent of their wealth in stock and received 82 percent of all dividend payments, a conservative estimate. The association between financial wealth and personal income was close: for the top 1 percent, capital returns were the largest component of income (50 percent in 1927). With concentrated wealth came sizable top 1 percent income shares.[34]

Market development in this era, including financial markets, did not occur in an autonomous economic realm but was abetted by the business community's reliance on political power. The result was "an enormous increase in continuous, centrally organized and controlled interventionism."[35] This included tariffs, subsidies, special charters, pro-business tax and spending policies, monetary and banking regulation, and suppression of labor unions. The most visible expression of financial politics was the prolonged effort to establish the gold standard, which subordinated worker and farmer concerns to financier interests in a strong currency. The battle came to a head during the 1896 presidential contest when John D. Rockefeller and J.P. Morgan each contributed vast sums to McKinley's campaign, as did other business leaders. Four years later the gold standard became law.

A strong central bank, free of Congressional purview and "special interests," was crucial for maintenance of the gold standard. The

---

American Economic Review; Jeffrey Williamson and Peter Lindert, *American Inequality: A Macroeconomic History* (New York: Academic Press, 1980), p. 50; Kevin Phillips, *Wealth and Democracy: A Political History of the American Rich* (New York: Broadway Books, 2002), p. 43; Kopczuk and Saez, "Top Wealth Shares"; Cedric B. Cowing, *Populists, Plungers, and Progressives: A Social History of Stock and Commodity Speculations, 1890–1936* (Princeton: Princeton University Press, 1965), p. 170.

[34] Adolf A. Berle and Gardiner C. Means, *The Modern Corporation and Private Property* (New York: Transaction Publishers, 1932), p. 106; Robert A. Gordon, *Business Leadership in the Large Corporation* (Washington, DC: The Brookings Institution, 1945); Dennis Leech, "Concentration and Control in Large U.S. Corporations" (1978) 35 *Journal of Industrial Economics*; Gardiner C. Means, "The Diffusion of Stock Ownership in the U.S." (1930) 44 *The Quarterly Journal of Economics* 599; Thomas Piketty and Emmanuel Saez, "Income Inequality in the United States," in A.B. Atkinson and T. Piketty (eds.), *Top Incomes over the Twentieth Century* (New York: Oxford University Press, 2007); Irving B. Kravis, "Relative Income Shares in Fact and Theory" (1959) 49 *American Economic Review*. In 1914, Scott Nearing, a socialist economist then teaching at the Wharton School, found similarity of labor's share in France, Germany, Switzerland, the UK, and the United States; it was about 60 percent. This is close to Kravis' figures. Scott Nearing, "Service Income and Property Income" (1914) 14 *Publications of the American Statistical Association*; Krueger, "Measuring Labor's Share."

[35] Polanyi, *Great Transformation*, p. 137.

deliberations over the Federal Reserve Act of 1913 were conducted by a small group of financiers, industrialists, and politicians led by Paul Warburg of Kuhn, Loeb. There was contention within this elite – between Wall Street and banks from outlying regions – that resulted in a compromise creating twelve district banks with New York at their apex. Warburg, who Woodrow Wilson later appointed to the first Federal Reserve Board, believed that the Act would insure that New York and the dollar, rather than London and the pound, had the upper hand in global finance. The financial elite understood the power of ideas and that they had to give the appearance of acting in the public interest, and so they "recruited, attracted, and developed the talents of leading economists, journalists and intellectuals."[36]

The courts became the shareholders' best friends. For much of the nineteenth century, jurists held that corporations were subject to regulation because they were public or quasi-public entities with powers derived from the state. But by the end of the century, the courts were asserting that corporations were islands of private property – like land – and had nothing to do with the state or any entity other than their owners. "Outside" interference with the corporation, whether by government or trade unions, was a taking, in the legal sense, whose harm could be measured by changes in the firm's market value. Eventually the theory developed that corporate power derived from shareholders – the principals – thereby allowing courts to "disaggregate the corporation into freely contracting individuals."[37]

V   The double movement in the past

From the 1870s through to the early 1900s, labor organizations were active in popular movements opposing the deflationary tendencies and tight credit associated with the gold standard. The movements ran the gamut from Greenbackers, radical Republicans, and free silverites

---

[36] Lawrence Goodwyn, *The Populist Movement: A Short History of the Agrarian Revolt in America* (New York: Oxford University Press, 1978), pp. 278–284; Phillips, *Wealth and Democracy*, p. 239; Bensel, *American Industrialization, passim*; Gabriel Kolko, *The Triumph of Conservatism* (New York: The Free Press, 1963); J. Lawrence Broz, *The International Origins of the Federal Reserve System* (Ithaca: Cornell University Press, 1997); James Livingston, *Origins of the Federal Reserve System: Money, Class and Corporate Capitalism, 1890–1913* (Ithaca: Cornell University Press, 1986), p. 228. *Haute finance* strong-armed other nations – in Asia and Latin America – to adopt the gold standard. Emily S. Rosenberg, *Spreading the American Dream: American Economic and Cultural Expansion, 1890–1945* (New York: Hill and Wang, 1982).

[37] Horwitz, *Transformation*, p. 90.

to the Knights of Labor and the People's Party. Labor's initial effort to promote the greenback, the "people's currency," came through the National Labor Union, the country's first amalgamation of trade unions. Trade unionists espoused the Republican ethos that direct producers were the source of value, whereas financiers were speculative parasites. This was an early expression of the idea that finance and the real economy operated in separate and conflicting realms. Labor not only had a distrust of concentrated financial power; it saw its interests as antithetical to those of finance. Labor opposed monetary stringency, condemned speculation that led to panics and depressions, and loathed the inequities associated with Gilded Age finance.[38]

Yet popular movements against the gold standard could neither unify nor sustain themselves, nor could they muster the resources to win elections. The Knights of Labor, the Populist Party, and the Bryan campaign of 1896 were valiant efforts. But Bryan's 1896 anti-gold campaign was run on a shoestring. The collapse of the Knights and later on of the Populist Party brought a halt to labor's financial activism.[39]

The political baton passed from agrarians and labor to Progressive reformers. Richard T. Ely, Thorstein Veblen, and Louis D. Brandeis were among the intellectuals who railed against financial monopoly. Brandeis criticized investment banking – "the money trust" – in a series of essays published in 1914 as *Other People's Money and How the Bankers Use It*. His ideas overlapped another strand in Progressive thought: an enthusiasm for social engineering. In a contemporaneous book, *Business – A Profession*, Brandeis predicted that corporations would become more efficient as a new class of technocratic managers separated itself from self-interested owners, eschewed class conflict, and adopted producerism in the form of scientific management and employee participation in both union and non-union forms.[40]

---

[38] Louis Hartz, *Economic Policy and Democratic Thought: Pennsylvania 1776–1860*, (Cambridge, MA: Harvard University Press, 1948); Mark Roe, *Strong Managers, Weak Owners: The Political Roots of American Corporate Finance* (Princeton: Princeton University Press, 1994), p. 68; David Montgomery, *Beyond Equality: Labor and the Radical Republicans, 1862–1872* (Urbana: University of Illinois Press, 1967), p. 445.

[39] Goodwyn, *The Populist Movement*, pp. 278–284; Phillips, *Wealth and Democracy*, p. 239; Bensel, *American Industrialization, passim*; Kim Voss, *The Making of American Exceptionalism: The Knights of Labor and Class Formation in the Nineteenth Century* (Ithaca: Cornell University Press, 1994).

[40] Louis D. Brandeis, *Other People's Money and How the Bankers Use It* (New York: Frederick A Stokes Company, 1914); Louis Brandeis, *Business – A Profession* (Boston: A. M. Kelley, 1914); Samuel Haber, *Efficiency and Uplift: Scientific Management in the Progressive Era, 1890–1920* (Chicago: University of Chicago Press, 1964).

Progressive jurists such as Brandeis advanced a pragmatic conception of the corporation that challenged conservative views. Ownership rights were held to be relative, not absolute. This required a balancing test to weigh claims made by shareholders against those of other claimants. Challenging assertions that the market was self-regulating, the legal realists argued that the market was embedded: "a social creation, a creature of law, government, and prevailing conceptions of legitimate exchange." The realists drew on a broad set of ideas, including those of the institutional economists, several of whom, like John R. Commons, had ties to the labor movement.[41]

Yet labor, or at least the AFL, mostly was silent on the era's financial issues, whether the 1912 Pujo investigations or the backroom negotiations over the Federal Reserve. One reason is that after the 1908 *Danbury Hatters* case, the AFL's political efforts were absorbed with undoing the judiciary's repressive interpretation of antitrust and other laws. Another is that organized labor, unlike farmers or small business, had options other than legislation to tame finance. Lloyd Ulman has well described the process by which unions formed national organizations in response to the extension and interpenetration of markets. Collective bargaining gave labor the power to privately challenge shareholder claims. A third reason for labor's silence was its electoral weakness. Compared to European unions, the AFL was small and did not form alliances with socialists, farmers, or the middle class. There were exceptions of course, chiefly at the local and state levels. Labor cooperated with the middle class in "sewer socialist" cities. And in the Midwest, labor participated in fusion parties or supported politicians like Wisconsin's "Fighting Bob" LaFollette, Jr., who opposed "Wall Street dictatorship" and demanded nationalization of banks.[42]

When it came to financial politics, European labor faced different incentives than the AFL. In much of Europe there was proportional instead of majoritarian voting, which gave labor a political voice through labor and other left-wing parties representing worker interests.

---

[41] Horwitz, *Transformation*, passim.
[42] Lloyd Ulman, *The Rise of the National Trade Union: The Development and Significance of Its Structure, Governing Institutions, and Economic Policies* (Cambridge, MA: Harvard University Press, 1955); James Weinstein, "Radicalism in the Midst of Normalcy" (1966) 52 *Journal of American History*; Cedric Cowing, "Sons of the Wild Jackass and the Stock Market" (1959) 33 *Business History Review*. The AFL had almost nothing to say about the gold standard during the 1910s and 1920s, whereas Britain's 1926 General Strike, in which 2.5 million workers participated, had at its heart the gold standard and the wage cuts attributed to it. Melvin C. Shefitz, "The Trade Disputes and Trade Unions Act of 1927: The Aftermath of the General Strike" (1967) 29 *Review of Politics*.

European labor was able to negotiate a political quid pro quo wherein it supported trade and financial openness in return for a social compact mitigating the risks that openness brought. The extensiveness of social insurance enacted before 1913 is positively related to a nation's level of openness in 1913. The United States, with majoritarian voting and a labor movement lacking political allies, was a social insurance laggard until the New Deal.[43]

Only at the midnight hour, in 1929, did the AFL weigh in on finance. Five months before the crash, its official magazine demanded that "growth of speculative credit shall not be permitted to undermine business stability." It warned that inaction would have deleterious effects on wage earners and, via underconsumption, on growth. When tax figures for 1929 were released, the AFL observed that the bulk of income gains since 1927 had gone to the top brackets. It blamed three factors: concentrated stock ownership, stock speculation that benefited the rich, and an uneven distribution of value-added due to excessively high dividends. But these words came late in the game, in fact, after the game was over.[44]

The Great Depression hit the United States especially hard, impoverishing the middle class along with workers and farmers. This created a broader political coalition than existed in 1896 and helped put Roosevelt into office. The belief was widespread that financial speculation and graft had caused the stock market crash and depression. Antipathy to finance led to a myriad of investigations and regulations. The official leadership of the AFL played a minor role in these events. But parts of

---

[43] Michael Huberman and Wayne Lewchuk, "European Economic Integration and the Labour Compact" (2003) 7 *European Review of Economic History*. Did social insurance expenditures have a redistributive effect on top shares? For the three northern European countries shown in Table 1 (Germany, Netherlands, Sweden), social spending as a share of national income rose from an average of 0.61 percent of national product in 1900 to 2.9 percent in 1930, nearly a five-fold gain; top shares declined after 1920. In France, social spending rose but only two-fold, and top shares did not change. In the United States, social spending did not change at all between 1900 and 1930 and top shares rose after 1920. The big changes in welfare expenditure and top shares did not occur in Europe or the United States until after World War II, however. In 1965, social expenditures in the three northern European countries stood at 21 percent of GDP, an expenditure that required substantial redistribution of pretax incomes. Peter Lindert, "The Rise of Social Spending, 1880–1930" (1994) 31 *Explorations in Economic History*; Jens Alber, "Is There a Crisis of the Welfare State?" (1988) 4 *European Sociological Review* 190.

[44] According to the AFL, between 1927 and 1928 capital gains rose by 70 percent, dividends by 7 percent, and wages by 1.5 percent. At International Harvester – a bellwether corporation in its day – wages barely budged during the 1920s despite the firm's record profits. (1929) 36 *American Federationist* 535; (1930) 37 *American Federationist* 339–341; Cowing, *Populists, Plungers*, pp. 155–186; Robert Ozanne, *Wages in Practice and Theory* (Madison: University of Wisconsin Press, 1968), p. 49.

the AFL, and of the urban working class more generally, were deeply involved in financial politics. Before the emergence of industrial unionism, the largest popular movements of the 1930s were led by demagogic populists like Senator Huey Long and Father Charles Coughlin. In a reprise of 1896, they blasted the money interests and called for the remonetization of silver.[45] Long attacked the nation's unequal distribution of wealth – "concentrated in the hands of a few people" – and tied it to the "God of Greed [worshipped] by Rockefeller, Morgan, and their crowd." Coughlin, too, attacked "bankers and financiers" and his heated rhetoric attracted millions of adherents from the same groups that had elected Roosevelt.[46]

In the Senate, Long disrupted the Glass–Steagall deliberations by filibustering for three weeks until the bill included limits on branch banking. Meanwhile Coughlin angrily testified to Congress about financial "plutocrats." He demanded a silver standard and nationalization of the Federal Reserve, which led Congressman Wright Patman to sponsor a bill along those lines. The AFL chimed in, asking that Congress erect safeguards "against speculation that destroys wealth and business structure."[47]

Congress and the Roosevelt administration spun a web of financial restraints, including the Securities Act of 1933 and suspension of gold convertibility, the Securities Exchange and Banking Acts of 1934, and the Investment Company Act of 1940. Some argue that these laws were designed by a New Deal brain trust that was deferential to finance and

---

[45] Roe, *Strong Managers*, p. 42. Said Coughlin, "God wills it – this religious crusade against the pagan of gold. Silver is the key to prosperity – silver that was damned by the Morgans." Members of the House and Senate pressured Roosevelt to send Coughlin to the 1933 London Conference on the gold standard and in 1934 Congress passed the Silver Purchase Act, a mostly symbolic gesture. William E. Leuchtenberg, *Franklin D. Roosevelt and The New Deal, 1932–1940* (New York: Harper & Row, 1963), 101; Daniel J.B. Mitchell, "Dismantling the Cross of Gold: Economic Crises and U.S. Monetary Policy" (2000) 11 *North American Journal of Economics & Finance* 77–104.

[46] *Ibid.*, p. 103; Alan Brinkley, *Voices of Protest: Huey Long, Father Coughlin, and the Great Depression* (New York: Knopf, 1982), pp. 140, 150, 171.

[47] Leuchtenberg, *Roosevelt*, pp. 54–56, 60; Cowing, *Populists, Plungers*, p. 223; Geisst, *Undue Influence*, p. 68; Paul Studenski and Herman E. Kroos, *Financial History of the United States* (New York: Beard Books, 1952), p. 363; Herbert M. Bratter, "The Silver Episode: II" (1938) 46 *Journal of Political Economy*; Ellis Hawley, *The New Deal and the Problem of Monopoly* (Princeton: Princeton University Press, 1966), p. 307; *New York Times*, December 13, 1937. Congressional Republicans and supply-side economists revived the gold-standard debate in the 1980s, leading to formation of the Gold Commission, which issued a pro-gold report in 1982. Nothing happened, although the idea has recurred since then, as in the 1996 presidential campaign of Steve Forbes. Mitchell, "Cross of Gold," p. 101.

thereby permitted regulatory capture. But limits on securities trading and financial centralization shrank the financial sector (see Table 13.1). Along with this came fewer opportunities for finance-derived incomes. The proportion of Harvard Business School graduates choosing Wall Street as their first position fell from 17 percent in 1928 to 1 percent in 1941. Not until the 1980s would fresh MBAs become as prevalent on Wall Street as they had been in the 1920s.[48]

Financial regulations also took hold in Europe and Japan. The world's industrialized nations experienced what John Ruggie calls "a common thread of social reaction against market rationality," which caused a contraction of global financial markets through 1980 (with a blip in the late 1960s). Top income shares in Europe, Japan, and the United States tracked these changes. They contracted from the 1930s through to the 1970s, at which point top shares in the United States and the UK started a steady climb that left Europe and Japan behind (see Table 13.1).[49]

VI Double movement redux

As the New Deal coalition broke down in the 1970s, labor found itself isolated. It was a Democrat, Jimmy Carter, who deregulated union strongholds such as the transportation and communications industries. But the situation went from bad to worse in the 1980s. Employer hostility to unions, encouraged by Reagan's PATCO actions, made it difficult for unions to retain members and gain new ones. Hostile takeovers and management buyouts were accompanied by downsizing on a massive scale. Labor's previous trifecta had transmogrified into a triple defeat.[50]

With its house collapsing, labor focused attention not on capital markets – though it criticized hostile acquisitions – but on product markets (trade) and on survival. In any event, it seemed that there was little labor could do with respect to finance because of its weak bargaining power and political influence, except at the state level, where it secured

---

[48] Vincent Carosso, "Washington and Wall Street: The New Deal and Investment Bankers" (1970) 44 *Business History Review*; Barry Eichengreen, *Golden Fetters: The Gold Standard and the Great Depression, 1919–1939* (New York: Oxford University Press, 1992); Steve Fraser, *Every Man a Speculator: A History of Wall Street in American Life* (New York: HarperCollins, 2005), pp. 444–447, 473.

[49] John G. Ruggie, "International Regimes, Transactions, and Change: Embedded Liberalism in the Postwar Economic Order" (1982) 36 *International Organization* 387.

[50] Daniel J.B. Mitchell, "Union vs. Nonunion Wage Norm Shifts" (1986) 76 *American Economic Review*.

passage of anti-takeover legislation in several states. The situation was eerily reminiscent of the 1920s. There was, however, at least one new factor: the trillions in pension assets over which unions had influence. In the late 1980s, labor awoke to the fact that these funds offered leverage to partially compensate for its deficiencies.

The development of labor's pension activism is a complicated story, involving the interplay between financial markets, state and local government pension funds (SLPFs), and union-affiliated pension funds (UAPFs). SLPFs changed in the 1980s as they were freed of limits on their equity allocations, which permitted them to raise their equity stakes to accommodate funding gaps and demographic shifts. In search of higher returns and influenced by shareholder-primacy doctrines, the SLPFs became leaders of the shareholder rights movement. The UAPFs were and are somewhat different. They came more slowly to shareholder activism and gave it a different twist.[51]

The largest and most active SLPF is CalPERS, which today has assets of almost $250 billion. (SLPFs have total assets of around $4 trillion.) CalPERS was one of the first institutional investors to pressure corporations to be more shareholder-friendly. It proposed what agency theorists saw as standard remedies for instantiating shareholder primacy: greater board independence, lower takeover barriers, larger payouts to shareholders, and tighter links between CEO pay and share performance. CalPERS relied on a variety of tactics, including proxy resolutions, public targeting of underperformers, lawsuits, and alliances with other owners, including corporate raiders. In 1985 CalPERS formed the Council of Institutional Investors (CII) to bolster its clout. The CII's initial members were other SLPFs. The CII later included UAPFs and corporate pension funds.

SLPFs professed to be interested in long-term performance but disgruntled corporate executives said that the funds abandoned their long-term philosophy whenever raiders offered sufficiently juicy premiums for their shares. The SLPFs supplied capital for financing hostile takeovers in the 1980s, which they justified in the same way as the raiders: that they were performing a public service by prodding underperforming companies to maximize shareholder value. CalPERS officially was on record that it preferred companies to improve shareholder returns without layoffs. But it was not averse to downsizing. Patricia Macht, a CalPERS official, told the *New York Times* in 1996,

---

[51] Teresa Ghilarducci, *Labor's Capital: The Economics and Politics of Private Pensions* (Cambridge, MA: The MIT Press, 1992).

"There are companies that are fat, that have not taken a good look at the number of employees they need."[52]

It would be a stretch to call SLPFs worker–owner coalitions. Although many of those enrolled in SLPFs are public-sector union members, there are limits on union and worker influence because ultimate control of an SLPF resides with the government entity that created it. Also, none of the "workers" covered by an SLPF is employed by companies in which their pension funds invest. Hence the SLPFs sometimes take positions that are pro-shareholder but harmful to private-sector employees. Union leaders from the private sector will state off the record that SLPFs can pursue shareholder primacy because doing so will never hurt their members. SLPF trustees retort that UAPFs ignore their fiduciary duties by favoring workers over retirees.[53]

The UAPFs are multiemployer funds that are jointly administered by unions and employers, also known as Taft–Hartley plans. UAPFs have combined assets that are only about 9 percent of the SLPFs', although their influence belies their size. They place greater emphasis than SLPFs on a corporation's employment responsibilities and on the negative aspects of financialization. For example, in 1989 the AFL-CIO opposed having pension funds invest in junk bonds whereas the CII, dominated by the SLPFs, supported it. Although UAPFs and SLPFs both criticize executive pay levels, the SLPFs are inclined to focus on damage to owners whereas UAPFs additionally emphasize any harm done to employees. Yet the funds overlap and work closely on many issues. UAPF staff funds include unions that represent public employees, such as AFSCME, while SLPFs from liberal regions stake out positions close to the UAPFs'. In fact, because the UAPFs' holdings are usually small, they must rely on friendly SLPFs to pressure companies and their boards to make desired changes.[54]

One architect of a distinctive UAPF approach was William B. (Bill) Patterson, field director for ACTWU in the 1970s. During the J.P. Stevens textile-workers organizing drive, Patterson helped to develop

---

[52] *New York Times* April 1, 1996. Jacoby, "Convergence by Design," p. 249. Note that one reason SLPFs could become equity-holders in LBOs was that they were, and are, exempt from ERISA, which continues to afford them greater investment flexibility than UAPFs.

[53] Sean Harrigan, former president of CalPERS, found out the hard way that SLPFs are not worker funds. At the time of his appointment to the CalPERS board by Governor Gray Davis, Harrigan was a union official. He staked out a laborist path for CalPERS during his tenure as board member and later chairman (1999–2004). But when Harrigan led CalPERS into conflict with California companies such as Disney and Safeway, Governor Arnold Schwarzenegger had him removed from the board.

[54] *Pensions & Investments*, February 6, 1989; *New York Times*, April 1, 1996.

the corporate campaign, in which unions pressure a company's major shareholders in hopes that the latter will restrain anti-union managers. It was a logical progression from pressuring managers via owners to deploying labor's own pension assets for similar ends. UAPFs began utilizing their pension assets tactically in support of traditional union objectives in organizing, negotiations, and strikes. Today that approach is still alive, especially at Change To Win (CTW) and the unions affiliated with it. CTW's unions have combined their pension assets to support organizing at companies such as Columbia Health Care, Manor Care (nursing homes), and Unicco (building services). Support from SLPFs has proven crucial in several of these efforts, as has support from large European pension funds.

As compared to the CTW, the AFL-CIO and its national unions are somewhat less likely to engage in tactical pension activities, that is, those in support of traditional union objectives. The AFL-CIO has more members in manufacturing, where most pension plans are provided by the employer and lack union influence. However, some AFL-CIO unions, such as the Steelworkers, regularly pursue the tactical approach. SLPFs have no members in the private sector but they occasionally refuse to invest in firms that benefit from privatization, such as bus companies.[55]

To avoid employer opposition, including RICO lawsuits, Patterson and others have tried to develop a pension model that will raise worker concerns, meet fiduciary standards, and attract support from other shareholders. What is called the "worker-owner" or "capital stewardship" philosophy has four parts. First is a search for investment criteria that promote worker interests while satisfying fiduciary law. For example, companies that overpay their executives are wasting money that could have gone to better purposes, including investments that enhance employee pay and security. Also, if two investments offer similar returns, labor will favor the company with better human resource management and human rights policies.[56] Second, UAPFs seek to persuade other investors that pro-worker policies promote long-term value.

---

[55] Paul Jarley and Cheryl Maranto, "Union Corporate Campaigns" (1990) 43 *Industrial and Labor Relations Review*; Stewart Schwab and Randall Thomas, "Realigning Corporate Governance: Shareholder Activism by Labor Unions" (1998) 96 *Michigan Law Review*; *Pensions & Investments*, April 4, 1994; *Pensions & Investments* September 29, 2003; Teresa Ghilarducci, James Hawley, and Andrew Williams, "Labour's Paradoxical Interests and the Evolution of Corporate Governance" (1997) 24 *Journal of Law & Society*; Interview with Carin Zelenko, March 24, 2008; *Boston Globe*, September 26, 2002; *The Deal*, April 30, 2007.

[56] On the relationship between human resource policies and firm performance, see Alex Edmans, "Does the Stock Market Fully Value Intangibles?" Working Paper, Wharton

Third, there is the hope that shareholder activism will give labor influence at the corporation's highest levels, a goal that has eluded it since the 1970s. Fourth, UAPFs espouse mainstream governance principles so as to establish common ground with other active investors.[57]

In this regard UAPFs have demanded that corporations limit executive pay; hold binding, not advisory, votes on shareholder resolutions; and minimize takeover defenses such as staggered boards. As noted, UAPF activism has eclipsed that of the SLPFs; UAPFs file more shareholder resolutions than any other investor group. The problem here is that UAPFs occasionally give the impression that they are in favor of shareholder primacy, governance principles that sometimes harm employee interests.[58]

A turning point came in 1997, when the AFL-CIO created an Office of Investment to coordinate labor's capital-market activities and hired Patterson to oversee it. Almost overnight, the AFL-CIO became the center of UAPF activism. One of the office's first moves was to create a website called PayWatch, which allows employees to compare their earnings to those of their CEO. The site was extremely popular, getting over four million hits in its first year. Later the website added a feature called "Pick-a-Pension," which divulges the value of egregious CEO retirement packages and calculates how much health insurance those packages could purchase for uninsured families.[59]

The AFL-CIO's Office of Investment and the CTW Investment Group have the freedom to be aggressively vocal on capital-market issues because neither has fiduciary obligations and therefore is free of legal actions by employer groups. The CTW Investment Group is closely linked to the tactical concerns of the CTW unions, especially SEIU. The AFL-CIO, because of the federation's long tradition of national-union autonomy, does less to directly support traditional objectives of its constituent unions and spends more time on strategic

---

School (2007). There are three mutual funds that invest in union-friendly companies. Two of the funds are above their benchmarks over the past five years; one is below by one-half of 1 percent. "Pro-Labor Mutual Funds Not Sacrificing Profits" (2007), www.thestreet.com/pf/mutualfundinvesting/10381202.html (last accessed February 22, 2011).

[57] *Pensions & Investments*, April 5, 1993; Interview with Damon Silvers, March 26, 2007; Thomas Kochan, Harry Katz, and Robert McKersie, *The Transformation of American Industrial Relations* (New York: Basic Books, 1986); Schwab and Thomas, "Realigning."

[58] Schwab and Thomas, "Realigning." *Houston Chronicle*, April 17, 1994; *Pensions & Investments*, April 13, 1995; *New York Times*, March 12, 1996.

[59] *Pensions & Investments*, April 23, 1998; Trumka in *Washington Post*, April 11, 1997; *Business Week*, September 29, 1997, December 8, 1997.

activities: gathering information, coordinating UAPFs, and lobbying on Capitol Hill. It issues "Key Votes" lists prior to proxy season that describe resolutions which various UAPFs intend to submit. The lists are circulated to UAPFs and SLPFs and to other institutional investors. Another coordinating effort is the AFL-CIO's Proxy Voting Guidelines, which are disseminated to UAPF trustees and their investment advisors. The guidelines identify good governance practices that also promote employee welfare, what is called "the high road to competitiveness."[60]

The AFL-CIO cast itself into the limelight during the corporate scandals epitomized by Enron. In January 2002, the federation's Executive Council was the first to respond to Enron when it demanded that companies refuse to renominate any Enron director serving on their boards. Two months later, Damon Silvers, the AFL-CIO's Associate General Counsel, appeared before the Senate Banking Committee and called for an omnibus law to insure directorial independence, tighter regulation of accountants and analysts, and repeal of the law shielding executives and auditors from lawsuits. Several of Silvers' proposals were included in the Sarbanes–Oxley Act of July 2002. The AFL-CIO hailed SOX and said the law was needed to reform financial markets which "once were well-regulated but are now trapped in a destructive cycle where short-term financial pressures combine with the greed of corrupt corporate insiders." Harking back to the 1890s, the AFL-CIO condemned markets for being "rigged to entrench and enrich speculators ... at the expense of employees, shareholders, and communities."[61]

---

[60] Interview with Rich Trumka, AFL-CIO, March 26, 2007; *IRRC Corporate Governance Bulletin*, April 2001; *Pensions & Investments*, March 23, 1998; AFL-CIO, *AFL-CIO Proxy Voting Guidelines: Exercising Authority, Restoring Accountablility* (2003); *Business Week*, April 15, 1993; Ron Blackwell and Bill Patterson, "The Crisis of Confidence in American Business," draft working paper, March 2003; *The Economist*, July 14, 2007. Long-term measures of performance make intuitive sense but many economists reject the claim that the long-term is anything more than a concatenation of multiple short-terms and that a focus on the long-term necessarily results in better long-term performance. They may be wrong but research contesting their claims is scanty at best, a problem that plagues not only pension activism but social investing more generally.

[61] *Financial Times*, January 26, 2002; Damon A. Silvers, Testimony, to the US Sen. Comm. on Banking, Housing, and Urban Affairs, "Hearing on Accounting and Investor Protection Issues Raised by Enron and Other Public Companies," 107th Cong., 2d. Sess., March 20, 2002; Skeel, *Icarus*, p. 175; Blackwell and Patterson, "Crisis of Confidence"; John C. Coates, "The Goals and Promise of the Sarbanes-Oxley Act" (2007) 21 *Journal of Economic Perspectives*. Labor's effort to capitalize on the scandals was undercut by revelations that Robert Georgine, a long-time building trades official, personally profited from Ullilco's investment in Global Crossing's IPO. *Business Week*, March 18, 2002.

In what follows, we focus on UAPF activism in four areas. Two of them – executive pay and board structure – are old chestnuts of the shareholder-rights movement. The other two are proxy access and regulation of private equity and hedge funds. In each of these areas, the labor movement since the late 1990s has been an outspoken advocate of change. While the financial crisis hastened adoption of these provisions, the labor movement's steady beating of the drum in the years before the crisis guided legislators in crafting provisions contained in the landmark financial regulation law enacted in July 2010.[62]

A Pay issues

Ever-higher CEO compensation and scandals such as options backdating have kept executive pay at the forefront of pension activism. The AFL-CIO and CTW have called for regulations to prevent backdating and to force executives to return pay if corporate earnings are revised. The proposals tap into public anger over stratospheric executive pay levels. In a recent survey of American households, 70 percent agreed with the statement, "When corporations are profitable, the benefits are not shared with workers but go only to the top."[63]

The SEC's new executive pay disclosure rules – for which the AFL-CIO lobbied – have uncovered numerous types of executive excess. The *New York Times* said that the rules brought to mind Brandeis' quip that "sunlight is said to be the best of disinfectants" (from his post-Pujo book, *Other People's Money*). In recent proxy seasons, UAPFs sponsored the vast majority of advisory pay resolutions. Some sought limits on golden parachutes and executive retirement benefits; others demanded that executive bonuses be awarded only if performance was superior to a peer group. By far the most popular of the UAPFs' resolutions are those urging a "Say on Pay" by holding advisory shareholder votes on a board's pay proposals. To avoid negative publicity, some companies have agreed to privately meet with activist shareholders, including labor, to discuss their pay policies. This has brought labor a measure of influence at strategic corporate levels. As one union official said, "Five years ago we would never have gotten in a corporate

---

[62] Schwab and Thomas, "Realigning"; Damon Silvers, William Patterson, and J.W. Mason, "Challenging Wall Street's Conventional Wisdom," in Archon Fung, Tessa Hebb, and Joel Rogers (eds.), *Working Capital: The Power of Labor's Pensions* (Ithaca: Cornell University Press, 2001).
[63] *San Diego Union Tribune*, January 31, 2007.

boardroom. Now we're regularly meeting with corporate directors about substantive issues."⁶⁴

The House in 2007 approved a bill backed by the SLPFs and UAPFs requiring companies to offer a say on pay. Although the Bush administration opposed the bill, the financial regulation law signed by President Obama in July 2010, nicknamed Dodd-Frank after its Congressional sponsors, gives shareholders the right to an advisory vote on executive pay every three year and the right to vote on golden parachutes. As noted, labor helped clear the way, through its ties to Congressman Barney Frank, who co-authored the law, and through regular blasting of executive pay both before the crisis and then after it, as with its criticisms of pay packages at Countrywide, Bear Stearns, Goldman Sachs, Bank of America, Citigroup, Morgan, and other firms.⁶⁵

B   Board reforms

Less dramatic but no less important has been the continuing emphasis on board reform. UAPF proposals include demands that originated with SLPFs to limit board interlocks, separate the CEO and chairman positions, and require boards to seek shareholder approval of takeover defenses. Again, the Dodd-Frank law requires modification of boards: compensation committees must be comprised of independent directors and companies with the same person serving as CEO and board chairman must explain the practice to shareholders.⁶⁶

C   Proxy access

UAPFs have proposed that long-term owners holding a minimum percentage of shares be given the right to nominate directors, what is called proxy access. Labor's hope is that owners will nominate directors who not only are independent in a meaningful sense but also knowledgeable about the company and the ingredients for its long-term success.⁶⁷ Rich Trumka is more ambitious. He wants directors who are

---

⁶⁴ *Business Week*, December 28, 2006; *New York Times*, April 8, 2007; Brandeis, *Other People's Money*, p. 92; AFL-CIO, "Key Votes Survey: How Investment Managers Voted in the 2006 Proxy Season" (2006); *L.A. Times*, April 21, 2007.
⁶⁵ *Atlanta Constitution*, June 6, 2007; *Financial Times*, April 1, 2007; *Business Week*, June 11, 2007; *New York Times*, March 7, 2008; *Wall Street Journal*, April 14, 2008.
⁶⁶ *Ibid.*; AFL-CIO, "Key Votes."
⁶⁷ Many corporate boards are comprised of CEOs from other companies who, although they are classified as independent, tend to be deferential to other CEOs. They also are prone to groupthink.

"worker-friendly," which might include employees, who, he notes, are relatively likely to be independent of management.[68]

Other institutional investors are allied with UAPFs on this issue; they see proxy access as an effective tool for board independence and executive accountability. It is also a way of making boards more transparent. As an AFL-CIO official says of proxy access, "You're opening up the kitchen inside these companies. That's a dark secret. That's a place where the insiders really play inside ball." In December 2007, under President Bush, the SEC voted along party lines to permit companies to deny proxy access. But Dodd-Frank now gives the SEC express authority to promulgate proxy-access rules. President Obama's appointment of Mary Schapiro to replace Christopher Cox as SEC head will likely bring proxy access to life.[69]

VII Private equity and hedge funds

Private equity funds (PE) are a throwback to earlier eras: to the LBOs of the 1980s and, because of their diversification, to the conglomerates of the 1960s. PE's modus operandi is to leverage its assets via debt, buy companies or their subsidiaries, take them private, dispose of corporate assets to pay off debt, and sell out. How PE makes money is a matter of dispute. PE funds say that, because they are blockholders aiming for a future sale, they have an incentive to manage corporate assets so as to raise efficiency and thereby earn capital gains. Critics charge that that the productivity effects of PE are undemonstrated and that PE derives its profits from the tax benefits of leveraged debt, from employee squeezing, from the sale to PE of companies at below-market value by incumbent executives seeking private benefits, and, last but not least, from aggressive cash withdrawals. Approximately 12 percent of PE investments are "quick flips" in which exit occurs in less than two years.[70]

---

[68] Lucian Bebchuk, "The Myth of the Shareholder Franchise" (2007) 93 *Virginia Law Review*; Silvers interview; *Daily Deal*, October 20, 2003; Damon Silvers and Michael Garland, "The Origins and Goals of the Fight for Proxy Access," in Lucian Bebchuk (ed.), *Shareholder Holder Access to the Proxy Ballot* (Cambridge, MA: Harvard University Press, 2005); Interview with Daniel Pedrotty, AFL-CIO, March 26, 2007; Trumka interview.
[69] Interview with Ron Blackwell, AFL-CIO, March 26, 2007; Bebchuk, "The Myth"; *LA Times*, February 17, 2003, July 26, 2007; *Financial Times*, April 1, 2007; Conference Board, "2007 Report"; *New York Times*, November 29, 2007. The SEC also has proposed doing away with nonbinding shareholder resolutions, which would eliminate advisory votes on executive pay and other issues.
[70] Patrick A. Gaughan, "How Private Equity and Hedge Funds Are Driving M&A," *Journal of Corporate Accounting and Finance* (2007); *The Economist*, February 10, 2007;

Low-wage service workers are especially vulnerable during and after a PE buyout because they are easier to replace. One of the first American unions to launch a public campaign against PE was SEIU, whose members – actual and potential – come from this sector. Blackstone, the largest PE fund, owns nearly 600 large office buildings whose janitors are or could be SEIU members; Cerberus and other PE funds are major players in the hotel industry; and Carlyle owns the nursing-home giant Manor Care, whose 60,000 employees the SEIU is seeking to organize. CTW uses a combination of tactics to put pressure on PE funds. It has organized street theater to personally embarrass PE executives and has released facts about PE funds that might hurt their public image, such as their heavy reliance on Chinese and Middle Eastern capital. Many of these activities are, however, a bargaining tactic. Andy Stern, head of SEIU and of CTW, has approached the funds, notably KKR, and offered to call off his attacks on PE tax breaks if the funds agree to treat workers fairly, including neutrality during organizing drives.[71]

The AFL-CIO's approach to PE is less tactical. After Blackstone announced its 2007 IPO, Rich Trumka filed two statements with the SEC criticizing the IPO as being motivated by tax evasion. As with other items in the Dodd–Frank law it was the labor movement that was partly responsible for provisions that will tamp down the excesses of private equity by requiring most derivatives to clear and trade on transparent exchanges and mandating that large managers of private equity funds register with the Securities and Exchange Commission.

The labor movement has also targeted hedge funds, which have assets of over $1.5 trillion. The figure understates their influence because they are the single largest trader in the equity markets. The funds have broadened their hedging strategies from stocks and foreign exchange to riskier assets like sub-prime debt, an investment that has caused the demise of several giant hedge funds since 2007. Dodd–Frank's provision for derivatives transparency and fund registration puts a crimp in hedge funds, as did the financial crisis itself, although it falls short of the full-bore proposals put forth by the labor movement.[72]

Business Week, February 10, 2007, October 30, 2006; *Washington Post*, April 4, 2007; *Wall Street Journal*, July 25, 2007; World Economic Forum, *Globalization*.

[71] World Economic Forum, *Globalization*; *Workforce Management*, May 7, 2007; *Independent*, April 2, 2007; SEIU, "Behind the Buyouts: Inside the World of Private Equity," April 2007; Andrew L. Stern to US House, Committee on Financial Services, May 16, 2007; *Washington Post*, April 4, 2007; *Washington Post*, April 18, 2008. The Chinese government recently purchased a $3 billion stake in Blackstone.

[72] *New York Times*, November 14, 2007. Hedge funds own 55 percent of Stelco, a unionized steel producer in Canada. Stelco's CEO is a former associate of Wilbur Ross, causing the union to fear that the funds will cut jobs and pensions. *Toronto Star*, June 2, 2007.

VIII Conclusion

Today, as in the past, conservatives proclaim that financial development is a free-market phenomenon unrelated to politics and best left free of them. Benefits of finance are touted; costs are ignored or portrayed as inevitable. The recurrence of financial crises, including the one that started in 2008, and of popular movements to restrain finance, suggest an opposite conclusion: that there *are* costs – inequality and volatility being two of them – and that they are neither trivial nor inevitable.

Sophisticated conservatives recognize a connection between finance and politics but it is the libertarian doctrine that financial development weakens the chokehold of vested interests such as unions, entrenched managers, and the state. In fact, as we have discussed, financial elites themselves are a vested interest. Financial markets flourish when elites can goad governments to favor finance, as was the case with the gold standard and the Federal Reserve system, and with post-1980 deregulation. Financiers not only are lobbyists; they also are norm entrepreneurs. To take one recent example, Wilbur Ross in 2006 funded a bipartisan group, the Committee on Capital Markets Regulations, which issued a highly publicized reports calling for "smarter" regulation, protective limits on financial litigation, and a rollback of Sarbanes–Oxley. One corporate law expert described the committee as "an escalation of the culture war against regulation." And then the crisis hit.[73]

It is difficult not to feel a touch of *schadenfreude* for those who, over the past twenty years, have confidently asserted the virtues of deregulation and the irrelevance of government in an era of globalization. Now is not a good time for libertarians, who are backpedaling furiously as governments around the world take dramatic steps to rescue financial markets from their follies. It is unclear what will be the long-term consequences of the rescue effort. For now, at least, the deregulatory impulse in finance is spent. Even conservatives accept that the quid pro quo for government assistance is tighter scrutiny and more regulation. But already financiers are demanding that any new regulations be removed when the crisis eases.

Conservatives portray financial markets as democratic; they help the masses, not only the elite. Financial regulation therefore has perverse

---

[73] Kaplan and Rauh, "Wall Street and Main Street"; Rajan and Zingales, *Saving Capitalism*; Marco Pagano and Paolo Volpin, "The Political Economy of Finance" (2001) 17 *Oxford Review of Economic Policy*; *New York Times*, October 20, 2006, December 1, 2006. The Committee is a blue-ribbon group whose roster includes prominent financiers, business leaders, and academics, such as R. Glenn Hubbard (Columbia), Hal C. Scott (Harvard), and Luigi Zingales (Chicago).

effects, they say, harming less affluent households who are the beneficiaries of financial development: "The financial revolution is opening the gates of the aristocratic clubs to everyone ... it puts the human being at the center of economic activity." (Identical claims about finance's democratizing effects were made in the 1920s.) An oft-cited example is the availability of credit for purchasing homes and smoothing consumption. Without doubt, a broad spectrum of households benefits from deeper credit markets, even from payday lending. However, the reality is that credit is not the great democratic leveler. Consumption inequality has risen, not fallen, since 1980. Housing credit has turned out to be a sham. Sub-median households face particular difficulties when their income shrinks due to job loss. The average high-school dropout facing unemployment has liquid assets worth only 5 percent of the income lost through unemployment – not much to borrow against – versus 124 percent for college graduates. For sub-median households, it is not credit but government safety nets such as unemployment insurance and food stamps that are their main resources for smoothing.[74]

Another benefit cited by conservatives is the spread of shareholding within the middle class, those straddling the median. Ostensibly it has made these households more affluent, tolerant of risk, and supportive of financial deregulation. The problem is that the median household is relatively disengaged from shareholding. In the United States, the middle quintile owns shares – directly or indirectly via pension plans – worth $7,500, which account for 5 percent of its assets. Its debt, mostly from mortgages but also from credit cards, stands at $74,000. Now take the average household from the top 1 percent. Its shares are worth $3.3 million and account for 21 percent of its assets. Debt stands at $566,000. So let's compare: The median household has a debt/equity ratio of 9.9; the top 1 percent has a ratio of 0.17. One need not be an economist to predict who will be leery of unregulated finance and who will welcome its risks. Efforts to rectify the imbalance between finance's costs and benefits are not "strange," as conservatives allege, nor are they evidence of an anti-market conspiracy.[75]

[74] Albert O. Hirschman, *The Rhetoric of Reaction: Perversity, Futility, Jeopardy* (Cambridge, MA: Harvard University Press, 1991); Adair Morse, "Payday Lenders: Heroes or Villains?" SSRN Working Paper 999408 (2007); Rajan and Zingales, "Great Reversals," p. 92; Cowing, *Populists, Plungers*, pp. 177–180; Claessens and Perotti, "Finance and Inequality"; Susan Dynarski and Jonathan Gruber, "Can Families Smooth Variable Earnings?" *Brookings Papers on Economic Activity* (1997), 229–230; David Cutler and Lawrence Katz, "Macroeconomic Performance and the Disadvantaged" (1991) 2 *Brookings Papers on Economic Activity* 1–74.

[75] Enrico C. Perotti and Ernst-Ludwig von Thadden, "The Political Economy of Corporate Control and Labor Rents" (2006) 114 *Journal of Political Economy* 169; Mishel et al., *Working America*, p. 261; Raghuram Rajan and Luigi Zingales, *Saving*

Conservatives assert that coordinated economies – where owners, executives, and workers cooperate in the pursuit of value creation – lack the discipline needed to sedulously pursue efficiency. Again the claim is a throwback, in this case to libertarian ideologues like Henry C. Simons of the University of Chicago, who criticized New Deal producerism as a "flagrant collusion between unions and employers." Yet the empirical evidence does not support the claim that relational corporate governance sacrifices growth. Between 1960 and 1980, CMEs on average grew faster than the liberal economies. If the period is narrowed to 1980–2000, the edge goes to the liberal economies. But even during those years, some liberal economies (Australia and Canada) grew less rapidly than some CMEs (Austria, Belgium, Finland, Norway, and the Netherlands).[76]

The financial meltdown has affected the entire global economy. But its impact has been uneven: the greater was a nation's involvement in the shadow banking system, the more heavily it has been hit. Most affected are the United States and the UK. The British are paying an enormous price for hitching their economic wagon to the financial services industry. Relatively less affected are the CMEs in Japan and continental Europe, as Angela Merkel liked to remind Gordon Brown, and countries that never went too far in the direction of financial deregulation, like Canada. Perhaps these differences will generate more support for a stakeholder approach to corporate governance in the United States. There are efforts along these lines but as yet they are straws in the wind.[77]

The conservatives' infatuation with finance has unintended (dare we say perverse?) effects. By causing a lopsided distribution of productivity

---

Capitalism from the Capitalists: Unleashing the Power of Financial Markets to Create Wealth and Spread Opportunity (Princeton: Princeton University Press, 2004), p. 18. After 2001, sub-prime mortgages also were touted as a democratizing force that would bring homes within the reach of those who previously could not afford them.

[76] Rajan and Zingales, *Saving Capitalism*, p. 247; Henry C. Simons, "For a Free-Market Liberalism" (1941) 206 *University of Chicago Law Review*; Jonas Pontusson, *Inequality and Prosperity: Social Europe vs Liberal America* (Ithaca: Cornell University Press, 2005), p. 5.

[77] A new realism is emerging in legal scholarship that challenges shareholder primacy and supports a more balanced approach. The neo-realists are at pains to point out that under law shareholders are not the corporation's sole residual claimants. They observe that corporations are cooperative teams rather than a nexus of arm's-length contracts. To produce wealth, team members invest in firm-specific assets that are worthless if the firm goes bust. Hence all team members – not only shareholders – bear residual risk. With illiquid investments and low diversification, employees have strong incentives to monitor agents and may be best placed to do so. See, for example, Margaret Blair and Lynn Stout, "A Team Production Theory of Corporation Law" (1999) 85 *Virginia Law Review*; Lynn LoPucki, "The Myth of the Residual Owner" (2004) 82 *Washington University Law Quarterly*.

gains, financial deregulation and shareholder primacy foster resistance to productivity improvements because employees think that the game is not worth the candle. Employee dissatisfaction and distrust in employers are at all-time highs. Moreover, financial development undermines public support for trade and financial openness. The direct effect is to raise employment risk so that individuals become wary of the additional risks associated with an open economy. While both types of risk can be mitigated with social insurance, efforts to strengthen the sagging social nets of the United States are being undermined by finance-induced inequality. This is the indirect effect. Rising top-income shares permit the rich to separate from the commonweal and withdraw their support for public spending. In the past, social compacts offered public education and social insurance as cushions against the volatility of an open economy. In our more inegalitarian age, the compacts are providing less in return for openness than before.[78]

The efforts of organized labor to reshape capital markets over the past twenty years have often been disappointing. There is a Janus-faced tendency among union-influenced pension funds to publicly embrace responsible investing while putting millions of dollars into socially retrograde investments. Then there is the problem of fissures in the labor movement: between the federations, between the federations and their unions, between SLPFs and UAPFs, and between local unions and their internationals. These splits hinder the coordination of labor's many separate pools of capital.

Nevertheless, an opening for labor has been created by the financial crisis. The middle class is worried about stagnant incomes and fearful of financial risk that has caused loss of homes, jobs, and retirement assets. Labor is one of the main groups connecting the dots between those concerns and the casino capitalism that is our financial system. It's striking how quickly labor's pre-crisis ideas have moved from the periphery to the center of political discourse. And during the worst of the financial crisis it was the AFL-CIO and CTW who were among the loudest voices alleging incompetence and greed on the part of the US financial industry. Just as business leaders and laissez-faire were

---

[78] Dani Rodrik, *Has Globalization Gone Too Far?* (Washington, DC: Institute for International Economics, 1997), pp. 62–63; Geoffrey Garrett and Deborah Mitchell, "Globalization, Government Spending, and Taxation in the OECD" (2001) 39 *European Journal of Political Research*; Kenneth Scheve and Matthew Slaughter, "A New Deal for Globalization" (2007) 86:4 *Foreign Affairs* 34. Concerned about declining support for financial and trade openness, the Financial Service Forum, representing the nation's twenty largest financial institutions, issued a report urging the government to do more to reduce risk and inequality in US labor markets. Peter Gosselin, *LA Times*, August 20, 2007

lionized in the 1920s and lampooned in the 1930s, so today we are witnessing a similar sort of delegitimation.

The outcome of the contests between financial elites and these new coalitions is uncertain. The elites have enormous monetary resources for lobbying, public relations, and other activities. And, as the logic of regulatory capture predicts, they will strive harder than the average citizen to influence the course of current regulatory efforts.[79] But a successful re-regulatory coalition, as emerged during the New Deal, can neutralize the power of financial elites. It is happening now.

The present does not repeat the past but it rhymes. The current financial crisis is putting government financial regulation back on the political agenda with a level of urgency not seen since the 1930s. Ironically, labor's engagement with financial markets before the crisis has put it in a leadership position during the crisis. Today finance is the master. Will it once again become the servant? The outcome depends on the politics of the double movement.

---

[79] Daron Acemoglu and James Robinson, "Persistence of Power, Elites, and Institutions" (2008) 96 *American Economic Review*. As during the Clinton years, donations by the financial services industry to Democrats in 2008 dwarfed contributions to the GOP. *LA Times*, March 21, 2008.

14 The conflicting logic of markets and the management of production

Suzanne Konzelmann and Frank Wilkinson

I   Introduction

Since the late 1990s, as the typical American family saw its income stagnate, the availability of easy credit and cheap imports fueled a consumer and real estate market boom. Households were able to use debt to supplement earnings and thereby live beyond their means, under the illusion of prosperity. The housing bubble and low interest rates added to the illusion as households were encouraged to increase borrowing, using the rising equity in their homes as collateral to fund additional consumption and investment in housing.

The conditions that produced this consumer boom were less comfortable for investors and financial intermediaries. Low interest rates and the large volume of Asian savings in the market not only depressed returns on traditional financial instruments. It also generated increasing pressure from investors for higher yields which could be achieved in essentially two ways: higher risk and higher leverage. Many opted for both, using the booming property markets as fuel.[1] In 2007, however, the US sub-prime bubble burst, plunging the global money markets and economy into crisis and revealing serious imbalances in the system as a whole.

Before the bubble burst, Strine argued that "both management and labor share an interest in the vitality of … equity markets" upon which their long-term retirement and savings incomes depend.[2] We would argue that managers and workers also share interests in production and in the long-term vitality of the *productive systems* for which they work, whose shares are traded on equity markets. In our view, the stock

---

[1] For a further discussion, see S. Konzelmann, M. Fovargue-Davies and G. Schnyder, "Varieties of Liberalism: Anglo-Saxon Capitalism in Crisis?" Working Paper, Cambridge Centre for Business Research (2010), pp. 30–40.
[2] L. Strine, "Towards Common Sense and Common Ground? Reflections on the Shared Interests of Managers and Labor in a More Rational System of Corporate Governance" (2007) 33 *Journal of Corporation Law* 4.

market maneuverings that are encouraged and justified by agency theory threaten this mutuality of interests and the productive efficiency it engenders by alienating workers, as well as other stakeholders (such as customers and suppliers), upon whom organizational performance ultimately depends. The wide reaching damage to the real economy that has been attributed to the global financial crisis suggests strongly that this extends further – to the broader local, national and regional productive systems in which individual firms are embedded

With the increasing globalization of product and capital markets – and in the absence of co-extensive regulation of corporate behavior and accountability – even greater pressure has been brought to bear on managers and workers at the local, national and regional levels. And as an increasing number of corporations engage in cross-border merger activity, the loss of any national identity means that there are economic incentives to relocate operations to localities (across the globe) where the greatest gains can be achieved, without regard for the impact this might have on the corporation's country of origin. The attractiveness of the geographically lowest-cost locations has set off a downward spiral, in which economic and social standards are driven to lower and lower levels globally, at the expense of localities with relatively higher standards and ultimately at the expense of the system as a whole.

This chapter examines the current role of the capital market and its effects, not only on operating companies, but also on society. Section II describes the growth of "worker capital" in the world's financial markets and, with it, the emergence of potential conflicts of interest among shareholder groups. Section III examines the relationship between corporate governance and labor management. Section IV considers the impact of labor management on productive system efficiency. Section V explores the influence of corporate governance on stakeholder relationships – and by extension, on cooperation within productive systems – as a way of understanding how corporate governance might impact the system's performance. In Section VI, the analysis is extended to global markets, where regulation is not co-extensive with the market. Section VII concludes.

II   The growth of "worker capital"

Until only recently there was a clear divide between investors and managers – who owned and controlled capital – and workers, who owned little if any capital. Security for the firm's employees in retirement rested on savings, social security and, for some, defined *benefits* from employer-provided pension plans. In effect, these are wages postponed until after retirement, the risk for the provision of which is carried by the employer.

These latter provisions have now largely disappeared for new entrants to the labor market and for job changers who, at best, have employer-provided supplements to their defined *contribution* plans. In these plans, regular sums of money are invested in the stock market to generate retirement income. Such schemes shift the risks of post-retirement income from the employer to the employee, creating a class of what Strine describes as "forced capitalists," whose interests are long-term, in the security of both their current employment and their financial prospects for retirement. This is in sharp contrast to the interests of shareholders seeking speculative gains, which ultimately threaten jobs.[3]

As a consequence of the growth of defined contribution plans there are rapidly growing quantities of *worker capital* available on the stock market. But forced capitalists find themselves in a potentially conflicted position because they mainly invest in the stock market though financial intermediaries; and it is these intermediaries who determine how their funds are placed and the degree of pressure exerted on the managers of productive enterprises to deliver value to shareholders.

Accompanying and related to these stock market trends has been the emergence of the corporate governance industry, comprised of pension fund administrators, stock market advisory agencies, corporate law scholars and business journalists.[4] Broadly speaking, the corporate governance industry has served to cement the prioritization of shareholder value into the management of public companies. The theoretical justification for this, in "agency theory," rests on the assumption that the stock market operates as an efficient market for corporate control. As such, it is the means by which shareholders can punish inefficient and malfeasant managers and reward successful and reliable ones by selling them their shares.[5]

A consequence of the prioritization of shareholder interests in corporate governance is increased demands for higher stock market prices and enhanced dividends. As a result, corporate managers face intensifying pressure to deliver such value to shareholders. The means by which this is most usually accomplished is through strategies designed to cut costs, including such approaches as downsizing, off-shoring existing

---

[3] Strine, "Towards Common Sense," pp. 5–7.
[4] Strine, "Towards Common Sense," pp. 9–10.
[5] M.C. Jensen, "Agency Costs of Free Cash Flow, Corporate Finance and Takeovers" (1986) 76 *American Economic Review* 323–329; A. Shleifer and R. Vishny, "A Survey of Corporate Governance" (1997) 52 *Journal of Finance* 737–783.

jobs, concentrating new job growth in low wage labor markets, and limiting domestic wage and benefit growth.[6] These measures have driven a wedge not only between labor and management but also between top management and lower-level managers who are required to implement the cost-cutting plans but are also its victims when management structures are de-layered.

In this context, while the agency costs resulting from the separation of the ownership and control of public corporations has been a focus of theory and research, precious little attention has been paid to the agency costs that arise from the "separation of ownership from ownership."[7] These are a consequence of the fact that, by and large, equity is owned and controlled not by the original investors, but by mutual funds and other institutional investors that handle their funds. This separation of ownership from ownership, and the preoccupation of institutional investors with short-term financial gains, drives a further wedge between labor and management, and between workers as the currently employed and workers as pensioners.

There is also a fundamental divergence in shareholder interests arising from the use of stock options and other forms of managerial remuneration designed to align the interests of senior managers and shareholders. In this context, the interests of managers are invariably short-term and invested in the performance of a single organization over which the executives have direct control. By contrast, worker capital has an inherently long-term perspective (building pension income). It is not directly related to the performance of the organization but rather of the market as a whole; and it is invested and managed by an intermediary who has to balance their own interests with those of workers, which themselves may be conflicted.[8]

III   Corporate governance and labor management

The 1990s was a period when corporate governance came to the fore as an issue both for public policy and management practice. The idea that managers should act as the agents of shareholders gained ground, particularly in the US and British systems. This was manifested in the

---

[6] L. Mishel, J. Bernstein and J. Schmitt, *The State of Working America* (Ithaca: Cornell ILR Press, 2001).
[7] Strine, "Towards Common Sense," p. 11; L. Strine, "Human Freedom and the Two Friedmans: Musings on the Implications of Globalization for the Effective Regulation of Corporate Behaviour," Research Paper No 07–26, University of Pennsylvania Law School, Institute for Law and Economics (2007), p. 30.
[8] For example, between those who have retired and those still working.

implementation of what might be considered *external* forms of governance, including the proliferation of corporate governance codes and the strengthening of shareholder protections; it also led to the widespread adoption of executive share option schemes and similar forms of managerial remuneration, designed to more closely align the interests and financial objectives of shareholders and top management. During this period, entire industries and sectors were restructured through the operation of the market for corporate control;[9] and in the process, long established mechanisms for the exercise of stakeholder voice – above all, employee representation in its various forms – were marginalized.

This was also an era when innovative forms of labor–management relations emerged in both the United States and the UK to capture the benefits of cooperation among corporate stakeholders. The background to this was rapid technological change and intensifying competition in product markets, brought about by globalization and, particularly in the case of the UK, privatization. Customers learned to exercise their choice more aggressively and shareholders became increasingly impatient for a quick and profitable return on their investments. In this process, the sustainable, long-term productive relationship between capital and production was increasingly compromised as a more speculative and volatile approach to investment gained favor.

In response to these pressures, firms were forced to re-examine their *internal* governance and organizational systems and structures in an effort to improve performance.[10] Although downsizing and business process re-engineering were part of the response, labor–management "partnerships" were also initiated, often in the very same companies that had undergone substantial restructuring. These arrangements led to innovations in the employment relationship, including a significant degree of self-management and autonomy for employees. However, outside the traditionally more cooperative industrial cultures such as those of Germany and Scandinavia, this involved very little, if any, real influence being vested in workers. As a result, the benefits of cooperation were essentially skewed in favor of management and by extension, shareholders. The German and Scandinavian systems had largely evolved in a context with supporting institutions and longer-term benefits and sustainability in mind. By contrast, the Anglo-American vision

---

[9] B. Holmstrom and S. Kaplan, "Corporate Governance and Merger Activity in the US: Making Sense of the 1980s and 1990s," Working Paper 01–11, MIT Department of Economics (2001).

[10] B. Burchell, D. Ladipo and F. Wilkinson (eds.), *Job Insecurity and Work Intensification* (London: Routledge, 2002).

of closer cooperation tended to have a much shorter horizon – and usually a purely financial motive.

Thus, as a means of enhancing the firm's competitiveness, corporate governance encouraged *internal* reforms aimed at fostering a higher degree of cooperation between management and labor. Yet it also intensified the pressure to prioritize short-term shareholder interests, thereby threatening to undermine the foundations upon which these very same forms of labor–management cooperation are dependent.

IV Efficiency in productive systems: cooperation and labor management

The logic of production is rooted in a recognition that *cooperation* is important for competitive performance. At the technical level this is obvious: relations within and between the units of production are technically interdependent and therefore need to be cooperative for operational efficiency. The sharing of information is also a necessarily cooperative activity. This is important in a technical sense to ensure that all participants are equally well informed about the best means of production and that components are designed and produced in such a way as best to fulfill their productive purpose. Success in production will also depend upon access to information on the latest products, processes and forms of organization. Here, cooperation pays off because of the problem-solving benefits of working together and because the sharing of information increases the pace of diffusion and development of new processes and products and hence the pace of technical progress. In this technical sense, therefore, business performance is importantly determined by the effectiveness of management in securing cooperation from its workforce, suppliers and customers.[11]

In management theory, growing appreciation of the increasing returns to greater worker involvement in the planning and execution of work, as well as to work group activities, worker self-regulation, closer involvement with management and a more democratic style of management, led to the development of the *human resource management* (HRM) school.[12] In this, insights of scientific management were integrated

---

[11] F. Wilkinson, "Co-operation, the Organization of Work and Competitiveness," Working Paper No. 85, Cambridge Centre for Business Research (1998).
[12] D. Guest, "Human Resource Management and Industrial Relations" (1987) 24 *Journal of Management Studies* 503–521; E. Appelbaum and R. Batt, *The New American Workplace: Transforming Work Systems in the United States* (New York: ILR Press, 1994); P. Blyton and P. Turnbull, "Debates, Dilemmas and Contradictions," in P. Blyton and P. Turnbull (eds.), *Reassessing Human Resource Management* (London: Sage Publications, 1992).

with those of the human relations school. The employing organization was re-conceptualized from pluralist to unitary, where all interests are shared; and the role of labor management was redefined from authoritarian to serving as facilitator of a participatory, cooperative and self-regulating system. In this process, the worker was no longer viewed as a factor of production in need of dragooning into compliance with contractual promise but rather was considered a full partner in cooperative production provided his or her psychological needs were fully met.

Broadly speaking, the purpose of HRM is to foster a pre-emptive rather than reactive approach to operational efficiency, quality control, and innovation by shifting responsibility and accountability for decision-making (on the part of both employees and managers responsible for employee related matters) toward the shop floor. Its adoption testifies to a shift in labor management practice "from coercion to the attempted production of self-regulated individuals."[13] For HRM to be effective, employees must be sufficiently trained, motivated and enabled in their work and satisfied with the terms and conditions of their employment.[14]

Models of HRM assign central importance to *commitment* to the objectives of the organization,[15] where commitment implies "strong acceptance of and belief in an organization's goals and values; willingness to exert effort on behalf of the organization; a strong desire to maintain membership of the organization."[16] Organizational commitment is important because it is seen to motivate workers to work harder and go "beyond contract;" to self-monitor and control, eliminating the need for supervisory and inspection personnel; to persist with the organization, thereby increasing the returns to investments in selection, training and development; and to avoid collective activities that might lower the quality and quantity of individual contributions to the organization.[17] This was taken a step further by the Japanese concept of Kaizen, where full cooperation as well as delegation of responsibility and the

---

[13] W. Hollway, *Work Psychology and Work Organisation* (London: Sage Publications, 1991), p. 20.
[14] Appelbaum and Batt, "The New American Workplace."
[15] Guest, "Human Resource Management," pp. 503–521; R. Walton, "Towards a Strategy of Eliciting Employee Commitment Based on Policies of Mutuality," in R. Walton and P. Lawrence (eds.), *Human Resource Management: Trends and Challenges* (Boston, MA: Harvard Business School Press, 1985); K. Legge, *Human Resource Management: Rhetorics and Realities* (London: Macmillan Publishers, 1995).
[16] Guest, "Human Resource Management," p. 513, quoting R. Mowday, L. Porter and R. Steers, *Employee Organization Linkages: The Psychology of Commitment, Absenteeism and Turnover* (London: Academic Press, 1982).
[17] Guest, "Human Resource Management," pp. 503–521.

ability to change and adapt processes were extended as far down the line as possible. This was on the premise that the organization working as a whole was stronger and more creative than one run exclusively by management. Thus, organizational performance depends upon the degree to which employees are willing and able to commit themselves to the organization, with cooperation being an essential requirement for effective production.

In the United States and Britain, however, the absence of formal institutions supporting labor management cooperation, relatively weak employment protection and the steady erosion of mechanisms for independent worker representation serve to undermine the foundations upon which employee commitment depends. The motivation behind this may well have been rooted in the more adversarial relationship inherent in a system where workers are not directly involved in strategic management. By contrast, in systems like Germany and Scandinavia, formal worker representation at the level of the board and in other key parts of the organization is commonplace and employment protection provisions are relatively strong. This has helped to build a strong tradition of trust through much greater transparency than exists in Britain and the United States. As a result, outside the more cooperative national industrial systems, not only was tangible employee involvement relatively rare; so, too, was real trust – which is hard to build in the short-term.

Over the long-term, cooperation and commitment – and hence long-term organizational performance – is importantly dependent on *trust*. Trust determines the degree to which employees commit themselves to the objectives of their employing organization. But this, in turn, depends upon their confidence that the commitments made to them by the organization are secure.

In production, the essence of trust is that it provides a guarantee that the agreed terms will be kept and that what is promised will be carried out to required specifications and quality standards. But it goes beyond contract fulfillment to include *goodwill* trust, which includes a willingness to share information and ideas, to honor informal understandings and be ready to renegotiate contracts and, in a more social sense, to be willing to give and take, to help in an emergency and to forgive occasional faults.[18] Goodwill trust gives the assurance that someone is so dependable that they can be trusted to take initiatives without the risk

---

[18] B. Burchell and F. Wilkinson, "Trust, Business Relationships and the Contractual Environment" (1997) 21 *Cambridge Journal of Economics* 217–237.

that they will take advantage;[19] and it is essential for full cooperation within productive systems.

The hallmark of high trust systems is that individuals and organizations working together provide open-ended commitments to cooperate, the returns from which are realized over an uncertain, long time period. Mutual trust acts to reduce uncertainty by increasing the confidence in truth, worth and reliability of people required to work together. The greater the trust each side has in the others, the greater will be the certainty that commitments made will not be abused. Trust, therefore, enables individuals to share expectations about the future, reducing uncertainty and allowing them to cooperate more effectively.[20] From the workers' perspective, trust is rooted in their perception of how they are treated by their employers and of the terms and conditions of employment; and they will respond negatively or positively, in terms of cooperation in production, depending upon how fair they consider these to be.

V Dominant stakeholders and cooperation

In a unitary view of the organization, conflicts of interest are minimized because the focus is on stakeholders' shared interests in successful organizational performance which forms the basis for their individual and collective economic security. In this context, collective action is viewed as dysfunctional and disruptive. However, organizations are not unitary. Interests necessarily diverge with respect to the distribution of jointly produced value and the use to which that value is put. Value, for example, can be distributed to stakeholders or it can be reinvested in productive activities, the choice of which will have short- and long-term implications for the various stakeholder groups.

The problem is augmented by the role played by corporate governance in designating a dominant stakeholder group and prioritizing interests accordingly. In cases where there is a dominant remote external stakeholder, such as shareholders in companies listed on a stock exchange, corporate governance has an important influence not only on the structure and nature of stakeholder relations but also on the level of commitment that stakeholders are willing and able to make to one another and the level of organizational commitment that is ultimately

---

[19] M. Sako, *Prices, Quality and Trust: Inter-Firm Relations in Britain and Japan* (Cambridge: Cambridge University Press, 1992).
[20] C. Lane and R. Bachman, "The Social Construction of Trust: Supplier Relations in Britain and Germany" (1996) 17 *Organization Studies* 365–395; N. Luhmann, *Trust and Power* (London: Wiley, 1979).

realized and sustained. This is because the commitments stakeholders make to one another are dependent on the requirements of the dominant stakeholder group. Thus, the ability to honor commitments is not entirely in the hands of those making them.

During the 1990s, the theorized role of the stock market as an efficient market for corporate control and the growing consensus that the agency problem lay at the heart of poor corporate performance meant that the consolidation of market power by hostile takeovers could be justified by the working of the market, which by definition serves the general interest.[21] Exclusive concern with the rights of shareholders rests on the assumption that they are motivated by *real* gain, based on expectations about the performance of the corporations whose shares are being traded, rather than *speculative* gain, based on expectations about what other shareholders might do.[22] It also rests on the assumption that stakeholders other than shareholders are relatively powerless. As a result, in response to pressure from shareholders, the incumbent managers (or some alternative team preferred by the stock market) will be able to readily improve the business's performance and as a consequence generate the higher returns demanded by shareholders.

However, outside the narrow focus of financial economics, it is recognized that organizational performance also depends upon the quality of its managers' relations with a wider range of stakeholders, including suppliers, consumers, communities and, especially, employees, which might be at risk if managers prioritize the short-term interests of shareholders. Gospel and Pendleton, for example, define corporate governance as encompassing "the relationship between three sets of actors or stakeholders – 'capital, management and labor' where the way the firm is financed acts as 'a set of constraints and opportunities which influence managerial choices, including in the labor area.'"[23] They suggest that when considering the "influence which capital and management have on labor and the systems of labor management which are put in place" it is necessary to consider the role of corporate ownership and patterns of financing alongside the HRM systems managements adopt.[24]

---

[21] S. Deakin and G. Slinger, "Hostile Takeovers, Corporate Law and the Theory of the Firm," Working Paper No. 56, ESRC Centre for Business Research (1997).
[22] J.M. Keynes, *The General Theory of Employment, Interest and Money, The Collected Writings of John Maynard Keynes, Volume III* (London: Macmillan Publishers, 1973), ch. 12.
[23] H. Gospel and A. Pendleton, *Corporate Governance and Labour Management: An International Comparison* (Oxford: Oxford University Press, 2005), pp. 3–4.
[24] Gospel and Pendleton, *Corporate Governance*, p. 5.

The possible "corporate governance constraint" on the quality of industrial relations, and hence cooperation between management and labor, arises because of the opportunities for low-cost exit on the part of shareholders, and the short-term time horizons this can impose. The ready availability of shares on the stock market, and the risk of hostile takeover this implies, increases the attention managers are obliged to pay to shareholders' interests, and risks compromising the commitment they can make to other stakeholders and to their workforce. This in turn risks breaching the *psychological contract*[25] managers have with their workforce, reducing the loyalty and commitment that can be expected from them, and their willingness to fully engage with management in ensuring high levels of productive performance.[26]

The upshot of this is the recognition that a dominant remote external stakeholder – shareholders in the case of quoted companies – can impose constraints on the ability of managers to adopt HRM practices designed to solicit from employees cooperation and involvement in the planning, managing and undertaking of production.[27] This raises the possibility of a conflict between the priority afforded shareholder interests and the long-term prospects of the corporation as a productive enterprise.

Nevertheless, research on UK-based stock exchange listed utilities and manufacturing companies has shown that some corporations' managers have been able, often with trade union support, to evolve strategies which encouraged shareholders to take a longer-term view of

---

[25] The notion of the psychological contract captures the *implicit* commitments made between employers and their employees. An important role of the psychological contract is that of helping to secure cooperation at work. In return for their loyalty, hard work and commitment, employee expects to be "looked after" through the course of their employment. In other words, employees expect employers to fill their side of the "bargain." But, where these expectations are not met, the likelihood of negative work attitudes increase, together with a decline in morale and motivation. B. Burchell, D. Day, M. Hudson, D. Ladipo, R. Mankelow, J. Nolan, H. Reed, I. Wichert and F. Wilkinson, *Job Insecurity and Work Intensification* (York: York Publishing Services, 1999); B. Burchell, D. Day, M. Hudson, D. Ladipo and F. Wilkinson (eds.), *Job Insecurity and Work Intensification* (London: Routledge, 2002).

[26] S. Deakin, R. Hobbs, D. Nash and G. Slinger, "Implicit Contracts, Takeovers and Corporate Governance: In the Shadow of the City Code," in D. Campbell, H. Collins and J. Wightman (eds.), *Implicit Dimensions of Contract* (Oxford: Hart, 2003); B. Burchell, D. Day, M. Hudson, D. Ladipo, R. Mankelow, J. Nolan, H. Reed, I. Wichert and F. Wilkinson, *Job Insecurity and Work Intensification* (York: York Publishing Services, 1999).

[27] S. Konzelmann, N. Conway, L. Trenberth and F. Wilkinson, "Corporate Governance and Human Resource Management" (2006) 44 *British Journal of Industrial Relations* 541–567; S. Konzelmann, N. Conway and F. Wilkinson, "Corporate Governance and Employment Relations," Working Paper No. 355, Cambridge Centre for Business Research (2007).

their investments; and this encouraged greater employee involvement.[28] Sector-specific factors, such as quality of services and consumer protection in utilities, also helped extend shareholder time horizons while the nature and intensity of product market competition (in particular whether it was price- or quality-orientated), the nature of the product, and the growth trajectory of firms had an impact on stakeholder commitment. This research suggests that there are ways by which the corporate governance constraint can be managed such that the requirements of shareholders in stock markets do not undermine the requirements of effective production.

VI Globalization and effective regulation

Compounding the consequences of the stock market constraint faced by managers and workers in listed companies, the globalization of capital, product and labor markets has served to intensify pressures, particularly in the absence of effective regulation.

During the postwar period in the United States and in the wake of the Great Depression, there was recognition of the need for a system of *national*-level regulations to protect the interests of workers, the environment and consumers. With expansion of the US market, corporations had grown to become increasingly national in scope; and their enormous political and economic strength grew to exceed the ability of individual states to constrain. During this period, the liberal response to market failure was the "New Deal," through which organized labor worked together with national government to protect the public interest in long-term economic and social welfare creation and to counter-balance the power of large corporations. This not only served to strengthen the US labor movement; it also produced national welfare provisions that raised and protected labor standards while at the same time improving access to such *public goods* as health care and security in retirement, many of these social benefits being provided by employers. In Europe, the creation of the European Union (EU) was a similar, though less coordinated, response to expansion of markets and of corporate productive systems.

During the 1990s, the growing *internationalization* of business gave rise to a European debate about the potentially destructive consequences

---

[28] S. Deakin, R. Hobbs, S. Konzelmann and F. Wilkinson, "Partnership, Ownership and Control: The Impact of Corporate Governance on Employment Relations" (2002) 24 *Employee Relations* 335–352; S. Deakin, R. Hobbs, S. Konzelmann and F. Wilkinson, "Anglo-American Corporate Governance and the Employment Relationship: A Case to Answer?" (2006) 4 *Socio-Economic Review* 155–174.

of international trade for labor standards within the EU.[29] The debate revolved around the possibility that unregulated markets might precipitate a "race to the bottom," in which lower labor standards in the developing world would ultimately drive down standards in the developed nations of which the EU formed a part. The result was the strengthening of internationally enforceable standards of practice within the EU, which with expansion, have been extended to all member states.

Undoubtedly, the increasing globalization of markets for products, labor and capital has contributed to economic growth in many developing countries; and it has generated benefits for consumers in the form of low price goods and services. But these short-term advantages have been gained at heavy cost. By lowering standards in the developed world, they effectively lower the floor that developing countries can hope to one day achieve. And whilst the availability of low price goods and services produced in the developing world has helped to reduce the daily cost of living for households in importing countries, the effect of globalization has been to make victims of labor and other immobile factors of production that can be outsourced to lower cost localities. In the process, the domestic demand base has been eroded. To some degree, the availability of cheap credit to fund current consumption, lower taxes and reductions in savings have masked the immediate effects of almost flat wage growth since the late 1970s on vulnerable groups.[30] But in the longer-term, spending on credit at a level exceeding disposable income has driven many households into poverty, serving to further undermine standards of living in much of the developed world.

In the absence of global financial regulation, pressure to deliver short-term shareholder gains has also led to fraudulent activities that have served to undermine confidence in capital markets, including the New York and London stock exchanges. The increasing globalization of equity holders means, further, that returns to equity will increasingly flow abroad, with a potentially destabilizing effect. Strine concludes that "the ability of any nation ... to address these emerging circumstances in isolation is ... minimal."[31] Just as cooperation is essential

---

[29] F. Wilkinson, "Equity, Efficiency and Economic Progress: The Case for Universally Applied Equitable Standards for Wages and Conditions of Work," in W. Sengenberger and D. Campbell (eds.), *The Role of Labour Standards in Industrial Restructuring* (Geneva: International Institute for Labour Studies, 1994); F. Wilkinson, "Co-operation, the Organization of Work and Competitiveness," Working Paper No. 85, Cambridge Centre for Business Research (1998).

[30] D. Silvers, "The Labor Movement's Views on Globalization," Remarks by Damon Silvers, Associate General Counsel, AFL-CIO to the Public Affairs Lecture Series, Farleigh Dickinson University, November 5, 2007.

[31] Strine, "Human Freedom and Two Friedmen."

for the long-term effectiveness of the corporate productive system, so it is for the broader productive system – both national and global – of which the corporation forms a part.[32] Thus, it is imperative that nations cooperate in developing a global institutional framework that extends *to* developing countries the corporate and financial regulations that have already proven effective in protecting social and economic standards.

VII   Conclusions

At the heart of the problem is a fundamental contradiction between the logic of the management of production and the logic of markets. Whereas production is a process for effectively combining and exploiting productive forces, markets are a mechanism for allocating resources and distributing income. For corporate governance, the logic of the market is that the threat of takeover, by helping to overcome agency problems, will deliver efficiency gains. But the implicit assumption is that there are no downstream costs to the organization associated with the negative effects that the market for corporate control and a change in business ownership might have on other corporate stakeholders. On the other hand, the logic of production suggests that prioritizing the interests of shareholders risks alienating workers and other stakeholders upon which organizations directly depend, with negative consequences for performance. The corollary is that employee protection and market regulation protecting the interests of suppliers and consumers may serve to reduce the expected short-term gains from speculative stock market activity whilst guarding against its potentially performance-damaging results.

In effect, there is a fundamental conflict between the theories of the *internal governance* of the corporation, as conceptualized by management theorists, and the theories of its *external governance*, as conceptualized by agency theorists. The former prioritizes production in assessing the quality of managers and the latter prioritizes trade. The reality is that to be effective, production and trade are necessarily complementary, although in the last analysis the market – both for products and corporations – is the judge of how effective corporations actually are. But these are markets that judge on the basis of the creation of long-term economic welfare rather than short-term speculative cash.

In terms of reform, what is needed is a level playing field that does not subordinate the requirements of production to the requirements

---

[32] Wilkinson, "Equity, Efficiency and Economic Progress"; Wilkinson, "Co-operation, the Organization of Work and Competitiveness."

of markets. In the context of globalization, what is needed are "global rules and real global enforcement mechanisms,"[33] which include effective regulation of global capital markets to counter-balance the economic power that global corporations and their shareholders might have over working people, wherever they are. Countries that have enforceable labor and social standards must not only enforce them but also exert leverage on countries that do not by refusing to do business with them. In this context, in the interest of trade and economic development, the requirement of global standards will reduce corporate incentives to base locational decisions on advantages achieved at the expense of the system's vulnerable stakeholders.

In the current system, "the only constituency with a vote is capital ... and the only other constituencies with real power are the Directors and top managers."[34] Because capital's "purpose" is the selfish pursuit of wealth, it logically follows that the regulations protecting the interests of constituencies other than capital (and those with power) – in particular workers, the environment and consumers – must also be global in scale. But the effective implementation and enforcement of such a framework requires *cooperation* among the nations involved. In our view, productive system efficiency is best achieved through the coordinated effort of the stakeholders involved, in pursuit of the interests and objectives that they have in common. But the effectiveness of collective action depends upon the acknowledgment of the reality of power imbalances and legitimate conflicts of interests and objectives. Only then can mutually satisfactory compromises be negotiated and agreed such that all parties are willing and able to fully cooperate in pursuit of their common interests in long-term social and economic welfare.

In the final analysis, the long-term health of the global economic system is dependent upon the recognition that despite differences in local, national and regional interests and objectives, there are important collective interests in the ability of the system to generate long-term economic and social welfare for all of its constituents, wherever they might be.

---

[33] D. Silvers, "The Labor Movement's Views on Globalization," Remarks by Damon Silvers, Associate General Counsel, AFL-CIO to the Public Affairs Lecture Series, Farleigh Dickinson University, November 5, 2007.

[34] Strine, "Human Freedom and the Two Friedmans," p. 42.

15 Organizing workers globally: the need for public policy to regulate investment

John Evans

I   Introduction

Organizing workers and collective bargaining are central activities of trade unions, but clearly they do not take place in a political or economic vacuum. With globalization, workers are increasingly part of global supply chains where companies can relocate investment to counter union pressure or undertake regulatory arbitrage. The thinking behind policy advocacy by unions covering the global economy is precisely to increase the leverage that unions have at all levels to organize workers, to negotiate with and have influence over multinational enterprises.

The financial crisis that deepened in September 2008 with the collapse of Lehman Brothers has mutated into a jobs crisis and sovereign debt crisis that has major social costs. However there was already a crisis of distributional justice, in part due to the impacts of market driven globalization before the onset of the financial crisis.

Since the fall of the Berlin Wall and the emergence of China and India as major producers on world markets, the number of potential participants in the global trade and investment system has doubled from three to six billion people.

The potential world labor force has at a conservative estimate also doubled – although the IMF suggests that when weighted by exports it has risen fourfold over the past two decades.[1] This initially affected the lower-skilled sectors of production and the workers employed in them, but technology is allowing international comparative advantage also to have an effect in the service sector and on professional jobs such as engineering and law, previously thought immune to international relocation. Moreover, foreign investment now drives or operates in

---

This chapter is a revised version of an analysis originally published by Unions 21 in the United Kingdom.

[1] International Monetary Fund, "World Economic Outlook: Globalization and Inequality," October 2007, ch. 5, available at: www.imf.org/external/pubs/ft/weo/2007/02 (last accessed February 22, 2011).

conjunction with trade. The growth of China's bilateral trade surpluses with the United States and most recently with the European Union have become a major policy issue. However 57 percent of China's exports are supplied to non-Chinese firms – many domiciled in the United States or Europe. Workers and their trade unions are therefore increasingly confronted by the same firms globally, either as their direct employers or indirectly through the expansion of global supply chains.

For trade unions the central priority for government policy with regard to the international investment system as a central component of the global market economy is that it sets a range of enforceable rules to ensure that workers' rights and core labor standards are taken out of competition and that the fruits of economic development are more fairly shared. A central part of this must be enforceable rules to cover the activities of multinational enterprises and supply chains.

II   The growing inequality of income

The effects of the globalization of investment on workers are mixed. Expanding investment flows give the opportunity to provide decent work for many of the billion people who are unemployed or underemployed and to relieve the poverty of the 1.4 billion people working for less than US$1.25 per day.[2] Few unions would dispute the potential benefits of inward investment in terms of jobs and technology transfer. Yet, unless governments manage this enormous expansion of the global labor force, it threatens to undermine the wages and working conditions of workers generally. The fact that workers are parts of global supply chains that have replaced multinational enterprises as the dominant form of business model has put pressure on employment standards across different categories of jobs. This issue therefore permeates significantly the daily relations between trade unions and employers. The attitudes of employers toward unions generally, including attitudes to union recognition, labor costs and technological change and work organization are increasingly dictated by international competitiveness. The threat of "exit" by an employer from a given labor market and relocation to an offshore site is now the growing feature of industrial relations when workers are seeking to organize trade unions and to negotiate.

Moreover, while workers may face the same employers in multiple jurisdictions they do not have rights to organize and bargain across

---

[2] UN Report on the Millennium Development Goals, 2010, http://unstats.un.org/unsd/mdg/Resources/Static/Products/Progress2010/MDG_Report_2010_En.pdf (last accessed February 24 2011).

jurisdictions. The rapid emergence of China as the dominant force and global location for manufacturing, where low wages in export sectors are based in part on the suppression of union freedoms and workers' rights, is having a chilling effect on the improvement of labor standards in East Asia and elsewhere. The most brutal examples of competition to attract investment by lowering labor standards are often found in export-processing zones (EPZs) where semi-manufactured products or raw materials are processed into goods for export by foreign companies operating outside normal laws and regulations of the host country. They may operate very differently in different parts of the world, but EPZs tend to have one overriding common characteristic: trades unions are tolerated in few of them.

The growing imbalance in the relative power of workers and their unions compared to employers in the global labor market is reflected in the changing functional distribution of income. This is evident in the falling share of wages as a proportion of national income throughout the OECD, as shown in Figure 15.1.

The ILO reports similar trends in the major emerging and transition economies. In addition, examining employment income one sees that the benefits of globalization in the industrialized countries have accrued disproportionately to the wealthiest families, while the majority of working families are excluded from sharing in increasing productivity and economic growth. As a result, the OECD notes that in seventeen of twenty countries surveyed, earnings inequality has risen (defined by the earnings of workers in the ninetieth percentile compared to workers in the tenth percentile).

III   Enforceable rules for the global labor market

The existing institutions and mechanisms of governance of global markets are imperfect. Although a caricature, it would be true to say that the institutions of "social" governance, such as the International Labour Organization (ILO), that bring together labor and social affairs ministers and those responsible for human rights, are weak, whereas those that deal with property rights, such as the World Trade Organization (WTO) or the International Financial Institutions, are strong. Moreover there is a lack of coherence between different parts of international governance. The same governments can profess support for labor rights at the ILO while undermining them in their activities at the WTO.

A range of governance mechanisms is potentially available to address the concerns of labor, from "hard" international regulations covering

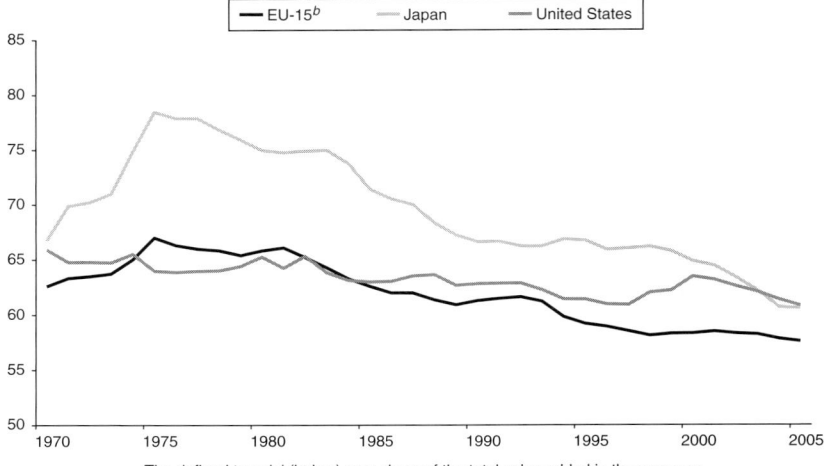

a) Total labor compensation, including employers' social security and pension contributions and imputed labor income for self-employed persons.
b) GDP-weighted average of the following countries: Austria, Belgium, Denmark, Finland, France, Germany, Ireland, Italy, the Netherlands, Spain, Sweden and the United Kingdom.
Source: OECD Economic Outlook database.

Figure 15.1 Wage share of national income EU-15, Japan and the United States, 1970–2005 (source: based on OECD Employment Outlook, 2007 Figure 3.7, available at: www.oecd.org/dataoecd/28/32/38798341.pdf (last accessed February 22, 2011))

specific fields to looser policy coordination, regional integration, continuing national regulation, and, at the most open-ended, regional or district level policies. Trade unions have pragmatically recognized that binding, "hard" mechanisms of regulation at a global level will only be able to cover a limited number of areas such as fundamental rights. They are therefore not an alternative for the looser forms of coordination and cooperation in other areas.

Unions' major objectives,[3] can be summarized as follows:

- to guarantee fundamental human rights at the workplace through binding international regulation as well as integrating "decent work" as an objective in development strategies;

---

[3] For a statement of international union policy see the resolution of the ITUC 2nd world congress, June 2010:www.ituc-csi.org/resolution-on-global-unions-global.html (last accessed February 22, 2011).

- to establish enforceable intergovernmental regulation covering the accountability of multinational enterprises and their employment practices;
- to create a negotiating space in international industrial relations through global framework agreements between global union federations and multinational enterprises;
- to use market power such as the influence of workers' savings or consumer pressure to ensure that there is a viable business case for socially responsible investment; and
- to use the regional space for regulation created by the European process of regional integration.

The following sections of the chapter will address each of these in turn.

IV Guaranteeing fundamental human rights at work

Globalization has drawn dramatic attention to the need to guarantee core workers' rights on a global basis. The agreement in the ILO in 1998 of the Declaration on Fundamental Principles and Rights at Work, focusing on core rights (freedom of association, rights to collective bargaining, freedom from forced labor or prison labor, freedom from child labor exploitation and non-discrimination), has provided a floor for employment regulation in the global economy and a standard that should be applied throughout the international governance system. Such rights are vital for human dignity and self-respect to be applied at the workplace. These are fundamental requirements that have to apply before more extensive employment regulation can be put in place. Without respect for freedom of association it is hard to apply even basic labor, or health and safety laws, or operate effective factory inspections. The core labor rights have also been agreed by the vast majority of countries operating in the global economy – the 177 members of the ILO – and it cannot be argued that they infringe upon national sovereignty. The issue is whether or not they are enforced in practice.

The international labor movement has for long advocated "workers' rights clauses" in trade and investment agreements and in the constitution of the WTO. The idea of a workers' rights clause is to ensure that fundamental workers' rights embodied in the ILO Declaration on Fundamental Principles and Rights at Work become an integral part of trade agreements. Such integration into trade agreements would require close cooperation on implementation between the WTO and the ILO. A workers' rights clause could make it easier for workers to form unions, and would help ensure that all governments took serious measures to tackle the abuses of basic workers' rights. It would provide a partial counterweight to the negative pressures on good labor relations in the global economy and could influence the behavior of corporations.

The issue has remained off the agenda in the WTO in the Doha round, although it is a live issue in many bilateral trade negotiations. If further trade liberalization is to regain public support, WTO members must recognize that trade is only one of the elements in the three pillars of sustainable development and give full attention to the social dimension of development, including the respect of fundamental workers' rights.

Other governmental institutions also have to treat core labor rights as criteria that they apply in their own activities. The World Commission on the Social Dimension of Globalisation[4] established by the ILO made in 2004 strong pleas for far more attention to be paid to the social dimension of globalization. It called for coherence to be established in the multilateral system to ensure respect for workers' rights by all international institutions including the lending and conditionality policies of the IMF and World Bank as well as the WTO. The Commission was followed up with Policy Coherence Initiatives by the different institutions.

But action must go beyond strengthening dialogue and coherence to:

- increase the ratification of the ILO's human rights conventions and strengthen the ILO machinery for the supervision of core labor standards;
- expand labor rights machinery in preferential trade arrangements;
- integrate obligations for core labor standards into all of the World Bank's lending policies;
- extend labor standards clauses in hemispheric and regional trade agreements;
- establish a forum to work on coherence between the ILO and the WTO;
- modernize the Article XX of the GATT to exclude from WTO disciplines goods made not just by prison labor, but any abuse of core labor standards;

---

[4] Report of the World Commission on the Social Dimension of Globalisation, International Labour Organization, *A Fair Globalisation, Creating Opportunities for All*, 2004, available at: www.ilo.org/fairglobalization/report/lang – en/index.htm (last accessed February 22, 2011).

- integrate the attainment of decent work and respect for core labor standards into development assistance programs.

V   The "social dimension" of investment agreements

The issue of social rules also arose in the ill-fated negotiations from 1995 to 1998 of the Multilateral Agreement on Investment (MAI) at the OECD. Trade unions were less single-minded in their approach to the MAI than the NGO campaign that was a significant factor in the derailment of the negotiations. As with the majority of the NGOs, unions had defensive objectives in seeking to ensure that governments' rights to regulate in the area of environment and social standards would not be compromised by the Agreement. As the details of the MAI texts emerged, the interaction of very wide definitions of "investment" and "expropriation" together with the investor to state dispute settlement arrangement gave very real cause for concern as to whether national and regional governments would be challenged and sued for legitimate attempts to regulate in the labor and environment area.

Unions also had affirmative objectives throughout the negotiations on the MAI, however. The trade unions represented in TUAC[5] argued that the development of a simple investment liberalization agreement, which guaranteed investors' rights but did nothing to protect workers' rights and establish corresponding obligations on multinational companies, would be unfair and unbalanced and would be opposed by trade unions.

Four mutually supportive elements were proposed for treating labor issues:

(1) the incorporation of the OECD Guidelines for Multinational Enterprises ("Guidelines") into the MAI through an extended reference in the Agreement's Preamble and the annexing of the full text of the Guidelines to the MAI;
(2) the incorporation into the MAI of the legal obligations on all the parties (OECD Members and non-Members alike) to set up National Contact Points to implement the Guidelines;
(3) a commitment in the Preamble of the MAI by governments to protect, enhance and enforce basic workers' rights;

---

[5] Trade Union Advisory Council to the OECD, for which this author is employed as an economist. The union positions on the MAI are set out in the "statements" section of the TUAC website: www.tuac.org (last accessed February 22, 2011).

(4) a specific provision in the MAI by which governments would undertake in a binding commitment subject to dispute settlement procedures not to seek to attract foreign investment by suppressing domestic labor standards or violating internationally recognized core workers' rights.

In April 1998 the MAI negotiations ended in much publicized failure and attempts to bring investment into the WTO as a new issue also were stopped dead. The spread of bilateral investment agreements and regional trade agreements with investment chapters has continued apace, however, and several of the same "social issues" have arisen. Bilateral investment agreements currently number more than 2,500 – or 5,500 if a broader definition of International Investment Agreements is used. Commentators close to trade unions have raised the concern that both the content of treaties and the rise in litigation under investor to state procedures may compromise legitimate and desirable government policies. A Friedrich Ebert Foundation report concludes:

Recent investor-state disputes have seen multinational firms seek to challenge the imposition of health and environmental measures, various forms of taxation, and even the introduction of affirmative action policies designed to promote certain disadvantaged racial or ethnic groups. There is a need for governments to scrutinize their existing treaties so as to ensure that they provide adequate safeguards for the exercise of legitimate government activity.[6]

Parallel to this has been the piecemeal development of what the OECD has called the "social dimension" of international investment agreements. Of the forty countries that are signatories to the OECD Declaration on International Investment and Multinational Enterprises (MNEs), an OECD survey[7] finds that fifteen countries have included labor, environmental or to a lesser extent anti-corruption language in one or more agreements. Much of the language reflects the issues that were current in the MAI negotiations, such as "not lowering standards," "the right to regulate," and the scope of "indirect expropriation" and promotion of "internationally recognised standards" such as labor rights.

What is not clear is the extent to which such language has moderated or conditioned the rise in investor to state litigation on environmental and social grounds. For unions, therefore, the current trend of

---

[6] Luke Eric Peterson, "The Global Governance of Foreign Direct Investment: Madly Off in All Directions," Friedrich Ebert Foundation, May 2005.
[7] Kathryn Gordon, "International Investment Agreements: Survey of Environmental, Labor and Anti-corruption Issues," 2007, available at: www.oecd.org (last accessed February 22, 2011).

international investment agreements would appear still to be increasing investor power versus states rather than balancing it with effective social responsibilities. More ambitious attempts to propose an alternative approach to bilateral agreements that blend rights and obligations of investors have been proposed by the International Institute for Sustainable Development (IISD) in the form of the 2005 IISD Model International Agreement for Sustainable Development. This has been looked at with interest by trade unions, in particular the extent to which the approach can "balance investor rights with a novel mix of voluntary and binding investor responsibilities, and with both host and home state rights and obligations."[8]

VI   More effective rules for multinational enterprises

The development of social elements in investment agreements has been far outpaced by the multifaceted initiatives of corporate social responsibility (CSR) and accountability. Governmental approaches have differed: while some governments see the complexity of globalization and a need for effective regulation, they realize that at the level of the nation-state or even that of the European Union it is difficult to implement regulation of global markets. They therefore see CSR as a way of trying to achieve those public objectives in a more global environment when more formal forms of regulation are not possible. But some governments have used voluntarism to argue that if companies are prepared to take the responsibility for sustainable development and social and environmental standards, then there are fewer responsibilities for the state. This approach carries the significant risk of initiatives that are driven by public relations goals and poorly enforced, rather than effective regulation.

Intergovernmental rules for multinational enterprises in the labor and social area have existed since the 1970s in the form of the OECD Guidelines on Multinational Enterprises ("Guidelines")[9] and the ILO Tripartite Declaration on principles concerning multinational enterprises and social policy.[10] In the wake of the failure of the MAI negotiations in 1998 the OECD undertook a significant Review of the Guidelines leading to revisions being adopted by the OECD Council

---

[8] The model agreement is available at: www.iisd.org (last accessed February 22, 2011).
[9] www.oecd.org/document/28/0,3343,en_2649_34889_2397532_1_1_1_1,00.html (last accessed February 22, 2011).
[10] www.ilo.org/public/english/employment/multi/tripartite/declaration.htm (last accessed February 22, 2011).

in 2000. In that context there was some willingness to develop the Guidelines into a more operational, more usable instrument that could be an important tool regulating multimationals' conduct. (The Guidelines are undergoing a further review in 2010–2011.)

Although not legally binding, the Guidelines nevertheless set out governmental expectations on how companies which are operating in (or from) the forty signatory countries should behave wherever they operate. They should not therefore be interpreted as purely optional; they are political commitments by governments as to their expectations of the behavior of their country's firms.

The Guidelines specify the need for companies to respect human rights and observe the core standards of the ILO, but they also set out prescriptions on attitudes to union recognition, relative employment conditions, procedures for plant closures, and health and safety issues, among others, in the Chapter on Employment and Industrial Relations. Significantly, they have an enforcement mechanism that was strengthened during the 2000 Review. Signatory governments are legally bound to establish a National Contact Point (NCP) to receive cases and attempt to conciliate between parties and, if they cannot resolve cases, successfully publish their recommendations. In the 1980s and 1990s many supposed NCPs were non-existent. In the 2000 Review governments re-committed themselves to establishing these NCPs, and articulated an expectation that the OECD would exert "peer pressure" to make the NCPs work.

Subsequent to the 2000 Review, and through 2009, unions have brought approximately 120 cases to the NCPs. TUAC affiliates and partners publish a regularly updated review of cases.[11] A majority of these cases concern violations of trade union rights, and roughly one-quarter concern restructuring (most often company closures), with the balance involving health and safety, environment, corruption or disclosure of information. Currently a little more than one-third of cases have arisen in countries whose governments have not adhered to the Guidelines.[12] On average, NCPs take thirteen months to deal with a case. Some cases have lasted for three years or more before they were closed by the NCPs.

Most closed cases have been resolved and/or led to public statements and recommendations by NCPs. Although the results of NCP

---

[11] See www.tuac.org/News/default.htm#1 (last accessed February 22, 2011).

[12] As of 2010 the thirty-four OECD countries and eight non-members have adhered to the OECD investment declaration that includes the Guidelines. Investment from these home countries is covered by the guidelines wherever they invest.

interventions are mixed, the fact that a case is submitted can sometimes have an impact on the outcome. In several cases an external trade union official making a site visit where there are ongoing cases, reporting on what is seen and then meeting with home country management has made a difference. Even when not the main factor in a case, sometimes the Guidelines have contributed to the solution as part of a wider union campaign. In about half of the trade union cases it is judged that the Guidelines have made a positive difference for the workers concerned.

However the excessive length of procedures indicates that far more work remains to be done to achieve effective implementation of the Guidelines and to fulfill the full potential of the Instrument. In successive submissions to the OECD, the TUAC has set out key elements of a reinvigorated agenda for implementing the Guidelines, including: clarification of the criteria by which the NCPs agree to deal with cases; government engagement in the promotion and awareness of the Guidelines; mainstreaming the Instrument in the OECD's other programs and beyond.

The first step in increasing government commitment to the Guidelines must be establishing soundly functioning NCPs. There have been some recent improvements. Since 2004 NGOs and their representative network at the OECD – the OECD Watch – have made a welcome step forward in the monitoring and awareness of the Guidelines.[13] However, the burden of developing the Instrument cannot rest upon trade unions and NGOs. The Guidelines are a far from perfect instrument, yet their governmental nature, the implementation mechanism and their content mean that strengthening them is an important priority for unions in the investment area. With more political will on the part of governments they could become a more effective tool. It was potentially significant that the Heiligendamm Summit conclusions in 2007 committed the G8 to the strengthening of the observance of the Guidelines through NCPs and called on emerging economies to adhere to the Guidelines.[14] A key test will be the extent to which the 2010–2011 Review becomes a real upgrade and raises the standard of NCP performance.

Unions would not see the OECD Guidelines as an alternative to legal regulation of companies, workers' capital strategies or collective bargaining, but they can be an important complement. The financial

---

[13] See www.oecdwatch.org (last accessed February 22, 2011).
[14] Heiligendamm Summit 2007 of the G8 plus Brazil, China, India, "Growth and Responsibility in the World Economy," paras. 22–24 (2007), available at: www.g-8.de/Content/EN/Artikel/__g8-summit/anlagen/2007–06–07-gipfeldokument-wirtschaft-eng,templateId=raw,property=publicationFile.pdf/2007–06–07-gipfeldokument-wirtschaft-eng.pdf (last accessed February 22, 2011).

crisis suggests that the excesses of markets need to be tamed by hard regulation. While several NGOs are campaigning for a binding code on human rights to be adopted by the United Nations, unions would agree with the report[15] of the United Nations special representative, John Ruggie, that decent work and enforcement of workers' rights have to progress by several routes at the same time.

VII Building international industrial relations

An international framework for balancing investor rights needs to include a framework for industrial relations. But just as the earliest trade unions and collective agreements preceded a national legal framework, international industrial relations are evolving as multinationals become engaged in different forms of negotiations with international trade union organizations.

Even though individual companies or industries are not legally obliged to recognize trade union organizations or engage in negotiations at the international level, limited international social dialogue has already started, notably with individual enterprises. On the trade union side, structures already exist – the Global Union Federations (GUFs) – which can form part of the basis for international industrial relations at both industry and company levels. Many GUFs have already established structures that deal with particular multinational enterprises, usually company councils. Many MNEs have recognized, formally or de facto, GUFs as their international counterparts. Some of this growing, global social dialogue has resulted in the negotiation of global agreements between global firms and GUFs.

By mid-2010 more than sixty global framework agreements have been concluded, covering several million workers. Unlike unilateral company initiatives, agreements are a way to resolve conflicts or problems before they become serious or damaging, based on the agreement, dialogue and the establishment of a certain amount of confidence inside the relationship. Unlike campaigns and other public action, the intention is to implement common, agreed principles in a way that leads to conflicts to be resolved or even anticipated. Whereas most CSR exercises are voluntary efforts – promises or claims – the adoption of framework agreements can be seen as the start of international collective bargaining.

In the maritime industry, an industry that has always been international, a full-fledged collective bargaining agreement covering wages,

---

[15] www.business-humanrights.org/Documents/SRSG-report-Human-Rights-Council-19-Feb-2007.pdf (last accessed February 22, 2011).

hours and working conditions has been negotiated and signed between the International Transport Workers Federation (ITF) and an association of ship-owners and ship-managers (IMEC). It is an important part of a larger effort to end the abuses of workers found in "flags of convenience."

In Europe, the law also requires a more formal structure for consultation. The process of European political and economic integration has also allowed cross-frontier regulation of labor standards to move well beyond the guarantee of core workers' rights. The European Trade Union Confederation (ETUC) has sought: (1) to establish a framework of standards to stop "social dumping"; (2) to achieve progress in the harmonization of social standards through both European legislation and social partner agreements; (3) to establish consultation, information and negotiation rights with multinational companies at a European level; (4) to expand the structural funds of the European Commission. One significant development in this process has been the passing of the European "Works Council" Directive and the subsequent creation of more than 700 European Works Councils in the multinational companies operating across the EU.

VIII   Using market and investor power

Some of the momentum behind the debate over CSR and socially responsible investment has resulted from the market pressures created by concerned consumers seeking to avoid buying products or services from firms seen to have negative social or environment practices. An industry has been created in social rating, certification, verification and labeling. Some of these initiatives are supported by unions and NGOs and may be valuable but many also have risks.

In sectors such as clothing and textiles, trade unions cooperate actively in some certification initiatives. The Ethical Trading Initiative represents a different but important approach. Certification bodies influence whether purchasers are prepared or not to buy products from certain factories. Trade unions have sought to be involved in what they are doing. On the other hand, some certification schemes can be misleading when information cannot be validated and verified properly. Inspectors may be present one day in a year but, even if they find every problem, they can't verify what happens on the other 364 days in the factory. Unions have adopted a pragmatic approach to each instrument to make sure that they are not mere public relations tools. There is no way to guarantee the effective respect of workers' rights unless workers can shift the balance of power at the workplace by having their own trade unions and are free to bargain collectively.

Market pressure for decent employment standards has also come from investors' concern over the potential risk of unsustainable social or environmental performance by companies in which they invest. With the growth of corporate governance scandals the quality of corporate governance has become a key issue for investors and unions.

A major campaign has developed in the trade union movement to mobilize the market pressure that potentially exists in workers' pension funds.[16] The total assets of the world's pension funds reached almost US$13,500 billion at a first peak in 1999. After falling back to US$10,800 billion in 2002, assets grew again in subsequent years to an estimated US$17,000 billion in 2007 prior to the onset of the crisis.

The ITUC, TUAC and the GUFs have created an international network to facilitate cooperation on workers' capital strategies. Socially responsible investment – and in particular the behavior of companies on workers' rights – is one of the main concerns of this Committee. Companies are increasingly vulnerable to direct shareholder actions, and are therefore more and more concerned about their reputation. Trade unions have been very active over the last few years in initiating these shareholder actions. The Committee raises support at the international level for these campaigns. Executive remuneration has been, next to workers' rights, one of the re-emerging issues.

IX The growth of financialization

Even prior to the financial crisis financial globalization posed major issues for unions beyond the stewardship of pension funds and socially responsible investment. Since 2004 the emergence of large and largely unregulated masses of financial capital at global level in the shape of "new investors" – notably private equity funds and hedge funds – has confronted traditional models of corporate governance.

One of the concerns unions have is the risk to financial stability and hence ultimately to jobs and incomes posed by the highly leveraged nature of the private equity investments and the lack of transparency of hedge funds. The financial crisis bore out these concerns. The financial shock created by sub-prime mortgage collapse in the United States has been a tragedy for many of the lower income families involved who lost their housing. However the contagion from the collapse of a series of hedge funds and the run on a UK bank,

---

[16] See also Chapters 13 and 16 in this volume.

Northern Rock, turned this into a world financial crisis. The US sub-prime markets were simply too small to account for the scale of disruption experienced. The accelerant has clearly been the rapidly growing and complex role of leverage in these markets. Given the scale of leverage and the complexity of financial products bankers simply no longer know what assets used as collateral on loans are worth any more.

These events reflect just one part of the concerns that have led unions to enter the world of discussion of hedge funds and private equity. In North America and in parts of Europe unions have had experience over a number of years of dealing with private equity investors at the venture capital end of the business as well as with some of the "distress funds" specializing in turning round companies in difficulty. Venture capital has traditionally been seen as a non-controversial part of the financial architecture – where high returns to some investors have reflected the high risk of supporting start-up companies and a necessary contributor to overall growth. With regard to "distress funds" unions, particularly in the United States, have on occasion adopted a proactive role in identifying investors and worked with them so as to restructure companies faced by severe problems and so safeguard jobs. Pension funds are also significant investors in this asset class, attracted by the high rates of return that funds advertised as a way of filling gaps in pension funding.

However, the spectacular growth of the leverage buyout end of the private equity business and the move by private equity to control very significant parts of the private sector economy has meant that important numbers of workers in several OECD countries are now employed by private equity controlled firms. Private equity transactions accounted for over one-quarter of all mergers and acquisitions in the United States and the EU in 2005. Private equity buyouts have expanded their reach to large-size companies, industries, household brands and even companies linked to public services. These alternative funds are largely debt financed, hence little-taxed and are exempt from many of the regulations that apply to traditional collective investment schemes, to banks and to insurance companies, notably in the areas of investment prudential rules and reporting requirements.

The impact of alternative investors on the real economy and sustainable development has yet to be impartially and comprehensively researched. However, trade unions' experiences with employment and working conditions linked to private equity are alarming. The high rates of return required to finance private equity debt-driven buyouts can jeopardize target companies' long-term interests and provision of decent employment conditions and security for employees. Studies, of which the most recent have been conducted in the UK,[17] suggest that wages in private-equity-backed companies grow more slowly than in the private sector as a whole, and that the private equity management culture is not consistent with quality employment. Rather than corporate restructuring for the purpose of shared productivity gains and increased competitiveness, private equity firms now appear to be looking at extracting maximum value over a short period before reselling the company at a substantial premium. As private funds have moved from niche market to a general form of corporate ownership and governance, the issue arises of how the very high rates of return are achieved and whether they are sustainable when the "real economy" at global level is growing at 3–4 percent per annum. Unions have concern at the business model based on high leverage, the pressures this puts on employment and working conditions as well as tax revenues. The predominant experience has been that the pressure for resale and capital gains over a relatively short time period are not consistent with the need for long-term investment in areas such as skill development, research and development, product innovation and patent registration.

The view of participants in the union movement is that the challenge for the post-crisis G20 is to restore financial markets to their legitimate role of funding real investment and supporting the real economy as opposed to running a casino.

X   Conclusion

If the fruits of growth are to be more equitably shared in what is now a global economy it has to be shown that it is possible to manage change in firms, industries, regions and labor markets in socially equitable ways. An industrial organization "model" has to be developed which is both competitive and socially acceptable. OECD countries have to restructure on the basis of a high set of labor standards and not on the basis of a low wage model of development whilst developing countries have to ensure that productivity growth is used to raise living standards, reduce poverty and contribute to sustainable development. The evolving investment regime will influence greatly whether this is indeed possible and whether some of the short-term excesses of financial capital

---

[17] Phil Thornton, "Inside the Black Box: Shedding Light on Private Equity" (The Work Foundation, March 2007).

can be reined in. The trade union movement is also having to become global in its reach where policy advocacy, assistance in capacity building and action on trade union rights and around multinational corporations is not seen just as a form of "solidarity" but rather the necessary daily activity of unions.

16 From governance to political economy: insights from a study of relations between corporations and workers

Harry W. Arthurs and Claire Mummé

I Introduction

Like public government, and for some of the same reasons, corporate governance is in crisis. Both seem unable to persuasively articulate their fundamental values; both have been losing legitimacy and credibility; both have been destabilized by rapid and complex socio-technical change; and both are finding it more difficult to accommodate the conflicting claims of internal constituencies and those of relevant 'others'.

However, workers are assigned very different roles in public government and corporate governance. Workers, like everyone else, are entitled to participate in the rites of public government. They may vote, run for office, and contribute to public debates either personally or as part of a collectivity of like-minded individuals. Moreover, workers can reasonably expect to have their voices heard and their rights respected. To be sure, they fare less well at the hands of the state than they ought to in theory.

Their interests are compromised by technocratic control of the policy process, by bureaucratic indifference, by the influence of corporate campaign contributions on government policy, by the clamour of competing claims, and by their own false consciousness. However, one rough measure of the democratic character of any state remains the extent to which workers are accommodated de jure and de facto within the processes and institutions of public government.

This is not the case in the context of corporate governance.[1] The presumption is that workers will not participate in the making of important decisions, including many which directly and dramatically affect their interests. This presumption may be rebutted under compulsion of law

---

This chapter originally appeared in 45 *Osgoode Hall Law Journal* 439 (2007), and has been re-printed by permission of the authors.

[1] For an insightful treatment of the dichotomy between labour and corporate policy, law, and scholarship, see Peer Zumbansen, 'The Parallel Worlds of Corporate Governance and Labor Law' (2006) 13 *Indiana Journal of Global Legal Studies* 261.

or by dint of economic pressure. It may be modified if corporate management deems it expedient to allow workers a larger role. However, the original presumption against participation remains the default position, and derogation from it is limited. Nor is departure from democratic principle viewed as problematic. Corporations, we assume, are market actors, not sites of political debate; they exist to make money, not to provide workers with opportunities for civic engagement.

However, public government and corporate governance are not so easily assigned to separate domains. Governments charter corporations, specify their governance structures, regulate the sale of their shares, require financial reporting, and prevent dishonest dealing. They create conditions which enable corporations to participate in markets by building infrastructure, educating the workforce, enforcing bargains, protecting property, ensuring honesty, and maintaining order. And, however reluctantly, they regulate the relationship between workers and their corporate employers. They specify minimum conditions of employment, protect (or at least acknowledge) the practices of collective bargaining and tax, and regulate corporations to ensure that the workers are somewhat buffered against the consequences of labour market fluctuations, accident, illness, discrimination, and old age.

Seen in this light, state intervention to ensure workers a formal role in the structures of corporate governance would not seem to represent a radical departure. Indeed, given the contemporary crisis of corporate governance, which has had such dire consequences for so many workers, it might even be regarded as a timely departure. After all, changes associated with technological developments, flexibilization, neo-liberalism, and globalization have altered the corporate structures and contractual arrangements governing work, as well as the content and character of work, the demography of the workforce, the regulatory environment, and the managerial cultures of corporations. Taken together, these changes have shifted the balance of power even more definitively in favour of employers and against unions and workers. Nonetheless, the assumption that owners, directors, and managers do – and should – exercise virtually unilateral control over corporate decision-making is as unlikely to be revisited now as at any time since corporations first came to dominate the economic landscape. It is buried too deeply in our labour, corporation, contract, tort, and criminal law; it is embedded too firmly in the social relations and cultural practices of corporate workplaces; it is justified too conclusively by ideology, economic science, and occasionally religion; it is a paradigmatic assumption about corporate governance so fundamental as to be almost beyond retrieval and, consequently, beyond reconsideration.

In the next section of this chapter, we describe four postwar attempts to re-imagine the role of workers within the corporation and their relation to the processes of corporate governance. Each has some descriptive power; each has some normative appeal; but each ultimately failed. Nonetheless, we believe that these four narratives provide important insights into the political economy of the corporation, which we develop at greater length in the third section of this chapter. To anticipate our conclusions, they reveal the corporation not only as it is usually imagined – as a site of orderly governance, rational decision-making, and purposeful coordination – but also as a site of conflict. Conflict is too seldom acknowledged in discussions of corporate governance, and when acknowledged, it is dismissed as pathological. But as the post-war experience of corporation–worker relations seems to demonstrate, conflict appears to be endemic to the political economy of corporations.

While acknowledging the dangers of extrapolation from this unique domain of corporate decision-making, we suggest that these insights may help to explain and predict how the political economy of corporations – not their governance structure – determines the fate of workers as it does of the shareholders, debt-holders and creditors, corporate managers and professional advisors, participants in corporate supply and distribution chains, consumers of corporate goods and services, and inhabitants of communities and environments which come within the corporate force field.

If our suggestion is sound, future attempts to re-imagine and reform the corporation should begin not with attempts to modify existing institutions of governance but with attempts to better comprehend its own political economy. To that end, we will conclude with a series of hypotheses which we hope will stimulate further debate and research.

II Employee interests and corporate governance

In this section we explore four attempts during the post-war period to influence corporate decision-making by reconceptualizing the status and rights of employees within corporations.

A Employees as 'citizens at work'

Collective bargaining makes certain implicit assumptions about corporate governance: that the interests of employers and employees are in tension; that this tension should be and can be resolved by negotiations between the two sides; that corporate managers will seek to maximize their interests by striking the most advantageous bargain; and that such bargains are evaluated and confirmed through the structures of corporate governance. Or to look at the matter the other way around, wages and working conditions will be determined unilaterally by corporate decision-makers – except to the extent that unions are able to influence such determinations through persuasion or power. In this sense unions under collective bargaining acquire influence within the corporate decision-making process comparable to that of the corporation's competitors, its most valued customers, or regulatory agencies: they are a force to be reckoned with, to be avoided if possible, and to be accommodated if not.

Moreover, an extensive literature reminds us that even without a formal system of collective bargaining, workplace normativity is shaped, to a significant extent, by 'the web of rule' which is spun through ongoing interactions among workers and managers.[2] Cooperation between and among them must be translated into well-understood and well-accepted routines and rituals to avoid constant renegotiation. Even where they appear to be acting unilaterally, supervisors must accommodate some worker preferences to maintain morale and productivity; and in knowledge-intensive industries especially, where workers must take many decisions on their own, routines and rituals often give way to explicit delegations of responsibility exercised through self-regulating teams.[3] Thus collective bargaining does not initiate but rather extends, makes explicit, and formalizes the involvement of workers in operational decisions in the corporate workplace, though seldom in the boardroom.

Formality is at its most extreme in North America, where collective bargaining from the 1930s onwards has been increasingly juridified. The legal right to organize and to bargain collectively was established by statute and enforced by an administrative agency.[4] Workplace disputes were adjudicated by arbitrators operating under a statutory mandate;[5] the rules of industrial conflict were defined by common law and legislation;[6] and judicial enforcement of rights and review of

---

[2] J.T. Dunlop, *The Industrial Relations System* (Carbondale: Southern Illinois University Press, 1958), at 7–18.

[3] P.K. Edwards and Hugh Scullion, 'Deviancy Theory and Industrial Praxis: A Study of Discipline and Social Control in an Industrial Setting' (1982) 16 *Sociology* 322; Stuart Henry, *Private Justice: Towards Integrated Theorizing in the Sociology of Law* (London: Routledge & Kegan Paul, 1983); and Otto Kahn-Freund, 'Intergroup Conflicts and their Settlement' (1954) 5 *British Journal of Sociology* 193.

[4] National Labor Relations Act, Pub. L. No. 74–198, 49 Stat. 449 (1935) (codified as amended at 29 USC § 151–169 (1994)) [NLRA].

[5] Canada Labour Code, R.S.C. 1985, c.-L.2 s.57.

[6] G.W. Adams, *Canadian Labour Law*, 2nd edn (Aurora: Canada Law Book, 1993+ looseleaf); Julius G. Getman, Bertrand B. Pogrebin, and David L. Gregory, *Labor Management Relations and the Law*, 2nd edn (New York: Foundation Press, 1999), ch. 4.

administrative and arbitral proceedings became commonplace.[7] Even the internal affairs of trade unions came under statutory regulation, especially in the United States.[8] Individual employment relations were treated similarly, though to a lesser degree. While the parties retain their contractual freedom to define the terms of the employment bargain, legislation has circumscribed its exercise to an extent. Minimum labour standards were introduced in the United States in the 1930s;[9] employers and workers were obliged to contribute to a social security fund;[10] and employers were required to provide safe and healthy working conditions and forbidden to engage in discrimination and harassment at work.[11] All of these statutorily compelled arrangements were to be enforced through judicial or administrative proceedings,[12] though recent decisions of the Supreme Court have allowed these proceedings to be displaced by private arbitration.[13]

These statutory regimes were rightly regarded by corporate employers as state-imposed limitations on their capacity to manage their workforces through unilateral managerial decisions – especially in the United States, in which the default presumption of 'employment-at-will' survives not only as an operative legal concept[14] but as a baseline condition of the new psychological contract between

---

[7] David A. Wright, '"Foreign to the Competence of Courts" Versus "One Law for All"': Labour Arbitrators' Powers and Judicial Review in the United States and Canada' (2002) 23 *Comparative Labor Law & Policy Journal* 967.

[8] The Labor–Management Reporting and Disclosure Act of 1959, 29 USC § 411, 501, provides legal protections for democratic practice and financial accountability within labour unions.

[9] Fair Labor Standards Act, Pub. L. No. 109–157 (1938) (codified as amended 29 USC § 201–219 (2005)).

[10] Social Security Act, 49 Stat. 648 (1935) (codified as amended by 42 USC § 301–1397j).

[11] The Occupational Health and Safety Act of 1970, 29 USCA 651–678; Title VII of the Civil Rights Act of 1964 (Pub. L. 88–352) (codified as amended by 42 USC § 2000e (2000)) [Title VII]; Racial Discrimination Act 1944, S.O. 1944, c. 51; and Canada Fair Employment Practices Act, S.C. 1952–53, c.19. See Paul H. Norgren and Samuel E. Hill, *Toward Fair Employment* (New York: Columbia University Press, 1964) for the early history of state Fair Employment Laws.

[12] The Occupational Health and Safety Act of 1970; Title VII.

[13] Katherine V.W. Stone, 'Mandatory Arbitration of Individual Employment Rights: The Yellow Dog Contract of the 1990s' (1996) 73 *Denver Law Review* 1017; Clyde W. Summers, 'Mandatory Arbitration: Privatizing Public Rights, Compelling the Unwilling to Arbitrate' (2004) 6 *University of Pennsylvania. Journal of Labour & Employment Law* 685.

[14] See, for example, Sanford M. Jacoby, 'The Duration of Indefinite Employment Contracts in the United States and England: An Historical Analysis' (1982) 5 *Comparative Labor Law Journal* 84; Clyde W. Summers, 'Employment at Will in the United States: The Divine Right of Employers' (2000) 3 *University of Pennsylvania Journal of Labor and Employment* 65.

workers and employers.¹⁵ How could all these intrusions on corporate decision-making be justified? In a country in which constitutional doctrine often acts as a proxy for political discourse, it is not surprising that the justification was expressed as an extended constitutional metaphor.

Workers, it was argued, should be entitled to rights in the workplace analogous to those enjoyed by them as citizens in a pluralist democracy. Thus, collective bargaining legislation came to be portrayed as the vindication of 'freedom of association'. The right of the majority of workers in an enterprise to vote to democratically 'elect' a union as their collective bargaining agent and the right of employers to exercise their 'freedom of speech' to solicit votes in opposition are both sheltered under obvious constitutional analogies. Collective agreements detailing wage scales, access to promotion, and other incidents of employment heralded the advent of 'the rule of law' in the workplace, while just cause for discharge and arbitration provisions ensured 'due process' for workers.

Explicit constitutional allusions were less common elsewhere, though some states did entrench labour and social rights. However, collective bargaining, labour standards, and anti-discrimination and social security legislations came to be regarded as a *grundnorm*, a fundamental premise, of the post-war social contract.¹⁶ Even when workers in those countries did not literally acquire rights of 'industrial citizenship',¹⁷ what emerged in the post-war settlement was indeed a new constitutional order – metaphorical rather than juridical – that decreed an end to unilateral managerial rule. But like so many other constitutional orders, this one proved easier to proclaim than to apply to the daily reality of life in the workplace.

---

¹⁵ Pauline T. Kim, 'Norms, Learning and the Law: Exploring the Influences on Workers' Legal Knowledge' (1999) *University of Illinois Law Review* 447, empirically demonstrates that employees believe – wrongly – that they have just cause recourse in law. Katherine V.W. Stone, *From Widgets to Digits: Employment Regulation for the Changing Workplace* (Cambridge and New York: Cambridge University Press, 2004), at 48–50 argues that the effect of the 'at will' doctrine was to an extent masked by the growth of internal labour markets which offered many workers de facto security in employment, even in the absence of legal protections. This security evaporated, she argues, when the digital economy destroyed these internal markets. See also Denise M. Rousseau and Snehal A. Tijoriwala, 'Assessing Psychological Contracts: Issues, Alternatives and Measures' (1998) 19 *Journal of Organizational Behavior* 679.
¹⁶ Milton Derber, *The American Idea of Industrial Democracy, 1865–1965* (Urbana: University of Illinois Press, 1970); Katherine V.W. Stone, 'The Post-War Paradigm in American Labor Law' (1981) 90 *Yale Law Journal* 1509 at 1514–1515.
¹⁷ H.W. Arthurs, 'Developing Industrial Citizenship: A Task for Canada's Second Century' (1967) 45 *Canadian Bar Review* 786.

Collective bargaining achieved some notable successes. Workers in unionized enterprises generally enjoyed better wages and working conditions, greater job security, and a more equitable regimen than their counterparts in enterprises without unions.[18] But in the United States, union membership levelled off at about one-third of the non-government workforce in the 1960s, and then in subsequent decades subsided to under 10 per cent.[19] In Canada, it had reached almost 40 per cent in the 1970s and now hovers around 30 per cent, about the average for OECD countries.[20] In part, this reflects the failure of unions – especially American unions – to reach out to new constituencies of workers. Other factors include the inherent constraints of highly juridified systems, the inability of collective bargaining to address the complex crises of a globalizing economy, and the dissolution of labour-dominated political coalitions.[21]

Mostly, however, collective bargaining in the United States did not so much expire of natural causes, as perish as a result of injuries suffered through aggravated assault by management. Since the 1970s, the corporate United States has waged wars of attrition to forestall unionization, litigating endlessly to avoid complying with labour laws, blocking legislative attempts to enhance workers' rights, neutering labour tribunals, and introducing Human Resources (HR) policies to reduce worker discontent.[22] And while collective bargaining suffered its greatest setbacks in the United States, it is also under siege pretty much everywhere else. American attitudes and strategies have been easily exported to branch plant economies, such as Canada.[23] Other countries – the United Kingdom under the Thatcher government, Australia,

---

[18] Richard B. Freeman and James L. Medoff, *What Do Unions Do?* (New York: Basic Books, 1984); Paul C. Weiler, *Governing the Workplace: The Future of Labor and Employment Law* (Cambridge, MA: Harvard University Press, 1990).

[19] United States: Labor Research Association (2000b) 'Union Trends and Data: Union Statistics', online: www.workinglife.org (formerly www.laborresearch.org).

[20] Clara Chang and Constance Sorrentino, 'Union Membership Statistics in 12 Countries' (December 1991) 114 *Monthly Labor Review* 46 at 48; Jelle Visser, 'Union Membership Statistics in 24 Countries' (January 2006) 129 *Monthly Labor Review* at 38.

[21] Cynthia Estlund, 'The Ossification of American Labor Law' (2002) 102(6) *Columbia Law Review* 1527; see also 'Symposium on the Future of Private Sector Unionism in the United States' (2001) 22 *Journal of Labor Research* 227ff.

[22] Freeman and Medoff, *What Do Unions Do?*, pp. 230–239; William Dickens and Jonathan Leonard, 'Accounting for the Decline in Union Membership, 1950–1980' (1985) 38 *Industrial & Labor Relations Review* 323; Thomas A. Kochan, Robert B. McKersie, and John Chalykoff, 'The Effects of Corporate Strategy and Workplace Innovations on Union Representation' (July 1986) 39 *Industrial & Labor Relations Review* 487; and Weiler, *Governing the Workplace*.

[23] Terry Thomason and Silvana Pozzebon, 'Managerial Opposition to Union Certification in Quebec and Ontario' (1998) 53 *Industrial Relations Law Journal* 750;

and New Zealand – launched their own ideological crusades against unions, often aided and abetted by elements of the corporate community.[24] Even in European countries, where collective bragaining has not been subjected to frontal attack, where 'citizenship' rights remain relatively entrenched, and where corporate leaders apparently remain committed to social market values, collective bargaining systems and labour market policies are being revised in response to real or perceived competition from the United States and, especially, from developing countries.[25]

In short, even allowing for considerable variation among the advanced economies, collective bargaining – the assertion of citizenship rights by workers – seems unlikely to contribute much to the current wave of corporate governance reforms.

B   Employees as 'stakeholders'

Some recent literature acknowledges, at least implicitly, the failure of collective bargaining to endow employees with the rights of citizens in the workplace. It seeks instead to characterize them as 'stakeholders', a generic concept that enables them to be analogized to shareholders. Workers, it is proposed, agree to an implicit contract under which they accept less than an opportunity wage in the early and middle part of their careers, when they first develop and then deploy skills and knowledge specific to the enterprise, in exchange for receiving a higher than opportunity wage in later years when their productivity is declining. Their initial sacrifice, it is argued, amounts to a sunk investment since they will not be able to sell enterprise-specific skills in the external labour market. Moreover, workers – 'stakeholders' – lack effective legal means to protect their investment, a vulnerability also suffered by individual shareholders, though in a less extreme form. It is on this basis that workers and other stakeholders claim to be entitled – like shareholders – to consideration of their interests in corporate decision-making. Their claims are especially cogent when stakeholder interests are adversely affected as a result of significant corporate restructuring.[26]

Karen Bentham, 'Employer Resistance to Union Certification: A Study of Canadian Jurisdictions' (Winter 2002) 57 *Industrial Relations Law Journal* 159.
[24] Paul Smith and Gary Morton, 'Union Exclusion and the Decollectivizing of Industrial Relations in Contemporary Britain' (1993) 31 *British Journal of Industrial Relations* 97.
[25] The European Employment Strategy has also concentrated on developing more flexible work labour market policies; see European Employment Strategy, online: http://ec.europa.eu/employment_social/employment_strategy/index_en.htm (last accessed 22 February 2011).
[26] Katherine V.W. Stone, 'Policing Employment Contracts within the Nexus-of-Contracts Firm' (1993) 45 *University of Toronto Law Journal* 353.

Within this overall characterization, the literature moves in several different directions. One tendency – embodied in legislation in many US states – seeks to liberate corporate directors from the duty to treat the 'interests of the corporation' as precisely congruent with the interests of its shareholders.[27] Directors are permitted, but not compelled, to consider the interests of stakeholders as well as those of the corporation. In the event of corporate restructuring, merger, or takeover, directors are allowed to negotiate arrangements which protect workers' rights and interests – even if the result is somewhat to reduce the financial gains of the shareholders. Proponents of this model of employment relations suggest that the permissive provisions of first-generation stakeholder statutes should be replaced by language that requires directors to consider the interest of all relevant groups.[28]

A second tendency – related to the first – is to extrapolate from the fiduciary duty owed by directors to shareholders to impose on corporate directors a comparable obligation to have regard for the interests of other stakeholders, including workers. This position has considerable moral cogency, not least because the power and wealth of corporate management have become so disproportionate to that of the workers employed by the corporation. However, the concept of a fiduciary duty has yet to win clear legal acceptance, and faces significant hostility from many corporate theorists and directors.[29] True, some legislation makes directors personally liable for workers' unpaid wages,[30] and for illness, injury,[31] or harassment[32] suffered in the workplace as a result of the corporation's failure to take reasonable measures to protect the workers, or of the directors' and management's failure to undertake due diligence to safeguard their workers from risk. Such provisions hint at the possible existence of a general legal obligation to workers based on their subordination to the governance structures of the corporation. However, that obligation has so far been derived from specific legislative provisions

---

[27] See 'Corporate Malaise – Stakeholder Statutes: Cause or Cure: Appendix' (1999) 21 *Stetson Law Review* 279.
[28] Katherine V.W. Stone, 'Employees as Stakeholders Under Non-Shareholder Constituency Statutes' (1991–1992) 21 *Stetson Law Review* 45; Margaret M. Blair, 'For Whom Should Corporations be Run? An Economic Rationale for Stakeholder Management' (1998) 31 *Long Range Planning* 195.
[29] Marleen A. O'Connor, 'Restructuring the Corporation's Nexus of Contracts: Recognizing a Fiduciary Duty to Protect Displaced Workers' (1991) 69 *North Carolina Law Review* 1189; Jonathan R. Macey and Geoffrey P. Miller, 'Corporate Stakeholders: A Contractual Perspective' (1993) 43 *University of Toronto Law Journal* 401.
[30] Employment Standards Act, R.S.O. 2000, c-41, s. 79, 81.
[31] Criminal Code, R.S.C. 1985, c. C-46, s.217(1) as amended by S.C. 2003, c. 21, s. 3.
[32] Guidelines on Discrimination Because of Sex, 29 C.F.R. § 1604.11(d), (e).

and, despite the impressive efforts of scholars to ground it in common law doctrines, has not yet been widely acknowledged or clearly articulated as a general legal duty.[33] Further, even if both these legal innovations were to receive clear legislative or jurisprudential approval, such an approach to the employment relationship has so far focused solely on the manner of its termination, rather than on other aspects of ongoing labour–management interaction.

A third approach acknowledges workers as stakeholders by introducing their representatives directly into the governance structures of the corporation. In the United Kingdom, for example, New Labour made 'partnership' the centrepiece of its workplace policy.[34] British unions generally responded positively, viewing partnership as a method of regaining relevance after the Thatcher years of labour market deregulation and waning membership.[35] However, it remains to be seen whether the initial positive response will be sustained.[36]

At a regional level, European experiments with worker participation in corporate management have reached their high-water mark in two institutions. The first is the Works Council, which may be established at the national level or, in the case of transnational companies, at the European Union regional level. These representative bodies are entitled to be informed about and/or consulted on important decisions such as plant closings and redundancies, as well as on more routine shop floor issues.[37] The second institution is co-determination, which

---

[33] Janis Sarra, 'Corporate Governance Reform: Recognition of Workers' Equitable Investments in the Firm' (1999) 32 *Canadian Business Law Journal* 384; Joseph W. Singer, 'The Reliance Interest in Property Rights' (1988) 40 *Stanford Law Review* 611.

[34] See Department of Trade and Industry, 'Fairness at Work', White Paper (London: HMSO, 1998) quoted in Nicholas Bacon and John Storey, 'New Employee Relations Strategies in Britain: Towards Individualism or Partnership?' (September 2000) 38 *British Journal of Industrial Relations* 407, at 407; Tony Dundon, Adrian J. Wilkinson, Mick Marchington, and Peter Ackers, 'The Meanings and Purpose of Employee Voice' (2004) 15 *International Journal of Human Resource Management* 1149.

[35] Nicholas Bacon and Paul Blyton, 'Co-operation and Conflict in Industrial Relations: What are the Implications for Employees and Trade Unions?' (1999) 10 *International Journal of Human Resources Management* 638, 638–639; Peter Ackers and Jonathan Payne, 'British Trade Unions and Social Partnership: Rhetoric, Reality and Strategy' (1998) 9 *International Journal of Human Resources Management* 529.

[36] See John Kelly, 'Social Partnership Agreements in Britain: Labor Cooperation and Compliance' (2004) 43 *Industrial Relations Law Journal* 267; Tonia Novitz, 'A Revised Role for Trade Unions as Designed by New Labour: The Representation Pyramid and "Partnership"' (2002) 29 *Journal of Law & Society* 487.

[37] See Paul L. Davies, 'Workers on the Board of the European Company?' (2003) 32 *Industrial Law Journal* 75; see also Joel Rogers and Wolfgang Streeck, *Works Councils: Consultation, Representation and Cooperation in Industrial Relations* (Chicago: University of Chicago Press, 1995).

under German law requires that worker-elected members comprise half of each company's supervisory board responsible for appointing and overseeing the management board. Unfortunately, although widely heralded as introducing a robust and non-symbolic form of social partnership into corporate management, German co-determination has not proved adaptable to non-manufacturing industries.[38]

In North America, the stakeholder/partnership model has been embraced, at least rhetorically, by many corporate leaders and has spawned a vast body of scholarship.[39] Partnership, it is claimed, will be the basis upon which American corporations will maintain their competitiveness in an increasingly competitive world,[40] and stakeholder-friendly management will be a strategy for corporations to regain the public trust.[41] Yet few North American corporations have actually moved to include stakeholders in their corporate governance processes. Indeed, even when workers secured participation, there was little evidence that they were willing or able to significantly influence company policies.[42]

The current North American 'stakeholder' discourse seems to be designed largely to convince workers that their interests are fundamentally aligned with those of the corporation.[43] At the rhetorical

---

[38] See Anke Hassel, 'The Erosion of the German System of Industrial Relations' (1999) 37 *British Journal of Industrial Relations* 483; John Grahl and Paul Teague, 'The German Model in Danger' (2004) 35 *Industrial Relations Law Journal* 557; and John T. Addison, Claus Schnabel, and Joachim Wagner, 'The Course of Research into the Economic Consequences of German Works Councils' (2004) 42 *British Journal of Industrial Relations* 255.

[39] Some leading examples include Blair, 'Stakeholder Management'; Archie B. Carroll and Ann K. Buchholtz, *Business and Society: Ethics and Stakeholder Management* (Cincinnati: South-Western, 1996); Max B.E. Clarkson, *The Corporation and Its Stakeholders: Classic and Contemporary Readings* (Toronto: University of Toronto Press, 1998); John C. Coffee, Jr., 'Shareholders Versus Managers: The Strain in the Corporate Web' (1986) 85 *Michigan Law Review* 1; Thomas Donaldson and Lee E. Preston, 'The Stakeholder Theory of the Corporation: Concepts, Evidence, and Implications' (1995) 20 *Academy of Management Review* 65; Katherine V.W. Stone, 'Employees As Stakeholders Under State Nonshareholder Constituency Statutes' (1991) 21 *Stetson Law Review* 45.

[40] US Department of Commerce and Labor, 'Employee Participation and Labor-Management Cooperation in American Workplaces: Commission on the Future of Work-Management Relations', reprinted in (1995) 38:5 *Challenge* 38 at 40.

[41] John A. Byrne, 'Restoring Trust in Corporate America: Business Must Lead the Way to Real Reform' (24 June 2002) 3788 *Business Week* 30; Thomas Clarke, 'Accounting for Enron: Shareholder Value and Stakeholder Interests' (2005) 13 *Corporate Governance: International Review* 598.

[42] Miguel Martinez Lucio and Mark Stuart, 'Assessing Partnership: Workplace Trade Union Representatives' Attitudes and Experiences' (2002) 24:3 *Employee Relations* 305, 314–316.

[43] Dave Ulrich, 'A New Mandate for Human Resources' (1998) 76:1 *Harvard Business Review* 124; Cathy A. Enz and Judy A. Siguaw, 'Best Practises in Human Resources'

level, workers are urged to enhance their 'human capital' through the opportunities for learning provided by their employer; they are told that they have been 'empowered' by participation in work teams and other strategies of self-discipline and peer management, and that they enjoy a privileged status within the enterprise as 'associates' with whom management can 'communicate openly'.[44] In similar fashion, directors and managers are urged to adhere to the principles of 'corporate social responsibility' (CSR) with its implied promise that employees – among others – will benefit from more enlightened corporate policies and become more loyal and efficient members of the corporate 'team'.[45] Combining this elevated moral sensibility with the threat that backsliding will be punished in the marketplace, some scholars predict that labour standards will be 'ratcheted' upwards, through a self-sustaining tendency which reflects the naturally reflexive propensity of corporate cultures and organizations to adhere to 'best practices'.[46] The intent, and the effect, of such rhetoric is obviously to encourage workers to think of themselves as 'stakeholders', with an interest in improving the company's productivity and profitability, which will bring its own rewards for them as for other stakeholders.

While honestly intended in many cases, and enthusiastically received by many workers, this vision of worker–employer partnership offers a promise of goodwill but no method of ensuring its delivery. Moreover, in some cases the same rhetoric has been used to co-opt organized workers so as to weaken their loyalty to their union, and to discourage them from advancing their interests through alternative, conflictual

(2000) 41 *Cornell Hotel & Restaurant Administration Quarterly* 48; and Paul S. Nadler, 'Empowerment: The Human Resources Goal for a New Century' (1999) 55:7 *The Secured Lender* 68.

[44] Wal-Mart, for example, describes its corporate culture as such: 'As a Wal-Mart Associate, you're part of a continuously growing, global family. The key to our culture's effectiveness is our Open Door Policy. Every Associate is encouraged to bring any suggestions to their supervisor. We also administer a company-wide Grass Roots Survey, which allows Associates to confidentially raise difficult issues about their Managers, policies and the company in general.' See online: www.walmartstores.com (last accessed 22 February 2011) under 'career information'.

[45] See Thomas O. Davenport, *Human Capital: What It Is and Why People Invest It* (San Francisco: Jossey-Bass, 1999); Karen Lawson, 'Build Your Business from the Inside Out: Four Keys to Employee Empowerment That Will Help Your Business Grow' (2001) 103 *Business Credit* 8; Susan G. Cohen and Diane E. Bailey, 'What Makes Teams Work: Group Effectiveness from the Shop Floor to the Executive Suite' (1997) 23 *Journal of Management* 239.

[46] Charles Sabel, Dara O'Rourk, and Archon Fung, 'Ratcheting Labor Standards: Regulation for Continuous Improvement in the Global Workplace' (23 February 2000), online: www2.law.columbia.edu/sabel/papers/ratchPO.html; Cynthia L. Estlund, 'Rebuilding the Law of the Workplace in an Era of Self-Regulation' (2005) 105 *Columbia Law Reiew* 319, 366–374.

strategies.⁴⁷ The current debate over the stakeholder model thus represents an attempt to shift the administration of the employment relationship away from state regulation of power towards self-regulation and/or market regulation. Well or ill intentioned, it is a strategy effected by persuading workers that their interests are either aligned with those of management or are best served by acquiescing in management's priorities. The consequence – intended or otherwise – is an erosion of workers' willingness and ability to rely on other courses of action should this community of interest prove illusory.

C   Employees as 'human capital'

If the notion of employees as 'citizens at work' seems anachronistic, and that of employees as corporate 'stakeholders' perhaps delusory or deceptive, is it more helpful to characterize their relationship to their corporate employer as one involving 'human capital'?[48]

Such an approach would require radical revision of labour law's traditional preoccupation with the redistribution of power and wealth within the employment relationship. That preoccupation included measures to prevent extreme forms of exploitation by corporate employers, to regulate the use of workers' countervailing power, and to provide a platform for contract-based benefits and for state welfare policies.[49] But all of these strategies worked largely because, during the post-war era, employment relationships had become relatively secure and enduring. Lengthy job tenure enabled workers to develop solidarity, justified their short-term sacrifices during strikes, and gave them reason to agree to complex collective agreements or corporate HR strategies. Without lengthy tenures, pensions and health insurance plans based on the accumulation of employer, employee, and state contributions would have been impossible, and new social institutions such as annual vacations and compassionate leave would be illogical. At the same time, tenure helped make these innovations affordable, because workers who became more skilled and more committed to the enterprise over time also became more productive and less militant.[50]

---

[47] John Kelly, 'Union Militancy and Social Partnership', in Peter Ackers, Charles Smith, and Paul Smith (eds.), *The New Workplace and Trade Unionism* (New York: Routledge, 1996), pp. 89–92.

[48] Symposium: The W. Irwin Gillespie Roundtables, 'Minister of Labour's Roundtable on Modernizing Labour Policy within a Human Capital Strategy for Canada' (2002) 28 *Canadian Public Policy* 71ff.

[49] Brian A. Langille, 'Labour Policy in Canada: New Platform, New Paradigm' (2002) 28 *Canadian Public Policy* 133, 137–139.

[50] Harry W. Arthurs, 'Labour Law Without the State?' (1996) 46 *University of Toronto Law Journal* 1.

This logic seems to have dissolved as the post-war Fordist regime gave way to a new liberalized and globalized economy in which the underlying relations of employment have become increasingly ephemeral, institutions of countervailing power have atrophied, state programmes of income maintenance have become less generous, and the Fordist social contract has fallen into disrepute.[51] The 1999 Supiot Report to the European Commission suggests that these fundamental dislocations of labour market policy and labour law were attributable to three developments: (1) rising skill levels among workers, (2) growing competition through increasingly open markets, and (3) rapid technological advances.[52] In response to these changes, corporate employers adopted flexible employment arrangements by redeploying personnel, operations, investments, and risks from the corporation's 'core' to alternate sites along the extended production and distribution chains, at many of which the corporation itself is not present. The result was not only attenuated links between the corporation and its employees,[53] but also the dissolving of worker solidarity and the disabling of the social innovations, legal mechanisms, and public policies which had been premised on the long-term employment contract.[54] Consequently, as Langille argues, the contract of employment no longer seems the logical site for regulatory intervention to guide our labour policies.[55]

The Supiot Report represents perhaps the most thorough and imaginative response to this challenge. It suggests that the employment relationship, narrowly defined, should no longer delimit the legal and social parameters of labour law. Rather, labour law should be organized

---

[51] Deborah A. DeMott, 'Fluid Relationships in Transitional Times: A Comment on Employees and Corporate Governance' (2000) 22 *Comparative Labor Law & Policy Journal* 149. DeMott estimates that workers born between 1957 and 1964 will have held an average of 9.2 jobs between age 18 and age 34. See also a survey by John J. Heldrich Center for Workforce Development, Rutgers University and Center for Survey Research and Analysis, University of Connecticut; K.A. Dixon and Carl E. Van Horn, 'The Disposable Worker: Living in a Job-Loss Economy' (2003) 6:2 *Work Trends*, online: www.heldrich.rutgers.edu/uploadedFiles/Publications/Disposable%20Worker.pdf. For a review of potential effects, see Stone, *From Widgets to Digits*, p. 4; Simon Deakin, 'The Evolution of the Employment Relationship', in Peter Auer and Bernard Gazier (eds.), *The Future of Work, Employment and Social Protection: The Dynamics of Change and the Protection of Workers* (International Labour Organization, 2002), online: www.ilo.org/public/english/bureau/inst/download/lyonang.pdf. Also, see generally William E. Scheuerman, *Liberal Democracy and the Social Acceleration of Time* (Baltimore: Johns Hopkins University Press, 2004), pp. 6–15.
[52] Alain Supiot, *Beyond Employment: Changes in Work and the Future of Labour Law in Europe* (Oxford: Oxford University Press, 2001) at 2 [Supiot Report].
[53] *Ibid.*, at 1–23.
[54] Linda Dickens, 'Problems of Fit: Changing Employment and Labour Regulation' (2004) 42 *British Journal of Industrial Relations* 595.
[55] Langille, 'Labour Policy in Canada', p. 140.

around a more general concept of work or career, or what Langille defines as the 'working life cycle'. This shift – Supiot, Langille and others agree – is needed to both create a labour market appropriate for a dynamic, flexible knowledge-based economy[56] and ensure that labour law can resume its historic protective functions in the context of such a market.[57]

As compensation for the loss of Fordist labour law's old familiar protections, the new regime would establish a system of social citizenship premised on labour market participation, and emphasizing the economic value of human capital.[58] Individuals, as socially productive citizens, would have access to a series of 'social drawing rights' which could be used to aid in their skills development or to spread the risks of a highly volatile labour market more evenly over time and across the polity. Drawing rights would include those which accrue from employment itself (wages, etc.), those generically associated with labour market participation (health and safety), those emerging from non-remunerated types of work (volunteer, self-training, and homework), and finally, the universal social rights not emerging from work but from one's social citizenship (health care and social security).[59] Thus the employment relationship would no longer provide the sole or dominant platform for labour market policy, but would serve instead as one among several.[60] This, presumably, would permit greater flexibility in employment relations and encourage the emergence of appropriate policies in other settings.

This new vision of labour law and employment relations has much to recommend it, including a credible diagnosis of the current realities

---

[56] 'Flexicurity' – a policy strategy that attempts, synchronically and in a deliberate way, to enhance the flexibility of labour markets, the work organization, and labour relations on the one hand, and to enhance security – employment security and social security – notably for weaker groups in and outside the labour market on the other hand – has attracted growing interest in Europe. See Ton Wilthagen and Ralf Rogowski, 'Legal Regulation of Transitional Labour Markets', in Gunther Schmid and Bernard Gazier (eds.), *The Dynamics of Full Employment: Social Integration Through Transitional Labour Markets* (Cheltenham: Edward Elgar, 2002), pp. 233, 250; Thomas Bredgaard, Flemming Larsen, and Per Kongshøj Madsen, 'The Flexible Danish Labour Market – a Review' (Aalborg, Denmark: Centre for Labour Market Research, 2005), online: www.tilburguniversity.nl/ faculties/frw/research/ schoordijk/flexicurity/publications/papers/fxp2005-12-larsenmadsenbredgaard. pdf; Gøsta Esping-Andersen and Marino Regini, *Why Deregulate Labour Markets?* (Oxford: Oxford University Press, 2000).

[57] Langille, 'Labour Policy in Canada', pp. 190–191.

[58] Gunther Schmid, 'Transitional Labour Markets and the European Social Model: Towards a New Employment Compact', in Schmid and Gazier, *Full Employment*, p. 393.

[59] Supiot Report, pp. 52–57.

[60] Langille, 'Labour Policy in Canada', p. 141.

of the labour market. However, it is also fraught with contradictions which may ultimately prove to be its undoing.

Clearly, it is in the interests of workers, employers, and society as a whole that workers be well trained and highly motivated, that their material needs and dignity be attended to, and that this be accomplished without placing undue reliance on the employment relationship. However, the protections and incentives provided in the new dispensation will not fall from the sky. Who will provide them? If it is employers, they must be persuaded to engage in an act of social benevolence: training workers who by definition are destined to leave them in the near future, which would cause them to lose their sunk investment in training. Not only that, workers would conceivably be taking away 'know-how' and other insider information which will be placed at the disposal of some other employer. If it is employees themselves, they must be convinced to take risks by investing in human capital – themselves – at the very moment when threats to their rights, earnings, benefits, and job tenure have made them risk-averse.[61] If it is the state, it must recover its capacity to raise taxes, invest in social infrastructure, and exercise at least a modicum of *dirigisme* in labour markets.[62] This requires a change in our political culture, which is not yet in evidence.

Thus, this exciting new vision is likely to remain only an elegant intellectual exercise until a wide variety of public and private actors abandon their traditional values, interests, perceptions, and behaviours.

D   *Employees as investors*

Perhaps half or more of American workers are investors either directly in their own right or indirectly through pension funds, benefit funds, credit unions, labour-sponsored venture capital funds, mutual funds, or other institutional investment pools.[63] However, for several reasons neither individual employee-shareholders nor worker-controlled investment funds have shown much inclination to intervene in corporate decision-making.

---

[61] Supiot Report, pp. 26–28; David Marsden and Hugh Stephenson (eds.), *Labour Law and Social Insurance in the New Economy: A Debate on the Supiot Report* (London: Centre for Economic Performance, 2001), p. 3, online: http://cep.lse.ac.uk/pubs/download/DP0500.pdf.

[62] Stone, *From Widgets to Digits*, pp. 5, 9; Supiot Report, pp. 24–26.

[63] One study estimated that 43 per cent of all American households owned stocks or mutual funds – and that the number was rising on a steep trajectory; Richard Nadler 'The Rise of Worker Capitalism' (1999) 359 *Policy Analysis* 1. It is unclear whether this number includes workers' interests in union-managed pension fund and benefit plan assets, estimated in 2003 to have a value of over $5 trillion. Testimony of

First, a considerable percentage of pension funds are not in fact controlled by workers or unions, but by employers or employers' nominees. Second, while Employee Stock Ownership Plans (esops) have increased in number since they were first introduced in the mid-1960s,[64] they are still not common. Third, the vast majority of workers still do not invest directly in the company which employs them, nor do union-managed funds often take strategic positions in such companies. As a result, while unions and union-owned investment funds do sometimes seek to advance workers' interests through shareholder resolutions,[65] non-union institutional investors, which hold the bulk of the workers' investment funds, seem to feel little compulsion to do likewise. Indeed, workers themselves mainly want institutional investors to produce reliably high rates of return, an outcome which might be put at risk if they pursued a secondary agenda of championing social causes.

As a result, corporate management rarely feels pressured to respond to the wishes of employee-investors. There are of course exceptions. Start-up companies may compensate their employees with shares or stock options, in lieu of market-level salaries; insolvent corporations may persuade employees and unions to exchange past or future wages for equity holdings, in order to keep the company afloat. But these are relatively rare occurrences and, in general, workers have not succeeded in aggregating their collective power as investors to advance their interests within the corporation that employs them.

Still, the reincarnation of employees as investors does appear to be having one potentially important consequence: the transformation of workers' identity and consciousness, and their incorporation into what has been described as a political system of 'market populism'[66] or 'worker capitalism'.[67] Critics and proponents seem to agree that stock ownership makes workers more inclined to favour reduced tax burdens

---

Daman A. Silvers, Associate General Counsel AFL-CIO to the Senate Committee on Commerce, Science and Transportation (20 May 2003), online: www.aflcio.org/mediacenter/prsptm/tm05202003.cfm.

[64] Centre for Economic and Social Justice, 'Employee Stock Ownership Plans', online: www.cesj.org/homestead/creditvehicles/cha-esop.htm. ESOPs provide tax credits for workers who invest in the firm which employs them.

[65] Marleen A. O'Connor, 'Labor's Role in the American Corporate Governance Structure' (2000) 22 *Comparative Labor Law & Policy Journal* 97; Stewart J. Schwab and Randall S. Thomas, 'Realigning Corporate Governance: Shareholder Activism by Labor Unions' (1997–1998) 96 *Michigan Law Review* 1018, 1022.

[66] Thomas Frank, *One Market Under God: Extreme Capitalism, Market Populism, and the End of Economic Democracy* (New York: Doubleday, 2000).

[67] Nadler, 'Empowerment'.

on wealth holders, and less inclined to favour costly government programmes for the delivery of health, education, or other public services which could be purchased privately.

In conclusion, the four dominant post-war strategies for ensuring recognition of workers' interests within the corporation all appear to have failed, both conceptually and practically. In each case, the problem appears to be, at least in part, a failure to comprehend the corporation as a political economy in itself, as well as an indispensable actor in the wider political economy.

III Political economy of the firm: cooperation and solidarity/divergence and conflict

Most theories of the corporation explicitly state or implicitly assume that its actions are ultimately motivated by the desire to enhance its profitability – that they represent a considered response to market and other conditions which may affect profitability positively or negatively – arrived at by human agents who act in accordance with mandates defined by its formal governance procedures. As Milton Friedman notoriously argued:

> [A] corporate executive is an employee of the owners of the business. He has direct responsibility to his employers. That responsibility is to conduct the business in accordance with their desires, which generally will be to make as much money as possible while conforming to the basic rules of the society, both those embodied in law and those embodied in ethical custom.[68]

Of course since corporate actions are the result of human judgments, they are by no means automatic or inevitable. But they are usually thought to emanate from a unitary corporate intelligence which is hierarchically controlled or, at the very least, coordinated through an established framework for consultation. To this general understanding there is one well-understood exception: decisions regarding labour. Conventional industrial relations literature postulates a bilateral relationship between the collectivity of workers (i.e. union, employee association, unorganized workers) and the collectivity of management (i.e. shareholders, directors, and managers). This bilateral relationship is generally understood to be one of conflictual cooperation.

---

[68] Milton Friedman, 'The Social Responsibility of Business is to Increase its Profits' (13 September 1970) *New York Times Magazine* 243.

However, contrary to general understandings concerning unitary corporate decision-making and bilateral conflictual worker–management relations, we argue that conflictual cooperation subsists not only between collectivities of labour and management, but also within them.

A   Management

It has long been understood – corporate governance theories to the contrary notwithstanding – that in practice directors are not mere agents of the shareholders, nor are managers mere servants of the directors.[69] What is less often understood is that managers themselves may operate according to the inconsistent logics or competing interests associated with their functional mandates (i.e. finance, marketing, sales, production, HR, technostructure) or their site of operations (head office or subsidiary, North America, Europe, or 'third world'). When choices have to be made, managers nominally respond to what appears to be 'the best interests of the firm'. But the firm's interests have an odd way of coinciding with their own, or at least of reflecting their individual way of looking at the world. This is implicitly acknowledged by the literature of corporate decision-making which stresses the need for coordination and the powerful influence of expertise. Finally, while coordination represents a challenge to corporations of all sizes and at all times, that challenge may be heightened both by internal developments such as growth in its size, complexity or modes of production, and by exogenous factors such as globalization, regulatory environment, or market conditions.[70]

Strategies for coordination range from the assertion of top-down hierarchical control to hetrarchical or team-building strategies, as well as from development of strong corporate cultures or values to information-sharing and better training. But each of these ultimately represents an attempt to ensure that the individual human agents who comprise 'management' respond to common or collective imperatives, and not to those which merely advance their own personal interests. This is an obvious source of the pathology which leads corporate managers to subordinate their own familial, psychological, and sometimes financial well-being when the corporation 'needs' them to do so.

---

[69] See Michael C. Jensen and William H. Meckling, 'Theory of the Firm: Managerial Behavior, Agency Costs and Ownership Structure' (1976) 3 *Journal of Financial Economics* 305.

[70] See, for example, John Kenneth Galbraith, *The New Industrial State* (Boston: Houghton Miflin, 1968) esp. ch. XIV.

Of course, the corporation achieves coordination by offering rewards (financial incentives and symbolic recognition, promises of promotion, immunity from redundancy) as well as by threatening sanctions (withholding of rewards, demotion, dismissal).[71] Rewards and sanctions are less effective when they are actually invoked than when they operate prospectively to shape values, influence perceptions, and condition behaviour. However, this is not always positive, even from the perspective of the corporation. Sometimes rewards and sanctions create extreme and harmful pathologies. Senior corporate actors forecast or report false financial success. Managers point the finger to deflect blame for their failures onto others. Lower level operatives adhere to dysfunctional but duly authorized procedures rather than risk censure by taking independent initiatives.[72]

Somehow, these internal contentions among managers are ultimately made to disappear. They are resolved by reasoned argument, by compromise, or by coercion; they are obfuscated by polite, placatory behaviour in conference rooms or executive offices; they are left to fester while events flow around them. But the fact remains that coordination within management is seldom perfect, and decisions are often taken on the basis of the personal preference, perception, or profit of individual managers, not because they are 'in best interests of the corporation'.

A practical example will illustrate the point. Suppose branch-plant management is faced with a directive from head office to reduce unit costs of production. A decision will have to be taken whether to ratchet down the price of locally purchased goods and services, to seek wage concessions from employees, to expand sales in order to achieve gains in marginal efficiency, or to ask for an expanded product mandate which will permit more intensive use of the existing plant and machinery. Different members of the management team may have very different views on which is the best strategy, and those views may be far from objective. Those concerned with procurement or contract administration may feel that to deliver the needed cost reductions will endanger their carefully cultivated relations with reliable long-term suppliers or the local community. IR/HR managers may be opposed to wage reductions which they know will provoke a strike or make it difficult to hire good workers in the local labour market – thus creating serious trouble

---

[71] John Parkinson, 'Models of the Company and the Employment Relationship' (2003) 41 *British Journal of Industrial Relations* 481.

[72] Margaret M. Blair, 'Post-Enron Reflections on Comparative Corporate Governance' (2003) 14 *Journal of Interdisciplinary Economics* 113; Robert W. Armstrong, Robert J. Williams, and J. Douglas Barrett, 'The Impact of Banality, Risky Shift and Escalating Commitment on Ethical Decision Making' (2004) 53 *Journal of Business Ethics* 365.

for themselves in the future. Sales managers may be pessimistic about the possibilities of expanding markets and fear that they may be forced to promise what they cannot deliver. And the local CEO may not wish to argue for an expanded mandate because this may engender conflict with peers or superiors, which will diminish his or her chances of climbing the corporate ladder. Or conversely, any of these managers may aggressively assert the opposite position, making the calculation that if they can achieve the objective set by head office – regardless of the consequences for colleagues, workers, suppliers, or the community – they will advance their own careers.

The point is that whatever strategy is adopted, it will not solely result from a considered consensus about how to advance the 'best interests of the corporation'. The decision will reflect a significant degree of jockeying for personal positional advantage, a central feature of the political economy of the corporation.

B   Workers and unions

Similar behaviour can be identified among rank-and-file workers. Unions are often 'managers of discontent': they routinely persuade or coerce individuals and small groups of workers into abandoning protests or grievances which might threaten the overall interests of the collectivity.[73] The result may well be, for example, that the introduction of new machinery or work practices acceptable to or acquiesced in by most workers may prejudicially affect the working lives of a small group, whose protests have been suppressed by their own union.

Unions are also often described as functioning as 'brokers' among various constituencies of workers. They must find a way to reconcile the legitimate expectations of skilled technicians in high demand in the external labour market with those of the wood-hewers and water-drawers who have fewer prospects outside the firm but who dominate the internal labour market and the union membership roster. They must persuade older workers trying to accumulate larger pensions to accept that the company will have to be able to devote significant funds to improving the wages of younger workers. They must balance the claims of workers whose legitimate expectation of promotion is based on a traditional seniority system with the claims of those most likely to benefit from affirmative action programmes designed to overcome

---

[73] C. Wright Mills, *The New Men of Power: American's Labor Leaders* (New York: Harcourt Brace, 1948); Diane H. Watson, *Managers of Discontent: Trade Union Officers and Industrial Relations Managers* (London: Routledge, 1988).

the embedded effects of old discriminatory hiring practices. And most poignantly, they must sometimes choose between sacrificing some members' jobs and keeping a plant open and all jobs if operations shut down.[74]

In the North American context, the competing interests and preferences of these individual employee and groups have somehow been mediated so that union negotiators can present a coherent package to management, and so that if and when a collective agreement is signed and submitted to a ratification vote, it will receive not only nominal majority support but a broad base of genuine acceptance.[75] European unions generally function at a greater distance from the individual workplace, but they too must somehow maintain industrial, social, and political solidarity among workers with often widely divergent interests.

Even (perhaps especially) in the absence of unions, employees develop ways of dealing with each other's competing demands and interests. Dunlop's famous insight that all workplaces are characterized by a 'web of rule' reminds us that in any complex relationship, such as a workplace, neither managers nor workers pursue their own interests without regard to the effect of their conduct on others, whether laterally across the same level of the organization (worker to worker, manager to manager) or vertically through the formal hierarchy (executive to manager to worker).[76] For example, workers may punish deviant conduct, such as 'rate busting', which produces pressures to speed up work, by informal grassroots sanctions such as ostracization or even sabotage.[77] Employer-sponsored work teams or quality circles may be used not only to disseminate know-how and improve productivity but to construct a system of worker self-discipline which enables conflicts to be resolved without direct managerial oversight or intervention.[78] Informal employee caucuses may emerge to advance the interests of specific constituencies – women, minorities, occupational groups – not

---

[74] Watson, *Managers of Discontent*, pp. 171–173.
[75] In North America, the principles of exclusivity and majoritarianism allow unions to negotiate this difficult terrain. A union with the support of a majority of the workers in a 'bargaining unit' may seek 'certification' as the bargaining agent; if granted, the union thereafter enjoys exclusive representation rights, tempered by the duty to 'fairly represent' all employees in the unit. See Roy J. Adams, *Industrial Relations under Liberal Democracy: North America in a Comparative Perspective* (Columbia: University of South Carolina Press, 1995) p. 4.
[76] Dunlop, *Industrial Relations*.
[77] Michael Burawoy, *Manufacturing Consent: Changes in the Labor Process Under Monopoly Capitalism* (Chicago: University of Chicago Press, 1979); Edwards and Scullion, 'Social Control'.
[78] Stuart Henry, 'Factory Law: The Changing Disciplinary Technology of Industrial Social Control' (1982) 10 *International Journal of Social Law* 365.

only vis-à-vis the employer, but in opposition to the interests of other groups.[79] And of course the existence of Works Councils in Europe and non-union employee associations in North America testifies to the need not only for a collective worker voice to convey employee views to management – itself the site of rival interests and perspectives – but also for a forum in which workers can reconcile their competing interests.[80]

C   The corporation and 'others'

It hardly needs saying that the 'best interests of the corporation' often conflict with the 'best interests' of competitors, even though all participants in a given market may have common interests in government policies which regulate them, consumer attitudes which define their market prospects, or interest rates and raw materials prices which determine their profit margins. What is somewhat less obvious is that 'the best interests of the corporation' often diverge from the best interests of its own workers, valued suppliers and customers, the community and ecosystems in which it functions, and also from the best interests of its nominal owners, the shareholders.

At first blush, this emphasis on conflict might seem to directly challenge the notion that a wide range of stakeholders contribute to and benefit from the success of any business enterprise, and that their views and interests ought therefore to be taken into account in corporate decision-making. It certainly brings into question the conventional assumption that shareholders are not only the ultimate beneficiaries of corporate success, but also the ultimate arbiters of all corporate conduct. Still, in the present context, attention to the conflictual dimension of all corporate decision-making ought to be uncontroversial. After all, as the old adage goes, 'to govern is to choose'. This, we will argue, is an essential step in comprehending the political economy of the corporation.

D   The political economy of the corporation

To reiterate a point we have now made several times, the corporation is not what it seems: a site of orderly activity in which rational economic actors identify with and act in response to 'the best interests of the

---

[79] Alan Stuart Hyde, 'Employee Caucuses: A Key Institution in the Emergent System of Employment Law' (1993–1994) 69 *Chicago-Kent Law Review* 149 at 172–173.
[80] Bruce E. Kaufman and Daphne Gottlieb Taras (eds.), *Nonunion Employee Representation: History, Contemporary Practice, and Policy* (Armonk: M.E. Sharpe, 2000).

corporation' – interests which are themselves hierarchically determined, clear, predictable, internally consistent, and normatively beyond challenge. On the contrary, the corporation is inevitably the site of contestation and incessant, inescapable, consequential choice by myriad actors with divergent mandates, interests, and frames of reference. It is therefore, inevitably, a site of conflict. A description of its political economy thus involves the identification of who makes which choices, on what basis, with what degree of regard for others, under what conditions of formal or practical constraint, and in which institutional context.

Without attempting definitive answers to these questions, we can at least propose that the political economy of the corporation indeed involves the exercise of power – both legal and economic – but that power is relatively widely disseminated both within and beyond the formal governance structures of the corporation.

However, its wide dissemination does not imply an equal distribution of this power. As recent experience has demonstrated, senior executives have the capacity to take important – even fateful – decisions relatively free from scrutiny by the board of directors, with much less accountability to shareholders, workers, and other stakeholders.[81] They also have the capacity to appropriate rewards much larger than those enjoyed by lower levels of management, and orders of magnitude greater than those assigned to workers[82] that are unrelated to performance and sometimes paid to the clear prejudice of shareholders.[83]

On the other hand, other actors – middle management, front rank supervisors, rank-and-file employees – have the capacity to take much smaller decisions which may nonetheless be fateful in their aggregation, if not individually. They too have the ability to claim rewards – to appropriate a share of corporate earnings – which may take the form of low visibility perks, favourable workplace conditions, or simply the space to act (or not act) opportunistically and according to their personal preferences. Nor are stakeholders – workers, suppliers and customers, the state, the community, and the environment – totally without influence. Even the most conventional accounts of corporate governance acknowledge that decision-making must be geared towards avoiding adverse

---

[81] Simon Deakin and Suzanne J. Konzelmann, 'After Enron: An Age of Enlightenment?' (2003) 10 *Organization* 583.
[82] Lucien Bebchuk and Jesse Fried, *Pay Without Performance: The Unfulfilled Promise of Executive Compensation* (Cambridge, MA: Harvard University Press, 2004); Louise Lavelle, 'A Payday For Performance' (18 April 2005) 3929 *Business Week* 78; Ellen M. Heffes, 'Compensation: Investors Troubled by Corporate Policies' (1 September 2005) *Financial Executive* 11.
[83] Ray Murrill, 'Stock Options Still the Preferred Incentive' (20 June 2005) 18:12 *Canadian HR Reporter* 12.

investor behaviour, consumer reactions, or regulatory consequences.[84] Shareholders and stakeholders – including workers – can significantly heighten the risk of such adverse consequences, if they are aggrieved, aggressive, well informed, and coordinated (which is to say if they can overcome their own governance problems), and if they insist that their voice be heard, despite not having a formal role in decision-making.

Our argument comes to this: corporate decision-making is not just the product of 'governance', of the formal institutions and processes assigned responsibility by law, or of custom. It is rather the outcome of a highly conflictual political economy, and of negotiations among myriad individual and collective actors whose influences operate within and around and, often, in opposition to or in disregard of the formal mechanisms of governance. Finally, the political economy of the corporation is embedded in – but also formative of – larger national and global political economies. This fact generates additional tensions.

On the one hand, 'globalization of the mind' – the worldwide dissemination of conventional wisdom among knowledge-based elites – has produced some convergence in the political perspectives, management structures, decision-making processes, and business strategies of major corporations.[85] To some extent this convergence has the effect of persuading influential public policy-makers and corporate actors that certain forms of labour market regulation, modes of production, corporate structures, and managerial 'best practices' are uniquely compatible with high productivity, national competitiveness, and, ultimately, corporate success.

On the other hand, notwithstanding globalization, differences persist. American, Japanese, French, and Swedish corporations display somewhat different attitudes towards the state, different formal governance systems, and different internal political economies from, say, corporations in the United Kingdom, Germany, Spain, or Korea (not to mention South Africa, India, and Brazil). Varieties of capitalism, in other words, produce varieties of corporate strategies for dealing with

---

[84] Richard M. Altman, *Investor Response to Management Decisions: A Research-Based Analysis of Actions and Effects* (Westport: Quorum Books, 1992); E. Frank Harrison, *The Managerial Decision-Making Process*, 5th edn (Boston: Houghton Mifflin, 1999).

[85] Harry W. Arthurs, 'Globalization of the Mind: Canadian Elites and the Restructuring of Legal Fields' (1997) 12 *Canadian Journal of Legal Studies* 219; Sanford Jacoby, Emily Nason, and Kazuro Saguchi, 'Corporate Organization in Japan and the United States: Is There Evidence of Convergence?' (15 June 2004), online: http://ssrn.com/abstract=559124; Christel Lane, 'Changes in Corporate Governance of German Corporations: Convergence to the Anglo-American Model?' (March 2003) ESCR Centre for Business Research, University of Cambridge Working Paper No. 259, online: www.cbr.cam.ac.uk/pdf/WP259.pdf.

workers, customers, suppliers, shareholders, regulators, and policy-makers.[86] Even major transnational corporations, closely identified with the political and business culture of the country where they originate and have their principal operations or head offices, are under considerable pressure to adjust to local labour market conditions and ways of ordering workplace relations.[87] Indeed, there is little evidence that they attempt to export their home country HR/IR policies holus-bolus to other jurisdictions where they conduct operations, except perhaps where the host country bears a close affinity to the home country, as with Canada and the United States.[88] Workplace regulation is often regarded as culture-, country-, and corporation-specific, and warnings abound concerning the non-exportability of labour laws and industrial relations systems and practices – along with powerful appeals to the horizon-expanding potential of the comparative approach.[89]

In short, globalization has revealed another dimension of the political economy of the corporation. The writ of its global board and management does not run everywhere, it cannot always be invoked to require elements of the corporation to conform to centrally determined policies, and it cannot always ignore or expect to transform local and specialized social systems.

---

[86] Robert Boyer and Pierre-François Souyri, *Mondialisation et régulations: Europe et Japon face à la singularité américaine* (Paris: Découverte, 2001); Robert Boyer, 'State and Market: A New Engagement for the Twenty-first Century', in Robert Boyer and Daniel Drache (eds.), *States Against Markets: The Limits of Globalization* (New York: Routledge, 1996), p. 84; Peter A. Hall and David Soskice, *Varieties of Capitalism: The Institutional Foundations of Comparative Advantage* (Oxford: Oxford University Press, 2001).

[87] Harry W. Arthurs, 'Who's Afraid of Globalization? Reflections on the Future of Labour Law', in John D.R. Craig and S. Michael Lynk (eds.), *Globalization and the Future of Labour Law* (Cambridge: Cambridge University Press, 2006); Tony Edwards, 'Corporate Governance, Industrial Relations and Trends in Company-Level Restructuring in Europe: Convergence Towards the Anglo-American Model' (2004) 35 *Industrial Relations Journal* 518.

[88] Harry W. Arthurs, 'The Role of Global Law Firms in Constructing or Obstructing a Transnational Regime of Labour Law', in Richard P. Appelbaum, William L.F. Felstiner, and Volkmar Gessner (eds.), *Rules and Networks: The Legal Culture of Global Business Transactions* (Portland: Hart, 2001), p. 273; but cf. Susan Bisom-Rapp, 'Exceeding Our Boundaries: Transnational Employment Law Practice and the Export of American Lawyering Styles to the Global Worksite' (2004) 25 *Comparative Labor Law & Policy Journal* 257.

[89] The locus classicus is Otto Kahn-Freund, 'On Uses and Misuses of Comparative Law' (1974) 37 *Modern Law Review* 1. But see, for example, Christopher J. Whelan, 'Labor Law and Comparative Law' (1985) 63 *Texas Law Review* 1425; Manfred Weiss, 'The Future of Comparative Labor Law as an Academic Discipline and as a Practical Tool' (2003) 25 *Comparative Labor Law & Policy Journal* 169; and see more generally, William Twining, 'Social Science and the Diffusion of Law' (2005) 32 *Journal of Law & Society* 203.

These insights, largely derived from an examination of corporate–worker relations, raise questions about current attempts to reform corporate governance roles, structures, and processes. As is well understood, these proposed reforms are fuelled by recent dramatic episodes in which corporations have inflicted grievous harms, not only on their workers (that is assumed), but on other constituencies – shareholders and bondholders – whose interests have traditionally been more carefully protected than workers' interests. Indeed, to the extent that the buoyancy of capital markets is often used as a proxy for a successful economy, a case can be made that all of us – including workers – have a stake in the proposed reforms. After all, if investors hesitate to invest and lenders to lend, businesses cannot expand and new jobs cannot be created. Tax revenues will stagnate, the value of pension funds and other collective investments will decline, and government expenditures will have to be curtailed. Thus, it can be argued, we all have a stake in the success of conventional corporate governance reforms. However, for reasons we have sketched above, and consolidate below in the form of a series of hypotheses, we believe that these reforms are likely to miss the mark.

IV Re-imagining corporate governance as political economy: seven hypotheses

We have so far focused largely on the roles of workers and managers in corporate decision-making, in suggesting that these roles are more accurately described in the discourse of political economy than that of governance. In this final section, we extrapolate from the experience of workers and managers in corporate governance to that of other groups which stand at a greater distance. In this regard, our work parallels that of Peer Zumbansen and others who have used labour law as both a microscope and a telescope with which to examine the micro- and macro-agenda of corporate reform.[90]

We propose seven very tentative hypotheses, not as firm conclusions but as provocations to further debate.

Hypothesis 1 Just as public governance is increasingly understood to involve processes beyond those formally or constitutionally designated as such, corporate governance must be understood to include the whole array of processes and institutions which shape corporate policy and action.[91]

---

[90] Zumbansen, 'Parallel Worlds'.
[91] Harry W. Arthurs, 'What Immortal Hand or Eye? – Who Will Redraw the Boundaries of Labour Law?', in Guy Davidov and Brian Langille (eds.), *Boundaries and Frontiers of Labour Law* (Oxford: Hart Publishing, 2006), p. 373.

Hypothesis 2 The claims of workers that their voices must be heard within corporate decision-making is as much a descriptive claim as it is a prescriptive claim. It does not stem from legal doctrines (the duty to bargain collectively, fiduciary obligations, implied contract, etc.), from moral or metaphorical claims (industrial citizenship), or from economic logic (worker empowerment reduces militancy and enhances productivity) – though all of these may have some validity. Rather it stems from the ineluctable fact that the actions of all human actors within the firm in some measure ultimately influence the course of corporate action.

Hypothesis 3 Public choice theory – like Marxism – sensibly assumes that rational self-interested actors will make governance decisions in their own interest.[92] If true, it is equally so for public and corporate governance. If politicians and public servants cannot or do not act 'in the public interest', corporate directors, officers, and managers cannot or do not act 'in the interests of the corporation'; or rather they act in that version of the corporation's interests which coincides with their own interests.

Hypothesis 4 How much and in what ways workers (and other actors) actually influence corporate action is determined not by the formal rules and structures of governance but by the extent and character of their power – by the political economy of the firm. Power, however, is determined by influences both indigenous and endogenous to the firm. Influences may include labour markets and markets for the firm's goods or services, corporate and general cultures, social and productive technologies, state and non-state normative regimes, and the global and national political economy within which the firm operates.

Hypothesis 5 Corporate governance is inherently conflictual and unstable because of the tendency of the groups of corporate actors denominated as labour and management to assert their own interests. While the reconciliation of competing claims does occur, it occurs at multiple levels, according to conflicting policy logics, within non-congruent time frames, and with varying degrees of explicitness.

Hypothesis 6 Proposals which rely on self-regulation, CSR, or 'best practices' to improve corporate governance assume a commonality of interest among corporate actors which is prima facie at odds

---

[92] James Buchanan and Gordon Tullock, *The Calculus of Consent: The Logical Foundations of Constitutional Democracy* (Ann Arbor: University of Michigan Press, 1962); Mancur Olsen, *The Logic of Collective Action* (New York: Schoken, 1965).

with the conflictual political economy which we have described.⁹³ They should be viewed with scepticism. Proposals to incorporate employees into the formal governance of the corporation at the level of the workplace and the boardroom – whether as citizens claiming democratic rights of participation, stakeholders claiming distributional consideration, or holders of human or financial capital claiming a return on their investment – should also be assessed in light of the complex, conflictual, and dynamic nature of the governance process.⁹⁴

Hypothesis 7   Though laws to prevent fraud and oppression and to promote accountability are clearly necessary, the "new" corporate governance must not focus exclusively or primarily on decision-making by boards of directors and managers. Rather, corporate governance can best be reformed by defining and structuring sites of conflict both inside and outside the corporation, and by emphasizing the means of mediating and managing, and occasionally promoting, conflict.

V   Conclusion

As noted, these seven hypotheses invite further investigation, challenge and, perhaps, revision. However, if they turn out to represent a more-or-less accurate account of the dynamic of corporate decision-making, they will have to be taken into account across a broad spectrum of current concerns: how can shareholders with modest holdings effectively register their views on proposed corporate actions that they perceive as contrary to their interests or values? How can directors, charged with the formal responsibility for corporate governance, discharge their responsibilities when they are almost wholly dependent on management for information and analysis? How can states influence decisions regarding the sale of domestic corporations to foreign parties, in order to avoid the loss of tax revenues, head office functions, production jobs, community well-being, or local control over valuable technologies and resources? How can corporations be held to account for failing to maintain an appropriate 'triple bottom line', which balances financial, environmental, and social outcomes? How can small businesses along the supply chains and distribution chains of dominant corporations protect themselves from abusive contractual practices? How can members

---

[93] Harry W. Arthurs, 'Corporate Self-Regulation: Political Economy, State Regulation and Reflexive Labour Law', in Brian Bercusson and Cynthia Estlund (eds.), *Regulating Labour in the Wake of Globalisation* (Portland: Hart Publishing, 2007).

[94] Allan C. Hutchinson, *The Companies We Keep: Corporate Governance For a Democratic Society* (Toronto: Irwin Law, 2005).

of minority or marginalized groups be guaranteed access to jobs and influence within the corporation commensurate with their talents? And of course, how can workers in general be assured decent and safe jobs, a measure of job security, and some voice in workplace and corporate decisions which affect them?

As yet, neither market discipline nor state regulation has produced satisfactory responses, and neither have traditional doctrines of corporate law or corporate 'best practices'. New strategies based on a better understanding of how corporations actually make decisions may prove more successful.

Part IV

The transnational embedded firm and the financial crisis

17 The intellectual foundations of the global financial crisis: analysis and proposals for reform

Frank Jan De Graaf and Cynthia A. Williams

I Introduction

The past two years' financial, and then economic, crises have led to widespread calls for rethinking market practices and regulation. A complex of specific market practices that have developed in the transition from an 'originate-and-hold' to an 'originate-and-distribute' model of banking[1] have been the focus of industry reports, domestic regulatory proposals and multilateral initiatives.[2] Many bank practices have been understood to have contributed to the crisis, and so are targeted for reform. These include, among others, excessive leverage; off-balance sheet accounting for special-purpose vehicles; securitization practices that left banks with few incentives to exercise careful credit screening; the complexity of financial products and lack of regulatory oversight or central clearing facilities for derivatives, especially credit default swaps;

We appreciate the permission of the *University of New South Wales Law Journal* to publish this chapter, which is revised from an earlier version that appeared in Volume 32:2 of that journal in 2009.

[1] For an excellent early discussion of this transition, see Treasury Committee, *Financial Stability and Transparency*, House of Commons Report No. 6, Session 2007–8 (2008).

[2] As of this writing, there are a number of quite comprehensive reports with suggestions for reform. Those that these authors particularly recommend for their clarity and depth of analysis include the Turner Review in the United Kingdom: Lord Adair Turner, *The Turner Review: A Regulatory Response to the Global Banking Crisis* (2009) Financial Services Authority, www.fsa.gov.uk/pubs/other/turner_review.pdf (last accessed 22 February 2011), and also Kern Alexander, J. Eatwell, A. Persaud and R. Reoch, *Financial Supervision and Crisis Management in the EU* (2007) European Securitisation Forum, www.europeansecuritisation.com/Market_Standard/Finance%20sector%20study.pdf (last accessed 22 February 2011), IP/A/ECON/IC/2007–069; Jacques de Larosière, Leszek Balcerovicz, Otmar Issing, Rainer Masera, Callum McCarthy, Lars Nyberg, José Pérez and Onno Ruding, *The High-Level Group on Financial Supervision in the EU: Report* (2009) European Commission, http://ec.europa.eu/internal_market/finances/docs/de_larosiere_report_en.pdf (last accessed 22 February 2011); Commission of Experts on Reforms of the International Monetary and Financial System, *Recommendations* (2009) United Nations, www.un.org/ga/president/63/letters/recommendationExperts200309.pdf (last accessed 22 February 2011).

pro-cyclical risk models adopted in Basel II; and conflicts of interest at credit ratings agencies. As this chapter is being written, the situation is in flux and what regulatory solutions will emerge is far from clear.

It is not surprising that the interrelated failings in the global financial markets are difficult to untangle and therefore to address, particularly since the economic crisis is not yet past and the regulatory challenges continue to evolve. Nor it is surprising that with the systematic deregulation of the financial markets, amongst other industries, over the past three decades in the United States and to a somewhat lesser extent the United Kingdom, the dramatic empirical demonstration of the results of that trend have convinced many that deregulation went too far, and that it is now time to restore an effective regulatory balance.

What is perhaps surprising, though, is the extent to which leading believers in 'light-touch' or 'no-touch' regulatory financial market approaches have publicly rejected at least some aspects of their prior catechism. Most notably, former chairman of the United States Federal Reserve Bank Alan Greenspan, a key architect of deregulation in the Reagan, Bush, Clinton and Bush administrations, has expressed surprise that one of the fundamental pillars of market self-regulation proved faulty. Thus, one axiom of orthodox economics is that individual self-interest will lead people and firms to make economically rational decisions. Another axiom is that market participants do a better job than government regulators in evaluating financial risk and thus determining the contours of necessary protection against that risk: protection that in a more regulatory environment would otherwise be provided by legal constraints. So it was a reversal for Greenspan to write in March of 2008 that '[t]hose of us who look to the self-interest of lending institutions to protect shareholder equity have to be in a state of shocked disbelief' since 'significant parts of [today's financial risk valuation system] failed under stress'.[3] And yet one must not overstate Greenspan's crisis of faith. In that same editorial in the *Financial Times* he also wrote that he hoped 'that one of the casualties [of the financial crisis] will not be reliance on counterparty surveillance, and more generally financial self-regulation, as the fundamental balance mechanism for global finance'.

A more searching critique was offered in the Turner Review for the United Kingdom's Financial Services Administration (FSA), issued days before the April 2009 London meeting of the G20 was convened to discuss financial system reform. Prior to the crisis the FSA had been celebrated for its principles-based 'light-touch' approach to financial regulation, and shared with the United States and Chairman Greenspan a

---

[3] Alan Greenspan, 'We Will Never Have a Perfect Model of Risk', *Financial Times*, 17 March 2008, p. 9.

faith in financial self-regulation. This is no longer the case. The Turner Review discusses in elegant detail 'the extent to which the crisis challenges past intellectual assumptions about the self-correcting nature of financial markets'.[4] Given the breadth of the critique in the Turner Review, we will discuss it in further detail below.

This is a moment in history which calls for reflection about the regulatory – and deregulatory – philosophy that has animated capital market regulation in the United States and United Kingdom. Section II takes that reflection forward. In Section III, we will discuss a number of important re-evaluations of capital market deregulation by regulators themselves. While the FSA in the United Kingdom goes further in challenging the intellectual underpinnings of existing capital market regulation than do the discussions yet forthcoming in the United States, we conclude Section III by observing that further insights on capital market regulation can be gained by comparing the theoretical and methodological commitments of different approaches to capitalism and corporate governance systems, which we do in Section IV. Thus, we discuss the neoclassical appreciation of liberal market systems and compare that to the Dutch and other European governance systems.

Having sketched out the problems created by translating unreconstructed neoclassical market theory into capital market regulation, we will then discuss Northern European alternatives for market regulation in Section V. We discuss existing European corporate governance models as an important starting point for the re-evaluation of capital market regulation, while recognizing that the European models also have their weaknesses. We discuss these corporate governance counterpoints to emphasize that alternative market models exist, models with different underlying assumptions in which, at least in theory, social values and long-term relationships get more attention. Thus, Northern European governance models can offer a source of ideas for market reforms that could lead to more stable markets with a longer-term investment orientation.[5] While corporate governance and capital market regulation are typically treated as separate subjects, we bring them together to argue that the same networked social values of the European corporate governance system should be incorporated into healthier capital market

---

[4] See the Introduction of *The Turner Review*, pp. 5–6.
[5] We recognize the difficulties of legal transplants and the institutional complementarities that undergird corporate governance systems, so we are not arguing that the Dutch or any other Northern European corporate governance system could be exported to the United States. What we do argue in this chapter is that the networked social *values* of these corporate governance systems should be emphasized in capital market reform efforts, and in Section VI we provide some policy proposals for how that could occur.

regulation. In Section VI we suggest some specific policy ideas for how to do that. Section VII concludes.

This chapter is deliberately ambitious, and as a result sketches out many points which could be discussed in greater detail. This is not a time for tinkering about the edges, however. Prevailing theory has created the worst global economic crisis since the Great Depression, yet bankers and many countries' leaders seem determined to return to business as usual, perhaps with a few extra regulatory bells and whistles but with no fundamental reform.[6] Yet fundamental reform is necessary, we argue, not only in how we regulate markets, but also in how we think about markets. This chapter seeks to advance that process.

II How mainstream economics led to market fundamentalism

The last thirty years have been dominated, in theory and practice, by a complex of beliefs about the operation of the capital markets and global financial integration that Nobel laureate and former International Monetary Fund (IMF) Chief Economist Joseph Stiglitz has called 'market fundamentalism'.[7] The macroeconomic version of the theory is that global 'capital-market liberalization should be good for economic growth and [reducing] the volatility of consumption' of developing economies.[8] In contrast to the theoretical predictions, by 2003 even the IMF Board recognized that 'it becomes difficult to make a convincing connection between financial integration and economic growth once other factors, such as trade flows and political stability are taken into account'.[9] Actual capital market liberalization and global integration have thus been associated with greater financial instability, more frequent currency crises, real economic dislocation and pro-cyclical flows of 'hot money' that do not necessarily lead to long-term growth.[10] In part this disconnect

---

[6] For one expression of concern about a return to 'business as usual' as the global financial crisis seemingly moderates, see Stefan Stern, 'We Need a Responsible Recovery, Not Business as Usual', *Financial Times*, 11 August 2009, p. 10.

[7] Joseph Stiglitz, 'Capital-Market Liberalization, Globalization, and the IMF' (2004) 20 *Oxford Review of Economic Policy* 57, 57.

[8] *Ibid.*, p. 59.

[9] Eswar Prasad, Kenneth Rogoff, Shang-Jin Wei and M. Ayhan Kose, *Effects of Financial Globalization on Developing Countries: Some Empirical Evidence* (2003) International Monetary Fund, www.imf.org/external/np/res/docs/2003/031703.pdf (last accessed 22 February 2011).

[10] See Dani Rodrik, *Has Globalization Gone Too Far* (Washington, DC: Institute for International Economics, 1997); Francisco Rodríguez and Dani Rodrik, 'Trade Policy and Economic Growth: A Skeptic's Guide to the Cross-National Evidence' (2000) 15 National Bureau for Economic Research *(NBER) Macroeconomics Annual* 261.

between neoclassical economic theory and real world results is because the underlying assumptions of the neoclassical model, assuming 'perfect information, perfect capital markets, and perfect competition' are 'a poor description of developed economies, and an even poorer description of developing countries and international capital markets'.[11]

Notwithstanding their weak descriptive validity, regulators in the developed economies of the United States and the United Kingdom have relied upon some of the same fundamental assumptions of neoclassical economic theory[12] in promoting capital market liberalization within domestic economies. As we interpret these underlying assumptions for capital market regulation, they include:

(1) Market prices of capital assets efficiently incorporate all available public information ('the efficient capital markets hypothesis') and reflect rational judgments about the discounted present value of future income streams from those assets ('the capital asset pricing model').
(2) So long as markets are transparent and do not suffer from information asymmetries then,
(3) self-interested investors will make rational economic decisions to maximize their own utility consistent with their preferences for risk, return and liquidity,
(4) which will lead to capital being allocated efficiently amongst a range of all possible productive uses of that capital; and
(5) as a result, social utility will be advanced, as the 'best' uses of productive intellectual and financial capital will prevail in the market.

Given such assumptions, governments have a number of important roles in capital market regulation. First, governments must establish the background conditions that are necessary for deep, liquid capital markets to thrive. These background conditions include well-developed rule of law norms; the potential for contracts to be enforced and property rights to be respected; sufficient securities law development and enforcement to protect against fraud. Second, governments have a role to play in addressing information asymmetries and other information imperfections so that investors can all have access to comparable information. Securities disclosure regimes are thus important, including the establishment of generally applicable, intelligent accounting standards that present a fair picture of a company's financial status.

---

[11] Stiglitz, 'Capital-Market Liberalization', p. 59.
[12] For an overview and critique of neo-classical methodology see Geoffrey M. Hodgson, *Economics and Institutions: A Manifesto for a Modern Institutional Economics* (Philadelphia: University of Pennsylvania Press, 1988), pp. 28–48.

Beyond that, though, as described by the Turner Review:

the predominant tendency of financial markets theory of the last twenty to thirty years has been to assert that:

(1) efficient and liquid financial markets deliver major allocative efficiency benefits [by the above means] ...
(2) markets are sufficiently rational as to justify a strong presumption in favour of market deregulation; and
(3) that even if markets are theoretically capable of irrational behaviour, policy-makers will never be able to judge when and how far they are irrational with sufficient confidence to justify market intervention.[13]

As a result of the efficient capital market assumptions and the 'predominant tendency' as described in the Turner Review, unregulated aspects of the financial markets have flourished. These include many derivatives markets, hedge funds, private equity funds, leverage ratios, securitizations and off-balance sheet accounting. All were deregulated or never regulated, given the underlying assumptions that sophisticated investors could fend for themselves,[14] and that sophisticated math would keep firm-level risk within acceptable bounds.[15]

---

[13] Turner, *The Turner Review*, p. 40.
[14] One clear example of this deregulatory trend in the United States concerned the attempts in 1998 of the Commodities Futures Trading Commission (CFTC) Chair Brooksley Born to regulate derivatives. The CFTC issued a concept release identifying a broad range of concerns that the unregulated derivatives markets posed, including those issues posed by the Credit Derivative Swaps that came to be so central in the global financial crisis: Commodities Futures Trading Commission, *Over the Counter Derivatives: Concept Release* (1998). The suggestion that the derivatives market might be regulated was met with resistance from senior Clinton administration officials, who under the auspices of the President's Working Group on Financial Markets, produced a report entitled *Over-the-Counter Derivatives Markets and the Commodity Exchange Act*, stating that: 'The members of the Working Group agree that there is no compelling evidence of problems involving bilateral swap agreements that would warrant regulation under the CEA [Commodities Exchange Act] ... The sophisticated counterparties that use OTC derivatives simply do not require the same protection under the CEA as those required by retail investors ... In general, private counterparty credit risk management has been employed effectively by both regulated and unregulated dealers of OTC derivatives, and the tools required by federal regulators already exist.' President's Working Group on Financial Markets, *Over-the-Counter Derivatives Markets and the Commodity Exchange Act* (1999) United States Department of the Treasury, 15–16, 34, www.ustreas.gov/press/releases/reports/otcact.pdf (last accessed 22 February 2011). For an overview of deregulatory initiatives during the late Clinton administration and the entirety of the George W Bush administration, see Joseph Stiglitz, 'Capitalist Fools' (2009) 51 *Vanity Fair* 48; Consumer Federation of America, *Reform of Financial Markets: The Collapse of Market Fundamentalism and the First Steps to Revitalize the Economy* (2009).
[15] See, for example, Basel Committee on Banking Supervision, *International Convergence of Capital Measurement and Capital Standards: A Revised Framework – Comprehensive*

This is not to suggest that there were no academic criticisms of market fundamentalism and its underlying assumptions, or that there were no qualifications that were made to the theory.[16] In fact, the relatively simple version of neoclassical economics that has been used to justify deregulation in the United States for the past thirty years has been under theoretical pressure from some important economists over that same period of time. Most of the assumptions have been tested by economic research, which has led to criticisms and in some cases modifications of the theory. A number of Nobel laureates have criticized parts of the neoclassical paradigm, including some, such as Amartya Sen (Nobel Prize 1998), Joseph Stiglitz (2001) and Paul Krugman (2008), who have advanced fundamental criticisms.[17] Yet neoclassical thinking still represents the mainstream in today's economics and almost every other theory starts from neoclassical reasoning. For example, transaction cost economics, institutional economics[18] and behavioural economics

---

Version (2006) Bank for Institutional Settlements, www.bis.org/publ/bcbs128.pdf (last accessed 22 February 2011).

[16] Here we refer to extensive debates on methodology in the outskirts of economics and between economics and management science. Joseph Stiglitz is well known for criticizing the influence of mainstream economic thinking on development policies; see, for example, Stiglitz, 'Capital-Market Liberalization'. Also, the thoughts of George M. Frankfurter on the current limited paradigm in modern finance are worth mentioning: see George M. Frankfurter, 'The Theory of Fair Markets (TFM) toward a New Finance Paradigm' (2006) 15 *International Review of Financial Analysis* 130. Methodologists such as Geoffrey M. Hodgson and D. Wade Hands have criticized almost every element of neoclassical economics, but especially the practice of economists of neglecting the theoretical and practical limitations of the underlying assumptions: see, for example, Hodgson, *Economics and Institutions*, pp. 42–49; D. Wade Hands, *Reflection without Rules: Economic Methodology and Contemporary Science Theory* (New York: Cambridge University Press, 2001). In comparative analysis see Bart Nooteboom, 'Voice- and Exit-Based Forms of Corporate Control: Anglo-American, European, and Japanese' (1999) 33 *Journal of Economic Issues* 845; Ruth V. Aguilera and Gregory Jackson, 'The Cross-national Diversity of Corporate Governance: Dimensions and Determinants' (2003) 28 *Academy of Management Review* 447; Gregory Jackson and Richard Deeg, 'Comparing Capitalisms: Understanding Institutional Diversity and Its Implications for International Business' (2008) 39 *Journal of International Business Studies* 540. Both methodological and comparative is the work of Nooteboom: see Bart Nooteboom, *Learning and Innovation in Organizations and Economies* (New York: Oxford University Press, 2000); Bart Nooteboom, 'Governance and Competence: How Can They Be Combined?' (2004) 28 *Cambridge Journal of Economics* 505.

[17] Besides Stiglitz (Noble Prize 2001), Amartya Sen is an example of a Nobel laureate (1998) who has a perspective on economics which goes further than neoclassical. Sen relates economic freedom with political freedom and states that economic and social development are intertwined and dependent of social preconditions: see, for example, Amartya Sen, *Development as Freedom* (New York: Knopf, 1999).

[18] Oliver Williamson can be seen as the main proponent of both transaction cost economics and new institutional economics. This latter economic perspective focuses on transactions in their institutional context. Institutional is here defined as legislative,

are directly linked to this thinking, as is current financial theory, such as modern portfolio theory, as it is taught in universities and practised in financial institutions.[19] On a microeconomic level, agency theory, in which the firm is modelled as a simple principal/agent relationship between shareholders, understood to be the principal, and management as their agents; and contract theory, in which firms are seen as a nexus of contracts, derive from the neoclassical economic theoretical perspective. Agency theory has been the bridge that law scholars and some economists, mainly in institutional economics and finance, have used to do comparative analysis between various economic models.[20] This is in contrast to a more sociological view of the economy in which normative and cognitive aspects of economic transactions are also taken into account.[21]

---

being the best and only relevant representation of social norms: see, for example, Oliver Williamson, *The Economic Institutions of Capitalism* (New York: Free Press, 1985); Oliver Williamson, 'The New Institutional Economics: Taking Stock, Looking Ahead' (2000) 38 *Journal of Economic Literature* 595.

[19] Slowly more critique is being brought to bear on modern portfolio theory. Alfred Slager and Kees Koedijk state that not much has been empirically proven in investment theory: see Alfred Slager and Kees Koedijk, 'Investment Beliefs, Every Asset Manager Should Have Them' (2007) 33:3 *Journal of Portfolio Management* 77, 78. Both Nassim Nicholas Taleb and George Soros criticize the non-reflective character of modern economic theory as it is applied in investment. This non-reflective character is seen as a critical driver for herding and other irrationalities on financial markets, which endanger long-term sustainable economic development. See Nassim Nicolas Taleb, *The Black Swan: The Impact of the Highly Improbable* (New York: Random House, 2007), pp. 3–21, 62–83, 295–298; George Soros, *The Crisis of Global Capitalism: Open Society Endangered* (New York: PublicAffairs, 1998), part 1; see generally George Soros, *The New Paradigm for Financial Markets: The Credit Crisis of 2008 and What It Means* (New York: PublicAffairs, 2008). This is directly related to the methodological critique of Hands, Hodgson and Bart Nooteboom that economic methodology does not take reflectivity into account or, in other words, neglects the social constructive dimension of much that is happening on financial markets. Frankfurter questions the unwanted consequences of current market practices and tries to outline some suggestions for a different market paradigm: Frankfurter, 'The Theory of Fair Markets'.

[20] Within this tradition the work of Rafael La Porta, Florencia Lopez-De-Silanes, Andrewi Shleifer and Robert Vishney is well known, even with their own acronym, LLSV. These authors compare economic systems by relating the legal protection of shareholders with the successful financial development of a country, often measured in stock price development, but, more recently, some GDP measures have also been taken into account. See Rafael La Porta, Florencio Lopez-De-Silanes and Andrei Shleifer, 'The Economic Consequences of Legal Origins' (2008) 46:2 *Journal of Economic Literature* 285–332; Rafael La Porta, Florencio Lopez-De-Silanes and Andrei Shleifer, 'Corporate Ownership Around the World' (1999) 24:2 *Journal of Finance* 471–517.

[21] See, e.g. Aguilera and Jackson, 'The Cross-national Diversity'; Jackson and Deeg, 'Comparing Capitalisms'.

Of course, parts of the criticisms of the neoclassical model have reached and been taken forward by mainstream economists themselves. Much economic research today is focused on further describing, detailing and specifying the assumptions of the neoclassical model and making clear when they work and when they do not. Behavioural finance can be seen as an example here. It has established the existence of common biases and heuristics in the way people process information; understanding these biases has informed and led to the modification of key rationality assumptions.[22] Information imperfections are now well understood to undermine the smooth functioning of real markets and to create credit and equity rationing.[23] Critical commentary has also shown that empirical results in real world financial markets and real world economies defied Panglossian economic predictions. Herding, asset bubbles, 'irrational exuberance' and momentum effects, just to name a few, have undermined theories of fundamental value efficiency.[24] Even the self-interest assumption was subject to empirical examination, and found to need significant qualification. Thus, people generally exhibit fairness constraints on their self-interested behaviour in laboratory experiments (less so economics students), in their relationships and even within firms, depending on the justice climate of the firm.

And yet an alliance of 'ideology and [economic] interests'[25] convinced regulators and policy-makers to continue promoting capital market deregulation based on simple neoclassical models, particularly in the last decade, and particularly in the United States. One result – before the global financial and economic crisis – has been the rapid expansion of the financial sector within the United States and the United Kingdom.[26] By 2006, approximately 40 per cent of corporate profits in the United States and United Kingdom were based on finance – producing 'activities internal to the banking system [that were] growing far more rapidly than end services to the real economy'.[27] (These profits have been shown to be ephemeral, as $7.2 trillion of public funds

---

[22] See Daniel Kahneman, Paul Slovic and Amos Tversky (eds.), *Judgment Under Uncertainty: Heuristics and Biases* (New York: Cambridge University Press, 1982).

[23] Stiglitz, 'Capital-Market Liberalization', p. 59. See also Taleb, *The Black Swan*, pp. 215–252.

[24] Robert Shiller's book *Irrational Exuberance* (Princeton: Princeton University Press, 2000) is the provenance for the quoted term. See Stiglitz, 'Capital-Market Liberalization' and Turner, *The Turner Review*, for discussion of herding, asset bubbles, momentum effects, home country biases and other real-world conditions inconsistent with neoclassical economic theory.

[25] Stiglitz, 'Capital-Market Liberalization'.

[26] See Turner, *The Turner Review*, p. 16.

[27] Ibid.

have been committed to shore up decimated bank balance sheets in the United States alone.[28]) Another result is that US investors, hungry for profits and with enormous pools of assets (pension funds, hedge funds and private equity) to invest increasingly (1) justified their search for yield by claiming that private, shareholder wealth-maximizing behaviour by firms and finance was the path to social wealth-maximizing and (2) increased the pressure on European firms and countries to adopt clearer allegiances to shareholders and to abandon 'old European' versions of stakeholder capitalism.[29]

III Deregulators as critics of deregulatory market theory

While theoretical debate and empirical evidence were not sufficient to challenge deregulatory capital market trends, the evident failings of finance and economics over the last three years have caused some re-examination of the efficacy of financial system self-regulation by even some quite prominent deregulators. The FSA, the United Kingdom's regulator of the financial markets, has put forward a thorough critique of financial market self-regulation. US authorities such as Alan Greenspan, former Chairman of the United States Federal Reserve Bank, and Judge Richard Posner, father of the influential United States-based law and economics movement, have also recognized that certain aspects of their fundamental preconceptions about markets were wrong. These developments are worthy of further exploration.

A Self-interest does not protect the market

As noted above, Alan Greenspan, for decades recognized as one of the most important global authorities on the financial markets, said in October 2008 to the United States House Committee on Oversight and Government Reform: 'Those of us who have looked to the self-interest of lending institutions to protect shareholders' equity, myself

---

[28] Judge Richard Allen Posner, *A Failure of Capitalism: The Crisis of '08 and the Descent into Depression* (Cambridge, MA: Harvard University Press, 2009), p. xi. The $7.2 trillion figure includes $5.2 trillion by the Federal Reserve in various standby arrangements and acceptance of unmarketable securities as collateral for prime rate loans; and $2 trillion by the Treasury Department.

[29] Marie-Laure Djelic and Jabril Bensedrine, 'Globalization and Its Limits: The Making of International Regulation', in Glenn Morgan, Peer Hull Kristensen and Richard Whitley (eds.), *The Multinational Firm: Organizing across Institutional and National Divides* (New York: Oxford University Press, 2001), p. 253.

included, are in a state of shocked disbelief.'[30] This admission suggests an acknowledgement that one of the foundational elements of deregulated capital markets cannot bear the weight given it. That individuals' pursuit of their own self-interest is an adequate regulatory mechanism to promote the well functioning of the markets is one justification for deregulation. If self-interest cannot be relied upon to develop capital markets that intelligently allocate capital to the best productive uses (and it is perhaps astonishing that it was thought to have that capacity, given all of the theoretical attention that has been paid for decades to the problems of self-interest within the firm, given the assumptions of agency theory), the fundamentals behind market thinking have to be redesigned.

Another prominent advocate of market self-regulation who has reversed course is Judge Richard Posner, Chief Judge of the United States Court of Appeals for the Seventh Circuit, Senior Lecturer at the University of Chicago Law School, and important architect and theorist in the development of the law and economics movement in the United States since the early 1970s. Law and economics theoreticians have generally, and vigorously, supported deregulation in a range of industries, including finance, as has Judge Posner. Yet, he now has the following to say about the current financial and economic crisis, which he is not shy to label a depression:

> Some conservatives believe that the depression is the result of unwise government policies. I believe it is a market failure. The government's myopia, passivity, and blunders played a critical role in *allowing* the recession to balloon into a depression, and so have several fortuitous factors. But without any government regulation of the financial industry, the economy would still, in all likelihood, be in a depression. We are learning from it that we need a more active and intelligent government to keep our model of a capitalist economy from running off the rails. The movement to deregulate the financial industry went too far by exaggerating the resilience – the self-healing powers – of laissez-faire capitalism.[31]

Further on, Judge Posner contrasts the system of American capitalism that has failed with its more resilient cousin, the European system:

> The point is only that excessive deregulation of the financial industry was a government failure abetted by the political and ideological commitments of mainstream economists, who overlooked the possibility that the financial markets seemed robust because regulation had prevented previous financial crises.

---

[30] Edmund Andrews, 'Greenspan Concedes Flaws in Deregulatory Approach', *New York Times*, 24 October 2008, B1.
[31] Posner, *A Failure of Capitalism*, p. xii (emphasis in original).

The depression is a failure of capitalism, or more precisely of a certain kind of capitalism ('laissez-faire' in a loose sense, 'American' versus 'European' in a popular sense), and of capitalism's biggest boosters.[32]

Notwithstanding this identification of the problems of American-style capitalism, in his review of Judge Posner's book, Nobel laureate Robert Solow concludes that Judge Posner has not come to any clear solutions to recommend, other than supporting a list of possible reforms that is shared by many other analysts (more transparency, limits on leverage, more control on managers, for instance).[33] Solow views the critical question in financial market reform as how to ensure the social function the financial system is meant to perform. 'Risks arise in the everyday business of economic life, and some human institution has to transfer them to those who are most willing to bear them', writes Solow, further stating that:

I find it hard to believe, and I suspect that Judge Posner shares my disbelief, that our overgrown, largely unregulated financial sector was actually fully engaged in improving the allocation of real economic resources. It was using modern financial technology to create fresh risks, to borrow more money, and to gamble it away.[34]

Indeed, Judge Posner wrote that '[a]s far as I know, no one has a clear sense of the social value of our deregulated financial industry, with its free-wheeling banks and hedge funds and private equity funds and all the rest',[35] about which Solow concludes that:

As Posner sees it, talk about greed and foolhardiness is comforting but not useful. Greed and foolhardiness were not invented just recently. The problem is rather that Panglossian ideas about 'free markets' encouraged, on one hand, lax regulation, or no regulation, of a potentially unstable financial apparatus and, on the other, the elaboration of compensation mechanisms that positively encouraged risk-taking and short-term opportunism.[36]

With this conclusion, both Solow and Judge Posner seem to ask for more fundamental ideas about how to restore the social value of financial markets. The authors of this chapter submit that the social value of financial markets is, at a minimum, allocating capital to socially productive uses so that new ideas and technologies can flourish, and so that

---

[32] Ibid., p. 260.
[33] Robert Solow, 'How to Understand the Disaster: Review of *A Failure of Capitalism* (2009)', *The New York Review of Books*, www.nybooks.com/articles/22655 (last accessed 22 February 2011).
[34] Ibid.
[35] Posner, *A Failure of Capitalism*, p. 295.
[36] Solow, 'How to Understand the Disaster'.

successful companies can continue to pursue effective long-term strategies. As we discuss below, combining the values of Northern European models of corporate organization with capital market regulation suggests a way forward to address the instabilities of deregulated markets and socially unproductive uses of capital, and thus provide some solutions to the problems of modern markets that both Judge Posner and Professor Solow perceive.

B   *Market regulators start questioning the fundamentals*

While the comments of Alan Greenspan and the commentary of Richard Posner are nothing less than astonishing to anyone schooled in law in the last three decades in the United States or familiar with US political debates, they fall short of sustained intellectual engagement with the underlying reasons for these failures of deregulatory policies. The Turner Review of the FSA in the United Kingdom addresses that gap. Thus, the Review concludes that each of the following five assumptions of the theory of efficient and rational markets 'is now subject to extensive challenge on both theoretical and empirical grounds':[37]

(1) Market prices are good indicators of rationally evaluated economic value.
(2) The development of securitized credit, since based on the creation of new and more liquid markets, has improved both allocative efficiency and financial stability.
(3) The risk characteristics of financial markets can be inferred from mathematical analysis, delivering robust quantitative measures of trading risk.
(4) Market discipline can be used as an effective tool in constraining harmful risk-taking.
(5) Financial innovation can be assumed to be beneficial since market competition would winnow out any innovations which did not deliver value added.[38]

From its careful canvassing of empirical evidence and evaluation of each of these assumptions, the Turner Review draws a number of conclusions that are relevant to reforming capital market regulation. First, the Turner Review recognizes that efficient markets can be irrational. While the assumption had been that independently acting market participants would react to new information based on rational assessments

---

[37] Turner, *The Turner Review*, p. 39.
[38] *Ibid.*

and that prices would tend towards a rational equilibrium, recent events have shown that efficient reactions to new information does not imply fundamental value rationality as there can be herd effects, momentum effects and price overshoots.[39] Moreover, and of more serious significance for regulatory policy, even if individuals act rationally, that does not imply collective rationality or that social welfare will necessarily be advanced. We see that today with concerns about the implications of the savings trap: the negative collective effects on an economy that can occur if every individual acts rationally and saves more money and spends less in light of insecure economic conditions, which drives demand down and further undermines collective economic security.[40] The Turner Review further concluded that allocative efficiency benefits have limits, so that 'beyond a certain degree of liquidity' the additional allocative efficiency benefits of further liquidity and market completion are outweighed by the risks of creating asset bubbles and additional instability – a risk it thought particularly prominent concerning securitization.[41] A major theme throughout the Turner Review was that stricter, countercyclical regulation is needed to promote collective market welfare, rather than relying upon notions of individual rationality, the accuracy of market signals and self-interest to advance important social goals. This countercyclical presumption extends, analogously, to the level of theory. Recognizing that accepting 'conventional wisdom' was part of the problem leading to excessive risk-taking, dangerous leverage levels and systemic instability, the Turner Review suggested considering instituting mechanisms for bringing in 'deliberately counter conventional wisdom views' to challenge regulators' and market participants' preconceptions.[42] Together with Greenspan and Judge Posner, the Turner Review acknowledges the limits of the theory that free, rational, well-informed market participants, by only striving for their own interest, create social welfare.

C   *What do the current evaluations by market regulators teach us?*

If we summarize these leading criticisms on current market thinking, we can draw the following conclusions.

First and foremost, many now seem to agree that self-interest cannot be the only value shaping market regulation. In our view, there should be better mechanisms for collective interests and social values

---

[39] Ibid., pp. 40–41.   [40] Ibid.
[41] Ibid., p. 41.   [42] Ibid., p. 85.

to supersede individual self-interest, since self-interest can promote conditions of excessive risk taking, short-term gratification and greed. The legitimate interests of market participants that regulation ought to promote should be defined to coincide with market conditions that will promote longer-term investment decisions and reduce systemic risk.

Second, current regulation does not lead to integrity per se, so governments (and educators) have to find other solutions to stimulate the integrity of both markets and market participants. This questions the fundamentals of regulatory design.

Third, stability is not something that is dependent on regulation only, but is an intrinsic characteristic of how market participants behave and which time horizon they use to express the reward of their actions. It is about how market participants interact when making transactions and what they take into account when they make these transactions.

These conclusions lead us to think it is necessary to develop a new perspective on the regulation of the capital markets, as do some of the authorities discussed above. Judge Posner's conclusion that American capitalism failed, while Europe's proved more resilient as a general matter, supports our view that there is much to learn from Europe, and specifically European corporate governance systems as we canvass for ideas for capital market reform.

IV Market fundamentalism and governance systems

In economics and management sciences, there is an extensive literature on corporate governance systems, the legal framework within which the relationship between stakeholders and a company may be constituted.[43] Most often, authors define two ideal types: an Anglo-American or market-based model, especially in the United States, the United Kingdom and Australia, and a network-based model common in Europe and Japan, as well as in some rapidly emerging economies such as Brazil, China and India.[44] In Table 17.1, the predominant characteristics of the two types of governance systems are displayed.

---

[43] Corporate governance systems go beyond legal requirements structuring the relationships between companies, the board, management, employees and shareholders. One can also consider legislation in the field of regulations protecting stakeholders, e.g. by legislation that organizes consumer protection and antitrust law as part of corporate governance.

[44] See, for example, La Porta *et al.*, 'Legal Origins'; Aguilera and Jackson, 'The Cross-national Diversity'. Within a tradition of comparative law, Pistor uses the terms 'liberal market economies' and 'coordinated market economies', following Peter Hall and David Soskice (eds.), *Varieties of Capitalism: the Institutional Foundations of Comparative Advantage* (Oxford: Oxford University Press, 2001): Katharina Pistor, 'Legal Ground

Table 17.1 *The characteristics of governance systems*

Governance system	Market-based	Network-based
General characteristics	Market orientation	Internal orientation
	Short-term relations	Long-term relations
	Competition	Cooperation
Governance structure	Capitalist form, focus on the financial markets, the shareholders	Collective form, focus on a group of stakeholders
Forms of corporate control	Exit-based: when dissatisfied, stakeholders leave	Voice-based: when dissatisfied, stakeholders complain in the network
Governance mechanism	Contract	Trust
Governance evaluation	Third parties	Networks
Theory	Agency theory	Stewardship theory/ normative stakeholder theory
Research orientation	Agency problems between the management and shareholders	Balancing stakeholder interest
Countries	US and UK	Continental Europe and Japan
Stakeholder influence strategies	Emphasis on indirect influence strategies (law)	Emphasis on direct influence-strategies (co-decision)
Characteristics of stakeholder influence-pathways	Regulation	Consultation

Source: Frank Jan de Graaf and Cor Herkströter, 'How Corporate Social Performance Is Institutionalized in the Governance Structure: the Dutch Governance Model' (2007) 74:2, *Journal of Business Ethics* 180

These characterizations have a highly theoretical nature and can be seen as idealized types on a continuum, in which the Market system defines one end of the continuum and the Network system defines the other. Thus, in every jurisdiction elements of both can be found, but the relative proportions of market versus social control of corporate and economic relationships vary.

Over the last decades, the agency perspective has been dominant in economic thinking about governance systems, concomitant with an emphasis on shareholders' interests. Agency issues began to draw academic attention with the recognition by Berle and Means of the separation of ownership from control in the modern American firm, a separation which gave rise in economic analysis to a preoccupation with agency issues at the core of the firm.[45] Clearly, as a matter of law whenever there is a principal/agent relationship, agency issues are central, and thus agency issues are important within every firm. Yet the 'agency perspective', as we are using the term, also encompasses the idea as it has been applied by many economists and law professors that shareholders are the principal in the relationship, and management and the board are the shareholders' agent. Contrary views, such as that the corporation is the principal, or that a team of stakeholders is the principal, are rejected within the dominant agency perspective.

The agency perspective has been supplemented by a conception of the firm as a 'nexus of contracts', operating in institutional environments in which governments set the framework in which capital flows freely.[46] Within an agency perspective on the market, since it is based on neoclassical economics, law has the somewhat minimalist remit described above: to safeguard a level playing field for all economic actors, mainly by ensuring transparency; and to create clear systems of property rights and contractual enforcement mechanisms.

Rules in Coordinated and Liberal Market Economies' (Working Paper No 30/2005, European Corporate Governance Institute, 2005). It is possible to make further distinctions. Weimer and Paape distinguish four systems: the Anglo-American model, the Rheinland model (state employee involvement with dispersed ownership), a Southern European model (large family-controlled holdings plus state involvement) and a Japanese system (state influence and many cross holdings): Jeroen Weimer and Joost Paape, 'A Taxonomy of Systems of Corporate Governance' (1999) 7:2 *Corporate Governance* 152; Richard Whitley, *Divergent Capitalisms: The Social Structuring and Change of Business Systems* (New York: Oxford University Press, 1999). Aguilera *et al.* further distinguish between the American corporate governance system and the British, contending that the corporate governance system in the United Kingdom has a stronger accountability mechanism in the board and a greater sensitivity to social responsibility concerns than does the American: Ruth Aguilera, Cynthia A. Williams, John M. Conley and Deborah E. Rupp, 'Corporate Governance and Corporate Social Responsibility: A Comparative Analysis of the United Kingdom and the United States' (2006) 14:3 *Corporate Governance: An International Review* 147.

[45] See, for example, Michael C. Jensen and William H. Meckling, 'Theory of the Firm: Managerial Behavior, Agency Costs and Ownership Structure' (1976) 3:4 *Journal of Financial Economics* 305; Eugene F. Fama, 'Agency Problems and the Theory of the Firm' (1980) 88 *Journal of Political Economics* 288.

[46] See, for example, La Porta *et al.*, 'Legal Origins'; Williamson, 'New Institutional Economics'; Michael C Jensen, 'Value Maximization, Stakeholder Theory, and the Corporate Objective Function', in Jörg Andriof, Sandra Waddock, Bryan Husted and Sandra Sutherland Rahman (eds.), *Unfolding Stakeholder Thinking* (Sheffield: Greenleaf Publications, 2002).

Ironically, in developing the 'nexus of contracts' view of the firm one important participant in the discussion, University of Chicago economist Eugene Fama, was clear that:

> ownership of capital should not be confused with ownership of the firm. Each factor in a firm is owned by somebody. The firm is just the set of contracts covering the way inputs are joined to create outputs and the way receipts from outputs are shared among inputs. In this 'nexus of contracts' perspective, ownership of the firm is an irrelevant concept.[47]

Fama also recognized that fully diversified shareholders do not have 'a special interest in [any one firm's] viability', even though they are residual claimants, since – unlike labour and management – shareholders can 'shift among teams [firms] with relatively low transaction costs and to hedge against the failings of any given team by diversifying their holdings across teams'.[48] Yet, shareholders' 'ownership' status, and/or position as residual claimants, have been the rationales for 'shareholder primacy' corporate governance theories. The emphasis on shareholders has excluded broader consideration of other team members' interests in most American law theory as well, the primary counter-example being Blair and Stout's team production model of the corporation.[49] Moreover, the emphasis on shareholders as residual claimants has not distinguished the short-term financial interests of fully-diversified portfolio investors from the long-term financial interests of stable, sustainable operating companies and economies. If markets promote fundamental value efficiency and the intelligent allocation of capital, there should be no difference between the short-term and long-term perspectives. But as recent events and evaluations have shown, markets are not operating in this way.

There are a number of problems with the agency-influenced view of corporate governance worth exploring. In these theories, business relationships are defined as if they only exist in bilateral contracts and within stable institutional arrangements. Political, technological, cultural and ethical influences are seen as stable, and not changing in relevant ways in decades.[50] Within the leading economic models radical changes, such as the current crisis, have not been taken into account,[51] nor have the influences of economic thinking on social and cultural

---

[47] Eugene F. Fama, 'The Disciplining of Corporate Managers' (Selected Paper No 56, Graduate School of Business University of Chicago, 1980), p. 4.
[48] *Ibid.*
[49] Margaret Blair and Lynn Stout, 'A Team Production Theory of Corporate Law' (1999) 85 *Virginia Law Review* 247.
[50] Hodgson, *Economics and Institutions*; Hands, *Reflection without Rules*.
[51] See generally Taleb, *The Black Swan*.

changes been subject to reflective examination within economics. In other words, finance and economics have been treated as distinct from social phenomenon, notwithstanding the seminal work of economic sociologist Mark Granovetter showing their interrelated status in modern market economies.[52] With the fundamental assumptions of market efficiency by self-interested economic actors under scrutiny, as in the Turner Review, we submit that shareholder dominated agency thinking should be re-evaluated as well. In the next section, we discuss the other major governance system, a network-based or stakeholder-oriented model, as a field to canvass for ideas on capital market reform. We recognize that this is quite familiar territory for many readers, but we use it to provide a context for developing the values that could influence the policy reforms suggested in the subsequent section.

V Network systems as inspiration in the development of reflective capitalist models

A *Alternative governance systems*

Within the outskirts of economics, in management science, the discussion about governance systems has been less decidedly shareholder dominated. Contrary to, or supplementary of, agency theory, stewardship theory and stakeholder theory have come into existence. Within this perspective, a company should not only be accountable to shareholders but also to a broader range of stakeholders.[53] The stakeholder perspective of a company supplements the agency theory, since no one disagrees that shareholders are a stakeholder of the firm.

Proponents of stakeholder views take issue with certain aspects of shareholder-dominated agency theories. One critique of agency theory is that too much emphasis has been placed on conflicts of interest between rationally operating actors within the firm, often simply construed as conflicts between the managers and the 'owners' of a company, the shareholders. In such a view, not enough emphasis has been placed on cooperation within the firm and on the optimal conditions for cooperation. In addition, economic exchange relations are most often

---

[52] Mark Granovetter, 'Economic Action and Social Structure: The Problem of Embeddedness' (1985) 91:3 *American Journal of Sociology* 481.
[53] See, for example, R. Edward Freeman, *Strategic Management: A Stakeholder Approach* (London: Pitman Publishing, 1984); James H. Davis, F. David Schoorman and Lex Donaldson, 'Toward a Stewardship Theory of the Firm' (1997) 22:1 *Academy of Management Review* 20; Thomas Kochan and Saul Rubinstein, 'Toward a Stakeholder Theory of the Firm: The Saturn Partnership' (2000) 11:4 *Organization Science* 367.

not one-to-one relationships, but occur in complex networks in which an agent is also hiring other agents, who in turn hires other agents. In a recent paper Johnson and De Graaf[54] describe this phenomenon for the pension fund industry. Pension fund trustees often hire investment consultants who hire a range of asset managers (corresponding to the range of asset classes in which the pension fund ought to be invested), creating such a complex network with so many agents within the supply chain, that a clear agency relationship between the pension beneficiaries and the companies in which their money is invested has disappeared. From a European perspective it is problematic that in such a network there is no clear connection between the social preferences of beneficiaries and the investment activities of their agents.

In Scandinavia, the Netherlands, Germany and Austria, economies can be seen as a social market system or network-based system[55] (see Table 17.1), which can have a positive impact on both the financial and social performance of companies in those countries, but has a positive effect on societies as well.[56] Although often overlooked by academics in economics, the stakeholder perspective of the firm can best be illustrated by business practices in Northern European countries. Whitley has collected numerous case studies showing how shareholders and other stakeholders shaped economic systems in these countries,[57] and Arndt Sorge has written about the impact of globalization on local communities, describing the Northern European systems, mainly by

---

[54] Keith L. Johnson and Frank Jan de Graaf, 'Modernizing Pension Fund Legal Standards for the 21st Century' (2009) 2 *Rotman International Journal of Pension Management* 44, 47 (Table 1).

[55] Network-based systems can be defined as systems in which reputational mechanisms in a network are seen as the most critical form of corporate control. This lies in contrast to market-based systems, in which 'exit' is the critical determinant for control. As such, it is the same distinction as market and social market governance systems, but with a different focus (corporate control). Network-based systems are most common in Europe and Japan; market-based systems predominate in the United States and the UK. See generally Frank Jan de Graaf and Cor Herkströter, 'How Corporate Social Performance is Institutionalized in the Governance Structure: The Dutch Governance Model' (2007) 74:2 *Journal of Business Ethics* 177.

[56] Jeffrey D. Sachs, *Common Wealth: Economics for a Crowded Planet* (New York: The Penguin Press, 2008), pp. 258–264 collects data that compares the economic and social outcomes of the social welfare economies (which he defines as Denmark, Finland, Norway and Sweden), with the mixed economies (Austria, Belgium, France, Germany, Italy and the Netherlands, which straddles both the mixed economies and the social welfare model), with the free market economies on such measures as economic equality, income security, poverty reduction, labour market outcomes (employment rates) and standard of living; and finds that the social market economies outperform the market economies on each measure.

[57] Whitley, *Divergent Capitalisms*.

using Germany as example, as long-term oriented, which created a social welfare system and a shared responsibility for sustainable economic development. Sorge relates the technological strength of the German economy, for example, to the system of guilds in that country in the Middle Ages. Craftsmanship has been an important value in Germany from the Middle Ages, which is now institutionalized in various measures.[58] The studies of business systems by Sorge, Whitley and many others relate the development of business models to historical and cultural determinants in which societies for long have been seen as organisms: social systems in which various economic actors are tied to each other by a large set of implicit and explicit rules. De Graaf and Herkströter describe the establishment of the Dutch governance system in depth, stating that in developing a system which balances stakeholder interests, corporate social responsibility is embedded in the governance structure of the company.[59] The assumption that a company is not only accountable to shareholders, but accountable to other stakeholders, is established in law by the development of a subtle system in which no stakeholder has, in the end, a disproportionate say in the company.

B   *The Dutch corporate governance system: an example of network interaction*

The Dutch network system was developed around 1970 by a group of lawyers strongly influenced by a 'corporatist' tradition, found in Roman Catholic and Protestant writing on economic development. They tried to bridge the tensions between labour and capital by helping employees and employers to understand their mutual dependencies. Within the 'corporatist' tradition, law functions differently than in (liberal) market systems. Within this perspective law is not (only) an instrument for ensuring proper economic transactions (assuming self-interest, creating transparency, within a market space with no interference of other parties), but lawmakers and lawyers are also serving the objective of building long-term sustainable relationships. In his work on the German economic governance system, Arndt Sorge attacks market thinking, stating that British banks care for the money of those who already have it, where German banks exist to make money available for those who do not have it yet.[60] He relates the German approach to 'metatraditions', a

---

[58] Arndt Sorge, *The Global and the Local: Understanding the Dialectics of Business Systems* (New York: Oxford University Press, 2005).
[59] De Graaf and Herkströter, 'Corporate Social Performance', p. 177.
[60] Sorge, *The Global and the Local*, p. 206.

specific institutional context in which there is a balance between individual and collective interests, driven by a mutual understanding of interdependency.[61]

In the two-tiered governance system in the Netherlands, the executive board is accountable to a supervisory board. The supervisory board is responsible by law to balance the interests of the different stakeholder groups.[62] To be able to do so, the supervisory board is independent: while both shareholders and the works council can nominate new members to the board, they were until 2004 appointed by cooptation (the sitting members appoint new members). Although shareholders have recently achieved more influence with the corporate governance arrangements, consensus is a key characteristic of decision-making in this system, and members of the board have a shared responsibility for all decisions taken.[63]

To balance the interests of different stakeholder groups, the supervisory board holds the executive board accountable for the 'general interest' and 'continuity' of the company. This balancing act limits the say of all stakeholders. For example, shareowners cannot instruct the supervisory board and executive board of a company.[64] They have a say in appointing or firing the supervisory board, remuneration, and must agree on the annual accounts and on major mergers and acquisitions.[65]

The resulting management stance is illustrated in a quote from a former CEO of a Dutch bank, ING, who commented on the reactions from stakeholder groups after a year with particularly good financial results:

---

[61] *Ibid.*
[62] The Code is based on the principle accepted in the Netherlands that a company is a long-term alliance between the various parties involved in the company. The stakeholders are the groups and individuals who, directly or indirectly, influence – or are influenced by – the attainment of the company's objects: i.e. employees, shareholders and other lenders, suppliers, customers, the public sector and civil society. The management board and the supervisory board have overall responsibility for weighing up these interests, generally with a view to ensuring the continuity of the enterprise, while the company endeavours to create long-term shareholder value. Corporate Governance Code Monitoring Committee, *Dutch Corporate Governance Code: Principles of Good Corporate Governance and Best Practice Provisions* (2009) 6[7], hwww.corpgov.nl/page/downloads/DEC_2008_UK_Code_DEF__uk_.pdf (last accessed 22 February 2011).
[63] *Dutch Civil Code*, art. 2:9.
[64] Being independent, the board can have another opinion than the controlling shareholders. In critical issues, the shareholders can vote against management and thereby question the functioning of the supervisory board. Also, the shareholders can vote against appointing a new member of the supervisory board: *Dutch Civil Code*, art. 2:142.
[65] *Dutch Civil Code*, art. 2:4.

All our stakeholders were disappointed. Shareholders had wanted more dividends, employees' higher wages, [borrowers] lower interest rates, and retail clients more interest on their savings. Such criticism was a signal that we had done a good job. We would have had a problem if one of the groups had not complained. That would have meant that we had favored one of the groups over the others.[66]

The stakeholder model leads to a delicate interaction model, which can be illustrated by the role of the works council in the Dutch system. Together with shareholders, who have in some circumstances more rights than in the United States,[67] works councils have (by law) a critical role in companies that have more than fifty employees: they represent employees in decision-making processes within the company, not only to safeguard employee interests, but also to be in defined circumstances partly responsible for long-term decisions and to represent the company's interests.[68] Moreover, the works council 'shall do all in its power to promote environmental care on the part of the enterprise'.[69] Along with shareholders, the works councils were given a special place in company law, although their main roles are defined in the Works Council Act.[70] First, the works council nominates the supervisory directors. Given this power, the works council received three other rights (1) the right of information, (2) the right of advice and (3) for some decisions, the right of approval. The last-mentioned right relates to decisions regarding reorganizations, investments that critically influence the characteristics of the firm[71] and changes affecting the legal

---

[66] See, for example, *Divergent Capitalisms*; De Graaf and Herkströter, 'Corporate Social Performance'. Recently, more attention is given to the role of stakeholders in governance structures and its impact on corporate social responsibility; see, for example, Frank Jan de Graaf and Jan Willem Stoelhorst, 'The Role of Governance in Corporate Social Responsibility: Lessons from Dutch Finance' (2009) *Business & Society* Sage Journals online, http://bas.sagepub.com/content/early/2009/05/27/0007650309336451.abstract (last accessed 22 February 2011).
[67] For instance, under Dutch corporate law, it is easier to block appointments to the board of directors or to call special meetings than under US corporate law. This is related to the difference between plurality voting (US) and majority voting in the EU. See, for example, J. Winter, 'Corporate Governance Handhaving in de VS, EU en Nederland', in M.J. Kroeze, C.M. Harmsen and M.W. Josephus Jitta (eds.), *Verantwoording: aan Hans Beckman* (Deventer: Kluwer, 2006), p. 621.
[68] *The Dutch Works Councils Act: English translation of the Dutch text of the Works Councils Act (Wet op de ondernemingsraden)* (2004) Social and Economic Council, art. 28, www.ser.nl/~/media/Files/Internet/Talen/Engels/2004/2004_or.ashx (last accessed 22 February 2011).
[69] *Ibid.*, art. 28.4. [70] *Ibid.*
[71] All these questions are related to the notion of the 'continuity' of the firm. If the shape of the firm would change importantly, for example, were a firm to sell all the key assets, the works council would have a say.

status of all employees, such as a spin-off where the resulting company would have fewer than fifty employees and thus no works council.

By giving the employees various ways to influence a company, an important interdependency came into existence.[72] For instance, the right of information may seem to be a toothless tiger, but it is not. It means that management has to explain its decisions, often on a monthly basis, to employees. If this is not done in a serious way, the works council could go to court.[73] Given the seriousness of this measure, today in the Netherlands management invests in stakeholder – in this case employee – relations. The management of a firm has to put serious energy into explaining its policies, which means it takes the perspectives of others into account in formulating those policies. The right of advice and the right of approval can be seen as similar measures, asking management to take the perspective of other groups into account. This is not done by strict regulation about how management should behave, or when it should disclose certain information. Rather what we see is reflectivity, organized by methods of dialogue.[74]

This Northern European thinking implies that courts are seen as a last resort. In a healthy relationship, people do not have the intention to go to court to solve their disputes. Rather, they try to create mutual understanding that provides ground for compromises, or, even better, for the best solution. Critical to understanding almost all European countries is that social values within markets and in between companies are not only set by regulation, but by 'voice', by the necessity of companies to be in dialogue with various stakeholders, formalized by corporate law. The nature of voice also implies that courts do not only decide on which individual is right, but make decisions guided by the society's interest as well.

There are, of course, criticisms that can be brought to bear on European stakeholder systems. In the last two decades these systems have been criticized both inside and outside the EU, mainly because national peculiarities block the development of free international markets, making it more difficult for outsiders to enter a specific national market. Furthermore, law that tries to ensure long-term relationships makes labour markets less flexible. Thus, network systems can get

---

[72] De Graaf and Herkströter, 'Corporate Social Performance', p. 184.
[73] If a group of shareholders, unions and works councils have a dispute with the management of a company, and regular influence pathways are not seen as effective, they can go to court. A special section of the Amsterdam court, de 'Ondernemingskamer' can decide in those circumstances whose opinion should prevail, although also in their rulings committees are often installed to bring the two parties on speaking terms again.
[74] De Graaf and Herkströter, 'Corporate Social Performance', p. 184.

sticky. The status quo is often more important than innovation and current positions can hinder necessary changes in corporate policies to adapt to challenging market conditions.

These weaknesses, however, do not give adequate reason to question the underlying principles of the stakeholder systems, in our view. Northern European countries have developed highly successful economies that nonetheless protect social welfare values. Germany is, for example, still the world's largest exporter and market leader in engineering, automotives and other high technology industries such as machine making for manufacturing. The automotive industries in Japan and Germany are enviable as the US automotive industry collapses. Scandinavia is leading in the development of mobile telephony, computer applications and renewable energy technology. While the United States is still a market leader in a number of industries (computers and biotech, for instance, and aviation in addition to the French), those are all fields in which the government has had a major funding and coordinating role through military spending and government grants to universities. In other words, these are fields with long-term, stable relationships between government and industry, much like the coordinated economies of Europe, and not fields where 'the market has decided' how to allocate funds.[75] The United States and UK are clearly market leaders in financial engineering and finance generally, but even Judge Posner and Lord Turner now question how socially valuable that leadership is.

C   *The implications of network thinking*

The creation of systems of interaction, i.e. network systems that help companies and stakeholders have dialogues, does not fit in neoclassical economic theory.[76] One critical difference is that within neoclassical economics the rational market actor makes decisions in a relationship between two parties. Social dynamics and social networks are not taken into account in the economic view of the market. A stakeholder or network view of the market assumes a different perspective on the market. In dialogue with relevant stakeholders, managers or other economic actors make decisions.

The Dutch corporate governance system is one example of a system that attempts to create conditions to encourage these values

---

[75] Ha-Joon Chang, *Bad Samaritans: The Myth of Free Trade and the Secret History of Capitalism* (New York: Bloomsbury Press, 2007).
[76] See, for example, Hodgson, *Economics and Institutions*; Nooteboom, 'Learning and Innovation'.

among parties with quite different perspectives and financial interests. Dialogue is critical in this system.

As has been stated above, the interaction between various stakeholders in economic decision-making provides an important contrast to the assumptions of neoclassical economics and agency theory. In network thinking, the key assumption is not that actors make deals on a market only striving for their own personal interests. The underlying principle is mutual long-term dependency between various stakeholders that act in close networks in which states set some limited guidelines for how and when various stakeholders should interact. At critical moments, stakeholders representing different interests (often related to different values and beliefs) have to discuss issues with each other. The regulatory structure is less specific about the outcomes of these interactions than that the interactions are required.

In European stakeholder systems, then, regulation sets standards for dialogue and in doing that it enables stakeholders to reflect on their own interests, the interests of others involved and the long-term interests shared by everyone. In focusing on dialogue, the legislator accepts the limitations of law. Law can never tackle all of the social implications of economic behaviour, because of the general nature of law and because new technologies and financial engineering can emerge to allow parties to engage in regulatory arbitrage. Therefore at critical moments stakeholders with diverse interests need to be able to influence a company.

Another contrary principle within these stakeholder systems is that markets are not considered 'value free' and it is understood that the economic decisions of even private actors such as companies have important consequences for the well-being of society. Because of these values, stakeholders should have a voice in companies' economic transactions. This is not only because the interests of stakeholders are better protected by giving them influence. At critical situations companies also need societies, as we see today in the United States in the banking, automotive, derivatives and insurance (AIG) industry. If there is mutual dependency, interaction is critical to safeguard the shared interests.

VI   Integrating social values and reflectivity into capital market regulation

We have discussed the Northern European system in detail as an approach to develop a broader perspective on market regulation than currently predominates. Within this perspective, when evaluating proposals for market reform a critical question should be if stakeholder interests are represented. We do not (naively) suggest that the Dutch or German or other European systems could be exported to the United States, given the historical and cultural roots of corporate governance systems. Neither is it our intention to idealize these systems, which have their flaws also. Comparative research can lead to important insights, though, and such insights are necessary in the current context, given the evident need for new regulatory approaches. When we try to extract from networked-based corporate governance systems some principles for thinking about embedded capital markets, we suggest that recognizing the interdependency of various stakeholders should be an important cornerstone of legislation. Interdependency not only requires transparency, but also recognizes the need for stakeholders to create long-term relationships to advance shared goals.

How might regulators take the values of reflective, stakeholder corporate governance into account in addressing capital market reform? We only begin the process of suggesting ideas here, a process we intend to take forward in more detail in further work.

Some context is in order to begin, though. These suggestions assume that certain regulatory changes will be taken forward by the international community in order to stabilize global finance. As this chapter is being written, it seems that countercyclical capital charges (as in Spain,[77] and as recommended by Lord Turner)[78] may be enacted, that there will be some greater regulation of the use of derivatives, particularly credit default swaps, and that there might be limits enacted to risk-creating executive compensation systems. Excessive leverage is another causal element of the global financial crisis that may be addressed. These authors consider each of these aspects to be necessary but not sufficient to create conditions for global financial stability. What is also needed is to put the world's financial system onto a more sustainable path, one that can project into the future with confidence that we are solving critical issues of systemic risk, misallocation of capital, underinvestment in human capital and accelerating depletion of critical natural resources. We sketch out below a number of other areas where global financial markets could be, and should be, reformed to incorporate more of the social and environmental values that European network structures work to include.

First, to moderate excess financial churning and to fund critical sustainable development worldwide, financial transactions should be assessed and taxed by their contribution to the economic benefit of a

---

[77] See 'Spanish Steps: A Simple Way of Curbing Banks' Greed', *The Economist*, 15 May 2008 (discussing Spanish bank regulation, including countercyclical capital charges), www.economist.com/specialreports/displaystory.cfm?story_id=11325484 (last accessed 22 February 2011).
[78] Turner, *The Turner Review*, pp. 53–67.

country, from currency transactions to mergers and acquisitions. Lord Turner has recently suggested a version of the Tobin tax could be used to tame financial speculation, a policy idea worthy of serious consideration.[79] While the Tobin tax on financial transactions was first suggested in 1972, it may be an idea whose time has finally come.

Second, creating mechanisms to incorporate social values into capital market functioning is critical. The language of markets is accounting. At a microeconomic level, International Financial Reporting Standards (IFRS) need to be revised to include measures for all of the positive and negative social and environmental externalities companies produce. So, for example, when companies invest in training their employees, that investment should be treated as a capital investment, not as a cost. When companies use water, produce greenhouse gas emissions or other pollution, or undermine habitats, those should be treated as costs. Measures such as Yale University environmental economist Robert Repetto's 'True Economic Value Added', which incorporates measures of environmental harm into an integrated measure of financial results, have been developed with intellectual rigour and are ready to be implemented into national and international accounting standards.[80]

Third, also at a microeconomic level, companies should be required to disclose specific environmental, social and governance data, including discussions of how boards of directors are evaluating human rights, social and environmental risks, and what stakeholder consultations inform the company's analysis. Requiring companies to disclose such data, with some potential liability consequences, can create conditions of reflexivity in smart companies.

Fourth, at a macroeconomic level, projects such as the French President's Commission on the Measurement of Economic Performance and Social Progress for replacing GDP as a measure of a country's economic health are of great value. Led by Nobel laureates Joseph Stiglitz and Amartya Sen, it attempts to address known issues with GDP measures, as well as to incorporate quality of life and sustainable development and environmental factors, into country level measures.[81] This suggested measure could be translated into domestic practice if adopted by the Financial Stability Board.

---

[79] *Ibid.*
[80] Robert Repetto and Daniel Dias, 'TRUEVA: A New Integrated Financial Measure of Environmental Exposure', Yale Center for Environmental Law and Policy, Working Paper No. 200602, 15 October 2006.
[81] Draft Summary, International Commission on the Measurement of Economic Performance and Social Progress, 2 June 2009, www.stiglitz-sen-fitoussi.fr/documents/draft_summary.pdf (last accessed 22 February 2011).

Each of these initiatives, albeit incomplete and imperfect, would start a process for incorporating stakeholder concerns into capital market financial values, and thus permit greater reflectivity at both company and country levels.

We recognize the irony of suggesting that social concerns and values be incorporated into the capital markets in significant part through the reductionist language of numbers. However, we think a stakeholder perspective on this language can overcome the reductionist tendencies. Within our assumption that markets have to serve people, new regulation has to be understandable for stakeholders and has to serve their common interests. This directly relates to the principle of fairness that is a cornerstone of every regulatory system. In the end, regulation is a framework that allows actors to make the best possible decisions. We are proposing that market regulation should no longer be conceptualized to serve the rational self-interest of individuals, but should help individuals – all within their own limited responsibility – to make the best decisions together, decisions that serve the common interest. This is not an idealistic plea only. It is a lesson we can learn from that other governance system, as it is active in some Northern European countries.

VII   Conclusion

In recent decades, an unrefined version of neoclassical economic thinking has been the primary influence on market regulation in the United States and, to a lesser extent, the United Kingdom. The market was assumed to be only a set of discrete transactions on interconnected submarkets. In this definition the market is a separate area of society, apart from social and cultural concerns, in which individual self-interest could be expected to advance both personal and social interests. That expectation has proved naïve. This chapter argues that the rigid use of neoclassical theory, defined, following Stiglitz, as 'market fundamentalism', has been one of the causes of the current financial crisis. In this market the self-interest of actors, which can develop into greed as a pathology, is the key driver of social progress; and under the assumption of full information, the market was assumed to develop towards a certain equilibrium between demand and supply on a consistent basis. By copying neoclassical economic thinking, methodological flaws have been incorporated in market regulation. The deterministic, individualistic, rational view of markets tending to equilibrium has led to neglecting the critical role of social values and change in economic progress.

Market regulators have accepted the role of neoclassical protagonists too easily. By focusing on self-interest within assumed value free markets, in the end every individual market participant is suffering and the well-being of societies is endangered.

If regulators want to facilitate sustainable and innovative economic growth, they should accept a more complex, less theoretical view of markets. In this view transactions are embedded in societies and must incorporate social values. Regulators could develop regulation that facilitates productive economic change by enabling informed transactions and interactions among market participants.

This chapter argues that Northern European market systems, although pressured by market fundamentalism, offer relevant perspectives for regulation that enables global financial markets in which economic development is driven by social values. In these Northern European countries, law facilitates a proper dialogue between companies and stakeholders on critical moments in economic progress. Law does not only protect individual interests, but also offers opportunities for companies and other actors to act in the interest of the collective, of society.

Dialogue is critical in this thinking, because within interaction ethical values come into existence. This dialogue should not focus on the limited self-interest of the stakeholders, but on objectives formulated in more general terms, for example 'the continuity of the firm' or 'the health of society'. What is critical within this perspective is that no one group's interest is thought to predominate. Besides shareholders, employees, customers, suppliers and governments are seen as critical partners in economic progress. If participants get the opportunity to take each other's interests into account and are offered pathways to exert influence, social values are institutionalized within economic processes.

When we compare the network perspective with the proclaimed measures the G20 wants to take, we see an under-defined set of suggestions in the G20 declaration. No preconditions are defined for more cooperation, no underlying principles are defined. It gives the impression that more supervision on a global level will help the financial markets out of the current crisis and that government support is critical for long-term development. The longer-term question of how to create sustainable long-term economic development has not even been asked.

18 Why executive pay matters to innovation and inequality

William Lazonick

I   Inequitable and unstable economic growth

The United States is the richest economy in the world. Yet in the 2000s the United States has been unable to deliver equitable and stable economic growth to its own population.[1] The national unemployment rate, which was over 6 percent in the "jobless recovery" of 2003, exceeded 10 percent in the "jobless recovery" of 2009. Even the jobs of well-educated and experienced members of the labor force have been vulnerable to downsizing and offshoring. Given that the financial meltdown of 2008 has not resulted in significant government regulation, there is reason to believe that financial chaos will return in the not-too-distant future.

The distribution of income has become increasingly unequal over the past three decades, with a disappearance of middle-income jobs.[2] As shown

---

Paper presented at the Workshop on Innovation & Inequality: New Indicators from Pharma and Beyond, sponsored by the European Commission's FINNOV and DIME projects, Sant'Anna School of Advanced Studies, Pisa, Italy, May 15–16, 2010. This chapter builds on research in William Lazonick, *Sustainable Prosperity in the New Economy? Business Organization and High-Tech Employment in the United States* (Kalamazoo: Upjohn Institute for Employment Research, 2009); William Lazonick, "The New Economy Business Model and the Crisis of US Capitalism" (2009) 4 *Capitalism and Society* 2; and William Lazonick, "The Explosion of Executive Pay and the Erosion of American Prosperity" (2010) 57 *Entreprises et Histoire* 141–164. The research is being funded by the FINNOV project through Theme 8 of the Seventh Framework Programme of the European Commission (Socio-Economic Sciences and Humanities), under the topic "The role of finance for growth, employment and competitiveness in Europe" (SSH-2007-1.2–03), and by the Ford Foundation project on "Financial institutions for innovation and development."

[1] William Lazonick, *Sustainable Prosperity in the New Economy? Business Organization and High-Tech Employment in the United States* (Kalamazoo: W.E. Upjohn Institute for Employment Research, 2009), ch. 1.
[2] See, for example, D. Autor, H. Lawrence, F. Katz and M. Kearney, "Trends in U.S. Wage Inequality: Revising the Revisionists" (2008) 90 *Review of Economics and Statistics* 300–325; Elizabeth Warren, "America without a Middle Case," *The Huffington Post*, December 3, 2009, available at: www.huffingtonpost.com/elizabeth-warren/america-without-a-middle_b_377829.html (last accessed February 22, 2011).

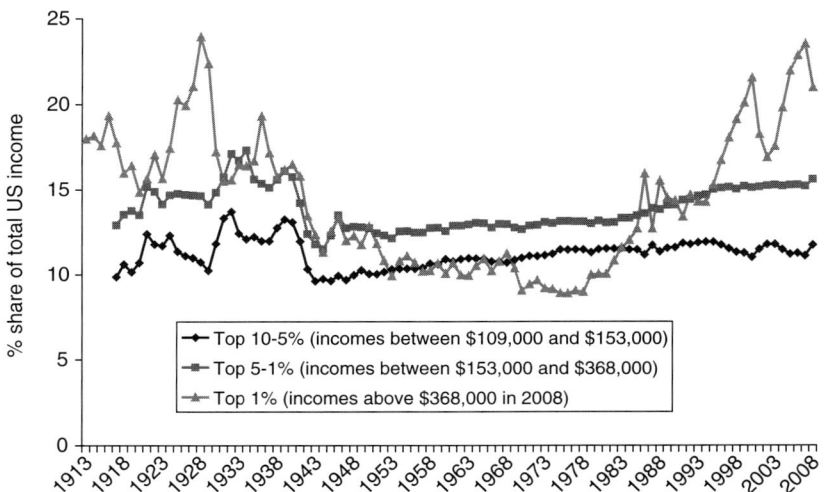

Figure 18.1 Shares of top income recipients in the United States, 1913–2007

in Figure 18.1, in the last half of the 2000s, the share of total income going to the top 1 percent of households rose to well over 20 percent.[3]

On the basis of data for the top 0.1 percent of the income distribution of the United States for 1916–2000, Thomas Piketty and Emanuel Saez observe in a paper entitled "The Evolution of Top Incomes: A Historical and International Perspective" that "[s]alary income has been driving up top incomes and has now become the main source of income at the very top," and that, across the advanced economies over the last quarter of the twentieth century, the income share going to the top 0.1 percent was largest in the United States.[4] Piketty and Saez conclude this paper with the statement: "Although cross-country analysis will always suffer from severe identification problems, our hope is that the database will renew the analysis of the interplay between inequality and growth."[5] Yet, as in their other work on concentration

---

[3] Emmanuel Saez, *Tables and Figures Updated to 2007 in Excel Format* (2009), http://elsa.berkeley.edu/~saez (last accessed February 27, 2011).

[4] Thomas Piketty and Emanuel Saez, "The Evolution of Top Incomes: A Historical and International Perspective" (2006) 96 *American Economic Review* 202. For data, 1916–2007, on the composition of the incomes of the top 0.1 percent in terms of salaries, business income, capital income and capital gains, Saez, *Tables and Figures Updated to 2007*.

[5] Piketty and Saez, "The Evolution of Top Incomes," p. 204.

of income at the top in the United States, Piketty and Saez ignore the role of stock-based compensation in general and stock options in particular in driving the increases in the "salaries" of the top income recipients.[6]

In this chapter I argue that a prime cause of the growing inequity and instability in the US economic system is the stock-based compensation of the executives who run the nation's leading industrial and financial corporations. In the 1980s and 1990s agency theorists advocated this type of compensation as an incentive for corporate executives to "maximize shareholder value" (MSV), and thereby improve the performance of the economy as a whole.[7] In the next section of this chapter, I argue that the basic tenets of agency theory are contradicted by the theory of innovative enterprise.[8] Then I show that in the corporate economy of the United States, the implementation of the incentives advocated by agency theory for the sake of MSV have over the past three decades resulted in an explosion of top executive pay. I go on to document the importance of stock buybacks in the United States as an instrument for MSV that, by manipulating a company's stock price, helps to boost executive pay. Finally I contend that in the United States the use of stock-based compensation, and in particular stock options, to motivate corporate executives to have a strong personal interest in the performance of their companies' stock prices has resulted in not only an inequitable distribution of income but also reduced investment in innovation and unstable economic performance.

---

[6] In a paper on top incomes in Canada that refers to stock-based compensation, Emmanuel Saez and Michael R. Beall Veall note: "In contrast to the United States, on Canadian tax returns, profits from stock-option exercises can be separated out from wages and salaries." Emmanuel Saez and Michael R. Beall, "The Evolution of High Incomes in Nothern America: Lessons From Canadian Evidence" (2005) 95 *American Economic Review* 841. For data that Saez adduces on stock-option remuneration as a share of total remuneration for the 100 highest-paid US CEOs, 1970–1999, see http://elsa.berkeley.edu/~saez, Table B4(CEOs) (last accessed February 27, 2011).

[7] Michael C. Jensen, "Agency Costs of Free Cash Flow, Corporate Finance and Takeovers" (1986) 76 *American Economic Review* 323–329, at 326; Michael C. Jensen and Kevin J. Murphy, "Performance Pay and Top Management Incentives" (1990) 98 *Journal of Political Economy* 225–264, at 226.

[8] See William Lazonick and Mary O'Sullivan, "Maximizing Shareholder Value: A New Ideology for Corporate Governance" (2000) 29 *Economy and Society* 13–35; William Lazonick, "Innovative Enterprise and Historical Transformation" (2002) 3 *Enterprise & Society* 35–54; William Lazonick, "The Chandlerian Corporation and the Theory of Innovative Enterprise" (2010) 19 *Industrial and Corporate Change* 317–349; William Lazonick, "The Explosion of Executive Pay and the Erosion of American Prosperity" (2010) 57 *Enterprises et Histoire* 141.

II   Maximizing shareholder value

Since the early 1980s corporate executives have justified their stock-based compensation as well as the corporate financial behavior that increases it by the dominant ideology that the role of the corporate executive is to "maximize shareholder value" (MSV).[9] At the same time, through agency theory, academic economists have supported this ideology by propounding a shareholder-value perspective on corporate governance that is consistent with the neoclassical theory of the market economy.[10] Especially in the United States, MSV remains the dominant ideology of corporate governance not only in business schools and economics departments but also in executive suites and corporate boardrooms.

For adherents of the theory of the market economy, "market imperfections" necessitate managerial control over the allocation of resources, thus creating an "agency problem" for those "principals" who have made investments in the firm. These managers may allocate corporate resources to build their own personal empires regardless of whether the investments that they make and the people whom they employ generate sufficient profits for the firm. They may hoard surplus cash or near-liquid assets within the corporation, thus maintaining control over uninvested resources, rather than distributing these extra revenues to shareholders. Or they may simply use their control over resource allocation to line their own pockets. According to agency theory, in the absence of corporate governance institutions that promote the maximization of shareholder value, one should expect managerial control to result in the inefficient allocation of resources.

The manifestation of a movement toward the more efficient allocation of resources, it is argued, is a higher return to shareholders. But why is it shareholders for whom value should be maximized? Why not create more value for creditors by making their financial investments more secure, or for employees by paying them higher wages and benefits, or for communities in which the corporations operate by generating more corporate tax revenues? Neoclassical financial theorists argue that among all the stakeholders in the business corporation only shareholders are "residual claimants." The amount of returns that shareholders

---

[9] Alfred Rappaport, "Selecting Strategies that Create Shareholder Value" (1981) 59 *Harvard Business Review* 139–149; Alfred Rappaport "Corporate Performance Standards and Shareholder Value" (1983) 3 *Journal of Business Strategy* 28–38.

[10] Eugene F. Fama and Michael C. Jensen, "Agency Problems and Residual Claims" (1983) 26 *Journal of Law and Economics* 327; Eugene F. Fama and Michael C. Jensen, "Separation of Ownership and Control" (1983) 26 *Journal of Law and Economics* 301.

receive depends on what is left over after other stakeholders, all of whom it is argued have guaranteed contractual claims, have been paid for their productive contributions to the firm. If the firm incurs a loss, the return to shareholders is negative, and vice versa.

By this argument, shareholders are the only stakeholders who have an incentive to bear the risk of investing in productive resources that may result in superior economic performance. As residual claimants, moreover, shareholders are the only stakeholders who have an interest in monitoring managers to ensure that they allocate resources efficiently. Furthermore, by selling and buying corporate shares on the stock market, public shareholders, it is argued, are the participants in the economy who are best situated to reallocate resources to more efficient uses.

Within the shareholder-value paradigm, the stock market represents the corporate governance institution through which the agency problem can be resolved and the efficient allocation of the economy's resources can be achieved. Specifically, the stock market can function as a "market for corporate control" that enables shareholders to "disgorge" – to use Michael Jensen's evocative term – the "free cash flow". As Jensen, a leading academic proponent of maximizing shareholder value, put it in a seminal 1986 article:

> Free cash flow is cash flow in excess of that required to fund all projects that have positive net present values when discounted at the relevant cost of capital. Conflicts of interest between share-holders and managers over payout policies are especially severe when the organization generates substantial free cash flow. The problem is how to motivate managers to disgorge the cash rather than investing it at below cost or wasting it on organization inefficiencies.[11]

How can those managers who control the allocation of corporate resources be motivated, or coerced, to distribute cash to shareholders? If a company does not maximize shareholder value, shareholders can sell their shares and reallocate the proceeds to what they deem to be more efficient uses. The sale of shares depresses that company's stock price, which in turn facilitates a takeover by shareholders who can put in place managers who are willing to distribute the free cash flow to shareholders in the forms of higher dividends and/or stock repurchases. Better yet, as Jensen argued in the midst of the 1980s corporate takeover movement, let corporate raiders use the market for corporate control for debt-financed takeovers, thus enabling shareholders to transform their corporate equities into corporate bonds. Corporate managers would

---

[11] Jensen, "Agency Costs," p. 323.

then be "bonded" to distribute the "free cash flow" in the form of interest rather than dividends.[12]

Additionally, as Jensen and Murphy, among others, contended, the maximization of shareholder value could be achieved by giving corporate managers stock-based compensation, such as stock options, to align their own self-interests with those of shareholders.[13] Then, even without the threat of a takeover, these managers would have a personal incentive to maximize shareholder value by investing corporate revenues only in those "projects that have positive net present values when discounted at the relevant cost of capital" and distributing the remainder of corporate revenues to shareholders in the forms of dividends and/or stock repurchases.

During the 1980s and 1990s, maximizing shareholder value became the dominant ideology for corporate governance in the United States. Top executives of US industrial corporations became ardent advocates of this perspective; quite apart from their ideological predispositions, the reality of their stock-based compensation inured them to maximizing shareholder value. The long stock market boom of the 1980s and 1990s combined with the remuneration decisions of corporate boards to create this pay bonanza for corporate executives.

To some extent, the stock market boom of the 1980s and 1990s was driven by New Economy innovation. By the late 1990s, however, innovation had given way to speculation as a prime mover of stock prices. Then, after the collapse of the Internet bubble at the beginning of the 2000s, corporate resource allocation sought to restore stock prices through manipulation in the form of stock buybacks. This massive "disgorging" of the corporate cash flow manifests a decisive triumph of agency theory and its shareholder-value ideology in the determination of corporate resource allocation.

Has this financial behavior led to a more efficient allocation of resources in the economy, as the proponents of maximizing shareholder-value claim? Quite apart from the empirical evidence that I present later in this chapter, there are a number of critical flaws in agency theory's analysis of the relation between corporate governance and economic performance. These flaws have to do with (1) a failure to explain how, historically, corporations came to control the allocation of significant amounts of the economy's resources; (2) the measure of "free cash flow"; and (3) the claim that only shareholders have "residual claimant" status. These flaws stem from the fact that agency theory, like the

---

[12] Jensen, "Agency Costs," p. 324.
[13] Jensen and Murphy, "Performance Pay," p. 226.

neoclassical theory of the market economy in which it is rooted, lacks a theory of innovative enterprise.[14]

Agency theory makes an argument for taking resources out of the control of inefficient managers without explaining how, historically, corporations came to possess the vast amounts of resources over which these managers could exercise allocative control.[15] From the first decades of the twentieth century, the separation of share ownership from managerial control characterized US industrial corporations. This separation occurred because the growth of innovative companies demanded that control over the strategic allocation of resources to transform technologies and access new markets be placed in the hands of salaried professionals who understood the investment requirements of the particular lines of business in which the enterprise competed. At the same time, the listing of a company on a public stock exchange enabled the original owner-entrepreneurs to sell their stock to the shareholding public. Thereby enriched, they were able to retire from their positions as top executives. The departing owner-entrepreneurs left control in the hands of senior salaried professionals, most of whom had been recruited decades earlier to help to build the enterprises. The resultant disappearance of family owners in positions of strategic control enabled the younger generation of salaried professionals to view the particular corporations that employed them as ones in which, through dedicated work effort over the course of a career, they could potentially rise to the ranks of top management.

With salaried managers exercising strategic control, innovative managerial corporations emerged as dominant in their industries during the first decades of the century. During the post-World War II decades, and especially during the 1960s conglomerate movement, however, many of these industrial corporations grew to be too big to be managed effectively. Top managers responsible for corporate resource allocation became segmented, behaviorally and cognitively, from the organizations that would have to implement these strategies. Behaviorally, they came to see themselves as occupants of the corporate throne rather than as members of the corporate organization, and became obsessed by the size of their own remuneration. Cognitively, the expansion of the corporation into a multitude of businesses made it increasingly difficult for

---

[14] See Lazonick, "Innovative Enterprise," p. 5; Lazonick, "The Chandlerian Corporation," pp. 320–324.
[15] William Lazonick, "Controlling the Market for Corporate Control: The Historical Significance of Managerial Capitalism" (1992) 1 *Industrial and Corporate Change* 445–488, at 449–451.

top management to understand the particular investment requirements of any of them.[16]

In the 1970s and 1980s, moreover, many of these US corporations faced intense foreign competition, especially from innovative Japanese corporations (also, it should be noted, characterized by a separation of share ownership from managerial control). An innovative response required governance institutions that would reintegrate US strategic decision-makers with the business organizations over which they exercised allocative control. Instead, guided by the ideology of maximizing shareholder value and rewarded with stock options, what these established corporations got were managers who had a strong personal interest in boosting their companies' stock prices, even if the stock-price increase was accomplished by a redistribution of corporate revenues from labor incomes to capital incomes and even if the quest for stock-price increases undermined the productive capabilities that these companies had accumulated in the past.

Agency theory also does not address how, at the time when innovative investments are made, one can judge whether managers are allocating resources inefficiently. Any strategic manager who allocates resources to an innovative strategy faces technological, market and competitive uncertainty. Technological uncertainty exists because the firm may be incapable of developing the higher-quality processes and products envisaged in its innovative investment strategy. Market uncertainty exists because, even if the firm succeeds in its development effort, future reductions in product prices and increases in factor prices may lower the returns that can be generated by the investments. Finally, even if a firm overcomes technological and market uncertainty, it still faces competitive uncertainty: the possibility that an innovative competitor will have invested in a strategy that generates an even higher-quality, lower-cost product that enables it to win market share.

One can state, as Jensen did, that the firm should only invest in "projects that have positive net present values when discounted at the relevant cost of capital." But, quite apart from the problem of defining the "relevant cost of capital," anyone who contends that, when committing resources to an innovative investment strategy, one can foresee the stream of future earnings that are required for the calculation of net present value knows nothing about the innovation process. It is far more plausible to argue that if corporate managers really sought

---

[16] William Lazonick, "Corporate Restructuring," in Stephen Ackroyd, Rose Batt, Paul Thompson and Pamela Tolbert (eds.), *The Oxford Handbook of Work and Organization* (Oxford: Oxford University Press, 2004), pp. 577–601.

to maximize shareholder value according to this formula, they would never contemplate investing in innovative projects with their highly uncertain returns.[17]

Moreover, it is simply not the case, as agency theory assumes, that all the firm's participants other than shareholders receive contractually guaranteed returns according to their productive contributions. Given its investments in productive resources, the state has residual-claimant status. Any realistic account of economic development must take into account the role of the state in (1) making infrastructural investments that, given the required levels of financial commitment and inherent uncertainty of economic outcomes, business enterprises would not have made on their own; and (2) providing business enterprises with subsidies that encourage investment in innovation. In terms of investment in new knowledge with applications to industry, the United States was the world's foremost developmental state over the course of the twentieth century.[18] As a prime example, it is impossible to explain US dominance in computers, microelectronics, software and data communications without recognizing the role of government in making seminal investments that developed new knowledge and infrastructural investments that facilitated the diffusion of that knowledge.[19]

The US government has made investments to augment the productive power of the nation through federal, corporate and university research labs that have generated new knowledge as well as through educational institutions that have developed the capabilities of the future labor force. Business enterprises have made ample use of this knowledge and capability. In effect, in funding these investments, the state (or more correctly, its body of taxpayers) has borne the risk that the nation's business enterprises would further develop and utilize these productive capabilities in ways that would ultimately redound to the benefit of the nation, *but with the return to the nation in no way contractually guaranteed.*

---

[17] Carliss Baldwin and Kim Clark, "Capabilities and Capital Investment: New Perspectives on Capital Budgeting" (1992) 5 *Journal of Applied Corporate Finance* 67–87; Clayton M. Christensen, Stephen P. Kaufman and Willy C. Shih, "Innovation Killers: How Financial Tools Destroy Your Capacity to Do New Things" (2008) 86 *Harvard Business Review* 98–105, at 100–101.
[18] William Lazonick, "Entrepreneurial Ventures and the Developmental State: Lessons from the Advanced Economies," Discussion Paper dp2008–01, United Nations University-World Institute of Development Economics Research (2008) 1–46, at 28–31.
[19] See, for example, National Research Council, *Funding a Revolution: Government Support for Computing Research* (Washington, DC: National Academies Press, 1999).

In addition, the US government has often provided cash subsidies to business enterprises to develop new products and processes, or even to start new firms. The public has funded these subsidies through current taxes, borrowing against the future, or by making consumers pay higher product prices for current goods and services than would have otherwise prevailed. Multitudes of business enterprises have benefited from subsidies without having to enter into contracts with the public bodies that have granted them to remit a guaranteed return from the productive investments that the subsidies help to finance.

Workers can also find themselves in the position of having made investments without a contractually guaranteed return. The collective and cumulative innovation process demands that workers expend time and effort now for the sake of returns that, precisely because innovation is involved, can only be generated in the future, which may entail the development and utilization of productive resources over many years. Insofar as workers involved in the innovation process make this investment of their time and effort in the innovation process without a contractually guaranteed return, they have residual claimant status.

In an important contribution to the corporate governance debate, Margaret Blair argued that, alongside a firm's shareholders, workers should be accorded residual-claimant status because they make investments in "firm-specific" human capital at one point in time with the expectation – but without a contractual guarantee – of reaping returns on those investments over the course of their careers.[20] Moreover, insofar as their human capital is indeed firm-specific, these workers are dependent on their current employer for generating returns on their investments. A lack of interfirm labor mobility means that the worker bears some of the risk of the return on the firm's productive investments, and hence can be considered a residual claimant. Blair goes on to argue that if one assumes, as shareholder-value proponents do, that only shareholders bear risk and residual-claimant status, there will be an underinvestment in human capital to the detriment of not only workers but the economy as a whole.

Investments that can result in innovation require the strategic allocation of productive resources to particular processes to transform particular productive inputs into higher-quality, lower-cost products than those goods or services that were previously available at prevailing factor prices. Investment in innovation is a direct investment that involves, first and foremost, a strategic confrontation with technological, market

---

[20] Margaret M. Blair, *Ownership and Control: Rethinking Corporate Governance for the Twenty-First Century* (Washington, DC: Brookings Institution Press, 1995).

and competitive uncertainty. Those who have the abilities and incentives to allocate resources to innovation must decide, in the face of uncertainty, what types of investments have the potential to generate higher-quality, lower-cost products. Then they must mobilize committed finance to sustain the innovation process until it generates the higher-quality, lower-cost products that permit financial returns.

What role do public shareholders play in this innovation process? Do they confront uncertainty by strategically allocating resources to innovative investments? No. As portfolio investors, they diversify their financial holdings across the outstanding shares of existing firms to minimize risk. They do so, moreover, with limited liability, which means that they are under no legal obligation to make further investments of "good" money to support previous investments that have gone bad. Indeed, even for these previous investments, the existence of a highly liquid stock market enables public shareholders to cut their losses instantaneously by selling their shares – what has long been called the "Wall Street walk."

Without this ability to exit an investment easily, public shareholders would not be willing to hold shares of companies over the assets of which they exercise no direct allocative control. It is the liquidity of a public shareholder's portfolio investment that differentiates it from a direct investment, and indeed distinguishes the public shareholder from a private shareholder who, for lack of liquidity of his or her shares, must remain committed to his or her direct investment until it generates financial returns. The modern corporation entails a fundamental transformation in the character of private property, as Adolf Berle and Gardiner Means recognized.[21] As property owners, public shareholders own tradable shares in a company that has invested in real assets; they do not own the assets themselves.

Indeed, the fundamental role of the stock market in the United States in the twentieth century was to transform illiquid claims into liquid claims on *the basis of investments that had already been made*, and thereby separate share ownership from managerial control. Business corporations sometimes do use the stock market as a source of capital for new investments, although the cash function has been most common in periods of stock market speculation when the lure for public shareholders to allocate resources to new issues has been the prospect of quickly "flipping" their shares to make a rapid speculative return. Public shareholders want financial liquidity; investments in innovation

---

[21] Adolf A. Berle and Means C. Gardiner, *The Modern Corporation and Private Property* (New York: Macmillan, 1932).

require financial commitment. It is only by ignoring the role of innovation in the economy, and the necessary role of insider control in the strategic allocation of corporate resources to innovation, that agency theory can argue that superior economic performance can be achieved by maximizing the value of those actors in the corporate economy who are the ultimate outsiders to the innovation process.

III Speculation and manipulation in the explosion of executive pay

The ideology of maximizing shareholder value is an ideology through which US corporate executives have been able to enrich themselves. In this they were aided in the 1980s and 1990s by academic proponents of the ideology such as Michael Jensen who argued that aligning the interests of top executives with those of public shareholders would result in a mode of resource allocation that would result in superior performance in the economy as a whole. The result has been an explosion and re-explosion of executive pay over the past three decades, fueled by stock-based compensation.

According to AFL-CIO Executive Paywatch, the ratio of the average pay of CEOs of 200 large US corporations to the pay of the average full-time US worker was 42:1 in 1980, 107:1 in 1990, 525:1 in 2000, and 319:1 in 2008.[22] As shown in Table 18.1, the average annual real compensation in 2008 dollars of the 100 highest paid corporate executives named in company proxy statements was $20.7 million in 1992–1995, $78.2 million in 1998–2001, and $62.0 million in 2004–2007.

As can be seen in Table 18.1, large proportions of these enormous incomes of top executives have come from gains from cashing in on the ample stock option awards that their boards of directors have bestowed on them.[23] The higher the "top pay" group, the greater the proportion of the pay of that group that was derived from gains from exercising stock options. For the top 100 group in the years 1992–2008, this

---

[22] AFL-CIO, *Executive PayWatch* (2009), www.aflcio.org/corporatewatch/paywatch/pay/index.cfm (last accessed February 22, 2011).

[23] A stock option award gives an employee the non-transferable right to purchase a certain number of shares of the company for which he or she works at a pre-set "exercise" price between the date the option "vests" and the date it "expires." Typically in US option grants, the exercise price is the market price of the stock at the date that the option is granted; vesting of the option occurs in 25 percent installments at each of the first four anniversaries from the grant date; and the expiration date of the option is ten years from the grant date. Unvested options usually lapse ninety days after termination of employment with the company.

Table 18.1 Total compensation of top executives of US-based corporations, average for 100, 500, 1,500 and 3,000 highest-paid executives, and the proportion of total compensation derived from gains from exercising stocks options (mean compensation in millions of 2009 US dollars)

	S&P 500 Index	NAS-DAQ Index	NAS-DAQ/S&P	Top 100 Mean $m.	% SO	Top 500 Mean $m.	% SO	Top 1500 Mean $m.	% SO	Top 3000 Mean $m.	% SO
1992	100	100	1.00	22.8	71	9.2	59	4.7	48	2.9	42
1993	109	119	1.10	21.0	63	9.0	51	4.7	42	3.1	36
1994	111	125	1.13	18.3	57	8.0	45	4.3	35	2.9	29
1995	131	155	1.18	20.6	59	9.6	48	5.2	40	3.4	34
1996	162	195	1.20	31.9	64	13.7	54	7.1	47	4.5	41
1997	210	243	1.16	43.5	72	18.3	61	9.3	55	5.8	49
1998	261	300	1.15	77.2	67	26.9	65	12.5	59	7.5	54
1999	319	462	1.45	69.0	82	27.5	71	13.2	63	7.9	57
2000	341	614	1.80	104.1	87	40.4	80	18.7	73	10.8	67
2001	284	332	1.17	62.3	77	23.7	66	11.3	58	6.8	53
2002	237	252	1.06	37.4	57	16.8	49	8.6	43	5.4	38

Table 18.1 (cont.)

	S&P 500 Index	NAS-DAQ Index	NAS-DAQ/S&P	Top 100			Top 500			Top 1500			Top 3000		
				Mean $m.	% SO		Mean $m.	% SO		Mean $m.	% SO		Mean $m.	% SO	
2003	232	275	1.18	48.4	64		21.0	55		10.7	48		6.7	43	
2004	272	330	1.21	54.6	75		24.6	62		12.8	55		8.0	50	
2005	290	348	1.20	66.5	78		28.2	63		14.3	56		8.9	51	
2006	316	463	1.47	67.3	68		29.0	58		15.1	51		9.5	46	
2007	354	428	1.21	59.6	69		27.4	58		14.6	50		9.3	45	
2008	291	356	1.22	39.2	62		16.6	48		8.3	38		5.0	33	
2009	227	307	1.35	29.6	44		13.9	27		7.7	17		5.0	12	

Notes: S&P 500 Index and the NASDAQ Composite Index set to 100 in 1992 for purposes of comparison.
Total compensation (TDC2 in the Compustat database) is defined as "Total compensation for the individual year comprised of the following: Salary, Bonus, Other Annual, Total Value of Restricted Stock Granted, Net Value of Stock Options Exercised, Long-Term Incentive Payouts, and All Other Total".
%SO means the percent of total compensation that the whole set (100, 500, 1,500 or 3,000) of highest-paid executives derived from gains from exercising stock options.
Note that company proxy statements (DEF 14A SEC filings) report the compensation of the company's CEO and four other highest paid executives. It is therefore possible that some of the highest-paid executives who should be included in each of the "top" categories are excluded. The mean compensation calculations are therefore lower bounds of actual average compensation of the highest paid corporate executives in the United States.
Sources: Standard and Poor's Compustat database (Executive Compensation, Annual); Yahoo! Finance at http://finance.yahoo.com (Historical Prices, Monthly Data).

Table 18.2 *Average annual US corporate stock and bond yields (%), 1960–2009*

	1960–1969	1970–1979	1980–1989	1990–1999	2000–2009
1. Real stock yield	6.63	−1.66	11.67	15.01	−3.08
2. Price yield	5.80	1.35	12.91	15.54	−2.30
Dividend yield	3.19	4.08	4.32	2.47	1.79
Change in CPI	2.36	7.09	5.55	3.00	2.57
3. Real bond yield	2.65	1.14	5.79	4.72	3.41

Note: Stock yields are for Standard and Poor's composite index of 500 US corporate stocks. Bond yields are for Moody's Aaa-rated US corporate bonds.
Sources: Updated from William Lazonick and Mary O'Sullivan, "Maximizing Shareholder Value: A New Ideology for Corporate Governance" (2000) 29 *Economy and Society* 13–35, at 27, using US Congress 2010, Tables B-62, B-73, B-95, B-96.

proportion ranged from a low of 57 percent in 1994, when the mean pay of the group was also at its lowest level in real terms, to 87 percent in 2000, when the mean pay was at its highest. In 2000 the mean pay of the top 3,000 was, at $10.8 million, only 10 percent of the mean pay of the top 100. Nevertheless, gains from exercising stock options accounted for 67 percent of the total pay of the top 3,000 group.

Note in Table 18.1 how the average pay of the highest paid corporate executives has risen and fallen with the fluctuations of major stock market indices. In the 1980s and 1990s, as shown in Table 18.2, high real stock yields characterized the US corporate economy. These high yields came mainly from stock-price appreciation as distinct from dividends yields, which were low in the 1990s despite high dividend payout ratios.[24] With the S&P 500 Index rising almost 1,400 percent from March 1982 to August 2000, the availability of gains from exercising stock options became almost automatic. Given the extent to which the explosion in US top executive pay over the past three decades has been dependent on gains from exercising stock options, there is a need to

---

[24] In the 1980s dividends paid out by US corporations increased by an annual average of 10.8 percent while after-tax corporate profits increased by an annual average of 8.7 percent. In the 1990s these figures were 8.0 percent for dividends (including an absolute decline in dividends of 4.0 percent in 1999, the first decline since 1975) and 8.1 percent for profits. The dividend payout ratio – the amount of dividends as a proportion of after-tax corporate profits (with inventory evaluation and capital consumption adjustments) – was 48.9 percent in the 1980s and 55.0 percent in the 1990s compared with 39.5 percent in the 1960s and 41.6 percent in the 1970s. From 2000 to 2009 the dividend payout ratio was 61.5 percent, including a record 70.4 percent in 2007.

understand the drivers of the stock-price increases that generate these gains.

The gains from exercising stock options depend on increases in a company's stock price. There are three distinct forces – *innovation*, *speculation* and *manipulation* – that may be at work in driving stock-price increases. Innovation generates higher-quality, lower-cost products (given prevailing factor prices) that result in increases in earnings per share, which in turn lift the stock price of the innovative enterprise. Speculation, encouraged perhaps by innovation, drives the stock price higher, as investors assume either that innovation will continue in the future (which, given that innovation is involved, is inherently uncertain) or that there is a "greater fool" who stands ready to buy the stock at yet a higher price. Manipulation occurs when those who exercise control over corporate resource allocation do so in a way that increases earnings per share despite the absence of innovation.

Figure 18.2 charts the roles of innovation, speculation and manipulation as *primary* drivers of US stock-price movements from the mid-1980s to the late 2000s. In the last half of the 1980s Old Economy companies that had run into trouble because of conglomeration in the United States and/or competition from the Japanese sought to manipulate stock prices through a "downsize-and-distribute" resource-allocation strategy.[25] This redistribution of corporate revenues from labor incomes to capital incomes often occurred through debt-financed hostile takeovers, with post-takeover downsizing enabling the servicing and retirement of the massive debt that a company had taken on. In addition, from the mid-1980s, many Old Economy companies engaged for the first time in large-scale stock repurchases in an attempt to support their stock prices. In the 1990s and 2000s stock buybacks would become a prime mode of corporate resource allocation. The main, and for most major US corporations only, purpose of stock buybacks is to manipulate stock prices.[26]

While Old Economy companies were manipulating stock prices in the 1980s and early 1990s, New Economy companies such as Intel, AMD, Microsoft, Oracle, Solectron, EMC, Sun Microsystems, Cisco Systems, Dell and Qualcomm were reinvesting virtually all of their incomes to finance the growth of their companies, neither paying dividends nor, once they had gone public, repurchasing stock.[27] It was *innovation* by

---

[25] Lazonick, "Corporate Restructuring," p. 577.
[26] William Lazonick, "The New Economy Business Model and the Crisis of U.S. Capitalism" (2009) 4 *Capitalism and Society* 2.
[27] Lazonick, *Sustainable Prosperity in the New Economy?* ch. 2.

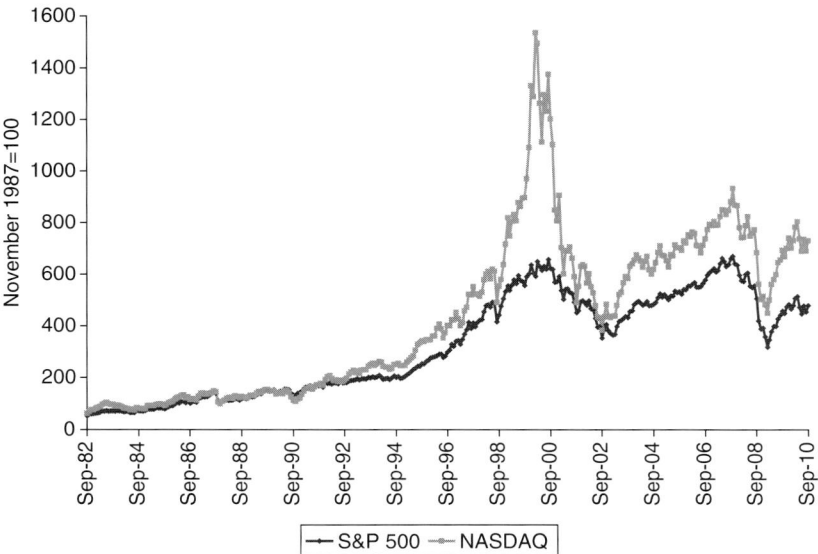

Figure 18.2 S&P 500 and NASDAQ Composite Indices, September 1982–April 2010

New Economy companies, most of them traded on NASDAQ, that culminated in the Internet revolution that provided a real foundation for the rising stock market in the 1980s and first half of the 1990s.

These New Economy companies had broad-based stock option programs that extended to non-executive employees. In the speculative boom of 1999–2000, the gains from exercising stock options of the average worker could be enormous. The most extreme example is Microsoft; in 2000 alone the gains across about 39,000 employees (not including the five highest paid executives) averaged an estimated $449,000.[28] During the same year, the gains from exercising stock options of the five highest paid Microsoft executives averaged $50.7 million – a ratio of "top 5" gains to average worker gains of 113:1.

In the late 1990s speculation took over, driving the stock market to unsustainable heights. As Figure 18.2 shows, the speculation in companies listed on NASDAQ was much more pronounced than in the companies that make up the S&P 500 Index, over 80 percent of which are listed on the New York Stock Exchange (NYSE). In 2000 the

---

[28] Lazonick, "The New Economy Business Model and the Crisis of U.S. Capitalism," p. 2.

average compensation of the top 100 NASDAQ executives was 19 percent higher than that of the top 100 NYSE executives, while in 2007 the compensation of the top 100 NYSE executives was 11 percent higher than that of the top 100 NASDAQ executives. In both years the proportion of the compensation that came from exercising stock options was higher for NASDAQ executives than for NYSE executives. Still, even for the NYSE executives, this proportion was 78 percent for the top 100 and 53 percent for the top 3,000 in 2000, and 65 percent for the top 100 and 43 percent for the top 3,000 in 2007. Whether their companies are listed on NASDAQ or NYSE, stock options give the top executives of US corporations a huge personal financial stake in a rising stock market.

In the 2000s the stock-option gains of these executives have come primarily through manipulation as distinct from innovation and speculation. The key instrument of stock-market manipulation is the stock repurchase. A stock repurchase occurs when a company buys back its own shares. In the United States, the Securities and Exchange Commission (SEC) requires stock repurchase *programs* to be approved by the board of directors. These programs authorize a company's top executives to do a certain amount of buybacks over a certain period of time. It is then up to the top executives to decide whether the company should actually do repurchases, when they should be done and how many shares should be repurchased at any given time. Repurchases are almost always done as open market transactions through the company's broker. The company is not required to announce the buybacks at the time they are actually done, although since 2004 it has been an SEC rule that, in their quarterly financial reports, companies must state the amount of repurchases in the past quarter and the average purchase price.

Data on 373 companies in the S&P 500 Index in January 2008 that were publicly listed in 1990 show that they expended an annual average of $106.3 billion (or $285 million per company) on stock repurchases in 1995–1999, representing 44 percent of their combined net income. These figures represented a significant increase from $25.9 billion in repurchases (or $69 million per company) in 1990–1994, representing 23 percent of their combined net income. Yet in the late 1990s the stage was being set for an even more massive manipulation of the market through stock repurchases, especially from 2003. Figure 18.3 shows the payout ratios and mean payout levels for 438 companies in the S&P 500 Index in January 2008 that were publicly listed from 1997 through 2008.[29]

---

[29] I treat data for companies with fiscal years ending January 1–June 30 as representing the previous calendar year, and for fiscal years ending July 1–December 31 as representing the current calendar year.

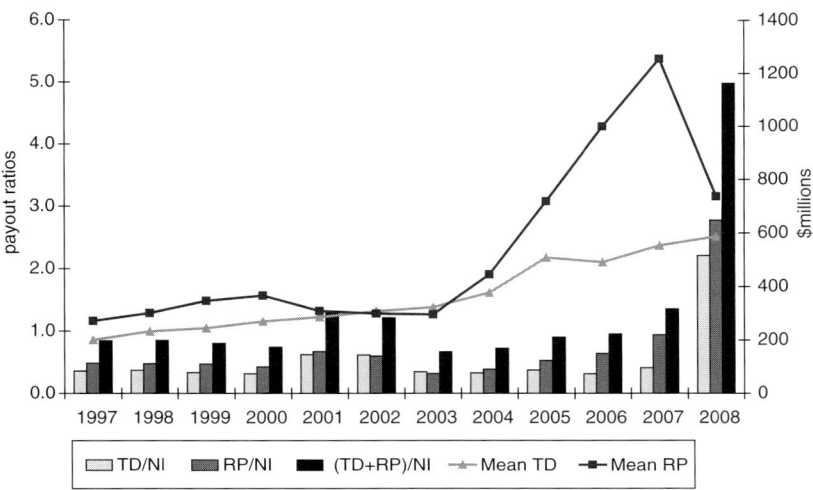

Figure 18.3 Ratios of cash dividends and stock repurchases to net income

From 1997 through 2008 these 437 companies expended $2.4 trillion on stock repurchases, an average of $5.6 billion per company, and distributed a total of $1.7 trillion in cash dividends, an average of $3.8 billion per company. Stock repurchases by these 437 companies averaged $323 million in 2003, rising to $1,256 million in 2007. Combined, the 500 companies in the S&P 500 Index in January 2008 repurchased $436 billion of their own stock in 2006, representing 64 percent of their net income, and $549 billion in 2007, representing 94 percent of their net income.

Figure 18.4 shows how the escalating stock repurchases from 2003 through 2007 helped to boost the stock market, driving the S&P 500 Index even higher in 2007 than its previous peak in 2000 before the 2008 financial debacle. In 2008 repurchases fell substantially for these 438 companies, constrained by a dramatic decline in combined net income from $583 billion in 2007 to $132 billion in 2008. Nevertheless, their combined repurchases only declined from $523 billion to $369 billion. As a result, the repurchase payout ratio more than tripled from 0.90:1 to 2.80:1. In addition, these companies paid out $5 billion more in dividends in 2008 than in 2007, with the result that the dividend payout ratio leapt from 0.41:1 to 1.86:1. Allocated differently, the billions spent on buybacks could have helped stabilize the economy. Instead, collectively, these companies not only spent all their profits on repurchases but also ate into their capital.

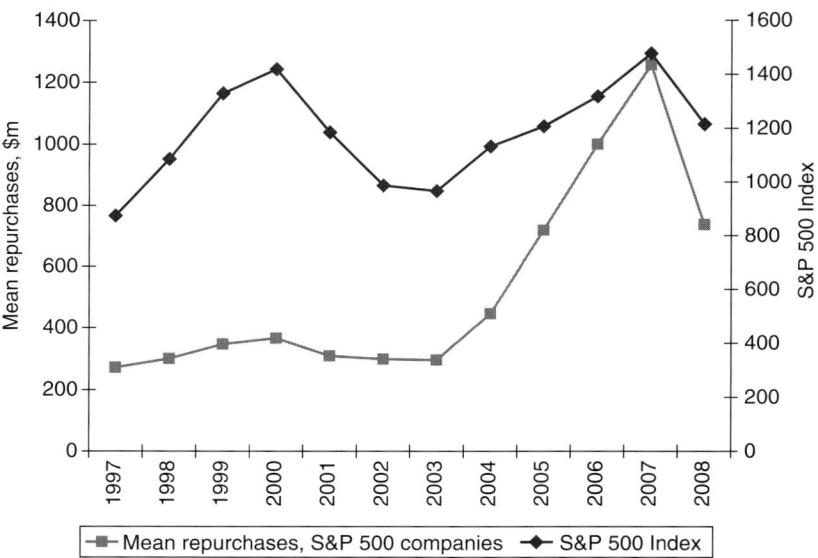

Figure 18.4 Stock repurchases by the S&P 500 (437 companies)

Why do corporations repurchase stock? Executives often claim that buybacks are financial investments that signal confidence in the future of the company and its stock-price performance.[30] In fact, however, companies that do buybacks never sell the shares at higher prices to cash in on these investments. To do so would be to signal to the market that its stock price had peaked. According to the "signaling" argument, we should have seen massive sales of corporate stock in the speculative boom of the late 1990s, as was in fact the case of US industrial corporations in the speculative boom of the late 1920s when corporations took advantage of the speculative stock market to pay off corporate debt or bolster their corporate treasuries.[31] Instead, in the boom of the late 1990s corporate executives as *personal investors* sold their own stock to reap speculative gains (often to the tune of tens of millions). Yet, if anything, these same corporate executives

---

[30] Henock Louis and Hal White, "Do Managers Intentionally Use Repurchase Tender Offers to Signal Private Information? Evidence from Firm Financial Reporting Behavior" (2007) 85 *Journal of Financial Economics* 205–231, at 207; Theo Vermaelen, *Share Repurchases: Foundations and Trends in Finance* (Hanover: Now Publishers, 2005), ch. 3.
[31] Mary O'Sullivan, "What Drove the U.S. Stock Market in the Last Century," Working Paper, INSEAD (2004).

as *corporate decision-makers* used corporate funds to repurchase their companies' shares in the attempt to bolster their stock prices – to their own personal gain. Given the extent to which stock repurchases have become a systematic mode of corporate resource allocation, and given the extent to which through this manipulation of their corporations' stock prices top executives have enriched themselves personally in the process, there is every reason to believe that, in the absence of legislation that restricts both stock repurchases as well as speculative and manipulative gains from stock options, executive behavior that places personal interests ahead of corporate interests will continue in the future.

There are a number of ways in which stock options as a mode of executive compensation can be abused. A company might reprice options that are underwater by canceling an existing option and replacing it with a new option with a lower exercise price.[32] As a result, an executive may be able to reap gains from stock-option grants even when the company's stock price declines. In 2006 a scandal broke out over the practice of backdating stock options – that is, granting option awards today as if they were granted at an earlier date when the market price of the stock and hence the exercise price of the options were lower.[33] Abuses can also occur in the timing of the exercise of options. Given the fact that in the United States companies are not required to announce the dates on which they actually do open market repurchases, there is an opportunity for top executives who have this information to engage in insider trading by using this information to time option exercises and stock sales.[34]

The more fundamental problem with US-style stock options, however, is that they are unindexed; that is, they virtually never carry any performance criteria that would only permit an executive to gain from the exercise of stock options when the company's stock-price increases

---

[32] Don M. Chance, Raman Kumar and Rebecca B. Todd, "The 'Repricing' of Executive Stock Options" (2000) 57 *Journal of Financial Economics* 129–154, at 130; Bruce R. Ellig, *The Complete Guide to Excecutive Compensation* (Columbus: McGraw-Hill, 2007), pp. 434–435.
[33] Erik Lie, "On the Timing of CEO Stock Option Awards" (2005) 51 *Management Science* 802–812; Charles Forelle and James Bandler, "The Perfect Payday: Some CEOs Reap Millions by Landing Stock Options When They are Most Valuable; Luck – or Something Else?" *Wall Street Journal*, March 18, 2006, p. A:1; Gennaro Bernile and Jarrell A. Gregg, "The Impact of the Options Backdating Scandal on Shareholders" (2009) 47 *Journal of Accounting and Economics* 2–26, at 3.
[34] Jesse M. Fried, "Insider Signaling and Insider Trading with Repurchase Tender Offers" (2000) 67 *University of Chicago Law Review* 421–473, at 464–468; Jesse M. Fried, "Open Market Repurchases: Signaling or Market Opportunism" (2001) 2 *Theoretical Inquiries in Law* 865–894, at 870–872.

are greater than those warranted by productive performance.[35] As a result, an executive, or any other employee with stock options, can gain from a speculative stock market as distinct from an improvement in the company's productive performance. In addition, as I have argued, executives can augment their stock-option gains by allocating corporate resources to do buybacks, the sole purpose of which is to manipulate the company's stock price. Some of the stock-based compensation of US executives is undoubtedly attributable to innovation, although even then there is the question of whether the stock-based compensation that executives secure is equitable relative to other contributors to the innovation process. Be that as it may, since the last half of the 1990s it has been speculation and manipulation that have been the main drivers of the explosion in the pay of US corporate executives.

IV Stock buybacks as "weapons of value destruction"

The theory that companies should be run to maximize shareholder value is based on false assumptions about who bears risk and who should reap rewards in the corporate economy. Yet, in the name of superior economic performance, this theory functions in the actual US economy to justify both unindexed stock options for top executives and massive stock buybacks to boost a company's stock price. The results, I argue, are not only outsized executive pay but also a failure of US business corporations to use their earnings to reinvest in innovation and high value-added jobs in the United States.

My analyses of different industries (some of which I have studied in more depth than others) strongly suggest that the explosions in executive pay are coming at the expense of innovation and the upgrading of employment opportunities in the US economy. In what follows, I present some pertinent evidence from key sectors of the US economy.[36]

Among the biggest stock repurchasers in the years prior to the financial crisis were many of banks that were responsible for the meltdown and were bailed out under the Troubled Asset Relief Program. They included Citigroup ($41.8 billion repurchased in 2000–2007), Goldman Sachs ($30.1 billion), Wells Fargo ($23.2 billion), JP Morgan Chase ($21.2 billion), Merrill Lynch ($21.0 billion) Morgan Stanley ($19.1 billion), American Express ($17.6 billion) and US Bancorp

---

[35] Lucian Bebchuk and Jesse Fried, *Pay without Performance: The Unfulfilled Promise of Executive Compensation* (Boston: Harvard University Press, 2004).
[36] See Lazonick, *Sustainable Prosperity in the New Economy?*; Lazonick, "The New Economy Business Model."

($12.3 billion). In the eight years before it went bankrupt in 2008, Lehman Brothers repurchased $16.8 billion, including $5.3 billion in 2006–2007. Washington Mutual, which also went bankrupt in 2008, expended $13.3 billion on buybacks in 2000–2007, including $6.5 billion in 2006–2007. Wachovia, ranked 38th among the Fortune 500 in 2007, did $15.7 billion in buybacks in 2000–2007, including $5.7 billion in 2006–2007, before its fire sale to Wells Fargo at the end of 2008. Other financial institutions that did substantial repurchases in the 2000s before running into financial distress in 2008 were AIG ($10.2 billion), Fannie Mae ($8.4 billion), Bear Stearns ($7.2 billion) and Freddie Mac ($4.7 billion). By spending money on buybacks during boom years, these financial corporations reduced their ability to withstand the crash of the derivatives market in 2008, thus exacerbating the jeopardy that they created for the economy as a whole.

Among the top ten repurchasers of stock in 2000–2008 were five of the leading ICT companies: Microsoft (the #2 repurchaser with $94.3 billion in buybacks), IBM (#3, $72.9 billion), Cisco Systems (#5, $53.6 billion), Intel (#8, $48.8 billion) and Hewlett-Packard (#10, $43.3 billion). All of these companies spent more on buybacks than they spent on R&D in 2000–2008. In the 2000s, all of these companies have been globalizing employment, and profiting through the creation of high-tech jobs in lower wage parts of the world such as China and India while using the profits of globalization to do stock buybacks at home.[37]

Meanwhile, US high-tech companies lobby the US government for more public investment in the US high-technology knowledge base, even as the companies allocate their own profits to huge stock buybacks. For example, in the 2000s Intel along with the Semiconductor Industry Association (SIA) has been lobbying the US Congress for more spending on the National Nanotechnology Initiative (NNI). At a press conference that the SIA organized in Washington, DC in March 2005, Intel CEO Craig Barrett warned: "U.S. leadership in the nanoelectronics era is not guaranteed. It will take a massive, coordinated U.S. research effort involving academia, industry, and state and federal governments to ensure that America continues to be the world leader in information technology."[38] In 2005 the annual

---

[37] Lazonick, "The New Economy Business Model"; William Milberg, "Shifting Sources and Uses of Profits: Sustaining U.S. Financializaton with Global Value Chains" (2008) 37 *Economy and Society* 420–451.

[38] Electronic News, "US Could Lose Race for Nanotech Leadership, SIA Panels Says," Electronic News, March 16, 2008, available at: www.nanotech-now.com/news.cgi?story_id=08495 (last accessed February 22, 2011).

NNI budget was $1.2 billion, just 11 percent of the $10.6 billion that Intel spent on stock repurchases in that year alone. Indeed, Intel's 2005 expenditures on stock buybacks exceed the total of $10.1 billion that has been spent on NNI since its inception in 2001 through 2009.[39] Given the extent to which the ICT industry in general, and a company like Intel in particular, has benefited from decades of government investments in the high-tech knowledge base, one might ask whether a portion of the massive funds that Intel allocates to buying back its own stock could not be more productively allocated "to ensure that America continues to be the world leader in information technology."

Among the largest repurchasers of stock in the 2000s have been pharmaceutical companies. For 2000–2008 Pfizer was the #7 repurchaser with $50.6 billion in buybacks, Johnson & Johnson #12 with $33.3 billion, Amgen #24 with $22.6 billion and Merck #31 with $18.7 billion. These and other US pharmaceutical companies charge higher drug prices in the United States than in other rich nations such as Japan, Canada and France because, their executives argue, they need the higher earnings to fund their R&D efforts in the United States. Yet the very same companies do massive stock buybacks for the sole purpose of manipulating their stock prices. Meanwhile, the United States is the world leader in biopharmaceuticals in large part because of $31 billion per annum that the National Institutes of Health spends (as of 2009) in support of the life sciences knowledge base, as well as numerous government subsidies to the pharmaceutical industry, including those under the Orphan Drug Act of 1983.[40] Instead of doing stock buybacks, the pharmaceutical companies could be contributing to the national life sciences effort, or lowering their drug prices to make their products more affordable to the American public.

There has been virtually no public policy debate in the United States over the practice of buybacks, its acceleration in recent years, or the implications for innovation, employment, income distribution and economic growth. Exceptionally, in the summer of 2008 four Congressional Democrats took aim at stock repurchases by the big oil companies, after Exxon Mobil, by far the largest repurchaser of stock

---

[39] The NNI budget was $1,554 million in 2008 and $1,695 million in 2009, and an estimated $1,781 million for 2010 (www.nano.gov/html/about/funding.html (last accessed February 22, 2011)).

[40] William Lazonick and Öner Tulum, "US Biopharmaceutical Finance and the Crisis of the Bioltech Indusry" (2009) *University of Massachusetts Lowell Center for Industrial Competitiveness* 1–32, at 12–13.

($144 billion in 2000–2008), had announced record second quarter profits of $11.7 billion, of which $8.8 billion went to stock buybacks.[41] In a letter to oil industry executives, the Congressmen asked them to "pledge to greatly increase the ratio of investments in production and alternatives to the amount of stock buybacks this year and next by investing much more of your profits into exploration and production on the leases you have been awarded in the U.S., and in the research and development of promising alternative energy sources."[42] Exxon Mobil did not pay much attention to this plea; in the last half of 2008 it repurchased another $17.5 billion for a total of $35.7 billion, or 79 percent of its net income, on the year. In the first three-quarters of 2009 Exxon Mobil did another $17.3 billion in buybacks, equivalent to 131 percent of its net income.

Recently, the United States engaged in a debate over health care reform, with the companies that provide health insurance in the forefront of opposition to progressive change, including the availability of a "public option" that would provide households with an alternative source of health insurance to that offered by the business corporations. Among the top fifty repurchasers for 2000–2008 were the two largest corporate health insurers: UnitedHealth Group at #23 with $23.7 billion in buybacks and Wellpoint at #39 with $14.9 billion.[43] For each of these companies, repurchases represented 104 percent of net income for 2000–2008. Over this period, repurchases by the third largest insurer, Aetna, were $9.7 billion, or 137 percent of net income, and the fifth largest, Cigna, $9.8 billion, or 125 percent of net income. Meanwhile the top executives of these companies typically reaped millions of dollars, and in many years tens of millions of dollars, in gains from exercising stock options. A serious attempt at health care reform would seek to eliminate the profits of these health insurers, given that these profits are used solely to manipulate stock prices and enrich a small number of people at the top.

---

[41] US Congress, "Democrats Tell Big Oil: Spend More on Production and Renewable Energy, Less on Stock Buybacks Before Making Demands for New Drilling Leases," US Congressional Documents and Publications, July 31, 2008, available at: http://menendez.senate.gov/newsroom/record.cfm?id=301639 (last accessed February 22, 2011).

[42] US Congress, "Democrats Tell Big Oil: Spend More on Production and Renewable Energy."

[43] William Lazonick, "Insurance Executives: A Big Part of Our Healthcare Problem," *The Huffington Post*, March 16, 2010, available at: www.huffingtonpost.com/william-lazonick/insurance-executives-a-bi_b_501093.html (last accessed February 22, 2011).

V Fighting financialization

In the United States, the problem of exploding executive pay has been around for a long time, and virtually nothing has been done about it. Indeed, in his 2008 book, *Supercapitalism*, Robert Reich, former Secretary of Labor in the Clinton administration and in general a critic of "financialization," justifies the explosion in executive pay by arguing that intense competition makes it much more difficult to find the talent who can manage a large corporation than it used to be.[44] In an interview in February 2010, President Barack Obama was quoted as saying that paying top corporate executives in stock rather than cash is a "fairer way of measuring CEO success and ultimately will make the performance of American business better." Referring specifically to the outsized remuneration of Lloyd Blankfein, CEO of Goldman Sachs and Jamie Dimon, CEO of JP Morgan, Obama went on to say: "I know both those guys; they are very savvy businessmen. And I, like most of the American people, don't begrudge people success or wealth. That is part of the free-market system."[45]

The one attempt in the 1990s by Democrats to control the rise of executive pay ended up doing just the opposite. In 1993, after Bill Clinton became President of the United States, his administration implemented a campaign promise to legislate a cap of $1 million on the amount of nonperformance-related, top-executive compensation that could be claimed as a corporate tax deduction. One perverse result of this law was that companies that were paying their CEOs less than $1 million in salary and bonus *raised* these components of CEO pay toward $1 million, which was now taken as the government-approved "CEO minimum wage." The other perverse result was that companies increased CEO stock-option awards, for which tax deductions were not in any case being claimed, as an alternative to exceeding the $1 million salary-and-bonus cap.[46]

A further irony of the Clinton legislation was that the high-tech lobby at the time was fighting against an attempt by the Financial Accounting Standards Board (FASB) to require companies to expense stock options. Especially for companies with broad-based stock-option

---

[44] Robert B. Reich, *Supercapitalism: The Transformation of Business, Democracy, and Everyday Life* (New York: Alfred A. Knopf, 2007), pp. 105–114.
[45] Jim Kuhnhenn, "Obama on CEO Bonuses: He doesn't 'Begrudge' Wealth; Compares to Athletes' Pay," Associated Press Newswires, February 10, 2010, available at:www.ksdk.com/news/local/story.aspx?storyid=195727 (last accessed February 22, 2011).
[46] John A. Byrne, "That's Some Pay Cap, Bill," *Business Week*, April 25, 1994, p. 57; John A. Byrne, "CEO Pay: Ready for Takeoff," *Business Week*, April 24, 1995, p. 87.

plans, this prospective regulatory change would have resulted in lower reported earnings that, it was thought, would result in lower stock prices. Hence, even though the proposed FASB regulation (which was ultimately decreed in 2004) would have reduced the corporate tax bill, corporate executives were against it. Why would these same executives have given much thought to the fact that there would be no *corporate* tax deductions for personal pay that exceeded the million-dollar cap?

Then as now, it is futile to talk about placing restrictions on executive compensation without limiting the extent to which executives can reap gains from stock options that result from either speculation or manipulation. Besides making manipulative stock repurchases illegal, legislation is needed to place limits on stock-option grants to individuals and to make the gains from the exercise of stock options dependent on achieving a variety of performance goals, including first and foremost ongoing contributions to high-quality job creation in the United States.

Economic activity entails both the creation of value, as goods and services are produced, and the extraction of value, as goods and services are consumed. Investment in innovation creates the potential for higher standards of living for those who contribute to the innovation process. Inequity occurs when certain groups in the economy – for example, top corporate executives – use their control over resource allocation to extract more than they create. Instability occurs when this excessive value extraction undermines innovation, and with it the potential for higher standards of living for the broader population. It is my contention that in the United States in the 2000s the stock-based compensation of corporate executives is a prime source of this instability, and the stock buyback is their most powerful "weapon of value extraction." Indeed, my research suggests that, by undermining innovation, stock repurchases have become "weapons of value destruction." Corporate stock repurchases should be banned, and stock-based compensation should be controlled so that executives cannot gain from speculation on and manipulation of the stock market. If not, we can expect that executive pay will continue to explode, and that, for lack of innovation and high-quality job creation, American prosperity will continue to erode.

19 Products, perimeters and politics: systemic risk and securities regulation

Mary Condon

I Introduction

Ever since Beck's observation that we live in a "risk society," the role of risk in structuring the activities of policy-makers and profit-seeking organizations has become ever more prominent.[1] A number of analysts have noted how risk management is a central preoccupation of businesses of all kinds, orienting both their internal activities and their external relations with their "stakeholders."[2] Indeed to the extent that the phenomenal growth of derivatives and credit default swap (CDS) trading is argued to have been one contributory factor in the global financial crisis of 2007–2009 (GFC), these financial products were sold to so-called "end user" businesses (airlines, commodities producers, etc.) as a risk mitigation strategy. As many have pointed out since the advent of the GFC, the financial services firms who packaged and sold these products appeared less adept at engaging in their own internal risk mitigation processes.[3]

Meanwhile "risk-based regulation" has increasingly captured the imagination of regulators, whether because of directives from politicians – as in the UK – as a response to resource shortages, or because it became synonymous with "smart regulation."[4] A number of commentators have observed that structuring regulatory activities in terms of a hierarchy of risk requires a different stance from a more traditional

---

[1] U. Beck, *Risk Society: Towards a New Modernity* (London: Sage Publications, 1992).
[2] M. Power, "Risk Management and the Responsible Organization," in R. Ericson and A. Doyle (eds.), *Risk and Morality* (Toronto: University of Toronto Press, 2003); M. Power, *Organized Uncertainty: Designing a World of Risk Management* (Oxford: Oxford University Press, 2007); B. Hutter, "Understanding the New Regulatory Governance: Business Perspectives," under review at *Law and Policy*.
[3] IOSCO, "Unregulated Financial Markets and Products," Final Report, September 2009, p. 12.
[4] J. Black and R. Baldwin, "Risk-Based Regulation" (2010) 32 *Law and Policy* 182; P. O'Malley, "Neoliberalism and Risk in Criminology," University of Sydney Legal Studies Research Paper, Sydney, Australia (September 2009), p. 1.

regulatory preoccupation with uniform adherence to legal norms.[5] Despite its increasing popularity as a form of meta-regulation,[6] Black and Baldwin point out that the risk-based regulation operationalized by the Financial Services Authority in the UK took part of the blame for a regulatory failure to protect the public during the GFC.[7] The attempt to identify which institutions and activities posed the most risk to the regulatory system with a view to concentrating regulatory effort there does not appear to have worked particularly well in the UK. Despite the lack of a ringing endorsement for contemporary practices of risk-based regulation, the discourse of "systemic risk" has nonetheless emerged as central to the activities of policy-makers and politicians globally in the wake of the financial crisis.

This chapter will probe the contours of the emergence of the language of systemic risk into broad public discourse. In particular I examine the encounter between this overarching discourse and a particular pre-existing subfield of financial regulation, that of securities regulation. In most jurisdictions, the scope of securities regulation (which begins by defining a "security"[8]) revolves around the regulation of the information disclosure provided to investors by issuers of securities, as well as the regulation of intermediaries interposed between buyers and sellers of securities (such as investment bankers, brokers, mutual fund salespeople, and in some cases, advisors), and the organized markets on which securities trade. Even more specifically, given that the financial crisis was global and continues to have global effects, I want to focus on the interaction between the discourse of systemic risk and the major institution involved in global securities governance, the International Organization of Securities Commissions (IOSCO). A brief account of IOSCO is provided in Section IV.

The chapter will proceed as follows: Section II will briefly describe the contours of the emerging architecture of international financial regulation following the GFC; Section III will attempt to describe the variety of meanings associated with the idea of systemic risk; Section IV will chart the initiatives begun by IOSCO to respond to the concern about systemic risk; Section V will speculate on the implications of

---

[5] Black and Baldwin, "Risk-Based Regulation," p. 184; Power, *Organized Uncertainty*; M. Condon, "Comparative Models of Risk-based Financial Services," Research Study (Project #5), Ontario Expert Commission on Pensions, 2007.
[6] B. Morgan, *Social Citizenship in the Shadow of Competition: The Bureaucratic Politics of Regulatory Justification* (Aldershot: Ashgate Press, 2003).
[7] Black and Baldwin, "Risk-Based Regulation," p. 182.
[8] The most traditional forms of security are company shares, units of trusts and debt instruments such as bonds and debentures.

the rise of systemic risk regulation for securities regulators and market participants. In particular it will address the possible repercussions of a shift to systemic risk for existing philosophies of securities regulation, such as its disclosure orientation, and the current debate about the role of so-called "new governance" or principles-based approaches to regulation.

II   The politics of international financial regulation

The GFC has prompted a great deal of attention to domestic and international arrangements for regulating the financial system, both in terms of the policy initiatives that needed to be embarked on, and the regulatory structures required to implement them. With respect to the latter, observations of domestic regulatory structures revealed that arrangements varied widely from jurisdiction to jurisdiction, with some having different regulatory arrangements for banking, insurance, securities markets and commodities markets, and others consolidating the regulation of the whole financial system into a single regulatory institution. The US represented probably the most extreme version of fragmentation of financial regulation, with a multiplicity of regulators at both the federal and state level responsible for portions of the financial system, while the UK had for almost a decade consolidated its financial regulatory arrangements in a single regulator.[9]

Both of these jurisdictions have embarked on far reaching legislative reform in the financial sector in the last several years. While the mosaic of US financial regulators has remained largely intact,[10] the UK is in the midst of dividing regulatory authority for components of the financial system among a number of new regulatory entities. These may include a new Financial Policy Committee of the Bank of England, a Prudential Regulatory Authority, a Consumer Protection and Markets Authority, and an Economic Crime Agency.

Meanwhile if the GFC was understood to require a direct political response from domestic legislators to stabilize their financial systems and their economies more generally, high priority was also given to

---

[9] It should be noted that this does not take account of the Bank of England's role in setting monetary policy.
[10] The Dodd–Frank Act abolishes the Office of Thrift Supervision and redistributes its functions among the Federal Reserve, the OCC and the FDIC (Davis Polk memo, July 2010, pp. 89–91 available at: www.davispolk.com/files/Publication/7084f9fe-6580–413b-b870-b7c025ed2ecf/Presentation/PublicationAttachment/1d4495c7-0be0–4e9a-ba77-f786fb90464a/070910_Financial_Reform_Summary.pdf (last accessed February 22, 2011)).

attempts to coordinate that response across jurisdictions. The G-20[11] group quickly emerged as the primary vehicle for attempts at high-level coordination of financial policy responses internationally.[12] It sponsored the further study of a variety of policy issues by the legacy international financial organizations (Bank of International Settlements [BIS], Basle Committee on Banking Supervision [BCBS], International Organization of Securities Commissions [IOSCO]) as well as a number of new networks of international and domestic regulators established following the crisis. These new networks include the Joint Forum (whose members are the BCBS, IOSCO and the International Association of Insurance Supervisors [IAIS]) and the European Systemic Risk Board. Domestically, there are similar proposals to establish entities such as the Financial Stability Oversight Council in the United States[13] and the Financial Policy Committee in the UK. It should be noted that, despite attempts at a coordinated approach, on some relevant policy issues (such as the regulation of credit rating agencies [CRAs]), schisms have appeared in the regulatory approaches preferred by North American policy-makers as opposed to those in the EU.[14]

The overarching issue that united, and justified attention to, a wide range of policy initiatives as well as the reformulation of the regulatory architecture for the financial system was the problem of systemic risk. Here the G-20 recommended that each of the IASB, BCBS, IAIS and IOSCO all take responsibility for this problem in their respective financial spheres, so that forms of regulatory response to systemic risk will become dispersed across a variety of international bodies. This raises challenging issues of coordination among those bodies, not to mention baseline issues of definitional and philosophical consistency. For example, a number of commentators have argued that the preferred philosophical stance of banking regulators toward the entities they regulate tends to be facilitative and cooperative, while focused substantively on ensuring the maintenance of adequate capital to support a typical bank's multiplicity of activities. Meanwhile, it is argued that the

---

[11] The members of the G-20 are: Argentina, Australia, Brazil, Canada, China, France, Germany, India, Indonesia, Italy, Japan, Mexico, Russia, Saudi Arabia, South Africa, South Korea, Turkey, the United Kingdom, the United States and the EU. See www.g20.org (last accessed February 22, 2011).

[12] J. Koppel, *World Rule: Accountability, Legitimacy, and the Design of Global Governance* (Chicago: University of Chicago Press, 2010).

[13] This council will be made up of ten federal financial regulators, an independent member and five non-voting members.

[14] S. Rousseau, "Regulating Credit Rating Agencies after the Financial Crisis: The Long and Winding Road toward Accountability," (2009), available at: http://papers.ssrn.com/sol3/papers.cfm?abstract_id=1456708 (last accessed February 22, 2011).

core mandate of securities regulators is capable of being more adversarial toward market participants in the interests of advancing a more explicit consumer protection mandate.[15] Thus, systemic risk has traditionally been seen as more consistent with the concerns of banking regulators, whereas securities regulators have tended to focus instead on the supposed "balance" to be drawn between achieving efficiency in capital raising and the operation of securities markets on the one hand, and protecting investors in the context of securities transactions on the other.[16]

III What is systemic risk anyway?

One interesting dimension of the emerging literature on systemic risk is how the definition ranges from the possibility of cataclysmic collapse of a whole financial system at one end of the spectrum to "increases in the cost of capital" on the other.[17] Thus, Karmel argues that "systemic risk is risk to an entire financial system or market, as opposed to the collapse of one firm within that market. This risk comes about because firms price only internal costs and benefits and not risks to the financial system."[18] Meanwhile, the Bank of International Settlements defines the term as the "risk that the failure of a participant to meet its contractual obligations may in turn cause other participants to default with a chain reaction leading to broader financial difficulties." Embedded here is the idea of an individual default or some other kind of trigger event having a domino-like effect on the stability of the broader financial system.

Schwartz's definition likewise focuses on a trigger event (economic shock or failure of a key institution), which causes a domino effect.[19] However, the risks to be avoided could encompass, for some

---

[15] E. Pan, "Structural Reform of Financial Regulation in Canada," A Research Study Prepared for the Expert Panel on Securities Regulation, 2009, available at:www.cardozo.yu.edu/pan (last accessed February 27, 2011); M. Condon, "Canadian Securities Regulation and the Global Financial Crisis" (2010) 42 *University of British Columbia Law Review* 489–490.
[16] See, for example, Ontario Securities Act s.1.1 where the purposes of the Act are identified as being (a) to "provide protection to investors from unfair, improper or fraudulent practices" and (b) "to foster fair and efficient capital markets and confidence in capital markets." Meanwhile the proposed Canadian Securities Act includes as one of three listed purposes the reduction of systemic risks.
[17] S. Schwartz, "Systemic Risk" (2008) 97 *Georgetown Law Journal* 198–199.
[18] R. Karmel, "The Controversy over Systemic Risk Regulation," Legal Studies Paper No. 179, Brooklyn Law School, Brooklyn, New York (2010), p. 4, available at: http://papers.ssrn.com/sol3/papers.cfm?abstract_id=1540691 (last accessed February 22, 2011).
[19] Schwartz, "Systemic Risk," p. 198.

commentators, both a decrease in the availability of capital or an increase in the cost of capital. Yet including an increasing cost of capital as a systemic risk to be managed or avoided is arguably casting the net too broadly, since a number of regulatory requirements in the securities area, now regarded as best practice, were initially resisted by market participants on the basis that they would increase the cost of raising capital.[20] This includes much of the apparatus of disclosure requirements imposed on issuers of securities. Schwartz points out that historically the regulation of systemic risk has focused largely on "preventing bank failure."

As a result of the GFC, however, the sources of systemic risk are taken to have broadened considerably. In a policy paper issued in early 2010, the Joint Forum (JF) provides a list of "major sources of systemic risk" on which it proposes to focus. These include: regulatory differences across financial sectors; supervision of financial groups; mortgage origination; hedge funds; and credit risk transfer products.[21] With respect to the first of these sources, the JF report notes that securities regulators are unique because of their mandate to regulate *markets* as well as institutions. On the other hand, securities regulators tend not to regulate their market participant *firms* on a group-wide as opposed to an individual basis, unlike many banking or insurance regulators. It is notable that the JF report also includes complex financial *products* such as mortgage products (asset-backed securities [ABS])[22] and credit risk transfer products (such as CDS and financial guarantee insurance) in its scoping of the sources of systemic risk. It is likely that the inclusion of both products and markets as sources of systemic risk is due to the involvement of IOSCO on the Joint Forum. However, both the academic and policy commentary reveals a lack of precision about the nature of systemic risk.

IV   The role of IOSCO in defining systemic risk

Roberta Karmel argues that the emergence of systemic risk as a key problem to be solved sparked a turf war among financial regulators in

---

[20] M. Condon, *Making Disclosure: Ideas and Interests in Ontario Securities Regulation* (Toronto: University of Toronto Press, 1998), pp. 64–66, 177–180.
[21] Joint Forum, "Review of the Differentiated Nature and Scope of Financial Regulation. Key Issues and Recommendations," Report, Bank for International Settlements (2010), p. 1, available at: www.bis.org/publ/joint24.htm (last accessed February 22, 2011).
[22] Here it singles out for attention the issue of the quality of underwriting of the component mortgages (i.e. origination) as a key issue in a "sound securitization" process.

the United States, a system that was already highly fragmented and disaggregated.²³ It is arguable that the same is evident at the international financial regulatory level. From the perspective of the IOSCO, it is possible to see that the organization has seized an opportunity to reinvent itself in the wake of the GFC and to emphasize its relevance. Thus, a number of recent speeches by high-ranking IOSCO officials have characterized the need for effective market regulation as the "virtuous twin" of prudential regulation.

The IOSCO was created in 1983 out of an earlier inter-American regional association, and a permanent General Secretariat for it was established in 1986. Over 100 jurisdictions are now members of the organization. There are three categories of membership: ordinary membership is open to a securities commission or similar government or statutory body; associate membership is open to public regulators of sub-national jurisdictions if the national regulatory body is also a member; affiliates are self-regulatory organizations, such as stock exchanges.²⁴ Only ordinary members have votes in the President's Committee, which meets annually.

The work of the IOSCO is accomplished through a number of committees. As noted above, the President's Committee is made up of all the members. The Executive Committee has nineteen members, including the Chairs of the Technical and Emerging Markets Committees, as well as the four regional committees. The Technical and Emerging Markets Committees are the two main "working committees" of the IOSCO. The Technical Committee (TC) approaches its review of major regulatory issues by dividing its work into six major subject areas,²⁵ while the Emerging Markets Committee (EMC) promotes the development of emerging markets, with similar working groups as the TC. Since the IOSCO has only a small permanent secretariat, much of the substantive work of these committees is accomplished by senior regulatory staff of domestic securities regulators from different jurisdictions. One of the IOSCO's overarching concerns is to promote greater regulatory convergence among its members. To this end, the work of the IOSCO revolves around the promulgation of policy papers and recommendations on securities market related issues. As will be discussed later in

---

[23] Karmel, "Systemic Risk Regulation," p. 1.
[24] The membership fee for all categories is 15,000 euro as at February 22, 2011. See www.iosco.org/about/index.cfm?section=membership (last accessed February 22, 2011).
[25] These are: multinational disclosure and accounting; regulation of secondary markets; regulation of market intermediaries; enforcement and exchange of information; investment management; credit rating agencies.

this chapter, the best practice recommendations of the IOSCO are taken up to varying degrees in different jurisdictions, although it is notable that the International Monetary Fund has begun to reference the extent of domestic compliance with IOSCO standards in the individual country reports it prepares. Apart from its policy work, the IOSCO also considers its Multilateral Memorandum of Understanding (MMOU), an enforcement-related protocol for information sharing among jurisdictions, to be one of its major achievements to date.

The current Secretary General of the IOSCO, Greg Tanzer, in a speech in May 2010, was quite explicit about characterizing the GFC as having had a transformative effect on the IOSCO. The GFC converted the IOSCO from being engaged in "a niche activity focused primarily on the needs of securities regulators, with a resolute focus on securities markets issues" to an organization with a radically different outlook involving being drawn into "the wider global effort to tackle the ills ravaging the financial system."[26] This includes the building of a "more resilient" financial system by way of building investor confidence.

In particular it appears that the IOSCO explicitly set itself the task of alerting the G-20 to the views of securities regulators on a number of issues, as "there had been a risk that solving the financial crisis was being viewed solely through the prism of assisting failing banks and insurers with insufficient regard to the need for an equal emphasis on the effective regulation of markets." Thus IOSCO Secretary General Tanzer points out that:

it was in the markets that much of the underlying behaviours that led to the crisis actually occurred, including the conflicts of interest, the profligate lending, excessive leveraging, inappropriate valuations, overvalued securitisations, off balance sheet vehicles, and extravagant compensation ... In other words, markets matter for systemic stability.[27]

This laundry list of ills in the capital markets certainly provides a broad policy canvas on which securities regulators may now paint, though it presumably also leaves them open to some culpability for this state of affairs having arisen in the first place.[28]

Meanwhile, the IOSCO's own working definition of systemic risk is a broad one, reminiscent of the slippage noted above between cataclysmic

---

[26] G. Tanzer, "The International Organization of Securities Commissions and the Future of Securities Regulation," Speech to Russian National Association of Securities Market Participants, May 12, 2010, available at: www.iosco.org/library/speeches/pdf/IOSCOSP04–10.pdf (last accessed February 27, 2011).
[27] Ibid.
[28] Black and Baldwin, "Risk-Based Regulation," p. 182.

events at one end of the spectrum and more arguably run-of-the-mill inadequacies on the other. Thus, Tanzer in May 2010 also says:

> In formulating its new Principles on Systemic Risk IOSCO has adopted the approach of viewing systemic risk as any widespread adverse impact on the financial system, and thereby the wider economy, caused by the design, distribution or behaviour under stressed conditions of certain investment products; the activities or failure of a regulated entity; a market disruption; or the impairment of a market's integrity. Systemic risk can also take the form of a more gradual erosion of market trust posed by inadequate protection standards, lax enforcement, or insufficient disclosure requirements.

The latter part of this definition places securities regulators front and center as primary contributors to the reduction of systemic risk. The IOSCO advises domestic securities regulators to continue to have processes in place to mitigate and manage risks and that "areas that require specific attention in this respect relate to investor protection, market integrity and the proper adherence to conduct of business standards." These are areas that are typically very familiar to domestic securities regulators and are generally consistent with their pre-GFC mandates. Tanzer further advises regulators to consider whether their "existing powers, operational structure and regulations are sufficient to meet any emerging risks" and to continue to monitor this. The IOSCO is clearly setting the stage here for a robust understanding of the role of securities regulators in solving the problems of the GFC.

Recent IOSCO deliberations on systemic risk in a transnational context

One of the major outcomes of the 2010 IOSCO annual meeting in Montreal was an "increased focus" on systemic risk by that organization. This development, according to Jane Diplock, the Chair of IOSCO's Executive Committee, accomplishes "a significant reform of the basis for global securities regulation."[29] It involves domestic securities regulators being encouraged to monitor and manage systemic risk, and to regularly review the "perimeter" of regulation. As discussed below, one manifestation of this is a new focus on the regulation of derivative products, which had tended not to be subject to regulation by securities regulators. IOSCO is also focused on a commitment to robust

---

[29] J. Diplock, "The Work of IOSCO and the Financial Regulatory Framework," Speech at the Global Financial Crisis Conference, Bond University, April 9, 2010, available at: www.sec-com.govt.nz/speeches/2010/090410.shtml (last accessed February 22, 2011).

clearing and settlement systems for derivatives trading and implicitly, to move over the counter (OTC) transactions into centralized clearing systems to the extent possible.

Overall, IOSCO recommends increased attention to markets as a location of systemic risk. It argues that "investor protection, market integrity, transparency and the proper conduct of business within markets (are) contributing factors to reducing systemic risk." The connection between markets and systemic risk implies a number of specific policy projects such as attention to the role of auditors, CRAs, entities offering analytical or evaluative services to investors, and hedge funds. Going forward, IOSCO has struck a "working group" on systemic risk to develop a discussion paper on the role of securities regulators with respect to systemic risk, as well as another group whose mandate is to "develop new IOSCO principles for disclosure ... for ABS."

Even prior to summer 2010, IOSCO's committees had been actively engaged in preparing policy recommendations touching on various aspects of the causes of the GFC. Such reports include both a consultation and a final report dealing with unregulated financial markets and products,[30] consultation and final reports on transparency of structured financial products[31] and more recently a report from the Emerging Markets Committee on OTC markets and derivatives trading in emerging markets.[32] We will see later that IOSCO also has an ongoing project dealing with hedge funds. Before providing a brief summary of the recommendations made in these various reports, one general point worth noting is that these reports collectively represent an enhanced concern for the regulation of investment *products*, in recognition of the increased variety and complexity of financial instruments now available to investors.

The UFMP final report focuses on two types of financial instrument, securitized products (including ABS, asset-backed commercial paper [ABCP], collateralized debt obligations [CDOs] and collateralized loan

[30] IOSCO, "Unregulated Financial Markets and Products," Consultation Report, May 2009, available at: www.iosco.org/library/pubdocs/pdf/IOSCOPD290.pdf (last accessed February 22, 2011); IOSCO, "Unregulated Financial Markets and Products," Final Report, September 2009, available at: www.iosco.org/library/pubdocs/pdf/IOSCOPD301.pdf (last accessed February 22, 2011).
[31] IOSCO, "Transparency of Structured Finance Products," Consultation Report, September 2009, available at: www.iosco.org/library/pubdocs/pdf/IOSCOPD306.pdf (last accessed February 22, 2011); IOSCO, "Transparency of Structured Finance Products," Final Report, July 2010, available at: www.iosco.org/library/pubdocs/pdf/IOSCOPD326.pdf (last accessed February 22, 2011).
[32] IOSCO, "OTC Markets and Derivatives Trading in Emerging Markets," Final Report, July 2010, available at: www.iosco.org/library/pubdocs/pdf/IOSCOPD330.pdf (last accessed February 22, 2011).

obligation [CLOs]) and CDSs. With respect to the former category of financial instrument, the Technical Committee which authored the Final Report identified three issues to address: (1) wrong incentives, (2) inadequate risk management practices and (3) regulatory structure and oversight issues. With respect to incentive issues, the Technical Committee encouraged domestic regulators to consider carefully the introduction of a retention requirement for securitized products (the idea that sponsors of the sale of securitized products should retain an ownership interest themselves), and should consider it alongside other recommendations being made dealing with enhanced disclosure, transparency and investor suitability. On the topic of enhanced disclosure, the Final Report encourages regulators to ensure that issuers render transparent to investors all verification and risk assurance practices that have been undertaken by the underwriter, sponsor and/or originator of the securitized investment vehicle. Finally, to acknowledge the possibility that investors might not have the capability to undertake an assessment of these products, the Report recommends that domestic regulators pay attention to the adequacy of their investor suitability standards and to consider strengthening them. Meanwhile, with respect to CDSs, the UFMP final report focuses on the need to establish central counterparties (CCP) to clear standardized CDSs, and to facilitate appropriate and timely disclosure of CDS data with respect to price, volume and interest levels.

In July 2010, the Emerging Markets Committee issued a report on OTC markets and derivatives trading in emerging markets. This report provided data on the use of derivatives and the extent of OTC trading in a number of emerging market jurisdictions and the regulatory issues that emerge from this data. The Report found that by far the most frequent type of derivative contract entered into, in the emerging markets studied, was interest rate contracts.[33] While ultimately this report included a recommendation that regulators should ensure that financial intermediaries trading in OTC derivatives have minimum regulatory capital, competent personnel, technical infrastructure and robust risk management standards, it argued that "investor protection can be achieved by full disclosure of information regarding all kinds of financial products to investors and especially applying a suitability test for

---

[33] This category had $449,793 billion of notional amounts outstanding, as compared to the next biggest identified category of $49,196 billion for foreign exchange contracts. The unallocated category amounted to $73,456 billion.

each of the investors." Interestingly, the report noted that "the most important implication" of the survey it conducted of emerging market regulators was "the data problem." Few jurisdictions could provide the data requested by the IOSCO committee, thus preventing a clear appreciation of "overall risk positions" in the OTC markets.

V Implications of systemic risk for securities regulation

What does the discovery of systemic risk by securities regulators mean for their existing practices and discourses? As indicated above, there are a wide variety of policy interventions possible for both domestic and international securities regulators in the name of systemic risk, including: regulation of the securitization process; regulation of the availability of specific financial products including derivatives; regulation of hedge funds using strategies such as registration, disclosure or conflict of interest requirements; the imposition of leverage limits on market participants; enhanced stability of clearing and settlement processes.

In general, the concept of systemic risk does seem to have given securities regulators a new legitimacy, and as we have seen above, IOSCO officials are acutely conscious of this. In particular, the idea that regulators should police the "perimeter of regulation" suggests a political and policy-maker willingness to contemplate increasing the ambit of regulation in the name of capturing activities that are designed strategically to avoid regulatory oversight. The mantra of deregulation seems to be deeply unpopular, if it ever was a feature of the financial regulatory landscape.[34] However several challenging issues arise from the marriage of securities regulation and systemic risk.

The future of disclosure: it seems likely that the discovery of systemic risk will have implications for the long-established commitment to *disclosure of information* as the central organizing principle of securities regulation. Domestic securities regulators have tended to operate on the assumption that if information is disclosed, investors can and should make their own individually-rational investment decisions. In this connection, we should pause to reflect on the point made earlier, which is that the GFC has prompted securities regulators to pay more attention to complex investment *products*. The disclosure orientation of securities regulation has historically operated from the perspective that issuers issue well-known types of financial instruments with similar properties (shares or bonds), so that what investors need is issuer-specific information, so

---

[34] J. Braithwaite, *Regulatory Capitalism: How it Works, Ideas for Making it Work Better* (Cheltenham: Edward Elgar Publishing, 2008).

as to assess the long-term prospects that their investment will prosper. In a financialized context in which complex investment products are sliced, diced and given different risk ratings according to underlying assets and other factors, the capacity of investors to understand any amount of disclosure provided about the product is questionable. At the least, the GFC has produced a need to reorient the disclosure strategies employed by securities regulators away from a focus on issuing firms and toward more fine-grained understanding of the features of investment products.

A related point is that it does seem likely that effective systemic risk regulation will require a robust commitment to market-wide data collection by regulators, as well as a capacity to interpret that data for surveillance purposes.[35] This process has been set in motion by IOSCO's Technical Committee with respect to the operations of hedge funds.[36] The Committee has issued a template for information collection by domestic regulators about the operations of hedge funds. It covers information such as, who the managers and service providers of the hedge funds are; fund performance; assets under management; asset class concentration; geographic exposure; liquidity of assets; extent of borrowing; credit counterparty exposure. While the data is being collected from individual funds, it is intended that it will be *aggregated* so that the information can be used by regulators to understand market trends and products as opposed to the historic commitment of securities regulation to issuer or firm-specific disclosure. Given IOSCO's access to domestic regulatory arrangements across the globe, it will clearly have a significant role to play in maintaining the infrastructure of this global market-wide data collection.[37] However the collection of such data raises the question of the capacities of securities regulators to interpret it so as to uncover whether systemic risks are present. This change in orientation for securities regulators will require them to augment the professional skill sets generally possessed by their staff, which often revolve around legal and accounting training.

More generally, the question may be posed as to what extent disclosure *can* be an adequate response to solving the systemic risk problems

---

[35] A. Lo, "The Feasibility of Systemic Risk Measurement," Written Testimony of Andrew Lo prepared for the US House of Representatives Financial Services Committee, Washington, DC (October 19, 2009).

[36] IOSCO, "International Regulators Publish Systemic Risk Data Requirements for Hedge Funds" media release, February 25, 2010, available at: www.iosco.org/news/pdf/IOSCONEWS179.pdf (last accessed February 22, 2011).

[37] In the United States the Dodd–Frank legislation has established an Office of Financial Research which is intended to support the collection and standardization of financial data, to conduct economic analysis and specifically to develop tools for risk management and monitoring.

enumerated by IOSCO as well as domestic policy-makers? Can systemic risk be contained primarily by requiring more disclosure of information about hitherto undisclosed activities, processes or products? It is the case that a disclosure strategy is the core of the proposals made domestically in the United States for the enhanced regulation of OTC derivatives trading (requiring such transactions to be submitted to a clearing agency), though exceptions to this requirement are also possible for "commercial end-users."[38] Similarly, IOSCO's Standing Committee on the Regulation of Secondary Markets has proposed an enhanced level of post-trade transparency for SFPs, in part because it was most consistent with a pre-existing regulatory commitment to transparency in the operation of markets.

Yet the debate about retention of "skin in the game" as a way of reducing risk-taking by originators of asset-backed securities suggests a willingness to go beyond disclosure, to orchestrate specific ownership parameters for ABS. On this issue, US legislators have been prepared to go further than the IOSCO, by prescribing levels of economic interest that must be retained by the originator. The IOSCO's report on this issue, noted above, simply exhorts domestic regulators to give this issue close attention. Similarly in some jurisdictions there has been a lively debate on the nature of incentive structures within financial services firms as highly relevant to the events that led to the GFC. This is also a thorny area for securities regulators, not just because compensation issues have tended to be framed in the United States and Canada as a matter of corporate law,[39] but because the trading-based incentive structures that are argued to have contributed to failures of risk management within financial firms reach further into organizations than regulators have up to now been prepared to venture.[40] Here it should be noted that under the Dodd–Frank legislation, the SEC along with other US federal regulators are empowered to prescribe rules prohibiting

---

[38] Davis Polk, "Summary of Dodd-Frank Wall Street Reform and Consumer Protection Act," p. 57. July 21, 2010 available at: www.davispolk.com/files/Publication/7084f9fe-6580–413b-b870-b7c025ed2ecf/Presentation/PublicationAttachment/1d4495c7-0be0–4e9a-ba77-f786fb90464a/070910_Financial_Reform_Summary.pdf (last accessed February 22, 2011).

[39] In the United States compensation issues have been framed as a matter of *state* corporate law, with federal jurisdiction centering around the role of the SEC in requiring disclosure of compensation levels for top executives. With respect to this approach, some commentators have argued that the effect of these SEC-imposed disclosure requirements has typically been to facilitate increases in executive compensation over time. In Canada, disclosure of compensation, imposed via securities law norms, has been limited to key executives.

[40] B. Sharfman, "Moving Beyond the Dodd-Frank Act: Reducing Systemic Risk by Cooling Wall Street's Bonus Culture," Working Paper (August 9, 2010) pp. 6–7, available at: http://ssrn.com/abstract=1623022 (last accessed February 22, 2011).

incentive-based executive compensation arrangements that encourage inappropriate risks or facilitate material financial loss.[41] Sharfman recommends the use of the tax system to discourage "front-end loaded" bonus plans as compensation for employees in financial firms.

Market participants and systemic risk: the concern raised above about the adequacy of disclosure as a regulatory response to systemic risk is connected to the issue of whether market participants themselves will embrace the project of regulating systemic risk. On this issue, analysts from the economics tradition argue that individual actors within a market cannot be expected to think about risks to the system as a whole, because they will not capture all those benefits of maintaining the system.[42] Indeed, the very acknowledgment of the need to police the "perimeter of regulation" suggests an acceptance that strategic, regulation-avoiding behavior by market participants will continue to be the norm. Regulators face the challenge of trying to enroll market actors in the project of paying attention to the possibility of systemic risk.[43] The Dodd–Frank legislation in the United States requires a broad range of financial institutions to have a risk committee which would be a sub-committee of the board of directors.[44] As noted above, regulators will require cooperation from market participants in sharing firm-specific information to allow them to scope more general market trends.[45] We have seen that IOSCO has found this to be a problem in emerging markets.

The GFC provides a renewed opportunity to consider a question long debated by law and society scholars and others about what motivates market participants to act in particular ways.[46] Why exactly do financial firms choose to operate at the perimeter of regulation? What factors influence the development of particular business models or products? For example, could financial firms like banks be prompted to create more fine-grained internal risk management processes in the absence of

---

[41] D. Nagy, R.W. Painter and M. Sachs, *An Overview of Securities Litigation and Enforcement: Cases and Materials* (Eagan: West Publishing Company, 2003), p. 2.

[42] Schwartz, "Systemic Risk"; Karmel, "Systemic Risk Regulation"; R.A. Posner, *A Failure of Capitalism: The Crisis of '08 and the Descent into Depression* (Cambridge, MA: Harvard University Press 2009), pp. 324ff.

[43] J. Black, "Enrolling Actors in Regulatory Processes: Examples from UK Financial Services Regulation" (2003) *Public Law* 62–90.

[44] Nagy *et al.*, *An Overview*, p. 2.

[45] In the United States the powers of the Office of Financial Research are backed by "the power to issue a subpoena to any financial company" (Davis Polk, "Summary of Dodd-Frank").

[46] D. Thornton, N. Gunningham and R. Kagan, "General Deterrence and Corporate Environmental Behavior" (2005) 27 *Law and Policy* 262–288; Posner, *Failure of Capitalism*, pp. 322–326.

being legislatively required to do so? Clearly, the Dodd–Frank legislation in the United States is taking no chances here; it requires financial firms to have risk committees. Similarly, on the issue of the retention of economic risk by ABS originators, Dodd–Frank requires them to retain an "unhedged economic interest" of not less than 5 percent of the credit risk in any such securities sold to third parties.

It should also be noted that IOSCO final report on Unregulated Markets and Products observed that industry self-governing initiatives would not be enough to avert another crisis with respect to such products. It quotes approvingly from a BIS paper asserting that the turmoil in the capital markets between 2007 and 2009 is "best seen as a natural result of a prolonged period of generalised and aggressive risk-taking."[47] All this suggests a degree of pessimism about the willingness of market participants to now embrace a role in the reduction of systemic risk, though more fine-grained and contemporary empirical research would be extremely helpful on this issue.[48]

A specific location of market participant involvement in the regulation of systemic risk is precisely in the area of regulatory design. The plethora of policy-making initiatives at both IOSCO and domestic regulatory levels offers the possibility for stakeholders to provide input so as to shape the ultimate substantive outcome of recommendations. Scholars in the "new governance" field preserve more faith in the ability of stakeholders to produce mutually acceptable and systemic outcomes through deliberative processes than do those who worry about the possibility of regulatory capture by influential market participants.[49] So one question that arises is whether an emphasis on designing *systemic risk* governance makes it more or less likely that collaborative and horizontal stakeholder-centerd regulatory deliberation could occur. Here it is noteworthy that IOSCO does have a practice of issuing consultation reports before making final recommendations, and in this sense its deliberative processes are broader than other international financial organizations.[50]

For example, when IOSCO's Standing Committee on the Regulation of Secondary Markets was examining the viability of a system for

---

[47] IOSCO, "Unregulated Financial Markets: Final Report," p. 12.
[48] Hutter, "New Regulatory Governance."
[49] C. Ford, "New Governance, Compliance, and Principles-Based Securities Regulation" (2008) 45 *American Business Law Journal* 1, 8–9; O. Lobel, "The Renew Deal: The Fall of Regulation and the Rise of Governance in Contemporary Legal Thought" (2004) 89 *Minnesota Law Review* 342–469; L. Snider, "Accommodating Power: The 'Common Sense' of Regulators" (2009) 18 *Social and Legal Studies* 179–197.
[50] Koppel, *Design of Global Governance.*

post-trade transparency for Structured Finance Products, it engaged in various deliberations with market participants, regulatory authorities and industry representatives (including meetings, presentations, roundtables and surveys). There was a clear divergence of opinion on the question of the desirability of post-trade transparency for SFPs between the "buy side" and the "sell side." Sell-side participants were concerned that the "non-standardised, complex and illiquid nature of structured finance products would make meaningful price comparability difficult or impossible."[51] The report ultimately recommended in favor of the buy side argument on the basis that greater information on traded prices would be a valuable source of information for market participants. The Technical Committee therefore recommended to member jurisdictions that they should "seek to enhance post-trade transparency of SFPs in their respective jurisdictions," and the report listed a series of factors to consider in developing such a regime.

But there is a remaining worry about just how many stakeholders will be in a position to comment knowledgeably, or in a non-self-interested manner, about the systemic risk implications of various initiatives.[52] The design and implementation of risk management processes has not generally been terrain that affords much opportunity for inclusivity in deliberation, but rather tends to be impenetrably technocratic and expertise-driven.[53] While the eruption of the GFC provided the opportunity to ask some basic questions about citizen participation in the design and operation of financial systems, the design of specific policy recommendations that followed has not been notably susceptible to broader public input.

VI Conclusion: IOSCO, soft law and international financial governance

This chapter has demonstrated that the policy-making profile of IOSCO has increased following the GFC. By its own reckoning, it should be credited with assertively broadening the discourse of systemic risk to embrace securities market infrastructure, processes and financial products. The network of international financial governors

---

[51] IOSCO, "OTC Markets: Final Report."
[52] J.M. Conley and C. Williams, "Global Banks as Global Sustainability Regulators: The Equator Principles," under review at *Law and Policy Review*.
[53] B. Hutter, "New Regulatory Governance," under review at *Law and Policy Review*; Power, *Organized Uncertainty*.

has acknowledged the role of IOSCO as a contributor of policy solutions in the financial area. This horizontal form of governance, in which policy-making is the subject of negotiation among a number of international financial organizations has been rendered more relevant, but also more visible, since the GFC. However, as a "soft law" institution, the other side of the coin of IOSCO's influence, of course, is its role with respect to domestic securities regulators. Here the scorecard so far, while preliminary, is rather more ambiguous. We have noted that it is the domestic regulators from the member jurisdictions (or their staff) who do much of the heavy lifting to produce the content of IOSCO policy documents. Yet IOSCO has limited power to require those same domestic regulators to accept and implement its policy recommendations, since its toolkit is limited to techniques of persuasion and best practice standard setting. It may be that this explains why many of IOSCO's recommendations, as we have seen above, are presented in terms of broad principles to consider rather than precise, rule-oriented mandates. As a principles-based site of financial governance, IOSCO may exhort, persuade or shame, but it does not have command and control capacity. One particular data point with respect to IOSCO's influence on domestic regulations concerns the current reforms to US domestic securities policy. Here, Howard Davies points out that "the Dodd-Frank debates over U.S. financial reform proceeded with almost no discussion of the global dimension of securities markets."[54] Specifically, IOSCO's recommendations about retention of an economic interest in ABS, as we have seen above, do not go as far as the recent US legislation, in the sense that they do not identify a particular target amount of economic interest that originators of securitized products must retain.

More generally, the argument of this chapter has been that the advent of systemic risk may turn out to be a game-changer for domestic securities regulators. In the short-term it may prompt them to revisit long-held understandings of the purpose and orientation of disclosure requirements, so as to focus more on the nuances of investment products on the one hand, and macro-issues of market structure on the other. The availability of financialized investment products creates new risks, as does the trading of these products. But it may also require securities regulators in many jurisdictions to confront more

---

[54] H. Davies, "Focus on the Meat and Two Veg of Reform," *Financial Times*, September 1, 2010, p. 11.

controversial issues of market operation and structure, such as the organization of financial firms themselves, or the scope of their activities in the capital markets – issues for which the disclosure of more information may be only part of the answer. This will be challenging, not least because the scope of the concept of systemic risk has yet to be completely understood.

20 Modernizing pension fund legal standards for the twenty-first century

Keith L. Johnson and Frank Jan De Graaf

> I made the mistake in presuming that the self-interests of organizations, specifically banks and others, were such that they were best capable of protecting their own shareholders and their equity of the firm.
>
>   Former Federal Reserve Board Chairman, Alan Greenspan, at a hearing of the House Committee on Oversight and Government Reform
>
> In other words, you found that your view of the world, your ideology, was not right, it was not working.
>   Chairman of the Committee, Rep. Henry Waxman
>
> Absolutely, precisely.[1]
>   Greenspan

I   Introduction

The growth of pension funds and retirement savings over the last three decades into a huge global block of capital has dramatically changed the effect that pension investment practices have on the global economy. Prevailing interpretations of fiduciary duty have encouraged this pension fund capital block to "herd" around similar investment practices that have become focused on the short term. This "lemming" behavior has contributed to the severity of economic booms and busts. It has also destroyed long-term economic value, transferred wealth from younger to older pension fund participants and raised questions about compliance with the fiduciary duty of impartiality.

The authors would like to thank all their Network for Sustainable Financial Markets [NSFM] colleagues who participated in discussions that led to the development of this chapter and who provided thoughtful comments on earlier versions. Network for Sustainable Financial Markets: www.sustainablefinancialmarkets.net (last accessed February 22, 2011). This chapter was first published by the Rotman International Centre for Pension management in the *Rotman International Journal of Pension Management* (Volume 3, Issue 1, Spring 2010), and has been re-printed by permission of the authors.

[1] October 23, 2008.

This chapter argues for a modernized interpretation of fiduciary duty that recognizes the symbiotic relationship between the sustainable success of both corporations and pension funds. It describes the impact that pension investment practices have on both the well-being of fund participants and health of the global economy. It also argues that fiduciaries should adopt pension fund governance practices found to be associated with improved investment performance, better align pension fund service provider incentives with the clients' long-term interests and expand risk identification and management practices to consider systemic and extra-financial factors that contributed to the current financial crisis. The authors recommend development of pension fund governance best practice guidelines, combined with adoption of a "comply or explain" reporting scheme, as a way to improve the ability of pension managers to meet their fiduciary obligations and promote economic stability.

II Mutual economic reliance between pension investors and corporations

At the end of 2008, economies throughout the world are spinning into recession, perhaps worse. Many stock markets have seen gains of the past decade completely wiped out. The value of pension fund equity holdings in the United States alone fell by $4 trillion over the past year.[2] Workers, consumers, taxpayers, companies and retirees are facing the worst economic crisis in nearly a century.

What initially seemed like an isolated Wall Street disaster has spread to Main Streets around the globe. It now appears that treatment of this pandemic will require systemic intervention on an international scale.[3] With the funding status of pension funds dropping fast, the future of pension promises is being re-evaluated worldwide in response to the

---

[2] Alicia Munnell, Jean-Pierre Aubry and Dan Muldoon, "The Financial Crisis and Private Defined Benefit Plans," Center for Retirement Research at Boston College, November 2008. Equity value in public and private defined benefit and defined contribution pension plans in the US fell by $3.8 trillion between October 9, 2007 and October 9, 2008, from a starting level of slightly over $15 trillion. The value of private pension funds in countries belonging to the Organization for Economic Co-Operation and Development (OECD) declined by $5 trillion during the first three quarters of 2008. *Pension Markets in Focus*, Issue 5, December 2008, OECD.

[3] Funding status of defined benefit pension plans at companies in the S&P 1500 dropped from 104 percent in December 2007 to 75 percent a year later. Jennifer Byrd, "A Brave New World for Pension Funding," *Pensions & Investments*, January 12, 2009, citing data from Mercer LLC.

crisis.⁴ Pension reform is likely to be considered as part of broader economic revitalization packages in many countries.

In considering reforms, changes in the role and influence of pension funds should be recognized.⁵ Many assumptions underlying the way economists, policy-makers and regulators have traditionally viewed pension systems no longer apply. Among the most important changes are the *growth of pension funds into huge pools of capital* and the correspondingly expanded influence that pension fund management practices now have on the larger economy.

For example, in the United States, institutional investor ownership of Fortune 1,000 companies has increased to 76 percent of outstanding equity.⁶ With retirement savings making up the largest block of those holdings, pension funds are central to the health of the financial system and are a primary source of capital.⁷ In some countries, the aggregate value of pension fund assets even exceeds the Gross Domestic Product.⁸ Pension fund management practices clearly matter to the global economy.

This combined influence of pension funds on the financial markets has not been widely examined in the context of pension fund governance practices. However, legal standards and governance of pension funds, including practices of the complex service provider network around pension funds, have grown into a major economic force. We expect the broader economic importance of pension funds to become even more evident as the economic crisis unfolds.

As pension fund assets and annuity payments decline, a chain reaction is triggered. Companies with defined benefit plans are forced to either make higher pension fund contributions, underfund or terminate their plans.⁹ Costs will likely be added to many government budgets to

---

⁴ For example, the Center for Retirement Research at Boston College estimates that funding status of private defined benefit pension plans has also declined from 98 percent to 85 percent over the first three quarters of 2008 and is still dropping. See Munnell et al., "The Financial Crisis and Private Defined Benefit Plans."

⁵ We recognize that circumstances vary from one country to another. Pension fund governance is not a "one size fits all" matter. Nevertheless, we believe that most of the issues which fiduciaries face are similar across markets.

⁶ C.K. Brancato and S. Rabimov, "The 2008 Institutional Investment Report: Trends in Institutional Investor Assets and Equity Ownership of U.S. Corporations," The Conference Board (September 2008).

⁷ Pension funds accounted for 38.3 percent of institutional investor public equity holdings in the United States during 2006, totaling $10.4 trillion.

⁸ In 2007, pension fund assets exceeded GDP in Iceland, the Netherlands, Switzerland and Australia. The average pension assets-to-GDP ratio in 2007 for all OECD countries was 76 percent. *Pension Markets in Focus*, Issue 5, December 2008, OECD.

⁹ Watson Wyatt estimates that companies in the United States with defined benefit plans will have to more than double their contributions during 2009. David Hilzenrath, "2008 Leaves Pensions Underfunded," *Washington Post*, January 8, 2009.

meet higher public sector defined benefit plan funding requirements in the wake of massive investment losses, with resulting tax increases or reductions in funding for other government programs. Pension savings levels, consumer confidence and buying power are likely to be affected. The knock-on economic effects for companies and the macro economy could be extensive.

The converse is also true. *Pension funds rely on growing creation of wealth by companies to cover future benefit obligations.* Defined benefit pension plans in the United States, on average, allocated 63 percent of their assets to corporate stocks at the end of 2007.[10] In countries like the Netherlands and Canada it is up to 50 percent.[11] As a result, the financial performance of pension funds is directly tied to stability and growth of the corporate sector and broader economy. The symbiotic nature of this relationship between pension funds and corporations means that neither can succeed without the success of the other. A healthy economy requires both.

This chapter focuses primarily on the pension fund side of the relationship. It highlights underlying systemic weaknesses of current pension fund legal and governance standards that are evident on a global basis. It also recommends changes designed to improve performance and sustainability of pension funds.[12] However, it must be emphasized that reforms to enhance sustainability of wealth creation are also required on the company side of the relationship. Without attention to reform and sustainability by both pension funds and corporations, each will underperform their potential.

III   Market changes have created a "lemming" fiduciary standard

Prevailing interpretations of fiduciary duty in Europe, Australia and the United States are mired in the 1960s and 1970s, when today's pension fund legal regimes were created. As a result, they are often ill-suited for

---

[10] Ilana Boivie and Beth Almeida, "Patience is a Virtue: Asset Allocation Patterns in DB and DC Plans," *National Institute on Retirement Security*, Issue Brief, July 2008. United States defined contribution plan allocations to stocks, at 37 percent during 2007, were also substantial.

[11] *Pension Markets in Focus*, Issue 5, December 2008, OECD.

[12] We recognize that there are critical differences between countries but believe that pension funds in most national systems struggle with comparable problems and have a similar collective effect on the financial markets. However, pension fund regulatory reform should be considered on a country by country basis, although in Europe there could still be a leadership role for the European Commission.

the complex investment instruments and the market-moving amount of assets being managed by pension funds in the twenty-first century.

Fiduciaries are generally advised, based on traditional legal assumptions about pension funds from financial markets of the twentieth century, to adhere to the same practices as are used by similar institutional investors.[13] Copycat investment behavior is encouraged by prevailing interpretations of the fiduciary duty legal standard. The result is a *magnification of natural investor tendencies to engage in herding behavior*, with pension funds pursuing the same strategies and investments. Given the exponential growth in pension assets since the 1970s, this produces added market volatility and new risks (even to the pension funds themselves). In effect, what functioned as a "prudent expert" fiduciary standard thirty years ago has become more of a "lemming standard" that increases the severity of booms and busts and discourages adoption of improved practices that are not yet used by peers.[14] Pension funds are often reluctant to pursue prudent strategies not being widely used by other pension funds for fear of exposure to liability from breach of the "lemming" standard.

One illustration of the damage contributed to by a legal standard interpreted so as to encourage lemming behavior has been the unrelenting focus on short-term results. This phenomenon was examined by the investment industry's leading global authority on investor protection and financial market ethics, the CFA Institute Centre for Financial Market Integrity, and the Business Roundtable Institute for Corporate Ethics, which represents CEOs from 160 global companies. After engaging thought leaders from the corporate issuer, investment

---

[13] Under 29 USC §18.1104, pension funds subject to the Employees' Retirement Security Income Act (ERISA) must be managed "with the care, skill, prudence, and diligence under the circumstances then prevailing that a prudent man acting in a like capacity and familiar with such matters would use in the conduct of an enterprise of a like character and with like aims." Under Dutch law, Pensioenwet Art. 105, the term professionalism is used. In regard to investment policies, the conduct of a prudent person is referenced as the applicable standard (art. 135). Furthermore, the law has delegated the interpretation of this law to the supervisory authority, the Dutch Central Bank.

[14] In the United States, little attention has been given to meaning of the ERISA introductory phrase in 29 USC §18.1104 which sets forth a separate, overarching requirement that fiduciaries *"shall"* discharge their duties *"in the interest of the participants and beneficiaries,"* imposing an obligation that is independent from the following phrase, *"and* for the exclusive purpose of providing benefits" (emphasis added). It appears that excessive investment herding behaviors, obsession with short-term performance and inattention to systemic risks, raises concerns about compliance with the first prong of the ERISA fiduciary duty clause cited above, because such practices may not be in the long-term interest of participants.

analyst, asset manager, institutional investor and individual investor communities, the study group concluded:

> The obsession with short-term results by investors, asset management firms, and corporate managers collectively leads to the unintended consequences of *destroying long-term value, decreasing market efficiency, reducing investment returns, and impeding efforts to strengthen corporate governance*. (Emphasis added)[15]

Indeed, academic research has found that pressure on corporate managers to deliver short-term investment results has become so strong that nearly 80 percent of them report they would sacrifice future economic value to manage short-term earnings so as to meet investor expectations.[16] CEOs who fail to meet two quarterly analyst consensus forecasts in a year suffer a 24 percent lower equity award and 14 percent lower bonus than CEOs who meet analysts' short-term expectations.[17]

This also raises questions about whether fiduciaries are adequately addressing their separate legal obligation to handle conflicting interests of different participant and beneficiary groups impartially (e.g. producing current income for retirees while generating future wealth for young participants).[18] Excessive focus on short-term investment horizons, use of short-term benchmarks and evaluation of portfolio managers primarily on short-term results, as well as inattention to risks associated with the potential long-term value destruction referenced above, should ring fiduciary duty alarms for pension funds that are managing assets to meet liabilities extending out over generations. The *fiduciary duty of impartiality*, which has been given little attention, needs to be dusted off and re-examined.[19]

---

[15] "Breaking the Short-Term Cycle," the CFA Institute Centre for Financial Market Integrity and Business Roundtable Institute for Corporate Ethics (July 2006).

[16] John Graham, Campbell Harvey and Shivaram Rajgopal, "Value Destruction and Financial Reporting Decisions" (September 6, 2006) at SSRN: http://ssrn.com/abstract=871215 (last accessed February 22, 2011).

[17] Richard Dean Mergenthaler, Shivaram Rajgopal and Suraj Srinivasan, "CEO and CFO Career Consequences to Missing Quarterly Earnings Benchmarks" (June 27, 2008), at SSRN: http://ssrn.com/abstract=1152421 (last accessed February 22, 2011).

[18] The duty of impartiality is summarized in official comments to §79(1) of the Restatement of Trusts, Third, as follows: "In what might be called the 'substantive' aspects of impartiality ... Subsection (1) directs trustees ... to make diligent and good-faith efforts to identify, respect, and balance the various beneficial interests when carrying out the trustees' fiduciary responsibilities in managing, protecting, and distributing the trust estate, and in other administrative functions."

[19] The *Code of Conduct for Members of a Pension Scheme Governing Body* which was published by the CFA Institute Centre for Financial Market Integrity in 2008 also recognizes that an effective trustee will "consider the different types of beneficiaries relevant to each pension scheme" and "engage in a delicate balancing act of taking sufficient risk to generate long-term returns high enough to support real benefit

One result of adopting a more balanced investment approach that considers long-term risks and future wealth generation, would be expansion of the risks and opportunities that are seen as relevant to a fund's investment strategy. The CFA Institute advises that pension fund governing boards, in addition to considering "typical financial measures," must consider "all relevant risk and value factors," which "may include environmental, social, and corporate governance issues."[20] Given the recent *impact of corporate governance, systemic and intangible factors* (e.g. risk management failure, automobile industry product obsolescence, regulatory agency inaction, loss of investor trust in market fairness) on pension funds in the economic crisis, there should be no doubt about the potential importance of extra-financial issues to long-term investors with broad market exposure.[21]

Unfortunately, most pension fund governance regulatory guidance on fiduciary and investment issues has taken a narrow view limited to quantitative measures. One by-product of the market crisis has been the realization that there are many investment risks that lie outside of what was traditionally quantified by mainstream investment consultants, advisors and portfolio managers. Systemic risks, which have been largely ignored, proved to be of great consequence. Now they need to be recognized and addressed as a fiduciary concern.

With most markets having eliminated statutory legal lists of allowed (or precluded) pension fund investments (a development which we heartily endorse), the task of determining appropriate investment risk exposures now falls completely on pension fund fiduciaries.[22] Their

---

increases for active participants who will become future beneficiaries while avoiding a level of risk that jeopardizes the safety of the payments to existing pensioners." In addition, in *Withers v. Teachers' Retirement System*, 447 F. Supp. 1248 (SDNY 1978), when the Court approved a New York City public pension fund investment in New York City bonds that were being issued to avoid the City's impending bankruptcy, it noted: "New York law imposes an obligation on trustees to accord impartial treatment to beneficiaries. It is more than evident, therefore, that the trustees of the TRS would have violated their fiduciary obligation had they exhausted the assets of an underfunded actuarially reserved pension system on a single class of beneficiaries (retirees). Their obligation, plainly, was to manage the fund so as to enable it to meet its obligations not only to current retirees, but also to those scheduled to retire in the future, whose pension and annuity rights would have been similarly earned over their years of active service and to whom the fund therefore had a legal responsibility."

[20] CFA Code of Conduct.

[21] Some regulators might need to revisit past interpretations of fiduciary duty in order to explicitly recognize risks that did not exist when fiduciary laws were originally written and pension funds had little collective influence on the markets or the broader economy.

[22] In Dutch law, the only investment restriction which still exists is a limit on investments in the company related to the fund (art. 135). In Britain, Lord Mackenzie of

collective effectiveness in fulfilling these duties will not only determine the future well-being of pension fund participants but will also play a major role in allocation of capital between companies and in the health of the economy. The importance of pension fund governance and investment practices in this regard cannot be overstated.

IV   Improving pension fund governance

In most European countries and in Japan, pension funds are generally established as a separate institutional entity with its own internal governing board. Many Eastern European countries, Spain and Mexico have developed more of a contractual arrangement, in which pension funds are segregated pools of assets without legal personality that are managed by a financial institution.[23] Aspects of the contractual form of pension fund management have also been extended to defined contribution arrangements, such as 401(k) and individual retirement accounts in the United States, where responsibility for selection of investment options is delegated to the participant, with limited duties held by the trustee and investment manager.

Historically, Anglo-Saxon pension fund law was founded on the law of trusts. Under that case law, trustees have generally been held to a higher standard of conduct than is required of corporate directors or parties to a contract.[24] In 1928, Justice Cardozo described the legal standard applicable to a trustee as follows:

> Many forms of conduct permissible in a workaday world for those acting at arm's length, are forbidden to those bound by fiduciary ties. A trustee is held to something stricter than the morals of the market place. Not honesty alone, but the punctilio of an honor the most sensitive, is then the standard of behavior.[25]

Luton, Parliamentary Under Secretary of State for the House of Lords, representing the Department of Work & Pensions, summarized the government's views on responsible investing by pension funds in October 2008, "There is no reason why trustees cannot consider moral and social criteria, in addition to their usual criteria of financial returns, security and diversification."

[23] F. Steward and J. Yermo, "Pension Fund Governance: Challenges and Potential Solutions," *OECD* Working Papers on Insurance and Private Pensions, No. 18 (2008), available at: http://econpapers.repec.org/paper/oecdafaab/18-en.htm (last accessed February 22, 2011).

[24] For example, trust law precludes fiduciaries from engaging in self-interested transactions with the trust, though corporate directors can usually enter into related party transactions with the company if disclosed and approved by disinterested directors as fair to the corporation. Compare Restatement of Trusts, Third, §78 to §144 of the Delaware General Corporation Law.

[25] *Meinhard v. Salmon* 249 NY 458 (1928).

All the forms of pension fund organization place substantial responsibility in the hands of agents who act on behalf of participants and beneficiaries. The legal standards and governance structures established to control these agents are critical to pension fund success.

Recent research on pension fund governance has established that *good governance is associated with increased returns*. A study published in the *Rotman International Journal of Pension Management* found that better-governed pension funds outperformed poorly-governed funds by 2.4 percent per annum during the four years ending December 2003.[26] The results confirmed a similar 1993–1996 study which found a 1 percent annual good governance performance dividend.[27]

Key factors found to be associated with good governance and pension fund success included:[28]

- selection of governing board members with relevant skills and knowledge;
- development of a board self-improvement culture;
- clear understanding of the board's mission and its investment beliefs;
- sufficient size to allow cost effective management of assets;
- competitive staff compensation to permit acquisition of internal expertise;
- insulation from conflicting political or third party agendas; and
- clarity of board and staff roles about delegation of management responsibilities.

The legal structure and governing principles within which pension funds must operate set critical decision-making boundaries. Legal rules that fail to encourage adoption of best practices, which have been found to be associated with pension fund success (i.e. that stress conformity to current practices), not only foster inferior results but also undermine the ability of pension funds to efficiently allocate capital in the marketplace. While different approaches might be required for the different

---

[26] Ronald Capelle, Hubert Lum and Keith Ambachtsheer, "The Pension Governance Deficit: Still with Us" (October 1, 2008) 1:1 *Rotman International Journal of Pension Management*, at SSRN: http://ssrn.com/abstract=1280907 (last accessed February 22, 2011).

[27] *Ibid.*

[28] For more insight about the critical role of board leadership, see Gordon L. Clark and Roger Urwin, "Making Pension Boards Work: The Critical Role of Leadership" (2008) 1:1 *Rotman International Journal of Pension Management* 38–45, Gordon L. Clark and Roger Urwin, "Best-Practices Pension Fund Governance" (2008) 9 *Journal of Asset Management* 1, 2–21.

pension fund structures being used in various markets, we see the high standard of fiduciary responsibility to the interests of all beneficiaries that was espoused by Justice Cardozo as a common guiding principle that is critical to maintaining pension fund integrity and fostering the trustworthy social networks that allow capital to flow efficiently within the global financial markets.

V Alignment of interests among agents and service providers

Conflicts of interest between pension fund participants/beneficiaries and their agents in the service provider chain, including pension fund governing board members, has been a major problem in the industry. A 2008 survey of European pension fund executives and asset managers provides some insight into challenges that need to be addressed.[29] When discussing the survey findings on alignment of interests, the report notes:

> There is a widespread perception in the pension world that the investment industry is perverse in one crucial sense: its food chain operates in reverse, with service providers at the top and clients at the bottom. Agents fare better than principals.

A key finding was that 65 percent of pension fund respondents believe that pension consultants do not understand the long-term needs of their clients, while only 15 percent of asset managers identify that as an issue.

The report concludes that pension consultants and asset managers should *develop forward-looking services that meet their clients' needs*, rather than selling what fits the manager's or consultant's own interests. That is seen as the basis for a new alignment of interests. Development of a *fee structure that is aligned with the value delivered* is also one of the top concerns cited by funds, with 67 percent noting it as important. More alarming is the finding that the vast majority of both pension fund executives and their fund managers see current pre- and post-retirement products as woefully inadequate to deliver adequate retirement incomes.

We believe that one of the reasons why the pension service provider supply chain has become inverted is the industry's high tolerance level for conflicts of interest. Table 20.1 summarizes some of the main

---

[29] Professor Amin Rajan, "DB & DC Plans: Strengthening Their Delivery," Create-Research 2008 at www.create-research.co.uk/pubRes/prTxt.html (last accessed February 22, 2011).

Table 20.1 *Main stakeholders in the pension fund service provider supply chain*

Stakeholder	Horizon (average)	Agency problem	General description
Participants and beneficiaries	Thirty+ years	Often have/exercise little control over either their contributions or investments.	Are neither involved or knowledgeable, which leads to mistrust in times of financial instability.
Trustees or governing board	Four to six years	Often union, employer or government representatives, with independent representatives in some countries. They are in the position for a limited time and typically have little financial or investment background.	May not have the necessary skills and are sometimes driven by other interests (e.g. in the Netherlands employee and employer representatives also negotiate working agreements); financial incentives are usually small.
Investment managers	One year	Work on short-term bonuses with clients who generally evaluate performance over one to three years.	Are incented by fees set on assets under management and evaluated relative to market benchmarks, which might not reflect pension funding needs.
Managers of companies	Three to twelve months	Only know a few vocal or active investors. In many countries less than 30 percent vote proxies. Little interaction.	Feel hunted and pressured to deliver quarterly returns by investors they do not know; are influenced by huge incentives based on stock price.

problems with the misalignment of interests in the pension fund stakeholder chain.

Given the prevalence of misaligned interests throughout the stakeholder chain, the importance of identifying, realigning and managing the interests of agents should be a priority. However, trustees often lack the skills to provide effective oversight of a complex financial organization and may not be aware of governance issues or have access to the expertise needed to address them.

Development of industry best practice standards would be one way to provide fiduciaries with practical guidance. Some markets combine best practice standards with a "comply or explain" reporting approach. This allows flexibility, while ensuring that best governance practices are considered. Comply or explain has been used in Britain and helped to improve pension fund governance practices there.[30] While not a panacea in and of itself, best practice regimens can be helpful.

VI   Six recommendations

Although different markets will have different issues, we provide the following recommendations as a general guide for modernization of pension fund legal standards. We recommend that regulators should:

(1) *Recognize the risks of excessive investment herding behavior* for both the economy and fund participants/beneficiaries. Regulators could clarify that practices of other similar investors are merely a reference point for establishment of a prudent investment program. Pension funds should be accorded the flexibility to pursue prudent investment strategies which differ from those that have been broadly adopted, as long as they are reasonably consistent with the fund's mission, investment outlook and risk tolerances and serve the interests of participants/beneficiaries.

(2) *Emphasize the duty of impartiality* and the need to balance short-term and long-term obligations. Guidance should stress the long-term, inter-generational nature of pension fund liabilities and recognize the impact of systemic risks.

(3) *Encourage fee structures that better align interests* of service providers with those of fund participants/beneficiaries. Portfolio managers and advisors should have a significant portion of remuneration that reflects the sustainable value received by the fund from their services. Boards should report on alignment of fees, with review by the fund's auditors.

---

[30] The Myners Report, issued in 2001 (and updated by the National Association of Pension Funds in 2008) provides a roadmap of best practices for British pension fund managers and could serve as a model for other jurisdictions. The Myners Report and 2008 update are available at: www.hm-treasury.gov.uk/myners_principles_review_of_progress.htm (last accessed February 22, 2011). Best practice recommendations have also recently been developed in the United States by the Stanford Institutional Investor Forum Committee on Fund Governance. They are available at: www.law.stanford.edu/program/executive/programs/Clapman_Report-070316v6-Color.pdf (last accessed February 22, 2011).

(4) *Confirm the importance of systemic and extra-financial risks* (i.e. items not reflected on the financial statements) that could affect the short- or long-term well-being of participants/beneficiaries. Clarify that the narrow and myopic view of risk and value that helped to fuel the current economic crisis is inappropriate for the management of pension fund assets. Encourage use of a forward-looking, comprehensive and interdisciplinary approach to the identification, valuation and management of risk and exercise of investor rights that is consistent with principles of inter-generational fairness.

We also put forth the following recommendations aimed at addressing the behavioral changes required to modernize pension fund governance practices. The appropriate oversight entities should:

(5) *Convene a market-specific best practices commission* to develop and maintain general standards aimed at improving the governance practices of pension funds. Consideration should be given to use of a "comply or explain" reporting approach on compliance with best practices to provide flexibility. Issues that should be considered include:

  a. *Development of governing board "fit for purpose" qualifications* for selection of governing board members and their continuing education. Implementation provisions could include annual board-specific inventories of trustee skills and capabilities needed to establish a "fit for purpose" pension fund board and maintain a culture of continuous improvement.[31] Annual reports to participants/beneficiaries and to the board's independent auditor could be required on each board's "fit for purpose" evaluation and plan.
  b. Creation of a process allowing beneficiaries to file a petition with the board (or with an appointing official or court) to seek resignation or *removal of an unfit trustee* who has been the subject of significant unresolved conflicts of interest or breaches of fiduciary duty.
  c. Representation of participants/beneficiaries on pension fund boards. To discourage diversion of fund assets and biased governance practices, consideration could also be given to mandating an *independent board chair* who is not affiliated with the plan sponsor.
  d. Required *periodic evaluation of plan design* and related regulatory, tax and legal requirements (by policy-makers, regulators and

---

[31] See the Myners and Stanford reports, above, for discussion of "fit for purpose" boards.

trustees), to encourage consideration of plan structures that best serve the interests of participants and beneficiaries.[32]

e. Annual board affirmation of a *statement of investment beliefs and mission* to provide appropriate focus. To encourage consistent implementation, an annual report could be required on how risk management and investment practices are designed to meet fund liabilities and foster participant/beneficiary long-term well-being.

f. *Collaboration between pension funds* to improve effectiveness in meeting mutual goals or provide the scale necessary to operate in a cost-effective manner. Smaller funds might be incented to merge or share staff resources.

g. Requirement that boards periodically evaluate and *report on their effectiveness in meeting best practices* and their plans for improvement.

h. Mandating regular external *audits of each fund's conflict of interest policy*, including compliance with it by the board, staff, investment managers and consultants/advisors.

i. Requirement that annual *cost reports be made on an unbundled basis* to facilitate management of expenses on a net result, transparent basis.

j. *Managing investor rights and proxy votes* to foster sustainable corporate success and economic stability. Require annual reports to be sent to the participants/beneficiaries and external auditor on responsible investment practices.

(6) *Organize educational programs* to promote fiduciary professionalism. Involve the pension fund industry in development of comprehensive educational programs to improve trustee skills and adoption of best practices.

VII   Conclusion

While trustee skills, legal standards and best practices are important, they are not the only considerations that matter. The pension promise

---

[32] In recent years, plan design alternatives to the traditional defined benefit (DB) and defined contribution (DC) options have been developed. For example, hybrid plans can combine features of DB and DC plans to offer individual accounts that are aggregated for cost-effective, professional management with oversight from a fiduciary board, provide full portability of accounts between employers and automatically convert individual accounts to life annuities upon retirement. Some countries (e.g. the Netherlands) have hybrid plans in place that could be examined as potential models for innovations in other markets.

is a shared responsibility that involves an inter-generational agreement with important implications for the economy and society at large.

Indeed, pension funds are *creatures of "trust" that involve long-term commitments and relationships* between beneficiaries, participants, trustees, managers, advisors, taxpayers, companies invested in, society, countries and different generations. Those relationships form networks that require mutual reliance, shared values and responsibilities within global economic and ecological systems.

Regulatory reform in the pension industry will be more effective if it looks beyond the surface and keeps the big picture context in focus. Reforms should eliminate incentives for fiduciaries to engage in short-term herding behavior and encourage development of long-term relationships that will foster sustainable economic growth.

Part V

Conclusion

21 Conclusion: evaluation, policy proposals and research agenda

Cynthia A. Williams and Peer Zumbansen

In this book we've brought together contributions from law, economics, sociology and politics in order to evaluate the effects of the shift to shareholder primacy in both the United States and the United Kingdom, in the context of a parallel shift in both countries to an economy in which finance has an increasingly central role. We have made a decision to include and even emphasize empirical evidence, rather than theory alone, in conscious rejection of the oft-stated view that "it takes a theory to beat a theory." For in evaluating the empirical effects of these decades-long trends in light of the global financial and economic crises – crises propagated from the United States – we submit that the problems inherent in American-style corporate governance have become manifest. The problem is not only one of corporate governance, since the shareholder wealth maximizing norm in the United States is embedded within economic and political institutions stripped of many social democratic norms and policies. But in conjunction with neoliberal economic and political norms, the result of shareholder primacy has been increasing economic volatility and inequality, systemic fragility, and financial risk that is increasingly being transferred to individuals to manage, particularly given the collapse of many collective bargaining agreements and collective arrangements for pensions.

The congruence of theory and evidence suggesting weaknesses in shareholder driven corporate governance gives rise to questions about what, instead, the goals of corporate governance should be, and how these goals may best be aligned with government policy. It is naïve to think that continental European stakeholder systems could be transplanted into the United States or the United Kingdom by legislative fiat. As the convergence debate has shown, corporate governance systems are sticky, being deeply embedded in complementary institutional frameworks, political constellations and social norms. Certainly aspects of stakeholder arrangements ought to be studied seriously and mined for their inherent values or regulatory approaches that could inform specific policy recommendations. But the embedded nature of firms and corporate governance arrangements does suggest caution, and encourages ever more serious, open-minded study in search of policy ideas. The following paragraphs seek to provide some ideas about what topics seem worthy of that further research.

First, as emphasized in a number of chapters, there are examples of both economically liberal economies such as Australia and Canada, and coordinated market economies such as Austria, Belgium, Finland, Germany, Norway and the Netherlands, that have either weathered the global financial crisis relatively unscathed, or have shown better economic performance than the United States and the United Kingdom over the last decades. (Chapter 13 is particularly instructive on these points, but see also Chapters 12 and 18.) Scandinavian corporate governance systems, as such, are worthy of greater study, having been relatively ignored in many comparative or international evaluations. More generally, evidence-based comparative study of the combinations of corporate governance, government policy and social norms to which these successes are owed would no doubt yield important insights.

One promising approach to developing corporate governance thinking that builds on the Varieties of Capitalism intellectual tradition is to more closely examine varieties of liberalism, as has been done recently by Konzelmann, Fovargue-Davies and Schnyder.[1] Their paper addresses the question of why Australian and Canadian banks fared so much better in the global financial crisis than did American and British banks, even though all four countries share an English common-law heritage and are market oriented economies. In addition to various government policies that did not permit imprudent mortgage lending or excessive leverage within financial institutions, the authors point to variations among the type of economic liberalism informing policy generally in Australia and Canada versus the United States and the United Kingdom. They construe Australian and Canadian economic policy as a variation of "ordoliberalism," an approach to economic regulation developed by the German Freiburg school of economists in the early decades of the twentieth century. This school of thought encourages a more active role for government than does laissez-faire liberalism, particularly with respect to inequalities or abuses of power among market actors. Not only is this economic theory worth further exploration and development and has, thus, been attracting attention well beyond the longstanding efforts to conceptualize European legal harmonization,

---

[1] S. Konzelmann, M. Fovargue-Davies and G. Schnyder, "Varieties of Liberalism" (2010), Centre for Business Research, University of Cambridge, Working Paper No. 403, available at" www.cbr.cam.ac.uk/pdf/WP403.pdf.

but the concept of "varieties of liberalism" is an important one for identifying further research trajectories, even as the specifics of banking (and pension) regulation in Canada and Australia are worthy of further examination.

Second, several of the market developments exposed in the financial crisis and discussed in this book give rise to further research questions and need for policy development. One, certainly, is the "systemic risk" concern identified in Chapter 19, particularly in conjunction with the derivatives market discussed by Sarra in Chapter 10. Various domestic regulators and transnational regulatory bodies have been grappling with the implications of this challenge, giving rise to a series of questions. "What is systemic risk? How is it created? How can it be addressed?" is just the beginning of questions that need attention. More fundamentally, we need to ask whether we have reached a level of financial complexity that is excessive, that is beyond the capacity of financial market participants themselves or regulators to understand and regulate. Is it simply a matter of distributed knowledge that needs to be mined more effectively by global regulatory "colleges" using better computers, or is there a limit to the types and number of derivative transactions that can be managed effectively in a world of hyper-connectivity and hyper-speed?

Research on systemic risk illustrates the intricate nature of this category of risk, something which is increasingly reflected, on the one hand, in interdisciplinary investigations on the constituting elements that make up systemic risk and, on the other, in an earnest revival of political economy and economic sociology work, as indicated in our introduction to this collection. A defining trait of this development is the distinct recognition that a better understanding of systemic risk is going to depend in a crucial manner on conceiving of it as a matter of comprehensive social theory, e.g. "governance," rather than through this or that economistic "model." Seen through this lens, the attention attracted by "systemic risk" is ample evidence of a decisive turn to social theory, conducted in an interdisciplinary manner.

Meanwhile, the crucial role of transparency and of "governance by disclosure" is increasingly seen as central to present debates over "good" corporate governance. This is nowhere felt more strongly than in the field of securities regulation, an area that in many liberal economies has relied primarily on disclosure of firm-specific information as the regulatory approach, connecting to views of well-informed, individual rational actors making economically intelligent investment decisions, with the assumption that this is the best way to promote allocational efficiency. Each of these premises is open to question in a world of systemic complexity and multiple redistributions of risk. As discussed in a number of chapters (and even by some regulators),[2] the premises of market efficiency, individual rationality leading to market rationality, allocational efficiency through capital markets, liquidity as always beneficial, even the role of capital markets as "capital providers to firms," need to be re-examined in light of the global financial crisis and empirical evidence of growing economic fragility, not resilience, in the financial system. Systems theory and chaos theory from engineering and physics are starting to be deployed to address these questions, which is a promising development. More fundamental and comprehensive research into systemic risk, derivatives transactions and complexity is still necessary, however, not only from these scientific traditions but also from cognitive psychology and regulatory theory.

Chapters 13, 15 and 18 also point to another complex of market developments that needs further research and more sustained policy development, concerning the implications from trends over the last three decades toward the ever spiraling upward distribution of compensation within the firm, particularly within shareholder driven corporate governance systems. Executive compensation systems designed to "align the interests of managers with the shareholders" as one or even the preferred solution to principal/agent problems, have exacerbated those problems, particularly, as we've seen, within financial firms. Excessive stock option compensation and bonus-driven compensation have been particularly pernicious in encouraging one-way bets in management's favor and excessive firm-level risk – risk that feeds into the systemic risk issues discussed above. As recognized by Roger Martin, the Dean of the Rotman School of Management in Toronto, Canada, executive compensation needs to be fundamentally re-designed to actually align the interests of management with that of the firm and its profitability or revenue, not its stock price.[3] Lazonick's work with Glimstedt and Xie on Swedish compensation systems provides another promising area of comparative study,[4] and there are no doubt other comparators valuable for study and to inform more subtle, and effective, policy interventions regarding executive compensation.

---

[2] The Turner Review of 2009, "A Regulatory Response to the Global Financial Crisis," Financial Services Authority (United Kingdom), section 1.4, available at: www.fsa.gov.uk/pubs/other/turner_review.pdf.

[3] Roger Martin, "Managers Must Be Judged On The Real Score," *Financial Times*, May 11, 2009, p. 9.

[4] Henrik Glimstedt, William Lazonick and Hao Xie, "The Evolution and Allocation of Employee Stock Options: Adapting US-style Compensation to the Swedish Business Model" (2006) 3 *European Management Review* 156–176.

Much of the above seems in our view to point directly to the firm as an entity, the organization and nature of which clearly exceeds its characterization as primarily an investment vehicle. The dramatic regulatory failure of corporate behavior which led to the crisis testifies to the inadequacy of the dominant descriptions of the firm. As alluded to in the introduction and spelled out in more detail in Chapter 7, there is much to be said for an approach which places the firm in the context of a volatile knowledge society, in which the demarcations between "public" and "private" have become porous and regulatory programs are faced increasingly with the challenge of dealing with constellations of extreme uncertainty. Such uncertainty pertains to the design of organizational frameworks as much as to finding the correct balance between interventionist and facilitative regulation. Uncertainty also pertains to the normative uncertainty of what firms should be allowed to do in a context where large portions of formerly "public" service provision, infrastructure development, finance and maintenance, as well as research and development, have been shifted over to the "private" sector. In this context of transformed statehood,[5] we need to rethink the fundamentals of our approaches to delineating public from private activity.[6]

Parallel and partially complementing work by scholars such as Lazonick, O'Sullivan or Zumbansen on the "learning" or the "innovative" firm, scholars such as Simon Deakin, Suzanne Konzelmann, Sanford Jacoby, Harry Arthurs but also Paddy Ireland and John Parkinson have been investigating, in particular, the role of the employee within the firm. Today, the disciplinary horizon has been widened even further. As employees within firms increasingly become critical to firms' knowledge bearing and knowledge creating capacities, insights from industrial and organizational psychology need to be brought to bear to connect those important disciplines' research with corporate governance and employment compensation design. Industrial and organizational psychology mechanisms to create high performance workplaces and enhance the justice climates within firms are well-understood in those disciplines, and the productivity gains of various mechanisms supported by extensive empirical evidence from both field and laboratory studies. This knowledge has been poorly integrated into corporate governance thinking on executive compensation, however, and as such provides fertile ground for interdisciplinary advance.

---

[5] See the interdisciplinary research program at www.sfb597.uni-bremen.de.
[6] For an early, provocative approach, see Bernard de Mandeville, *The Fable of the Bees, or Private Vices, Public Benefits* (1714).

Finally, the capital market interventions of pension funds, and the fiduciary duties of pension fund trustees, need further research and careful policy consideration given the importance of these collective welfare institutions to the health of both societies and capital markets. As Chapters 9, 13 and 20 explore, pension funds of various kinds (public, private and/or labor-oriented) have become key market actors, owning large swathes of the market and becoming invested in every asset class and type of financial transaction. Given their long-term promises to beneficiaries they ought to be the ultimate patient capitalists. Decades of under-funding by political actors have created acute short-term pressures, however. Moreover, pension funds interact with an entire supply chain of advisors and asset managers whose incentives may not, and often do not, align with the interests of the ultimate beneficiaries. Thus many funds have become anything but patient capitalists. How this situation could be addressed requires a fundamental re-evaluation of the nature of funds' fiduciary duties, recognizing that funds own the whole market and thus need to be concerned with the health of the whole market and the societies in which they are embedded. Moreover the problems associated with the funds' investment supply chain are well understood, as Chapter 20 discusses. It is time to consider in more detail policy solutions to address those problems. As with each of the topics discussed here, the present collection suggests that such solutions ought to be pursued through a close dialogue between "theory" and "practice."

Index

agency costs, 24, 55, 75, 166–167, 235, 321

banking regulation, 244, 297
bankruptcy, 4, 31, 34, 207, 229, 285, 434, 465
behavioral economics, 15
Berle and Means, 23–24, 56, 63–66, 93, 123, 151, 154, 157–158, 160, 163–166, 171–173, 175, 246, 399, 423
board of directors, 60–61, 67, 68, 70–74, 80–81, 84, 86, 91, 96, 126, 373, 430, 454
business judgment rule, 61, 74, 78–79, 84–85, 96–99, 102, 103

capital markets, 1–2, 4, 5–8, 10, 24, 26–27, 38, 46, 75, 84, 87, 89–90, 94–96, 151, 158, 161, 162, 165, 171, 172, 178–180, 183, 185, 187, 192, 195, 200, 201–204, 206, 210, 229, 232, 267, 277, 280, 303, 313, 316, 319, 330, 332, 385–393, 395, 397, 401, 408–411, 447, 455, 458, 480, 482
capitalism, 2, 3, 12, 42–51, 54, 58–59, 74, 119, 126–128, 130, 136–137, 153–155, 157, 163, 164, 165, 167, 170–174, 236, 258, 260, 262–263, 265, 293–294, 316, 366, 374, 385, 392, 393, 394, 397, 437, 478
co-determination, 5, 10, 359
collateralized debt obligations, 49, 206–207, 212, 213, 285, 449
Companies Act (UK), 32–33, 246–247
coordinated market economy, 7, 257, 294, 315
corporate democracy, 61, 69–70
corporate finance, 53, 119, 138, 261
corporate governance
  Dutch, 385, 403–408, 409
  French, 23, 259, 374

  German, 23, 237, 259, 294, 322, 360, 374, 402, 403, 409
  Japanese, 8, 214, 260, 294, 374
  UK, 5, 8, 25, 35, 37, 39, 234, 237, 270, 323, 359, 374
  US, 5, 8, 25, 35, 82–103, 214, 234, 237, 294, 315, 323, 360, 374, 409, 418, 477
corporate governance codes, 17, 322
corporate governance reform, 8, 24, 25, 117, 141, 357, 376
corporate social responsibility, 4, 66, 119, 120, 122, 123, 126–134, 140–144, 147, 154, 165, 168, 202, 341, 344–345, 361, 377, 403
credit default swaps, 4, 50, 205–212, 217, 222, 226–230, 232, 383, 409, 440, 445, 449–450

debt, 25, 29–30, 36–37, 49, 51–52, 57, 59, 62, 71, 109, 121, 152, 156, 160–163, 169–171, 174–175, 183, 191, 207, 212–217, 223, 229, 230, 231, 232, 235, 277, 279, 284–285, 288, 291, 311–312, 314, 318, 333, 347, 352, 417, 428, 432
Delaware, 3, 16, 61, 62, 74, 76–81, 96–102, 104, 106–118, 253
deregulation, 12, 33–34, 44, 46, 51, 56, 58, 92, 102, 121, 139, 271, 289–290, 292, 303, 313–316, 359, 384–395
derivative suit, 72, 87
derivatives, 39, 45, 49, 51–52, 57–58, 205–232, 280, 312, 383, 388, 408, 409, 435, 440, 448–451, 453, 479, 480
director primacy, 81
Disney case (US), 99
dividends, 25, 28, 39, 46, 52–53, 59, 65, 66, 70–71, 86, 153, 156, 169, 283, 295, 297, 301, 320, 405, 417–418, 427, 428, 431, 467

483

duty of care, 61, 74, 78, 84, 87, 97–99

economic crisis, 12, 384, 386, 391, 393, 460–461, 465, 471, 477
economic model, 45, 390, 400
economic sociology, 4, 8–12, 106, 257, 266, 274, 479
efficient capital market hypothesis, 94, 102, 387
embeddedness, 3, 8–12, 104–107, 115–116, 119, 124, 127, 130, 138, 139, 140–141, 144, 145, 147, 179, 278, 292, 300, 319, 351, 371, 374, 381, 403, 409, 412, 444, 477–478, 482
employees, 16, 18–21, 31, 34–39, 59, 68, 129, 143, 151, 158, 170, 175, 177, 184, 197, 214–215, 226, 227, 229, 234, 237, 244–254, 256, 262, 265, 277, 284, 286–289, 299, 304–312, 316, 319–329, 331, 348, 352, 357, 361–373, 378, 403–406, 410, 412, 416, 429, 434, 454, 481
end of history, 1, 5, 127, 280
Enron, 30–34, 80, 111, 113, 154, 163, 167, 207, 264, 308
European corporate governance regulation, 233, 385, 397
executive compensation, 5, 46, 55, 99, 193, 409, 433, 438–439, 454, 480

fiduciary duty, 7, 21, 72, 84, 86, 87, 96, 98, 100, 158, 246, 248, 253, 254, 305, 358, 459, 460, 462, 463, 464, 471, 482
finance capitalism, 2, 3, 12
financial capitalism, 119, 128, 136–137, 153
financial crisis, 3, 7, 12, 15, 17, 33, 34, 39, 43, 81, 82, 119, 122, 138, 177, 198, 203, 205, 217, 234, 247, 261, 272, 280, 285, 291, 309, 312, 313, 316, 319, 333, 344, 346–347, 381–384, 393, 409, 411, 434, 440–441, 447, 460, 478–480
financial paradigm, 4, 120, 137, 144
financial regulation, 12, 303, 310, 313, 317, 330, 384, 441–442
financialism, 121–122, 138
financialization, 3, 4, 118, 121, 125–126, 154, 170–171, 173, 176, 272–273, 274, 277, 280, 293, 305, 437

Glass–Steagall Act (US), 34, 261, 289, 302
globalization, 3, 170, 259, 263, 289, 313, 319, 322, 329–332, 333–341, 346, 351, 356, 363, 368, 374, 375, 435

Gramm–Leach–Bliley Act (US), 51, 56, 58
Great Depression, 46, 58, 61, 89, 301, 329, 386

hedge fund, 4, 24, 38–39, 49, 56, 102–103, 158–159, 161, 171, 175, 180, 186, 198, 199, 208, 209, 279, 283, 285, 288, 309, 311–312, 346, 388, 392, 394, 445, 449–452

independent directors, 17, 61, 67, 74, 78, 80, 310
industrial relations, 6, 130, 181, 187, 328, 334, 342, 344, 367, 375
industrial revolution, 22, 33, 83, 87
inequality, 6, 29, 30, 40, 277–281, 282, 289, 313, 314, 316, 334, 335, 413, 414
insolvency, 21, 188, 206, 209, 213, 217, 225–232
institutional investors, 2, 8, 16, 18, 27, 37, 46, 48, 53–56, 93–95, 101, 102, 122, 158, 167, 175, 180, 193, 195, 202, 259, 260, 261, 262, 270, 284–286, 292, 304, 308, 311, 321, 366, 461–464
institutions, 3, 4, 8, 11–12, 15, 22, 42–59, 62, 74, 80, 82–84, 90, 102–103, 105, 123, 129, 146, 154, 158, 166, 175, 178–183, 187, 190, 192, 204, 218, 221, 227, 232, 247, 259–261, 264–266, 271, 284–285, 290, 322, 325, 335–338, 350, 352, 359, 362, 363, 374, 376, 384, 390, 392, 416, 420, 421, 434, 441, 445, 454, 477, 478, 482
interdisciplinarity, 9, 120, 471, 479, 481
investment banking, 2, 49–51, 57–59, 60–63, 68, 103, 151, 153, 154, 160, 161, 174, 180, 213, 283, 299, 441

Keynes, 171, 172, 289
Keynesian economics, 74, 120, 123
knowledge, 2–3, 35, 80, 88, 122–123, 128, 138–148, 174–175, 209, 228, 263, 265, 266, 353, 357, 364, 374, 421, 435–436, 467, 479, 481
knowledge management, 139, 147
knowledge society, 2, 4, 119, 142–148, 481

labor law, 68, 269
laissez-faire, 278, 316, 393
law and economics, 9–12, 164, 292, 392, 393

Index

Lehman Brothers, 34, 208, 230, 264, 333, 434
leverage, 34, 49, 57, 96, 151, 154, 159–163, 177, 180, 187, 192, 201, 279, 285, 287, 291, 304, 311, 318, 332, 333, 346, 347, 348, 383, 388, 394, 396, 409, 451, 478
liberal market economy, 7, 257
limited liability, 21–22, 49, 61, 74, 159, 423
Long Term Capital Management, 51

managerialism, 70, 84, 88, 96, 109, 114, 118
mortgage, 49, 57, 121, 151, 186, 195, 205, 234, 266, 314, 346, 445, 478

neoliberalism, 477
New Deal, 32, 56, 61, 64, 68, 74, 113, 152, 165, 166, 172, 290, 301, 302, 303, 315, 317, 329
new institutional economics, 9, 12, 105
non-governmental organization, 1–2, 146, 225, 339, 343, 344, 345
Northern Rock, 33–35, 347

ownership and control, 24, 55, 124, 152, 153–154, 157, 165, 167, 171, 190, 202, 204, 246, 262, 321

paradigm, 4, 75, 88, 91, 120–123, 128–129, 134–139, 142–144, 147, 151, 157, 163, 171, 194, 198, 289, 351, 389, 417
path-dependency, 11, 129
Polanyi, Karl, 3, 8–9, 11, 104–106, 117, 122, 128, 135, 146, 278
private equity, 4, 38–39, 56, 102, 151–176, 186, 189, 198, 201, 203, 279, 283–288, 294, 309, 311–312, 346–348, 388, 392, 394
private ordering, 143, 167
property rights, 19, 118, 165, 267, 268, 335, 387, 399
public good, 74, 95, 121, 329

race-to-the-bottom, 108, 111, 113
regulatory competition, 112
regulatory state, 92

salary, 70, 160, 283, 288, 366, 415, 419, 438

Sarbanes–Oxley Act, 31, 35, 113, 114, 117, 167, 308, 313
Securities and Exchange Commission, 57, 66, 82, 159, 209, 312, 430
securities law, 32, 67, 166, 387
securitization, 24, 57, 59, 121, 128, 212, 266, 277, 290, 451, 457
settlor, 37
shareholder value, 18, 26, 27, 30, 31, 41, 114, 119, 121, 127, 137, 236, 246, 252, 254, 256, 259, 260, 264, 271, 291, 304, 320, 424, 434
shareholder voting, 5, 101, 309
social norms, 12, 477, 478
social welfare, 6, 95, 124, 141, 270, 273, 329, 332
special purpose vehicle, 32, 34, 207
state competition, 116
stock options, 283, 287, 292, 293, 321, 366, 415, 418, 420, 439
stockholders, 16, 47, 51, 52, 55, 68, 70, 73, 121
system of production, 170
systemic risk, 7, 216, 218, 222, 397, 409, 458, 465, 470, 480

takeover, 4, 17, 18, 21, 23, 25, 27, 29, 34, 38, 76, 78, 96, 109, 111, 113, 160, 161, 168, 172, 174, 198, 233–255, 287, 290, 291–292, 294, 303–304, 307, 310, 327, 328, 331, 358, 417, 418, 428
theory of the firm, 4, 16, 75, 76, 122, 123, 127, 141
trade union, 5, 157, 167, 169, 170, 297–299, 328, 333–337, 339–346, 347, 349, 354
trustee, 36–38, 60–61, 65–66, 68–69, 72, 77, 158, 166, 181, 187, 215, 305, 308, 402, 466, 471–473, 482

Van Gorkom case (US), 96, 99
varieties of capitalism, 7, 130, 258, 374, 478
varieties of liberalism, 478
venture capital, 6, 27, 158, 159, 161, 186, 201, 347, 365

welfare state, 12, 35, 123, 131, 139, 142, 143, 263, 273, 274